INTERACTIONS

A Thematic Reader

INTERACTIONS

A Thematic Reader

EIGHTH EDITION

Ann Moseley
Texas A&M University-Commerce

Jeanette Harris
Texas Christian University

WADSWORTH
CENGAGE Learning™

Australia • Brazil • Japan • Korea • Mexico • Singapore • Spain • United Kingdom • United States

WADSWORTH
CENGAGE Learning™

Interactions: A Thematic Reader, Eighth Edition
Ann Moseley and Jeanette Harris

Publisher/Executive Editor: Lyn Uhl

Director of Developmental English and College Success: Annie Todd

Assistant Editor: Melanie Opacki

Editorial Assistant: Matthew Conte

Media Editor: Amy Gibbons

Marketing Manager: Kirsten Stoller

Marketing Coordinator: Brittany Blais

Marketing Communications Manager: Courtney Morris

Project Management: PreMediaGlobal

Art Director: Jill Ort

Print Buyer: Mary Beth Hennenbury

Rights Acquisitions Specialist—Text: Katie Huha

Rights Acquisitions Specialist—Image: Jennifer MeyerDare

Cover Designer: Nancy Goulet

Cover Image: "Web of Executives" by Frederic Joos—Getty Images

Compositor: PreMediaGlobal

For product information and technology assistance, contact us at **Cengage Learning Customer & Sales Support, 1-800-354-9706**.

For permission to use material from this text or product, submit all requests online at **www.cengage.com/permissions**

Further permissions questions can be emailed to **permissionrequest@cengage.com**

Library of Congress Control Number: 2010941137

ISBN-13: 978-0-495-90829-6

ISBN-10: 0-495-90829-0

Wadsworth
20 Channel Center Street
Boston, MA 02210
USA

Cengage Learning is a leading provider of customized learning solutions with office locations around the globe, including Singapore, the United Kingdom, Australia, Mexico, Brazil and Japan. Locate your local office at **international.cengage.com/region**.

Cengage Learning products are represented in Canada by Nelson Education, Ltd.

For your course and learning solutions, visit **www.cengage.com.**

Purchase any of our products at your local college store or at our preferred online store **www.cengagebrain.com.**

Instructors: Please visit **login.cengage.com** and log in to access instructor-specific resources.

Printed in the United States of America
1 2 3 4 5 6 7 14 13 12 11 10

For my husband, Fred, as always—A. M.
For Henry—J. H.

CONTENTS

RHETORICAL TABLE OF CONTENTS   xix

PREFACE   xxviii

INTRODUCTION   1

UNIT ONE
THE SELF   13

■ My Name   SANDRA CISNEROS   15
Unhappy with her Spanish name, a young girl selects a new name for herself.

■ The Name Is Mine   ANNA QUINDLEN   17
Quindlen reflects on her decision to keep her own name when she married.

Born Black, White, and Jewish   REBECCA WALKER (NEW)   20
The daughter of a famous African American novelist and a Jewish civil rights lawyer describes her birth and her struggle to find her identity as a person of mixed race.

I'm Just Me   LYLAH M. ALPHONSE   23
Alphonse explores society's reaction to people who do not fit neatly into a single category.

───────

■ Brackets indicate paired or grouped readings.

■ Between Two Worlds   DIANA ABU-JABER (NEW)   26

*The daughter of a Jordanian father and an American mother, Abu-Jaber
emphasizes the importance of finding self-respect and personal identity.*

■ Living in Two Worlds   MARCUS MABRY   31

*Mabry tells of a trip home to New Jersey when he was a student at
Stanford.*

The Jacket   GARY SOTO   35

Soto tells the story of how an ugly green jacket affected his life.
Focus: Narration

On Being 17, Bright, and Unable to Read   DAVID RAYMOND   39

*A student describes what it is like to have the learning disability of
dyslexia.*

■ The Need for Achievement   DOUGLAS A. BERNSTEIN (NEW)   43

*In this textbook selection, a psychology professor identifies some distin-
guishing characteristics of people who have high and low achievement
motivation.*

■ Zero   PAUL LOGAN (NEW)   48

*A college freshman learns from the mistakes that resulted in a "zero" grade
point average during his first semester and becomes a successful student.*

CRITICAL THINKING, READING, AND WRITING   **54**

*Annotating a Text   54
Example: "Growing Up Asian" by Kesaya E. Noda   55
Exploring Ideas Together   59
Exploring the Internet   60
Writing Essays   61*

UNIT TWO
FAMILY   63

■ What Is This Thing Called Family?   LEE HERRICK (NEW)   65

*Herrick describes not only the difficulties of being a Korean adoptee in a
Caucasian community but also the love and valuable traits he gained in his
Caucasian adoptive family.*

■ Defining Family   BRYAN STRONG, CHRISTINE DEVAULT, AND THEODORE F.
COHEN (NEW)   69

*The authors of this selection from a sociology textbook provide both
formal and informal definitions of the modern family.*

Mother and Freedom   MAYA ANGELOU   73

Liberated by her mother when she was 17, Angelou cares for her cancer-stricken mother and prays for the strength to let go when the time comes.

The Old Man   LARRY L. KING   76

King recalls conflicts he had with his father when he was a teenager.

Only Daughter   SANDRA CISNEROS   80

Cisneros receives affirmation from her father when he praises one of her stories.

A Daughter's Journey   SHARON LIAO   84

On a trip to China, Liao learns more about her parents and their culture—and therefore more about herself.

A Parent's Journey Out of the Closet   AGNES G. HERMAN   92

A mother describes her long, difficult struggle in learning to accept her son's homosexuality.

Sibling Imprints   FRANCINE KLAGSBRUN   99

Klagsbrun argues that sibling rivalry has long-lasting effects on an individual's personality and development.

Brothers   BRET LOTT   106

Lott describes the relationship between himself and his brother and how it evolved as they grew older, and then connects this relationship to that of his own two sons.
Focus: Description

No Snapshots in the Attic: A Granddaughter's Search for a
    Cherokee Past   CONNIE MAY FOWLER   112

Fowler's search for her Native American heritage leads her to the ancient oral art of storytelling.

Hold the Mayonnaise   JULIA ALVAREZ   120

Alvarez describes the process of adjustment she underwent as a Latina stepmother to two blond, Anglo stepdaughters.

The Family That Stretches (Together)   ELLEN GOODMAN   124

Goodman asserts that the concept of family must stretch to include many different types of families.

CRITICAL THINKING, READING, AND WRITING   **128**

Writing a Personal Essay   128
Example: "Who Am I? Reflections of My Parents" by Roderick Hartsfield,
    student   130

Exploring Ideas Together   133
Exploring the Internet   133
Writing Essays   134

UNIT THREE
FRIENDS AND MATES   137

College Friends   JENNIFER CRICHTON   139
The writer describes her need for friendship during her first semester at college and what her college friends have meant to her since then.

A Small Act   JIMMY CARTER   143
Carter remembers how a small act changed his relationship with friends when he was a child.

A Boyhood Friendship in a Divided Valley   BEN KAMIN   146
This essay tells of an unlikely friendship between an Israeli and a Palestinian.

Oil and Water   VALERIE OWEN   149
A student tells of two very different people who become good friends.

Vinnie's Jacket   ANNA NUSSBAUM   152
Written when she was a college student, Nussbaum's essay describes a friend who died but is fondly remembered.

The Difference between Male and Female Friendships   ELLEN GOODMAN AND PATRICIA O'BRIEN   155
The authors discuss the different roles that communication plays in male and female friendships.

What Are Friends For?   MARION WINIK   159
The author categorizes different kinds of friendships she has experienced.
Focus: Classification

Great Expectations   STEPHANIE COONTZ (NEW)   163
Coontz and Bhalla argues that people today expect more out of marriage than ever before.

My Home, My World   ARCHENA BHALLA   167
As a student, Bhalla compares the Indian custom of arranged marriages to more informal American courtship customs.

Marriage and Divorce American Style   E. MAVIS HETHERINGTON   172

Hetherington identifies different types of marriages and argues that there are both good and bad divorces just as there are good and bad marriages.

Gay Marriage Looms as "Battle of Our Times"   JANE LAMPMAN   178

Lampman predicts that the issue of gay marriage will become increasingly divisive in the future.

Why Isn't a Nice Person Like You Married?   ELSIE BLISS   183

The author argues that remaining single is a choice that should be respected.

CRITICAL THINKING, READING, AND WRITING   **186**
Writing a Summary   186
Example: "Summary of 'The Difference between Male and Female Friendships"   187
Exploring Ideas Together   188
Exploring the Internet   188
Writing Essays   189

UNIT FOUR
WORK   191

Work, Mind, and Identity   MIKE ROSE (NEW)   193
Rose argues that it takes thought and intelligence to do physical work.

What You Do Is What You Are   NICKIE MCWHIRTER   199
McWhirter argues that "Americans . . . tend to define and judge everybody in terms of the work they do, especially work performed for pay."

Girl in an Oven   SARAH JEANETTE SMITH   202
A female student tells of her struggle "to act like a girl while working like a man" during the summer she spent fighting wildfires in New Mexico.

One Man's Kids   DANIEL MEIER   207
This writer describes his experience as a first-grade teacher in an urban classroom.

The Psychic Satisfactions of Manual Work   MATTHEW B. CRAWFORD
   (NEW)   211
*Crawford describes the pleasure and satisfaction that can result from
physical work.*

W-O-R-K   BRIAN BRAAKSMA   214
*This student writer gives a vivid example of the hard and distasteful phys-
ical labor that his father expected of him on the family's farm in Iowa.*

Big Russ and Me   TIM RUSSERT   218
*Tim Russert, the late moderator of Meet the Press, remembers how hard
his father worked and is grateful for the work ethic he learned from "Big
Russ."*

Regular Work for an Irregular Economy   CARMEN MARTINO AND
   DAVID BENSMAN (NEW)   226
*The authors describe the unrewarding and even demeaning process of
finding work through a temporary work agency.*
Focus: Process

Easy Job, Good Wages   JESUS COLON   229
*A Puerto Rican writer recalls an important lesson he learned when he first
looked for a job as a young immigrant.*

Salvaging an Interview   TAMEKIA REECE (NEW)   232
*Reece identifies four unexpected problems that can occur in an interview
and makes recommendations for solving them.*

The Way We Worked   TOM BROKAW   235
*Brokaw argues that a defining characteristic of the World War II genera-
tion was their great capacity for work.*

The Future of Work   ROBERT B. REICH   239
*A former secretary of labor predicts which careers will need workers
in the future.*

CRITICAL THINKING, READING, AND WRITING   **244**
Responding to a Text   244
*Example: "The McDonald Image" (Response to "What You Do Is What
   You Are" by Nickie McWhirter)   245*
Exploring Ideas Together   247
Exploring the Internet   248
Writing Essays   248

UNIT FIVE
A Diverse Society 251

A Passion for Diversity   ANN POMEROY (NEW)   253

Pomeroy tells how Deborah Dagit, even though she has a serious disability herself, has fought not only for disability rights but also for diversity in all areas.

Getting to Know about You and Me   CHANA SCHOENBERGER   257

As a student, this writer describes how it feels to be the victim of religious stereotyping.
Focus: Cause and Effect

Mother Tongue   AMY TAN (NEW)   261

Tan describes the different "Englishes" she speaks and the effects these different forms of English have had on her life and writing.
Focus: Cause and Effect

Black Men and Public Space   BRENT STAPLES (NEW)   268

A black journalist describes the fear that some people have shown when they encounter him in a public place.

Indian Education   SHERMAN ALEXIE   272

This Native American author gives a year-by-year account of his experiences during 12 years of schooling.

People Like Us   DAVID BROOKS   280

Brooks suggests that "we all pay lip service to the melting pot, but we really prefer the congealing pot."

Mongrel America   GREGORY RODRIGUEZ   286

Rodriguez points out that intermarriage may ultimately erase America's racial divisions.

Two Ways to Belong to America   BHARATI MUKHERJEE (NEW)   292

One of two Indian sisters who came to the United States for an education, Mukherjee contrasts her own decision to become a citizen with her sister's decision to remain an expatriate.

Anonymous Victims of Dreams and a River   VICTOR LANDA   297

Landa remembers immigrants who died trying to cross the Rio Grande.

I Have a Dream   MARTIN LUTHER KING, JR.   300

The famous civil rights leader dreams that African Americans will eventually enjoy the rights promised by the U.S. Constitution to all Americans.

CRITICAL THINKING, READING, AND WRITING   **305**

Analyzing a Text   305
Example: "An Analysis of Audience in Martin Luther King's 'I Have a Dream' Speech"   306
Exploring Ideas Together   309
Exploring the Internet   310
Writing Essays   310

UNIT SIX
NATURE AND ENVIRONMENT   313

A Sense of Place   GEORGE J. DEMKO   315

A geographer emphasizes the importance of a personal "sense of place" even though places change.

Weather Reports   KATHLEEN NORRIS   319

The author gives poetic examples of "weather reports" for the year she spent on the border between North and South Dakota.
Focus: Example

Storm Country   PAUL CRENSHAW   325

Remembering nights in his family's Midwestern storm cellar, Crenshaw describes the formation, destructiveness, and "terrible beauty" of a tornado.

Dispatch from the Edge: Katrina   ANDERSON COOPER   332

Reporting from Baton Rouge on the night Katrina hit, Cooper concludes that the aftermath of a storm can be more difficult than the storm itself.

Rescuing Oiled Birds   JOHN FLESHER AND NOAKI SCHWARTZ (NEW)   337

This essay describes the efforts to rescue birds soaked with oil from the 2010 Gulf spill and discusses the pros and cons of these efforts.

ANWR: The Great Divide   SCOTT WALLACE (NEW)   341

Wallace contrasts the lifestyle of the traditional Gwich'in Indians in the southern part of ANWR, who depend on the caribou for subsistence, with that of the Inupiat Eskimos on the northern edge, who have used oil money to bring modern improvements to their village.

Seven Myths about Alternative Energy   MICHAEL GRUNWALD (NEW)   347

Grunwald argues that, although alternative energy sources will eventually contribute to an energy solution, we must look to more immediate solutions, such as efficiency and conservation.
Focus: Example

■ The True Cost of Carbon   AL GORE (NEW)   355

Gore argues that global warming will destroy "the habitability of the planet" and proposes a price on carbon as a solution to the problem.

■ Is Humanity Losing the Global Warming Debate?   S. FRED SINGER AND DENNIS T. AVERY (NEW)   360

The authors argue that although moderate global warming exists, it is part of a "natural 1,500-year-climate cycle (plus or minus 500 years)."

Waste   WENDELL BERRY   365

Berry describes the contamination of our countryside and explores the relationship between this waste and the decline in human potential and achievement.

It's Inconvenient Being Green   LISA TAKEUCHI CULLEN (NEW)   369

In this humorous essay, Cullen explores her own "eco-anxiety."

CRITICAL THINKING, READING, AND WRITING **372**

Writing a Persuasive Essay   372
Example: "Dice or Doves?" by Cindy Camburn, student   373
Exploring Ideas Together   378
Exploring the Internet   379
Writing Essays   379

UNIT SEVEN
TECHNOLOGY AND MEDIA   381

■ Literacy Debate Online: R U Really Reading?   MOTOKO RICH (NEW)   383

Rich compares and contrasts literacy development through books with that through the Internet.
Focus: Comparison and Contrast

■ Games and Literacy   LIZ DANFORTH (NEW)   389

Danforth argues that games and literacy "go hand in hand."

Fraternities of Netheads: Internet Addiction on Campus   KIMBERLY S. YOUNG   393

A psychologist identifies factors that contribute to Internet overuse on campus and warns of the negative effects of Internet addiction on students.

We ALL Pay for Internet Plagiarism   ELLEN LAIRD   399

A college English professor describes an instance of Internet plagiarism and discusses the negative societal effects of such plagiarism.

Facebook in a Crowd   HAL NIEDZVIECKI (NEW)   404

Although he had 700 Facebook "friends," the author found himself almost alone when he decided to invite his online friends to a party.

Bad Connections   CHRISTINE ROSEN   407

Analyzing the negative effects of cell phones and digital video recorders, Rosen argues that we should sometimes just "turn our machines off."

Buckle Up and Stop Texting: One Teen's Legacy   MARGIE JACINTO (NEW)   412

This essay tells the sad story of a young woman who died while driving and texting and the life-giving legacy that others have created from her death.

The Real Digital Divide   SHARI CAUDRON   415

Caudron contrasts two different types of computer users.
Focus: Comparison and Contrast

The Distorting Mirror of Reality TV   SARAH COLEMAN   420

Coleman defines, analyzes, and critiques reality television.

YouTube: The People's Network   LEV GROSSMAN   424

A reporter analyzes reasons for the phenomenal success of YouTube.

The Blogs Must Be Crazy   PEGGY NOONAN   428

Noonan defends bloggers, analyzing the reasons for their power and predicting their future.

In iPad We Trust   DANIEL LYONS (NEW)   434

A journalist analyzes the high expectations we have for technology today, even suggesting that technology has become a kind of religion to some people.

Could You Live with Less?   STEPHANIE MILLS   437

Distinguishing between needs and wants, Mills concludes that she can live a happier, more ecological life with less technology.

CRITICAL THINKING, READING, AND WRITING   **441**

Writing a Report   441

Example: "Technology and the Hearing Impaired" by Tammy Holm, student   443

Exploring Ideas Together   447

Exploring the Internet   448

Writing Essays   448

UNIT EIGHT
■ HEROES AND ROLE MODELS   451

Larger than Life   PHILIP TOSHIO SUDO   454

Sudo defines the word hero and comments on its meaning in societies of the past and present.

Focus: Definition

■ Risking Your Life for Another   JOHN QUIÑONES (NEW)   457

The author tells the story of 20-year-old Jeremy Hernandez, who risked his life to save the other adults and 52 children on a bus hanging over a collapsed bridge on the Mississippi River.

My Right Hand   MICHAEL WEISSKOPF   463

A reporter tells the story of losing his hand in a grenade explosion in Baghdad and his realization that this loss saved his life and the lives of his three companions.

Ferguson   MICHAEL NORMAN (NEW)   469

The author remembers Ferguson, a replacement he knew for only a minute in Viet Nam before the young man was killed.

■ September 11, 2001: Answering the Call   BILL MOON   472

A student expresses his admiration for the heroic response of the New York firefighters and police officers and the passengers of Flight 93 to the September 2001 terrorist attacks.

■ Hero Inflation   NICHOLAS THOMPSON   477

Thompson asks whether the word hero has been used too frequently and too loosely since September 11, 2001.

Giving Students the Heroes They Need   PETER H. GIBBON   482

Gibbon argues not only that young people today still need heroes but also that a hero can be imperfect and still be great.

Rosa Parks through a New Lens   PAUL ROGAT LOEB   486

Loeb argues that understanding the larger context of Parks's actions increases her heroism.

The New Heroes and Role Models   TYLER COWEN   492

Cowen explores the distinction between heroes and role models as well as the changing nature of fame and celebrity.

I Am Not a Role Model   CHARLES BARKLEY   500

Barkley argues that family members, not celebrities, are the best role models for young people.

True Grit   BARRY TARGAN   505

In this autobiographical essay, Targan describes the quiet heroism of his father, a hardworking grocer who truly devoted his life to his family.

CRITICAL THINKING, READING, AND WRITING   **509**

Writing a Movie Review   509
Example: "Review of Hero"   511
Exploring Ideas Together   514
Exploring the Internet   514
Writing Essays   515

CREDITS   517

INDEX   523

RHETORICAL TABLE OF CONTENTS

ANALYSIS

My Name   SANDRA CISNEROS   15

I'm Just Me   LYLAH M. ALPHONSE   23

The Need for Achievement   DOUGLAS A. BERNSTEIN   43

Growing Up Asian   KESAYA E. NODA   55

The Family That Stretches (Together)   ELLEN GOODMAN   124

Who Am I? Reflections of My Parents   RODERICK HARTSFIELD   130

College Friends   JENNIFER CRICHTON   139

Great Expectations   STEPHANIE COONTZ   163

Marriage and Divorce American Style   E. MAVIS HETHERINGTON   172

Why Isn't a Nice Person Like You Married?   ELSIE BLISS   183

Work, Mind, and Identity   MIKE ROSE   193

The Future of Work   ROBERT B. REICH   239

Mother Tongue   AMY TAN   261

People Like Us   DAVID BROOKS   280

Mongrel America   GREGORY RODRIGUEZ   286

Anonymous Victims of Dreams and a River   VICTOR LANDA   297

An Analysis of Audience in Martin Luther King's "I Have a Dream" Speech   306

A Sense of Place   GEORGE J. DEMKO   315

The True Cost of Carbon   AL GORE   355

Is Humanity Losing the Global Warming Debate?   S. FRED SINGER
      AND DENNIS T. AVERY   360

It's Inconvenient Being Green   LISA TAKEUCHI CULLEN   369

Games and Literacy   LIZ DANFORTH   389

Fraternities of Netheads: Internet Addiction on Campus   KIMBERLY
      S. YOUNG   393

Bad Connections   CHRISTINE ROSEN   407

The Distorting Mirror of Reality TV   SARAH COLEMAN   420

YouTube: The People's Network   LEV GROSSMAN   424

The Blogs Must Be Crazy   PEGGY NOONAN   428

Technology and the Hearing Impaired   TAMMY HOLM   443

Rosa Parks through a New Lens   PAUL ROGAT LOEB   486

The New Heroes and Role Models   TYLER COWEN   492

I Am Not a Role Model   CHARLES BARKLEY   500
Review of Hero   511

CAUSE AND EFFECT

The Name Is Mine   ANNA QUINDLEN   17

Born Black, White, and Jewish   REBECCA WALKER   20

Between Two Worlds   DIANA ABU-JABER   26

Living in Two Worlds   MARCUS MABRY   31

The Jacket   GARY SOTO   35

On Being 17, Bright, and Unable to Read   DAVID RAYMOND   39

The Need for Achievement   DOUGLAS A. BERNSTEIN   43

Zero   PAUL LOGAN   48

Growing Up Asian   KESAYA E. NODA   55

What Is This Thing Called Family?   LEE HERRICK   65

The Old Man   LARRY L. KING   76

Only Daughter   SANDRA CISNEROS   80

A Daughter's Journey   SHARON LIAO   84

A Parent's Journey Out of the Closet   AGNES G. HERMAN   92

Sibling Imprints   FRANCINE KLAGSBRUN   99

No Snapshots in the Attic: A Granddaughter's Search for a
      Cherokee Past   CONNIE MAY FOWLER   112

Hold the Mayonnaise   JULIA ALVAREZ   120

Who Am I? Reflections of My Parents   RODERICK HARTSFIELD   130

College Friends   JENNIFER CRICHTON   139

A Small Act   JIMMY CARTER   143

Vinnie's Jacket   ANNA NUSSBAUM   152

Marriage and Divorce American Style   E. MAVIS HETHERINGTON   172

Gay Marriage Looms as "Battle of Our Times"   JANE LAMPMAN   178

Why Isn't a Nice Person Like You Married?   ELSIE BLISS   183

What You Do Is What You Are   NICKIE MCWHIRTER   199

The Psychic Satisfactions of Manual Work   MATTHEW B. CRAWFORD   211

W-O-R-K   BRIAN BRAAKSMA   214

Easy Job, Good Wages   JESUS COLON   229

Salvaging an Interview   TAMEKIA REECE   232

The Way We Worked   TOM BROKAW   235

The Future of Work   ROBERT B. REICH   239

The McDonald Image   MCWHIRTER   245

A Passion for Diversity   ANN POMEROY   253

Getting to Know about You and Me   CHANA SCHOENBERGER   257

Mother Tongue   AMY TAN   261

Black Men and Public Space   BRENT STAPLES   268

People Like Us   DAVID BROOKS   280

Mongrel America   GREGORY RODRIGUEZ   286

Anonymous Victims of Dreams and a River   VICTOR LANDA   297

A Sense of Place   GEORGE J. DEMKO   315

Dispatch from the Edge: Katrina   ANDERSON COOPER   332

Rescuing Oiled Birds   JOHN FLESHER AND NOAKI SCHWARTZ   337

ANWR: The Great Divide   SCOTT WALLACE   341

Seven Myths about Alternative Energy   MICHAEL GRUNWALD   347

The True Cost of Carbon   AL GORE   355

Is Humanity Losing the Global Warming Debate?   S. FRED SINGER AND DENNIS T. AVERY   360

Waste   WENDELL BERRY   365

It's Inconvenient Being Green   LISA TAKEUCHI CULLEN   369

Dice or Doves?   CINDY CAMBURN   373

Literacy Debate Online: R U Really Reading?   MOTOKO RICH   383

Fraternities of Netheads: Internet Addiction on Campus   KIMBERLY S. YOUNG   393

We ALL Pay for Internet Plagiarism   ELLEN LAIRD   399

Facebook in a Crowd   HAL NIEDZVIECKI   404

Bad Connections   CHRISTINE ROSEN   407

Buckle Up and Stop Texting: One Teen's Legacy   MARGIE
    JACINTO   412
The Distorting Mirror of Reality TV   SARAH COLEMAN   420
YouTube: The People's Network   LEV GROSSMAN   424
In iPad We Trust   DANIEL LYONS   434
Could You Live with Less?   STEPHANIE MILLS   437
Technology and the Hearing Impaired   TAMMY HOLM   443
My Right Hand   MICHAEL WEISSKOPF   463
Ferguson   MICHAEL NORMAN   469
September 11, 2001: Answering the Call   BILL MOON   472
Hero Inflation   NICHOLAS THOMPSON   477
Rosa Parks through a New Lens   PAUL ROGAT LOEB   486

CLASSIFICATION

The Need for Achievement   DOUGLAS A. BERNSTEIN   43
College Friends   JENNIFER CRICHTON   139
What Are Friends For?   MARION WINIK   159
Marriage and Divorce American Style   E. MAVIS HETHERINGTON   172
What You Do Is What You Are   NICKIE MCWHIRTER   199
The Real Digital Divide   SHARI CAUDRON   415

COMPARISON AND CONTRAST

Between Two Worlds   DIANA ABU-JABER   26
Living in Two Worlds   MARCUS MABRY   31
Brothers   BRET LOTT   106
The Difference between Male and Female Friendships   ELLEN
    GOODMAN AND PATRICIA O'BRIEN   155
My Home, My World   ARCHENA BHALLA   167
Gay Marriage Looms as "Battle of Our Times"   JANE
    LAMPMAN   178
Two Ways to Belong to America   BHARATI MUKHERJEE   292
ANWR: The Great Divide   SCOTT WALLACE   341
Literacy Debate Online: R U Really Reading?   MOTOKO RICH   383
The Real Digital Divide   SHARI CAUDRON   415
The Blogs Must Be Crazy   PEGGY NOONAN   428
The New Heroes and Role Models   TYLER COWEN   492

Definition

Growing Up Asian   KESAYA E. NODA   55

What Is This Thing Called Family?   LEE HERRICK   65

Defining Family   BRYAN STRONG, CHRISTINE DEVAULT, AND THEODORE
F. COHEN   69

The Family That Stretches (Together)   ELLEN GOODMAN   124

College Friends   JENNIER CRICHTON   139

The Difference between Male and Female Friendships   ELLEN
GOODMAN AND PATRICIA O'BRIEN   155

Great Expectations   STEPHANIE COONTZ   163

A Sense of Place   GEORGE J. DEMKO   315

Fraternities of Netheads: Internet Addiction on Campus   KIMBERLY
S. YOUNG   393

We ALL Pay for Internet Plagiarism   ELLEN LAIRD   399

The Distorting Mirror of Reality TV   SARAH COLEMAN   420

YouTube: The People's Network   LEV GROSSMAN   424

The Blogs Must Be Crazy   PEGGY NOONAN   428

Larger than Life   PHILIP TOSHIO SUDO   454

My Right Hand   MICHAEL WEISSKOPF   463

September 11, 2001: Answering the Call   BILL MOON   472

Hero Inflation   NICHOLAS THOMPSON   477

Giving Students the Heroes They Need   PETER H. GIBBON   482

Rosa Parks through a New Lens   PAUL ROGAT LOEB   486

The New Heroes and Role Models   TYLER COWEN   492

I Am Not a Role Model   CHARLES BARKLEY   500

True Grit   BARRY TARGAN   505

Description

My Name   SANDRA CISNEROS   15

Born Black, White, and Jewish   REBECCA WALKER   20

I'm Just Me   LYLAH M. ALPHONSE   23

Between Two Worlds   DIANA ABU-JABER   26

Living in Two Worlds   MARCUS MABRY   31

The Jacket   GARY SOTO   35

Growing Up Asian   KESAYA E. NODA   55

The Old Man   LARRY L. KING   76

A Daughter's Journey   SHARON LIAO   84

Sibling Imprints   FRANCINE KLAGSBRUN   99

Brothers   BRET LOTT   106

No Snapshots in the Attic: A Granddaughter's Search for a
   Cherokee Past   CONNIE MAY FOWLER   112

Work, Mind, and Identity   MIKE ROSE   193

Girl in an Oven   SARAH JEANETTE SMITH   202

Easy Job, Good Wages   JESUS COLON   229

Anonymous Victims of Dreams and a River   VICTOR LANDA   297

A Sense of Place   GEORGE J. DEMKO   315

Weather Reports   KATHLEEN NORRIS   319

Storm Country   PAUL CRENSHAW   325

Dispatch from the Edge: Katrina   ANDERSON COOPER   332

Waste   WENDELL BERRY   365

Fraternities of Netheads: Internet Addiction on Campus   KIMBERLY
   S. YOUNG   393

Risking Your Life for Another   JOHN QUIÑONES   457

My Right Hand   MICHAEL WEISSKOPF   463

Ferguson   MICHAEL NORMAN   469

True Grit   BARRY TARGAN   505

EXAMPLE AND ILLUSTRATION

Sibling Imprints   FRANCINE KLAGSBRUN   99

Brothers   BRET LOTT   106

The Family That Stretches (Together)   ELLEN GOODMAN   124

College Friends   JENNIFER CRICHTON   139

Work, Mind, and Identity   MIKE ROSE   193

What You Do Is What You Are   NICKIE MCWHIRTER   199

One Man's Kids   DANIEL MEIER   207

W-O-R-K   BRIAN BRAAKSMA   214

Big Russ and Me   TIM RUSSERT   218

Easy Job, Good Wages   JESUS COLON   229

Salvaging an Interview   TAMEKIA REECE   232

The Way We Worked   TOM BROKAW   235

A Passion for Diversity   ANN POMEROY   253

Getting to Know about You and Me   CHANA SCHOENBERGER   257

Mother Tongue   AMY TAN   261

Black Men and Public Space   BRENT STAPLES   268

People Like Us   DAVID BROOKS   280

A Sense of Place   GEORGE J. DEMKO   315

Weather Reports   KATHLEEN NORRIS   319

Storm Country   PAUL CRENSHAW   325

Dispatch from the Edge: Katrina   ANDERSON COOPER   332

Seven Myths about Alternative Energy   MICHAEL GRUNWALD   347

Waste   WENDELL BERRY   365

Literacy Debate Online: R U Really Reading?   MOTOKO RICH   383

Fraternities of Netheads: Internet Addiction on Campus   KIMBERLY
    S. YOUNG   393

We ALL Pay for Internet Plagiarism   ELLEN LAIRD   399

Bad Connections   CHRISTINE ROSEN   407

The Blogs Must Be Crazy   PEGGY NOONAN   428

In iPad We Trust   DANIEL LYONS   434

Larger than Life   PHILIP TOSHIO SUDO   454

September 11, 2001: Answering the Call   BILL MOON   472

Hero Inflation   NICHOLAS THOMPSON   477

Giving Students the Heroes They Need   PETER H. GIBBON   482

The New Heroes and Role Models   TYLER COWEN   492

True Grit   BARRY TARGAN   505

NARRATION

Born Black, White, and Jewish   REBECCA WALKER   20

Between Two Worlds   DIANA ABU-JABER   26

Living in Two Worlds   MARCUS MABRY   31

The Jacket   GARY SOTO   35

On Being 17, Bright, and Unable to Read   DAVID RAYMOND   39

Zero   PAUL LOGAN   48

Growing Up Asian   KESAYA E. NODA   55

What Is This Thing Called Family?   LEE HERRICK   65

Mother and Freedom   MAYA ANGELOU   73

The Old Man   LARRY L. KING   76

Only Daughter   SANDRA CISNEROS   80

A Daughter's Journey   SHARON LIAO   84

A Parent's Journey Out of the Closet   AGNES G. HERMAN   92

Sibling Imprints   FRANCINE KLAGSBRUN   99

Brothers   BRET LOTT   106

No Snapshots in the Attic: A Granddaughter's Search for a
   Cherokee Past   CONNIE MAY FOWLER   112

A Small Act   JIMMY CARTER   143

A Boyhood Friendship in a Divided Valley   BEN KAMIN   146

Vinnie's Jacket   ANNA NUSSBAUM   152

My Home, My World   ARCHENA BHALLA   167

Work, Mind, and Identity   MIKE ROSE   193

Girl in an Oven   SARAH JEANETTE SMITH   202

One Man's Kids   DANIEL MEIER   207

W-O-R-K   BRIAN BRAAKSMA   214

Big Russ and Me   TIM RUSSERT   218

Easy Job, Good Wages   JESUS COLON   229

Getting to Know about You and Me   CHANA SCHOENBERGER   257

Mother Tongue   AMY TAN   261

Black Men, Public Space   BRENT STAPLES   268

Indian Education   SHERMAN ALEXIE   272

Weather Reports   KATHLEEN NORRIS   319

Storm Country   PAUL CRENSHAW   325

Dispatch from the Edge: Katrina   ANDERSON COOPER   332

We ALL Pay for Internet Plagiarism   ELLEN LAIRD   399

Facebook in a Crowd   HAL NIEDZVIECKI   404

Buckle Up and Stop Texting   MARGIE JACINTO   412

Risking Your Life for Another   JOHN QUIÑONES   457

My Right Hand   MICHAEL WEISSKOPF   463

Ferguson   MICHAEL NORMAN   469

September 11, 2001: Answering the Call   BILL MOON   472

Rosa Parks through a New Lens   PAUL ROGAT LOEB   486

PERSUASION

Great Expectations   STEPHANIE COONTZ   163

What You Do Is What You Are   NICKIE MCWHIRTER   199

Regular Work for an Irregular Economy   CARMEN MARTINO AND
   DAVID BENSMAN   226

Getting to Know about You and Me   CHANA SCHOENBERGER   257

Indian Education   SHERMAN ALEXIE   272

People Like Us   DAVID BROOKS   280

Mongrel America   GREGORY RODRIGUEZ   286

Anonymous Victims of Dreams and a River   VICTOR LANDA   297

I Have a Dream   MARTIN LUTHER KING, JR.   300

Seven Myths about Alternative Energy   MICHAEL GRUNWALD   347

The True Cost of Carbon   AL GORE   355

Is Humanity Losing the Global Warming Debate?   S. FRED SINGER
      AND DENNIS T. AVERY   360

Waste   WENDELL BERRY   365

Dice or Doves?   CINDY CAMBURN   373

Games and Literacy   LIZ DANFORTH   389

Bad Connections   CHRISTINE ROSEN   407

Buckle Up and Stop Texting: One Teen's Legacy   MARGIE
      JACINTO   412

The Distorting Mirror of Reality TV   SARAH COLEMAN   420

The Blogs Must Be Crazy   PEGGY NOONAN   428

Could You Live with Less?   STEPHANIE MILLS   437

Hero Inflation   NICHOLAS THOMPSON   477

Giving Students the Heroes They Need   PETER H. GIBBON   482

I Am Not a Role Model   CHARLES BARKLEY   500

True Grit   BARRY TARGAN   505

PROCESS

Great Expectations   STEPHANIE COONTZ   163

Regular Work for an Irregular Economy   CARMEN MARTINO AND
      DAVID BENSMAN   226

Easy Job, Good Wages   JESUS COLON   229

Salvaging an Interview   TAMEKIA REECE   232

Storm Country   PAUL CRENSHAW   325

Dispatch from the Edge: Katrina   ANDERSON COOPER   332

Technology and the Hearing Impaired   TAMMY HOLM   443

September 11, 2001: Answering the Call   BILL MOON   472

Hero Inflation   NICOLAS THOMPSON   477

PREFACE

OVERVIEW OF THE TEXT

Like the previous seven editions of *Interactions: A Thematic Reader,* this eighth edition is designed to help students discover meaning in what they read and to convey meaning in what they write. The text's readings and accompanying apparatus—which have been class tested and proven effective through seven previous editions—guide students from a consideration of self to an awareness of how the self interacts with other people and phenomena. We hope the diverse reading selections in *Interactions* will not only create a stimulating context for reading and writing but also help students find their own voices by providing them with new perspectives on the individual within an increasingly diverse and technologically sophisticated society.

NEW TO THIS EDITION

- Twenty-eight readings completely new to *Interactions* and six favorite readings from the first six editions
- Discussion questions accompanying the photographs at the beginning of each unit
- At least one reading in each unit that focuses on a particular method of development: narration, description, classification, process, example, cause and effect, comparison and contrast, and definition. (Additional instruction and student models of these methods of development are provided on the *Interactions,* eighth edition, student website, available at www.cengagebrain.com.)
- Increased emphasis on vocabulary in all units

Key Features of the Text

The following features deserve special attention:

- Thematic focus on the self throughout the text
- Strong reading–writing connections throughout the text
- Paired and/or grouped readings in each unit
- Student essay in each unit
- Emphasis on both critical thinking and collaborative learning
- Group discussion activities at the end of each unit
- Internet activities that connect to the unit topic at the end of each unit
- Writing assignments at the beginning and end of each reading selection and at the end of each unit
- Reading and writing lessons in each unit that provide students with detailed instruction and models on the following topics: annotating a text, writing a personal essay, writing a summary, responding to a text, analyzing a text, writing a persuasive essay, writing a report, and writing a movie review

Reading Selections

The reading selections are organized into thematic units that guide students from a consideration of self to an examination of close human relationships and finally to more abstract topics such as work, society, nature and environment, technology and media, and heroes and role models. This edition includes nearly ninety reading selections. About one-third (twenty-eight) of these readings are completely new to *Interactions*. All other readings have proven to be successful in the seventh and/or earlier editions of the book.

The reading selections represent a wide range of voices, topics, and sources, including a balance of male and female authors and significant contributions by culturally diverse writers. This authorial diversity allows students to encounter new voices and to identify with familiar ones. The readings also provide students with effective models and styles of writing. At least one essay in each unit is by a student writer. (*Note*: These student essays sometimes appear as examples in the **Critical Thinking, Reading, and Writing** sections.) In addition, each unit has at least two sets of paired (or grouped) readings that present related, parallel, or different (even contrasting) viewpoints, thus encouraging students to view subjects from more thoughtful, varied, and complex perspectives.

Apparatus

The Introduction explains to students the process and interdependence of reading and writing, stressing the connections that students can make between their own experiences and what they read. It also introduces them to prewriting techniques such as freewriting, brainstorming, mapping, clustering, and journals. Finally, it emphasizes the importance of considering audience and purpose in all reading and writing activities.

Each reading selection is accompanied by the following apparatus:

- **Headnotes** precede the reading selections. Their purpose is to introduce the author and give students a brief overview of the selection.

- **Before You Read** activities involve students in prewriting and prereading activities. Before reading a selection, students are asked to **THINK** critically about its main idea or topic, **EXAMINE** specific elements of the text (including vocabulary), and **WRITE** a journal entry reacting to the topic of the essay.

- **As You Read** activities encourage students to interact with the reading selection by determining its main idea, annotating the text, focusing on specific information, or relating what they read to their own experiences.

- **After You Read** sections reflect the format of the **Before You Read** sections, encouraging students to **THINK** about the ideas and opinions presented in the reading, **EXAMINE** specific features of the text, and **WRITE** a response to what they have read (usually an essay of some type).

CRITICAL THINKING, READING, AND WRITING

At the end of each unit is a section that provides specific reading and writing instruction and examples for the following assignments:

Unit 1: **Annotating a Text**

Unit 2: **Writing a Personal Essay**

Unit 3: **Writing a Summary**

Unit 4: **Responding to a Text**

Unit 5: **Analyzing a Text**

Unit 6: **Writing a Persuasive Essay**

Unit 7: **Writing a Report**

Unit 8: **Writing a Movie Review**

This section also includes activities and assignments that help students analyze, make connections among, and explore topics introduced in the readings in the unit. For example, **Exploring Ideas Together** asks students to collaborate on topics suggested by the readings in the unit, synthesizing and analyzing information orally and/or in collaborative writing activities. **Exploring the Internet** suggests ways in which students can expand and enrich their knowledge of subjects introduced in the readings by searching the Internet for related topics and information. And **Writing Essays** provides additional writing assignments that require students to write different types of essays. Many of these assignments give students the opportunity to synthesize topics from the readings in the unit with their own experiences and opinions, whereas others ask students to draw information from outside sources.

SUPPORT FOR INSTRUCTORS

The *Interactions*, eighth edition, website includes materials for both instructors and students.

The *Interactions* Instructor Website provides not only brief quizzes (with answers) for each reading selection but also an Instructor's Manual containing the following instructional material:

- Additional suggestions for additional activities based on the **Before You Read, As You Read,** and **After You Read** sections
- Suggestions for teaching vocabulary
- Additional reading and writing activities
- Two additional tables of contents, one emphasizing genre and one identifying alternate themes

The student site provides instruction and model student essays for the following methods of development, with each lesson being tied to one or more readings in the corresponding unit of *Interactions*, eighth edition:

Lesson 1: Narration

Lesson 2: Description

Lesson 3: Classification

Lesson 4: Process

Lesson 5: Cause and effect

Lesson 6: Example

Lesson 7: Comparison and contrast

Lesson 8: Definition

This student site also lists Related Links for students to research websites related to unit topics, reading selections and authors, and writing instruction—especially citing sources in Modern Language Association style.

You may access the *Interactions*, eighth edition, website at www.cengagebrain.com by typing the full title—*Interactions: A Thematic Reader*—into the search line.

ACKNOWLEDGMENTS

We are indebted to the following reviewers for their suggestions in revising *Interactions* for its eighth edition: Clark Draney, College of Southern Idaho; Susan McDowall, Central Community College; Carol Myers,

Athens Technical College; Maryanne Patulski, Syracuse University; Timothy Quigley, Salem State College; Rhonda J. Ray, East Stroudsburg University; Cynthia L. Walker, Faulkner University; Lance Weldy, Francis Marion University.

We would also like to thank our children, Davy Moseley and Elaine Harris, who have guided us through various technological complexities and difficulties with this and previous editions.

Finally, we would like to thank our students, who inspired the first edition of *Interactions* and who taught us how to teach.

Ann Moseley and Jeanette Harris

INTRODUCTION

What is the young woman doing in the photograph above? How can you tell? From the expression on her face, how focused is she on her task? Where do you most like to study, read, and write—in your room, in a library or laboratory, or outside like this young woman?

■ ■ ■

This book is about you—about the individual self that you are and how you *interact* with other people and the world. Each unit explores a different relationship. Beginning with the first unit, which focuses on your relationship to yourself, the book moves from close, intimate relationships with family, friends, and mates to more distant, abstract relationships with the society and the world in which you live. We hope you will enjoy the readings in this book and will learn more about yourself and your relationships from them.

But this book has another purpose as well: to help you become a better reader and writer. We believe that you can do this by reading, discussing, and writing about the selections in this book.

BECOMING A BETTER READER

Reading, like writing, is a process of constructing meaning. When you read, you do not merely take meaning from the text by recognizing the words on the page; you *create* meaning. That is, your existing ideas, information, and experiences *interact* with the ideas and information you discover in the text. No one knows exactly what happens when a person reads, but we do know that you are more likely to discover meaning in what you read if you view reading as a process that includes what you do *before you read, as you read,* and *after you read.*

BEFORE YOU READ

Although you may think of reading and writing as lonely tasks, neither readers nor writers operate in isolation. A piece of writing is a site where readers and writers interact. Thus, before you even begin to read something, you should consider the *purpose* and intended *audience* of the writer. Becoming aware of the writer's purpose and audience, as well as your own purposes for reading, will automatically make you a better reader. For example, in the following paragraph from *How to Study in College,* Walter Pauk writes to an audience of college freshmen to convince them of the importance of establishing a study schedule that suits their particular needs:

> It is important for each individual to choose the type of schedule that fits his or her circumstances best. Some students work better with a detailed schedule, whereas others work better with a brief list of things to do. Circumstances also influence the type of schedule a student should make. There are on-campus students, commuting students, married students, employed students, night-class students, and part-time students, and each has different scheduling requirements. Every student should *adapt* the principles of schedule building to his or her personal circumstances, rather than *adopt* some ideal model which fits hardly anybody.

Notice that the writer of this paragraph makes no attempt to amuse or entertain his readers or to reveal anything about himself in his writing. His tone and style are clear, matter-of-fact, and direct because his purpose is primarily to instruct and advise.

Although he is also writing about schedules, the writer of the following paragraph about Larry McMurtry, the well-known Texas writer, has a very different purpose and intended audience. In this paragraph, David

Streitfeld provides an entertaining description of McMurtry's daily work schedule.

> He gets up very early in the morning, reads for a bit—he's now working his way through a large chunk of the critic and diarist Edmund Wilson—then writes briskly, without notes or anguish. ("Some writers are bleeders. I'm not.") Then he likes to drive out to a restaurant in one of the surrounding towns. Before an early bed, he reads a little more. "A perfect life," he calls it.

The purpose of this paragraph is not to teach readers the importance of making a schedule but to give them insight into McMurtry as a writer by focusing on his daily schedule. Its purpose is thus to inform and entertain rather than to instruct. And because the article appeared in a newspaper, it is obviously intended for a more general audience.

As a reader, you will have a better understanding of what you read if you are aware of the writer. In fact, one of the major differences between experienced and inexperienced readers is not level of skill (how many words are in their vocabulary, how many words per minute they can read, or how much grammar they know) but awareness of purpose and audience.

Before you read, you should also clearly understand your own purpose for reading. In performing different reading tasks, your purposes will vary widely. If you are looking for an apartment, you will read the classified ads by scanning them very quickly, looking for certain words or phrases (furnished, 2 bedrooms, washer/dryer, and so on). You do not need to read every word or to remember everything you read in such cases. Rather, because you are searching for specific information, you will read in a highly selective fashion. If you are reading a letter from a friend, instructions for operating a new DVD player, an article in a magazine, a bestselling novel, or a biology text, you will read in very different ways because in each case your purpose for reading is different.

When you are assigned a selection to read in a textbook, you do not always have a real purpose for reading (other than complying with the teacher's assignment). In fact, you often have no idea of what you are going to read until you have begun to read it. In this text, we give you some information about each selection so that you will know in a general way what it is about before you begin reading. We also suggest activities that will better help you to understand what you are about to read and to relate your reading to your own experiences.

Any method of retrieving information (writing, discussing, or thinking) is valuable to you as a reader because it enables you to make connections and see relationships that you would not otherwise recognize. For example, suppose your history professor has assigned a section of your textbook that discusses the beginning of labor unions in this country. If you write a journal entry about working conditions that you have observed or experienced before you begin to read the assignment, you will comprehend and retain more of what you read because you will mentally connect the new information in your textbook with your previous experiences. In fact, what you do before you read an assignment can be the key to understanding what you read. Thus, one of the most effective ways to begin reading is to recall what you know about the subject before you even begin to read the new material.

AS YOU READ

As you read, you need to distinguish between *main ideas* and *supporting ideas.* Readers, like writers, need to recognize what is primary, or most important, and what is secondary, or less important. Every sentence has a main idea, which is often expressed by the *subject* and *verb;* most paragraphs have a main idea, which may be stated in a *topic sentence;* and larger pieces of discourse, such as essays or reports, usually have a *thesis,* which may be stated explicitly as a *thesis statement* or simply implied. Identifying main ideas and relating them to the details that support them are important reading skills that will help you comprehend and remember what you read.

For example, look at the following passage. These paragraphs are from nature writer Edward Abbey's book *Desert Solitaire: A Season in the Wilderness* (1968), which recounts Abbey's experiences as a ranger in Utah's Arches National Park. Although it is part of a longer work, this passage is a miniature essay in itself. Notice, as you read, that we have underlined the main ideas for you.

> I like my job. The pay is generous; I might even say munificent: $1.95 per hour, earned or not, backed solidly by the world's most powerful Air Force, biggest national debt, and grossest national product. The fringe benefits are priceless: clean air to breathe (after the spring sandstorms); stillness, solitude and space; an unobstructed view every day and every night of sun, sky, stars, clouds, mountains, moon, cliffrock and canyons; a sense of time enough to let thought and feeling range from here to the end of the world and back; the discovery of something intimate—though impossible to name—in the remote.
>
> The work is simple and requires almost no mental effort, a good thing in more ways than one. What little thinking I do is my own and I do it on government time. Insofar as I follow a schedule it goes about like this:
>
> For me the work week begins on Thursday, which I usually spend in patrolling the roads and walking out the trails. On Friday I inspect the campgrounds, haul firewood, and distribute the toilet paper. Saturday and Sunday are my busy days as I deal with the influx of weekend visitors and campers, answering questions, pulling cars out of the sand, lowering children down off the rocks, tracking lost grandfathers and investigating picnics. My Saturday night campfire talks are brief and to the point. "Everything all right?" I say, badge and all, ambling up to what looks like a cheerful group. "Fine," they'll say; "how about a drink?" "Why not?" I say.
>
> By Sunday evening most everyone has gone home and the heavy duty is over. Thank God it's Monday, I say to myself the next morning. Mondays are very nice. I empty the garbage cans, read the discarded newspapers, sweep out the outhouses and disengage the Kleenex from the clutches of cliffrose and

cactus. In the afternoon I watch the clouds drift past the bald peak of Mount Tukuhnikivats. (*Someone* has to do it.)

Tuesday and Wednesday I rest. Those are my days off and I usually set aside Wednesday evening for a trip to Moab, replenishing my supplies and establishing a little human contact more vital than that possible with the tourists I meet on the job. After a week in the desert, Moab (pop. 5500, during the great uranium boom) seems like a dazzling metropolis, a throbbing dynamo of commerce and pleasure. I walk the single main street as dazed by the noise and neon as a country boy on his first visit to Times Square. (Wow, I'm thinking, this is great.)

Although you cannot count on finding all main ideas expressed in exactly the same place in everything you read, the main idea often occurs as the first or second sentence of a paragraph (as in the first paragraph in this passage), but it may also be a middle sentence or even the last sentence in a paragraph. And the main idea of a paragraph or the thesis of a longer piece may not be stated at all but merely implied. In such instances, you must infer the main idea from the information given. For example, Abbey states several main ideas but doesn't supply an explicit thesis for the passage as a whole. However, the main reason he likes his job is clearly not money or prestige but his undemanding, relaxed schedule, which permits him to lead an isolated, uncomplicated life. Thus, this idea functions as the thesis for the passage. And, by extension, Abbey may be suggesting that everyone should choose a job (or career) on the basis of values other than money or prestige.

As both a reader and a writer, you need to be aware of the importance of main ideas and to understand how all discourse is a series of relationships between these main ideas and the more specific details that support and develop them. You probably noticed as you read the selection by Abbey that his main ideas are supported by specific details about what he does on his job and when he does these different tasks. These specific details explain and develop his more general main ideas and elaborate on why Abbey likes his job.

As a reader, you not only need to distinguish between main ideas and supporting details but also to write as you read—to underline, highlight, circle, and draw pictures; to mark between the lines; and to write in the margins. If you are going to get your money's worth from the books you buy and the courses you take, you must be willing to write in your books. In this book you will find white space and enough room to mark the text and write in the margins. We designed the book in this way because we want you to annotate, or mark, your text. (For additional instruction on how to annotate a text, see Unit One, pages 54–59.)

AFTER YOU READ

When you write, you often go back and rewrite what you have written, editing and revising your ideas so that they are more accessible to your reader. When you read, you also need to revise—to reconstruct and add to the meaning that you created as you read. After each reading selection, we provide questions and writing activities that help you in this process of revising your understanding of what you have read. The suggestions below will also help you rethink and remember what you have read.

- *Write about what you have read.* Writing in response to what you have read is one of the most effective ways to make it your own. For example, after reading the essay by Edward Abbey on his weekly job schedule, you could summarize it or write a journal entry about your own job or college schedule. Or you could outline the essay, or map the relationships among main ideas and their major supporting ideas.

- *Discuss what you have read with others.* Discussing what you have read with others nearly always helps you to discover meaning in what you read. Therefore, we suggest that you talk frequently with your classmates about what you have read. After reading the selection by Abbey, for example, you could compare your own experiences and schedules with those of a group of your classmates, and then discuss how schedules give shape to a person's life. Talking, like writing, helps you to see new connections, arrive at different interpretations, and discover new meanings.

- *Reread what you have read.* Rereading is another effective way of ensuring that your interaction with a text is productive. Each time you read something, you gain a new understanding of it; rereading what you have already read enables you to build on your prior knowledge of the text as well as your own increased knowledge of the subject. So do not hesitate to reread. Whether it is a single word, a line or sentence, a paragraph, or even an entire selection, rereading not only clarifies and reinforces the meaning you discover in a text but also helps you discover new meanings.

■ WRITE a journal entry about your own reading process, comparing and contrasting it with the one described here.

BECOMING A BETTER WRITER

Writing begins as an idea. The most informal note, like the most complex report or essay, originates as an idea that anticipates and shapes the completed piece of writing. But writing is not as simple as this statement suggests. You do not simply come up with an idea and then transfer it directly onto paper or a computer screen. Writing, like reading, is a process—often messy and nonlinear, but still a process. In order to become a better writer, you need a general understanding of this process—what you should do *before you write, as you write,* and *after you write.*

BEFORE YOU WRITE

Before you begin to write, you usually need to plan—to think about what you are going to write, discover new ideas, make connections with what you already know, perhaps even look for additional information, and generally organize your thoughts. One of the most important parts of this preliminary process is to think about your purpose and audience—your own purpose in writing as well as the knowledge and reading skills of those who will read what you write.

Purpose. Writers have multiple reasons for writing. When you have a writing assignment, you probably write primarily because the assignment is required, but you may also have other purposes: to communicate information, to express your ideas, to impress your teacher and classmates, to demonstrate knowledge, and to improve your skills as a writer. These multiple purposes inform your writing process and shape the resulting piece of writing. But you also have more specific purposes for writing that are often determined by the assignment or your choice of a topic. For example, you may write to explore (journal writing), to reconstruct your own experiences (memoir or personal experience essays), to teach or advise (instructions), to inform (reports), or to persuade (editorials or persuasive essays). These different purposes do not usually exist in isolation. You may write to inform *and* instruct or to explore *and* reconstruct your own experiences. And because all writing is to some extent persuasive, you are always trying to persuade your reader to accept your point of view. For example, in addition to providing you with the information you need to put a product together, the writer of a set of instructions may also be trying to persuade you to perform the task in a specific way, to take certain precautions, and to value and trust the company that produced the product.

In determining your purpose for writing, you also need to consider your *thesis* (the particular point you are trying to make or the primary impression you want your reader to gain from reading what you have written). Thus, before you begin to write anything, you need to formulate your thesis. It is a good idea to begin writing with a thesis clearly in mind to guide your writing, even if you decide later to change your thesis or not to state it explicitly.

Audience. Your audience consists of the people for whom you are writing —those who will read what you have written. Audience, like purpose, shapes the form that a piece of writing takes. Good writers begin a writing project not only by identifying who their readers will be but also by *analyzing* their readers. For example, they think about how much information their readers have as well as their educational level, their interests, the time they will devote to reading, and their purpose, or purposes, in reading. In other words, they write *for* specific readers.

Prewriting. When faced with a writing assignment, you may need to spend some time thinking about what you want to write and how to structure your ideas before you actually begin to write your paper or essay. If this is the case, you may benefit from some preliminary writing activities— some warm-up exercises to help you collect your thoughts and focus on the writing project at hand. A few of the most common preliminary writing strategies are defined and illustrated for you below:

1. *Freewriting.* In its purest form, freewriting is the practice of writing whatever comes into your head on a topic without worrying about form or correctness. Because this technique is a loosening-up exercise, it is important to continue writing even if you write only meaningless phrases such as "I can't think of anything to write." As you write, you should not be concerned with formal matters of organization, sentence structure, spelling, or punctuation. When you freewrite, you are letting associations lead you from one idea to another, drifting back in time to retrieve information and sensations that are buried in your long-term memory. These long-buried, half-forgotten ideas and experiences can often be recalled once you begin writing.

    As illustrated below, a related strategy is focused freewriting, which helps prepare you to read or write about a particular subject by rapidly recording as many ideas as you can think of about the topic.

    > Let's see, schedules, schedules. What kind of schedules do I know about? I check plane schedules when I visit Dad or get ready to go back to campus. I had to follow a really strict schedule when I worked at McDonald's last summer. The boss really lost it when I came in late! Just looked at the spring schedule to figure out what classes I want to take next semester. I really don't think I like schedules. I'm not sure if I even have a schedule. Guess I better start thinking about one.

2. *Journal entries.* Writing a journal entry differs from freewriting in that you are exploring a topic rather than giving immediate reactions to it. Journal entries allow you to examine a topic and to discover not only what you think but also how you feel. As illustrated in the following example, a journal entry also has more structure than does freewriting, and the ideas in it are more closely connected. Therefore, producing a journal entry will take more time and thought than freewriting. In fact, in a journal entry you often express ideas that you can later use in compositions for audiences other than yourself. Like freewriting, however, a journal entry is personal and informal, and most instructors simply respond to journal entries by commenting on them rather than evaluating such entries for organization, spelling, and punctuation.

    > My life seems to be run by schedules. Each morning when I get up I have to think about what day it is, and then I know the schedule I have to follow. I have one schedule for Mondays, Wednesdays, and Fridays and another one for Tuesdays and Thursdays. On MWF days I go to class from 9:00 to 12:00 and work at the library from 1:00 to 5:00. On T/TH days I go to class from 9:30 to 12:15, but I have a lab from 2:00 to 4:30, so I have to work at the library from 6:00 until 10:00. Needless to say, I

have to study every night. Since I usually go to church on Sunday mornings and study in the afternoons, Saturday is the only day I have that isn't run by a schedule. Perhaps it's the freedom of that day that makes it so great to me. I can visit friends, go to the movies, or just sleep in if I want. If it wasn't for this day, I couldn't face another week of schedules.

3. *Brainstorming and Clustering.* Brainstorming works in much the same way as freewriting. However, when you brainstorm, you simply select a topic and make a *list* of ideas related to that topic, instead of writing connected ideas. As the following brainstorming on schedules shows, it is important to generate as long a list as possible, writing down everything that comes into your mind.

Time	*Katie's theater schedule*
family schedules	*Tina's ballet schedule*
no extra time	*Brad's soccer schedule*
Rigid	*daily schedule*
my college schedule	*weekly schedule*
MWF classes	*study schedule*
T/TH work schedule	*study nights/weekends*
no time to sleep	*study 2 hrs/1 hr class*

After you have generated a fairly lengthy list, you may want to select and "cluster" related ideas by circling and connecting them, perhaps discarding the other ideas. For example, as shown here, you might select one idea that seems especially relevant or interesting to you, such as "family schedules" and then, as shown here, circle and draw lines to cluster related ideas.

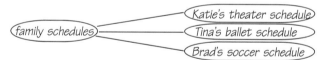

You might even want to brainstorm again, this time focusing on the new narrowed topic.

4. *Mapping.* Another means of visualizing relationships is through mapping. If you are mapping a topic, you begin with the topic itself in the center of a blank piece of paper and then branch out from the topic with related ideas. You can continue this branching process as long as you can think of related ideas, examples, and details. A map is a good way of generating ideas because after you get your map started, you can select one idea from the map that interests you or triggers other ideas and continue to develop that idea while ignoring the rest. This technique encourages you to delve deep into your memory to discover specific ideas. From the following map, for example, you might discover that you want

to write a journal entry or an essay about what you enjoy doing during your free time.

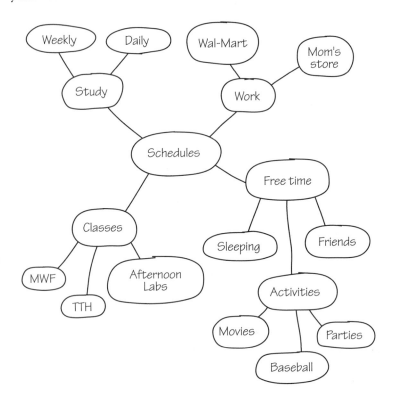

AS YOU WRITE

Neither writing nor reading is a neat, orderly process. Although the final product may appear to be neat, writing is a process in which the writer's mind shuttles back and forth between a mental image and the written text that is emerging on the page. Both reading and writing involve going backward (retrieving information from your mental data bank) as well as going forward (discovering new information and making new connections).

Although the messiness of these processes is often hidden from view, discreetly tucked away inside the reader's or writer's mind, there are times when the mess needs to show, times when it needs to spill out on the clean white page. Writers often need to rewrite what they have written. They may need to create several disorganized drafts before they can produce something they want to share with a reader.

When you have some idea of what you want to write, you are ready to begin drafting your paper. Throughout this part of the writing process, you will often move backward as well as forward. For example, even though you have formulated a thesis beforehand, you may discover when you actually begin to write that you need to revise this thesis or even change it completely. Because writing often leads to new insights and discoveries, these early drafts are sometimes referred to as *discovery drafts*. Don't be concerned if your initial mental image of your text changes significantly as you continue to write. The early part of this process often involves reading and revising as well as writing. As you write, you will be rethinking what you want to write. This is a normal, productive part of the process. Ultimately, you will produce a piece of writing that satisfies you.

AFTER YOU WRITE

Once you have a completed draft, you should try to put it aside for a time and then focus on revising the entire paper. Even as you write, you are rethinking and revising what you want to say. However, you always need to revise the completed draft as well. Revising involves rereading a draft carefully and critically. To do this, you must try to see your paper through the eyes of your reader. You must also be willing to make major changes—to generate new material, to move information from one place to another, and even to delete large portions if necessary. In general, at this point you want to focus on the following questions:

- Do I have a clear thesis, and is my paper focused on this thesis?
- Have I supported my thesis adequately?
- Are my major points effectively supported?
- Are my paragraphs unified and well structured?
- Are my introduction and conclusion effective?

After you have written and revised your paper, you need to turn your attention to preparing the final draft—the one you will submit to a reader (even, or especially, if that reader is your instructor). This final stage in the process involves editing, proofreading, and formatting what you have written so that it is as readable and correct as possible. By the time you begin this stage, you are focusing primarily on the accuracy and appearance of your paper. This is the time to make sure that each sentence is well structured, each word correctly used, and each mark of punctuation appropriate. If you are using a computer, you will need to make final decisions about format and run the spell-checker. Do not underestimate the importance of this final effort to make your paper as readable and correct as possible.

■ **WRITE** a journal entry about your own writing process, comparing and contrasting it with the one described here. You may want to meet with a group of your classmates to discuss your writing processes.

CONCLUSION

You not only use your own experiences to discover meaning when you read and write, but you also make sense of your experiences and yourself through reading and writing. As you read the selections and do the assignments in this book, we hope you will increase your understanding of yourself and how you interact with the people and phenomena in your world. In this process of self-discovery, we believe, you will also become a more experienced and effective reader and writer.

THE SELF

Jeff Greenberg/PhotoEdit

Look carefully at the young man in this photograph and imagine what he might be thinking. What details led you to your interpretation? Do you enjoy spending time alone like this young man? How can such an experience help you know yourself?

■ ■ ■

I t is not always easy to know yourself—to know who you are and how you came to be that person. And just when you think you know yourself, you change. You get older, form different relationships, develop new interests, go to college, change jobs, or move to a new community, and the process of knowing yourself begins again. So your

13

entire life is spent trying to figure out who you are and how to be happy being that person.

One of the ways to examine who you are is to look at the important relationships in your life—especially those with your family and friends. Another way to gain insight into yourself is to think about the experiences you have had and how they have shaped who you are. The language and culture of your particular community also help determine who you are. From birth you absorb and are shaped by the language, values, and patterns of behavior that characterize your own small, immediate group.

This first unit focuses on these factors and how they may shape a person. The unit also includes readings that explore issues of self-esteem and motivation—how factors such as your name, age, gender, family, ethnic background, physical appearance, and school performance influence your self-perception and your actions. As you read these selections, think about your self-image. How would you describe yourself to someone who did not know you? Compare yourself to the child you once were, analyze why you have become the person you are today, or predict the kind of person you will be.

As you read the selections in this unit, also keep in mind the similarities between reading and writing discussed in the Introduction. Remember that the process you go through in reading these selections is much like the process that the writers went through in writing them. Both you and the writers are discovering and constructing meaning. When you read, you are adding to and modifying what you already know. You are also evaluating another person's ideas and information and opinions.

Also remember that reading, like writing, is a messy process. To increase your understanding, underline the sentences that state main ideas or have some other importance to you, circle unfamiliar words, and write notes to yourself in the margins (see "Annotating a Text," pages 52–56). Don't just read these selections; interact with the ideas and information in them. You will not understand yourself any better or improve as a reader unless you actively engage in a dialogue with the writers and their texts.

Finally, remember that you need to write in response to what you read if you want to make the information and ideas your own. In addition to annotating the text, you may want to summarize, outline, or write a journal about what you have read. Throughout this book, you will also write essays responding to and developing ideas from your reading. Some of these essays are based on a particular method of development—narration, description, classification, process, cause and effect, exemplification, comparison and contrast, or definition. In Unit One, for example, the assignment for Gary Soto's "The Jacket" is to write a narrative. Remember, however, that although an essay may have one primary method of development, most essays combine two or more methods.

My Name

■ ■ ■

SANDRA CISNEROS

Sandra Cisneros, the only daughter in a large Mexican American family, writes stories and poems that reflect her own experience with conflicting cultures and languages. She addresses such issues as poverty, cultural suppression, self-identity, and gender roles in her poetry and fiction. This reading selection is taken from *The House on Mango Street* (1984), a prize-winning collection of narratives about a Mexican American family struggling to adjust to life in an English-speaking culture. Loosely based on the life of the author, the selection below tells of a young girl's reaction to her name, Esperanza, which means "hope."

BEFORE YOU READ

■ **THINK** about your given name, the one you "go by." Is it a family name? Or were you named after a famous person? Do you know why your parents chose to name you as they did? Do you have a nickname? If so, what is its origin?

■ **EXAMINE** the words *esperanza* and *hope,* both of which have been used as female names. Although both words mean the same thing, they look and sound very different. The Spanish word *esperanza* is much longer and more musical; the English word *hope* is not only shorter but also almost blunt sounding.

■ **WRITE** in your journal the name you would have chosen for yourself, and tell why you would have chosen this name.

AS YOU READ

Think about the importance we attach to names and why.

■ ■ ■

In English my name means hope. In Spanish it means too many letters. 1
It means sadness, it means waiting. It is like the number nine. A
muddy color. It is the Mexican records my father plays on Sunday
mornings when he is shaving, songs like sobbing.

It was my great-grandmother's name and now it is mine. She was a 2
horse woman too, born like me in the Chinese year of the horse—which

is supposed to be bad luck if you're born female—but I think this is a Chinese lie because the Chinese, like the Mexicans, don't like their women strong.

My great-grandmother. I would've liked to have known her, a wild   3
horse of a woman, so wild she wouldn't marry until my great-grandfather threw a sack over her head and carried her off. Just like that, as if she were a fancy chandelier. That's the way he did it.

And the story goes she never forgave him. She looked out the window   4
all her life, the way so many women sit their sadness on an elbow. I wonder if she made the best with what she got or was she sorry because she couldn't be all the things she wanted to be. Esperanza. I have inherited her name, but I don't want to inherit her place by the window.

At school they say my name funny as if the syllables were made out of   5
tin and hurt the roof of your mouth. But in Spanish my name is made out of a softer something like silver, not quite as thick as sister's name Magdalena which is uglier than mine. Magdalena who at least can come home and become Nenny. But I am always Esperanza.

I would like to baptize myself under a new name, a name more like the   6
real me, the one nobody sees. Esperanza as Lisandra or Maritza or Zeze the X. Yes. Something like Zeze the X will do.

■   ■   ■

AFTER YOU READ

■ **THINK** about the young girl's reaction to her name. Why does she want another name? Does a person's name make a difference in the way you perceive that person? Does your own name affect how you feel about yourself? Do the names of others affect how you react to them? Why does exchanging names seem important when you first meet someone? Could you feel that you really knew someone whose name you did not know?

■ **EXAMINE** the name "Zeze the X," which Esperanza chose for herself. Why do you think she liked this name?

■ **WRITE** an essay about your own name—where it came from, whether you like it, how you think others perceive it, and what other name you might choose for yourself if you were free to do so.

The Name Is Mine

■ ■ ■

ANNA QUINDLEN

Winner of the 1992 Pulitzer Prize for Commentary, Anna Quindlen has been a columnist for both *The New York Times* and *Newsweek*. She has published three collections of her columns and six novels. One of her novels, *One True Thing*, was made into a movie starring Meryl Streep and William Hurt. Her latest novel, *Every Last One*, was released in April 2010. Quindlen and her husband, Gerald Krovatin, live in New York City. In the following essay, Quindlen tells the story of her name and how that name has helped to shape her various identities.

BEFORE YOU READ

■ **THINK** about the custom of married females adopting the surnames of their husbands. What problems or advantages are associated with this custom?

■ **EXAMINE** the preceding essay, "My Name," by Sandra Cisneros. Even though the purpose, content, and tone of the selections by Cisneros and Quindlen differ significantly, both authors clearly believe that names play an important role in a person's sense of identity.

■ **EXAMINE** the words *matriarchal* and *patriarchal* (paragraph 8). From Latin, *-archy* means "rule"; *matri-* means "mother"; and *patri-* means "father." Therefore, in a matriarchy, the mother is the head of the household; in a patriarchy, the father is the head of the household. To help you remember these and other words you will learn in this book, we suggest that you keep a vocabulary journal, perhaps on your computer, so that you can add words and alphabetize them. See the example below:

Word:	Hint:	Meaning:
matriarchal	*-archy* means rule	ruled by the mother (or a woman)

■ **WRITE** a journal entry stating your opinion on the issue of married women keeping their own surnames rather than taking their husbands' surnames.

AS YOU READ

Annotate this essay by using several different types of annotations. For instructions on how to annotate, see "Annotating a Text" at the end of this unit (pages 52–56).

■ ■ ■

I am on the telephone to the emergency room of the local hospital. My elder son is getting stitches in his palm, and I have called to make myself feel better, because I am at home, waiting, and my husband is there, holding him. I am 34 years old, and I am crying like a child, making a slippery mess of my face. "Mrs. Krovatin?" says the nurse, and for the first time in my life I answer "Yes." 1

This is a story about a name. The name is mine. I was given it at birth, and I have never changed it, although I married. I could come up with lots of reasons why. It was a political decision, a simple statement that I was somebody and not an adjunct of anybody, especially a husband. As a friend of mine told her horrified mother, "He didn't adopt me, he married me." 2

It was a professional and a personal decision, too. I grew up with an ugly dog of a name, one I came to love because I thought it was weird and unlovable. Amid the Debbies and Kathys of my childhood, I had a first name only my grandmothers had and a last name that began with a strange letter. "Sorry, the letters I, O, Q, U, V, X, Y and Z are not available," the catalogues said about monogrammed key rings and cocktail napkins. Seeing my name in black on white at the top of a good story, suddenly it wasn't an ugly dog anymore. 3

But neither of these are honest reasons, because they assume rational consideration, and it so happens that when it came to changing my name, there was no consideration, rational or otherwise. It was mine. It belonged to me. I don't even share a checking account with my husband. Damned if I was going to be hidden beneath the umbrella of his identity. 4

It seemed like a simple decision. But nowadays I think the only simple decisions are whether to have grilled cheese or tuna fish for lunch. Last week, my older child wanted an explanation of why he, his dad and his brother have one name, and I have another. 5

My answer was long, philosophical and rambling—that is to say, unsatisfactory. What's in a name? I could have said disingenuously. But I was talking to a person who had just spent three torturous, exhilarating years learning names for things, and I wanted to communicate to him that mine meant something quite special to me, had seemed as form-fitting as my skin, and as painful to remove. Personal identity and independence, however, were not what he was looking for; he just wanted to make sure I was one of them. And I am—and then again, I am not. When I made this decision, I was part of a couple. Now, there are two me's, the me who is the individual and the me who is part of a family of four, a family of four in which, in a small way, I am left out. 6

A wise friend who finds herself in the same fix says she never wants to change her name, only to have a slightly different identity as a family member, an identity for pediatricians' offices and parent-teacher conferences. She also says that the entire situation reminds her of the women's movement as a whole. We did these things as individuals, made these decisions about ourselves and what we wanted to be and do. And they were good decisions, the right decisions. But we based them on individual choice, not on group dynamics. We thought in terms of our sense of ourselves, not our relationships with others.

Some people found alternative solutions: hyphenated names, merged names, matriarchal names for the girls and patriarchal ones for the boys, one name at work and another at home. I did not like those choices; I thought they were middle grounds, and I didn't live much in the middle ground at the time. I was once slightly disdainful of women who went all the way and changed their names. But I now know too many smart, independent, terrific women who have the same last names as their husbands to be disdainful anymore. (Besides, if I made this decision as part of a feminist world view, it seems dishonest to turn around and trash other women for deciding as they did.)

I made my choice. I haven't changed my mind. I've just changed my life. Sometimes I feel like one of those worms I used to hear about in biology, the ones that, chopped in half, walked off in different directions. My name works fine for one half, not quite as well for the other. I would never give it up. Except for that one morning when I talked to the nurse at the hospital, I always answer the question "Mrs. Krovatin?" with "No, this is Mr. Krovatin's wife." It's just that I understand the down side now.

■   ■   ■

AFTER YOU READ

- **THINK** about the different perspectives Quindlen includes in her essay. She is careful to say that her decision about keeping her own name is not the only or necessarily the best answer to this complex problem. What are some of the factors that she includes in her discussion? Is her essay more or less satisfactory because she does not argue strongly for a single answer? Would you describe Quindlen as a feminist because she has not chosen to take her husband's name? Why or why not?

- **EXAMINE** the second sentence in paragraph 6 ("What's in a name?"), which is an allusion to a line in Shakespeare's *Romeo and Juliet*. Did you recognize the line or at least find it familiar? In Shakespeare's play, the response to the question is "A rose by any other name would smell as sweet." Does Quindlen include this reference to Shakespeare's words because she agrees with the sentiment expressed in them? What other reasons might she have for including this allusion to Shakespeare?

- **WRITE** a paragraph or essay in which you argue for or against the custom of women taking their husbands' names.

Born Black, White, and Jewish

■ ■ ■

REBECCA WALKER

A feminist activist, Rebecca Walker is a contributing editor to *Ms.* magazine; the editor of *To Be Real: Telling the Truth and Changing the Face of Feminism;* and a contributor to numerous periodicals, including *Essence, Mademoiselle,* and *Harper's.* The daughter of Pulitzer Prize-winning novelist Alice Walker and Jewish civil rights attorney Mel Leventhal, Walker is also the author of two autobiographical books, *Black, White, and Jewish: Autobiography of a Shifting Self* (2001) and *Baby Love: Choosing Motherhood after a Lifetime of Ambivalence* (2007). In *Black, White, and Jewish,* from which the following selection is taken, Walker describes her struggles to find her identity as a person of mixed race and to relate to both of her parents, who divorced in 1976.

BEFORE YOU READ

■ **THINK** of stories you have heard of your own birth or adoption. What is special, unusual, or important to you about this very personal story?

■ **EXAMINE** the title of the selection. What challenges and rewards would likely come with being "Black, White, and Jewish"? How does the subtitle of Walker's book, "Autobiography of a Shifting Self," reflect the likely result of such a complex heritage?

■ **EXAMINE** the words *ineffable* and *stoic* that Walker uses to describe her parents in paragraph 7. Describing the parents' humanness, *ineffable* can mean either "indescribable, beyond expression" or "something that is not to be uttered, taboo." (In your opinion, which meaning is Walker using here? Or is she using both meanings?) To be *stoic* is to be brave, enduring, impassive, and indifferent to pleasure or pain.

■ **WRITE** a journal entry in which you follow the directions and answer the questions that Walker poses in her first paragraph.

AS YOU READ

Compare the story of Walker's birth to the story of your own birth or adoption.

Y ou may want to ask about the story of your birth, and I mean 1
down to the tiniest details. Were you born during the biggest
snowstorm your town had seen in fifty years? Did your father
stop at the liquor store on the way to the hospital? Did you refuse to appear, holding on to the inside of your mother's womb for days? Some sin-
ewy thread of meaning is in there somewhere, putting a new spin on the
now utterly simplistic nature-nurture debate. Your job is to listen carefully
and let your imagination reconstruct the narrative, pausing on hot spots
like hands over a Ouija board.

I was born in November 1969, in Jackson, Mississippi, seventeen months
after Dr. King was shot. When my mother went into labor my father was
in New Orleans arguing a case on behalf of black people who didn't have
streetlights or sewage systems in their neighborhoods. Daddy told the judge
that his wife was in labor, turned his case over to co-counsel, and caught
the last plane back to Jackson.

When I picture him, I conjure a civil rights Superman flying through a 2
snowstorm in gray polyester pants and a white shirt, a dirty beige suede
Wallabee touching down on the curb outside our house in the first black
middle-class subdivision in Jackson. He bounds to the door, gallantly gathers up my very pregnant mother who has been waiting, resplendent in her
African muumuu, and whisks her to the newly desegregated hospital. For
his final leg, he drives a huge, hopelessly American Oldsmobile Toronado.

Mama remembers long lines of waiting black women at this hospital, 3
screaming in the hallways, each encased in her own private hell. Daddy
remembers that I was born with my eyes open, that I smiled when I saw
him, a look of recognition piercing the air between us like lightning.

And then, on my twenty-fifth birthday, Daddy remembers something 4
I've not heard before: A nurse walks into Mama's room, my birth certificate in hand. At first glance, all of the information seems straightforward
enough: mother, father, address, and so on. But next to boxes labeled
"Mother's Race" and "Father's Race," which read Negro and Caucasian,
there is a curious note tucked into the margin. "Correct?" it says. "Correct?" a faceless questioner wants to know. Is this union, this marriage,
and especially this offspring, correct?

A mulatta baby swaddled and held in loving arms, two brown, two 5
white, in the middle of the segregated South. I'm sure the nurses didn't
have many reference points. Let's see. Black. White. Nigger. Jew. That
makes me a tragic mulatta caught between both worlds like the proverbial
deer in the headlights. I am Mammy's near-white little girl who plunges to
her death, screaming, "I don't want to be colored, I don't want to be like
you!" in the film classic *Imitation of Life*. I'm the one in the Langston
Hughes poem with the white daddy and the black mama who doesn't

know where she'll rest her head when she's dead: the colored buryin' ground behind the chapel or the white man's cemetery behind gates on the hill.

But maybe I'm being melodramatic. Even though I am surely one of   6 the first interracial babies this hospital has ever seen, maybe the nurses take a liking to my parents, noting with recognition their ineffable human-ness: Daddy with his bunch of red roses and queasiness at the sight of blood, Mama with her stoic, silent pain. Maybe the nurses don't load my future up with tired, just-off-the-plantation narratives. Perhaps they don't give it a second thought. Following standard procedure, they wash my mother's blood off my newborn body, cut our fleshy cord, and lay me gently over Mama's thumping heart. *Place infant down on mother's left breast, check blankets, turn, walk out of room, close door, walk up hall-way,* and so on. Could I be just another child stepping out into some un-known destiny?

■ ■ ■

AFTER YOU READ

■ **THINK** about Walker's narrative of her birth in paragraphs 2–5. In your opinion, how much of this narrative is factual, and how much is fic-tional? Give examples of both factual and imaginary elements in the story. What incident in the narrative is most disturbing to Walker, and why?

■ **EXAMINE** paragraph 6, in which Walker uses two significant allusions. Based on Fannie Hurst's novel of the same name, the 1959 film classic *Imitation of Life* starred Lana Turner as a white widowed mother, Lora Meredith, who has ambitions of becoming a famous actress. Meredith and her daughter are paralleled by a black widowed single mother, Annie Johnson, who has a nearly white daughter, Sarah Jane. Walker specifically refers to Sarah Jane's attempts to pass for white and her rejection of her mother and her blackness. The Langston Hughes poem to which Walker refers is probably "Cross" (1925), which begins, "My old man's a white old man / And my old mother's black" and ends, "I wonder where I'm gonna die, / Being neither white nor black?"

■ **WRITE** an essay telling the story of your own birth or adoption. Use Walker's suggestions and questions in paragraph 1 to guide your essay.

I'm Just Me

■ ■ ■

LYLAH M. ALPHONSE

Lylah Alphonse, whose mother is from India and whose father is from Haiti, was born and raised in Princeton, New Jersey. She is a news editor at the *Boston Globe* and the author of *Triumph over Discrimination: The Life Story of Farhang Mehr.* Unlike Rebecca Walker, who struggled with her mixed identity, Alphonse makes it clear in the following essay from the *Boston Globe* that she is very comfortable with who she is, even though our society occasionally makes life difficult for people who do not belong to a single ethnic group.

BEFORE YOU READ

■ **THINK** about what it is like to be part of two different cultures and to have physical characteristics derived from both. How does a mixed racial heritage complicate life for a person? How do other people react to someone whom they cannot assign to a single race?

■ **EXAMINE** the title of this essay. Although the author seems proud of her mixed background, she is eager to be perceived as an individual— someone who is unique and distinctive. Why do you think she is determined to be perceived as an individual rather than simply as the product of the two cultures represented by her parents?

■ **EXAMINE** also the word *aptitude,* which occurs in paragraph 6. Alphonse is using this word to mean intelligence or understanding, but certain aptitude tests also help determine an individual's natural talents or inclinations. Such tests can sometimes help individuals select college majors or careers.

■ **WRITE** a journal entry in which you analyze the various ethnic, religious, and/or racial elements of your own background. Try to determine how each of these elements is reflected in you—what it contributes to your appearance, physique, personality, and so on.

AS YOU READ

Try to distinguish among the concepts of culture, ethnicity, and race.

■ ■ ■

—————————

T his is me: caramel-colored skin, light-brown eyes, brown-black hair   1
with a few silver threads just to the right of my temple. I have a
few freckles, like cocoa powder dusted under my right eye. I'm
5 foot 3, 115 pounds, was a field hockey goalie, still am a fencer.

This is me: I have my mother's Persian features, my father's Haitian   2
coloring, and curly hair that's somewhere in between. When I was little,
I desperately wanted my younger brother's graceful hands and my youngest brother's huge green eyes.

This is me: On census forms, aptitude tests, and applications, whenever   3
possible I check the box for "other" after the question about race. When
there's no "other" option, I check four boxes: white (German and French
on my father's side), Asian (Persian Indian on my mother's side), Native
peoples (Arawak Indian on my father's side), and black (an African great-
grandfather on my father's side). If the instructions limit me to only one
box, I skip it entirely.

One would think that institutions could have come up with a different   4
method of classifying people by now. According to 1990 census information, the number of "other" people has grown to 9.8 million—a 45 percent
increase since 1980—and it's still on the rise. "Mixed" marriages doubled
between 1980 and 1992, when 1.2 million were reported. And "mixed" is
more than just black and white, though those unions have increased also—
by 50 percent, to 250,000, since 1980.

"Mixed" relationships are nothing new, even though the media still   5
sometimes treat them as though they are. My family's been doing it for
four generations. Five, if you count me and my blond-haired, blue-eyed
boyfriend.

There's a massive push to include a "mixed-race" box on the census   6
for the year 2000, but SATs, GREs, and other aptitude tests can surely rethink their designations more than once a decade. Why isn't there a
"mixed" box on all those other forms yet? Or instructions that tell us to
"check all that apply"? Or, better still, a new question, "What group do
you identify with?"

Natives of Zimbabwe, which used to be Rhodesia, who are descended   7
from that country's British settlers are just as African as natives of Ethio-
pia, but in the United States we wouldn't call them African Americans. Yet
we would give that label to the child of a Caucasian woman and a man
from the West Indies, even though the child's connection to the African
continent is distant, if it exists at all.

Why do we call mixed marriages "interracial?" Isn't it your ethnicity—   8
the culture in which you are raised—that defines who you are more so
than your race? Race is part of the equation, of course, but the color of
your skin doesn't necessarily dictate the culture and traditions that sur-
round you while you're growing up.

I grew up in Princeton, N.J. It was very sheltered—kind of like grow-   9
ing up wrapped in cotton, which I think was a good thing. When I left

Princeton to go to college in Syracuse, N.Y., I was naive about racial matters. I still think I am. I was surprised by the looks I'd get when I walked around on campus at night with my friends and by the fliers I got year after year inviting me to attend the "African American Orientation" at the student center. I didn't understand why, when I was reporting a stalker, the campus police officer told me that I spoke English very well.

Then I realized that people were looking at my skin and deciding that 10 I was African American; or looking at my features and deciding I was Indian; or listening to me talk and not being able to place me at all.

People still try to figure out my background. But now, instead of just 11 looking at me and wondering, they ask me questions like "So, were you born here?" Or "Where in India are your parents from?" And "What do you consider yourself?" A friend's father once asked, point-blank, "What exactly *is* Lylah?" ("Female," my friend replied.)

These are the answers I give them: I was born and raised in Princeton, 12 N.J. My mother is from India. My father is from Haiti. As for what I consider myself ...

I'm just me.   13

■ ■ ■

AFTER YOU READ

■ **THINK** about the two arguments that Alphonse includes in her essay. The first, and more explicit, is her argument that race is not a simple concept and that many people derive from not only more than one race but also more than one ethnic or cultural background. But she is also implicitly arguing for acceptance of people as they are—for not classifying people according to their racial or ethnic backgrounds. Which argument do you think is stronger, and why?

■ **EXAMINE** the distinctions Alphonse makes among race, ethnicity, and culture in paragraph 8. Do you agree with these distinctions? Look up these three terms in a dictionary and see whether the definitions support Alphonse's distinctions.

■ **WRITE** an essay entitled "I'm Just Me" in which you describe yourself in terms of your own ethnic, racial, and/or cultural background.

Between Two Worlds

■ ■ ■

DIANA ABU-JABER

The daughter of a Jordanian father and an American mother, Diana Abu-Jaber teaches at Portland State University. She has drawn on her dual heritage for three novels—*Arabian Jazz, Crescent,* and *Origin* (2007)—and for the memoir *The Language of Baklava* (2005). She has also contributed to various periodicals, including *Southern Review, The New York Times,* and *The Washington Post.* Her memoir, like the following 2009 essay from *Self* magazine, uses food symbolically to represent culture. Like Walker and Alphonse, Abu-Jaber finds herself between two worlds of culture and/or race, but she emphasizes her struggle to find self-respect and her own personal identity.

BEFORE YOU READ

■ **THINK** about what you know about the Bedouin people of the Middle East. These desert-dwelling Arabians were originally nomadic, but in recent years many of them have become seminomadic or have settled in villages and urban areas. Famous for their hospitality, the Bedouins are the largest cultural group in Jordan, where they live mostly in the desert areas in the southern and eastern parts of the country.

■ **EXAMINE** the title of this essay, "Between Two Worlds." How do you think it would feel—or how does it feel—to be a child caught between different cultures, ethnic groups, or races of your family? How do Walker and Alphonse in the preceding selections deal with living between different worlds? How do you predict Abu-Jaber will handle her own dual heritage?

■ **EXAMINE** the Jordanian terms—many of which relate to food—that Abu-Jaber uses in her essay. *Mensaf* (paragraph 2) is Jordanian lamb stew, and *baklava* (paragraph 3) is a rich, sweet pastry made from layers of phyllo dough sweetened with honey or syrup and filled with chopped nuts. The term *yella imshee* [*yalla imshee*] (paragraph 11) means "Let's go," and the words *jellabia* (paragraph 4) and *min eedi* (paragraph 6) are defined in the context of the essay.

■ **WRITE** a journal entry in which you describe your culture's, specifically your own family's, eating rituals. Is there anything special or unusual about your customs?

AS YOU READ

Underline words, phrases, and passages that specifically describe Jordanian Bedouin customs. Identify the point at which Abu-Jaber's attitude toward these customs changes.

■ ■ ■

My father's Bedouin family ate standing up at a communal tray ₁ under a tent thundering with wind. I first joined their outdoor feasts when I was 7. He transplanted our family from Syracuse, New York, back to his homeland, Jordan, intending it to be a permanent move, a homecoming. But my sisters and I had been growing up in the States: We were softies, familiar only with a watered down, Americanized version of Arab traditions. Dad thought he'd raised us to be native Jordanians, but there were all sorts of surprises awaiting us in this new world—like learning to eat with our hands.

My mouth and fingers stung from the heat of the food for the first few ₂ weeks in Jordan. I was instructed to eat the *mensaf* quickly—as soon as the meat, bread and steaming, rich, oniony yogurt sauce were poured from the pot to the tray. I'd often watched my father and his brothers eat with their hands, while my mother, sisters and I ate mostly with a knife and fork. It felt exciting and adventurous to cross over to my father's side, like taking on a new world of eating. There was an art to scooping the lamb, rice, and bread into the hand, palming it to the fingertips and pushing the fragrant morsel into the mouth. I learned to eat from the section of the communal tray before me—no roaming or second-guessing allowed. Everyone said, "Thanks be to God," upon finishing—grace coming after the meal instead of before: the gratitude of a full stomach.

There were other changes: fresh mint in the tea; marble courtyards and ₃ birds kept outside in wire cages; a ripe, dusky, desert-dry sun. Jordan was a lovely, sensuous world to turn a child loose in, but the novelty didn't last. After a year, Dad gave up on his project of making us Arabs. The truth was, America already had a grip on his heart, and we returned to the United States. Suddenly, though, cutlery seemed cumbersome. I wondered aloud if it was truly possible to enjoy your food if you couldn't touch it. My mother, who is Anglo-American, firmly reminded me that we were home again and silverware was part of the deal. She'd been a good sport about mastering Arabic and learning to make baklava, but we were back on her turf now. To my child's mind, it followed a sort of cosmic reasoning: In Jordan, we did it Dad's way; in Mom's country, we followed Mom's rules.

So it was a pleasure when, a couple of years later, my forkless Uncle Saeed ₄ moved his entire family—wife, kids and grandkids—from Jordan to a big, noisy house on the other side of Syracuse. Saeed was actually a distant relation, a relative of someone's cousin, but we all called him Uncle Saeed to show respect. He was "a real, old-time Bedouin," according to my dad—a traditionalist and a throwback to the days of the refined nomad, his ancient codes of behavior governing everything, including the proper welcoming of guests and the correct slaughtering of goats. He might have worn slacks while cruising around town in his Crown Victoria, but as soon as he got home, he'd exchange the confining Western clothes for his white *jellabia*, a robelike shift with a long, swishing skirt.

Our families visited each other constantly, and the elders always prepared mensaf for our gatherings. This was Uncle Saeed's favorite dish, so it had to be everyone's favorite. It reminded Dad and his family of their long-lost home; it was the closest any of them could come not only to that place but also to a time when the family squeezed together at one table—Dad, his seven brothers and one sister and their exhausted parents. All of them eating hot food from one big, round tray: What greater intimacy could they ask for? It was a little slice of Jordan in snowy Syracuse.

Uncle Saeed also adhered to the custom of expressing affection by feeding his nearest and dearest, young and old, *min eedi*, meaning "from my hand." Growing up in the warm bath of my family's adoration, I was accustomed to being treated as community property. My Arab relatives routinely fretted over and finger-combed my hair, examined my teeth and tested my reflexes. Accepting food from their fingertips was a natural extension of this physical ownership. For my father, this meant picking up the crispy bits of chicken from the bottom of the pan and feeding us shreds with the tips of his fingers. But for Uncle Saeed, it meant trying to stuff us full of the same great mouthfuls he was accustomed to. For him, the equation was simple: The more food you pour into children and the more you love them, the bigger and stronger they'll grow.

Before long, I dreaded weekly meals with my boisterous uncle. I hated being called to his side, where, with one arm scooped around my narrow shoulders, he'd shape a dumplinglike palmful of meat and rice intended especially for me. The size of it was overwhelming. Breathing was difficult with my mouth filled to capacity; my eyes filled and my head swam as I struggled to gulp it all down. But then, at least, I was free of the awful min eedi—until the next family gathering.

It never occurred to me that there was anything optional about Uncle Saeed's offerings. They were simply part of our ritual. To refuse seemed like refusing love, the nutrient of life itself. But one day when I was 11 or 12, I overheard my mom on the phone with one of my American aunts complaining: "I'm really sick of it. I don't want all that food in my mouth or my kids'. It's gross!" Uncle Saeed often beckoned my mother to his side, feeding her in the same joshing, affectionate way he fed the younger generation. This was normal, right? Caught between cultures, I wasn't sure. My mother was a soft-spoken only child who had married into a sprawling, boisterous Arabic clan, and sometimes the sheer chaos they created seemed to weigh on her.

A week or two later, my mom took me aside. "Listen," she said, her 9
eyes intent. "Do you like it when Uncle Saeed offers you food?" I really
had to consider my answer. For me, anything to do with the family had
never been a matter of like or dislike. The min eedi ritual was a fact of
existence, like the color of the sky. I dreaded the moment when Saeed
brandished a great heaping palm in my direction, but I couldn't explain
exactly why. I wasn't well-versed on subjects such as control, boundaries
or intrusion. I thought it was my job as a child to obey and fatten up and
be respectful to everyone, just as I knew I'd be expected to get married and
nurture a family and be respectful some more when I grew up.

So when my mother asked her impossible question, I had no idea how 10
to answer it. Besides, the adults in my family rarely conferred with the children. Unaccustomed to being consulted for my opinions, I said, honestly,
"I don't know."

The next time our families gathered for dinner, something had shifted. My 11
mom sat moodily through the long meal, eating little, talking less, her eyes
set on some internal middle distance. The dreaded min eedi moment arrived midway through the dinner. Uncle Saeed fed whichever of his children who happened to be sitting closest to him at the table; then his eyes
lit on me: "Diana, *yella, imshee!*" He held up a great bolus of food.

Suddenly I felt my mother's restraining hand on my arm. She shook her 12
head firmly and looked Uncle Saeed in the eye. "No," she said, her voice
smooth as stone.

It's very possible that up until that day in his 73rd year, my Uncle 13
Saeed had never heard the word *no* from a woman. I remember that a fris-
son of astonishment seemed to pass through his neck and shoulders, and
his eyes refocused, as if he were having trouble figuring out who had spoken. Then his mouth opened in the shape of a great laugh as he asked,
"How else can I fatten her up?"

"I don't want my daughters fattened up."   14

I was relieved. But now when I look back on the day my mother said 15
no to Uncle Saeed, I remember a sense of underlying grief in that room as
well. This was the very moment when my family started mourning an inevitable loss, of connection to the world we'd all left, of our heritage. Uncle
Saeed, who from what I could tell had never before really seen me as an
individual—as anything apart from a member of a mass of children—
allowed his gaze to sharpen. He glanced from me to my defiant mother.
"OK," he said mildly. In his world, it was undignified to argue or become
angry with a woman.

Not long after that, Uncle Saeed moved his family back to Jordan. 16
America was too cold, he told my dad, as if Syracuse represented the entire
nation, as if winters in Jordan weren't also sharp and windy and biting.
I would never again stand under my uncle's arm and be fed too much
food. At the time, I felt a twinge of guilty relief at being freed from this
burden: There was no pleasure in eating without having any say in the

matter. But, in her own reserved and determined way, my mother had demonstrated that I should have control over my own body and what went into it. Much later, I came to understand that having jurisdiction over myself would make everything else possible in life. Respect for others was important, but self-respect would fuel important decisions about my place in the world. In this sense, I am my mother's daughter.

Still, I was very sorry to see my uncle go. It was hard for me to realize 17 that some choices aren't simple or easy to make—like the choice between being fed by a loving hand and doing it for myself. But, of course, some of the hardest decisions are the most important ones of all.

■ ■ ■

AFTER YOU READ

■ **THINK** about Abu-Jaber's changing feelings toward Jordanian eating rituals. How does she come to feel about these customs when she first visits the "lovely, sensuous world" of Jordan with her family? At what point do her feelings begin to change? Describe her confusion about these changing feelings. How and why does her mother stop Uncle Saeed from using the *min eedi* ritual with Abu-Jaber? Do you think that Abu-Jaber's mother—and Abu Jaber herself—made the right decisions? Explain.

■ **EXAMINE** paragraph 16. What did Abu-Jaber's mother's actions demonstrate about her desires for her daughter's life? What did Abu-Jaber learn about herself and what is important for her?

■ **WRITE** an essay about your family's (or your culture's) eating customs, perhaps focusing on one special meal or custom. Be sure to show the significance of the custom(s) you are describing on you and/or on family or cultural life.

Living in Two Worlds

■ ■ ■

MARCUS MABRY

Award-winning journalist Marcus Mabry was a correspondent for *Newsweek* for nineteen years, the last five of which he was chief of correspondents. In July 2007 he became the international business editor of *The New York Times*. He is the author of *Twice as Good: Condoleezza Rice and Her Path to Power* (2008) as well as *White Bucks and Black-eyed Peas: Coming of Age Black in White America* (1995), a memoir of his experiences growing up poor in a black section of Trenton, New Jersey, before winning a scholarship to a prep school. The following essay about a trip from Stanford University back to his home in New Jersey—a journey that he describes as "travel between the universes of poverty and affluence"—was published in *Newsweek* as part of its "Newsweek on Campus" series.

BEFORE YOU READ

■ **THINK** about the transitions you faced when you started college. Are transitions also required when you return to your previous life?

■ **EXAMINE** the title of this essay. How many different worlds do you live in, and how do these worlds differ from one another?

■ **EXAMINE** also paragraphs 1–3 of the essay, which introduce you to the contrasts in the essay. Whereas the previous essays by Walker, Alphonse, and Abu-Jaber focus on different racial or cultural heritages, Mabry is concerned here with differences in class and lifestyle represented by his wealthy college friends and his poor family.

■ **EXAMINE** also the word *tenacity* (paragraph 11), which means "persistent, holding firmly." How much tenacity do you think Mabry needs to finish his college degree while remaining aware of his family's poverty?

■ **WRITE** a journal entry comparing and contrasting your life as a college student with your life before you started college or your life in two different economic situations.

AS YOU READ

Indicate in the margin beside each paragraph whether it focuses on Mabry's experiences at home or at school.

■ ■ ■

A round, green cardboard sign hangs from a string proclaiming, 1
"We built a proud new feeling," the slogan of a local supermarket. It is a souvenir from one of my brother's last jobs. In addition
to being a bagger, he's worked at a fast-food restaurant, a gas station, a
garage and a textile factory. Now, in the icy clutches of the Northeastern
winter, he is unemployed. He will soon be a father. He is 19 years old.

In mid-December I was at Stanford, among the palm trees and weighty 2
chore[s] of academe. And all I wanted to do was get out. I joined the rest
of the undergrads in a chorus of excitement, singing the praises of Christmas break. No classes, no midterms, no finals ... and no freshmen! (I'm a
resident assistant.) Awesome! I was looking forward to escaping. I never
gave a thought to what I was escaping to.

Once I got home to New Jersey, reality returned. My dreaded fresh- 3
men had been replaced by unemployed relatives; badgering professors had
been replaced by hard-working single mothers; and cold classrooms by di-
lapidated bedrooms and kitchens. The room in which the "proud new feeling" sign hung contained the belongings of myself, my mom and my
brother. But for these two weeks it was mine. They slept downstairs on
couches.

Most students who travel between the universes of poverty and afflu- 4
ence during breaks experience similar conditions, as well as the guilt, the
helplessness and, sometimes, the embarrassment associated with them.
Our friends are willing to listen, but most of them are unable to imagine
the pain of the impoverished lives that we see every six months. Each time
I return home I feel further away from the realities of poverty in America
and more ashamed that they are allowed to persist. What frightens me
most is not that the American socio-economic system permits poverty to
continue, but that by participating in that system I share some of the
blame.

Last year I lived in an on-campus apartment, with a (relatively) mod- 5
ern bathroom, kitchen and two bedrooms. Using summer earnings, I added
some expensive prints, a potted palm and some other plants, making the
place look like the more-than-humble abode of a New York City Yuppie.
I gave dinner parties, even a *soirée française*.

For my roommate, a doctor's son, this kind of life was nothing ex- 6
traordinary. But my mom was struggling to provide a life for herself and
my brother. In addition to working 24-hour-a-day cases as a practical
nurse, she was trying to ensure that my brother would graduate from
high school and have a decent life. She knew that she had to compete for
his attention with drugs and other potentially dangerous things that can
look attractive to a young man when he sees no better future.

Living in my grandmother's house this Christmas break restored all the 7
forgotten, and the never acknowledged, guilt. I had gone to boarding
school on a full scholarship since the ninth grade, so being away from poverty was not new. But my own growing affluence has increased my

distance. My friends say that I should not feel guilty: what could I do substantially for my family at this age, they ask. Even though I know that education is the right thing to do, I can't help but feel, sometimes, that I have it too good. There is no reason that I deserve security and warmth, while my brother has to cope with potential unemployment and prejudice. I, too, encounter prejudice, but it is softened by my status as a student in an affluent and intellectual community.

More than my sense of guilt, my sense of helplessness increases each 8 time I return home. As my success leads me further away for longer periods of time, poverty becomes harder to conceptualize and feels that much more oppressive when I visit with it. The first night of break, I lay in our bedroom, on a couch that let out into a bed that took up the whole room, except for a space heater. It was a little hard to sleep because the springs from the couch stuck through at inconvenient spots. But it would have been impossible to sleep anyway because of the groans coming from my grandmother's room next door. Only in her early 60s, she suffers from many chronic diseases and couldn't help but moan, then pray aloud, then moan, then pray aloud.

This wrenching of my heart was interrupted by the 3 A.M. entry of a 9 relative who had been allowed to stay at the house despite rowdy behavior and threats toward the family in the past. As he came into the house, he slammed the door, and his heavy steps shook the second floor as he stomped into my grandmother's room to take his place, at the foot of her bed. There he slept, without blankets on a bare mattress. This was the first night. Later in the vacation, a Christmas turkey and a Christmas ham were stolen from my aunt's refrigerator on Christmas Eve. We think the thief was a relative. My mom and I decided not to exchange gifts that year because it just didn't seem festive.

A few days after New Year's I returned to California. The Northeast 10 was soon hit by a blizzard. They were there, and I was here. That was the way it had to be, for now. I haven't forgotten; the ache of knowing their suffering is always there. It has to be kept deep down, or I can't find the logic in studying and partying while people, my people, are being killed by poverty. Ironically, success drives me away from those I most want to help by getting an education.

Somewhere in the midst of all that misery, my family has built within 11 me, "a proud feeling." As I travel between the two worlds it becomes harder to remember just how proud I should be—not just because of where I have come from and where I am going, but because of where they are. The fact that they survive in the world in which they live is something to be very proud of, indeed. It inspires within me a sense of tenacity and accomplishment that I hope every college graduate will someday possess.

■   ■   ■

AFTER YOU READ

■ **THINK** about how this experience of going back and forth between two worlds has shaped the person Mabry has become. In your opinion, which world has influenced him more? Explain.

■ **EXAMINE** the number of paragraphs that focus on New Jersey and those that focus on Stanford. Which place does Mabry describe in more detail? Why?

■ **EXAMINE** also the following statement, which is found in paragraph 10:

"Ironically, success drives me away from those I most want to help by getting an education."

Explain what you think Mabry means by this statement. Do you agree or disagree with him? Why?

■ **WRITE** an essay comparing and contrasting two different "worlds" in which you live or between which you travel. (For instruction about writing comparison and contrast essays, see Lesson 7 on the *Interactions*, eighth edition, student website at www.cengagebrain.com.)

FOCUS ON NARRATION

The Jacket

■ ■ ■

GARY SOTO

Gary Soto, a prolific writer and former university professor, is perhaps most critically acclaimed for his poetry. He received the Award of the International Poetry Forum in 1976 for his book-length poem *The Elements of San Joaquin,* and his collections *Black Hair* has been praised for its portrayal of Soto's Mexican American childhood. Soto has written a number of young adult novels and is also well known for his collections of autobiographical essays, including *Living Up the Street* (1985), *Small Faces* (1986), and *The Effects of Knut Hamsun on a Fresno Boy* (2000). In this narrative essay from *Small Faces,* he recounts his experience with an extremely ugly jacket he was forced to wear when he was a child and the effects, both real and imagined, of this jacket on his life.

BEFORE YOU READ

■ **THINK** about the experience of wearing some article of clothing that you did not like when you were a child and about how wearing this garment made you feel. Do the clothes you wear still affect the way you feel about yourself on a particular day or occasion?

■ **EXAMINE** the first sentence of this essay: "My clothes have failed me." What do you think Soto means by this statement? What are different ways that clothes can "fail" someone? In the remainder of his essay, Soto narrates the events that led him to this general impression or conclusion.

■ **WRITE** in your journal a description of some garment you remember wearing as a child, and tell how that garment made you feel.

AS YOU READ

Try to determine the thesis of Soto's essay by looking for the answer to why his jacket "failed" him and considering whether his family's economic situation contributed to this failure and thus to his low self-esteem.

■   ■   ■

My clothes have failed me. I remember the green coat that I wore   1
in fifth and sixth grades when you either danced like a champ
or pressed yourself against a greasy wall, bitter as a penny toward the happy couples.

When I needed a new jacket and my mother asked what kind I wanted,   2
I described something like bikers wear: black leather and silver studs with
enough belts to hold down a small town. We were in the kitchen, steam on
the windows from her cooking. She listened so long while stirring dinner that
I thought she understood for sure the kind I wanted. The next day when I got
home from school, I discovered draped on my bedpost a jacket the color of
day-old guacamole. I threw my books on the bed and approached the jacket
slowly, as if it were a stranger whose hand I had to shake. I touched the vinyl
sleeve, the collar, and peeked at the mustard-colored lining.

From the kitchen mother yelled that my jacket was in the closet. I closed   3
the door to her voice and pulled at the rack of clothes in the closet, hoping the
jacket on the bedpost wasn't for me but my mean brother. No luck. I gave up.
From my bed, I stared at the jacket. I wanted to cry because it was so ugly and
so big that I knew I'd have to wear it a long time. I was a small kid, thin as a
young tree, and it would be years before I'd have a new one. I stared at the
jacket, like an enemy, thinking bad things before I took off my old jacket
whose sleeves climbed halfway to my elbow.

I put the big jacket on. I zipped it up and down several times, and   4
rolled the cuffs up so they didn't cover my hands. I put my hands in the
pockets and flapped the jacket like a bird's wings. I stood in front of the
mirror, full face, then profile, and then looked over my shoulder as if
someone had called me. I sat on the bed, stood against the bed, and
combed my hair to see what I would look like doing something natural.
I looked ugly. I threw it on my brother's bed and looked at it for a long
time before I slipped it on and went out to the backyard, smiling a "thank
you" to my mom as I passed her in the kitchen. With my hands in my pockets
I kicked a ball against the fence, and then climbed it to sit looking into the
alley. I hurled orange peels at the mouth of an open garbage can and when
the peels were gone I watched the white puffs of my breath thin to nothing.

I jumped down, hands in my pockets, and in the backyard on my knees   5
I teased my dog, Brownie, by swooping my arms while making bird calls. He
jumped at me and missed. He jumped again and again, until a tooth sunk
deep, ripping an L-shaped tear on my left sleeve. I pushed Brownie away to
study the tear as I would a cut on my arm. There was no blood, only a few
loose pieces of fuzz. Damn dog, I thought, and pushed him away hard when
he tried to bite again. I got up from my knees and went to my bedroom to sit
with my jacket on my lap, with the lights out.

That was the first afternoon with my new jacket. The next day I wore   6
it to sixth grade and got a D on a math quiz. During the morning recess
Frankie T., the playground terrorist, pushed me to the ground and told me
to stay there until recess was over. My best friend, Steve Negrete, ate an
apple while looking at me, and the girls turned away to whisper on the

monkey bars. The teachers were no help: they looked my way and talked about how foolish I looked in my new jacket. I saw their heads bob with laughter, their hands half-covering their mouths.

Even though it was cold, I took off the jacket during lunch and played kick- 7
ball in a thin shirt, my arms feeling like braille from goose bumps. But when I returned to class I slipped the jacket on and shivered until I was warm. I sat on my hands, heating them up, while my teeth chattered like a cup of crooked dice. Finally warm, I slid out of the jacket but a few minutes later put it back on when the fire bell rang. We paraded out into the yard where we, the sixth graders, walked past all the other grades to stand against the back fence. Everybody saw me. Although they didn't say out loud, "Man, that's ugly," I heard the buzz-buzz of gossip and even laughter that I knew was meant for me.

And so I went, in my guacamole jacket. So embarrassed, so hurt, 8
I couldn't even do my homework. I received Cs on quizzes, and forgot the state capitals and the rivers of South America, our friendly neighbor. Even the girls who had been friendly blew away like loose flowers to follow the boys in neat jackets.

I wore that thing for three years until the sleeves grew short and my 9
forearms stuck out like the necks of turtles. All during that time no love came to me—no little dark girl in a Sunday dress she wore on Monday. At lunchtime I stayed with the ugly boys who leaned against the chainlink fence and looked around with propellers of grass spinning in our mouths. We saw girls walk by alone, saw couples, hand in hand, their heads like bookends pressing air together. We saw them and spun our propellers so fast our faces were blurs.

I blame that jacket for those bad years. I blame my mother for her bad 10
taste and her cheap ways. It was a sad time for the heart. With a friend I spent my sixth-grade year in a tree in the alley waiting for something good to happen to me in that jacket, which had become the ugly brother who tagged along wherever I went. And it was about that time that I began to grow. My chest puffed up with muscle and, strangely, a few more ribs. Even my hands, those fleshy hammers, showed bravely through the cuffs, the fingers already hardening for the coming fights. But that L-shaped rip on the left sleeve got bigger; bits of stuffing coughed out from its wound after a hard day of play. I finally scotch-taped it closed, but in rain or cold weather the tape peeled off like a scab and more stuffing fell out until that sleeve shriveled into a palsied arm. That winter the elbows began to crack and whole chunks of green began to fall off. I showed the cracks to my mother, who always seemed to be at the stove with steamed-up glasses, and she said that there were children in Mexico who would love that jacket. I told her that this was America and yelled that Debbie, my sister, didn't have a jacket like mine. I ran outside, ready to cry, and climbed the tree by the alley to think bad thoughts and watch my breath puff white and disappear.

But whole pieces still casually flew off my jacket when I played hard, 11
read quietly, or took vicious spelling tests at school. When it became so spotted that my brother began to call me "camouflage," I flung it over the fence into the alley. Later, however, I swiped the jacket off the ground and went inside to drape it across my lap and mope.

I was called to dinner: steam silvered my mother's glasses as she said   12
grace; my brother and sister with their heads bowed made ugly faces at
their glasses of powdered milk. I gagged too, but eagerly ate big rips of
buttered tortilla that held scooped up beans. Finished, I went outside with
my jacket across my arm. It was a cold sky. The faces of clouds were piled
up, hurting. I climbed the fence, jumping down with a grunt. I started up
the alley and soon slipped into my jacket, that green ugly brother who
breathed over my shoulder that day and ever since.

■ ■ ■

AFTER YOU READ

■ **THINK** about Soto's thesis and write it in your own words. Certainly the
opening sentence forms part of this thesis, but Soto also shows how his
experience with his jacket affected his self-concept. Do you think the
jacket caused other people to shun him or think less of him, as he believed? Or did Soto simply blame the jacket for problems he had during
those years? (As these questions suggest, Soto's narrative essay also has
elements of cause and effect.)

■ **EXAMINE** the following definition of the word *symbol*:

Symbol: One that represents something else by association, resemblance, or
convention, especially a material object representing something invisible. (*The American Heritage College Dictionary,* 4th ed. Boston:
Houghton Mifflin, 2002)

The jacket in Soto's story functions as a symbol, representing something
more than simply an article of clothing? What do you think it
represents?

■ **EXAMINE** also Soto's essay with a group of your classmates to determine whether it has each of the four qualities of a good narrative or
story: (1) high interest, (2) a clear chronological organization, (3) effective descriptive details, and (4) a stated or suggested thesis or general
impression. First, was the story interesting to you? If so, identify the
most interesting elements. Then, identify and list the major chronological events and determine if this organization is clear. Next, circle particularly effective details—those that give facts or appeal to your senses.
Finally, identify Soto's general impression or thesis.

■ **WRITE** an essay narrating an experience that made you feel particularly
bad or particularly good. Like Soto, you may want to tell the story of an
object or piece of clothing that was important to you. In either case, include in your personal narrative the four qualities listed in the last section. (For help with writing narratives, see Lesson 1 of the *Interactions,*
eighth edition, student website at www.cengagebrain.com.)

On Being 17, Bright, and Unable to Read

■ ■ ■

DAVID RAYMOND

When David Raymond wrote this essay, he was a high school student in Connecticut. The essay, which tells of Raymond's frustrations because he could not read, was published in *The New York Times*. In this essay he describes what it is like to have a learning disability and to experience the low self-esteem that can result from such a disability.

BEFORE YOU READ

■ **THINK** about how you feel when you do not know the correct answer to a question a teacher asks you or cannot do what a teacher expects you to do.

■ **EXAMINE** the word *dyslexia* (paragraph 2). The word has two parts: *dys-* is a prefix meaning abnormal or impaired; *lexia* comes from a Greek word (*lexis*), meaning speech. However, the word *dyslexia* means an impairment of the ability to read rather than to talk.

■ **WRITE** in your journal a definition of the word *dumb*. Can you think of more than one definition? Which usage do you hear most often? Is the word often used cruelly?

AS YOU READ

Notice the reaction of Raymond's parents and teachers to his learning disability. Identify these reactions by underlining the passages and writing the word *parents* or *teachers* in the margins.

■ ■ ■

One day a substitute teacher picked me to read aloud from the textbook. When I told her "No, thank you," she came unhinged. She thought I was acting smart, and told me so. I kept calm, and that got her madder and madder. We must have spent 10 minutes trying to solve the problem, and finally she got so red in the face I thought she'd blow up. She told me she'd see me after class.

Maybe someone like me was a new thing for that teacher. But she wasn't new to me. I've been through scenes like that all my life. You see, even though I'm 17 and a junior in high school, I can't read because I have dyslexia. I'm told I read "at a fourth-grade level," but from where I sit, that's not reading. You can't know what that means unless you've been there. It's not easy to tell how it feels when you can't read your homework assignments or the newspaper or a menu in a restaurant or even notes from your own friends.

My family began to suspect I was having problems almost from the first day I started school. My father says my early years in school were the worst years of his life. They weren't so good for me, either. As I look back on it now, I can't find the words to express how bad it really was. I wanted to die. I'd come home from school screaming, "I'm dumb. I'm dumb—I wish I were dead!"   3

I guess I couldn't read anything at all then—not even my own name— and they tell me I didn't talk as good as other kids. But what I remember about those days is that I couldn't throw a ball where it was supposed to go, I couldn't learn to swim, and I wouldn't learn to ride a bike, because no matter what anyone told me, I knew I'd fail.   4

Sometimes my teachers would try to be encouraging. When I couldn't read the words on the board they'd say, "Come on, David, you know that word." Only I didn't. And it was embarrassing. I just felt dumb. And dumb was how the kids treated me. They'd make fun of me every chance they got, asking me to spell "cat" or something like that. Even if I knew how to spell it, I wouldn't; they'd only give me another word. Anyway, it was awful, because more than anything I wanted friends. On my birthday when I blew out the candles I didn't wish I could learn to read; what I wished for was that the kids would like me.   5

With the bad reports coming from school, and with me moaning about wanting to die and how everybody hated me, my parents began looking for help. That's when the testing started. The school tested me, the child-guidance center tested me, private psychiatrists tested me. Everybody knew something was wrong—especially me.   6

It didn't help much when they stuck a fancy name onto it. I couldn't pronounce it then—I was only in second grade—and I was ashamed to talk about it. Now it rolls off my tongue, because I've been living with it for a lot of years—dyslexia.   7

All through elementary school it wasn't easy. I was always having to do things that were "different," things the other kids didn't have to do. I had to go to a child psychiatrist, for instance.   8

One summer my family forced me to go to a camp for children with reading problems. I had a good time. I met a lot of kids who couldn't read and somehow that helped. The director of the camp said I had a higher I.Q. than 90 percent of the population. I didn't believe him.   9

About the worst thing I had to do in fifth and sixth grade was to go to a special education class in another school in our town. A bus picked me up, and I didn't like that at all. The bus also picked up emotionally disturbed kids ... I was always worried that someone I knew would see me on that bus. It was a relief to go to a regular junior high school.   10

Life began to change a little for me then, because I began to feel better 11
about myself. I found the teachers cared; they had meetings about me and
I worked harder for them for a while. I began to work on the potter's wheel,
making vases and pots that the teachers said were pretty good. Also, I got a
letter for being on the track team. I could always run pretty fast.

At high school the teachers are good and everyone is trying to help me. 12
I've gotten honors some marking periods and I've won a letter on the
cross-country team. Next quarter I think the school might hold a show of
my pottery. I've got some friends. But there are still some embarrassing
times. For instance, every time there is writing in class, I get up and go to
the special education room. Kids ask me where I go all the time. Sometimes
I say, "to Mars."

Homework is a real problem. During free periods in school I go into 13
the special ed room and staff members read assignments to me. When I get
home my mother reads to me. Sometimes she reads an assignment into a
tape recorder, and then I go into my room and listen to it. If we have a
novel or something like that to read, she reads it out loud to me. Then
I sit down with her and we do the assignment. She'll write, while I talk
my answers to her. Lately I've taken to dictating into a tape recorder, and
then someone—my father, a private tutor or my mother—types up what
I've dictated. Whatever homework I do takes someone else's time, too.
That makes me feel bad.

We had a big meeting in school the other day—eight of us, four from 14
the guidance department, my private tutor, my parents and me. The subject
was me. I said I wanted to go to college, and they told me about colleges
that have facilities and staff to handle people like me. That's nice to hear.

As for what happens after college, I don't know and I'm worried about 15
that. How can I make a living if I can't read? Who will hire me? How will
I fill out the application form? The only thing that gives me any courage is
the fact that I've learned about well-known people who couldn't read or
had other problems and still made it. Like Albert Einstein, who didn't
talk until he was 4 and flunked math. Like Leonardo de Vinci, who everyone seems to think had dyslexia.

I've told this story because maybe some teacher will read it and go easy 16
on a kid in the classroom who has what I've got. Or, maybe some parent
will stop nagging his kid, and stop calling him lazy. Maybe he's not lazy or
dumb. Maybe he just can't read and doesn't know what's wrong. Maybe
he's scared, like I was.

■   ■   ■

AFTER YOU READ

■ **THINK** about the source of Raymond's low self-esteem and compare it to the cause of Soto's low self-concept. In your opinion, which basic problem would be easier to deal with?

■ **THINK** also about Raymond's skill as a potter and his athletic ability. How did these successes improve his self-confidence?

■ **EXAMINE** Raymond's confession that he fears going to college. Do most people fear a new experience such as starting college? How does having a handicap of any kind make such experiences even more frightening? What fears do you have about college?

■ **WRITE** a paragraph or brief essay in which you discuss the effect of school performance on self-concept. Be sure you emphasize the cause and effect. (See Lesson 5 on the *Interactions* student website, available at www. cengagebrain.com, for instruction on cause-and-effect essays.)

The Need for Achievement

■   ■   ■

DOUGLAS A. BERNSTEIN

A professor of psychology at the University of Illinois at Urbana-Champaign, Douglas A. Bernstein has contributed to numerous psychology journals and to several books on psychology. The following selection is taken from his introductory psychology textbook, *Essentials of Psychology,* 5th ed. (2011).

BEFORE YOU READ

■ **THINK** about your own goals for achievement. What are your personal, college, and career goals? Do you think you have set worthwhile but realistic goals for yourself, or do you need to adjust some goals up or down?

■ **EXAMINE** the title of the selection "Need for Achievement." How great is your need for achievement? How much time and effort do you spend trying to achieve your goals? Do you need to work harder to achieve some of your goals? Explain.

■ **EXAMINE** also the organization of the selection. Notice that, like many textbook selections, Bernstein puts his main idea in his introduction and then restates this idea in a slightly different way in his conclusion. Notice also that he divides the content of the selection into sections with subtitles to help guide your reading.

■ **WRITE** a journal entry with three lists, one each identifying your primary personal, college, and career goals.

AS YOU READ

Underline words, phrases, and sentences that suggest Bernstein's thesis, or main idea.

■   ■   ■

Many athletes who already hold world records still train intensely; many people who have built multimillion-dollar businesses still work fourteen-hour days. What motivates these people? One answer is **achievement motivation,** or the *need for achievement* (Murray, 1938). People with high achievement motivation seek to master tasks—such as sports, business ventures, occupational skills, 1 intellectual puzzles, or artistic creation—and feel intense satisfaction from doing so. They work hard at striving for excellence, enjoy themselves in the process, and take great pride in achieving at a high level.

INDIVIDUAL DIFFERENCES

How do people with strong achievement motivation differ from others? To find out, researchers gave children a test to measure their need for achievement and then asked them to play a ring-toss game. Most of the children who scored low on the need-for-achievement test stood either so close to the ring-toss target that they couldn't fail or so far away that they could not succeed. In contrast, children scoring high on the need-for-achievement test stood at a moderate distance from the target, making the game challenging but not impossible (McClelland, 1958).

Experiments with adults and children suggest that people with high achievement needs tend to set challenging but realistic goals. They actively seek success, take risks when necessary, can wait for rewards, and are intensely satisfied when they do well (Mayer & Sutton, 1996). Yet if they feel they have tried their best, people with high achievement motivation are not too upset by failure (Winter, 1996). Indeed, there is some evidence that the differing emotions—such as anticipation versus worry—that accompany the efforts of people with high and low achievement motivation can affect how successful those efforts will be (Pekrun, Elliot, & Maier, 2009).

Differences in achievement motivation also appear in the kinds of goals people seek in achievement-related situations (Molden & Dweck, 2000). Some tend to adopt *learning goals*. When they play golf, take piano lessons, work at problems, go to school, and engage in other achievement-oriented activities, they do so mainly to get better at these activities. They realize that they may not yet have the skills necessary to achieve at a high level, so they tend to learn by watching others and to struggle with problems on their own rather than asking for help (Mayer & Sutton, 1996). When they do seek help, people with learning goals are likely to ask for explanations, hints, and other forms of task-related information, not for quick, easy answers that remove the challenge from the situation. In contrast, people who adopt *performance goals* are usually more concerned with demonstrating the competence they believe they already possess. They tend to seek information about how well they have performed compared with others rather than about how to improve their performance (Butler, 1998). When they seek help, it is usually to ask for the "right answer" rather than for tips on how to find the answer themselves. Because their primary goal is to display competence, people with performance goals tend to avoid new challenges if they are not confident that they will be successful, and they tend to quit in response to failure (Grant & Dweck, 2003; Weiner, 1980). Those with learning goals tend to be more persistent and less upset when they don't immediately perform well (Niiya, Crocker, & Bartmess, 2004).

DEVELOPMENT OF ACHIEVEMENT MOTIVATION

Achievement motivation develops in early childhood under the influence of   5
both genetic and environmental factors. Children inherit general behavioral
tendencies such as impulsiveness and emotionality, and these tendencies
may support or undermine the development of achievement motivation.
The motivation to achieve is also shaped by what children learn from
watching and listening to others, especially their parents. Evidence for the
influence of parental teachings about achievement comes from a study in
which young boys were given a task so difficult that they were sure to
fail. Fathers whose sons scored low on achievement motivation tests often
became annoyed as they watched their boys work on the task, discouraged
them from continuing, and interfered or even completed the task themselves (Rosen & D'Andrade, 1959). A much different response pattern
emerged among parents of children who scored high on tests of achievement motivation. Those parents tended to (1) encourage the child to try
difficult tasks, especially new ones; (2) give praise and other rewards for
success; [and] (3) encourage the child to go on to the next, more difficult
challenge (McClelland, 1958). Parents' influence on achievement reaches
well beyond their physical presence. Research with adults shows that even
the slightest cues that bring a parent to mind can boost some people's efforts to achieve a goal (Shah, 2003) and that college students—especially
those who have learning goals—feel closer to their parents while taking
exams (Moller et al., 2008).

More general cultural influences also affect the development of achieve-   6
ment motivation. Subtle messages about a culture's view of the importance
and value of achievement often appear in the books children read, the stories
they hear, and the programs they see on television. Does the story's main
character work hard and overcome obstacles, thus creating expectations of a
payoff for persistence? Or does a lazy main character drift aimlessly and then
win the lottery, suggesting that rewards come randomly, regardless of effort?
And if the main character succeeds, is it the result of personal effort, as is typical of stories in individualist cultures? Or is success based on ties to a cooper-
ative and supportive group, as is typical of stories in collectivist cultures?
These themes appear to act as blueprints for reaching one's goals. It is not surprising, then, that ideas about achievement motivation differ from culture to
culture. In one study, individuals from Saudi Arabia and from the United
States were asked to comment on short stories describing people succeeding
at various tasks. Saudis tended to see the people in the stories as having succeeded because of the help they got from others, whereas Americans tended to
attribute success to the internal characteristics of each story's main character
(Zahrani & Kaplowitz, 1993).

In short, achievement motivation is strongly influenced by social and   7
cultural learning experiences and by the beliefs about oneself that these experiences help create. People who come to believe in their ability to achieve
are more likely to do so than those who expect to fail (Dweck, 1998;
Greven et al., 2009; Wigfield & Eccles, 2000).

REFERENCES

Butler, R. (1998). Information seeking and achievement motivation in middle childhood and adolescence: The role of conceptions of ability. *Developmental Psychology, 35,* 146–163.

Dweck, C. S. (1998). The development of early self-conceptions: Their relevance for motivational processes. In J. Heckhausen & C. S. Dwech (Eds.), *Motivation and self-regulation across the life span.* New York: Cambridge University Press.

Grant, H., & Dweck, C. S. (2003). Clarifying achievement goals and their impact. *Journal of Personality and Social Psychology, 85,* 541–553.

Greven, C. U., Harlarr, N., Kovas, Y., Chamorro-Premuzic, T, & Plomin, R. (2009). More than just IG: School achievement I predicted by self-perceived abilities—but for genetic rather than environmental reasons. *Psychological Science, 20,* 753–762.

Mayer, F. S., & Sutton, K. (1996). *Personality: An integrative approach.* Upper Saddle River, NJ: Prentice-Hall.

McClelland, D. C. (1958). Risk-taking in children with high and low need for achievement. In J. W. Atkinson (Ed.), *Motives in fantasy, action, and society* (pp. 306–329). Princeton, NJ: Van Nostrand.

Molden, D. C., & Dweck, C. S. (2000). Meaning and motivation. In C. Sansone & J. M. Harackiewicz (Eds.). *Intrinsic and extrinsic motivation: The search for optimal motivation and performance.* San Diego: Academic Press.

Moller, A. C., Elliot, A. J., & Friedman, R. (2008). When competence and love are at stake: Achievement goals and perceived closeness to parents in an achievement context. *Journal of Research in Personality, 42,* 1386–1391.

Murray, H. A. (1938). *Explorations in personality.* New York: Oxford University Press.

Niiya, Y., Crocker, J., and Bartmess, E. N. (2004). From vulnerability to resilience: Learning orientations buffer contingent self-esteem from failure. *Psychological Science, 15,* 801–805.

Pekrun, R., Elliot, A. J., & Maier, M. A. (2009). Achievement goals and achievement motivation: Testing a model of their joint relations with academic performance. *Journal of Educational Psychology, 10*(1), 115–135.

Rosen, B. C., & D'Andrade, R. (1959). The psychosocial origins of achievement motivation. *Sociometry, 22,* 188–218.

Shah, J. (2003). Automatic for the people: How representations of significant others implicitly affect goal pursuit. *Journal of Personality and Social Psychology, 84,* 661–681.

Weiner, B. (1980). *Human motivation.* New York: Holt, Rinehart & Winston.

Wigfield, A., & Eccles, J. S. (2000). Expectancy-value theory of achievement motivation. *Contemporary Educational Psychology, 24,* 68–81.

Winter, D. G. (1996). *Personality: Analysis and interpretation of lives.* New York: McGraw Hill.

Zahrani, S. S., & Kaplowitz, S. A. (1993). Attributional biases in individualistic and collectivist cultures: A comparison of Americans with Saudis. *Social Psychology Quarterly, 56*(3), 223–233.

■   ■   ■

AFTER YOU READ

■ **THINK** about Bernstein's main idea, writing his thesis in your own words. Pay particular attention to the introduction and the conclusion and to your underlining.

■ **EXAMINE** the section entitled "Individual Differences," which focuses on setting goals. What kind of goals do people with high achievement motivation set? Why is it important for individuals to set this kind of goals? What happens if individuals set goals that are way too high or way too low? Also, what is the difference between *learning goals* and *performance goals?* Which is usually better, and why?

■ **EXAMINE** also the section on "Development of Achievement Motivation." How do both societal—especially parental—and cultural influences affect the development of achievement motivation?

■ **EXAMINE** also citations to sources in the selection and the References section at the end. Bernstein uses American Psychological Association style. You will have the opportunity to see samples of Modern Language Association style on pp. 373–376 and 443–445. These models will help you in citing sources in your own essays.

■ **WRITE** an essay discussing your own goals. You may focus on personal, college, or career goals, but describe and evaluate each goal. Determine whether each goal is a learning goal or a performance goal, and consider also whether each goal is worthwhile and realistic. (For help with writing personal essays, see pages 128–133.)

Zero

■ ■ ■

PAUL LOGAN

Like many beginning freshmen, Paul Logan coasted through his first semester of college—as he had through high school. He soon discovered, however, that without self-discipline and what Douglas Bernstein calls "achievement motivation," he was doomed to failure. After a chance encounter with some old high school friends who were doing well in college, Logan decided to get serious and take control of his life by approaching college in a different way. Logan's narrative essay was published in *Making the Most of Your life: Eight Motivational Stories and Essays* (2008), edited by John Langan.

BEFORE YOU READ

■ **THINK** of your own first semester of college. Did you—or do you—exercise self-discipline and establish and achieve both short-term and long-term goals in your classes? What grades did you—or do you expect to—make?

■ **EXAMINE** the title and the first three paragraphs of the essay. How would you feel if you received a semester report of three F's and two Incompletes, which would give you a zero grade point average?

■ **EXAMINE** also the words *mediocre* (paragraph 3) and *apathetic* (paragraph 24) from the essay. Deriving from a Latin word meaning "middle," *mediocre* is average or commonplace; to be apathetic is to be uninterested.

■ **WRITE** a journal entry about your first semester—or even your first few weeks—of college. What academic goals have you set for yourself? Have you met these goals? Why or why not?

AS YOU READ

Underline passages that deal with the subjects of goal motivation and achievement and of success and failure. Also identify and mark the incident that transforms Logan's attitude and approach to college.

■ ■ ■

THREE F'S AND TWO I'S.

My first semester grades hit me like a kick in the stomach. The *F*'s were for classes where my work was poor. The *I*'s were "incompletes"—for courses in which I never finished my assignments. They eventually became *F*'s too.

I crumpled the report card and shoved it deep in a trash can. I can't say I was surprised. A zero grade point average was what I deserved, no question about it. But seeing my name in print on the worst possible report card still hurt. It also lit a spark in me, one that changed my life.

I was nineteen when I bombed out my first year of college. I hadn't always been a poor student. During elementary and middle school, I was consistently at the top of my class. But when I transferred into a huge regional high school, everything changed. I started "underachieving." Guidance counselors, teachers, and members of my family noticed. "You have potential," they'd say when they heard of my mediocre performance. "You just don't apply yourself."

They didn't understand. The truth was I *did* apply myself—just not to academics. As a shy, acne-prone teenager thrown into an enormous and unfamiliar high school, grades were not my priority; survival was. During my freshman year, I was constantly hassled and teased by a group of older guys at my school. They shoved and threatened me on the bus, teased me in the halls, and mocked me during lunchtime. *Nerd. Geek. Loser.* These insults were fired at me like bullets. Sometimes they came with fists. I got scared.

This fear transformed me. Constantly stressed and distracted, I stopped worrying about classes. Too embarrassed to admit to teachers or my family what was happening, I quietly dropped from an A student in 8th grade to C student just a year later. My definition of success changed dramatically. To me, a good day at school was no longer about doing well in class. It was simply about getting home without being hassled. To achieve this goal, I learned to blend in to the crowd—to look, talk, and act like the popular kids. First, I changed my clothes and hairstyle. Then I started behaving differently, hanging out with new "friends" and teasing the few kids who fit in worse than me. By the end of my freshman year, I escaped being at the bottom of the social ladder, but I also gave up on being a good student.

Instead, my focus was on following the crowd and being a social success. In 10th grade, I got a job at a nearby mall, so I could buy what seemed important: name-brand clothes, expensive sneakers, the latest CDs, and movie tickets—things I thought I needed to be popular. So what if my grades tumbled because I neglected my studies? At least no one was laughing at me anymore. By 11th grade a new girlfriend and my used car were what I cared most about. Classes were a meaningless activity I endured weekdays. Senior year was more of the same, though I took the SAT and applied to a few colleges—because classmates were doing it. Despite my mediocre grades, I managed to get accepted. The following

September, thanks to my family's savings, I followed the crowd and floated straight to college.

That's when I started to sink. Years of putting social time and my job   7
ahead of school left me without study habits to deal with college work. Years of coasting in class left me unready for assignments that required effort and time management skills. Years of following others left me unequipped to make smart choices about my education. In addition to lacking skills, I also lacked motivation. College felt as meaningless to me as high school. Though I'd gotten accepted at a four-year university, nothing pushed me to succeed there. I arrived on campus in September without skills, goals, and a plan. I figured I could continue doing what I had done for years: coasting. It was a recipe for disaster.

My first week on campus, I coasted through freshman orientation, skip-   8
ping activities because I didn't take them seriously. My second week, I attended a few parties, got home late, and overslept, missing a bunch of classes. No big deal, I thought. I'd just float by and hand in my homework late. But I quickly discovered, unlike high school, catching up was difficult in college. Readings in my English and History classes were longer and more complicated than I was used to—too difficult for me to skim. Writing assignments were more numerous and required more time than I'd expected. Unaccustomed to the workload, I started cutting "easy" classes to complete overdue assignments from other courses. This strategy made me fall further behind, which, in turn, made it even more difficult to motivate myself to attend class.

Why bother if you're already behind? I thought.   9

Deadlines passed and work kept piling up, and I began to realize I was   10
over my head. Halfway through the semester, I stopped going to classes regularly, hoping instead that I could score well on final exams to offset my missing assignments. But without attending class and taking notes, there was no way I could adequately prepare for tests. While coasting worked in high school, it didn't work in college. By the end of ten weeks, I knew I was done. No longer able to float, I'd sunk. My family was stunned and disappointed at my failure. I was, too, though the lesson hadn't yet fully sunk in.

That happened a few months later when I was working at a large ware-   11
house store called Sam's Club—the one place near home that would hire an unskilled college dropout in the middle of winter. My job was to retrieve shopping carts from the store's massive parking lot and stack them in rows for customers. Days and nights, I trudged across the dismal asphalt, collecting carts and cleaning up piles of garbage and soiled diapers shoppers left behind. On this March afternoon, it was raw and stormy, and I was wearing a used yellow Sam's Club raincoat that made me stink of sweat and vinyl. My hair was dripping, and my shoes squished like soaked sponges with each step.

The store was crowded with shoppers, and I'd just shoved a heavy train   12
of carts next to the front door when a cluster of young people walked out.

I recognized them immediately; four popular classmates who'd gone to my high school. They were giggling about something—a sound that brought me back to the time, years earlier, when I'd feared being laughed at by my peers. My face began to burn.

"Oh my God, it's *Paul*," said one of them. They all looked at me. I felt 13 trapped.

"What are *you* doing here?" said Ken, a guy who'd been in my English 14 class in 10th grade. He glanced at my rain-soaked jacket.

"Working," I said. There was an awkward silence. I had spent years 15 trying to fit in with people like them, and now I only wanted to get away. "What about you?" I asked, hoping to change the subject.

"We're home for spring break," Ken replied.   16

The burning on my face suddenly grew hotter. They were already finish- 17 ing their first year of college, and I was pushing carts in the rain—pushing carts for them.

"Paul, we need more carts in here! Hurry up!!!" my supervisor yelled 18 from inside the store.

My former classmates looked uncomfortable and embarrassed. I could 19 see the questions in their eyes. *What happened to you? Weren't you in college too?* I felt as if my first grade point average was written across my face and they were reading it.

ZERO POINT ZERO.

I nodded a quick goodbye and turned away. My eyes stung as the truth of 20 my mistakes poured down on me like the rain. I had allowed myself to become what my grade point average said: a failure—a dropout without a plan, a goal, or a real future. A zero. Coasting wasn't going to carry me any further. Neither would the CD's, the parties, or the brand name sneakers I'd so valued in high school. By pursuing them and nothing else, I'd closed doors in my life. If I kept following the same path, I could spend years struggling in that dreary parking lot or some other menial job while my peers moved forward. I wanted to do more with my life than push shopping carts.

The spark which ignited at the sight of my report card erupted into a 21 burning flame in my chest. Watching my friends drive off that afternoon, one thing was suddenly clear to me: it was time to get serious and take control of my life. College could help me do that, I realized. It could be a lifeline; I just had to grab it—no more coasting.

The following fall, with money saved from working nine months in the 22 parking lot, I paid for classes at a local community college. This time, I attended every orientation activity—and I took notes. Learning from past mistakes, I also bought a calendar and jotted down each assignment, so I could see deadlines well in advance and plan accordingly. Instead of skipping classes for social time, I arranged social events after class with peers who seemed serious about their work. No longer a follower, I became a study group leader! This actually helped me become a popular student—the thing I had chased for so long in high school.

I am not going to say it was easy. After long days on the job, I spent   23
longer nights at home doing my coursework. It took months of practice for me to learn the skills I'd missed in high school: how to take good notes, how to take tests, how to write an effective essay, and how to get help when I needed it. But gradually I learned.

Throughout my second attempt at college, I sat beside many students   24
who reminded me of myself during my first semester. I recognized them right away—students who seemed distracted or apathetic in class or who were frequently absent. They usually disappeared after a few weeks. Some were dealing with full lives that made it difficult to focus on their courses. Others, especially the ones straight out of high school, were coasting, unsure of why they were there or what they were doing. For these students, college is especially tough.

To thrive in college, you have to want to be there, and you have to be   25
ready to focus on work. Some people aren't ready. They're likely to fail, just as I did. But even failure, as painful as it is, doesn't have to be an ending. It can be a learning experience—one that builds strength and gives direction. It can also serve as a wake-up call that turns a floating student into a serious one. It can even light a spark that sets the stage for future success. Take it from me, a former zero, who graduated from community college with a perfect 4.0 grade point average!

■   ■   ■

AFTER YOU READ

■ **THINK** about the effectiveness of Logan's narrative. Use the questions in the second "AFTER YOU READ—EXAMINE" section of Soto's essay (page 38) to evaluate Logan's essay. Note also that—like many good narratives—Logan's essay includes not only description but also dialogue. Find examples of both.

■ **THINK** also about why Logan began underachieving (paragraph 3-6) in high school. How did his focus and definition of success change at this time? Have you or any of your friends gone through this downward spiral? What advice would you give someone to prevent them from underachieving and setting superficial goals in this way?

■ **EXAMINE** paragraphs 6 and 7. Why did Logan take the SAT and apply for college? How might you explain the lack of motivation that he admits to in paragraph 7? Then look at paragraphs 20–22 and 24. How was Logan's second attempt at college different from his first?

How did his goals change? How did he learn to set realistic learning goals? (See Bernstein's definition of learning goals on page 44.)

■ **EXAMINE** also the incident in the Sam's Club parking lot (paragraphs 12–21) that finally made him realize that he "wanted to do more ... than push shopping carts" for the rest of his life. Why did this incident have such an impact on him?

■ **WRITE** an essay in which you set goals for yourself for the rest of the semester. Introduce your essay by briefly evaluating your self-discipline and use of goals thus far in the term. Then identify three realistic goals that you think you can achieve by the end of the term.

UNIT ONE

■ ■ ■

Critical Thinking, Reading, and Writing

■ ANNOTATING A TEXT

Annotations are the tracks you leave in a text you are reading. They should reveal what was going on in your mind as you read. Your annotations should, of course, indicate the author's main ideas and supporting details. But you might also indicate words you don't know or ideas with which you agree or disagree. Annotating as you read will not only help you understand what you read but also enable you to remember the content longer. Annotating a text is in some ways like carrying on a dialogue with the author of the text. You are responding to his or her ideas. But annotating can also be viewed as talking to yourself—asking yourself questions, reminding yourself of what you think is important, marking words or phrases you don't know, and making comments to yourself. In addition, annotating helps you become a stronger writer by making you aware of how texts are constructed and by making it easier for you to use a text as a source for your own writing.

How you choose to annotate is, of course, up to you. You may want to draw illustrations or diagrams, highlight with colored markers, circle words you do not know, number information, underline or put asterisks beside ideas you consider important, or write notes to yourself about what you are reading. You may also want to connect what you are reading to previous experiences or jot down questions to ask your instructor. Although some reading selections do not require a written response, it is usually helpful to communicate with yourself in writing as you read. The more difficult the material you are reading, the more important it is that you respond to it in writing.

BEFORE YOU READ

Some students make the mistake of making too many annotations when they read. Instead, you should be selective and discriminating so that your marks provide clear signals to guide you when you later return to the text to review it or study for a test. If you have underlined or highlighted almost everything, you will simply be rereading the entire text.

Thus, the first step in annotating is to have a plan. If you use only one type of annotation—say, underlining or highlighting—your annotations will be less useful to you than if you use different types of annotations for different purposes. For example, you might circle words you don't know and write comments in the margins to indicate disagreement or agreement. The plan is up to you, but having a plan is an important step in learning to annotate effectively. At times you may depart from your plan, but it is best to have one in mind and to follow it generally. You may want to include some of the following strategies in your plan:

- Circle words you don't know.
- Highlight passages you find especially interesting or informative (perhaps even using different colors).
- Underline main ideas.
- Write comments in the margins.
- Put question marks in the margin next to statements you are unsure about or don't understand.
- Put plus signs in the margin when you especially agree with the author.
- Put minus signs in the margin when you disagree with the author.
- Use asterisks to indicate ideas you find most significant.

Ideally, you should read through the material once and then annotate it on a second reading when you have a better sense of which ideas and information are significant. But even on a first reading, you will better understand what you are reading if you annotate as you read.

Example
We have marked the following essay by Kesaya E. Noda to illustrate how a reader might annotate a passage.

Growing Up Asian

Introduction:
Personal
background

Definition: To
prolong the
existence of
something

Sometimes when I was growing up, my identity   1
seemed to hurtle toward me and paste itself right to
my face. I felt that way, encountering the
stereotypes of my race (perpetuated) by non-Japanese
people (primarily white) who may or may not have had
contact with other Japanese in America. "You don't
like cheese, do you?" someone would ask. "I know your
people don't like cheese." Sometimes questions came
making allusions to history. That was another aspect
of the identity. Events that had happened quite
apart from the me who stood silent in that moment
connected my face with an incomprehensible past.
"Your parents were in California? Were they in those
camps during the war?" And sometimes there were
phrases or nicknames: "Lotus Blossom." I was
sometimes addressed or referred to as racially
Japanese, sometimes as Japanese-American, and

How will she
resolve these?

sometimes as an Asian woman. Confusions and
distortions abounded.

*Two ways to
know oneself:
inside and
outside

How is one to know and define oneself? ① From the   2
inside—within a context that is self-defined, from a
grounding in community and a connection with culture
and history that are comfortably accepted? ② Or from

the outside—in terms of messages received from the media and people who are often ignorant? Even as an adult I can still see two sides of my face and past. I can see from the inside out, in freedom. And I can see from the outside in, driven by the old voices of childhood and lost in anger and fear.

Are these 2 sentences part of her thesis?

I Am Racially Japanese

History of Japanese Americans

[A voice from my childhood says: "You are other. You are less than. You are unalterably alien." This voice has its own history. We have indeed been seen as other and alien since the early years of our arrival in the United States. The very first immigrants were welcomed and sought as laborers to replace the dwindling numbers of Chinese, whose influx had been cut off by the Chinese Exclusion Act of 1882. The Japanese fell natural heir to the same anti-Asian prejudice that had arisen against the Chinese. As soon as they began striking for better wages, they were no longer welcomed.]   3

Main idea of paragraph

I can see myself today as a person historically defined by law and custom as being forever alien. Being neither "free white," nor "African," our people in California were deemed "aliens, ineligible for citizenship," no matter how long they intended to stay here. Aliens ineligible for citizenship were prohibited from owning, buying, or leasing land. They did not and could not belong here. The voice in me remembers that I am always a *Japanese-American* in the eyes of many. A third-generation German-American is an American. A third-generation Japanese-American is a Japanese-American. Being Japanese means being a danger to the country during the war and knowing how to use chopsticks. I wear this history on my face.   4

Her tone changes— becomes more poetic

I move to the other side. I see a different light and claim a different context. My race is a line that stretches across ocean and time to link me to the shrine where my grandmother was raised. Two high white banners lift in the wind at the top of the stone steps leading to the shrine. It is time for the summer festival. Black characters are written against the sky as boldly as the clouds, as lightly as kites, as sharply as the big black crows I used to see above the fields in New Hampshire. At festival time there is   5

liquor and food, rituals, discipline, and
abandonment. There is music and drunkenness and
invocation. There is hope. Another season has come.
Another season has gone.

Main idea

*Definition:
religion of Japan
(worship of
nature &
ancestors)*

I am racially Japanese. I have a certain claim to   6
this crazy place where the prayers intoned by a
neighboring Shinto priest (standing in for my
grandmother's nephew who is sick) are drowned out by
the rehearsals for the pop singing contest in which
most of the villagers will compete later that night.
The village elders, the priest, and I stand
respectfully upon the immaculate, shining wooden
floor of the outer shrine, bowing our heads before
the hidden powers. During the patchy intervals when
I can hear him, I notice the priest has a stutter. His
voice flutters up to my ears only occasionally
because two men and a woman are singing gustily into a
microphone in the compound, testing the sound
system. A prerecorded tape of guitars, samisens, and
drums accompanies them. Rock music and Shinto

*Word defined in
context*

prayers. That night, to loud applause and cheers, a
young man is given the award for the most netsuretsu—
passionate, burning—rendition of a song. We roar our
approval of the reward. Never mind that his voice had
wandered and slid, now slightly above, now slightly
below the given line of the melody. Netsuretsu.
Netsuretsu.

**Conclusion
suggests thesis
that Noda is
inside &
outside, past &
present,
Japanese &
American*

In the morning, my grandmother's sister kneels at   7
the foot of the stone stairs to offer her morning
prayers. She is too crippled to climb the stairs, so
each morning she kneels here upon the path. She shuts
her eyes for a few seconds, her motions as matter of
fact as when she washes rice. I linger longer than she
does, so reluctant to leave, savoring the connection
I feel with my grandmother in America, the past, and
the power that lives and shines in the morning sun.

The annotations we have made reflect our reading of these paragraphs.
We have underlined topic sentences in paragraphs and sentences that suggest
Noda's thesis that her life encompasses both the inside and the outside, the
past and the present, Japan and America. We have circled words we need to
define. We have highlighted information we reacted to or wanted to remember, and we have put asterisks by particularly important ideas. Different readers discover different meanings as they read, and the same reader may even

discover different meanings upon rereading. But annotating what you read enables you to understand and remember what is most useful and important to you at the time. Your annotations also provide you a record of your reading so that you can easily review the material at a later time. Even more important, annotations force you to think about what you are reading as you read.

Assignment

Using the suggestions on page 55 and your own ideas, write out your own annotation plan—what you intend to do when you annotate. Although you may decide to change this plan later or vary from it as you actually annotate a selection, you will benefit from having a detailed plan to which you can refer as you read.

AS YOU READ

In addition to the plan you have constructed, the following guidelines will help you annotate a text effectively:

- Keep your annotation plan handy so that you can refer to it if necessary.
- Don't let your plan inhibit you; just use it as a guideline.
- Don't stop to look up unfamiliar words as you read; instead, just mark the words and look them up later. (At that time, you can add a brief definition to your annotations.)
- Remember you are the only reader for your annotations, so your marks do not have to make sense to anyone but you. (Just be sure that you will be able to make sense of them a few days or even a few weeks after you have read the selection.)

Assignments

1. Choose one of the reading selections in Unit One of *Interactions* that you have not previously read. Using your annotation plan, read and annotate the selection you have chosen.

2. Select a reading selection from Unit One that interests you (one you have already read). Choose a topic from this selection that you would like to know more about and, using a search engine such as Google or Yahoo!, run a search on the topic you have chosen. For example, if you found the essay "I'm Just Me" by Lylah M. Alphonse interesting, you could look up the author's name or her references to topics such as Haiti, Arawak Indians, people of mixed race, or interracial marriage. Next, select one of the sources you find and print out a copy. Then, using your annotation plan, read and annotate it.

AFTER YOU READ

Review the reading selection you have annotated, focusing on your annotations. Can you remember what each annotation means? Do you need to look up some words that were unfamiliar to you? Can you now answer some of the questions you may have had? Are there additional questions or comments you have now that you would like to add to your annotations? Then discuss your annotation experience with your instructor or a group of your classmates. Did annotating the text as you read improve your attention or comprehension? Do you remember what you read in more detail? What would you do differently next time? What would you do the same, and why?

■ EXPLORING IDEAS TOGETHER

1. Using one or more of the selections from this unit—especially those by Soto, Raymond, Bernstein, and Logan—as reference points, discuss with a group of your classmates the concept of self-esteem and how it is formed.

2. With a group of your classmates, discuss the effects of physical appearance on a person's self-image. Do you know an attractive person who has low self-esteem or an unattractive person who has high self-esteem? Is it important that others consider a person attractive, or is it only how the person feels about his or her own appearance that matters? Consider in your discussion the essays by Alphonse, Soto, and Logan.

3. In a small group, discuss whether a person should set extremely high, perhaps even unattainable, goals or realistic goals.

4. Compare the selection by Cisneros with the one by Quindlen. Focusing on the attitudes of the two writers toward their names, make two lists: one list stating the ways in which the two writers agree and the other list stating the ways in which they disagree.

5. There are different theories about how human personalities are constructed. Some theorists believe that genetic factors are most important, others believe that parental influence is what shapes a person, and a new theory argues that peer influence is the most important element in determining who a person becomes. Still others argue that people are the products of the language and culture of the community in which they are reared. Working with a group of your classmates, discuss these theories and decide which one you find most convincing. Consider relevant essays in this unit.

6. Discuss how and why a person may change while passing from one stage of life to another. Consider the reading selections in this unit that focus on different rites of passage (e.g., "Between Two Worlds" by Abu-Jaber, "Living in Two Worlds" by Mabry, and "Zero" by Logan).

■ EXPLORING THE INTERNET

You can find more information related to these exercises at the *Interactions* website: www.cengagebrain.com.

1. The website "Behind the Name: The Etymology and History of First Names" provides you with information about names—their derivations, meaning, popularity, and so on. Explore this website to learn more about your own name and the effect that a person's name may have on that individual. Relate this information to "My Name" by Cisneros and "The Name Is Mine" by Quindlen.

2. Diana Abu-Jaber begins her essay "Between Two Worlds" by describing her family's brief stay in her father's home country of Jordan. If you don't know much about Jordan and its people, you may want to look at the websites of the "Natural Map of the Kingdom of Jordan" as well as "The People of Jordan" and "Bedouin: Wikipedia." You can access this information most easily from the Related Websites section of the student website for *Interactions*, eighth edition.

3. From 5% to 10% of the population has some kind of learning disability, with dyslexia being the most common. For more information on dyslexia, go to the Dyslexia Foundation website, or look up "dyslexia" on WebMd. If you or someone you know has dyslexia, this information will be particularly interesting to you.

4. In the model essay "Growing Up Asian" in the "Critical Thinking, Reading, and Writing" section of this unit, Noda refers to the Japanese internment camps in paragraph 1 ("Were they in those camps during the war?"). To learn more about World War II internment camps on the West Coast and how they affected Japanese Americans, Google the topic "Japanese-American Internment." You will find several sites that provide historical information about the internment camps and the people who were in them. How does learning about the internment camps help you understand the discrimination experienced by Noda and other Japanese Americans?

5. Go to the Related Websites section of the *Interactions*, eighth edition, student website and click on the link for "Steve Jobs's Stanford Commencement Speech." As you read this speech, notice that it is divided into three separate narratives, or stories. Although all three connect to Job's thesis, found in his statement that "You've got to find what you love" (paragraph 15), each separate story has its own main point about life and the self. State these three main ideas in your own words. (Or your instructor may want to divide your class into three main groups, with each group working on one story.) After you finish reading and discussing this speech, write a journal entry or narrative essay explaining how you found, or hope to find, "what you love" and why you love it. You may focus on college, a person or persons, a career, a hobby, or a place. (For help with writing narrative essays, see Lesson 1 on the *Interactions*, eighth edition, student website.)

6. Select one or two authors from this unit whose essay(s) you particularly enjoyed. Use a search engine to look up this person on the Web to see what additional information you can find. Some authors have personal websites.

■ WRITING ESSAYS

1. Write a narrative essay in which you define yourself by focusing on either a conflict in your life or an incident that served as a rite of passage toward your adulthood. (See Lesson 1 on narration on the *Interactions*, eighth edition, student website).

2. Reread the essays by Cisneros and Quindlen. Then write an essay about how your own name does or does not reinforce your concept of who you are.

3. In this unit, several selections share the theme of isolation (for example, the essays by Cisneros, Soto, Raymond, and Logan). Write an essay in which you focus on some way in which you feel isolated from others, using at least one of the selections in this unit as a source.

4. Describe the environment in which you grew up in a way that suggests how it shaped you and/or your image of yourself. You may want to refer to one of the essays by Cisneros, Walker, Abu-Jaber, Mabry, Soto, or Noda.

5. Write an essay in which you compare the challenges and rewards of a mixed heritage, such as those described by Walker, Alphonse, and Abu-Jaber.

6. Using the essay by Mabry as a model, write an essay in which you discuss the role that education plays in shaping and/or changing a person's life.

7. Write an essay in which you discuss the effects of goal setting— successful and/or unsuccessful—on self-esteem. You may want to refer to one of the essays by Raymond, Bernstein, or Logan, but be sure to use examples from your experiences and observations as well.

8. Write an essay in which you compare two of the essays in this unit, focusing on the theme of identity or self-concept. Lesson 7 on the *Interactions*, eighth edition, student website, www.cengagebrain.com, provides guidelines for writing comparison and contrast essays.

Note: You can find helpful suggestions for essay assignments 1–4, and perhaps 7, in the lesson on "Writing a Personal Essay" (pages 128–133).

FAMILY

Monkey Business Images/Shutterstock.Com

What is the family in this photograph doing? How do they feel about this activity—bored, happy, or excited? How many generations are represented in the photograph? Does your family play games, have dinner, and do other activities together? How important is it for families to spend time together?

■ ■ ■

One of the first and most important relationships that you establish is with your family of origin. In fact, to a great extent you are defined in terms of your initial family experiences. Who you become depends on who you were—your position in your family, your

63

relationship with different members of your family, and your perception of yourself as part of your family. As you grow older, you will probably establish a new family, but that family will almost certainly be a reflection of the one in which you grew up. Even if you choose consciously and deliberately to change the old patterns, they will still be there at some level.

This unit includes reading selections that encourage you to explore the relationships within your family and to define yourself more clearly in terms of these relationships. You will read about traditional and nontraditional families, positive and negative relationships, and changing families. All of the selections encourage you to think about how you define a family and how a family defines you.

For many years, our ideas of family were based on what sociologist Ian Robertson calls the "middle-class 'ideal' family so relentlessly portrayed in TV commercials, one that consists of a husband, a wife, and their dependent children." To incorporate the complexity of modern family structures, Robertson more openly defines a family as "a relatively permanent group of people related by ancestry, marriage, or adoption, who live together, form an economic unit, and take care of their young."* How does this definition compare with your own? Does it describe your own family as well as the families of your friends? Can you think of families that it does not describe? Explain.

Before you begin this unit, take a few minutes to write about your own family. Use one or more of the following questions to guide your writing:

1. Describe the family in which you grew up. Was it traditional or nontraditional, small or large, wealthy or poor, happy or unhappy?
2. If you have already established a family of your own, how is it similar to or different from the one in which you grew up?
3. To which member of your family are you closest? Why?
4. Which member of your family do you most resemble? In what way(s)?
5. What would you change about your family if you could?
6. What would you not want to change?
7. What role(s) do you play in your family?
8. How is your family different from other families? How is your family like other families?

As you read the selections in this unit, remember to annotate the text—to underline important or interesting ideas, to circle words that you do not know, and to write questions and comments in the margins. This unit also gives you the opportunity to read and write descriptive essays (see Bret Lott's "Brothers"), and the "Critical Thinking, Reading, and Writing" section provides instruction in writing personal essays.

---

*Ian Robertson, *Sociology*, 3rd ed. (New York: Worth, 1987), pp. 348–349.

What Is This Thing Called Family?

■   ■   ■

LEE HERRICK

An instructor of English at Fresno City College and the founding editor of the literary magazine *In the Grove,* Lee Herrick
has published poems and essays in numerous journals, including
the *Berkeley Poetry Review,* the *Hawaii Pacific Review,* and
The Bloomsbury Review. He was the guest editor for the special
issue of *Asian American Poetry and Writing* entitled *New
Truths: Writing in the 21st Century by Korean Adoptees,* and
his book of poems, *This Many Miles from Desire* (2007), has
received favorable reviews. Born in Daejeon, South Korea, Herrick was adopted by American parents when he was ten months
old. In the following essay, he tells his personal story as a Korean adoptee.

BEFORE YOU READ

■ **THINK** about what it would be like to be adopted by a family of another ethnic group or race. What would be some of the challenges and
difficulties? What would be some of the rewards?

■ **EXAMINE** the title of this essay. What is your answer to the question
"What Is This Thing Called Family"?

■ **EXAMINE** also the word *taunting* (paragraph 4), which means "insult-
ing" or "mocking." (Have you ever been taunted by someone, and if so,
how did it make you feel?) Also look at the words *mantra* and *kimchi.*
In Hinduism, a mantra is a sacred phrase or formula, but more generally it means a repetitive phrase or saying. Kimchi is a traditional Korean food, a pickled dish of various vegetables and seasonings.

■ **WRITE** a journal entry in which you answer the question "What Is This
Thing Called Family?"

AS YOU READ

Underline passages that show the "unique perspective on the notion of
family" that Herrick's experience has given him.

■ ■ ■

As a Korean adoptee raised by Caucasian parents, I have a unique   1
perspective on the notion of family. It is not defined by physical
similarity. I look nothing like them. I am Asian and they are Caucasian, as is my sister (adopted as well, from Alameda). But the subtle similarities one acquires through family are inevitable—the signs, the way one
lifts her eyebrows in curiosity or disdain. We joke about having each
other's traits, but they are habits or quirks, not the same shape of nose or
chin.

My sister and I were raised in California's East Bay Area and later in   2
the Central Valley. In the 1970's, the towns weren't as diverse as they are
now. But we had great childhoods. We had a sibling rivalry for the ages,
but deep down there was a whole lot of love. I remember her defending me
when racial slurs would come my way.

"He's Korean," Holly would say, when the other kids would tell me   3
"Go back where you came from, Chinaman." She would intervene and
change the subject when I was asked irritating questions like "What *are*
you?" and "How can *she* be your sister?" I think of my sister like a defender, a protector. I also now realize that as much as she was defending
me, she was defending herself and her right as an adoptee to have a
brother who looked like me.

I remember an incident when I came home from grade school one day,   4
sniffing and trying to conceal my tears after a day of particularly aggressive
taunting—the subject at hand was my "flat face." It was hurtful and
brought me to tears on the long walk home after the bus dropped me off.
But it was also very strange to me because I was raised in a Caucasian
family, so the boy taunting me looked like my cousins ... why was he so
mean? It was also confusing because I didn't have an Asian accent, nor did
I speak Korean or any other Asian language. My favorite baseball team
was the Oakland A's, my favorite player was Reggie Jackson. I loved *Star
Wars,* Batman, and eventually Atari—all things 70's. I felt normal (whatever that is). Many well-intentioned people also told me "you're an American!" or "you're not like other Asians I've met." To this day I am wary of
all these suspect declarations.

I walked in the front door, Phil Donahue's inquisitive lisp coming from   5
the television. My mother noticed I had been crying. She bent down like a
baseball catcher and took my face into her open hands, wiping my tears
with her thumbs. "Oh, honey, what's *wrong*?" she asked.

I sniffed and wiped my nose with the back of my hand. "Nothing," I   6
said.

"Honey, I'm your mom. You can tell me," she said.   7

"My face isn't flat, is it?" I asked, feeling the small mound of my nose   8
on my face, proving it wasn't flat. I was still sniffing.

I can still remember the hurt look on her face, the sadness. I can't remem-   9
ber exactly what she said, but it was something about how some people are
just ignorant and to let it "roll right off" my back. I felt better that day, and

time after time throughout my life as I encountered difficult times I would often repeat her mantra in my head. She gave me something to use. Years later, as I was defining the term *idiot* in high school, acting out some of my anger, she would often be the one to spell out the conditions of my grounding. Of course, years later I came to appreciate the support (and discipline) she and my father gave me. Some things just take a while.

My father is a quiet man. I think of him as the model for giving of 10 yourself as much as you can. Once, when I was fifteen or sixteen, at the height of my selfish teen years, he asked me if I wanted to help him volunteer serving hot dogs at the local Peach Fair.

"Do I get paid?" I asked, clearly not hearing the word *volunteer*.   11

"No," he said. He left, no doubt wondering what kind of person I was 12 becoming.

He is also the kindest, most soft-spoken, modest person I know. I have 13 never heard him scream, not even when my sister and I were raising all kinds of hell as teenagers. Sure, he gets mad, but his calm demeanor is a trait I have always admired (probably never successfully emulated).

Being a Korean adoptee has been wonderful but undoubtedly challeng- 14 ing. Anger, kindness, forgiveness have all been a part of my life. To varying degrees I have to believe they are a part of all families. To say the least, being separated from one's birth mother is not easy to come to terms with, and it is complicated further by being in an interracial family. But that is what we are—a family.

I have come to believe that family goes far beyond a child's eyes look- 15 ing like her mother's and father's, or a child having the same mannerisms as her parents (which we do, in fact, have). It is more than a name or a number of bedrooms in a home. I have come to believe that family is about love and struggle and adapting. That there are many different types of family and that they evolve—2.5 kids and a white fence, single parent families, those involving incarceration, illness (or a combination of all of these)—family is a wide term with plenty of room for interpretation.

Yes, I think about my birth parents from time to time, although I have 16 not met them. But several years ago I returned to Seoul, the capital city where I was born. It felt like going home—no one staring at me because I was the only Asian in a room, eating barbecued squid and kimchi from the street vendor, shopping in Lotte World and the Namdaemun Market, seeing the ancient temples and modern skyscrapers downtown.

But while it felt like home, it really wasn't. Home is about family, the 17 people who will stand up for you and say "He's Korean." It is about people who comfort you and tell you that your face is *not* flat. It is not about perfection; it is about trying to be a good person (I realize this now when I am volunteering). It is about getting opportunities and support, discipline and the chance to fail and be responsible. No family member, no matter how present or absent, fills just one role. My sister is the protector but also an inspiration for kindness. My mother is a support system but also the creative force. My father is a role model but also a support system.

They are all hilarious and have great work ethics. I can only hope just an ounce of this rubbed off on me.

I still find it interesting when children look just like their parents. Of 18 course biology dictates that likelihood, but not in my family. It is second nature that we don't look the same. Currently, my wife (part German-Irish, part Filipina) and I are adopting. We will soon welcome our daughter into our lives (and vice versa), aware of some of the many challenges of an international adoption, the beauty and hard work involved in family, and a foundation of unconditional love from which we should always begin.

■ ■ ■

AFTER YOU READ

■ **THINK** about Herrick's dual heritage—Korean and American. What did he discover about himself and his sense of home and family when he visited Seoul, Korea? For a better understanding of Herrick's feelings on this subject, read his poem "Korean Adoptee Returns to Seoul" on the "Samples" section of his website. (See the list of related websites at www.cengagebrain.com on the student site for *Interactions,* eighth edition.)

■ **EXAMINE** the first and last paragraphs—paragraphs 1 and 18. How do these paragraphs show the "unique perspective" on family that Herrick developed through his experience as a Korean adoptee of a Caucasian family? In contrast to the physical similarities that connect most families, what "traits," actions, and feelings does Herrick have in common with other members of his family?

■ **EXAMINE** the essay to find the challenges and difficulties that Herrick had as a "Korean adoptee" in a Caucasian family. Then examine the essay to find the joys and rewards that resulted from his experience. Discuss your ideas with a group of your classmates, making two lists—one of Herrick's challenges and difficulties, and one of his joys and rewards.

■ **WRITE** an essay in which you give your personal definition of family by answering the question "What Is This Thing Called Family?" Include in your essay references to Herrick's definition of family as well as your own ideas, both those in your earlier journal and those that you developed during or after reading Herrick's essay.

Defining Family

■ ■ ■

BRYAN STRONG,
CHRISTINE DEVAULT, AND
THEODORE F. COHEN

Originally written by Bryon Strong and then cowritten with Christine DeVault, *The Marriage and Family Experience: Intimate Relationships in a Changing Society* has been revised and updated for the eighth through tenth editions by Theodore F. Cohen. A professor of sociology and anthropology at Ohio Wesleyan University, Cohen earned his MA and PhD in sociology from Boston University. He teaches and researches in the areas of family life and gender, focusing on the family lives of men and on emerging family lifestyles. In addition to being the author of the latest edition of *The Marriage and Family Experience* (2008), Cohen is also the coauthor of *Perspectives on Political Communication: A Case Approach* (2007) and the editor of *Men and Masculinity: A Text Reader* (2000).

BEFORE YOU READ

■ **THINK** about the definition of family you wrote for the previous reading selection by Lee Herrick. Do you think your definition is general enough to incorporate all families in the United States? How might you change it to fit all of these families?

■ **EXAMINE** the first paragraph in the selection and try to answer the two questions posed at the end. Do these questions complicate your own personal definition of family? If so, how?

■ **WRITE** a list of the individuals whom you consider to be members of your family.

AS YOU READ

Identify and underline the definitions of *family* in the selection. Also, determine how the tone and purpose(s) of this selection differ from those of the previous essay by Herrick.

■   ■   ■

As contemporary Americans, we live in a society composed of many   1
kinds of families—married couples, stepfamilies, single-parent
families, multigenerational families, cohabiting adults, child-free
families, families headed by gay men or by lesbians, and so on. With such
variety, how can we define family? What are the criteria for identifying
these groups as families?

For official counts of the numbers and characteristics of American fami-   2
lies, we can turn to the U.S. Census Bureau. The Census Bureau defines a **family** as "a group of two or more persons related by birth, marriage, or adoption
and residing together in a household" (U.S. Census Bureau 2001). A distinction is made between a family and a **household**. A household consists of "one
or more people—everyone living in a housing unit makes up a household"
(Fields 2003). Single people who live alone, roommates, lodgers, and live-in
domestic service employees are all counted among members of households, as
are family groups. *Family households* are those in which at least two members
are related by birth, marriage, or adoption (Fields 2003). Thus, the U.S. Census reports on characteristics of the nation's households *and* families. Of the
111,278,000 households in the United States in 2002, 75,596,000, or 68%,
were family households. Among family households, 76% (57,320,000) consisted of married couples, either with or without children (Fields 2003).

In individuals' perceptions of their own life experiences, *family* has a   3
less precise definition. For example, when we asked our students whom
they included as family members, their lists included such expected relatives as mother, father, sibling, spouse, as well as the following:

best friend	lover	priest
boyfriend	minister	rabbi
girlfriend	neighbor	and teacher
godchild	pet	

Most of those designated as family members are individuals related by   4
descent, marriage, remarriage, or adoption, but some are **affiliated** kin—
unrelated individuals who feel and are treated as if they were relatives.

Furthermore, being related biologically or through marriage is not al-   5
ways sufficient to be counted as a family member or kin. One researcher
(Furstenberg [and Spanier] 1987) found that 19% of the children with biological siblings living with them did not identify their brothers or sisters
as family members. Sometimes an absent or divorced parent was not
counted as a relative. Stepparents, stepsiblings, or stepchildren were the
most likely not to be viewed as family members (Furstenberg [and Spanier]
1987; Ihinger-Tallman and Pasley 1987). Emotional closeness may be more
important than biology or law in defining family.

There are also ethnic differences as to what constitutes family. Among   6
Latinos, for example, *compadres* (or godparents) are considered family
members. Similarly, among some Japanese Americans the *ie* (pronounced
"ee-eh") is the traditional family. The *ie* consists of living members of the

extended family (such as grandparents, aunts, uncles, and cousins), as well as deceased and yet-to-be-born family members (Kikumura and Kitano 1988). Among many traditional Native American tribes, the **clan,** a group of related families, is regarded as the fundamental family unit (Yellowbird and Snipp 1994).

A major reason we have such difficulty defining *family* is that we tend   7 to think that the "real" family is the **nuclear family,** consisting of mother, father, and children. The term "nuclear family" is [at the time of this writing] less than 60 years old, coined by anthropologist Robert Murdock in 1949 (Levin 1993). What most Americans consider to be the **traditional family** is a mostly middle-class version of the nuclear family in which women's primary roles are wife and mother and men's primary roles are husband and breadwinner. The traditional family exists more in our imaginations than it ever did in reality.

Because we believe that the nuclear or traditional family is the real family,   8 we compare all other family forms against these models. To include these diverse forms, the definition of family needs to be expanded beyond the boundaries of the "official" census definition. A more contemporary and inclusive definition describes family as "two or more persons related by birth, marriage, adoption, or choice. Families are further defined by socio-economical ties and enduring responsibilities, particularly in terms of one or more members' dependence on others for support and nurturance" (Allen, Demo, and Fine 2000). Such a definition more accurately and completely reflects the diversity of contemporary American family experience.

BIBLIOGRAPHY

Allen, Katherine R., David H. Demo, and Mark A. Fine. *Handbook of Family Diversity*. New York: Oxford University Press, 2000.

Fields, Jason. *America's Families and Living Arrangements: 2003*. Current Population Reports, P20-553. U.S. Census Bureau, Washington, D.C., 2003.

Furstenberg, Frank F., Jr., and Graham Spanier, eds. *Recycling the Family: Remarriage after Divorce*, rev. ed. Newbury, Park, CA: Sage, 1987.

Ihinger-Tallman, Marilyn, and Kay Pasley. "Divorce and Remarriage in the American Family: A Historical Review." In *Remarriage and Stepparenting: Current Research and Theory*, edited by K. Pasley and M. Ihinger-Tallman. New York: Guilford Press, 1987.

Kikumura, Akemi, and Harry Kitano. "The Japanese American Family." In *Ethnic Families in America: Patterns and Variations*, 3rd ed., edited by C. Mindel et al. New York: Elsevier North Holland, 1988.

Levin, Irene. "The Model Monopoly of the Nuclear Family." Paper presented at the National Conference on Family Relations, Baltimore, November 1993.

U.S. Census Bureau. "Marital Status of the Population 15 Years and Over, by Sex and Race: 1950 to Present." MS-1. Washington, DC: U.S. Government Printing Office, 2001.

Yellowbird, Michael, and C. Matthew Snipp. "American Indian Families." In *Minority Families in the United States: A Multicultural Perspective*, edited by R. L. Taylor. Englewood Cliffs, NJ: Prentice Hall, 1994.

■ ■ ■

AFTER YOU READ

- **THINK** also about the tone and purposes of this selection. How do they differ from the tone and purpose of the previous essay by Herrick?

- **THINK** also about the ethnic differences that exist in families. How does the composition of many Latino, Japanese American, and Native American families differ from that of many Caucasian families?

- **EXAMINE** carefully the U.S. Census Bureau definition of a family in sentence 1 of paragraph 2. Like all formal definitions, this one puts the term to be identified—*family*—in a larger class of related institutions and then shows how it differs from other members of the class. According to the U.S. Census Bureau, how does a family differ from other households? Look also at the definition of family provided in paragraph 8. Which definition is more like your own personal definition of family? Which definition better fits all families in the country? Which definition do you prefer and why do you prefer it?

- **EXAMINE** also the definition of a household and the U. S. Census statistics given in paragraph 2 and in the accompanying figure about households and families. How are households and families related? How are they different? Of the total households in the country, how many (and what total percent) are considered family households? How many family households (and what percent) consist of married couples, with or without children? How many (and what percent of) family households do not include a married couple? Finally, what percentages of households are composed of (1) non-family households and (2) of persons living alone? How do you interpret these categories? Do any of these figures surprise you? Explain.

- **WRITE** an essay in which you define *family*. (If you wrote an earlier essay giving your personal definition of family, you may want to use it as a draft, revising it for this assignment.) Begin this essay with your own formal definition, but include also your personal definition of family as well as specific supporting examples. If you would like further information about writing a definition essay, go to Lesson 8 on the *Interactions*, eighth edition, student website at www.cengagebrain.com.

Mother and Freedom

■ ■ ■

MAYA ANGELOU

A renowned singer, dancer, actor, and poet, Maya Angelou has written six volumes of memoirs, beginning with *I Know Why the Caged Bird Sings* in 1970 and concluding with *A Song Flung Up to Heaven* in 2002. Her honors include the National Medal of Arts, a Grammy, the Quill Award for poetry, and selection by *Writer's Digest* in 1999 as one of the 100 best writers of the twentieth century. In 1993, she read her poem "On the Pulse of Morning" at Bill Clinton's first inauguration. The following selection was published in Angelou's autobiographical collection of essays, *Even the Stars Look Lonesome* (1997).

BEFORE YOU READ

■ **THINK** about how you felt at age seventeen, and reflect on your relationship with your parent(s) at that time. Did you sometimes feel, or act, in an independent or rebellious manner? What caused you to feel and act in this way, and what were the results?

■ **EXAMINE** the title of this selection. How do you think a mother can develop a sense of freedom or liberation in her child? How might a child also liberate a parent? Explain.

■ **EXAMINE** also the words *concessions* (paragraph 8), *compromises* (paragraph 8), and *feisty* (paragraph 11). A concession is something that is yielded, perhaps a point in an argument; and a compromise is a settlement of differences in which both sides make concessions. Angelou uses the term *feisty* to indicate that her mother is high-spirited and excitable.

■ **WRITE** a journal entry describing your need for independence and even your rebellion toward your parent(s) when you were a teenager.

AS YOU READ

Notice how the roles of mother and daughter become reversed over the years. Underline passages that suggest this role reversal.

■ ■ ■

S he stood before me, a dolled-up, pretty yellow woman, seven inches   1
shorter than my six-foot bony frame. Her eyes were soft and her voice
was brittle. "You're determined to leave? Your mind's made up?"

I was seventeen and burning with passionate rebelliousness. I was also   2
her daughter, so whatever independent spirit I had inherited had been nurtured by living with her and observing her for the past four years.

"You're leaving my house?"   3

I collected myself inside myself and answered, "Yes. Yes, I've found a   4
room."

"And you're taking the baby?"   5

"Yes."   6

She gave me a smile, half proud and half pitying.   7

"All right, you're a woman. You don't have a husband, but you've got   8
a three-month-old baby. I just want you to remember one thing. From the
moment you leave this house, don't let anybody raise you. Every time you
get into a relationship you will have to make concessions, compromises,
and there's nothing wrong with that. But keep in mind Grandmother Hen-
derson in Arkansas and I have given you every law you need to live by.
Follow what's right. You've been raised."

More than forty years have passed since Vivian Baxter liberated me   9
and handed me over to life. During those years I have loved and lost,
I have raised my son, set up a few households and walked away from
many. I have taken life as my mother gave it to me on that strange graduation day all those decades ago.

In the intervening time when I have extended myself beyond my reach   10
and come toppling Humpty-Dumpty-down on my face in full view of a
scornful world, I have returned to my mother to be liberated by her one
more time. To be reminded by her that although I had to compromise
with life, even life had no right to beat me to the ground, to batter my teeth
down my throat, to make me knuckle down and call it Uncle. My mother
raised me, and then freed me.

And now, after so many eventful years of trials, successes and failures, 11
my attention is drawn to a bedroom adjoining mine where my once feisty
mother lies hooked by pale blue wires to an oxygen tank, fighting cancer
for her life.

I think of Vivian Baxter, and I remember Frederick Douglass's mother,   12
enslaved on a plantation eleven miles from her infant son, yet who, after
toiling a full day, would walk the distance to look at her child hoping
that he would sense a mother's love, then return to the plantation in time
to begin another day of labor. She believed that a mother's love brought
freedom. Many African Americans know that the most moving song created during the centuries of slavery was and remains "Sometimes I Feel
Like a Motherless Child."

As a mother and a daughter myself, I have chosen certain songs and 13 poems to take to my mother's room, and there we will laugh and cry together.

I pray I shall have the courage to liberate my mother when the time 14 comes. She would expect that from me.

■ ■ ■

AFTER YOU READ

■ **THINK** about how Angelou felt when she left her mother's house at the beginning of this essay. What responsibilities did she have? Do you think it was easier for her to leave, or would it have been easier for her to stay with her mother? Would you have made the same decision as Angelou? Why or why not?

■ **EXAMINE** the first two paragraphs of the essay. What qualities and feelings are suggested by Angelou's description of her mother? What qualities, both stated and implied, does Angelou have in common with her mother?

■ **EXAMINE** also Angelou's statements that her mother "raised" her and then "freed" her (paragraph 10). Are these statements contradictory or logical? In determining your response, look up the word *raise* in a dictionary and discuss its meaning fully with a group of your classmates. Also discuss how—and why—Angelou connects a mother's love with freedom. Finally, how does Angelou herself play the liberating role of a mother at the end of the essay?

■ **WRITE** a personal essay in which you describe your own individual "graduation day" (paragraph 9)—the day you first began to establish your independence. Why did you want to become more independent? What problems did you face? How did you solve these problems? Ultimately, how successful were you in establishing your independence? (See pages 120–124 for help with writing a personal essay; see Lesson 1 on the *Interactions*, eighth edition, student website at www.cengagebrain. com for guidelines for writing narrative essays.)

The Old Man

■ ■ ■

LARRY L. KING

Larry King is probably best known for his play *The Best Little Whorehouse in Texas* (1982), which was not only one of the longest running musical comedies on Broadway but also a successful film starring Dolly Parton and Burt Reynolds. However, King has also written serious nonfiction. For example, his classic autobiography, *The Old Man and Lesser Mortals* (1974), not only relates his own experiences with his father but also suggests larger truths about generational conflicts and familial ties. Although King's book is a collection of essays, it exhibits the unity and character development of a well-written novel. This particular selection focuses on the relationship between King and his father as the son is asserting his independence, just as Angelou does in the previous selection. King grew up in West Texas, which is the setting for this narrative.

BEFORE YOU READ

■ **THINK** about an argument that you had with your parents or some other authority figure when you were younger. How did this argument make you feel?

■ **EXAMINE** this sentence from paragraph 1: "By the time I entered the troublesome teen-age years, we were on the way to a long, dark journey." From this statement, how would you describe the journey that King and his father are starting? (The essays by Sharon Liao and Agnes G. Herman also deal with journeys of self-discovery.)

■ **EXAMINE** also the last sentence of paragraph 3, in which King relates that before he was eighteen years old, he had escaped his family situation by joining the army. How does King's age at this time compare to Angelou's age when she left her mother's home? Comment on these ages as typical times for "rites of passage," or growing up.

■ **EXAMINE** also the words *hedonist* (paragraph 1), meaning one who seeks pleasure; *eschew* (paragraph 2), meaning to shun or avoid; and *neophyte* (paragraph 6), meaning a novice or beginner.

■ **WRITE** a journal entry listing and briefly discussing several issues about which you and your parents (or parent figures) have argued or still argue.

AS YOU READ

Determine what you think Lawrence realizes when he and his father are saying goodbye in the bus station.

■ ■ ■

The Old Man was an old-fashioned father, one who relied on corporal punishments, biblical exhortations, and a ready temper. He was not a man who dreamed much or who understood that others might require dreams as their opium. Though he held idleness to be as useless and as sinful as adventure, he had the misfortune to sire a hedonist son who dreamed of improbable conquests accomplished by some magic superior to grinding work. By the time I entered the troublesome teen-age years, we were on the way to a long, dark journey. A mutual thirst to prevail existed—some crazy stubborn infectious contagious will to avoid the slightest surrender.

The Old Man strapped, rope whipped, and caned me for smoking, drinking, lying, avoiding church, skipping school, and laying out at night. Having once been very close, we now lashed out at each other in the manner of rejected lovers on the occasion of each new disappointment. I thought The Old Man blind to the wonders and potentials of the real world; could not fathom how current events or cultural habits so vital to my contemporaries could be considered so frivolous—or worse. In turn, The Old Man expected me to obediently accept his own values: show more concern over the ultimate disposition of my eternal soul, eschew easy paths when walking tougher ones might somehow purify, be not so inquisitive or damnfool dreamy. That I could not (or would not) comply puzzled, frustrated, and angered him. In desperation he moved from a "wet" town to a "dry" one, in the foolish illusion that this tactic might keep his baby boy out of saloons.

On a Saturday in my fifteenth year, when I refused an order to dig a cesspool in our backyard because of larger plans downtown, I fought back: it was savage and ugly—though, as those things go, one hell of a good fight. But only losers emerged. After that we spoke in terse mumbles or angry shouts, not to communicate with civility for three years. The Old Man paraded to a series of punishing and uninspiring jobs—night watchman, dock loader for a creamery, construction worker, chicken butcher in a steamy, stinking poultry house, while I trekked to my own part-time jobs or to school. When school was out I usually repaired to one distant oil field or another, remaining until classes began anew. Before my eighteenth birthday I escaped by joining the army.

On the morning of my induction, The Old Man paused at the kitchen table, where I sat trying to choke down breakfast. He wore the faded old crossed-gallus denim overalls I held in superior contempt and carried a lunch bucket in preparation of whatever dismal job then rode him. "Lawrence," he said, "is there anything I can do for you?" I shook my head. "You need any money?" "No." The Old Man shuffled uncertainly, causing the floor to creak. "Well," he said, "I wish you good luck." I nodded in the direction of my bacon and eggs. A moment later the front door slammed, followed by the grinding of gears The Old Man always accomplished in confronting even the simplest machinery.

Alone in a Fort Dix crowd of olive drab, I lay popeyed on my bunk at   5
night, chain smoking, as Midland High School's initial 1946 football game
approached. The impossible dream was that some magic carpet might
transport me back to those anticipatory tingles I had known when bands
blared, cheerleaders cart-wheeled sweet tantalizing glimpses of their pant-
ies, and we purple-clads whooped and clattered toward the red-shirted
Odessa Bronchos or the Angry Orange of San Angelo. Waste and desola-
tion lived in the heart's private country on the night that opening game
was accomplished on the happiest playing field of my forfeited youth.
The next morning, a Saturday, I was called to the orderly room to accept
a telegram—a form of communication that had always meant death or
other disasters. I tore it open with the darkest fantasies to read MIDLAND
26 EL PASO YSLETA 0 LOVE DAD. Those valuable communiqués arrived on ten consecutive Saturday mornings.

With a ten-day furlough to spend, I appeared unannounced and before   6
a cold dawn on the porch of that familiar frame house in Midland. The
Old Man rose quickly, dispensing greetings in his woolly long-handles.
"You just a first-class private?" he teased. "Lord God, I would a-thought
a King would be a general by now. Reckon I'll have to write ole Harry
Truman a postcard to git that straightened out." Most of the time, however, (when I was not out impressing the girls with my PFC stripe) a cautious reserve prevailed. We talked haltingly, carefully, probing as
uncertainly as two neophyte premed students might explore their first skin
boil.

On the third or fourth day The Old Man woke me on the sleeping porch,   7
lunch bucket in hand. "Lawrence," he said, "your mother found a bottle of
whisky in your suitcase. Now, you know this is a teetotal home. We never had
a bottle of whisky in a home of ours, and we been married since 19-and-11.
You're perfectly welcome to stay here, but your whisky's not." I stiffly mumbled something about going to a motel. "You know better than that," The
Old Man scolded. "We don't want you goin' off to no blamed motel."
Then, in a weary exasperation not fully appreciated until dealing with trans-
gressions among my own off-spring: "Good God, son, what makes you want
to raise ole billy hell all the time?" We regarded each other in a helpless silence. "Do what you think is right," he said, sighing. "I've done told you
how me and your mother feel." He went off to work; I got up and removed
the offending liquids.

The final morning brought a wet freeze blowing down from Amarillo   8
by way of the North Pole. The Old Man's car wouldn't start; our family
had never officially recognized taxis. "I'll walk you to the bus station," he
said, bundling in a heavy sheepskin jumper and turning his back, I suspect,
so as not to witness my mother's struggle against tears. We shivered down
dark streets, past homes of my former schoolmates, by vacant lots where I
played softball or slept off secret sprees, past stores I remembered for their
bargains in Moon Pies and then Lucky Strikes and finally Trojans. Nostalgia and old guilts blew in with the wind. I wanted to say something healing
to The Old Man, to utter some gracious good-bye (the nearest thing to

retroactive apologies a savage young pride would permit), but I simply knew no beginnings.

We sat an eternity in the unreal lights of the bus station among crying babies, hung over cowboys, and drowsing old Mexican men, in mute inspection of those dead shows provided by bare walls and ceilings. The Old Man made a silent offering of a cigarette. He was a vigorous fifty-nine then, still clear eyed, dark haired, and muscular, but as his hand extended that cigarette pack and I saw it clearly—weather cured, scarred, one finger crooked and stiff jointed from an industrial accident—I suddenly and inexplicably knew that one day The Old Man would wither, fail, die. In that moment, I think, I first sensed—if I did not understand—something of mortality; of tribes, blood, and inherited rituals.

■   ■   ■

AFTER YOU READ

■ **THINK** about what young Lawrence realizes in the bus station. This realization functions as the main idea, or thesis, of the essay. State this main idea in your own words.

■ **THINK** also about how King's experience with his father is similar to Angelou's with her mother. How does each assert independence? How are the relationships in the two essays different?

■ **EXAMINE** the father's attitude toward his son and the son's attitude toward his father. How are they the same, and how are they different? With which one do you identify more closely? Why?

■ **EXAMINE** also the large number of references to specific objects, people, and events that King includes in the essay. How do these specific details help you to visualize the time (late 1940s) and place (West Texas) in which the narrative is set? What are some of the most effective details? How do they help you understand the son's reactions to his father?

■ **WRITE** a character sketch of King's father. Identify and discuss at least three of his major characteristics, supporting each characteristic with specific examples from the story.

■ Or **WRITE** a personal essay in which you describe a specific argument or disagreement you had with a parent or some other authority figure when you were young. Include specific details in your narrative, and discuss or imply in your first or last paragraph what this event meant to you. (For help with writing personal essays, see pages 128–133. You may also want to review the qualities of good narration on p. 38 of Unit One and the lesson on narration on the *Interactions*, eighth edition, student website at www.cengagebrain.com.)

Only Daughter

■ ■ ■

SANDRA CISNEROS

Sandra Cisneros, whose "My Name" from *The House on Mango Street* (1984) opens this textbook, is a widely read and highly acclaimed Chicana author. Cisneros has also published the multigenerational family novel *Caramelo* (2002), four collections of poems, and a children's book. The following essay appeared in *Glamour* magazine a few months before the publication of her collection of stories, *Woman Hollering Creek and Other Stories* (1991).

BEFORE YOU READ

- **THINK** about how parents view the gender of their children. Do you think parents sometimes make different plans and have different expectations for sons and daughters? Should they? Why or why not?

- **EXAMINE** the title and the first two paragraphs of the essay, especially Cisneros's declaration that the circumstances of her being "the only daughter in a family of six sons ... explains everything." What do you think Cisneros means by this statement? What does she mean when she adds the phrases "Mexican" and "working-class" family to her description? How does culture affect the way families view the gender of children?

- **EXAMINE** also the words *retrospect* (paragraph 5) and *philandering* (paragraph 7), both of which can be defined by their word parts. The Latin prefix *retro-* means "back," and the Latin root *spectāre* means "to look at," so "in retrospect" means looking backward. Based partly on the Greek *phil(o)*, *philandering* means having casual love affairs. (Also look at the italicized Spanish words in the essay. Cisneros defines most of these words in context, but can you decipher the others?)

- **WRITE** a journal entry in which you explore the relationship between the gender of a child and the parents' expectations for that child.

AS YOU READ

Identify and underline passages that specifically describe the relationship between Cisneros and her father, particularly the feelings they have for each other.

■ ■ ■

Once, several years ago, when I was just starting out my writing 1
career, I was asked to write my own contributor's note for an
anthology I was part of. I wrote: "I am the only daughter in a
family of six sons. *That* explains everything."

Well, I've thought about that ever since, and yes, it explains a lot to 2
me, but for the reader's sake I should have written: "I am the only daughter in a *Mexican* family of six sons." Or even: "I am the only daughter of a
Mexican father and a Mexican-American mother." Or: "I am the only
daughter of a working-class family of nine." All of these had everything
to do with who I am today.

I was/am the only daughter and *only* a daughter. Being an only daugh- 3
ter in a family of six sons forced me by circumstance to spend a lot of time
by myself because my brothers felt it beneath them to play with a *girl* in
public. But that aloneness, that loneliness, was good for a would-be
writer—it allowed me time to think and think, to imagine, to read and prepare myself.

Being only a daughter for my father meant my destiny would lead me 4
to become someone's wife. That's what he believed. But when I was in the
fifth grade and shared my plans for college with him, I was sure he understood. I remember my father saying, "*Que bueno, mi' ja,* that's good."
That meant a lot to me, especially since my brothers thought the idea hilarious. What I didn't realize was that my father thought college was good for
girls—good for finding a husband. After four years in college and two
more in graduate school, and still no husband, my father shakes his head
even now and says I wasted all that education.

In retrospect, I'm lucky my father believed daughters were meant for 5
husbands. It meant it didn't matter if I majored in something silly like English. After all, I'd find a nice professional eventually, right? This allowed
me the liberty to putter about embroidering my little poems and stories
without my father interrupting with so much as a "What's that you're
writing?"

But the truth is, I wanted him to interrupt. I wanted my father to un- 6
derstand what it was I was scribbling, to introduce me as "My only daughter, the writer." Not as "This is only my daughter. She teaches." *Es
maestro*—teacher. Not even *profesora*.

In a sense, everything I have ever written has been for him, to win his 7
approval even though I know my father can't read English words, even
though my father's only reading includes the brown-ink *Esto* sports magazines from Mexico City and the bloody *¡Alarma!* magazines that feature
yet another sighting of *La Virgen de Guadalupe* on a tortilla or a wife's
revenge on her philandering husband by bashing his skull in with a *molca-
jete* (a kitchen mortar made of volcanic rock). Or the *fotonovelas,* the little
picture paperbacks with tragedy and trauma erupting from the characters'
mouths in bubbles.

My father represents, then, the public majority. A public who is disinterested in reading, and yet one whom I am writing about and for, and privately trying to woo.

When we were growing up in Chicago, we moved a lot because of my father. He suffered bouts of nostalgia. Then we'd have to let go our flat, store the furniture with Mother's relatives, load the station wagon with baggage and bologna sandwiches and head south. To Mexico City.

We came back, of course. To yet another Chicago flat, another Chicago neighborhood, another Catholic school. Each time, my father would seek out the parish priest in order to get a tuition break, and complain or boast: "I have seven sons."

He meant *siete hijos,* seven children, but he translated it as "sons." "I have seven sons." To anyone who would listen. The Sears Roebuck employee who sold us the washing machine. The short-order cook where my father ate his ham-and-eggs breakfasts. "I have seven sons." As if he deserved a medal from the state.

My papa. He didn't mean anything by that mistranslation, I'm sure. But somehow I could feel myself being erased. I'd tug my father's sleeve and whisper: "Not seven sons. Six! And *one daughter.*"

When my oldest brother graduated from medical school, he fulfilled my father's dream that we study hard and use this—our heads, instead of this—our hands. Even now my father's hands are thick and yellow, stubbed by a history of hammer and nails and twine and coils and springs. "Use this," my father said, tapping his head, "and not this," showing us those hands. He always looked tired when he said it.

Wasn't college an investment? And hadn't I spent all those years in college? And if I didn't marry, what was it all for? Why would anyone go to college and then choose to be poor? Especially someone who had always been poor?

Last year, after ten years of writing professionally, the financial rewards started to trickle in. My second National Endowment for the Arts Fellowship. A guest professorship at the University of California, Berkeley. My book, which sold to a major New York publishing house.

At Christmas, I flew home to Chicago. The house was throbbing, same as always; hot *tamales* and sweet *tamales* hissing in my mother's pressure cooker, and everybody—my mother, six brothers, wives, babies, aunts, cousins—talking too loud and at the same time, like in a Fellini film, because that's just how we are.

I went upstairs to my father's room. One of my stories had just been translated into Spanish and published in an anthology of Chicano writing, and I wanted to show it to him. Ever since he recovered from a stroke two years ago, my father likes to spend his leisure hours horizontally. And that's how I found him, watching a Pedro Infante movie on Galavisión and eating rice pudding.

There was a glass filmed with milk on the bedside table. There were several vials of pills and balled Kleenex. And on the floor, one black sock and a plastic urinal that I didn't want to look at but looked at anyway. Pedro Infante was about to burst into song, and my father was laughing.

I'm not sure if it was because my story was translated into Spanish, or 19 because it was published in Mexico, or perhaps because the story dealt with Tepeyac, the *colonia* my father was raised in and the house he grew up in, but at any rate, my father punched the mute button on his remote control and read my story.

I sat on the bed next to my father and waited. He read it very slowly. 20 As if he were reading each line over and over. He laughed at all the right places and read lines he liked out loud. He pointed and asked questions: "Is this So-and-so?" "Yes," I said. He kept reading.

When he was finally finished, after what seemed like hours, my father 21 looked up and asked: "Where can we get more copies of this for the relatives?"

Of all the wonderful things that happened to me last year, that was the 22 most wonderful.

■   ■   ■

AFTER YOU READ

■ **THINK** about the relationship between Cisneros and her father. What upsets Cisneros about this relationship? How does Cisneros's distinction between "only daughter" and "*only* a daughter" (paragraph 3) reveal much of what concerns her? What kind of relationship, or reaction, does she want from her father?

■ **EXAMINE** the passages that you underlined describing Cisneros's relationship with her father. What particular experience creates a significant improvement in that relationship? Why do you think this experience is so important not only to Cisneros but also to her father?

■ **WRITE** a personal essay—perhaps a narrative essay—about "the most wonderful" experience you have had with your father (or another close relative). Be sure that you not only describe the experience fully but also explain its importance. (For help with writing personal essays, see pages 128–133; for help with narrative essays, see Lesson 1 on the *Interactions*, eighth edition, student website at www.cengagebrain.com.)

■ Or **WRITE** an essay comparing and contrasting the expectations that parents—especially fathers—have for daughters in contrast to sons. (See Lesson 7 on the *Interactions* student website at www.cengagebrain.com for help with writing comparison and contrast essays.)

A Daughter's Journey

■ ■ ■

SHARON LIAO

This reading, like the ones that precede and follow it, narrates an individual's journey to a greater understanding of, and closeness with, family. On a trip to China with her parents, Sharon Liao came to understand more about her parents and their culture—and therefore more about herself. A graduate of the University of North Carolina at Chapel Hill, Liao has worked in various journalistic positions for *The Washingtonian*, *Reader's Digest*, *Fitness Magazine*, and *Prevention*. The following essay appeared in the January 2001 issue of the *Washingtonian*.

BEFORE YOU READ

■ **THINK** about the title, "A Daughter's Journey." A person taking a journey moves from one place to another, but, as in the experience of Sharon Liao, a journey can be emotional and intellectual as well as physical. Have you ever taken a physical or emotional journey in which you learned more about yourself or some member of your family? What did you learn?

■ **EXAMINE** the word *enigma* in this sentence: "My parents' pre-American life was an *enigma* to me" (paragraph 10). An enigma is something that is puzzling or difficult to explain.

■ **WRITE** a journal entry about something in the life of one or both of your parents that has been difficult for you to understand. Or write a journal entry about a physical or emotional journey you took in which you learned more about yourself and/or some member of your family.

AS YOU READ

Underline passages that show Liao is developing a greater understanding of and respect for her parents.

■ ■ ■

I should have been just another face in the blur of bodies that circled 1
through the hotel lobby in Zhang Jia Jie, a city in central China. But my words singled me out.

"Yun dou," I repeated to the red-capped clerk. Maybe he understood 2
English: "Do you have a gym here?"

The clerk blinked, studying the incongruity between English words and ₃ my half-moon eyes, rounded nose, and midnight hair. Then he reached behind the counter and pulled out an iron, as if laundry could substitute for exercise.

I smiled blankly. My brain rooted through my limited Chinese vocabu- ₄ lary. After a minute of silence, my dad strolled up, his eyebrows arched in amused triangles.

"She wants to know where the gym is," he supplied in rapid Mandarin ₅ Chinese, his native language. He turned to me and explained gently, "Yun dong is exercise, Sharon. Yun dou means iron."

I mumbled a sheepish apology to the laughing clerk and glanced at my ₆ dad. A look of recognition flashed through his eyes: We had gone through this before.

Only this time, the tables were turned. For the first time, I realized how ₇ my parents must have felt throughout their 27 years as American citizens. Like strangers in their own country.

When I was younger, I would sometimes close my eyes and try to ₈ imagine my parents as children. What were they like growing up in China and Taiwan?

But I could only envision them in the grainy black-and-white of their ₉ faded childhood pictures. It was not until I saw a photo from 1973, when my dad was 38 and my mom was 24, that I could finally visualize them in vivid color, clad in bell-bottoms and smiling in front of our North Carolina house.

My parents' pre-American life was an enigma to me. Their childhood 10 stories didn't match the people I knew. I couldn't picture my domestic mom, unsure of her halting English, studying international economics at a Taiwanese university. I laughed at the image of my stern father, an electrical engineer, chasing chickens in his Chinese village.

I related to my parents' pre-American lives as only a series of events, 11 like facts for some high-school history exam. My dad fled to Taiwan in 1949 as a 14-year-old, after the Communists won the civil war. His father fought for the losing side, the Nationalists. My mom's father, a Nationalist navy captain, also retreated to Taiwan. My mom grew up thinking that her family would eventually return to China, after the Nationalists reclaimed their homeland.

That didn't happen, and my parents did not step onto Chinese soil for 12 more than 50 years—after spending half their lives in the United States and raising both of their children as Americans. When they finally returned to the "mainland," they brought along a product of their American life. They brought me, their 22-year-old daughter.

For the past three years, my parents' circle of friends has arranged an 13 annual trip to a different region of China. Like my parents, the majority fled to Hong Kong and Taiwan as children. As young adults, they moved to the United States to lead better lives. Now they return to China as a reminder of the past.

This was the first year my parents decided to participate in the trip. They 14 asked my older brother, Tim, and me to join them on their six-city tour across the middle of China.

I almost said no. There were plenty of reasons not to accompany my parents. My brother couldn't go because of medical-school courses. I recently graduated from college and was itching to move from North Carolina to Washington. I wanted to start my new job at *The Washingtonian* and settle in my Rosslyn apartment. 15

Besides, I had already traveled through China; I spent five months in Beijing on a study-abroad program my sophomore year of college. My next dream vacation was a backpacking trip across India, not a two-week sightseeing tour with my parents and 30 of their friends. 16

I cringed when Mom described details of the trip, which was shaping up to be straight out of one of Chevy Chase's "family vacation" movies. 17

"Everyone wear bright pink or blue hat," she said excitedly. "So no one get lost. Such good idea, don't you think, Sharon?" 18

"Uh, yeah, Mom," I replied, thankful she couldn't see my grimace over the phone. 19

I debated whether I could spend two 17-hour flights trapped next to my parents, who shout stomach-sinking questions like "Sharon, need to go pee-pee?" in public places. The trip seemed like an impossible challenge. Those flights plus 17 more days of travel: Could I make it out with my sanity intact? 20

But something inside urged me to go. I couldn't explain why, after my jam packed list of why-nots, I wanted to spend all my vacation time on my parents. 21

When the plane jerked to a stop in Shanghai, our first destination, all of those reasons I decided to go materialized in the expressions on my parents' faces. My mom folded and unfolded her hands impatiently in her lap. My dad craned over my seat for a glimpse out the porthole window. 22

I was surprised and slightly scared to see my stoic dad's eyes glimmering with emotion. He slipped his hand, soft and spotted with age, in mine. 23

"Last time I was here, more than 50 years ago," he said. "My parents going from north to south, away from the Communists. So much bombing. A lot of people starving." He leaned close and nodded. "You very lucky, Sharon." 24

That was my dad's line. When I would whine as a child, my dad's response was inevitable: "Some people not lucky as you." My brother and I would mimic those words in imitation of him, smothering our giggles. 25

But I never cared about being lucky. I just wanted to be normal. I wanted to be like the other American kids. 26

My parents, however, intended my brother and me to become model Chinese-Americans. They planned for us to speak fluent Mandarin and switch from American to Chinese culture with the ease and grace of diplomats. 27

It didn't happen. My parents struggled to teach us their culture. Starting from age six, they would drag me away from Saturday cartoons to a Chinese church. 28

I would squirm in my seat while a teacher recited Chinese vocabulary. I dutifully recited my "bo po mo fo's"—the ABCs of speaking Chinese. But 29 in my head, I rearranged the chalk marks that made up characters into pictures of houses and trees.

When four o'clock inched by, I dashed out to the front of the church 30 to meet my parents. For me, Saturday Chinese school wasn't the culturally enriching experience it was intended to be. It was a major drag.

When I turned nine, I declared I wasn't going to Chinese school any 31 more.

"This stinks," I yelled. "None of my friends have to go to extra school 32 and have extra homework. Why do I have to go?"

"Because you Chinese," my mom replied coolly.   33

"Then I don't want to be Chinese," I shouted back, my face turning pink. 34 "It's not fair. I just want to be normal." I almost stopped, but the words were already out of my mouth. "Why can't you and Dad be normal? Why can't you be like everybody else's parents? I wish I was someone else's kid."

I waited for my mom to shout at me or drag me to my room. But she 35 just stared at me with tired eyes. "If you don't want to go, don't have to," she said, turning away.

I opened my mouth to say anything that would erase that deflated look 36 in her eyes. But it was too late.

As an adult, I wince when I remember my behavior. I want to lecture 37 who I was then: Tell her not to yell at her parents because they were different, because that is who they are. Tell her to listen when they teach her Chinese, because that is who she is.

...

As I grew older, my parents often turned to me with questions about 38 American culture and language. Sometimes I felt like the parent, teaching my mom and dad about an American tradition or slang phrase.

I envied my friends' relationships with their parents. It seemed so easy 39 for them. My friends didn't have to worry that their parents would embarrass them with questions like "Is this good price?" and "What's this meaning?"

Their parents chatted easily with each other and our teachers. Their 40 parents understood dating, the prom, and what it was like to grow up with the pressures of drinking, drugs, and sex. Their parents asked them about their social and love lives.

My parents discussed only my grades, career, and prospective salary.   41

Their parents knew the right things to say. My parents spoke in thickly 42 accented English. My stay-at-home mom speaks English like I speak Chinese: slowly, halting, and punctuated by "um"s and "ah"s. She becomes confused when someone speaks English too rapidly.

I recognize my mom's I-don't-get-it look instantly. Her mouth freezes 43 in a polite smile. Her eyes cloud with confusion, and a thin line traces across her forehead. When her face molds into that blank stare, I know it's time to explain something.

About a month before we left for China, I helped my mom return a pur- 44 chase to Wal-Mart. The clerk rudely ignored my mom's slow English, speaking to me instead.

In the car, my mom thanked me for my help. "Xie xie, Sharon," she   45
said.

I kept my eyes on the road. "It's nothing, Mom."   46

She patted my shoulder. "I have good daughter," she said. "Good   47
American daughter."

In the airport before we departed for China, my parents' friends—   48
many of whom I was meeting for the first time—herded around me. As is
Chinese custom, they fired off one compliment after another.

"Such pretty daughter," they crowed to my beaming dad. "Good swim-   49
mer. So smart."

One man, my "Uncle" Liu, pulled me aside. "Your parents," he said,   50
wagging a finger in my face. "So proud of you. Always talking about
you."

His words surprised me.   51

I felt like I barely spoke with my parents. Did they really know who   52
I was?

Then the question, the one I skirted throughout my adolescent and col-   53
lege years, surfaced in my conscience. Of course I loved my parents. But
did I really know who these people were? Did I even come close to understanding them?

The tour was a 17-day whirlwind beginning in Shanghai. We snaked   54
across the middle of China. We toured lakes laden with lotus flowers,
snapped pictures of jagged mountains rising out of the Yellow River, and
hiked up stone stairs to intricately painted temples.

I saw beautiful things, such as rice paddies cut like square emeralds   55
into the mountainside. I toured interesting places, like a factory where the
employees spun silk into sheets of gloss.

But the best part of the trip was watching my parents. They carried   56
themselves with an ease unfamiliar to me. They blended into the throngs
of Chinese people instead of sticking out as two small dark figures in the
crowd. Even my parents' clothes, tacky and out of date by American standards, fit in.

Their voices swelled with authority. My mom would translate the tour   57
guide's Chinese in her girlish, unwavering voice. She whispered historical
anecdotes she learned in school as we fell in step behind the tour group.

At meals, my parents answered my constant questions. "What's this?"   58
I asked suspiciously about each colorful bowl that would rotate by on the
lazy Susan.

My parents chuckled at my response when a waiter placed a bowl of   59
soup on the table. I was horrified to see the remnants of a turtle floating in
a clear yellow broth. But the rest of the table shouted with excitement.

"Turtle soup, so fragrant!" exclaimed my dad. He ladled a generous   60
portion into his bowl. "I haven't had this since I was young." The other
adults chimed in their stories about the last time they tasted turtle soup.

My table cried in dismay when I let the soup circle past me.   61

"But this is the only time you can have turtle soup," Mr. Bai said,   62
blinking indignantly.

I placed my hand over my soup bowl. "That's okay. Really." 63

"Strange," Mr. Bai said in Chinese, shaking his head. "Such good soup." 64

As in most third world nations, scenes of poverty offset China's exqui- 65 site beauty. Although the nation's economy is developing rapidly, the base standard of living lags behind what I'm accustomed to.

It was hard for me to step off our air-conditioned tour bus into a 66 crowd of dusty children clutching begging cups. Sometimes I felt guilty as I boarded our cruise ship with my arms full of souvenirs. I felt the employees sizing up my purchases.

It reminded me of a conversation my dad and I had near the beginning 67 of the trip. "Guess how much our tour guide makes in one year," he'd said. "No? She makes 400 yuan a year. Can you believe it?"

I calculated the figures. The guide, a cute girl just out of college, earned 68 50 US dollars a year.

Later, our group toured a college campus in Nanjing. A student let me 69 inside her dorm so I could use the bathroom. As I walked down the hall to the toilet, I gaped at the dorm rooms. They reminded me of my two-person college room, about the same size with poster-covered walls. But six beds were crammed into each room.

The student rambled on about her aspirations. "Everyone here studies 70 computer science, minor in English," she said. "We all hope to move to America one day. I study all day so I can make good score on GRE. Do you know GRE?"

I looked at this fresh-faced girl, barely out of her teens. "I could be this 71 girl," I thought. Then I wondered, "What if I was this girl? What would I be like if I grew up here?"

How very different I would be. Maybe more like my parents. 72

My experience in China pieced together the puzzle I knew as my par- 73 ents. For the first time, I saw them in their entirety. I saw them in their culture, not in mine.

I realized that many things I found embarrassing or frustrating about 74 my parents were normal in China.

I understood why my parents moved, talked, and acted the way they 75 did. I understood why my dad constantly reminded me I was lucky. My own face molded into my mom's I-don't-get-it look. Even her attempts at birthday cake made sense.

Halfway through the trip, I craved cookies and sweets. In China, meals 76 typically end with a plate of sliced oranges or pears.

I was thrilled when I discovered one hotel restaurant that offered West- 77 ern cuisine. I beckoned the waiter and ordered a slice of cake. It was picture perfect: pale vanilla swirled with chocolate frosting. I dug in.

My dad asked me how it tasted. 78

I made a face. "Gross," I said, managing to swallow the dry mouthful. 79 "It tastes like Mom's."

He nodded in agreement. "No butter in Chinese cooking," he said. 80 "Not like the soft kind of cake you used to in America. Better stick to fruit."

During the trip I befriended Rachel, the daughter of friends of my parents'. We laughed over feelings we experienced as Chinese-Americans and griped about the toilets.   81

Rachel spoke flawless Chinese and read off the characters on the karaoke screen with ease.   82

"Your daughter speaks such good Chinese," my dad complimented Rachel's dad, Mr. Chow. "And even reads it, too. You must be so proud."   83

I felt awkward standing next to my dad. In Chinese tradition, Mr. Chow was supposed to brush off the compliment and return it heartily. In this case, he slapped his hand on my dad's shoulder and started talking about the next tour stop.   84

I bit my lip. The interaction touched an insecure spot, something I developed in college. Was I not Chinese enough?   85

When I first arrived at the University of North Carolina at Chapel Hill in 1996, the number of Asians on campus shocked me. I had never seen so many people like me before. My classes included other sleek black heads. It was a complete contrast to elementary school.   86

There were Asian clubs, classes, sororities, and events. Here my Chinese-American background didn't isolate me. I took pride in who I was.   87

I enrolled in a number of Chinese- and Asian-studies classes to compensate for the many years I ignored my heritage. I read books on history and culture. I traveled to Beijing in a language program, where I learned so many things about China and myself.   88

But through it all, I still doubted myself as a Chinese-American when I couldn't answer a Chinese-history question or speak fluently. I felt like an imposter in Chinese skin.   89

Near the end of the trip, my parents and I decided not to hike up the Zhang Jia Jie mountain range. We sat and talked on a bench overlooking the towering stone monoliths.   90

It was a few days after "the iron incident," as my confused run-in with the hotel clerk became known in our tour group.   91

"Too bad I don't speak fluent Chinese," I said wistfully. "I should have learned it when I was little. I should have listened when you tried to teach it to me."   92

Other apologies surfaced in my mind but didn't make it out of my lips. I wanted to tell my parents that if I could go back in time, I would act differently. I would accept myself for who I was and them for who they were.   93

But my dad looked at me with understanding. He gently covered my hand with his. "It's okay," he said. "You learning it now."   94

My mom smiled supportively. "Never too late," she said.   95

I have struggled to put that trip, 19 days in total, into words. When I look back, I realize how much it changed my life.   96

When I speak to my parents on the phone from my Rosslyn apartment, there is a mutual understanding. Our conversations extend past the two-dimensional questions about where they went out to eat or how my job is going. I talk about my life. My parents talk about what they were doing when   97 they were my age, and I can imagine them with crystal clarity: fresh young students at Taiwanese universities.

Moving to Washington, with its large Asian population, completes the 98
picture. I look in admiration at children on the street, babbling in Chinese to their parents. I can't wait for my parents to visit so I can show them Chinatown and the Chinese artifacts at the Freer Gallery of Art.

I reflected on these things one day while waiting for the Metro about a 99
week after I returned from China.

A middle-aged Asian man clutching his young son leaned over to me. 100
He made friendly conversation, pointing to my jade pendant threaded on a bright red string around my neck.

"Where did you get this?" he asked, his words slanting in a familiar 101
accent.

"Oh, my mom bought it for me in China," I replied, sliding the cool 102
bit of green between my fingers. "I was there just last week."

"I am from Hong Kong," he said. "You are Chinese?"   103

"I was born here, but my parents are from China and Taiwan," I ex- 104
plained. We chatted about the places and sights I saw on my trip. The Metro squealed into the stop.

"Nice that you went to China with your parents," he said.   105

It was nice, I reflected, as I stepped onto a Metro car.   106

I am very lucky.   107

■ ■ ■

AFTER YOU READ

■ **THINK** about how Liao felt as a child growing up in the United States. Which was more important to her—being like her peers or being like her parents? Do you think most young people have similar feelings? Do you think Liao's Asian heritage initially drew her closer to her parents or separated her from them? Support your opinions.

■ **THINK** also about the effect that Liao's trip to China with her parents had on her. How did this journey help Liao to develop a greater understanding of and respect for her parents?

■ **EXAMINE** the sentence with which Liao concludes her narrative: "I am very lucky." Identify and comment on similar statements earlier in the essay. How does this last sentence show the importance of Liao's trip with her parents and what she has learned about herself from this journey?

■ **WRITE** a personal essay in which you explain how your relationship with one or both of your parents—or parent figure(s)—has changed over time. (See "Writing a Personal Essay," pages 128–133.)

A Parent's Journey Out of the Closet

■ ■ ■

AGNES G. HERMAN

This essay, like the preceding one by Sharon Liao, describes a personal journey in which an individual develops a greater understanding of her family and herself. As a social worker and the wife of a rabbi, Agnes Herman thought she was prepared for being a mother. But discovering that her nineteen-year-old son was gay forced her to come to terms with some difficult issues. In this essay she tells of her "journey"—the long struggle she underwent in order to accept her son's sexuality without blame or guilt.

BEFORE YOU READ

■ **THINK** about what it means to be gay or lesbian in a society such as ours. How do most cultures view homosexuality? How does our culture view homosexuality? How have attitudes toward this sexual orientation changed in recent years?

■ **EXAMINE** the title of this essay. What does "coming out of the closet" usually mean today? How has our perception of this phrase and the process to which it refers changed in recent years? From the title, what do you expect the parent's attitude and situation to be?

■ **EXAMINE** also the traditional Jewish words from Herman's essay that are discussed in this paragraph. The *kiddush* (paragraph 1) is the blessing of the bread and wine at the beginning of a Jewish Sabbath or holy day, and a *challah* (paragraph 1) is a leavened and plaited loaf of bread used in celebrating the Sabbath. *Bris* (paragraph 1) refers to the circumcision of a male infant when he is about eight days old, and a *bar mitzvah* (paragraph 7) is the ceremony that a boy undergoes at age thirteen to indicate that he has reached adulthood. The *seder* (paragraph 39) is the ritual and ceremonial dinner held on the first evening of Passover, the spring Jewish festival recalling the freeing of the ancient Israelites from Egypt.

■ **WRITE** a journal entry in which you explore your position on the issue of homosexuality. Has your position changed in some way? If so, why and how?

AS YOU READ

Trace Herman's journey out of the closet, indicating in the margins each step forward in her struggle to accept her son's sexual orientation.

■ ■ ■

When we agreed to adopt seven-month-old Jeff, we knew that his life as a member of a Jewish family would begin the moment we brought him to our home. We celebrated that joyous homecoming with appropriate religious ritual, with blessings recited by Jeff's rabbi father as our gurgling, happy baby teethed on his infant kiddush cup and enjoyed his challah. There, in the warmth of our extended family circle of grandparents, an aunt, an uncle, and the Temple Board, our small son passed comfortably through his bris, his initial Jewish milestone. There would be many more.

By the time he was two, Jeff ate an ice cream cone without spilling a drop; his face came out of the sticky encounter clean. At five, he watched other kids play ball in the alley, standing aside because he had been told not to play there. Besides, he seemed more comfortable playing with the little girl next door. There were awkward moments as he began to grow up, such as the times when the baseball bat, which his father insisted upon, was not comfortable in his hands, but the rolling pin, which his father decried, was. His grandmother, whom he adored, remarked, "Jeff is too good."

I knew she was right, and privately I felt a nagging fear I could hardly express to myself. Was Jeff a "sissy"? That archaic term was the only one I dared whisper to myself. "Gay" only meant "lively and fun-loving"; "homosexual" was a label not to be used in polite society and certainly never to be mentioned in the same sentence with a child's name. Such a term would certainly stigmatize a youngster and humiliate a family.

Jeff continued to be an eager volunteer in the kitchen and a reluctant participant on the ballfield. We fought the former and pressed to correct the latter, frustrating our son while we all grew tense. As to our silent fears, we repressed them.

Jeff developed reading problems in school. We worried, but accepted the in-appropriate assurance offered by his teacher. "He is such a good boy—don't confuse him with counseling." We bought it, for a while. As the reading problems continued, Jeff did enter therapy and was helped to become less anxious and learn how to read all over again. At our final parental consultation with the psychiatrist, I hesitantly asked, "Doctor, I often worry that Jeff is effeminate. What do you think?" I held my breath while he offered his reassurance: "There is nothing wrong with your son. He is a sensitive boy—not aggressive or competitive. So he likes girls! In a few years you will be worrying about that for other reasons."

Jeff looked forward eagerly to religious school. He accompanied his dad, helped around the temple, and received many kudos. He was quick, efficient, and willingly took instructions. In later years, even after his father was no longer in the pulpit, Jeff continued his role as a temple volunteer. He moved chairs and carried books; later, he changed fuses, focused spotlights, and handled sound equipment. Jeff was comfortable; it was "his" temple. Other children there shared his interests and became his friends, later forming the temple youth group.

Bar mitzvah class, however, was a difficult obstacle. When Hebrew be- 7
came a daily family battle, we withdrew him from Hebrew school to be tutored instead by his father. He spent a substantial amount of time, which otherwise was not available, with his dad. As a result, a potential failure was transformed into another family milestone. Jeff yawned his way through formal bar mitzvah training, but when his big day arrived, he was prepared, and pleased even himself.

During confirmation and youth group years, Jeff seemed to be strug- 8
gling to be like his peers. Temple became the center of his life. He worked and played there, dated, went steady, and attended meetings and dances. He shared with no one—not his parents, his friends, or his rabbi—his own feelings of being "different."

When Jeff was sixteen, we moved from New Rochelle to Los Angeles. It 9
was a difficult move for him, cutting off relationships and sources of recognition and acceptance. As we settled into our new home, Jeff began to explore the San Fernando Valley, enrolled in high school, and tried to make new friends. At our insistence, he attended one meeting of the local temple youth group, but felt rejected by the youngsters there. That marked the unfortunate beginning of Jeff's disenchantment with synagogues and withdrawal from family religious observances and celebrations.

Jeff gradually acclimated to his new environment. He took Amy, a 10
Jewish girl his own age, to the senior prom; he cruised Van Nuys Boulevard on Wednesdays with Ann. He was always on the move—coming home to eat, shower, change clothes, and zip out again. We blamed it on the fast pace of California and the novelty of having his own "wheels": first a motorcycle, and then a car. There were several accidents—none serious, thank heavens! Again, in retrospect, the furious struggle with his identity must have played a part in his fast-paced behavior. At the time, though, we buried our heads in the sand, believing that Jeff was merely behaving like every other teenager.

After high school, the pace seemed to slow down a bit. So when Jeff 11
was nineteen and we decided to leave him in charge for the six months of our sabbatical world tour, we had no hesitation. Conscientious and cautious, he could handle the cars and the checkbook. He would continue in college and be available to his sister Judi, also attending college. We flew off to Europe and Israel, confident and secure.

When an overseas call came three months later in Jerusalem, my heart 12
beat fast, and my sense of well-being faltered slightly. "Everything is fine, no problem. I have quit college. Now don't get excited.... I want to go to business school and study interior design. Jobs are plentiful; I know a guy who will hire me the minute I graduate."

Jeff had always shown a creative flair for color and design. He con- 13
stantly rearranged our furniture, changing one room after another. All this raced through my mind as I held the phone, separated from him by

9000 miles. Erv and I looked at each other, wished Jeff luck, and told him to write the check for his tuition.

When we finally returned home, Jeff was obviously depressed. His an- 14 swers to our questions were surly, clipped, and evasive. Behaving unlike his usual loving self, he ran in and out of the house silently, furtively, always in a hurry. He seemed uninterested in our trip and was clearly trying to avoid us.

One day during Passover, Erv was searching for a favorite cantorial 15 record that Jeff often appropriated. He checked Jeff's record collection and poked about among the torn jeans. Speechless and ashen, Erv returned to the breakfast room and dropped a book into my lap: *Homosexuality in Modern Society.* "This was hidden in Jeff's room." My heart raced and skipped. Confrontation was finally at hand, not only with Jeff, but with my own fears as well.

Then our son came through the front door on the run: "I'm late ... can't 16 stop ... talk to you later."

The tone of our response and expressions on our faces stopped him 17 mid flight. "Son, stand still! Something is going on, you are not yourself! Are you in trouble? Drugs, maybe? Is one of your girlfriends pregnant? Or, are you, is it possible that you are ... homosexual?"

I waited, trembling. The faces of my beloveds were creased with anger 18 and worry. I could barely breathe.

"Yes, I am gay." A simple sentence, yet I did not understand. Nothing 19 was "gay"!

We asked in unison, "What does that mean?"   20

"I am homosexual," he explained. After long minutes of uncomfort- 21 able conversation, we sent Jeff on his way with "we'll talk later." I ran from the room to what was to become my comfort zone, the cool tile of the bathroom floor, and I cried my eyes out. I guess Erv went to work. All we can recall now is that neither of us could face the reality right then.

That evening and the next, we did an enormous amount of soul- 22 searching. What did I, a social worker, know about homosexuality? What did my husband, the rabbi, know? Our academic credentials were impressive—professionally we were both well-trained to help other people in pain. But in our personal distress, we felt helpless.

Everything I had ever heard about homosexuality destroyed all my 23 dreams about our son's future. He would never marry and have children. His warmth, caring, good looks, and so many other wonderful traits would not be passed along to a son or daughter, a grandchild. We wondered whether we could keep him in our family circle, or would we lose him to "that other world" of homosexuality, a world that was foreign to us.

We wracked ourselves with self-blame—what did we do wrong? I ac- 24 cepted all the myths about homosexuality. First, the myth of the strong mother—I was a strong mother, but what mother doesn't overexert her influence on her children? Second, the myth of the absent father—Erv spent so much time crisscrossing the country, berating himself for not being at home enough. Third was the myth of seduction—had someone lured Jeff into this awful lifestyle? And then, finally, I believed the myth of "the cure"—that the right therapist could change Jeff's sexual orientation.

We did seek help from a therapist. He was patient, caring, and accept-   25
ing of Jeff and his lifestyle. He helped us begin to sort out myth from real-
ity and guided us through a tangled web of grief, pain, and disappointment. He gently destroyed our unrealistic hope of "changing" Jeff. Our abiding love for our son was, of course, the key to this difficult yet hopeful journey.

I did not like Jeff's lifestyle at that time, but that did not interfere with   26
my love for him. Understanding and acceptance gradually grew, but the path to real comfort continued to be bumpy.

Jeff sought help, too. At nineteen, he admitted that there was much   27
that he wanted to know about himself. During that time, he offered a com-
ment that we gratefully accepted: "Please stop blaming yourselves. It is not your fault that I have grown up gay." With those words, Jeff erased our most devastating, yet unspoken, anxiety.

Time moved along for all of us. We grieved the loss of deeply held ex-   28
pectations for our son's life. We experienced inner turmoil. Jeff struggled to make peace with himself. We learned to support one another.

Over time, we came to understand that a child who is homosexual   29
needs no less understanding, support, and acceptance than one who is het-
erosexual. Clearly, our gay son has the same human needs that his straight sister has: for empathy and patience, for security and success, for caring and love. Rejection is difficult for both our children, yet perhaps more so for our gay child. Society has taught him that he will experience less vali-
dation and more unnecessary pain. He, and all of us who love him, are vulnerable to that pain.

It became clear that Jeff's sexual orientation was only one part of his   30
life. There remained the ordinary concerns and controversies intrinsic to raising any child. Jeff rode the roller coaster of financial and vocational problems. We provided advice, which he sometimes accepted, and loans, which he often repaid. Jeff's married sister behaved in much the same manner.

Jeff became ill and required the usual chicken soup and tender care in   31
his apartment. He preferred receiving that attention from friends, but also expected Mother and Dad to stop by regularly with reassurance and love. His sister behaved the same way when she broke her leg and was living alone.

When a love affair went sour, Jeff became depressed and sad. We wor-   32
ried and tried to be especially sensitive to his pain. The same support was called for when his sister faced divorce with sadness and depression. We were happier when Jeff was living with a friend who cared about him and about whom he cared, and we felt the same way about his sister, now happily remarried.

During all this time, it never occurred to us to turn to the Jewish com- 33
munity for support, though we knew its resources well. We kept our concerns about Jeff's lifestyle to ourselves: We were in the closet. A child's
homosexuality was not something one discussed in 1969 and throughout
the 1970s. And sharing intimacies with others was not our way—these
were matters we had to work out ourselves. We had decided alone, together, to marry each other; we decided alone, together, to have children.
And we decided alone, together, to tough out our son's homosexuality,
confront it, embrace him, and then face the world together.

I recall sitting with close friends one evening. Naturally, the conversa- 34
tion turned to our kids. At one point, someone said, "I think we have
something in common." We all agreed, but even then, none of us could
articulate it. In fact, on the way home, Erv asked, "Are you sure their oldest son is gay?"

Finally we came "halfway out," sharing only with family. We found 35
almost unanimous acceptance; affection for Jeff did not falter. But it was
seventeen long years before we went public in the Jewish community.
Even during the years when my husband was deeply involved in supporting
the establishment of a gay outreach synagogue in Los Angeles, when he
was busy teaching others that Judaism must not turn its back on any of
its children, we did not share our son's homosexuality with the Jewish
public.

I "came out" for us, with Jeff's permission, in 1986, with an article in 36
The Re-constructionist, a national Jewish magazine. The response was
overwhelming. Support from rabbis, lay leaders, and friends poured in
from around the country. Even at that late date, comfortable as we had
become with Jeff's lifestyle, we found those messages heartwarming and
reassuring.

Some of our friends were angry that we had not shared our pain with 37
them. Perhaps we did not trust people to practice compassion and acceptance. Perhaps we did not trust them to understand that we are not failures
as parents. We did not want our son to suffer rejection from those we
loved. We did not want to be rejected by those we loved!

The pressure was greater on Jeff. Because he is a rabbi's child, he felt, 38
correctly, that the expectations of him were high. Jeff was not alone in
fearing the expectations of others; he had learned that sensitivity from us.
Every family feels a need to be without flaws: a nonsensical, impossible attitude, but it is real. Among rabbis' families it is often exaggerated.

Should we have trusted our friends and colleagues from the beginning? 39
Could we have dared to test the support of the synagogue leaders with
whom Erv worked daily? Should we have risked our own self-image and
left the closet earlier? Would any of that have made our son more comfortable at our seder table or at services? I do not have the answers. I believe
we came out only when we were ready; getting ready took a long time.

■ ■ ■

AFTER YOU READ

■ **THINK** about Herman's reaction to the discovery that her son is gay. What are some of the emotions that she experiences? Does she ever question the decision that she and her husband made to adopt Jeff? How does she finally learn to be comfortable with her son's homosexuality? Why would many parents (especially in 1969) have difficulty accepting a child's homosexuality?

■ **EXAMINE** paragraph 29, especially the sentence in which Herman states that "we came to understand that a child who is homosexual needs no less understanding, support, and acceptance than one who is heterosexual." Do you think that Jeff's need for acceptance may actually have been greater than that of most heterosexual children? Why or why not?

■ **EXAMINE** closely the titles of this essay and the previous one by Sharon Liao. How are the journeys of Liao and Herman similar? How are they different?

■ **WRITE** an essay in which you tell of an experience you have had that involved a lengthy process of acceptance. This experience might be a divorce—your own or that of someone close to you, such as your parents; the loss of a family member, perhaps through death or a long-distance move; gaining a new sense of identity, perhaps through sexual awareness or career determination; the acquisition of a new family member, such as a younger sibling, stepparent, or stepsibling; a major setback or failure; or a significant disappointment. Briefly describe the experience, but focus on the process of recovering and adjusting rather than on the experience itself. For guidelines for writing narrative essays, see Lesson 1 on the *Interactions*, eighth edition, student website at www.cengagebrain.com.

■ Or **WRITE** an essay in which you compare the journeys of Herman and Liao, explaining their similarities and differences. Be sure to use specific supporting examples from both essays. See Lesson 7 on comparison and contrast on the *Interactions* student website at www.cengagebrain.com.

Sibling Imprints

■ ■ ■

FRANCINE KLAGSBRUN

A successful editor and writer, Francine Klagsbrun has contributed to both the *Encyclopedia Americana* and *The World Book Encyclopedia*. She has written many informative books for children, published essays in *Ms.* and *Newsweek,* and explored the Jewish faith in her two most recent books, *Jewish Days* (1996) and *The Fourth Commandment* (2002). In the following selection, which is an excerpt from her book *Mixed Feelings: Love, Hate, Rivalry, and Reconciliation among Brothers and Sisters,* Klagsbrun draws on her personal experiences with her brother, Robert Lifton, whose success as a businessman parallels Klagsbrun's own success as a writer.

BEFORE YOU READ

■ **THINK** about your personal experiences with (or observations of) sibling relationships. What feelings were dominant in these relationships— love, jealousy, competition, or some other feeling?

■ **EXAMINE** the title of the selection. How can siblings "imprint" one another?

■ **EXAMINE** also the following phrases and italicized words from Klagsbrun's essay and the definitions provided for you.

1. "psychological *jargon*" (paragraph 22): specialized or technical language

2. "*potency* of sibling influence" (paragraph 33): strength

3. "feel *despondent*" (paragraph 34): depressed, dejected

4. "*empathy*" among young children" (paragraph 39): such complete understanding that one almost feels like the person for whom the understanding is felt

5. "*oblivious* of one's parents" (paragraph 45): unaware, forgetful

■ **WRITE** a journal entry about your experiences with (or observations of) a sibling relationship.

AS YOU READ

Identify and mark in some way each anecdote (brief narrative) that Klagsbrun includes in her essay. What purposes do these anecdotes serve in the essay?

■ ■ ■

One Sunday afternoon of my childhood stands out in sharp relief   1
from all others. It's a grueling hot day in mid-July. We are on the
way home—my father and mother, my brother Robert, and I—
from a day at Jones Beach, about an hour's drive from our Brooklyn apartment. I am around six years old and my brother around ten.

We have been inching along, stuck in a massive traffic jam. Perspiring   2
from the stifling heat (air conditioners in cars as yet unknown), our bodies
raw from the mixture of sunburn and dried ocean salt and itching from the
tiny grains of sand we have not bothered to wipe away with our towels,
Robert and I fight constantly in the back seat. Irritated, my father finally
pulls off the road and rearranges the seating, my brother in back with my
mother, and I with my father up front. To quiet us, he also buys each a
Dixie cup—those little round containers filled with equal amounts of chocolate and vanilla ice cream.

I begin nibbling at my ice cream with the flat wooden spoon that ac-   3
companies it, and in nibbling I hatch a delicious plan. I will eat slowly, so
slowly that I will finish *last*. I'll have ice cream left after Robert has gulped
down all of his, and just when he might be wishing for more, I'll produce
mine. "Look," I'll say, "*I* still have ice cream to eat." What I will mean is
that I have something he doesn't have, that this time I will have beaten
him, this older brother whom I adore and idolize, but who has always be-
sted me.

So I nibble slowly at my ice cream with my wooden spoon, and it be-   4
gins to melt.

"Are you finished with your ice cream?" I call out every few minutes.   5

"No, not yet," he answers.   6

On we drive, and the heat becomes more intense, and the ice cream   7
melts and melts until the chocolate runs into the vanilla, and the cup turns
warm and sticky.

"Are you finished yet?" I turn around to try to see how much ice   8
cream he has left, but he holds his cup close to his chest.

"Not yet." And my ice cream is now warm liquid, the chocolate and   9
vanilla completely blended.

Then, finally, triumph.   10

"I'm finished," he says.   11

"Ha-ha," I shout in glorying delight just as I had imagined it. "*I* still   12
have *my* ice cream." I hold up my cup, crushed and leaking now, to show
him. "I scream, you scream, we all scream for ice cream," I chant, and in
the next moment quickly gulp down the syrupy mixture. It bears little resemblance to the cool treat it had once been, yet nothing I have ever tasted
is as pleasing to me as this victory.

"Ha-ha yourself." My brother's voice, rocking with laughter, rises   13
from the back seat as I swallow the last drop. "I fooled you. I still have
mine." Leaning forward, he shows me the leftover in his own cup, then

proceeds to drink slowly, all the while bending close to my face so that my utter defeat will not for one second be lost on me.

Tricked! But worse. He has won again. I cannot make my mark. I can- 14 not get a leg up on him, not even with a cup of ice cream soup. I bellow with the pain only a child knows who has been totally outwitted.

"It's not fair!" I scream. "He always gets what he wants. He always 15 has more than I have. I can never win. I can never have anything of my own."

My brother roars with glee. "I scream, you scream, we all scream for 16 ice cream," he mocks as I bawl uncontrollably. My parents laugh also, scolding me for acting like a baby. Why all this fuss? It's nothing more than ice cream, after all. What difference does it make who ate it first?

But I know what the fuss is about. It's about much more than ice 17 cream. It's about coming out ahead for once. It's about establishing myself and holding my own. It's about being recognized.

Decades pass.   18

I am now a writer and my brother a businessman.   19

"You know, don't you," my husband says to me one evening when 20 I'm describing to him some of my research and findings about adult siblings, "that I make a point of trying to avoid putting myself into situations with you that you would perceive as competitive?"

"What do you mean?" I ask cautiously.   21

Although my husband is a psychiatrist, there has long been an unspo- 22 ken agreement between us that he not apply the tools of his profession to our family life. Little psychological jargon ever gets tossed around our home, and few of our discussions—or arguments—serve as sources for analytic interpretations. Now, however, I feel a worm of suspicion gnawing within. What is he trying to tell me?

"You've been talking about the influence of siblings," he says, "and 23 I was thinking that I try to steer clear of situations that would stir up in you the old feelings of competition you have with Robert."

"First of all," I reply, "Robert and I get along just fine. Secondly, my 24 old competitions with him have nothing to do with anything that goes on between us—you and me. Third of all ..." I hesitate. "So what kinds of situations have you avoided that you think would make me feel competitive toward you?"

"Well," he says slowly, "I haven't written a book, even though I've 25 thought about doing so from time to time."

"Written a book!" I explode. "Why should you write a book? *I'm* the 26 writer in the family. You run a hospital, you hold academic appointments. You have everything you want. Why should you move in on my turf ? Why can't I ever have anything of my own?" Echoing that long-forgotten wail of childhood, I add with fervor, "It's not fair!"

I stop, astonished at the vehemence of my reaction.   27

"Okay," I say, trying to laugh. "You made your point. Maybe I do 28 repeat with you some of the competitive feelings I had with Robert. Let's drop this subject."

"Sure."   29

"Want some ice cream?"   30

I have never been unaware of the importance my brother holds in my   31
life. That awareness, in fact, motivated this book, with its goal of exploring
and unraveling the mysteries of sibling attachments. But it was not until
I was well into my investigations, not until my conversation with my husband, that I became truly conscious of the lasting imprint my relationship
with my brother has had on all aspects of my existence, including my
marriage.

What I discovered in myself I have seen operating in others as well.   32
The effects of our early experiences with brothers and sisters remain with
us long after childhood has ended, long after the experiences themselves
have faded into the past, influencing us as adults in ways we rarely recognize, from the intimate relationships we establish with lovers and spouses,
to the attitudes we carry into the workplace, to our behavior toward our
children.

The woman who, twice, married and divorced "exciting, dynamic and   33
irresponsible" men much like her younger brother is an example of the potency of that sibling influence. So is the corporate executive who time and
again, without realizing it, stops himself from going after the top position
in his company because somewhere within he believes that only his older
brother and not he is capable of filling such a role. And so too—to take
one more example—is the lawyer who describes growing up with a domi-
neering older sister who physically and emotionally grabbed everything
from her: clothes, toys, eventually even her friends.

"My sister dominates my life," the lawyer says, although they live   34
miles apart and have little contact. She explains: "I still can't deal with
any kind of rivalry. If I know someone else is competing with me for a
client, I pull back. But at the same time, I feel despondent if the client
doesn't come to me, as if I've lost out to my sister again. I have the same
reaction to love triangles. I get into a terrible state if I think another
woman is at all interested in a man I'm going out with. I don't want someone I care about to be taken away from me the way my sister took everything that meant something. But neither can I fight for what I want."

More aware of such inner conflicts, perhaps, than many people, she   35
says, "In every relationship that I encounter, I reenact what I had with my
sister."

We usually associate such reenactments with our parents, and certainly   36
both professional and popular literature have made us conscious of the
dominant and lasting impact of our parents on our lives. Yet the more
closely one examines the sibling experience, the more evident it becomes
that the bond between brothers and sisters leaves its own stamp, separate
and apart from the mark parents make, and, in turn, demands scrutiny on
its own.

Unlike the ties between parents and children, the connection among   37
siblings is a horizontal one. That is, sibs exist on the same plane, as peers,
more or less equals. Although one may be stronger or more dominant than

others, brothers and sisters rarely exert the kind of power and authority over one another that parents hold over their children. Nor are there rules, codes of behavior for different stages of life or biblical commandments mandating siblings to respect and honor one another as they must respect and honor parents. As a result they are freer, more open, and generally more honest with each other, than they are with parents, and less fearful of punishment or rejection. As children, they say what is on their minds, without censoring their words or concerning themselves about the long-range effects of their emotions on one another. Even as adults, many sibs speak more bluntly to each other than they dare to friends or colleagues.

The freedom siblings enjoy with one another and the peer status they 38 hold also allow them greater intimacy than they have with their mothers or fathers. In growing up, sisters and brothers often spend more time alone together than they do with parents, and they get to know each other in ways that their parents never know them. An older child reexperiences her own past in playing with a younger one. The younger learns from sharing the older's activities, and in the process comes to understand both his sib and himself.

Together, siblings become experts in penetrating each other's thoughts 39 and feelings. Studies of empathy among young children have found that toddlers as young as two or three are able to interpret for their parents baby siblings' expressions and noises and explain a baby's wishes that a mother or father doesn't understand. "He wants to go out," an older child will say, or, "She's hungry," or, "Pick her up, Mommy," and usually the information will be correct.

Siblings have a compelling need to accumulate the knowledge they 40 have of each other. Each *wants* to know what makes the other tick. Each *wants* to know which buttons to press to make the other cry or cringe. Each also wants to know how to make the other laugh and how to win the other's love and approval. In its intensity, their mutual knowledge becomes all-embracing—a naked understanding that encompasses the very essence of the other's being.

Once gained, that gut understanding remains a crucial part of the link 41 between siblings for life. Even after years of separation, an adult brother or sister may quickly, intuitively, pick up on another's thoughts, sympathize with the other's needs, or zero in—unerringly—on the other's insecurities.

The intimate knowledge siblings hold is not limited to themselves; it 42 also includes knowledge of their parents. Sibs are able to validate for one another realities about their parents. They may be the only ones who know, for instance, that beneath the wit and charm the world sees in their parents lies a cold, mutual anger that causes the family great suffering. More important, children often blame themselves for a parent's cruel or disturbed behavior. A brother or sister helps free the other from his guilt and blame, helps define family conditions for the other.

Discussing the pain of growing up with an abusive, alcoholic father, one 43 man said, "My older sister was like an oasis I could escape to. I could bounce things off her and say, 'Hey, what's happening?' and she would reassure me that none of it was my fault, that it had nothing to do with me. I'll always be grateful to her for that."

But even in happy homes young siblings become allies. They may fight 44 and scream at each other, but they also offer one another solace and safety in a world that appears overwhelmingly stacked in favor of adults. They share secrets parents never hear, and communicate with each other through signals and codes, private languages whose meanings only they know.

One of my sweetest recollections of the past is that of lying in bed late 45 at night, speaking to my brother through the wall of our adjoining rooms. We speak loudly, oblivious of our parents in their bedroom down the hall. We ... talk "silly talk," making up nonsense words and sounds that send us into peals of laughter and affirm for me that nobody is as clever and funny as my big brother.

"Shush," my mother quiets us angrily. "Go to sleep, both of you." 46

We snort as we try to squelch the waves of giggles that envelop us, 47 dizzyingly conscious of our superiority to the parents we have excluded from our club.

"Are you asleep?" we continue to call out to each other in stage whispers 48 until the voice down the hall sounds as though it means business, and one of us drifts off.

Through their clubby confidences and shared secrets, through the time 49 they spend alone and the knowledge they gain, siblings learn to cooperate and get along together. They discover the meaning of loyalty, and master skills in defending one another against the outside even in the midst of their own angers or vicious battles. They cultivate their ability to have fun, to laugh and make jokes. They gain their first experiences in knowing themselves as individuals but also as persons connected to others. In short, they learn what it means to be "we" and not just "I."

Eventually what siblings learn with each other gets transferred to their 50 dealings with the world beyond the family, to schoolmates and friends, later to adult peers.

With their learning and knowledge siblings also build a personal his- 51 tory that serves as a reference point through the years. That is not to say that brothers and sisters have identical histories. Each child in a family experiences life differently, relates differently to parents, and creates a different and unique environment for the other. Yet there is a family ethos and a pool of memories—of parental attitudes, of humor and expectations, of vacations and hard times—that transcend individual experiences and form a common past for siblings.

The pull of memory and history and the rewards of sibling companion- 52 ship draw adult brothers and sisters to each other in spite of their differences.

■ ■ ■

AFTER YOU READ

- ■ **THINK** about how one sibling can "imprint" or influence another sibling's life. In class discussion, give examples of such imprints from the reading as well as from your personal experience and observation.

- ■ **EXAMINE** the author's conversation with her husband in paragraphs 20 to 30. What discovery does she make about herself as well as about her relationships with her brother and her husband?

- ■ **EXAMINE** also the final paragraph (52), which provides a partial statement of the essay's thesis. In your opinion, what other element(s) form part of the thesis? State Klagsbrun's thesis in your own words.

- ■ **WRITE** a summary of this selection. (*Hint:* Before you begin your summary, be sure to determine the thesis and main ideas of the essay. Remember that most examples should be omitted in a summary, although you may include brief versions of important extended examples. For additional help with writing summaries, see pages 186–188.)

- ■ Or **WRITE** a brief essay describing a particular relationship between siblings. Be sure your essay includes a clear thesis, or main point, about that relationship.

FOCUS ON DESCRIPTION

Brothers

■ ■ ■

BRET LOTT

Not only have the stories of Bret Lott, editor of *The Southern Review*, appeared in publications such as *Story, The Iowa Review,* and *The Southern Review,* but many of them have also been widely anthologized. He has published several novels and two collections of stories as well as two memoirs, *Before We Get Started: A Practical Memoir of the Writer's Life* (2006), and *Fathers, Sons, and Brothers: The Men in My Family* (1997); in the latter, he analyzes the relationships among the male members of his family. Like the preceding essay by Francine Klagsbrun, Lott's essay focuses on the relationship between siblings. Both authors emphasize the antagonism that often characterizes sibling relationships as well as the real affection that siblings usually feel for each other, and both use anecdotes, or brief narratives, to develop their essays. However, Klagsbrun is direct and explicit, stating her arguments clearly, while Lott implies, or suggests, the thesis of his primarily descriptive essay.

BEFORE YOU READ

■ **THINK** about family pictures and how they are a type of family history, giving a glimpse of the past and prompting memories that might otherwise lie buried. How do pictures differ from verbal records? Which are "truer"?

■ **EXAMINE** the different sections of this essay. How many sections do you identify? Why do you think a writer would divide a brief essay into different sections?

■ **EXAMINE** the final sentence of this essay: "And here are my own two boys, already embarked." To *embark* means to set forth, as on a journey or a venture. As you read, try to identify the venture on which Lott's two sons are embarking.

■ **WRITE** in your journal about a family picture or photograph that you remember well. Describe in detail the photograph and what it reveals.

AS YOU READ

Try to determine how the author, as an adult, feels about his brother. Also, underline descriptive phrases, both those that state facts and those that appeal to your senses (sight, sound, touch, etc.).

■ ■ ■

This much is fact: 1

There is a home movie of the two of us, sitting on the edge of the swim- 2
ming pool at my grandma and grandpa's old apartment building in Culver
City. The movie, taken sometime in early 1960, is in color, though the color
has faded, leaving my brother Brad and me milk-white and harmless children,
me a year and a half old, Brad almost four. Our mother, impossibly young, is
in the movie, too. She sits next to me, on the right of the screen. Her hair, for
all the fading of the film, is coal black, shoulder length and parted in the middle, curled up on the sides. She has on a bathing suit covered in purple and
blue flowers, the color in them nearly gone. Next to me, on the left of the
screen, is Brad in his white swimming trunks, our brown hair faded to only
the thought of brown hair. I am in the center, my fat arms up, bent at the
elbows, fingers curled into fists, my legs kicking away at the water, splashing
and splashing. I am smiling, the baby of the family, the center of the world at
that very instant, though my mother is pregnant, my little brother Tim some
six or seven months off, my little sister Leslie, the last child, still three years
distant. The pool water before us is only a thin sky blue, the bushes behind us
a dull and lifeless light green. There is no sound.

My mother speaks to me, points at the water, then looks up. She lifts a hand 3
to block the sun, says something to the camera. Her skin is the same white as
ours, but her lips are red, a sharp cut of lipstick moving as she speaks.

I am still kicking. Brad is looking to his right, off the screen, his feet in 4
the water, too, but moving slowly. His hands are on the edge of the pool,
and he leans forward a little, looks down into the water.

My mother still speaks to the camera, and I give an extra hard kick, 5
splash up shards of white water.

Brad flinches at the water, squints his eyes, while my mother laughs, 6
puts a hand to her face. She looks back to the camera, keeps talking, a
hand low to the water to keep more from hitting her. I still kick hard, still
send up bits of water, and I am laughing a baby's laugh, mouth open and
eyes nearly closed, arms still up, fingers still curled into fists.

More water splashes at Brad, who leans over to me, says something. 7
Nothing about me changes: I only kick, laugh.

He says something again, his face leans a little closer to mine. Still I kick. 8

This is when he lifts his left hand from the edge of the pool, places it on 9
my right thigh, and pinches hard. It's not a simple pinch, not two fingers
on a fraction of skin, but his whole hand, all his fingers grabbing the flesh
just above my knee, and squeezing down hard. He grimaces, his eyes on his
hand, on my leg.

And this is when my expression changes, of course: in an instant I go from   10
a laughing baby to a shocked one, my mouth a perfect O, my body shivering
so that my legs kick even harder, even quicker, but just this one last time.
They stop, and I cry, my mouth open even more, my eyes all the way closed.
My hands are still in fists.

Then Brad's hand is away, and my mother turns from speaking to the   11
camera to me. She leans in close, asking, I am certain, what's wrong.

The movie cuts then to my grandma, white skin and silver hair, seated on   12
a patio chair by the pool, above her a green and white striped umbrella. She
has a cigarette in one hand, waves off the camera with the other. Though
she died eight years ago, and though she, too, loses color with each viewing,
she is still alive up there, still waves, annoyed, at my grandpa and his camera, the moment my brother pinched hell out of me already gone.

This much is fact, too: 13

Thumbtacked to the wall of my office is a photograph of Brad and me,   14
taken by my wife in November 1980, the date printed on the border. In it
we stand together, I a good six inches taller than he, my arm around his shoulder. The photograph is black and white, as though the home movie and its
sinking colors were a prophecy, pointed to this day twenty years later: we
are at the tide-pools at Portuguese Bend, out on the Palos Verdes Peninsula;
in the background are the stone-gray bluffs, to the left of us the beginnings of
the black rocks of the pools, above us the perfect white of an overcast sky.

Brad has on a white Panama hat, a gray hooded sweatshirt, beneath it a   15
collarless shirt. His face is smooth-shaven, and he is grinning, lips together,
eyes squinted nearly shut beneath the brim of the hat. It is a goofy smile,
but a real one.

I have on a cardigan with an alpine design around the shoulders, the   16
rest of it white, the shawl collar on it black, though I know it to have
been navy blue. I have on a button-down Oxford shirt, sideburns almost
to my earlobes. I have a mustache, a pair of glasses too large for my face,
and I am smiling, my mouth open to reveal my big teeth. It isn't my goofy
smile, but a real one, too.

These are the facts of my brother: the four-year-old pinching me, the   17
twenty- four-year-old leaning into me, grinning.

But between the facts of these two images lie twenty years of the play of   18
memory, the dark and bright pictures my mind has retained, embroidered
upon, made into things they are, and things they are not. There are twenty
years of things that happened between my brother and me, from the
fist-fight we had in high school over who got the honeybun for breakfast,
to his phone call to me from a tattoo parlor in Hong Kong, where he'd
just gotten a Chinese junk stitched beneath the skin of his right shoulder
blade; from his showing me one summer day how to do a death drop
from the jungle gym at Elizabeth Dickerson Elementary, to his watching while
his best friend and our next-door neighbor, Lynn Tinton, beat me up on
the driveway of our home, a fight over whether I'd fouled Lynn at basketball.

I remember—memory, no true picture, certainly, but only what I have made the truth by holding tight to it, playing it back in my head at will and in the direction I wish it to go—I remember lying on my back, Lynn's knees pinning my shoulders to the driveway while he hit my chest, and looking up at Brad, the basketball there at his hip, him watching.

I have two children now. Both boys, born two and a half years apart. 19

I showed the older one, Zeb—he is almost eight—the photograph, asked 20
him who those two people were.

He held it in his hands a long while. We were in the kitchen. The bus 21
comes at seven-twenty each morning, and I have to have lunches made,
breakfasts set out, all before that bus comes, and before Melanie takes off
for work, Jacob in tow, to be dropped off at the Montessori school on her
way to her office.

I waited, and waited, finally turned from him to get going on his lunch. 22

"It's you," he said. "You have a lot of hair," he said. 23

"Who's the other guy?" I said. 24

I looked at him, saw the concentration on his face, the way he brought 25
the photograph close, my son's eyes taking in his uncle as best he could.

He said, "I don't know." 26

"That's your Uncle Brad," I said. "Your mom took that picture ten 27
years ago, long before you were ever born."

He still looked at the picture. He said, "He has a beard now." 28

I turned from him, finished with the peanut butter, now spread jelly on the 29
other piece of bread. This is the only kind of sandwich he will eat at school.

He said from behind me, "Only three years before I was born. That's 30
not a long time."

I stopped, turned to him. He touched the picture with a finger. 31

He said, "Three years isn't a long time, Dad." 32

But I was thinking of my question: *Who's the other guy?* and of the 33
truth of his answer: *I don't know.*

Zeb and Jake fight. 34

They are only seven and a half and five, and already Zeb has kicked out 35
one of Jake's bottom teeth. Melanie and I were upstairs wrapping Christmas presents in my office, a room kept locked the entire month of December because of the gifts piled up in there.

We heard Jake's wailing, dropped the bucket of Legos and the red and 36
green Ho! Ho! Ho! paper, ran for the hall and down the stairs.

There in the kitchen stood my two sons, Jacob with his eyes wet, whim- 37
pering now, a hand to his bottom lip.

I made it first, yelled, "What happened?" 38

"I didn't do it," Zeb said, backing away from me, there with my hand 39
to Jacob's jaw. Melanie stroked Jacob's hair, whispered, "What's wrong?"

Jacob opened his mouth then, showed us the thick wash of blood be- 40
tween his bottom lip and his tongue, a single tooth, horribly white, swimming up from it.

"We were playing Karate Kid," Zeb said, and now he was crying. 41
"I didn't do it," he said, and backed away even farther.

One late afternoon a month or so ago, Melanie came home with the 42
groceries, backed the van into the driveway to make it easier to unload
all those plastic bags. When we'd finished, we let the boys play outside,
glad for them to be out of the kitchen while we sorted through the bags
heaped on the counter, put everything away.

Melanie's last words to the two of them, as she leaned out the front 43
door into the near-dark: "Don't play in the van!"

Not ten minutes later Jacob came into the house, slammed shut the front 44
door like he always does. He walked into the kitchen, his hands behind
him. He said, "Zeb's locked in the van." His face takes on the cast of the
guilty when he knows he's done something wrong: his mouth was pursed,
his eyebrows up, his eyes looking right into mine. He doesn't know enough
yet to look away. "He told me to come get you."

He turned, headed for the door, and I followed him out onto the porch 45
where, before I could even see the van in the dark, I heard Zeb screaming.

I went to the van, tried one of the doors. It was locked, and Zeb was 46
still screaming.

"Get the keys!" he was saying. "Get the keys!" 47

I pressed my face to the glass of the back window, saw Zeb inside jump- 48
ing up and down. "My hand's caught," he cried.

I ran into the house, got the keys from the hook beneath the cupboard, 49
only enough time for me to say to Melanie, "Zeb's hand's closed in the
back door," and turned, ran back out.

I made it to the van, unlocked the big back door, pushed it up as quick 50
as I could, Melanie already beside me.

Zeb stood holding the hand that'd been closed in the door. Melanie and 51
I both took his hand, gently examined the skin, wiggled fingers, and in the
dull glow of the dome light we saw that nothing'd been broken, no skin
torn. The black foam lining the door had cushioned his fingers, so that
they'd only been smashed a little, but a little enough to scare him, and to
make blue bruises there the next day.

But beneath the dome light there'd been the sound of his weeping, then 52
the choked words, "Jacob pulled the door down on me."

From the darkness just past the line of light from inside the van came 53
my second son's voice: "I didn't do it."

I have no memory of the pinch Brad gave me at the edge of an apart- 54
ment complex pool, no memory of my mother's black hair—now it's a sort
of brown—nor even any memory of the pool itself. There is only that bit of
film.

But I can remember putting my arm around his shoulder, leaning into 55
him, the awkward and alien comfort of that touch. In the photograph we
are both smiling, me a newlywed with a full head of hair, he only a month
or so back from working a drilling platform in the Gulf of Mexico. He'd

missed my wedding six months before, stranded on the rig, he'd told us, because of a storm.

What I believe is this: that pinch was entry into our childhood; my arm 56 around him, our smiling, the proof of us two surfacing, alive but not unscathed.

And here are my own two boys, already embarked.   57

AFTER YOU READ

■ **THINK** about the six different sections of the essay and how each functions. The first section describes an event that took place beside the pool of Lott's grandparents' apartment when he and his brother Brad were both small; the second section describes in detail a photograph of the brothers twenty years later, focusing first on the two brothers in the center and then moving outward; the third section comments on that twenty-year span; the fourth section describes Lott showing his photograph to his older son; the fifth section is a descriptive narration of two fights between Lott's sons, Zeb and Jake; and the sixth gives Lott's overall impression of the two sets of brothers, connecting their growth experiences.

■ **THINK** about facts versus fiction. Lott includes many facts in his essay, beginning each section with references to facts (i.e., "This much is fact") or with statements of fact ("Zeb and Jake fight"). What types of facts does he include? How does he interpret these facts? Is his interpretation entirely nonfiction? Is it fiction? Even in an essay such as this one based on real people and events, is it possible to stick just with facts? Based on the facts and the implications in the essay, how would you characterize Lott's attitude toward his brother?

■ **EXAMINE** the descriptive details that you underlined while reading the essay. Some of these details are factual; some are sensory. In paragraph 1, for example, the brothers' ages of one and a half and "almost four" are factual, but the description of their "milk-white" skin and their mother's "bathing suit covered in purple and blue flowers" is sensory, appealing to the sense of sight. Work with a group of your classmates to make two lists, one of factual details and one of sensory details, from either section 1 or section 2 of the essay.

■ **WRITE** a descriptive essay of a particular family video or photograph. In describing a video, you will be describing people and an action; in describing a photograph, you will be describing people and an object (the photograph). Be sure to organize your description logically (by time for the video and by space for the photograph) and to include both factual and sensory details. State your thesis, or overall impression, at the beginning or end of your essay. (See Lesson 2 on the *Interactions*, eighth edition, student website available at www.cengagebrain.com for more help with writing a descriptive essay.)

No Snapshots in the Attic: A Granddaughter's Search for a Cherokee Past

■ ■ ■

CONNIE MAY FOWLER

The Irving Bacheller Professor of Creative Writing at Rollins College and an award-winning author, Connie May Fowler has published several novels, the most recent being *The Problem with Murmur Lee* (2006). Much of her work—including the novels *Sugar Cage*, *Before Women Had Wings*, and *Remembering Blue*—was inspired by her childhood experiences in the St. Augustine area of Florida; however, it is her second novel, *River of Hidden Dreams* (1995), that is most closely related to her personal experiences. When her father's early death left her living in poverty with her alcoholic mother, Fowler looked to her paternal grandmother, Oneida Marie Hunter May, for aid and inspiration not only in her life but also in her writings. Frustrated by her grandmother's having hidden her Native American past and by the lack of physical and factual evidence of her own personal heritage—both Native American and European—Fowler begins a physical and mental journey that leads her back to the ancient oral art of storytelling.

BEFORE YOU READ

- ■ **THINK** about your own sense of family heritage. Do you feel that you "know" your ancestors—your grandparents and even great-grandparents whom you may not have ever met? If so, how did you learn about these ancestors? Do you feel that your life is richer for this knowledge? If you do not feel that you know your ancestors, do you believe that you have lost something valuable? Explain.

- ■ **EXAMINE** the title, "No Snapshots in the Attic." Fowler expands this idea in paragraph 2, when she declares that "our attics are empty." What do you think she means by these statements? How does the presence or absence of physical objects, or mementos, in Fowler's family differ from the family situation described by Brett Lott? What, besides snapshots, might be missing from Fowler's life?

- ■ **EXAMINE** also the following phrases and italicized words from Fowler's essay and the definitions provided for you.

  1. "stories *stymied* behind the mute lips" (paragraph 1): stumped, obstructed

  2. "*excise* her Indian heart" (paragraph 6): cut out, remove

3. "*raucous* laughter" (paragraph 7): rough, harsh

4. "strange *elocution*" (paragraph 7): public speaking, sometimes artificial

5. "*ephemeral* recitation" (paragraph 8): short-lived, fleeting

6. "*empirical* evidence" (paragraph 9): based on experiment or observation

7. "*xenophobic* society" (paragraph 11): racist, fearful or contemptuous of foreigners

8. "doomed to *oblivion*" (paragraph 13): state of being completely forgotten

9. "*incarceration* of Plains Indians" (paragraph 13): imprisonment

10. "historical *genocide*" (paragraph 16): planned killing of a racial, political, religious, or cultural group

11. "culture had been *obliterated*" (paragraph 16): completely destroyed

12. "*manipulation* of our past" (paragraph 17): shrewd or devious management

■ **WRITE** a journal entry about the ancestor who intrigues you the most. Are you more interested in what you *know* or in what you *do not know* about this person? How have you acquired the information that you have? What additional information would you like to have?

AS YOU READ

Trace the physical and mental journey that Fowler makes in search of her Cherokee past. What roadblocks does she encounter in this search? How does she finally achieve a sense of this past?

■ ■ ■

For as long as anyone can remember, poverty has crawled all over the hearts of my family, contributing to a long tradition of premature deaths and a lifetime of stories stymied behind the mute lips of the dead. The survivors have been left without any tangible signs that evoke the past: no photographs or diaries, no wedding bands or wooden nickels. 1

This absence of a record seems remarkable to me since our bloodline is diverse: Cherokee, Irish, German, French; you would think that at least a few people would have had the impulse to offer future generations a few concrete clues as to who they were. But no; our attics are empty. Up among the cobwebs and dormer-filtered light you will find not a single homemade quilt, not one musty packet of love letters. 2

Lack of hard evidence of a familial past seems unnatural to me, but I have developed a theory. I believe that my relatives, Indians and Europeans alike, couldn't waste free time on preserving a baby's first bootee. There were simply too many tales to tell about each other, living and dead, 3 for them to be bothered by objects that would only clutter our homes and our minds.

The first time I noticed this compulsion to rid ourselves of handed-down possessions was in the summer of my eighth year when my mother decided to fix the front screen door, which was coming off its hinges. As she rummaged through a junk drawer for a screwdriver, she came upon a dog-eared photograph of her father. He stood in front of a shack, staring into the camera as though he could see through the lens and into the eyes of the photographer. "Oh, that old picture," my mother said disdainfully. "Nothing but a dust catcher." She tossed the photo in the trash, pulled up a chair, lit a cigarette and told me about how her Appalachian-born daddy could charm wild animals out of the woods by standing on his front porch and singing to them.

The idea that my family had time only for survival and storytelling takes on special significance when I think of my grandmother, my father's mother, Oneida Hunter May, a Cherokee who married a white man. Hers was a life cloaked in irony and sadness, yet 30 years after she died her personal history continues to suggest that spinning tales is a particularly honest and noble activity.

Throughout her adult life, the only time Oneida Hunter May felt free enough to claim her own heritage was in the stories she told her children. At all other times, publicly and privately, she declared herself white. As both a writer and a granddaughter, I have been haunted by her decision to excise her Indian heart and I have struggled to understand it. Of course, her story would work its way into my fiction, but how it did and what I would learn about the truth of cultural and familial rumors when they contradict the truth of our official histories would change the way I see the world, the way I write, and how and whom I trust.

Until I became an adult this is what I accepted as true about my grandmother: She was a Cherokee Indian who married a South Carolinian named John May. Early in the marriage they moved to St. Augustine, Fla. They had three children, two boys and a girl. Shortly after moving to Florida, John May abandoned his wife and children. The family believed he joined the circus. (When I was a child my family's yearly pilgrimage to the Greatest Show on Earth took on special significance as I imagined that my grandfather was the lion tamer or the high-wire artist.) Grandmama May was short and round. While she was straightforward with the family about her Indian ancestry, she avoided instilling in us a shred of Native American culture or custom. Through the use of pale powder and rouge, she lightened her skin. Her cracker-box house on the wrong side of the tracks was filled with colorful miniature glass animals and hats and boots, all stolen from tourist shops downtown. According to my father, she was "run out of town on a rail" more than once because of the stealing, and she even spent time in the city jail. Her laughter was raucous. She tended to pick me up by putting her hands under my armpits, which hurt, and it seemed as if every time I saw her she pinched my cheeks, which also hurt. My grandmother mispronounced words and her syntax was jumbled.

I've since realized that her strange grammar patterns and elocution were the results of having no formal education and of speaking in a language that was not her native tongue.

For me, growing up was marked not only by a gradual loss of inno- 8 cence but by the loss of the storytellers in my life: grandparents, aunts and uncles, parents. With them went my ability to believe and know simple truths, to accept the face value of things without needless wrestling. As the cynicism of adulthood took hold, I began to doubt the family stories about my grandmother and I even decided my recollections were warped by time and the fuzzy judgment of childhood, and that the stories were based on oral tradition rooted in hearsay. What is this ephemeral recitation of our lives anyway? A hodgepodge of alleged fact, myth and legend made all the more unreliable because it goes unchecked by impartial inquiry. After all, don't scholars dismiss oral histories as anecdotal evidence?

I told myself I was far too smart to put much stock in my family's Homeric 9 impulses. In choosing to use my grandmother's life as a stepping-off point for a new novel, I decided that everything I knew as a child was probably exaggerated at best and false at worst. I craved empirical evidence, irrefutable facts; I turned to government archives.

I began my inquiry by obtaining a copy of my grandmother's death certifi- 10 cate. I hoped it would provide me with details that would lead to a trail back to her early life and even to her birth. The document contained the following data: Oneida Marie Hunter May was born Aug. 14, 1901, in Dillon, S.C. She died June 8, 1963, of diabetes. But from there her history was reduced to no comment. Line 13, father's name: five black dashes. Line 14, mother's maiden name: five dashes. Line 16, Social Security number: none. The most chilling, however, because it was a lie, was line 6, color or race: white.

Her son, my uncle J. W., was listed as the "informant." Perhaps he 11 thought he was honoring her by perpetuating her longstanding public falsehood. Perhaps, despite what he knew, he considered himself white—and therefore so was she. Perhaps in this small Southern town he was embarrassed or frightened to admit his true bloodline. Did he really not know his grandparents' names? Or did he fear the names would suggest his Indian lineage? Whether his answers were prompted by lack of knowledge or a desire to be evasive, the result was that the "facts" of the death certificate were suspect. The information recorded for posterity amounted to a whitewash. The son gave answers he could live with, which is what his mother had done, answers that satisfied a xenophobic society.

Thinking that perhaps I had started at the wrong end of the quest, 12 I went in search of her birth certificate. I contacted the proper office in South Carolina and gave the clerk what meager information I had. I realized that without a Social Security number, my chances of locating such a document were slim, but I thought that in its thirst for data the government might have tracked Indian births. "No, I'm sorry," I was told over the phone by the clerk who had been kind enough to try an alphabetical search. "South Carolina didn't keep detailed files on Indians back then.

You could try the Cherokees, but I don't think it will help. In those days they weren't keeping good records either."

I was beginning to understand how thoroughly a person can vanish   13
and how—without memory and folklore—one can be doomed to oblivion. But I pursued history, and I changed my focus to Florida. I began reading accounts of St. Augustine's Indian population in the last century, hoping to gain insight into my grandmother's experience. There is not a great amount of documentation, and most of what does exist was written by long-dead Roman Catholic missionaries and Army generals, sources whose objectivity was compromised by their theological and military mandates. Nevertheless, I stumbled on an 1877 report by Harriet Beecher Stowe about the incarceration of Plains Indians at Castillo de San Marcos (then called Fort Marion) at the mouth of the St. Augustine harbor.

During their imprisonment, which lasted from 1875 to 1878, the Indians   14
were forced to abandon their homes, religions, languages, their dress and all other cultural elements that white society deemed "savage"—a term used with alarming frequency in writings of the time. Calling the Indians in their pre-Christian state "untamable," "wild" and "more like grim goblins than human beings," Stowe apparently approved of what they became in the fort: Scripture-citing, broken-spirited Indians dressed like their tormentors, United States soldiers. She writes, "Might not the money now constantly spent on armies, forts and frontiers be better invested in educating young men who shall return and teach their people to live like civilized beings?"

The written record, I was discovering, was fabulous in its distortion,   15
and helpful in its unabashedness. It reflected not so much truth or historical accuracy as the attitudes of the writers.

The most obvious evidence of the unreliable nature of history is the cultural   16
litany set down in tourist brochures and abstracted onto brass plaques in parks and on roadsides across America. My family has lived for three generations in St. Augustine, "The Oldest Continuously Inhabited City in America. Founded in 1565." What this proclamation leaves out is everything that preceded the town's European founding. Like my uncle's carefully edited account of my grandmother's life, St. Augustine's official version amounts to historical genocide because it wipes away all traces of the activities and contributions of a specific race. For hundreds of years this spit of land between two rivers and the sea was the thriving village of Seloy, home to the Timucuan Indians. But while still aboard a ship, before ever stepping onto the white and coral-colored shores of the "New World," Pedro Menéndez renamed Seloy in honor of the patron saint of his birthplace. Then he claimed this new St. Augustine and all of "La Florida" to be the property of Spain; the Timucuans and their culture had been obliterated by a man at sea gazing at their land.

These distinctions between European facts and Indian facts are not   17
trivial. The manipulation of our past is an attempt, unconscious or not, to stomp out evidence of the success and value of other cultures. My grandmother's decision to deny her heritage was fueled by the fear of

what would happen to her if she admitted to being an Indian and by the belief that there was something inherently inferior about her people. And the falsehoods and omissions she lived by affected not just her; her descendants face a personal and historical incompleteness.

But when the official chronicles are composed of dashes and distortions 18 and you still hunger for the truth, what do you do? For me, the answer was to let my writer's instincts take over. I slipped inside my grandmother's skin and tried to sort out her motives and her pain. I imagined her birth and what her mother and father might have looked like. I gave them names, Nightwater and Billy. I called the character inspired by my grandmother Sparrow Hunter. She would bear a daughter, Oneida. And it would be Oneida's offspring, Sadie Hunter, who would uncover the stories that revealed the truth.

But I needed to know how a young Indian woman with three babies to 19 feed survives after she's been abandoned in a 1920's tourist town that promoted as its main attraction an ancient and massive fort that had served as a prison for Comanches, Kiowas, Seminoles, Apaches, Cheyennes, Arapaho, Caddos and others. The writer-granddaughter listened to her blood-born voices and heard the answers. Her grandmother made up a birthplace and tried to forget her native tongue. She stayed out of the sun because she tanned easily, and she bought the palest foundations and powders available. She re-created herself. For her children and grandchildren never to be called "Injun" or "savage" must have been one of her most persistent hopes. And what bitter irony it must have been that her children obeyed and took on the heritage of the man who had deserted them. I was discovering that my novel would be far better served if I stopped digging for dates and numbers and instead strove to understand my grandmother's pain.

My research had another effect, one far more important than causing me 20 to question our written record. It pushed me forward along the circle, inching me back to where I had started: the oral history. My family has relentlessly nurtured its oral tradition as though instinctively each of us knew that our attics would be empty for generations but our memory-fed imaginations could be filled to overbrimming with our tales of each other. And certainly, while the stories are grandiose and often tall, I decided they are no more slanted than what is fed to us in textbooks.

I have come to view my family's oral history as beautifully double- 21 edged, for in fiction—oral or written—there is a desire to reveal the truth, and that desire betrays my grandmother's public lie. It is in the stories shared on our beloved windy porches and at our wide-planked pine tables, under the glare of naked moth-swept light bulbs, that the truth and the betrayal reside. Had my grandmother not felt compelled to remember her life before John May stepped into it and to relate to little Henry and J. W. and Mary Alice what times were like in South Carolina in the early 1900's for a dirt-poor Indian girl, then a precious link to her past and ours would have been lost forever. And while she raised her children to think of themselves as solely white, she couldn't keep secret who she really was.

Those must have been wondrous moments when she tossed aside the 22
mask of the liar to take up the cloak of the storyteller. It was a transformation rooted in our deepest past, for she transcended her ordinary state and
for a brief time became a shaman, a holy person who through reflection,
confession and interpretation offered to her children an opportunity to become members of the family of humankind, the family that traces its history not through DNA and documents but through the follies and
triumphs, the struggles and desires of one another. So I turn to where the
greatest measure of truth exists: the stories shared between mother and
child, sister and brother, passed around the table like a platter of hot biscuits and gravy and consumed with hungry fervor.

My attempt to write about my grandmother's life was slow and often 23
agonizing. But turning a tangle of information and inspiration into a novel
and into a facet of the truth that would shine was the process of becoming
a child again, of rediscovering the innocence of faith, of accepting as true
what I have always known. I had to believe in the storyteller and her stories again.

The novel my grandmother inspired is fiction, for sure, but it reinforces 24
the paradox that most writers, editors and readers know: fiction is often truer
than nonfiction. A society knows itself most clearly not through the allegedly
neutral news media or government propaganda or historical records but
through the biased eyes of the artist, the writer. When that vision is tempered
by heaven and hell, by an honesty of the intellect and gut, it allows the reader
and viewer to safely enter worlds of brutal truth, confrontation and redemp-
tion. It allows the public as both voyeur and safely distanced participant to
say, "Aha! I know that man. I know that woman. Their struggles, their temp-
tations, their betrayals, their triumphs are mine."

One of my favorite relatives was Aunt Emily, J. W.'s wife. I saw her 25
the night of my father's death in 1966 and—because my aunt and uncle
divorced and because my father's death was a catastrophic event that
blew my family apart—I did not see her again until 1992. She was first in
line for the hometown book signing of my debut novel, "Sugar Cage." We
had a tearful and happy reunion, and before she left she said, "I remember
the day you were born and how happy I was that you were named for
your Grandmother Oneida."

I looked at her stupidly for a moment, not understanding what she was 26
saying. Then it dawned on me that she misunderstood my middle name
because we pronounced Oneida as though it rhymed with Anita. "Oh no,"
I told her. "My name is Connie Anita." Aunt Emily smiled and said,
"Sweetheart, the nurse wrote it down wrong on your birth certificate. All of
us except for your grandmother got a big laugh out of the mistake. But believe
me, it's what your parents said: you're Connie Oneida."

I loved that moment, for it was a confirmation of the integrity of our 27
oral histories and the frailties of our official ones. As I go forward with a
writing life, I accept that my creative umbilical cord is attached to my ancestors. And to their stories. I've decided to allow their reflective

revelations to define me in some measure. And I have decided not to bemoan my family's bare attics and photo albums, because as long as we can find the time to sit on our porches or in front of our word processors and continue the tradition of handing down stories, I believe we will flourish as Indians, high-wire artists, animal charmers and writers all. And the truth will survive. It may be obscured occasionally by the overblown or sublime, but at least it will still be there, giving form to our words and fueling our compulsion to tell the tale.

■ ■ ■

AFTER YOU READ

■ **THINK** about Fowler's two different heritages: European and Native American. Does she find these heritages to be complementary or contradictory? How does she become reconciled to both? With which does she ultimately identify? If, like Fowler, you have a mixed heritage, how have you reconciled the different elements of your ancestry?

■ **EXAMINE** the description of Fowler's grandmother as storyteller found in paragraph 22. As this passage suggests, family stories provide not only family history but also important family beliefs and values. Which images in this passage are the most effective and why? What does this passage tell you about Native American life in particular?

■ **WRITE** a summary of this reading selection. Structure your summary around the four main sections in the reading, but remember to include in your summary only main ideas and not the specific details that you would include in an essay. (For help with writing summaries, see pages 186–188.)

■ Or **WRITE** a story about your family—one that reveals something about your family's history, values, or goals. Your story might be one of those "passed around the table like a platter of hot biscuits" from family member to family member, or it might be one that you make up from clues that you have about one of your ancestors. Like Fowler in her search for her Cherokee grandmother, you can try to "slip inside the skin" of this person and tell the story through his or her eyes.

Hold the Mayonnaise

■ ■ ■

JULIA ALVAREZ

The distinguished Latina poet and novelist Julia Alvarez is the author of numerous books of poetry and fiction and the recipient of many awards, including the American Library Association's Notable Book Award for her first book, *How the Garcia Girls Lost Their Accents* (1991). Alvarez was born in New York but raised in the Dominican Republic; her family returned to the United States in 1960 for political reasons. Her experiences of finding her place in an unfamiliar homeland and her interest in family relationships involving different cultures are major subjects in her work, including her autobiographical collection of essays, *Something to Declare* (1999). In this selection Alvarez focuses specifically on the relationship between a Latina stepmother and her American stepdaughters.

BEFORE YOU READ

■ **THINK** about the stereotype of "the stepmother" as found in stories such as "Hansel and Gretel." Have such stories caused you to form a negative opinion of stepmothers in general? Do you have a (or have you known someone's) stepmother? How do your personal experiences and observations compare or contrast with the stereotype?

■ **EXAMINE** the title of the selection. With what culture is mayonnaise most closely associated? Can you think of any Latino foods that use mayonnaise?

■ **EXAMINE** the following words from the essay and their definitions:

1. *aficionado* (paragraph 4): enthusiastic follower or admirer

2. *condiment* (paragraph 4): sauce or seasoning, such as mustard or ketchup

3. *usurp* (paragraph 11): to take and keep another's power or position

4. *assimilationist* (paragraph 15): one who supports an individual's culture being absorbed into a broader national culture

■ **WRITE** a journal entry in which you discuss your reaction—positive or negative—to a particular cultural food.

AS YOU READ

Note in the margin each time Alvarez uses mayonnaise as a symbol of American culture. How do her reactions to this food parallel her reactions to American culture in general and to her new American stepdaughters in particular?

■ ■ ■

"If I die first and Papi ever gets remarried," Mami used to tease 1 when we were kids, "don't you accept a new woman in my house. Make her life impossible, do you hear?" My sisters and I nodded obediently, and a filial shudder would go through us. We were Catholics, so of course, the only kind of remarriage we could imagine had to involve our mother's death.

We were also Dominicans, recently arrived in Jamaica, Queens, in the 2 early 60's, before waves of other Latin Americans began arriving. So, when we imagined who exactly my father might possibly ever think of remarrying, only American women came to mind. It would be bad enough having a *madrastra,* but a "stepmother."

All I could think of was that she would make me eat mayonnaise, a 3 food I identified with the United States and which I detested. Mami understood, of course, that I wasn't used to that kind of food. Even a madrasta, accustomed to our rice and beans and tostones and pollo frito, would understand. But an American stepmother would think it was normal to put mayonnaise on food, and if she were at all strict and a little mean, which all stepmothers, of course, were, she would make me eat potato salad and such. I had plenty of my own reasons to make a potential stepmother's life impossible. When I nodded obediently with my sisters, I was imagining not just something foreign in our house, but in our refrigerator.

So it's strange now, almost 35 years later, to find myself a Latina step- 4 mother of my husband's two tall, strapping, blond, mayonnaise-eating daughters. To be honest, neither of them is a real aficionado of the condiment, but it's a fair thing to add to a bowl of tuna fish or diced potatoes. Their American food, I think of it, and when they head to their mother's or off to school, I push the jar back in the refrigerator behind their chocolate pudding and several open cans of Diet Coke.

What I can't push as successfully out of sight are my own immigrant 5 childhood fears of having a *gringa* stepmother with foreign tastes in our house. Except now, I am the foreign stepmother in a gringa household. I've wondered what my husband's two daughters think of this stranger in their family. It must be doubly strange for them that I am from another culture.

Of course, there are mitigating circumstances—my husband's two 6 daughters were teen-agers when we married, older, more mature, able to understand differences. They had also traveled when they were children with their father, an eye doctor, who worked on short-term international projects with various eye foundations. But still, it's one thing to visit a foreign country, another altogether to find it brought home—a real bear plopped down in a Goldilocks house.

Sometimes, a whole extended family of bears. My warm, loud Latino   7
family came up for the wedding: my tia from Santo Domingo; three dramatic, enthusiastic sisters and their families; my papi, with a thick accent I could tell the girls found hard to understand; and my mami, who had her eye trained on my soon-to-be stepdaughters for any sign that they were about to make my life impossible. "How are they behaving themselves?" she asked me, as if they were 7 and 3, not 19 and 16. "They're wonderful girls," I replied, already feeling protective of them.

I looked around for the girls in the meadow in front of the house we   8
were building, where we were holding the outdoor wedding ceremony and party. The oldest hung out with a group of her own friends. The younger one whizzed in briefly for the ceremony, then left again before the congratulations started up. There was not much mixing with me and mine. What was there for them to celebrate on a day so full of confusion and effort?

On my side, being the newcomer in someone else's territory is a role   9
I'm used to. I can tap into that struggling English speaker, that skinny, dark-haired olive-skinned girl in a sixth grade of mostly blond and blue-eyed giants. Those tall, freckled boys would push me around in the playground. "Go back to where you came from!" "*No comprendo!*" I'd reply, though of course there was no misunderstanding the fierce looks on their faces.

Even now, my first response to a scowl is that old pulling away. (My   10
husband calls it "checking out.") I remember times early on in the marriage when the girls would be with us, and I'd get out of school and drive around doing errands, killing time, until my husband, their father, would be leaving work. I am not proud of my fears, but I understand—as the lingo goes—where they come from.

And I understand, more than I'd like to sometimes, my stepdaughters'   11
pain. But with me, they need never fear that I'll usurp a mother's place. No one has ever come up and held their faces and then addressed me, "They look just like you." If anything, strangers to the remarriage are probably playing Mr. Potato Head in their minds, trying to figure out how my foreign features and my husband's fair Nebraskan features got put together into the two tall, blond girls. "My husband's daughters," I kept introducing them.

Once, when one of them visited my class and I introduced her as such,   12
two students asked me why. "I'd be so hurt if my stepmom introduced me that way," the young man said. That night I told my stepdaughter what my students had said. She scowled at me and agreed. "It's so weird how you call me Papa's daughter. Like you don't want to be related to me or something."

"I didn't want to presume," I explained. "So it's O.K. if I call you my   13
stepdaughter?"

"That's what I am," she said. Relieved, I took it for a teensy inch of   14
acceptance. The takings are small in this stepworld, I've discovered. Sort of
like being a minority. It feels as if all the goodies have gone somewhere
else.

Day to day, I guess I follow my papi's advice. When we first came, he   15
would talk to his children about how to make it in our new country. "Just
do your work and put in your heart, and they will accept you!" In this age
of remaining true to your roots, of keeping your Spanish, of fighting from
inside your culture, that assimilationist approach is highly suspect. My Latino students—who don't want to be called Hispanics anymore—would
ditch me as faculty adviser if I came up with that play-nice message.

But in a stepfamily where everyone is starting a new life together, it   16
isn't bad advice. Like a potluck supper, an American concept my mami
never took to. ("Why invite people to your house and then ask them to
bring the food?") You put what you've got together with what everyone
else brought and see what comes out of the pot. The luck part is if everyone brings something you like. No potato salad, no deviled eggs, no little
party sandwiches with you know what in them.

■ ■ ■

AFTER YOU READ

- ■ **THINK** about how Alvarez felt not only as a new stepmother but also as
  a stepmother to children of a different culture. Describe her feelings toward her new stepdaughters. During the story, how do these feelings
  change and why?

- ■ **EXAMINE** the phrase "my husband's daughters," which Alvarez uses to
  introduce her stepdaughters. What does this phrase show about her feelings about herself as well as about her stepdaughters? What prompts her
  to change the way she introduces her stepdaughters, and how does this
  simple change improve her relationship with them?

- ■ **WRITE** an essay in which you first identify one or more problems of
  adjustment that are common to stepfamilies such as Alvarez's family.
  Then propose a solution for the problem(s) that you have identified.

- ■ Or **WRITE** an essay in which you discuss some particular foods or types
  of foods to which your family has an especially positive or negative reaction. Your essay should include a thesis statement explaining why
  your family feels as it does about this food or how it is associated with
  your family's identity or traditions.

The Family That Stretches (Together)

■ ■ ■

ELLEN GOODMAN

This essay, like the previous one by Julia Alvarez, discusses families extended through divorce and remarriage. Ellen Goodman is a Pulitzer Prize–winning journalist chiefly known for her syndicated newspaper columns, many of which have been collected in books (*Close to Home, At Large, Keeping in Touch, Making Sense,* and *Value Judgments*). Goodman writes primarily out of her own experiences. In the following essay, she begins by describing her conversation with a young girl who is part of a family that has been formed and expanded by divorce, continues by telling of another nontraditional family that she knows, and, on the basis of these personal experiences, comes to some conclusions about modern families. It is perhaps useful to know that Goodman herself has experienced divorce.

BEFORE YOU READ

■ **THINK** about the different types of families you know and have read about—those that have a traditional husband and wife plus mutual children, those that consist of a single parent and child, and those that include remarried adults, each with children from previous marriages. Based on your reading, observation, and experience, can you think of families that consist of still other combinations?

■ **EXAMINE** the title of the selection. How do you think families can "stretch" and still keep "together"? Can certain types of families accomplish stretching and keeping together better than others? If so, which ones?

■ **EXAMINE** also the following words from the essay and their definitions:

1. *genealogist* (paragraph 1): one who studies the ancestry of a family or families

2. *configurations* (paragraph 5): arrangements

3. *nomenclature* (paragraph 13): system of naming

■ **WRITE** a journal entry listing as many different types of family combinations as possible. Include not only the types of families that you know personally but also those you have read about, heard about, or can imagine.

AS YOU READ

Underline phrases and sentences that suggest the thesis, or main idea, of the article.

■ ■ ■

Casco Bay, Maine—The girl is spending the summer with her ex- 1
tended family. She doesn't put it this way. But as we talk on the
beach, the ten-year-old lists the people who are sharing the same
house this month with the careful attention of a genealogist.

First of all there is her father—visitation rights awarded him the month 2
of August. Second of all there is her father's second wife and two children
by her first marriage. All that seems perfectly clear. A stepmother and two
stepbrothers.

Then there are the others, she slowly explains. There is her step- 3
mother's sister for example. The girl isn't entirely sure whether this makes
the woman a stepaunt, or whether her baby is a stepcousin. Beyond that,
the real puzzle is whether her stepaunt's husband's children by his first
marriage have any sort of official relationship to her at all. It does, we
both agree, seem a bit fuzzy.

Nevertheless, she concludes, with a certainty that can only be mustered 4
by the sort of ten-year-old who keeps track of her own Frequent Flier cou-
pons, "We are in the same family." With that she closes the subject and
focuses instead on her peanut butter and jelly.

I am left to my thoughts. My companion, in her own unselfconscious 5
way, is a fine researcher. She grasps the wide new family configurations
that are neglected by census data takers and social scientists.

After all, those of us who grew up in traditional settings remember 6
families which extended into elaborate circles of aunts, uncles, and cousins.
There were sides to this family, names and titles to be memorized. But they
fit together in a biological pattern.

Now, as my young friend can attest, we have fewer children and more 7
divorces. We know that as many as 50 percent of recent marriages may
end. About 75 percent of divorced women and 83 percent of divorced
men then remarry. Of those remarriages, 59 percent include a child from
a former marriage.

So, our families often extend along lines that are determined by de- 8
crees, rather than genes. If the nucleus is broken, there are still links forged
in different directions.

The son of a friend was asked to produce a family tree for his sixth- 9
grade class. But he was dissatisfied with his oak. There was no room on it
for his step grandfather, though the man had married his widowed grandmother years ago.

More to the point, the boy had to create an offshoot for his new baby 10
half- brother that seemed too distant. He couldn't find a proper place for

the uncle—the ex-uncle to be precise—whom he visited last summer with his cousin.

A family tree just doesn't work, he complained. He would have pre-   11
ferred to draw family bushes.

The reality is that divorce has created kinship ties that rival the most   12
complex tribe. These are not always easy relationships. The children and
even the adults whose family lives have been disrupted by divorce and remarriage learn that people they love do not necessarily love each other.
This extended family does not gather for reunions and Thanksgivings.

But when it works, it can provide a support system of sorts. I have   13
seen the nieces, nephews—even the dogs—of one marriage welcomed as
guests into another. There are all sorts of relationships that survive the
marital ones, though there are no names for these kinfolk, no nomenclature for this extending family.

Not long ago, when living together first became a common pattern,   14
people couldn't figure out what to call each other. It was impossible to introduce the man you lived with as a "spouse equivalent." It was harder to
refer to the woman your son lived with as his lover, mistress, housemate.

It's equally difficult to describe the peculiar membership of this new   15
lineage. Does your first husband's mother become a mother-out-law? Is
the woman no longer married to your uncle an ex-aunt? We have nieces
and nephews left dangling like participles from other lives and stepfamilies
entirely off the family tree.

Our reality is more flexible and our relationships more supportive than   16
our language. But for the moment, my ten-year-old researcher is right.
However accidentally, however uneasily, "We are in the same family."

■　■　■

AFTER YOU READ

- ■ **THINK** about the thesis of Goodman's essay, which is suggested primarily in the final five paragraphs. What is this thesis? Compare Goodman's
  thesis and her conclusions about modern families with your ideas and
  those of your classmates on the subject. Do you think Goodman's attitude toward the modern family can best be described as optimistic or
  pessimistic? Do you agree or disagree with her opinion? Why or why
  not?

- ■ **EXAMINE** Goodman's statement in paragraph 8 that today families are
  often "determined by decrees, rather than genes." Then restate and explain Goodman's meaning.

- ■ **EXAMINE** also paragraphs 9–11, in which Goodman discusses the advantages of family "bushes" over family "trees" for many modern

families. Which format do you think is more accurate and realistic for most families?

- ■ **WRITE,** or diagram, your own family "tree" or "bush." Which format works better for your family? Then compare your diagram with those of a group of your classmates.

- ■ Or **WRITE** an essay arguing for or against the idea that a family expanded and shaped by divorce can function as well as a family expanded only by biology.

UNIT TWO

■ ■ ■

Critical Thinking, Reading, and Writing

■ WRITING A PERSONAL ESSAY

An **essay** is a short nonfiction composition on a single topic. Although other types of essays primarily inform or persuade their readers, a **personal essay** treats a topic from the author's personal viewpoint. This unit includes personal essays by Lee Herrick, Maya Angelou, Larry L. King, and Sandra Cisneros as well as longer personal narratives by Sharon Liao, Agnes G. Herman, and Connie May Fowler. Because the personal essay allows writers to use their own experiences and observations and to express their own opinions about a variety of subjects, it has become a popular assignment in many composition classes.

BEFORE YOU WRITE

Planning and preparing to write a personal essay involve at least three steps: (1) thinking about your subject, your purpose, and your audience; (2) prewriting to generate ideas on your subject; and (3) organizing your essay.

Subject, Purpose, and Audience

In writing a personal essay, your subject is essentially yourself—what you have experienced and observed or what you think about a particular subject. Many of the reading and writing assignments in Unit Two focus specifically on your relationship with your family and how your family affects your sense of self. Your general purpose in writing a personal essay will be to express yourself as well as to entertain or inform your audience. For each personal essay you write, however, you will also develop a more specific purpose, which you will state (or imply) in your **thesis**. In his personal essay about his family, Roderick Hartsfield wrote the following thesis:

> Thinking about my physical reflection, I realize that I am the person I am today primarily because of the influence of my parents.

As stated in this thesis, Roderick wants to inform his readers about the influence his parents have had on his life and his identity.

Many personal essays are written for general audiences. In your composition class, however, you are also writing for your instructor and your classmates. Thus, you should not only follow your instructor's guidelines carefully, but also keep in mind the preferences and interests that he or she has expressed in class. Any composition instructor will expect an interesting, clearly organized, and well-edited essay.

Prewriting

Often, the most important writing is that which you do before you actually begin to draft your essay. In this stage, you explore and focus your ideas, and you think about what information will achieve your purpose and interest your audience. The "Introduction" to this textbook describes and provides examples of several types of prewriting, including freewriting, journal entries, brainstorming, clustering, and mapping. If you aren't familiar with some of these methods, review them now. (See pages 7–9.)

Organization

Like most well-organized writing, a personal essay includes three main parts: an introduction, a body, and a conclusion.

Although students often spend little time thinking about or writing an **introduction,** it is actually one of the most important elements of an essay. If your introduction doesn't clearly state the main idea of your essay and capture the interest of your readers, they are likely to stop before finishing the essay. On the other hand, if your introduction interests your reader, gives necessary background information, and provides a clear thesis (main idea), you will have created a sympathetic reader for the remainder of your essay.

The **body** of your essay is the longest and, ultimately, the most important element. A good introduction leads your readers to expect clear and sufficient support for your main idea, so be sure that the body of your essay adequately develops and clearly supports your thesis.

Although many models suggest that an essay must have five paragraphs, including three body paragraphs, you actually have a great deal of flexibility in the number of paragraphs you include in your essay, especially in its body. It is better to have two well-developed body paragraphs than three skimpy ones. However, it is important to include enough information to develop your thesis (specific examples and details) and to divide this information into well-developed, coherent paragraphs—with each paragraph developing a major point in an expository essay, an important part of the chronology in a narrative, or an important element of a descriptive essay. You should also be sure that you arrange these paragraphs in a logical order (general to specific, least important to most important, chronological, nearest to farthest, or the like).

Your **conclusion** should bring your essay to a satisfactory sense of completion for your readers. Conclusions often restate (not repeat) your main idea, but the conclusion to a personal essay may also comment on the importance to the writer of the person or experience being discussed. If your personal essay is descriptive, you may want to end with your general impression of the place, person, or thing being described. If it is narrative, you may want to comment on the importance of the event—on what you learned from it or on the effect it had on your life.

Example

To help you in writing your own personal essay, read the following sample student essay by Roderick Hartsfield.

Who Am I? Reflections of My Parents

After reading several essays about the self and the self's relation to family, I have been brought face-to-face with an important question: Who am I? Looking in the mirror gives me a small clue to the answer to this question, for reflected back at me I see my father's height and build as well as many of my mother's facial features. Thinking about my physical reflection, I realize that I am the person I am today primarily because of the influence of my parents. [1]

The character traits that I have gained from my father are more important than the physical traits that my mirror shows. My father has taught me determination of purpose and respect for others. From the moment I took my first step as a small child, he pushed and encouraged me to always follow through with whatever I was doing. One example of his encouragement occurred when I played my first game of junior high football. Because I misread a play, the opposing team scored a touchdown on my side of the field. That experience hurt my self-confidence so much that I found it hard to continue to play, but at half-time my father spoke to me and told me to keep my head up no matter how the game turned out. My father has also taught me respect for other people, their belongings, and their opinions even if I do not agree with them. When I was a youngster, I attentively observed my father as he conversed with other people. If he disagreed with something a person said, he would politely say, "I respect your opinion, but I must disagree." As a result of observing his reactions, I will to this day listen to another person's opinion, whatever it is, and then let that person know that I respect that opinion before I say that I disagree. [2]

More than my mother's facial features are reflected in my life also. Indeed, she has provided me with some very valuable teachings that have sculpted me into the person I am today. Just as my father taught me to be tough on the outside, she taught me to be tough on the inside. I have gained from my mother not just a strong will and a broad mind but also a willingness to listen to people who have personal problems. While I was living at home, I often saw her make time to listen to the problems of her friends, family, or anyone else who needed help no matter what she was doing. It is from her, I think, that I have developed a sort of sixth sense that allows me to feel, in some way, when someone close to me is troubled. As a result, I have sat up countless hours of the night comforting and listening to the problems of my friends, family, and at times my friend's friends. Since I have been on the college football squad, I have become a kind of informal counselor to many of my teammates. These people know that I will always be there to listen. Thanks to my mother, I now know the importance of caring about the feelings of other people and of keeping my ears open to hear their troubles. [3]

<u>I also have other qualities that are reflections of both of my par-</u>   4
<u>ents: my stubbornness and my temper</u>. Although my parents are two totally
different people, they react very similarly when they get upset—and if I
don't watch myself, I react in the same way. I am particularly tempted to
be stubborn and quick-tempered when I am involved in the competitive
sport of football. Sometimes I believe that I know more than the coach
does about what play will work best in a particular situation, but I know
that if I stubbornly do the play "my way," I may not get to play the next
set of downs. Also, it is natural to get angry when someone on the other
team takes a dirty shot at me while the referee's back is turned, but I
have learned that if I let my temper get the better of me and fight back, I
am likely to be the one who receives the foul and hurts my team.

So who am I? My mirror shows that I have physical characteristics of   5
both of my parents, but my life itself shows that I have their personal
qualities as well. I have the strength of my father's determination and
respect for others as well as the spirit of my mother's wisdom and caring.
But while my life reflects the qualities of my parents, I have also tried
to develop my character by curbing my stubborn and temperamental reactions. As a result, I believe that I am truly becoming my own person.

————

The introduction of this essay captures reader interest with the mirror image and provides a clear thesis; each paragraph includes a topic sentence
(underlined) developed with relevant examples and analysis; and the conclusion returns to the idea of the mirror image, restates the thesis, and
draws a logical conclusion.

Assignments

Select one of the following assignments about family as the subject of a
personal essay.

1. Write an essay that, like Hartsfield's, shows how one or more of your
    family members have influenced you, molding you into the person you
    are today.

2. Several of the assignments in the "Writing Essays" section at the end
    of this unit also provide good assignments for personal essays. Con-
    sider especially assignment 1, which requires you to explore your fam-
    ily heritage; assignment 2, which asks you to describe a personal
    journey to greater understanding of a family member; assignment 3,
    which focuses on youthful rebellion against a parent or parent figure;
    and assignments 4 and 5, which ask you to describe in some way one
    of your family members. (For assignments 4 and 5, see the guidelines
    for writing descriptive essays on Lesson 2 of the *Interactions*, eighth
    edition, student website at www.cengagebrain.com.)

AS YOU WRITE

After you select (or your instructor specifies) a particular assignment, spend some time prewriting about your chosen subject. Use your prewriting and any feedback you receive from your instructor or your classmates to help you write a preliminary thesis statement—the main idea that you want to develop in your essay. (Remember that you may change this thesis as you write.)

After you decide on your specific subject and preliminary thesis, you are ready to organize and draft your essay. Some writers like to write an outline before they actually begin writing; other writers prefer to write what is often called a *discovery draft,* finding their organization as they write. In either case, as you write your draft be sure to include the three main parts of an effective personal essay:

- An introduction that captures the interest of your reader, provides necessary background, and states your thesis
- Several body paragraphs, each of which has a clear topic sentence and supports your thesis with relevant examples and details
- A conclusion that provides a sense of closure, perhaps restating your thesis

When you finish your draft, save it and print a copy for yourself. You may also want to print multiple copies for discussion in a peer revision group.

AFTER YOU WRITE

After you have written a draft of your personal essay, reread it carefully to make sure that it includes an introduction, body, and conclusion that are clear and well developed. Also determine whether the paragraphs in the body of the essay are organized in the most logical arrangement; if not, rearrange these paragraphs as needed, being sure to change transitions to match your reorganization.

After you (and perhaps your peer group) have evaluated the content of your essay, make any revisions that you believe are necessary to improve it. When you have revised the content, organization, and development of your personal essay, edit it for problems in grammar, usage, sentence structure, and style. Here are some of the questions you might want to ask yourself or discuss with your group:

- Does my essay have a consistent point of view (first person, third person, etc.)?
- Is tense used consistently in my essay (present, past, etc.)?
- Have I corrected any major sentence errors (fragments, comma splices)?

- Have I corrected errors in grammar (subject-verb agreement, pronoun reference) and usage (spelling, capitalization, punctuation)?
- Do I need to make any stylistic changes in my essay?

After you have edited your essay for the problems listed above, reread it one final time to eliminate careless errors.

■ EXPLORING IDEAS TOGETHER

1. The essay by Lee Herrick gives an informal definition of family, and the textbook selection "Defining Family" provides a more formal, objective definition. With a group of your classmates, review the definitions in both selections and then discuss which definition you prefer individually and as a group. Make a list of the reasons you selected the definition that you chose.

2. The essays by Angelou and King describe individuals seeking independence and selfhood by rebelling against their parents. Do you think rebellion is a natural part of growing up and establishing a position in one's family? Why or why not? Do you think that most people, like Angelou and King, ultimately reconcile with their families? Discuss these issues with a group of your classmates.

3. Both Liao and Herman write about the expectations that parents have for their children. Make a list of expectations that your parents had (or have) for you. Then compare your list with those of a group of your peers, discussing potential positive and negative effects.

4. Two selections in this unit—Fowler's "No Snapshots in the Attic" and Lott's "Brothers"—explore the importance of family photographs and home movies in reconstructing family histories. How does the essay by Fowler confirm or contradict the essay by Lott? Discuss the roles that family pictures play, according to these two writers. Then discuss the role and importance of family photographs and movies in your own experience.

5. In their respective essays, Alvarez describes her remarriage and her relationship with her stepdaughters, and Goodman discusses how divorce and remarriage often extend families. With a group of your peers, discuss how these authors view the effects of divorce and remarriage on a child. Compare and/or contrast the two viewpoints.

■ EXPLORING THE INTERNET

You can find more information related to these exercises at the *Interactions*, eighth edition, student website: www.cengagebrain.com

1. Several of the authors represented in this unit have official Internet sites. To view photographs and find out more about Lee Herrick,

Maya Angelou, Sandra Cisneros, Connie May Fowler, and Julia Alvarez, refer to the list under "Related Websites" at the *Interactions* student website.

2. Lee Herrick's essay describes his experiences as a Korean adoptee of a Caucasian family. To find out more about adoption, explore the *About Adoption* website found as a link on the *Interactions* student site. You may find out more about Korean adoption and adoptees by putting these terms in the search line.

3. Klagsbrun and Lott describe the intense conflict and competition often felt between siblings. A good source for further exploration of sibling relationships is Tufts University's *Child and Family Web Guide,* available under "Related Websites" on the *Interactions* site. Under the major category of "Parenting," you will find the subtopic "Siblings," which has direct links to several articles on sibling relations. After you explore this topic further, you may want to write your own essay exploring the causes or effects of sibling rivalry.

4. Two additional links about families and family life that you can find on the *Interactions* website are *Parents Magazine* and *Working Mother.*

■ WRITING ESSAYS

1. Fowler's essay focuses on family heritage—on searching for or maintaining connections with previous generations as a way of understanding oneself and passing on one's family heritage to future generations. Write a personal essay about one of your ancestors, perhaps a grandparent. Do you have physical evidence of this ancestor, or was your knowledge of this person transmitted orally? If you do not know about one or more of your ancestors, discuss why this knowledge is missing in your life and what you have lost or gained as a result. (See pages 128–133 for help with writing personal essays.)

2. Several of the essays in this unit—those by King, Liao, Herman, Lott, and Fowler—use the metaphor of a journey, either explicitly or implicitly, to explain an individual's developing understanding of one or more family members. If you have experienced such a personal journey, write an essay about it. What was the question or incident that started you on your journey of exploration? What did you find out? And how did your journey change you as a person as well as a member of your family? (See pages 128–133 for guidelines for writing personal essays.)

3. The readings by Angelou, King, and Liao focus on a child's rebellion against a parent. In your opinion, does the kind of rebellion described by these writers ultimately have a positive or a negative effect on the child? Write an essay for a specific audience (perhaps for parents of adolescents or for adolescents themselves) in which you explain your

position, supporting it with your own personal experience(s). (You may be able to use ideas from your discussion of assignment 2 in "Exploring Ideas Together.")

4. Write a descriptive essay about a particular family member. Along with describing how this family member looks and acts, provide a thesis at the beginning or end of your essay that gives your overall impression of this person. (See Lesson 2 on the *Interactions*, eighth edition, website for guidelines for writing descriptive essays.)

5. The readings by Klagsbrun and Lott rely on descriptive anecdotes, or brief stories, to portray a family member. Write an essay in which you use two or three brief anecdotes to characterize one of your family members.

6. Write an essay on *one* particular family relationship: mother-daughter, mother-son, father-daughter, father-son, grandmother-granddaughter, grandfather-grandson, brother-sister, and so on. Refer to at least one essay in this unit and provide support from your own experiences and observations.

7. Alvarez and Goodman discuss families that have been extended and complicated through marriage, divorce, and remarriage. Write an essay in which you take a position on the positive or negative effects that relationships with in-laws or steprelatives can have on a family or an individual.

8. Write an essay in which you show how the family has changed during the past ten, twenty, or thirty years. You might simply identify and explain some of these changes, you might focus on the causes of the changes, or you might discuss the effects (positive or negative) of the changes. In your essay, use specific support from at least two essays in this unit. (For help with writing cause and effect essays, see Lesson 7 of the *Interactions* student website.)

FRIENDS AND MATES

This photograph shows a group of college students enjoying being together. For what activity are they preparing? What activities, such as tailgating, do you enjoy doing with your friends? Do you think friendship is the primary relationship shared by this group of people? Does friendship sometimes lead to a romantic interest?

■ ■ ■

Although your family relationships may be largely predetermined by biology and circumstances, you reach beyond your family to choose your friends and mates. In this unit you will read about these important relationships and about the individual and cultural factors that affect how these relationships are formed.

137

Throughout your lifetime, you will have a great many friends. Unlike your family ties, which remain basically the same, your friendships will change. That is, your friends in college may be different from those you had as a child, or your relationship with a particular friend may change. A friend may move away, drift away, or even die. Sometimes, a relationship that starts as a friendship may develop into a romantic attachment.

Of all the relationships you form in your lifetime, perhaps the most important is the one that you establish with a mate or partner. Your decision to share your life with a particular person, whether you choose carefully and deliberately or hastily and impulsively, tells more about you and how you perceive yourself than almost any other decision you make. It is therefore not surprising that most people spend a great deal of time and energy thinking about, planning for, and establishing these relationships.

The process of selecting a mate varies greatly from society to society. A number of contemporary societies still follow the age-old custom of arranged marriages, which was once practiced even in European countries. In our society, however, the process of choosing a mate typically involves a person dating a variety of potential partners and then deciding, on the basis of these experiences, which one is "right." Ideally, this choice results in a long and happy life together—a life in which the two people love and support each other, share an intimate emotional and physical relationship, have children and cooperate in rearing them, and grow old together.

In reality, however, choosing a mate is seldom as tidy and uncomplicated as this description suggests. Finding a mate or partner often involves luck and circumstances as much as—or more than—love and wisdom. And although the ideal in our society continues to be that two people meet, fall in love, get married, and live happily ever after, that ideal is often not realized. You will be joining an increasingly small minority if you spend your entire life happily married to one person. It is possible, perhaps even likely, that you will have a series of partners, each of whom will play a significant role in your life. Increasingly, people in our society may live with an individual, or a sequence of individuals, before deciding to marry; may divorce and remarry one or more times; or may outlive one mate and choose another. In addition, some individuals select mates of the same sex, and other individuals—sometimes by chance, but often by choice—remain single.

As the variety and richness of the reading selections in this unit show, making friends and finding a suitable mate or partner—while always challenging and sometimes discouraging—are still important goals for most people. We hope that the readings in this unit will increase your understanding of yourself and how you form these relationships.

College Friends

■ ■ ■

JENNIFER CRICHTON

Jennifer Crichton is the author of the nonfiction books *Family Reunion* and *Delivery: A Nurse-Midwife's Story*, and her work has appeared in *Parents* magazine. In 1986 Crichton married David Emil, who ran the elegant Windows on the World restaurant at the top of the World Trade Center. When the restaurant was destroyed on September 11, 2001, the couple escaped death themselves only by the fortunate coincidences that neither had yet reached work.

The following essay, which Crichton published in the "Campus Times" section of *Ms. Magazine*, is directed primarily at college women. College students of both sexes, however, will identify with Crichton's loneliness and need for friendship during her first semester and with her enthusiasm for the valued friendships she formed in college.

BEFORE YOU READ

■ **THINK** about how you felt when you first entered college. Did you feel lonely, afraid, and in need of a friend? Who was the first friend you met in college? How did you form that friendship? Was it—or is it still—a close friendship?

■ **EXAMINE** the following words by reading the sentences in which they occur in the essay. Then read the definitions provided.

1. *Cataclysmic* (paragraph 2): Like *catastrophe*, this word begins with the Greek prefix *cata-*, which means "down." A *cataclysm* is, literally, a "down wash"; the adjective *cataclysmic* means "pertaining to a major disaster."
2. *Platonic* (paragraph 6): This word is defined by its context as a nonphysical or spiritual relationship. *Platonic* friendships are being contrasted here with sexual relationships. The word derives from the classical Greek philosopher, Plato, who viewed the physical as an imperfect reflection of an ideal world.
3. *Spontaneous* (paragraph 16): This word is defined in context by its synonym "unplanned."

■ **WRITE** a journal entry agreeing or disagreeing with Crichton's opening sentence: "As far as I'm concerned, the first semester away at college is possibly the single worst time to make friends."

AS YOU READ

Identify and underline Crichton's attitude(s) toward college friendships in general as well as toward specific college friends.

■ ■ ■

As far as I'm concerned, the first semester away at college is possibly the single worst time to make friends. You'll make them, but you'll probably get it all wrong, through no fault of your own, for these are desperate hours.

Here's desperation: standing in a stadium-like cafeteria, I became convinced that a thousand students busy demolishing the contents of their trays were indifferent to me, and studying me with ill-disguised disdain at the same time. The ability to mentally grasp two opposing concepts is often thought of as the hallmark of genius. But I credit my mind's crazed elasticity to panic. Sitting alone at a table, I see the girl I'd met that morning in the showers. I was thrilled to see her. The need for a friend had become violent. Back at the dorm, I told her more about my family's peculiarities and my cataclysmic summer fling than I'd ever let slip before. All the right sympathetic looks crossed her face at all the right moments, whereupon I deduced that through the good graces of the housing department, I'd stumbled upon a soulmate. But what seemed like two minds mixing and matching on a cosmic place was actually two lonely freshmen under the influence of unprecedented amounts of caffeine and emotional upheaval. This wasn't a meeting of souls. This was a talking jag of monumental proportions.

By February, my first friend and I passed each other in the hall with lame, bored smiles, and now I can't remember her name for the life of me. But that doesn't make me sad in the least.

Loneliness and erosion of high school friendships through change and distance leave yawning gaps that beg to be filled. Yet, I never made a real friend by directly applying for the position of confidante or soulmate. I made my best friendships by accident, with instant intimacy marking none of them—it wasn't mutual loneliness that drew us together.

I met my best friend Jean in a film class when she said Alfred Hitchcock was overrated. I disagreed and we argued out of the building and into a lifelong friendship where we argue still. We became friends without meaning to, and took our intimacy step by step. Deliberate choice, not desperate need, moved us closer. Our friendship is so much a part of us now that it seems unavoidable that we should have become friends. But there was nothing inevitable about it. It's easy to imagine Jean saying to me in that classroom, "Hitchcock's a hack, you're a fool, and that's all I have to say." But that was not all she had to say. Which is why we're friends today. We always have more to say.

Friendship's value wasn't always clear to me. In the back of my mind, I believed that platonic friendships were a way of marking time until I struck the pay dirt of serious romance. I'd managed to digest many romantic notions by my first year of college, and chief among them was the idea that I'd meet the perfect lover who would be everything to me and make me complete. I saw plunging into a relationship as an advanced form of friendship, friendship plus sex. Lacking sex, platonic friendships seemed like a lower standard of living. As long as my boyfriend offered me so much in one convenient package, women friends were superfluous. I thought I was the girl who had everything.

But what made that relationship more—the sex—made it a bad re- 7
placement for friendship. Sexual tension charged the lines of communication between us. White noise crackled on the wire as desire and jealousy, fear of loss, and the need to be loved conspired to cloud and distort expression. Influenced by these powerful forces, I didn't always tell the truth. And on the most practical level, when my boyfriend and I broke up, I had lost more than my lover, I lost my best friend.

"You can't keep doing this," Suzanne told me later that same year.   8

"What?"   9

"Start up our friendship every time your relationship falls apart."   10

"I don't do that," I said. It was exactly what I did.   11

"Yes, you do, and I'm sick of it. I'm not second best. I'm something 12 entirely different."

Once you see that relationships and friendships are different beasts, 13 you'll never think of the two things as interchangeable again, with friendships as the inferior version. . . .

Friendships made in college set a standard for intimacy other friendships 14 are hard-pressed ever to approach. "I've become a narrow specialist in my friendships since graduation," says Pam. "With one friend I'll talk about work. With another, we're fitness fanatics together. But I don't really know much about them—how they live their lives, what they eat for breakfast, or if they eat breakfast at all, who their favorite uncle is, or when they got their contact lenses. I don't even know who they voted for for President. There will be a close connection in spots, but in general I feel as if I'm dealing with fractions of people. With my college friends, I feel I know them whole."

In college, there's time to reach that degree of intimacy. One night, my best 15 friend and I spent hours describing how our respective families celebrated Christmas. My family waited until everyone was awake and caffeinated before opening presents, hers charged out of bed to rip open the boxes before they could wipe the sleep out of their eyes. We were as self-righteous as religious fanatics, each convinced our own family was the only one that did Christmas right. Did we really spend an entire night on a subject like that? Did we really have that much time?

Operating on college time, my social life was unplanned and spontane- 16 ous. Keeping a light on in our rooms was a way of extending an invitation. We had time to hang out, to learn to tell the difference between ordinary crankiness and serious depression in each other, and to follow the digressions that were at the heart of our friendships. But after college, we had to change, and in scheduling our free-form friendships we felt, at first, self-conscious and artificial.

When I had my first full-time job, I called my best friend to make a dinner 17 date a week in advance. She was still in graduate school, and thought my planning was dire evidence that I'd tumbled into the pit of adult convention. "Why don't you have your girl call my girl and we'll set something up?" she asked. Heavy sarcasm. While the terms of the friendship have shifted from digressive, spontaneous socializing to a directed, scheduled style, and we all feel a certain sense of loss, the value of friendship has, if anything, increased.

If my college journals were ever published in the newspaper, the   18
headline would most likely read, "FEM WRITER PENS GOO," but I did find
something genuinely moving while reading through my hyper-perceptions the
other day. Freshman year I'd written: "I am interested in everything. Nothing
bores me. I hope I don't die before I can read everything, visit every place, and
feel all there is to feel."

The sentiment would be a lot more poignant if I'd actually gone ahead   19
and died young, but I find it moving anyway because it exemplifies what's
good about being young: that you exist as the wide-eyed adventurer, fueled
by the belief that you might amount to something and anything, and
that your possibilities are endless. When I feel this way now, I'm usually
half-dreaming in bed on a breezy Saturday morning. Or I'm with a college
friend—someone with whom I'd pictured the future, back when the future
was a dizzying haze viewed with the mind's eye from the vantage point of a
smoky dorm room. Together we carved out life with words and hopes. When
I'm with her now, I remember that feeling and experience it all over again,
because there's still a lot of hazy future to imagine and life to carve. With my
friend, I can look to my future and through my past and remember who I am.

■ ■ ■

AFTER YOU READ

■ **THINK** about how college friendships differ from friendships formed in
other circumstances and other times. How rewarding were Crichton's
college friendships in comparison to other friendships? How rewarding
are your own college friendships as compared to other friendships?
What do you do and talk about with each different group? How are
these friendships similar? How are they different?

■ **EXAMINE** Crichton's statement about relationships and friendships in
paragraph 13. How does she compare the two? Do you agree or disagree with her comparison? Explain.

■ **EXAMINE** also Crichton's statement that "friendships made in college set a
standard for intimacy other friendships are hard-pressed ever to approach"
(paragraph 14). How does she support this statement? Like her friend Pam,
Crichton also believes that "with my college friends, I feel I know them
whole." What do you think she means by this statement? From your own
experiences, do you agree or disagree with these statements?

■ **WRITE** an essay about a particular college friendship of your own.

■ Or **WRITE** an essay comparing and contrasting your friendship with another college student and a friendship you made in other circumstances—
in childhood, in high school, or at work, for example. For instructions
about writing comparison and contrast essays, see Lesson 7 on the
Interactions, eighth edition, website, at www.cengagebrain.com.

A Small Act

■ ■ ■

JIMMY CARTER

Winner of the 2002 Nobel Peace Prize, Jimmy Carter (James Earl Carter, Jr.) was the thirty-ninth president of the United States, but his greatest legacy may well be the work he has done as an ex-president. Since leaving the White House, Carter and his wife, Rosalynn, have dedicated themselves to working for social justice and basic human rights. The nonprofit Carter Center, based in Atlanta, promotes peace and health in nations around the globe. And each year for one week, the Carters lead the Jimmy Carter Work Project for Habitat for Humanity International. In addition, Carter has written more than a dozen books, including *An Hour before Daylight: Memories of a Rural Boyhood* (2001). The reading selection below is taken from this memoir.

BEFORE YOU READ

■ **THINK** of your own early childhood and the playmates you had. Which of these playmates do you remember most vividly and why?

■ **EXAMINE** the title of this selection. Think of a small act that affected a relationship you had with a friend. Was the effect positive or negative? Was the act intentional or unintentional?

■ **EXAMINE** also the following words and definitions: to *emulate* (paragraph 2) is to imitate, a *surrogate* (paragraph 2) is a substitute, and *deference* (paragraph 6) is courteous yielding.

■ **WRITE** a journal entry about a friendship you had as a child. Include in your account how and why that relationship changed as you grew older.

AS YOU READ

Be aware of the prejudices built into our society during Carter's childhood, and notice how and why his relationships with his black friends change as he grows older.

■ ■ ■

From the first day we moved to the farm in Archery, my primary playmate was Alonzo Davis, always known as A.D., who lived on our farm with his uncle and aunt. During my first four years in Plains I had known only white children, and it must have been quite a change for me to meet this very timid little black boy with kinky hair, big eyes, and a tendency to mumble when he talked. I soon learned that A.D.'s bashfulness evaporated as soon as we were out of the presence of adults and on our own together, and it took me about an hour to forget, once and for all, about any racial differences between us. Since our other play-mates on the farm were also black, it was only natural for me to consider myself the outsider and to strive to emulate their habits and language. It never seemed to me that A.D. tried to change, except when one of my parents was present. Then he just became much quieter, watched what was going on with vigilance, and waited until we were alone again to re-sume his more carefree and exuberant ways.

I was soon spending most of my waking hours on the farm with him,   2
except when I was alongside Daddy or Jack Clark. Although his surrogate parents didn't know exactly when he was born, A.D. was close to my age, and it was not long after we met that he and his aunt adopted my birthday as his own, so we could share whatever celebrations there might be. A.D. was slightly larger and stronger than I, but not quite as fast or agile, so we were almost equal in our constant wrestling, running, and other contests. I was perfectly at ease in his house, and minded his uncle and aunt as though they were my own parents. At least during our younger years, I believe that he felt equally comfortable in our house; he and I didn't think it was anything out of the ordinary in our eating together in the kitchen, rather than at the table where my family assembled for meals.

When I had a choice of companions, I always preferred A.D. We   3
worked, played, fished, trapped, explored, built things, fought, and were punished together if we violated adult rules. Our other regular playmates were A.D.'s cousin Edmund Hollis and Milton and Johnny Raven, two brothers who lived a half-mile down the road....

Until my last two years of high school, the black boys at Archery were   4
my closest friends; I had a more intimate relationship with them than with any of my white classmates in town. This makes it more difficult for me to justify or explain my own attitudes and actions during the segregation era. A turning point in my relationship with A.D. and my other friends oc-curred when we were about fourteen years old. Until then, there had never been any distinction among us, despite the great difference between our economic circumstances. I lived in the "big house" and they lived in tenant shacks; I had a bicycle, my parents owned an automobile, and we went to separate churches and schools. I was destined to go to college, and few of them would finish their high school work. But there were no acknowledged differences of rank or status when we were together in the fields, on the creek banks, or playing in our yard or theirs, and we never thought about being of different color.

Around age fourteen, I began to develop closer ties with the white com-   5
munity. I was striving for a place on the varsity basketball team and

developed a stronger relationship with my classmates, including a growing interest in dating girls. One day about this time, A.D., Edmund, and I approached the gate leading from our barn to the pasture. To my surprise, they opened it and stepped back to let me go through first. I was immediately suspicious that they were playing some trick on me, but I passed through without stumbling over a tripwire or having them slam the gate in my face.

It was a small act, but a deeply symbolic one. After that, they often 6 treated me with some deference. I guess that their parents had done or said something that caused this change in my black friends' attitude. The constant struggle for leadership among our small group was resolved, but a precious sense of equality had gone out of our personal relationship, and things were never again the same between them and me.

It seems strange now that I never discussed this transition in our lives with 7 either my black friends or my own parents. We still competed equally while on the baseball field, fishing, or working in the field, but I was not reluctant to take advantage of my new stature by assuming, on occasion, the authority of my father. Also, we were more inclined to go our separate ways if we had an argument, since I was increasingly involved with my white friends in Plains. I guess all of us just assumed that this was one more step toward maturity and that we were settling into our adult roles in an unquestioned segregated society.

■ ■ ■

AFTER YOU READ

- ■ **THINK** about the circumstances that led to the change in Carter's relationship with his black friends. Remember that Carter was born in 1924 in a small southern town. Were friendships between white and black children common at this time? Were such friendships more or less likely to occur in the South than in the North? Why do you think Carter's relationships with his black playmates changed as they grew older? Are relationships between children of different races or ethnic backgrounds more or less common today? Why or why not?

- ■ **EXAMINE** Carter's description of the "small act" that changed his relationship with his black playmates (paragraphs 5 and 6). What was the act? Why do you think Carter calls this act "deeply symbolic"? What did the act symbolize for him and his friends?

- ■ **WRITE** an essay about a friendship you have (or have had) with someone who is different from you in some way or who is looked at differently by society. Did your different backgrounds ultimately create difficulties in your friendship? Why or why not? Did outside forces put a strain on your friendship? If so, how? If your friendship encountered problems because of your differences, were you successful in resolving those problems? If so, how? If not, why?

- ■ Or **WRITE** an essay about a friendship that has changed significantly over time.

A Boyhood Friendship in a Divided Valley

■ ■ ■

BEN KAMIN

Israeli-born Ben Kamin is both a rabbi and a writer. He is also the author of several books, the most recent of which are *The Spirit behind the News* (2009) and *Nothing Like Sunshine: A Story in the Aftermath of the MLK Assassination* (2010). In addition, Kamin is a frequent contributor of essays and editorials to newspapers, including *The New York Times*, which published this essay in 2002. Like Carter's "A Small Act," this essay tells the story of a boyhood friendship that is destroyed by racial discrimination as the boys grow older. In Kamin's essay, the loss of the friendship is because one boy is an Israeli and the other a Palestinian.

BEFORE YOU READ

■ **THINK** about the Israeli-Palestinian conflict and what it would be like to live side by side with people whom you feared and hated. How difficult would it be to reach out to someone on the other side, knowing that your families had been engaged in a deep and ongoing conflict for many years?

■ **EXAMINE** the word *carnage*, which appears in the first sentence of the essay. It means a massive slaughter or a massacre. Do you think this word is overly dramatic, or is Kamin justified in using it, given the history of events in Israel and Palestine? What do you know about the Israeli-Palestinian conflict? (For more information about this conflict, see the second assignment of "Exploring the Internet," page 189.)

■ **WRITE** a journal entry in which you describe a friend you once had who was different from you in a significant way.

AS YOU READ

Compare this essay to "A Small Act" by Jimmy Carter. How are the situations in the two essays similar? How are they different?

■ ■ ■

The carnage from Palestinian suicide bombings in Tel Aviv and the ambush of a bus in the West Bank this week make hope for peace between Israel and the Palestinians seem impossible. Yet each outrage, followed by unending grief and fierce response, makes me think even more about a little dialogue I had long ago with a Palestinian neighbor of mine.

1

Every morning now I read about the Palestinian town of Qalqilya and 2
terrorists who might be seeking shelter there. But Qalqilya is not just a
passing news reference for me.

In the fall of 1961, I was eight years old and living in the Israeli hamlet 3
of Kfar Saba, where my parents had also been born. We could see the Sa-
marian Mountains from our porch, and the town of Qalqilya, then part of
Jordan, with its minarets and stone streets, just a mile or so away. A valley
of orchards and wild brush hung between us and was forbidden; the border was more or less defined by an old rail path left behind by the British,
who had quit their mandate in Palestine five years before I was born.

But exactly because the citrus-scented valley between Kfar Saba and 4
Qalqilya was off limits to us, it was enticing to me one Saturday afternoon
that fall. I rode my bicycle past the village square, beyond the old bus station, and into the valley that unfolded against the biblical mountains. Qalqilya was close by where I walked in the thick groves that divided the two
worlds. And then I realized that I was not alone. Standing by and staring at
me was an Arab boy, about my age, as surprised by this encounter as I.

We both froze in fear. But curiosity quickly prevailed and we began to 5
talk. It was a halting mixture of Hebrew and English; I did not know any
Arabic. I still remember that he knew words from both of my languages
and I did not know any from his. And I still remember his face very clearly,
particularly the way that he smiled.

I told him about my village and described my father as a war hero and 6
a mighty man who had once fought in that valley. He told me that his father was very tall and strong and was chieftain of his village. We talked
about the orange trees and agreed to meet again in a week at the same
spot. I told him my name. He told me his—Ahmed. We parted, the sons
of fathers who may have battled each other in that valley.

Our second appointed meeting was washed out by an autumn rain, 7
but we did again meet several days later. I had not told my parents about
the first meeting because they would certainly have disapproved. Ahmed
stood waiting for me. We barely touched shoulders. There was a tension
we did not understand. But we were driven by something very good that
we also did not understand.

We both knew that this second meeting would confirm the first but 8
necessarily be the last. Nevertheless, it was truly friendly. We taught each
other words from each other's languages, simple words like "goat," "bicycle" and "rain." We compared notes on siblings. And then the time grew
short. Before leaving, we did something together, reaching almost simultaneously for the same large orange hanging down from the tree above us,
we opened it and shared the slices. How sticky and sweet it tasted. We
buried the peels and the seeds in the ground under the tree.

I remember Ahmed's face. In the television footage of rage coming to 9
us from that same valley, I look for that face. We are both middle-aged
men now and, on a visit two years ago, I saw that few trees were left in
that valley. Israeli tanks rolled into Qalqilya this spring. Unforgivable
bombings have killed children in my birth village. I wonder where Ahmed

is and what we would say to each other if we were to meet again. Might it be possible for us to reach a reconciliation now? Would he remember that we once knew more about peace than all of the grownups on either side of our valley?

■ ■ ■

AFTER YOU READ

■ **THINK** about a time in your life when you had a friend who was different from you in significant ways or of whom your parents disapproved. In both this story and the one by Jimmy Carter, the older generation subtly or openly discourages the friendship of the two boys. Why do you think young people are more open than adults to friendships with people who do not share their own cultural, linguistic, and/or racial background?

■ **EXAMINE** the reasons why Kamin and his Palestinian friend, Ahmed, found it difficult to be friends. Were the obstacles to their friendship more or less significant than the obstacles to the friendship that Carter shared with his black neighbors? As adults, how did Carter and Kamin feel about the loss of these friends?

■ **EXAMINE** also paragraph 8. What did Kamin and Ahmed do together, and how is this act symbolic?

■ **WRITE** an essay in which you tell of one of your friendships that has ended or changed in significant ways. You should not only describe your friend but also analyze why the friendship did not last and what your feelings are about that person now.

Oil and Water

■ ■ ■

VALERIE OWEN

In contrast to the two previous essays, Valerie Owen's experiences with a friend who was different to her proved to be positive and longlasting. Born and raised in Oklahoma, Owen examines the radical personality differences between her friend and herself, relating how these differences not only brought two people together and helped seal a lifelong friendship but also helped to shape the person she is today. In her essay, written in her freshman English course, Owen illustrates that even the most unlikely people can end up being the best of friends.

BEFORE YOU READ

■ **THINK** about the title "Oil and Water." What happens when you pour oil and water together? How might two friends be like oil and water?

■ **EXAMINE** the first paragraph of the essay. How does this paragraph capture your interest? How does it introduce the subject of the essay? Then look at the second paragraph. What makes the first sentence especially surprising? After reading this statement, how unlikely was a friendship between these two young women?

■ **WRITE** a journal entry about your best friend. Are you and your best friend more like each other or more different? How do your similarities or differences contribute to your friendship?

AS YOU READ

Look for the connection between the title "Oil and Water" and the subject of the essay. Does the friendship between Valerie and Gayla seem at first to be as unlikely as a blend of oil and water?

■ ■ ■

Even though we are separated by 265 miles of long, desolate high- 1
way, I know exactly what she's doing right now. She's punching
the snooze button for the third time in a row and muttering a few
choice words. Her name is Gayla Holcomb, and she's my best friend.

We met in junior high school, and it was hate at first sight. I was not 2
able to pinpoint her most annoying habit, because she had so many. While

I had been brought up to be quiet and reserved, she enjoyed burping at will and often felt compelled to whistle at the boys. Indeed, her backwoods mannerisms were as shocking to me as a slap in the face.

If I could have, I would have avoided her. This proved to be impossible, 3 for when we compared our class schedules, I realized that they were identical. Even so, had it not been for a certain incident in our chemistry class, Gayla and I might have never looked past our differences long enough to form a friendship of any kind.

Our chemistry was conducting experiments in the laboratory, and 4 I had the honor of being Gayla's lab partner. She was horsing around as usual and accidentally started a fire. The entire student body had to evacuate the building, and the fire department was called. Gayla and I were the only ones who found any humor in the whole situation. Apparently, we found too much humor in it, because our teacher called our parents, and we were both grounded. From that day forward, every time I saw Gayla, I would think of the "Bunsen Burner Mishap," and I would have to laugh. It was the beginning of a beautiful friendship.

I began to enjoy spending time with Gayla and even sat next to her 5 during the lunch hour on purpose. In no time at all, we were walking home from school together on the weekdays and tying up our parents' phone lines on the weekends. I caught myself admiring the same outspoken personality that had caused me to shudder just a few short weeks earlier. As time went on, I even chose to adopt some of her footloose ways.

My poor parents didn't know what to think. I went from a quiet, re- 6 served honor student who spent her spare time playing the violin and writing poetry to a full-blown adolescent girl who was painting her room purple and dragging on Main Street until the wee hours of the morning with some awful girl who liked to burp in public. Fortunately, they also noticed I seemed to be happier and decided not to interfere with my newfound friendship.

As the school days lapsed into summer, our friendship grew. We spent 7 many afternoons in the shade under the old pear tree in my backyard. There we shared many secrets that had never before been told. I now knew that John Denver made her weak in the knees, and she knew that I thought my father was demented. We trusted one another with our secrets, confident that neither one of us would ever breathe a word to another living soul, because we believed we would never, ever fight.

To our surprise, we found that even the best of friends fight. Not only 8 did we fight, but we fought hard and often over stupid things like boys. We also found that even while we were spitting mad at one another, we wouldn't break the trust that held us so dearly. Secrets remained secrets, and we always found the road back to our friendship.

After graduation we both went our own ways. I moved to Kansas and 9 started a family. Gayla moved to Edmond, Oklahoma, and started a family of her own. Although marriage, miles, and years have slowly pulled us apart, we are as close as we have ever been.

While we were once too different to be friends, it was our differences 10 that drew us together and built the memories that have kept us together through all of these years. I find the time to phone Gayla once or twice a month, and from time to time she finds her way into my dreams.

■ ■ ■

AFTER YOU READ

■ **THINK** about the thesis, or main point, of Owen's essay. In which paragraph is it most clearly stated. Write this thesis in your own words.

■ **THINK** also about the "Bunsen Burner Mishap" that Owen describes in her essay. Do you think she and Gayla would have become friends if it had not been for this accident? How did this incident bring them together? Have you ever had a similar experience in forming a friendship? Explain.

■ **EXAMINE** carefully the language of the essay, pointing out how Owen's vivid word choice makes the friends and their friendship seem real to you. Examples of her vivid and effective language include her comparison of Gayla's "backwoods mannerisms" to "a slap in the face" (paragraph 2). What other effective uses of language do you find in the essay?

■ **WRITE** an essay about one of your friends who is very different from you. How has this difference affected your friendship?

■ Or **WRITE** an essay about your "best friend." How did you meet? How did you first become friends? What qualities and experiences contribute to your friendship? Has this friendship been, or do you believe it will be, a lasting friendship? Explain.

Vinnie's Jacket

■ ■ ■

ANNA NUSSBAUM

Anna Nussbaum started writing when she was still a student in high school in Colorado Springs, Colorado. She continued to publish as a college student at the University of Notre Dame, winning *Commonweal*'s 2001 Young Writers Contest for "Vinnie's Jacket," which was then published in *Commonweal* in 2003. This essay tells of a close friendship that remains real to the author even after its unexpected and tragic end.

BEFORE YOU READ

■ **THINK** about a time when you lost someone for whom you cared a great deal. What was your reaction to this loss? Do you think that writing about this person would have eased your grief? Why or why not?

■ **EXAMINE** the following sentence from the essay: "He was the person with whom I was my best self" (paragraph 7). Do you have friends who make you feel this way? Is this sentence a good definition of a friend? Why or why not?

■ **EXAMINE** also the word *disaffected* (paragraph 3), which means withdrawn, isolated, or uninterested.

■ **WRITE** in your journal about a friend who makes you feel good about yourself.

AS YOU READ

Underline the details Nussbaum includes in describing both her friend and herself.

■ ■ ■

Vinnie loaned me his jacket one night when we were sitting in his basement bedroom listening to the Fugees and catching up. He'd been smoking in the stairwell leading into his room. Because the door had been open, it was cold. Vinnie let me pick out a jacket. I chose the red and blue plaid. It was one of his purchases from Goodwill. "That was only a dollar seventy-five," he told me smiling. 1

The jacket smelled like him, like Marlboros and sweat and Calvin Klein cologne. It had a grease stain on the sleeve from when he'd worn it 2 while repairing his old Ford. Its cotton exterior and nylon lining were worn and smooth. It felt good and I wore it home.

The next weekend I went to a party in my hometown wearing Vinnie's 3 jacket. Vinnie couldn't come. I walked in and surveyed the scene. I felt sure I was the youngest person there. It was full of twentysomethings who for whatever reason had hung around Colorado Springs after high school either to work or go to community college or both. Everyone looked ironic and beautiful and disaffected. Women had elaborate tattoos that hung like necklaces across their collarbones and dipped into their bosoms. People had piercings in their cheeks and lips and tongues and eyebrows and bellies and noses. I shoved my hands in the pockets of Vinnie's jacket and breathed deeply. I slouched confidently through the crowd. I danced to the punk band in the basement, and smiled at people who didn't smile back. Vinnie's jacket made me feel safe and loved and cool, the way he made me feel.

I told him all about the party the next morning on the phone. At first he 4 laughed 'cause it was funny, but he kept laughing at the sound of his own laughter. It took off. He let me keep wearing the jacket through April and into May until he decided I might as well keep it. Forever. That's what I did.

I saw Vinnie the night before he died. I rode my bike over to his house. I 5 signed his yearbook. I hugged him close, all warm and alive. He'd lifted me off my feet and held me in the air for a long time. We'd promised never to lose touch.

Vinnie died in June, right after graduation. He had been in pain, but 6 he wasn't a complainer. No one knew exactly what was wrong. He'd been losing much weight. He'd had exploratory surgery and had been seeing various doctors, one of whom suggested a psychiatrist. He thought the weight loss might have been caused by anxiety. Vinnie took too many of the painkillers he'd been given by the shrink and they stopped his heart. It was an unintentional overdose. That's what we were told.

The night he died I had gone to the movies. I saw a movie about a man 7 who blew up the world, and I came home to find my mother waiting on the front porch. She called me inside and said, "Anna, Vinnie Franz is dead." All I could do was sob and scream "No. Don't tell me this!" because Vinnie was my best friend. He was the person with whom I was my best self. With Vinnie I was funnier, smarter, braver, kinder, more beautiful, more faithful. Or at least that's how I felt. He was the last person with whom I could still be a kid, long after I could no longer be a kid with myself. He was fun. I called Vinnie every day, and he called me. We didn't even say hello anymore, we just picked up the phone and started talking where we'd left off. He was the one who made me laugh so hard I couldn't see. He was the one I yelled with. He watched out for me. He kept all my secrets. And he was dead.

Adults want to focus on why Vinnie died. They want to know who 8 was at fault. But that doesn't interest me so much. What interests me is how one friendship can teach you about loyalty and laughter, and how one friendship can carry you from one road to the next.

When Vinnie died I wanted to go back to the days when I first met him 9 in sixth grade. The kid was crazy in love with God. He sent me notes in class about how much Jesus loved me. He went to Mass on foot every Sunday in middle school; his mom and sister didn't attend. He sat in the back. Afterward he got doughnuts and ate them on the roof of the nearby hospital looking at the sky, and smoking.

This past summer everything started burning. My state. My church.   10
My world. Wild fires raged in Colorado. The hard part at such times is waiting to see what will be consumed, what will endure, and what will change forever. They say that death is a part of life but for much of my life it wasn't. Now I go to Vinnie's grave at Evergreen Cemetery and I sing to the sod. I take long walks and converse with the air, but the subject isn't there. I walk at night wearing Vinnie's jacket and search the sky. Dry lightning illuminates the muddy red clouds at dusk and the blue gray clouds at night. I'm looking for my friend.

My jacket no longer smells of him. It smells like me now. Sometimes I   11
think there's nothing left. Then I tell a joke he told me and people laugh; or I check my oil the way he showed me, or I let a guy pay for lunch the way he used to do, or I put on mascara Jersey style and I know he'd approve. I think about all those days and nights spent in each other's friendship, and the days when he was my only friend. We loved each other; that's what I take with me.

This has been a hard story to tell. Because I don't want to sell out my   12
friend and I also don't want him to be forgotten. But I do want you to know his name.

■   ■   ■

AFTER YOU READ

- ■ **THINK** about the title of this essay. Why do you think Nussbaum chose this particular title? Why is her friend's jacket so important to her? Think also about the ways in which Nussbaum and her friend Vinnie were different. Identify and discuss these differences. Were they also similar in some important ways? If so, how? Do you think it is unusual for a male and female to be close friends? Why or why not?

- ■ **EXAMINE** details that you underlined as you read Nussbaum's essay. Which ones gave you the best sense of Vinnie and Nussbaum?

- ■ **WRITE** an essay about a friend who makes you feel good about yourself, using your journal as a rough draft. Focus especially on adding specific details and incidents that will help your reader understand what your friend is like and why he or she makes you feel good about yourself.

- ■ Or **WRITE** an essay in which you argue for or against the idea that a male and female can have a close friendship without a romantic or sexual attraction.

The Difference between Male and Female Friendships

■ ■ ■

ELLEN GOODMAN AND

PATRICIA O'BRIEN

Ellen Goodman is a successful novelist, and Patricia O'Brien has written several novels. The two women are good friends who cowrote *I Know Just What You Mean: The Power of Friendship in Women's Lives* (2000). Although this book focuses on female friendships—how they work and how they affect the lives of women—the authors also explore the differences between male and female friendships. The following selection from their book attempts to answer the question "Why do men and women, on the topic of friendship, puzzle each other so much?"

BEFORE YOU READ

■ THINK about your own perceptions of male and female friendships. Do you see them as different? In what ways?

■ EXAMINE the last sentence of the first paragraph, in which the authors state, "While women tend to *be* together, men tend to *do* together." Do you agree with this statement? Why or why not? If this observation is accurate, what does it indicate about the difference between male and female friendships?

■ EXAMINE also the word *prototypical* (paragraph 10), which means a "typical example or model." Identify the prototypical pictures of women friends and men friends that the authors provide. Do you agree that these are the most common pictures of female and male friendships?

■ WRITE a journal entry in which you list some of the differences that you have observed between male and female friendships.

AS YOU READ

Underline and number the differences between male and female friendships that you find in this selection.

■   ■   ■

Why do men and women, on the topic of friendship, puzzle each other so much? Let us start with the obvious: women do friendship differently than men. Among women, friendship is conducted face-to-face. But as Carolyn Heilbrun once wrote, "Male friends do not always face each other: they stand side by side, facing the world." While women tend to *be* together, men tend to *do* together.   1

We have thought about this friendship divide ever since [the] ... time when sex differences were just beginning to go under an intense cultural microscope. We know that men's feelings of closeness and connection are real; that painting a house or watching a ball game together can be an act of friendship. But we also know we would feel lonely if we couldn't talk to each other about everything, through good and bad times.   2

The two of us have wondered over the years just what is going on between men. And the truth is, we have disagreed with each other about whether men are missing something so central to friendship that it amounts to almost a fatal flaw, or whether they are handling friendship just fine—in their own, mysterious way. Do men, as Letty Pogrebin wrote in *Among Friends*, deserve "Incompletes" in the subject of friendship? Are women in the business of grading?   3

"What on earth do you have to say to each other?" men ask. Women have their own counterquestion for male friends: "You spent all day together on the golf course and never told him you were worried about your job?"   4

When we first began telling people that we were writing about women and friendship, the second or third question would invariably be, "What about men? Are you writing about them, too?" Sometimes it was asked with a smile or a teasing challenge; sometimes defensively. We could hear a distinct subtext: if you're writing only about women, are you saying your friendships are better than ours?   5

We answered that we were writing about women because, if you write about what you know, what we know are women's friendships. We would leave it to men to write about their own friendships. The contradictory, complex differences between the two sexes in a time of such change is a topic for a different kind of book. Yet here we are, looking across the gender divide with curiosity and sometimes bewilderment.   6

Let's give comedian Rob Becker the first take on this subject. Becker plays Darwin to the sexes in the theatrical hit, *Defending the Caveman*. He announces to his audiences at one point that—at last—he has the gender-friendship gap all figured out.   7

So, here's how it works, he says. Men were the hunters, see? They were required to stand side by side without talking for fear they'd scare off the prey. Women? They were gatherers, out there foraging in the jungle for food. So they HAD to talk while they worked, for safety.   8

You get the picture? "If a woman goes for very long without hearing the voice of another woman, she knows she's been eaten by an animal,"   9

Becker announces. So women are genetically allotted some five thousand words a day, while men are allotted only two thousand. No wonder women talk more, he triumphantly concludes.

Well, hunters and gatherers aside, if there is one prototypical image of 10 women sharing friendship, it's that of two friends sitting across a table from each other, clutching their coffee cups, talking feelings. If there is a similar image of men, it is of buddies sitting together watching television, talking football.

We know these images are simplistic and women and men are both 11 guilty of stretching them to make assumptions about each other's friendships that range from the stereotypic to the bizarre. Men never talk about anything but sports, women say in frustration. Women talk only about clothes, men retort. Both sexes get trapped in vast generalizations. But the differences between the same-sex friendships of men and women are real. Decades of research can't be ignored.

A long list of studies tell[s] men and women what they already know: 12 men and women talk about different things in different ways. Men are less likely to talk about personal subjects with other men than women are with other women. As Pogrebin summed it up, "The average man's idea of an intimate exchange is the average woman's idea of a casual conversation."

What else do the researchers show? Men's friendships are based on 13 shared activities, women's on shared feelings. Men who do things together, paint that house, change that tire, feel close; women who share secrets, troubles, relationships, feel close.

If you had a camera you could videotape the gender gap. Women liter- 14 ally touch each other more; they sit closer together, focus on one-to-one sharing. But when men talk about what they do with their friends, you get a different portrait: men doing things together in groups.

The research list goes on. Men do not criticize their friends as much as 15 women, but neither do they communicate the kind of acceptance women count on from their friends. Men put shared interests highest among the reasons they bond with a friend, while women first want friends who share their values. And even men tend to view their friendships with women as closer and more intimate than those with other men.

And yet—here's the counterweight—at least among grade school boys, 16 a study shows that a relative lack of intimacy and affection doesn't affect the importance or the satisfaction boys get from their friends.

Every friendship is as different as the people involved, and not all men 17 are caveman hunters and not all women are cavewoman gatherers. But differences between male and female friendships have remained constant and consistent. What has shifted are the values placed on those differences. What's striking now is that the culture has gone from seeing men's friendships as superior to seeing women's friendships as superior. Is that just a swing of the pendulum?

It's not surprising that philosophers in the past routinely dismissed 18 women as incapable of true friendship. They were certain that, because women led more "trivial" lives, they had limited capacity for elevated feelings. The classical idea of friendship was heroic, and the greatest thing a man could give a friend was his courage and loyalty. Montaigne once wrote in a spirit of superior regret, "To speak truly, the usual capacity of women is not equal to the demands of the communion and intercourse which is the sustenance of that sacred bond; nor do their minds seem firm enough to sustain the pressure of so hard and so lasting a knot."

Women, on the other hand, often idealized their relationships with   19 each other. Historian Nancy Cott describes how educated women in the nineteenth century passionately poured out their feelings, often expressing their firm belief in the superiority of female relationships. "I do not feel that men can ever feel so pure an enthusiasm for women as we can feel for one another," wrote one woman to another. "Ours is nearest to the love of angels."

The idea that friendship is defined by intimacy has become, in our   20 time, less fervently defined—but more solidly understood. As a result, the gender gap has been focused on the intimacy gap. And men's friendships are indeed often given an "incomplete" grade.

■   ■   ■

AFTER YOU READ

■ THINK about the authors' argument that women friends communicate with each other while men friends simply do things together. In your experience, do you find this to be true? If so, what does it say about men and women?

■ EXAMINE the quotation from Pogrebin in paragraph 12: "the average man's idea of an intimate exchange is the average woman's idea of a casual conversation." Do you agree with this assertion? Why or why not? Do you believe that men's friendships are inferior to women's simply because men do not communicate in the way women do? Why or why not? What other significant differences do you think exist between male and female friendships?

■ WRITE an essay in which you compare and/or contrast male and female friendships. Use this reading selection as a source along with your own experiences and observations. Lesson 7 of the *Interactions*, eighth edition, website at www.cengagebrain.com provides instruction in writing comparison and contrast essays.

FOCUS: CLASSIFICATION

What Are Friends For?

■ ■ ■

MARION WINIK

Marion Winik, who teaches writing at the University of Balti-more, is known not only as a writer but also as a reflective and witty commentator on National Public Radio; her commen-taries for *All Things Considered* are collected on the National Public Radio website (see Related Websites on the *Interactions*, eighth edition, student site). Her essays have appeared in *The New York Times Magazine*, *Parenting*, *Cosmopolitan*, and *Sa-lon*. She has also authored eight books of poetry and creative nonfiction, the most recent of which are *Rules for the Unruly* (2001), *Above Us Only Sky* (2005), and *The Glen Rock Book of the Dead* (2008). This essay, in which Winik categorizes dif-ferent kinds of friendships, appears in her collection entitled *Telling: Confessions, Concessions, and Other Flashes of Light* (1994).

BEFORE YOU READ

- ■ **THINK** about the question posed in the title of this essay: "What Are Friends For?" How would you answer this question?

- ■ **EXAMINE** the first paragraph of this essay. What can you tell about this essay from this brief, one-sentence introductory paragraph? Examine, especially, the author's tone. How would you describe her tone? What does it suggest about the essay that is to follow?

- ■ **EXAMINE** also the words *accentuates* (paragraph 6), meaning "em-phasizes"; and *indispensable* (paragraph 8), meaning "necessary, essential."

- ■ **WRITE** a journal entry in which you answer the question posed in the title. That is, based on your life and experience, what are friends for?

AS YOU READ

Circle (or highlight) each different category of friends that the author includes in her essay.

■   ■   ■

I was thinking about how everybody can't be everything to each other,   1
but some people can be something to each other, thank God, from the
ones whose shoulder you cry on to the ones whose half-slips you borrow to the nameless ones you chat with in the grocery line.

Buddies, for example, are the workhorses of the friendship world, the   2
people out there on the front lines, defending you from loneliness and
boredom. They call you up, they listen to your complaints, they celebrate
your successes and curse your misfortunes, and you do the same for them
in return. They hold out through innumerable crises before concluding
that the person you're dating is no good, and even then understand if you
ignore their good counsel. They accompany you to a movie with subtitles
or to see the diving pig at Aquarena Springs. They feed your cat when you
are out of town and pick you up from the airport when you get back.
They come over to help you decide what to wear on a date. Even if it is
with that creep.

What about family members? Most of them are people you just got   3
stuck with, and though you love them, you may not have very much in
common. But there is that rare exception, the Relative Friend. It is your
cousin, your brother, maybe even your aunt. The two of you share the
same views of the other family members. Meg never should have divorced
Martin. He was the best thing that ever happened to her. You can confirm
each other's memories of things that happened a long time ago. Don't you
remember when Uncle Hank and Daddy had that awful fight in the middle
of Thanksgiving dinner? Grandma always hated Grandpa's stamp collection; she probably left the windows open during the hurricane on
purpose.

While so many family relationships are tinged with guilt and obliga-   4
tion, a relationship with a Relative Friend is relatively worry free. You
don't even have to hide your vices from this delightful person. When you
slip out Aunt Joan's back door for a cigarette, she is already there.

Then there is that special guy at work. Like all the other people at the   5
job site, at first he's just part of the scenery. But gradually he starts to
stand out from the crowd. Your friendship is cemented by jokes about
coworkers and thoughtful favors around the office. Did you see Ryan's
hair? Want half my bagel? Soon you know the names of his turtles, what
he did last Friday night, exactly which model CD player he wants for his
birthday. His handwriting is as familiar to you as your own.

Though you invite each other to parties, you somehow don't quite fit   6
into each other's outside lives. For this reason, the friendship may not survive a job change. Company gossip, once an infallible source of entertainment, soon awkwardly accentuates the distance between you. But wait.
Like School Friends, Work Friends share certain memories which acquire
a nostalgic glow after about a decade.

A Faraway Friend is someone you grew up with or went to school   7
with or lived in the same town as until one of you moved away. Without

a Faraway Friend, you would never get any mail addressed in handwriting. A Faraway Friend calls late at night, invites you to her wedding, always says she is coming to visit but rarely shows up. An actual visit from a Faraway Friend is a cause for celebration and binges of all kinds. Cigarettes, Chips Ahoy, bottles of tequila.

Faraway Friends go through phases of intense communication, then 8 may be out of touch for many months. Either way, the connection is always there. A conversation with your Faraway Friend always helps to put your life in perspective: when you feel you've hit a dead end, come to a confusing fork in the road, or gotten lost in some crackerbox subdivision of your life, the advice of the Faraway Friend—who has the big picture, who is so well acquainted with the route that brought you to this place—is indispensable.

Another useful function of the Faraway Friend is to help you remem- 9 ber things from a long time ago, like the name of your seventh-grade history teacher, what was in that really good stir-fry, or exactly what happened that night on the boat with the guys from Florida.

Ah, the Former Friend. A sad thing. At best a wistful memory, at worst 10 a dangerous enemy who is in possession of many of your deepest secrets. But what was it that drove you apart? A misunderstanding, a betrayed confidence, an unrepaid loan, an ill-conceived flirtation. A poor choice of spouse can do in a friendship just like that. Going into business together can be a serious mistake. Time, money, distance, cult religions: all noted friendship killers. You quit doing drugs, you're not such good friends with your dealer anymore.

And lest we forget, there are the Friends You Love to Hate. They call 11 at inopportune times. They say stupid things. They butt in, they boss you around, they embarrass you in public. They invite themselves over. They take advantage. You've done the best you can, but they need professional help. On top of all this, they love you to death and are convinced they're your best friend on the planet.

So why do you continue to be involved with these people? Why do 12 you tolerate them? On the contrary, the real question is, What would you do without them? Without Friends You Love to Hate, there would be nothing to talk about with your other friends. Their problems and their irritating stunts provide a reliable source of conversation for everyone they know. What's more, Friends You Love to Hate make you feel good about yourself, since you are obviously in so much better shape than they are. No matter what these people do, you will never get rid of them. As much as they need you, you need themtoo.

At the other end of the spectrum are Hero Friends. These people are 13 better than the rest of us, that's all there is to it. Their career is something you wanted to be when you grew up—painter, forest ranger, tireless doer of good. They have beautiful homes filled with special handmade things presented to them by villagers in the remote areas they have visited in their extensive travels. Yet they are modest. They never gossip. They are always helping others, especially those who have suffered a death in the family or an illness. You would think people like this would just make you sick, but somehow they don't.

A New Friend is a tonic unlike any other. Say you meet her at a party. In 14 your bowling league. At a Japanese conversation class, perhaps. Wherever, whenever, there's that spark of recognition. The first time you talk, you can't believe how much you have in common. Suddenly, your life story is interesting again, your insights fresh, your opinion valued. Your various shortcomings are as yet completely invisible.

It's almost like falling in love. 15

■ ■ ■

AFTER YOU READ

■ **THINK** about the tone of the essay. How would you describe it? Does the first paragraph give you an accurate impression of what to expect? Do you think that the author is serious about her classification of friends even though she uses a casual, humorous tone? Why or why not?

■ **THINK** also about the qualities that make a good classification essay. Besides having a clear purpose and thesis, an effective classification essay should have a clear basis of classification, and each category should clearly fit that basis. For example, Winik seems to be classifying her friends based on the friendship situation, such as being a relative, a coworker, and so on. Which of her categories fit this criterion most clearly? Do any of her categories stretch the basis of classification? (You might even identify the most interesting and well-developed categories and discuss them in small groups, comparing Winik's friends to some of your own.) What is your overall evaluation of "What Are Friends For?" as a classification essay?

■ **EXAMINE** more carefully the eight categories of friends that the author discusses. How would you describe each category? What categories would you add or delete to improve the essay as classification?

■ **WRITE** an essay in which you classify the different friends in your life. Be sure to select one basis of classification, such as what you do with these friends, how each friend fits on a "closeness" scale, and the like. Identify 3–5 categories of friends that fit your chosen basis of classification. Then give one or two examples of friends in each category, showing how these friends clearly belong in the category into which you have placed them. Lesson 3 on the *Interactions*, eighth edition, website at www.cengagebrain.com provides additional instruction on and examples of classification.

Great Expectations

■ ■ ■

STEPHANIE COONTZ

A specialist on marriage and the family, Stephanie Coontz teaches history and family studies at Evergreen State College in Olympia, Washington. She is the author of several books, including the related books *The Way We Never Were: American Families and the Nostalgia Trap* (1992) and *The Way We Really Are: Coming to Terms with America's Changing Families* (1997). Her most recent book, *Marriage, a History: From Obedience to Intimacy, or How Love Conquered Marriage*, was named by *The Washington Post* as one of the best books of 2005. Coontz has appeared on *Oprah Winfrey, The Today Show, 20/20*, and other television venues. The article below appeared in the *Baltimore Sun* in June 2005.

BEFORE YOU READ

■ **THINK** about the title, "Great Expectations"—which is an allusion to the title of a novel by Charles Dickens. In her essay Coontz is referring to the expectations many people today have for marriage. Do you think that "great expectations" for marriage are justified today? Why or why not?

■ **EXAMINE** the humorous quotation at the end of the first paragraph. What word did the student mean instead of *vowels*? Do you agree or disagree with Coontz's follow-up statement? Then examine the word *covenant* in paragraph 7. A *covenant* is a binding agreement or contract, such as a marriage.

■ **EXAMINE** also the length of the paragraphs in the essay. Look especially at paragraphs 2–7, 14, and 15. How many sentences does each of these paragraphs have? Other paragraphs in the essay have only two or three sentences, and the longest paragraphs (10 and 18) have only four sentences. This style of short paragraphs is consistent with newspaper articles, such as this one.

■ **WRITE** a journal entry in which you discuss your expectations for marriage or a long-term relationship.

AS YOU READ

Underline phrases and sentences that suggest the thesis of the essay.

■ ■ ■

T he problem with modern marriage, according to conventional wisdom, is that today's couples don't make marriage their top priority and put their relationship above all else. As one of my students once wrote, "People nowadays don't respect the marriage vowels." Perhaps she meant IOU. 1

But my research on the history of marriage convinces me that people now place a higher value on marriage than ever before in history. In fact, that's a big part of the problem. 2

One reason marriage is fragile today is that we expect so much more of it than we used to, and many of our expectations are contradictory. 3

Most people recognize that marriage takes sacrifice, hard work and the ability to put up with the bad in your partner as well as the good. 4

But they also expect marriage to be the ultimate source of their happiness and the most fulfilling, passionate relationship in their lives. 5

When Arkansas Gov. Mike Huckabee "upgraded" his marriage vows on Valentine's Day before an audience of 5,000 enthusiastic marriage advocates, a banner reading "Passion Transformation Intimacy Oneness Covenant" summed up their case for marriage. 6

Unfortunately, people who expect to find passion, transformation, intimacy and oneness in their marriages often end up disappointed in their covenant, and the higher their expectations, the greater their disappointment. 7

Europeans and Americans used to view marriage as a work relationship in which passion took second place to practicality and intimacy never interfered with male authority. As that view of marriage has changed over the past 100 years, the divorce rate has risen steadily. 8

For most of history, people had modest expectations of marital happiness. The upper middle classes of Europe in the Middle Ages, who arranged their marriages for political and economic gain, believed that true love and passion could only exist outside marriage, in an adulterous affair. 9

In the 18th and 19th centuries, conventional wisdom among middle-class men was that the kind of woman you'd want for a wife was incapable of sexual passion. One marital advice expert even wrote that frigidity was a virtue to be cultivated in women. When wives wrote about their husbands in diaries, they were much less likely to describe intimate conversations than to record a persistent feeling of loneliness. A successful marriage was more often based on resigned acceptance than on transformation. 10

In the early 20th century, people came to expect marriage to be based on love, sexual attraction and personal fulfillment. But women often settled for less because of their economic dependence on men. 11

As late as the 1960s, polls found that nearly three-fourths of college women said they would marry a man they didn't love if he met their other criteria. In the 1970s, the working-class women interviewed by psychologist Lillian Rubin defined a good husband in terms that had little to do 12 with intimacy or passion. "He's a steady worker; he doesn't drink; he doesn't hit me. That's a lot more than my mother had."

Today, by contrast, the desire for a "soul mate" is nearly universal. Eighty percent of women say it's more important to have a husband they can confide in than one who earns a good living. And more than two-thirds of men say they want a more rounded relationship with their wife than their father had with their mother, one marked by passion, intellectual equality, intimacy and shared interests. 13

Recognizing the potential for disillusion in such high hopes, some people counsel couples to tamp down their expectations of personal fulfillment and happiness. 14

Certainly, anyone who expects each day with his or her spouse to be filled with passion, joy and transcendent oneness will be disappointed a lot of the time. 15

But having spent many years researching the low-expectation marriages of the past, I don't think high expectations are such a bad thing. True, they raise the risk of disappointment and disillusionment when one or both partners refuse to work on problems in the relationship. But they also motivate many people to put more energy into their relationships than couples did in centuries past. 16

When a marriage works well today, it works better than anyone in the past ever dared to dream. When it doesn't work well, people have more options to leave. And when people have doubts about their future, they have the option not to marry at all. 17

We may not always approve of the choices people make and the relations they aspire to. But in marriage, as in politics, that is the price of democracy. People have the right to change their minds. We cannot foreclose people's choices and tamp down their aspirations without losing most of the things that make modern marriage so rewarding. 18

■ ■ ■

AFTER YOU READ

■ **THINK** about the thesis of Coontz's essay and then formulate it in a sentence. In your opinion, are the higher expectations for marriage today a positive or a negative change? Do you think these expectations will create happier or unhappier marriages? Support your opinion with reasons and examples.

■ **EXAMINE** Coontz's discussion of the history of marriage in paragraphs 8–12. How were marriages made and viewed in the Middle Ages? What kind of relationship did most middle-class men and women expect—and have—in the eighteenth and nineteenth centuries? How did most Americans view marriage 100 years ago? What changes took place in marriage in the early twentieth century? Even with these changes, what surprising results showed up in polls of women in the 1960s and 1970s?

■ **WRITE** an essay about the expectations you have (or had) for marriage or a lifelong relationship (for yourself or for someone else). Begin your essay with an introduction and a clear thesis statement, and then identify and discuss from three to five of your most important expectations. You may want to include ideas from the THINK questions for your conclusion.

My Home, My World

■ ■ ■

ARCHENA BHALLA

The following student essay won first prize in the 1998–1999
student essay competition sponsored annually by Friends of
the Miami University Libraries. The daughter of Indian immigrants to the United States, Bhalla grew up in America. As a
result, she has been exposed to both the Indian custom of arranged marriages and the more informal American customs of
romance and marriage described by Stephanie Coontz in the
previous selection. In 2010 Bhalla married an American of
mixed race, part black and part white. She currently practices
law in New York City.

BEFORE YOU READ

■ **THINK** about how you would feel if your parents' culture didn't allow
you to date. How would you react to being required to follow courtship
customs different from those of your friends? Would you understand
that your parents thought they were doing what was best for you?
Why or why not?

■ **EXAMINE** the following Indian words that occur in Bhalla's essay. Each
of these words has been defined for you.

1. *betis* (paragraph 3)	Daughters
2. *rajma chaval* (paragraph 6)	An Indian dish consisting of kidney beans, spices, and rice
3. *Hindi* (paragraph 6)	India's national language
4. *Punjabi* (paragraph 6)	A North Indian language
5. *Poojas* (paragraph 6)	Religious Hindu ceremonies

■ **WRITE** a journal entry about how you would feel if you were not (or
had not been) allowed to date.

AS YOU READ

Consider the two cultures, Indian and American, in which Bhalla grew up.
Which culture do you think will ultimately influence her more? Or do you
think she can somehow balance these influences?

■ ■ ■

The anticipation of going home for the holidays was killing me.   1
I hadn't been home since that dark day my parents dropped me
off to start college: August 22, 1996. It was a day that I will never
forget. After all, it was a day that would change my life forever. A day that
would mark the beginning of me; I would learn to achieve my independence in a world that was so American. By being away from my family,
I was secretly afraid that I would lose my culture. I am sure my parents
felt the same way. I know this because my mother would always say to
me: "Remember who you are and where you come from. You are Indian
and will always be Indian." Nevertheless, my parents left me in my gloomy
room in 336 Symmes. It smelled of newness, like a new car that hadn't
been broken in yet. My parents decided to leave me early so that I could
unpack and gather my thoughts, but what they didn't realize was that they
were leaving behind a daughter not ready to begin her life. Someone who
desperately longed to stay in her parents' security blanket for the rest of
her life. Someone who needed something to hold onto. Almost three years
later, I shudder at the thought of being a lonely freshman. Not only was
I leaving behind my family, as many freshmen had to do, but I was also
leaving a vital part of my life—my Indian culture. However, I have come
to realize that searching for my identity wasn't as hard as I thought it
would be. The Indian culture was always, and will always be, engraved
on me for the rest of my life.

I grew up in two cultures: an Indian one and an American one. My   2
parents immigrated to the United States over 25 years ago from India, but
they didn't leave behind their Indian upbringing. Instead, they passed it on
to me, as well as to my other three siblings. We were always taught that
being Indian was a part of us—a way of life that would be with us for
the rest of our lives, whether we liked it or not. Growing up I remember
my mother always telling me that I had to deal with "different" parents.

"You cannot choose your parents. Whether you like it or not, we are   3
your parents." My mother would continue to tell me this over and over
again. She always had a way of shoving Indian culture down my throat.
When I was a preteen and even as a teenager, she would often tell me
just how different being Indian in America was. I couldn't participate in
slumber parties because my parents didn't see the point in spending the
night in someone's house, especially since they didn't know the parents.
I would always have to be brought home at night, before all the fun began.
To make matters worse, I would have to hear all about who slept first, on
Mondays at school. When I entered my teen years, I wasn't allowed to date
because Indians were supposed to have arranged marriages. After all, you
don't marry the person you love, but you love the person you marry. *Betis*
were taught to be obedient to their parents, when it came to issues such as
boys. Since dating was never an option when I was growing up, I found
other ways of being "American."

I would talk on the phone for hours with my girlfriends. We would 4 giggle and gossip about boys, and about our sixth-grade teacher, Miss Love. I would dress up like a punk-rocker, listen to Madonna, and eat American food. I guess my parents dealt with this time in my life, but only if my grades remained good. After all, if I did well in school, they were happy. Being well educated was always a huge part of my life. This included being at the top of my class, studying constantly, and hardly having any time at all to play. I grew up watching *Sesame Street*, not *Winnie the Pooh* or *Cinderella*. If I wanted to know about fairy tales, I was given the option of reading the storybooks, instead of watching the movies. Money, games, books, and whatever else I wanted was given to me as an incentive to do well in school. A 'B' was bad; an 'A' was excellent; and anything lower than a 'B' was deemed inappropriate. When I entered high school, studying school subjects and doing my homework was not enough. I was encouraged to study for the SATs, since this was crucial to my parents. My father's pet phrase was: "Education is the key to success. No one can ever take that away from you." I still hear him saying that to me. My parents would constantly tell me that they didn't want me to do well in school for their sake, but for my own. However, being in my twenties, I can see other motivations behind their eagerness for me doing well in school.

My parents had an arranged marriage. My mother was nineteen when 5 she married my dad, who was twenty-eight at the time. They met for five minutes before the marriage was agreed on, and ten days later they were married. Growing up I have been taught that marriage isn't two people getting married, but two families getting together. My parents have instilled this thought into me and I respect this aspect of the culture. However, I am disturbed by the credentials that come along with "arranging" an arranged marriage. Education, caste, socioeconomic status, religion, family background, and even family name are only some of the characteristics that are used to unite a couple in marriage. While the parents are arranging a marriage with the right frame of mind, it is still difficult to accept for someone who is so used to the American way of dating. Still, it is virtually impossible to have an arranged marriage being American. This is where my parents [and I] come into conflict. I am Indian *and* American, and this disturbs my parents. They want me to adhere to Indian culture and have an arranged marriage. At the same time, they fail to realize that I have been raised in a culture where love is what marriage is all about. What they fail to see is that I was raised with Indian culture, but when I step out of my house, I am inherently stepping out of the culture. This doesn't mean that my Indian values will be tarnished, but it does mean that I will want to, and maybe even need to, assimilate to the American, popular culture.

Coming to college, I have realized just how vital being an individual 6 becomes. I know that my identity is unique because of two clashing, and sometimes, opposing cultures. At the same time, I know that this will only make me stronger because I have chosen to take the best of both worlds, and to create my own individuality out of this. I am Indian *and* American. When I am in my home, I am a different person, and must assimilate myself to total Indian culture. This means I will respect my heritage and eat *rajma chaval*, speak in *Hindi* or *Punjabi*, and participate in *Poojas*. When I step out of my house, I will, at the same time, adapt to the American culture. I will listen to English music, go dancing with my friends uptown, and speak in English. Nevertheless, I will maintain my Indian heritage because it is such a large part of who I am. I have a greater respect for my elders, those who are less fortunate than I am, and for people who are disabled. I understand the value of an education, family, and friends. I combine all of these characteristics into my everyday American way of life, hence making me the person I am today.

Immigration is critical when discussing America's national identity. 7 This is the only real way we, as Americans, can learn about other cultures. After all, nearly all of Americans are immigrants to the country. Therefore, in a sense we are all different in terms of our heritage. Our national identity is indeed based on our openness to accept immigrants into the country. Without this feeling of hospitality, we would never have become the strong, independent nation that we are today. Our economy is thriving, and we are powerful in the global market. Still, to sustain this healthy economy in the 21st century, we must continue to deem immigration as a critical part of our country's issues. I have learned that being an individual, regardless of religion, nationality, and race, is essential in the United States. I know that I am individualistic because of my authenticity, but more so because of the way that I have dealt with my bi-culturalism. Our national identity will never be specifically defined because of its individual differences. Still, if we as the people of the United States strive to search for our own identities, this can, and will, benefit us as a nation now, and in the long run.

When I returned home for the holidays after completing my first year at 8 Miami, I began to see how I had changed. I longed to go back to school, to be able to do what I wanted, when I wanted to. I struggled with my parents' strict Indian culture that I always dealt with in the past. However, now I wanted my own self to be able to come through. I wanted to be able to be American *and* Indian. I was able to do this by teaching my parents what it is like to be me—how the challenges I face sometimes clash with my Indian heritage. Slowly they are beginning to understand how a child raised by two Indian people cannot be completely Indian in a nation full of Americans.

■ ■ ■

AFTER YOU READ

■ **THINK** about the arranged marriage of Bhalla's parents. Based on the comments that Bhalla makes about her parents, how would you describe their marriage? Do you think it has been successful? Do you think an arranged marriage like that of Bhalla's parents could be successful if it began here in the United States?

■ **EXAMINE** the phrase "you don't marry the person you love, but you love the person you marry" (paragraph 3). This philosophy is one of the primary beliefs on which arranged marriages are based. What do you think of this philosophy? Do you think you could come to love someone in an arranged marriage? Why or why not?

■ **EXAMINE** also paragraph 5, in which Bhalla discusses the different marriage customs in India and the United States. Focus especially on Bhalla's statement that "marriage isn't two people getting married, but two families getting together." How true is this statement for marriages in the United States? How important are families in a marriage? Can they help a marriage to succeed or fail? How? Based on this paragraph and on the information in the introduction, which do you think influenced Bhalla more in selecting a mate—Indian or American customs? In other words, what were her "expectations" for marriage?

■ **WRITE** an essay in which you compare today's U.S. custom, in which "romantic love" is the basis for marriage, with the Indian custom of arranged marriages. For instructions about writing comparison and contrast essays, see Lesson 5 on the student website for *Interactions*, eighth edition, available at www.cengagebrain.com.

Marriage and Divorce American Style

■ ■ ■

E. MAVIS HETHERINGTON

A professor of psychology at the University of Virginia, E. Mavis Hetherington has published numerous articles and has edited or coauthored more than a dozen books on family psychology. Her most recent coauthored books are *For Better or Worse: Divorce Reconsidered* (2002) and *Child Psychology: A Contemporary Viewpoint* (2005). In the following essay, based on a large, long-term study of the effects of divorce and remarriage, Hetherington identifies different types of marriages and argues that there are both bad and good divorces, just as there are both bad and good marriages.

BEFORE YOU READ

■ **THINK** about the institution of divorce in the United States. How common is it? Do you think that divorce occurs more frequently in the United States than in other societies? Does our society generally consider divorce a good or a bad situation? Have you experienced divorce directly, as either a child or an adult? What were the effects—short term and long term—on you and other family members?

■ **EXAMINE** the two major subheadings of the article. In your opinion, what are the major differences between good marriages and bad marriages? What are the major differences between good divorces and bad divorces? Specifically, how can a divorce be a good thing?

■ **EXAMINE** also the following words from the essay. Definitions have been provided for you.

1. *salutary* (paragraph 1): beneficial, constructive
2. *longevity* (paragraph 3): long life
3. *cohesive* (paragraph 4): holding or sticking together
4. *individuated* (paragraph 4): individualized
5. *endemic* (paragraph 7): common, prevalent
6. *belligerence* (paragraph 7): hostile, aggressive, or warlike attitude or actions
7. *dysfunctional* (paragraph 14): disordered or impaired in functioning
8. *contentious* (paragraph 15): quarrelsome
9. *neurotic* (paragraph 15): having a mental or emotional disorder with anxiety, phobia, or the like
10. *efficacy* (paragraph 15): ability to produce desired effect; effectiveness
11. *exacerbated* (paragraph 15): aggravated; increased severity of
12. *laudable* (paragraph 18): praiseworthy, commendable

■ **WRITE** a journal entry in which you react to the idea that there can be good divorces as well as bad divorces.

AS YOU READ

Identify specific qualities that make a good marriage by placing a check mark in the left margin and qualities that contribute to a bad marriage by putting a check mark in the right margin.

■   ■   ■

On average, recent studies show, parents and children in married families are happier, healthier, wealthier, and better adjusted than those in single-parent households. But these averages conceal wide variations. Before betting the farm on marriage with a host of new government programs aimed at promoting traditional two-parent families and discouraging divorce, policy makers should take another look at the research. It reveals that there are many kinds of marriage and not all are salutary. Nor are all divorces and single-parent experiences associated with lasting distress. It is not the inevitability of positive or negative responses to marriage or divorce that is striking, but the diversity of them.

Men do seem to benefit simply from the state of being married. Married men enjoy better health and longevity and fewer psychological and behavioral problems than single men. But women, studies repeatedly have found, are more sensitive to the emotional quality of the marriage. They benefit from being in a well-functioning marriage, but in troubled marriages they are likely to experience depression, immune-system breakdowns, and other health related problems.

We saw the same thing in the project I directed at the Hetherington Laboratory at the University of Virginia, which followed 1,400 divorced families, including 2,500 kids—some for as long as 30 years—interviewing them, testing them, and observing them at home, at school, and in the community. This was the most comprehensive study of divorce and remarriage ever undertaken; for policy makers, the complexity of the findings is perhaps its most important revelation.

GOOD MARRIAGES, BAD MARRIAGES

By statistical analysis, we identified five broad types of marriage—ranging from "pursuer-distancer" marriages (which we found were the most likely to end in divorce), to disengaged marriages, to operatic marriages, to "cohesive-individuated" marriages, and, finally, to traditional marriages (which had the least risk of instability).

To describe them briefly: 5

- Pursuer-distancer marriages are those mismatches in which one spouse, usually the wife, wants to confront and discuss problems and feelings and the other, usually the husband, wants to avoid confrontations and either denies problems or withdraws.
- Disengaged marriages are ones where couples share few interests, activities, or friends. Conflict is low, but so is affection and sexual satisfaction.
- Operatic marriages involve couples who like to function at a level of extreme emotional arousal. They are intensely attracted, attached, and volatile, given both to frequent fighting and to passionate lovemaking.
- Cohesive-individuated marriages are the yuppie and feminist ideal, characterized by equity, respect, warmth, and mutual support, but also by both partners retaining the autonomy to pursue their own goals and to have their own friends.
- Traditional marriages are those in which the husband is the main income producer and the wife's role is one of nurturance, support, and home and child care. These marriages work well as long as both partners continue to share a traditional view of gender roles.

We found that not just the risk of divorce but also the extent of   6
women's psychological and health troubles varies according to marriage
type—with wives in pursuer-distancer and disengaged marriages experiencing the most problems, those in operatic marriages significantly having
fewer, and those in cohesive-individuated and traditional marriages the
fewest. Like so many other studies, we found that men's responses are
less nuanced; the only differentiation among them was that men in
pursuer-distancer marriages have more problems than those in the other
four types.

The issue is not simply the amount of disagreement in the marriage;   7
disagreements, after all, are endemic in close personal relations. It is *how*
people disagree and solve problems—how they interact—that turns out to
be closely associated with both the duration of their marriages and the
well-being of wives and, to a lesser extent, husbands. Contempt, hostile
criticism, belligerence, denial, and withdrawal erode a marriage. Affection,
respect, trust, support, and making the partner feel valued and worthwhile
strengthen the relationship.

GOOD DIVORCES, BAD DIVORCES

Divorce experiences also are varied. Initially, especially in marriages involv-   8
ing children, divorce is miserable for most couples. In the early years, ex-
spouses typically must cope with lingering attachments; with resentment
and anger, self-doubts, guilt, depression, and loneliness; with the stress of
separation from children or of raising them alone; and with the loss of social
networks and, for women, of economic security. Nonetheless, we found that

a gradual recovery usually begins by the end of the second year. And by six years after divorce, 80 percent of both men and women have moved on to build reasonably or exceptionally fulfilling lives.

Indeed, about 20 percent of the women we observed eventually 9 emerged from divorce enhanced and exhibiting competencies they never would have developed in an unhappy or constraining marriage. They had gone back to school or work to ensure the economic stability of their families, they had built new social networks, and they had become involved and effective parents and socially responsible citizens. Often they had happy second marriages. Divorce had offered them an opportunity to build new and more satisfying relationships and the freedom they needed for personal growth. This was especially true for women moving from a pursuer-distancer or disengaged marriage, or from one in which a contemptuous or belligerent husband undermined their self-esteem and child-rearing practices. Divorced men, we found, are less likely to undergo such remarkable personal growth; still, the vast majority of the men in our study did construct reasonably happy new lives for themselves.

As those pressing for government programs to promote marriage will 10 no doubt note, we found that the single most important predictor of a divorced parent's subsequent adjustment is whether he or she has formed a new and mutually supportive intimate relationship. But what should also be noticed is that successful repartnering takes many forms. We found that about 75 percent of men and 60 percent of women eventually remarry, but an increasing number of adults are opting to cohabit instead— or to remain single and meet their need for intimacy with a dating arrangement, a friendship, or a network of friends or family.

There is general agreement among researchers that parents' repartner- 11 ing does not do as much for their children. Both young children and adolescents in divorced and remarried families have been found to have, on average, more social, emotional, academic, and behavioral problems than kids in two-parent, non-divorced families. My own research, and that of many other investigators, finds twice as many serious psychological disorders and behavioral problems—such as teenage pregnancy, dropping out of school, substance abuse, unemployment, and marital breakups—among the offspring of divorced parents as among the children of nondivorced families. This is a closer association than between smoking and cancer.

However, the troubled youngsters remain a relatively small proportion 12 of the total. In our study, we found that after a period of initial disruption 75 percent to 80 percent of children and adolescents from divorced families are able to cope with the divorce and their new life situation and develop into reasonably or exceptionally well-adjusted individuals. In fact, as we saw with women, some girls eventually emerge from their parents' divorces remarkably competent and responsible. They also learn from the divorce experience how to handle later stresses in their lives.

Without ignoring the serious pain and distress experienced by many 13 divorced parents and children, it is important to underscore that substantial research findings confirm the ability of the vast majority to move on successfully.

It is also important to recognize that many of the adjustment problems 14 in parents and children and much of the inept parenting and destructive family relations that policy makers attribute to divorce actually are present *before* divorce. Being in a dysfunctional family has taken its toll before the breakup occurs.

Predicting the aftermath of divorce is complex, and the truth is ob- 15 scured if one looks only at averages. Differences in experience or personality account for more variation than the averages would suggest. A number of studies have found, for instance, that adults and children who perceived their predivorce life as happy and satisfying tend to be more upset by a marital breakup than those who viewed the marriage as contentious, threatening, or unfulfilling. Other studies show that adults and children who are mature, stable, self-regulated, and adaptable are more likely able to cope with the challenges of divorce. Those who are neurotic, antisocial, and impulsive—and who lack a sense of their own efficacy—are likely to have these characteristics exacerbated by the breakup. In other words, the psychologically poor get poorer after a divorce while the rich often get richer.

The diversity of American marriages makes it unlikely that any one- 16 size-fits-all policy to promote marriage and prevent divorce will be beneficial. Policy makers are now talking about offering people very brief, untested education and counseling programs, but such approaches rarely have long-lasting effects. And they are generally least successful with the very groups that policy makers are most eager to marry off—single mothers and the poor.

In their recent definitive review of the research on family interventions, 17 Phil Cowan, Douglas Powell, and Carolyn Pape Cowan find that the most effective approaches are the most comprehensive ones—those that deal with both parents and children, with family dynamics, and with a family's needs for jobs, education, day care, and health care. Beyond that, which interventions work best seems to vary, depending on people's stage of life, their ethnic group or the kind of family they are in, and the specific challenges before them.

Strengthening and promoting positive family relationships and improv- 18 ing the many settings in which children develop is a laudable goal. However, policies that constrain or encourage people to remain in destructive marriages—or that push uncommitted couples to marry—are likely to do more harm than good. The same is true of marriage incentives and rewards designed to create traditional families with the husband as the economic provider and the wife as homemaker. If our social policies do not recognize the diversity and varied needs of American families, we easily could end up undermining them.

■   ■   ■

AFTER YOU READ

■ **THINK** about the personal qualities found in a good marriage that were listed in paragraph 7. What are these qualities, and how do they strengthen a relationship? Think also about the qualities listed by the author as causes of a bad marriage. Give an example of a marriage in which one or both spouses exhibit positive qualities. Then give another example in which one or both spouses show negative behaviors.

■ **EXAMINE** paragraph 5, in which Hetherington classifies different types of marriages. Can you identify one or more of these types among the married couples that you know? Into which category, or categories, would you place most marriages you have observed? Can you think of some marriages that do not fit easily into any of these categories? Explain.

■ **WRITE** an essay in which you classify marriages, husbands, or wives. If you select marriage as your topic, you may use or adapt the categories in paragraph 5 of this article, or you may create your own classifications. (You don't have to use the same number of categories that Hetherington uses.) Be sure to provide at least one good example of each category you discuss. For instruction on writing classification essays, see Lesson 3 on the *Interactions*, eighth edition, student website, at www.cengagebrain.com.

■ Or **WRITE** an essay on the subject of remarriage. You might focus on the reasons that so many people remarry after a divorce, on some potential problems with remarriage, or on what couples can do to increase the likelihood of success for a second, third, or even fourth marriage.

Gay Marriage Looms as "Battle of Our Times"

■ ■ ■

JANE LAMPMAN

The author of this article, Jane Lampman, is a staff writer for the *Christian Science Monitor*, a journal that reports on and explores religious issues. In this article Lampman addresses the controversial issue of gay marriage, focusing on the possibility of a compromise between those who claim that gay marriage is an equal rights issue and those who argue that the increasing acceptance and promotion of gay marriage endangers their freedom to practice their religion according to their beliefs. This selection appeared in 2006 in the *Christian Science Monitor*.

BEFORE YOU READ

■ **THINK** about your own position on the issue of gay marriage. Is your position primarily influenced by religious beliefs, family tradition, ideas about individual liberty, or personal experience?

■ **EXAMINE** the first paragraph of this article, in which the author states that the issue of gay marriage is "becoming a conflict of equality vs. religious liberty." Have you thought of this issue in these terms before? Do you think this is a productive way to address this controversial issue? Why or why not?

■ **EXAMINE** also the following phrases, italicized words, and definitions:

1. "religious *waiver*" (paragraph 2): a document putting aside a requirement or a right
2. "*ameliorate* such conflict" (paragraph 4): to improve, make better (i.e., reduce conflict)
3. "*sanctify* marriages" (paragraph 9): to make sacred or holy
4. "*litigation* battles" (paragraph 12): legal processes or actions
5. "*advocates* on both sides" (paragraph 13): (noun) supporter or defender of a cause

■ **WRITE** a journal entry in which you agree or disagree with the idea that viewing the issue of gay marriage as a conflict between equality and religious liberty is productive.

AS YOU READ

Underline the different sources that Lampman cites in her article. Note in the margins whether each of these sources supports the idea that gay marriage is a matter of equality or views it as an issue of religious liberty.

■ ■ ■

The battle over same-sex marriage is shaping into something more than deep societal tradition vs. civil rights. It is becoming a conflict of equality vs. religious liberty.

As gays make gains, some religious institutions are coming under pressure. For instance:

- A Christian high school in Wildomar, Calif., is being sued for expelling two students on suspicion of being lesbian. The parents' suit claims that the school is a business under state civil rights law, which prohibits discrimination based on sexual orientation.

- Catholic Charities in Boston, where same-sex marriage is legal, recently shuttered its adoption agency rather than serve gay and lesbian couples in conflict with church teaching. The church's request for a religious waiver from state antidiscrimination rules has made no headway.

- Christian clubs at several universities are fighting to maintain school recognition while restricting their leadership to those who conform to their beliefs on homosexuality.

Meanwhile, the Christian Legal Society and similar groups are mounting a national effort to challenge antidiscrimination policies in court, claiming they end up discriminating against conservative Christians.

"The fight over same-sex marriage—and two very different conceptions of the ordering of society—will be a knock-down, drag-out battle," predicts Marc Stern, a religious liberty attorney at the American Jewish Congress. Both sides are pursuing their agendas in state legislatures, courts, and public schools. Both sides tend to view the struggle as a zero-sum, society-defining conflict. For supporters of gay marriage, it represents the last stage in America's long road to equality, from racial to gender to sexual equality. For opponents, traditional marriage stands as the God-ordained bedrock of society, essential to the well-being of children and the healthy functioning of the community. While no one expects the courts to force unwilling clergy to perform weddings for same-sex couples, some see a possibility that religious groups (other than houses of worship) could lose their tax-exempt status for not conforming to public policy, as did fundamentalist Bob Jones University, over racial issues in 1983.

Legal experts of various views met last December, hosted by the Becket Fund, a nonpartisan institute promoting religious free expression, to consider the implications of same-sex marriage for religious liberty. Writing about the conference in *The Weekly Standard*, Maggie Gallagher quoted participants as seeing the coming litigation as "a train wreck," "a collision course," and "the battle of our times." To ameliorate such conflict, some insist that, given the nation's commitment to both equal rights and religious liberty, accommodations must be found.

"This set of issues tests us in new ways, and I don't think either side is going to win the day," says Charles Haynes, of the First Amendment Center in Washington, in an interview. "For the foreseeable future, we are going to be living with two important claims, and we have to find ways to protect the rights of people on all sides."

Douglas Laycock, of the University of Texas Law School, suggests a   6
modification to the current joint administration of marriage by the state and religious groups: "We can never resolve the debate over same-sex marriage until we separate legal marriage from religious marriage," he says in a conference paper. "The state should administer legal marriage, and its rules … should be made through the political process. Religious organizations should administer religious marriages," making their own rules. The legal relationship "could be called 'civil union' for gays and straights alike."

Ms. Gallagher, head of the Institute for Marriage and Public Policy,   7
worries about any delegalizing of marriage. "That would be a good solution if there weren't a great public purpose to marriage that needs legal support to sustain.… If you chop it into pieces, that's a powerful statement by the law that there's no important purpose to marriage as a public institution."

…

Religious leaders on both sides of the Marriage Protection Amendment   8
have formed coalitions, demonstrating that religious perceptions vary considerably. Some 50 leaders from Roman Catholic, Mormon, Southern Baptist, Orthodox, Evangelical, and Orthodox Jewish traditions formed the Religious Coalition for Marriage, focused on strengthening its traditional role in society. They see the amendment as essential to protect "marriage from … activist courts determined to reinterpret this fundamental institution … against the will of the American people," says Richard Land, a leader of the Southern Baptist Convention. (A recent Gallup poll found 58 percent of Americans opposing same-sex marriage and 39 percent favoring it. The country is split on a constitutional amendment: 50 percent in favor, 47 percent opposed.)

On the other side, Clergy for Fairness—including leaders from main-   9
line Protestant and Reform Jewish denominations—says that people of faith disagree on same-sex marriage and that religious denominations, not the federal government, should decide whether they'll sanctify marriages. The group also says it opposes the amendment because it would mark the first time the Constitution would be used "to restrict the rights of an entire group of Americans."

Chai Feldblum, a Georgetown University law professor active on gay   10
rights issues, argues that the government should view both heterosexuality and homosexuality as morally neutral—"though how you 'deploy' your sexual activity can be very morally laden," she says. "It's an incredible stain on the government that it is denying governmental structures for loving relationships and families," she adds. Yet she acknowledges the genuine difficulty that same-sex marriage presents for some religious people. "I'd like gay people to understand that when religious people have to do something against their belief," Professor Feldblum says, "that impinges on their deep sense of self, just as I would like religious people to

understand that when gay people are told they ... can't marry their loved one, that impinges on that person's deep sense of self." She's wary of granting religious waivers on these issues, however.

In Gallagher's view, "We are in a situation where courts are declaring 11 our great historic, cross-cultural understanding of marriage to be a form of bigotry. That's a very destructive message," when research shows that children do much better in households with a mother and a father.

Others worry about the harm litigation battles could do. "People on 12 both sides see this as good vs. evil," says the First Amendment Center's Dr. Haynes, "and those positions are going to tear us apart, deeply hurt the nation and our commitment to civil rights and religious freedom." Haynes has just worked with groups on both sides to develop sexual-orientation guidelines for public schools. "I've been involved in brokering nine different guidelines on issues like the Bible and religious holidays, and this has been the hardest," Haynes says. After eight months, Christian educators and a gay group involved in school issues did agree on a process for local districts to use that each side thought was fair. Whether local districts pick up on the guidelines remains to be seen. Clamor over textbooks, for example, has erupted in Massachusetts and in Canada, where kindergartners are being introduced to stories about families with same-sex parents. Although schools must reflect the legal status of such relationships in the curriculum, some parents are demanding notice and protections. "Some will ask why those parents should be given consideration," Haynes says. "The answer is that this is America, and we try to do the best we can to protect the religious liberty of even the smallest minority.... This takes more work than simply saying 'winner takes all.'"

Yet who is going to broker common ground is the question as advo- 13 cates on both sides seek complete victory. Legal experts expect a patchwork of legislation and court decisions to emerge. "Then we will have to worry about how to deal with the fact we have different rules in different states," Mr. Stern says. "If two or three big states move to same-sex marriage, however, it's not going to work to have different definitions across the U.S."

■ ■ ■

AFTER YOU READ

■ THINK about the opinion of the author of this article. Is Lampman taking a position on whether gay marriage *should* be an issue of equality or of religious liberty? Or is she simply arguing that this is the direction in which this conflict is headed? Does she present the two sides of this issue fairly? Support your opinion.

■ EXAMINE the sources you have underlined and note which side each represents. Is there an equal number of sources from each side—those who see the conflict as a matter of equality versus those who view it as a matter of religious liberty? Can you detect any bias in the author's use of sources or in the way she presents each side of this issue?

■ **WRITE** a persuasive essay in which you argue one side of this issue— either that gay marriage is a matter of equality (i.e., homosexuals are equal to heterosexuals and thus should be allowed to marry) or of religious freedom (i.e., churches and religious institutions should have the freedom to determine their position on this issue and to limit those who are allowed to marry). Guidelines for writing persuasive essays are provided on pages 372–378 at the end of Unit Six.

■ Or **WRITE** a response to Lampman's article, focusing on whether you think she is balanced and fair in presenting the two sides of this issue. (See "Responding to a Text" on pages 244–247 at the end of Unit Five for help with this assignment.)

Why Isn't a Nice Person
Like You Married?

■ ■ ■

ELSIE BLISS

This essay, which was first published in a magazine entitled *Single Parent*, expresses a viewpoint that is often ignored—the idea that some people prefer a single life to marriage or any other relationship. The author, Elsie Bliss, is a Washington writer-editor who has often written and spoken on topics related to successful living for singles.

BEFORE YOU READ

■ **THINK** about the reasons someone might prefer to remain single in our society rather than marrying. Have you considered this choice? Why or why not? What are the advantages of being single? What are the disadvantages?

■ **EXAMINE** the title of the essay. Why is it a "loaded" question? How would you respond if someone asked you this question?

■ **EXAMINE** also the French phrase "C'est moi!" (paragraph 8) This phrase means, "It's me!" You may also need to know that *inordinately* (paragraph 3) means without restraint or moderation; *besieged* (paragraph 6) means aggressively surrounded, hemmed in, or harassed; *angst* (paragraph 9) means a serious feeling of apprehension or anxiety; and a *deterrent* (paragraph 13) is something that prevents an action.

■ **WRITE** in your journal a list of reasons why being single might be better than being married or in a long-term relationship. Then make another list of reasons why being married or in a long-term relationship could be better than being single. Which list is longer?

AS YOU READ

Underline the reasons the author gives for preferring to remain single.

■ ■ ■

I am asked THE QUESTION by friends at every wedding reception. Also at every party and family gathering by well-meaning relatives and sometimes strangers. If it were not for this question and my creative response, some of the people I meet wouldn't find anything to say to me. But the time it hurts most is that moment when an eligible man I've just met wonders aloud, "Gee, it's a wonder you aren't married."

Am I supposed to admit that I am very insecure yet demanding? That   2
no one I have ever met who was available was sufficiently desirable to justify giving up my precious independence? That no matter how I searched (while appearing not to be searching) there has not been anyone who met my rather rigid list of criteria? Am I expected to actually unload this emotional baggage on some poor schnook who might himself prove to be truly desirable? Or course not. Because then I would frighten him off.

Speaking for many nice, attractive, loving, and desirable single people,   3
I'd like to climb up on my soapbox and explain a few things. What I say may not hold true for all single people, but for some who have stayed single for an inordinately long time....

Being single is quite respectable. It is a valid way of life. It is not a   4
tragedy or a handicap. It is being the boss; the captain of your ship. I quite like it, even though I readily admit that I frequently miss what married people have when their marriage is going well; just as they miss the freedom I have to decide my own goals and priorities.

I am sorry to say that statistics are against their marriages going well, unfor-   5
tunately. Marriage in the 20th century is in trouble. Single is not in trouble, despite its bad press and your Aunt Sophie's opinion. Single has a lot going for it.

If you took a poll of your friends and their feelings about marriage, and   6
if they responded candidly, you'd find that (as some brilliant mind once noted) marriage is like a besieged fortress; those who are inside want to get out and those who are outside want to get in. Perhaps the question should be put to married people, "Why is a nice person like you married?"

Some day I may find a partner who will allow me to be me and who   7
will even respect and admire my need to be myself. He won't criticize my liking health foods or tell me I'm uptight because I won't go to a nude beach. He'll think I am fine, quirks and all even though I love sitcoms and hate game shows and violent movies. If I am lucky, he will have the same desire to be himself and I'll respect and love him for it. Our two selves may join and become a couple of happy individuals. Note, I did not say we would become ONE, but a couple of individuals. Where did the myth originate that you become part of another? Better half, indeed.

Until that happens, no matter how long it takes (maybe never), I will   8
not be categorized as a liberated woman or a Jewish Mother or anything else. I am all of these and none of them. I am the product of years of development and growth, including experiences of joy and sorrow. I am like fine chocolate—bitter-sweet. I was liberated long before it was fashionable and I was a Jewish Mother type as a ten-year-old child. You don't have to be Jewish or a mother or even a female to be a J.M. If the definition is a protective, assertive, overly sensitive, deeply involved, demonstrative person, then hallelujah! C'est moi!

Probably what causes the greatest angst among single people is some-   9
one looking at us with a mixture of wonder and pity and saying, "You are so attractive, it's a shame you aren't married."

Would I gaze at anyone and say, "You are such an attractive person; 10
it's a shame you are overweight"? Or, "How come a couple like you who
argue so much are not divorced?" Or, "You seem so nice; why can't you
find a good job?"

Of course no civilized person would ask these things. But there are 11
those who consider being single a national dilemma and one that permits
constant probing into the single person's psyche to learn the causes.

As with most things, being single is a trade-off. It is a mixed blessing of 12
being private with time of your own to use as you see fit plus the occasional twinge of being left out as you observe hand-holding couples strol-
ling down life's road together. To some single people, the fear of failure is
a great deterrent to marriage, especially if they have feelings of insecurity
born of being the children of perfectionist parents. This can color all
decision-making for them.

If you are single, and none of the above applies to you, then you will 13
have no trouble replying easily when you hear that ageless question, "Why
isn't a nice person like you married?" You'll smile sweetly at Aunt Minnie
and say, "Gee, I've been too busy to notice it, but gosh, you're right, I'm
not married; I didn't realize. I'll give it some thought and get back to you."

That ought to hold her, but only until the next time you meet. 14

■ ■ ■

AFTER YOU READ

■ **THINK** about the advantages of being single that the author gives.
Which of Bliss's reasons are the most convincing? Why are these particular reasons convincing? Do you think Bliss would like to get married if
she met a person who met her criteria? Support your opinion with specific statements from the essay.

■ **EXAMINE** the author's argument that an ideal marriage is a union of
two individuals who remain individuals (paragraph 7). How realistic is
this expectation? If you can, give an example of a couple in a marriage
or long-term relationship who have retained their separate identities and
individualities. How successful is their relationship?

■ **WRITE** an essay comparing life as a single person with life in a marriage
or long-term relationship. Before you begin your essay, examine the lists
you made before you read Bliss's essay and revise them to reflect any
changes in your thinking that occurred as a result of your reading and
discussion of this topic. In your introduction or conclusion (or both),
state clearly which kind of life you prefer. Develop the major reasons
for your preference in the body of your essay. Lesson 7 on the *Interactions*, eighth edition, student website (www.cengagebrain.com) provides
instruction for writing comparison and contrast essays.

UNIT THREE
■ ■ ■

Critical Thinking, Reading, and Writing

■ **WRITING A SUMMARY**

The ability to summarize is one of the most useful skills a student can have. It is an essential skill for both reading and writing. Instructors may require a summary as an independent assignment or may ask for a summary in the context of a larger assignment. For example, any time you are asked to review a book or movie, you must summarize. Likewise, summaries are required for essay exams, research assignments, response essays, and reports. The ability to summarize succinctly and clearly is of great value whatever your major or career goal.

Students often confuse summaries and paraphrases. In both, you use your own language, but summaries condense the original material while paraphrases do not. Thus, a summary is much shorter than the material being summarized. In fact, you can even summarize an entire book in one or two sentences. A paraphrase, in contrast, is essentially the same length as the original material because, when you paraphrase, you simply put the source material in your own words, keeping all of the information and ideas that are in the original. For example, see the following paraphrase of paragraph 10 of Goodman and O'Brien's essay "The Difference between Male and Female Friendships":

> A common image of female friends is two women at a table
> drinking coffee together and discussing how they feel. In a
> typical friendship situation, men friends discuss football
> while they watch TV.

Compare this paragraph to the original paragraph on page 146. Note that wording and word order are changed, but that the length of the two paragraphs is similar. Thus, a paraphrase is more appropriate for very brief passages—a few sentences at most.

Do not underestimate the difficulty of summarizing. It requires first of all basic comprehension of the selection to be summarized. Second, you must be able to discriminate between main ideas and supporting material such as details and examples. Finally, you must know how to convert these main ideas into your own words and yet reflect accurately the source you are summarizing.

BEFORE YOU WRITE

Sometimes you will be summarizing a long text, such as a book; at other times you may need to summarize only a paragraph or two. Whatever you are summarizing, the following guidelines will help you begin:

- Read and annotate the text you are summarizing.
- Identify the author's thesis and main supporting points.
- Review your annotations and reread sections of the text as needed.

Note: Those by Carter, Kamin, Winik, Coontz, and Hetherington are most easily summarized. If the piece you are summarizing is primarily narration, you may want to identify major events in chronological order rather than try to identify a thesis and major supporting points.

Example

Summary of "The Difference Between Male and Female Friendships"

In their essay entitled "The Difference between Male and Female Friendships," Ellen Goodman and Patricia O'Brien point out that males and females view friendship in very different ways. According to the authors, female friendships tend to be based on communication, especially communication about feelings. In contrast, male friendships usually focus on "shared activities." If men communicate at all, they usually talk about what they are doing rather than what they are feeling. In other words, men value relationships based on common interests while women usually select friends on the basis of common values. The authors conclude that male and female friendships have probably remained fairly constant throughout history but that recently society has become more critical of the type of friendship typical of that between males. Whereas in the past male friendships were considered superior, today female friendships are idealized because they are more intimate.

AS YOU WRITE

Once you are confident you understand the material to be summarized, you are ready to begin writing. The following guidelines will help as you write:

- As a general rule, you should begin any summary by identifying the title and author.

  Example: In her article "Understanding Family Relationships," June Taylor, a professor of social sciences at Columbia University, explores sibling rivalry.

- Always use your own words. (It's better not to look at the text as you write so that you will not be tempted to borrow the language of the original. But if you do quote a phrase, be sure to enclose it in quotation marks.)
- Focus on main ideas. (Omit details, descriptions, examples, etc.)
- Keep it brief because the whole point of a summary is to reduce the size of the original text while conveying its main ideas.

Assignment

Following the guidelines given above, read (or reread) one of the essays in Unit Three. (*Note*: Those by Carter, Kamin, and Winik are most easily summarized.) Then write a brief summary of the essay you have read.

AFTER YOU WRITE

You will need to revise your summary as you would any written assignment. Remember, your summary must be clear to someone who has not read the original material. Thus, you should reread your summary carefully to be sure someone who is unfamiliar with the original text will understand not only your summary but also the original source. In addition, you should do the following:

- Eliminate all unnecessary material; your summary should be much briefer than the text you are summarizing.

- Be sure your summary reflects the substance of the source but does not rely on the words of the source. (You may quote brief phrases or passages but you must enclose them within quotation marks.)

■ EXPLORING IDEAS TOGETHER

1. Meet with a group of your classmates to discuss and define the term *friendship*. Then compare your group's definition with those by other groups. Which elements in the definitions are similar? Which are different?

2. In small groups, discuss how dating and marriage have changed not only in the past 100 years but also just since your parents were dating. To aid your discussion, review the readings by Coontz and Bhalla, but include your own observations also. (You may even want to interview your parents, or someone of their generation.)

3. Some of the essays in this unit emphasize the importance of communication in a good relationship. Identify and discuss one or more of the essays that illustrate how effective communication can strengthen a relationship and one or more that illustrate how a breakdown in communication can result in a damaged relationship.

4. Organize a discussion or debate about which is preferable—married life or single life.

■ EXPLORING THE INTERNET

You can find links to most of the sites in the following exercises on the *Interactions*, eighth edition, student website, available at www.cengage brain.com:

1. Explore "The Friendship Page" found as a link in the Related Websites section of the *Interactions*, student site. On it you will find quotations, poetry, movies, and other information on friendship.

2. Some knowledge of the Israeli-Palestinian conflict is helpful in understanding Kamin's "A Boyhood Friendship in a Divided Valley." For information about this conflict, Google Wikipedia and search for "The Arab-Israeli Conflict," where you will find a summary of this ongoing conflict.

3. Two websites on marriage are "Smart Marriages" and "About Marriage," both available as links on the *Interactions* student website. Explore these sites, select an interesting article, and share a summary with your classmates.

4. To research the causes and effects of divorce, you may want to explore the general site for *Divorce* magazine as well as the more specific sites "What Are Common Causes of Divorce?" and "Children and Divorce: The Effects of Divorce on Children." All are links on the Related Websites page of the *Interactions*, student website.

5. The essay by Jane Lampman argues that "Gay Marriage Looms as 'Battle of Our Times.'" To learn more about this issue, use a search engine such as Google to access websites that argue for and against gay marriage. Then work in small groups to evaluate the arguments on these sites.

6. Two online sites for singles are *Singles* magazine and the *Online Dating Magazine*, both available as links on the *Interactions*, student website.

■ WRITING ESSAYS

1. Write an essay defining the word *friend* or *friendship*. You may want to refer to one or more of the first seven essays in this unit as you draft your essay. (See Lesson 8 on the *Interactions*, eighth edition, student website for help with writing a definition essay.)

2. Write an essay arguing that good friendships are based primarily on either similarities or differences. Consider gender, ages, careers, interests, backgrounds, ethnicity, and so on, but limit your points of comparison to two, three, or four points. You may want to review the essays by Crichton, Carter, Kamin, and Owen before planning your essay. (See pages 372–378 for guidelines for writing persuasive essays.)

3. Interview someone who is considerably older than you about the process of mate selection that existed when that person was young. Write an essay for an older or younger audience comparing and contrasting the process as you know it with that described by the older person. (See Lesson 7 on the *Interactions* student website for help with writing comparison and contrast essays.)

4. The essay by Bhalla describes a type of courtship and marriage very different from modern American marriage as described by Coontz and from those with which you are probably familiar. Write an essay in which you compare these two types of courtship and marriage, identifying the strengths and weaknesses of each. (For help with writing comparison and comparison contrast essays, see Lesson 7 on the Interactions, eighth edition, student website.)

5. Write an essay in which you describe the ideal partner or mate. (You may draw some ideas from the essays by Hetherington or Bliss.)

WORK

Daniel Laflor/iStockphoto.com

Is the image above a "real photograph" or a "set shot" meant to illustrate an ideal view of work? How can you tell? How many different types of work are represented in this photograph? How much diversity in gender, race, and ethnicity do you see? In spite of the staging of this photograph, what does it show you about work and careers?

■ ■ ■

P eople are often defined by the work they do. Individuals are identified as teachers or lawyers or accountants in the same way they are identified by their names. In fact, once we have asked a person's name, we next want to know what he or she does. Even before children become adolescents, they are asked what they want to do or be when they grow up. In our society it is assumed that everyone, or almost everyone,

191

will work. However, the nature of work has changed. Our ancestors often worked long hours at tasks that required great physical strength and endurance. Both men and women (and often children as well) accepted physical labor as a fact of life. Although many people in our society still work in jobs that are physically demanding, much heavy labor has been taken over by machines. While many people still work long hours and are on their feet all day, others spend more time operating a machine, thinking, or talking. But whether we use our minds, our hands, or both, we still call what we do work.

Not only is work less physically demanding than it once was, but it is also less defined in terms of gender differences. Fifty years ago some types of work were typically performed by males while other types were per- formed by females. Nurses and secretaries were nearly always females, while doctors, construction workers, and mail carriers were almost inevi- tably males. Today most of those distinctions have been erased. In fact, it is difficult to think of any job that is associated exclusively with either males or females. Women pilot airplanes while men serve snacks to the passen- gers; men take care of small children while women serve as presidents of universities. Both men and women are lawyers, doctors, senators, astro- nauts, and truck drivers. Women have already served as secretary of state and speaker of the House of Representatives, and in the near future a woman may well become president of the United States.

Even though the kind of work we do has changed, working has not become less important. Work is still how we define ourselves and how we spend most of our time. When technology began to make work less physi- cally demanding and production faster, many people predicted that Amer- icans would work fewer hours—but this has not happened. Most people still work eight hours a day, and many people work far more, bringing work home or holding two jobs instead of one. Couples often come home from their jobs to face child-rearing and housekeeping responsibilities. In- stead of becoming a society in which people work less, we have become a society in which people work more.

We continue to redefine what it means to work: more people work at home as well as at offices and factories, technology plays an increasingly important role in work, and people share jobs. But the importance of work will not change. Children will continue to pretend they are working, young people will continue to worry about what career to pursue, and adults will continue to focus on their jobs as a major feature of their lives. Perhaps most important, people will continue to define themselves in terms of their work.

The reading selections in this unit describe the connections among work, the mind, and identity; reversed gender roles in work; the satisfaction as well as the agony of hard physical labor; problems of unemployment and temporary work in a weak economy; the process of getting a job; and the past and future of work.

Work, Mind, and Identity

■ ■ ■

MIKE ROSE

One of the most respected experts on language and literacy in the country, Mike Rose was the child of an immigrant family who was tracked into vocational studies until a special teacher took an interest in him and encouraged him to go to college. In his autobiographical classic *Lives on the Boundary* (1989), Rose describes his youth and his work as director of the tutoring center at the University of California, Los Angeles. He earned his PhD in education from UCLA in 1994 and is currently a professor at UCLA's Graduate School of Education and Information Studies. The winner of several prestigious awards, Rose has also authored numerous other books, including *Possible Lives: The Promise of Public Education in America* (1995) and *Why School? Reclaiming Education for All of Us* (2009). In the following selection from *The Mind at Work: Valuing the Intelligence of the American Worker* (2004), Rose argues that it takes thought and intelligence to do physical work.

BEFORE YOU READ

■ **THINK** about the title of this selection. How are work, mind, and identity connected? Give specific examples.

■ **EXAMINE** the last sentence of Rose's first paragraph. How does this sentence relate to the title of the selection? How do we decide "who's smart and who isn't"? How does "the work someone does...feed into that judgment"? And what is "the effect such judgment has on our sense of who we are and what we can do"?

■ **EXAMINE** the following italicized words, their context, and their definitions:

1. "*erratic* scheduling" (paragraph 4): irregular
2. "cultural *iconography*" (paragraph 6): system of pictures or representations
3. "*cacophony* of customer's voices" (paragraph 8): jarring, harsh, discordant sound
4. "word was *coveted*" (paragraph 11): desired
5. "I craved *competence*" (paragraph 12): capability, ability to do well

■ **WRITE** a journal entry in which you describe the thought processes that you believe go into some kind of physical or "blue-collar" work such as welding, carpentry, plumbing, waitressing, hairdressing, and so forth.

AS YOU READ

Underline effective descriptive passages and bracket passages in the selection in which Rose refers to the intelligence required to do physical work.

■ ■ ■

I grew up a witness to the intelligence of the waitress in motion, the reflective welder, the strategy of the guy on the assembly line. This, then, is something I know: the thought it takes to do physical work. Such work put fod on our table, gave shape to stories of affliction and ability, framed how I saw the world. I come from a family of immigrants who, with two exceptions, did not finish high school, and who worked in blue-collar or service jobs all their lives. I did not do so well in school myself, spent several years in the vocational track, and squeaked my way into a small college on probation—the first in the family to go beyond high school. Measures of intellectual ability and assumptions about it are woven throughout this history. So I've been thinking about this business of intelligence for a long time: the way we decide who's smart and who isn't, the way the work someone does feeds into that judgment, and the effect such judgment has on our sense of who we are and what we can do. 1

It was tough work that my family did. I would later come to understand the dynamics of occupational status and social class, but I could sense early on how difficult the work was, and that without it, we'd starve. I also saw that people knew things through work. And they used what they learned. This experience was all very specific to me, not abstract, emerging from the lived moments of work I had witnessed, from all sorts of objects and images, from sound and smell, from rhythms of the body. These sensory particulars stay with me, resonant. 2

There was a table covered with slick plastic in the center of my grandmother's kitchen. Anyone who visited drank a cup of coffee there, wooden chair turned sideways to talk to her as she cooked. All meals were eaten at this table. My uncle Frank, a welder for the Pennsylvania Railroad, has come in from work, soiled denim, the smell of machinist's oil in it, his face smeared with soot. He washes at the kitchen sink, sleeves rolled up, scrubbing his arms, full lather, angling them under the faucet. He settles in at the table; there's a radio at its edge, and he turns it on to hear the evening news. My grandmother sets a large plate of steaming macaroni before him, deep red sauce; there is a bowl of chops, cooked earlier, in the center of the table. Frank's hands are huge, and as he talks to us—a deep voice that can quickly rise in amazement—he tears off a big chunk of Italian bread and begins to eat with a focus and capacity that made its way into the comic tales told about him by his brothers, stories I would acquire through the hearing. After a while, he pushes the chair back, but not too far, unbuttons the top of his trousers, says he's eaten way too much, dear Lord, and reaches for a chop, or for that loaf of bread, and leans in again, a deep pleasure against the bitter cold and exhaustion of the roundhouse. 3

Frank was a guy who made it a point to know things; he read a lot 4
and inquired until he understood how something worked. It felt good to
be with him. I remember him, his well-spoken voice, guiding me through
the Railroader's Museum: cutaways of running gear; diagrams and technical information on steam, diesel, and electric locomotives; photos of
wooden freight cars, cabooses, the interiors of luxury passenger cars; posed
workmen; lots of repair equipment; an operational model railroad. I knew
of Frank's many complaints about the railroad: layoffs and erratic scheduling, the brutal hours, the biting cold or sweltering heat, the burns over his
arms and legs. But Frank also saw himself as a "railroad man," someone
who had made his contribution to this major American industry. Doing a
job well mattered. "Work hard," he wrote to his son, away in the army.
"No one likes a half-assed man." One of the moments I remember from
that day at the museum, a simple but lasting one, is Frank standing before
a display case, pointing to some miniature assembly of cable and gear, explaining in detail how it worked, taking his time until I got it.

Many testaments have been written, both in fiction and memoir, about 5
the physical labor of our forebears: from accounts of the prairie farm, the
mills, and the mines to tales of immigrant life—the Lower East Side to the
agricultural fields of Central and Southern California. One of the most stirring moments in Mario Cuomo's keynote address to the 1984 Democratic
National Convention is the memory of his father working long and hard
hours in the family grocery store, teaching the young Mario "all I needed
to know about faith and hard work by the simple eloquence of his
example." Such invocation speaks powerfully to Americans, stirs things
deep in our cultural and personal histories. How interesting it is, though,
that our testaments to physical work are so often focused on the values
such work exhibits rather than on the thought it requires. It is a subtle
but pervasive omission. Yet there is a mind at work in dignity, and values
are intimately related to thought and action.

It is as though in our cultural iconography we are given the muscled 6
arm, sleeve rolled tight against biceps, but no thought bright behind the
eye, no image that links hand and brain. I find myself here wondering
about Cuomo's father. I imagine the many decisions he had to make, the
alternatives large and small he weighed, the moments when he had to think
quickly through his fatigue.

My mother shaped her adult identity in the restaurant business and, all 7
the while I was growing up, worked as a waitress in coffee shops and
family-style restaurants. My father and I would sometimes visit her at
Coffee Dan's, waiting for her shift to end, riding the bus home together,
her feet killing her. When she worked the counter and took cash, we would
find two stools by the register; when she had the main room, we sat at the
back booth where the waitresses took their break. We would pass the time
with her once the lunch or dinner rush had faded. There wasn't much for a
child to do, the hours stretched out, so I listened to the cooks and waitresses. They talked about the customers, or the boss, or each other; about

the things going on at home with their kids; about how tired they were. And I watched what they did.

I remember particular people, like my mother's coworker Rose Gold- 8 stein, a gentle woman whose house across town we visited, and Bobbi, the new hire just out of high school, on whom I had a desperate crush. And there was a cook whose name I've forgotten, but who would sit in the booth on break, smoking, solemn, food splattered all over his white uniform, down to the shoes. At the back booth, you would catch the thick smell of the grill and the whiff of stale food and cigarettes, scraped and dumped. These odors hung in my mother's uniform and hair. When things got busy, there was a heightened clatter of kitchen and dishwasher, and I could feel the rise in the pulse of the place: the cacophony of customers' voices; waitresses weaving in and out, warning "behind you" in a voice both impassive and urgent; all these people eating separately in one big public space.

I remember the restaurant's lingo, remember liking the code of it. 9 Tables were labeled by the number of chairs—and, thus, customers— around them: *deuces, four-tops, six-tops.* Areas of the restaurant had names: the *racetrack* was the speedy front section. Orders were abbreviated for the cook: *fry four on two,* my mother would call out as she clipped a check onto that little rotating wheel. To speak this language gave you a certain authority, signaled know-how.

I have many images of my mother at work, distinct from the other do- 10 mains of her life: her walking full-tilt with an armload of plates along one arm and two cups of coffee somehow cradled in her other hand; her taking orders, pencil poised over pad; her flopping down in the booth by my father, the whoosh of the cushion; "I'm all in," she'd say, and whisper something quickly to us about a customer. She would stand before a table, her arm stacked with those plates, picking one order off for this person, then another, then another—always seeming to get it right, knowing who got the hamburger, who got the fried shrimp. She'd argue with the cook over a returned order; "he gave me lip," she'd tell us, rushing by. I remember her sitting sideways at the back booth, talking to us, her one hand gripping the outer edge of the table, watching the floor, and noting, in the flow of our conversation, who needed something, who was finishing up, whose order was taking longer to prepare than it should.

What did I come to know about work like Frank's or my mother's, 11 mechanical-industrial or life in the restaurant? Surely, that it was hard, physically taxing, dirty, injurious. I never knew my grandfather—he died of pneumonia before I was born—but I heard, with some frequency, a story about him losing his leg in the railroad stockyards, the same place where Frank worked. This was not the kind of work my parents and uncles and aunts wanted their kids to do. I knew, as well, that work was unsteady; you could lose your job, with disastrous consequences. Hard as it was railed against as it occasionally was, work was coveted, for it was a stay against poverty. One reason my mother valued waitressing was that she knew she could always find work. I also got the clear sense from observing people in my family or in the neighborhood that having work, though you'd be wiped out at day's end, affected your overall mood, your bearing. The men in the neighborhood who were out of work were unhappily at loose ends, sitting around, listless, time on their hands. My mother bemoaned the physical punishment of her job, but she spoke as well about "being among the public." The phrase carried for her a claim of achievement. The Pennsylvania Railroad had Frank—had much of the town—in its grip, and he cursed it often. But he was, finally, a railroad man—hard work, masculine, with national consequence. The work that my uncle and my mother did affected their sense of who they were, and, though limiting in so many ways, it provided a means of doing something in the world.

Doing something in the world. I couldn't have expressed it this way 12 when I was growing up, but the work I saw connected in my mind with agency and competence—that's what being an adult meant to me, and it was intimately tied to physical work. And as does any child, I craved competence. Special terminology caught my ear, the idiom of freight trains or food orders, because not everyone could speak it, especially speak it the right way, and it made things happen. Particular movements of the body made things happen, too, in the restaurant or the stockyard. And there was knowledge of tools and devices, wrenches and hacksaws and measures, but the cash register, too, and the whirring blender. Tied to this knowledge were tricks of the trade. And what a kick it was when one of my uncles or a cook or a waitress showed me how to do something a little more effectively, with a little less effort and a little more finesse. Hold it this way. Move it in, like this. See? I became the work's insider, if just for a moment....

Labor, as a political and social force, has diminished in power and has 13 less immediate grab on the national imagination. The work that currently captures our fancy involves high technology, electronic media, and "symbolic analysis." Trumpeted as an unprecedented kind of work, such "knowledge work" represents emerging opportunity. It is associated with advanced education, and there is no doubt that work of this type requires high levels of analytic skill.... But, though identified with another era, work of body and hand continues to create the material web of daily life. As with any human achievement, such work merits our understanding: the way we talk about it matters. And the dimension of it that is least discussed and appreciated—and that we can continue to learn from—is the thought it takes to do it well.

■   ■   ■

AFTER YOU READ

- **THINK** about the thought and intelligence required for the skilled physical work that Rose describes in his essay. Identify these particular jobs and discuss with your classmates the mental processes behind the work that Rose describes or that you can imagine.

- **THINK** also about Rose's thesis and formulate it in your own words. (Hint: Pay particular attention to the first and last paragraphs.)

- **EXAMINE** Rose's statement that the "sensory particulars [of work] stay with me, resonant" (paragraph 2). *Resonant* means reverberating, echoing, or reflecting meaningfully. Then locate sentences and paragraphs that are particularly resonant with descriptive details that appeal to your senses. Which details relate especially to the connection between thought and physical work?

- **EXAMINE** carefully paragraph 11. Why did Rose's mother value waitressing? How does Rose contrast the feelings of the people in the neighborhood who were "out of work" and those of people who had work?

- **WRITE** an essay discussing the "lingo" (paragraph 9) or "special terminology" (paragraph 12) of a particular job or type of work. You may refer to—or respond to—Rose's essay, but base your content on your own experiences and observations. (See pp. 244–247 at the end of this unit for instructions for "Responding to a Text.") You may want to expand your knowledge by interviewing someone about the terminology particular to his or her line of work

What You Do Is What You Are

■ ■ ■

NICKIE McWHIRTER

A reporter and columnist for the *Detroit News* and the *Detroit Free Press*, Nickie McWhirter—like Rose—associates work with identity. In the following essay, first published in the *Detroit Free Press,* she argues that "Americans ... tend to define and judge everybody in terms of the work they do, especially work performed for pay." However, McWhirter further argues that defining a person by how that person "earns his or her rent money" is not always accurate or fair.

BEFORE YOU READ

■ **THINK** about someone you know who holds a prestigious job but whom you do not respect. Think also about someone you know who holds a menial job but whom you do respect. If you were describing these two people to someone, would you identify them by their job titles or in some other way?

■ **EXAMINE** the first sentence of this essay. Do you agree with McWhirter that the practice of defining people in terms of the work they do is prevalent among Americans? If you agree, why do you think this is true? If not, how might you refute this assertion?

■ **EXAMINE** the following words and their definitions:

1. *validate* (paragraph 1): verify, declare sound and valid
2. *dynastic* (paragraph 4): referring to a succession of rulers from the same family
3. *anthropologist* (paragraph 6): one who studies the origin, development, and behavior of man
4. *entrepreneur* (paragraph 7): one who establishes and assumes risk for a business venture, often in an innovative way

■ **WRITE** a journal entry in which you explore the idea that young people choose a profession on the basis of how it will define them rather than on the basis of their qualifications for or interest in that profession.

AS YOU READ

Underline and number in the margin each of McWhirter's major assertions about the effects of defining someone on the basis of how that person earns a living. (*Hint*: Pay particular attention to McWhirter's topic sentences.)

■ ■ ■

Americans, unlike people almost everywhere else in the world, tend
to define and judge everybody in terms of the work they do, especially work performed for pay. Charlie is a doctor; Sam is a car-
penter; Mary Ellen is a copywriter at a small ad agency. It is as if by
defining how a person earns his or her rent money, we validate or reject
that person's existence. Through the work and job title, we evaluate the
worth of the life attached. Larry is a laid-off auto worker; Tony is a retired
teacher; Sally is a former showgirl and blackjack dealer from Vegas. It is as
if by learning that a person currently earns no money at a job—and maybe
hasn't earned any money at a job for years—we assign that person to
limbo, at least for the present. We define such non-employed persons in
terms of their past job history.

This seems peculiar to me. People aren't cast in bronze because of the
jobs they hold or once held. A retired teacher, for example, may spend a
lot of volunteer time working with handicapped children or raising money
for the Loyal Order of Hibernating Hibiscus. That apparently doesn't
count. Who's Tony? A retired teacher. A laid-off auto worker may pump
gas at his cousin's gas station or sell encyclopedias on weekends. But who's
Larry? Until and unless he begins to work steadily again, he's a laid-off
auto worker. This is the same as saying he's nothing now, but he used to
be something: an auto worker.

There is a whole category of other people who are "just" something. To
be "just" anything is the worst. It is not to be recognized by society as having
much value at all, not now and probably not in the past either. To be "just"
anything is to be totally discounted, at least for the present. There are lots of
people who are "just" something. "Just" a housewife immediately and pain-
fully comes to mind. We still hear it all the time. Sometimes women who have
kept a house and reared six children refer to themselves as "'just' a
housewife." "Just" a bum, "just" a kid, "just" a drunk, bag lady, old man,
student, punk are some others. You can probably add to the list. The "just"
category contains present non-earners, people who have no past job history
highly valued by society and people whose present jobs are on the low end of
pay and prestige scales. A person can be "just" a cab driver, for example, or
"just" a janitor. No one is ever "just" a vice-president, however.

We're supposed to be a classless society, but we are not. We don't recognize a titled nobility. We refuse to acknowledge dynastic privilege. But
we certainly separate the valued from the valueless, and it has a lot to do
with jobs and the importance or prestige we attach to them.

It is no use arguing whether any of this is correct or proper. Rationally
it is silly. That's our system, however, and we should not only keep it in
mind but we should teach our children how it works. It is perfectly swell
to want to grow up to be a cowboy or a nurse. Kids should know, however, that quite apart from earnings potential, the cattle breeder is much
more respected than the hired hand. The doctor gets a lot more respect
and privilege than the nurse.

I think some anthropologist ought to study our uncataloged system of 6
awarding respect and deference to each other based on jobs we hold.
Where does a vice-president–product planning fit in? Is that better than
vice-president–sales in the public consciousness, or unconsciousness? Writers earn diddly dot, but I suspect they are held in higher esteem than
wealthy rock musicians—that is, if everybody older than 40 gets to vote.

How do we decide which jobs have great value and, therefore, the job- 7
holders are wonderful people? Why is someone who builds shopping centers called an entrepreneur while someone who builds freeways is called a
contractor? I have no answers to any of this, but we might think about the
phenomenon the next time we are tempted to fawn over some stranger because we find out he happens to be a judge, or the next time we catch ourselves discounting the personal worth of the garbage collector.

■ ■ ■

AFTER YOU READ

■ **THINK** about the American work ethic—the high value we traditionally
place on work. Do you see a relationship between this work ethic and
the practice of defining people on the basis of what they do to earn a
living? Explain. What other causes can you identify for what McWhirter
believes is a typically American practice?

■ **EXAMINE** McWhirter's assertion (in paragraph 4) that "We're supposed to be a classless society, but we are not." Do you agree or disagree with this assertion? Do you think McWhirter supports this
assertion adequately in this essay? Why or why not?

■ **WRITE** an essay in which you respond to McWhirter's essay by either
agreeing or disagreeing with *one* of her assertions. You may want to
consult "Responding to a Text" at the end of this unit (pages
244–247).

■ Or **WRITE** an essay in which you classify the jobs of people who work
at your college or university according to the respect they earn from the
student body based on the type of work they do. See Lesson 3 on the
Interactions, eighth edition, student website at www.cengagebrain.com
for information about writing classification essays.

Girl in an Oven

■ ■ ■

SARAH JEANETTE SMITH

Sarah Jeanette Smith, who is from Silver City, New Mexico, wrote this essay when she was a sophomore interior design student. During the summer after her freshman year of college, Smith worked as a firefighter for the U.S. Forest Service in New Mexico. As a rookie and the only woman on her crew, Smith spent the summer "trying to act like a girl while working like a man." In her essay she describes the danger of firefighting and the challenge of being the only female in a "man's world," as well as how this experience helped her to define herself.

BEFORE YOU READ

■ **THINK** about different professions that are traditionally associated with either males or females. Are there fewer of these today than there used to be? Are there any professions today that are exclusively male or female?

■ **EXAMINE** the title of this essay. What image does it evoke? Knowing that firefighters refer to a forest fire as an "oven" may help you understand the title better.

■ **EXAMINE** the italicized words in the following phrases from Smith's essay. The words are defined for you.

1. "I *pondered* the unknown" (paragraph 2): thought about; considered carefully
2. "his *intimidating* presence" (paragraph 3): frightening; threatening
3. "wind conditions and *topography*" (paragraph 9): physical description of a geographical region
4. "macho *pyromaniac*" (paragraph 11): one who has an uncontrollable desire to start a fire

■ **WRITE** two lists—one of professions or jobs that have traditionally been associated with females, and one of professions or jobs that have traditionally been associated with males.

AS YOU READ

Mark the descriptive passages that communicate most vividly to you what it is like to fight forest fires.

■   ■   ■

I tasted the smoke curling into my lungs, I blinked as the dancing flames 1
tried to snatch my eyelashes, and I felt my boots melt on the smoldering ground. And then I looked at the guys around me—a hippie boss
and his recruits—a redneck cowboy, a gangster, a macho snowboarder and
an overweight father. And then there was me: the girl.

I had been hired as a summer wildland firefighter with the Forest Ser- 2
vice, and this New Mexico wildfire was my first near-kabob experience.
For a split second, I pondered the unknown impulse that caused me to
strap on a pair of massive black boots and confront a flaming force that
danced and sparked, daring me to challenge it. Then I heard the urgent
yell of my crew boss, jerking my mind back to the char-grilling force.

Evan Sota was a seasoned firefighter, and his beady eyes were just the 3
beginning of his intimidating presence. The hazel points seemed to detach
from his face and drill right through me, exposing my naked inexperience
beneath the green and yellow Nomex fire wear. Evan's thick gray mustache
fell over his mouth, and he seemed to enjoy the ambiguity of his hidden
facial expressions. Long summers on the fire line had sculpted a man of
solid muscle and big hands, and experience was even tied into the knot of
the bandanna covering his bald head. A sense of military formality gave
order and precision to his mannerisms and instructions; he was the only
person on the fire to have his last name monogrammed on his pack and
shirt pocket. If there was anything Evan successfully conveyed to us, it
was the sizzling uncertainty of the fire and our need to perform accordingly
with "aggressive caution."

Safety was always of utmost concern, and we were loaded down with 4
hard hats, huge black boots, safety glasses, gloves and the most sacred object in the lives and deaths of firefighters: the fire shelter. It could supposedly save your life if you could bury yourself under the taco-like shelter in
less than 30 seconds. But if the fire got hotter than 500 degrees Fahrenheit,
the aluminum laminate would melt, sealing your baked-potato fate. After
practice in training, I was confident about the procedure, but I hoped that
I wouldn't ever face the last-resort.

Equipping us with one last encouraging comment, Evan squinted with 5
serious emphasis and pronounced, "This is the closest thing to war you'll
see as a civilian. I want you to go out there and rock this oven!"

My crew's first order was to dig a "fire line" down a dry creek bot- 6
tom, in order to connect with another crew coming to tie in the last corner.
Surrounding the fire with a line of fresh dirt put a halt to the blazing furnace, and once the line was dug, it was only a matter of "mopping-up"
and watching the flames slowly burn out. We grabbed our *Pulaskis*—the
fire axe with a hoe opposite the blade. I lined up with my crew, and we
fell into the staccato rhythm of chinking rocks and shoveling dirt. In
hunched-over positions, we wore our packs at all times, even when nature
called us to take a break. Dehydration was a problem on the line, and the
hot sun, hotter fire and dripping sweat made it necessary to carry at least a

gallon of water. Not only did I look forward to the refreshing wetness on my lips, but I also guzzled the water to lighten my heavy pack. I took a break after working for an hour, and Evan warned me that we might have to continue digging line until midnight.

It was 10 a.m. I took another drink.   7

I wasn't the only rookie on the crew; all the other guys were first-time   8
forest firefighters, with the exception of Jake. As the token cowboy of the group, Jake had endless stories of ropin' and ridin' across his father's ranch in Wyoming. Jake and I patrolled the fires during late nights, making coffee on the warm smoldering coals and sharing our own stories of college life. Jake had a story about the time he got kicked out of college—he and some buddies stole a pickup-load of fish from a hatchery and then scattered them all over campus—and it was so good that we didn't care if it was a lie. His cowboy background made him the biggest gentleman on the crew, and I spent most of my time working on fires with him. Jake was like a big brother to me; he was encouraging and strong when I needed him to be, made me laugh when tears were beginning to fall, and stood ready to bash anyone who doubted I could "hang."

As I leaned against the sloping creekbed during the break, I remem-   9
bered that frantic morning of loading gear into helicopters and then flying to the fire. It was my first helicopter flight, my first fire and the first time that I didn't have the option of making a collect call home. The helicopter's low flying altitude intensified my anticipation, and the waxy pine smears below me looked almost close enough to touch. The beautiful green shine of the untouched pine needles was in sharp contrast to the burned ruin of charred sticks, drifting smoke and billowing flames. Fires were more than just burning wood, though. In training, I learned about fuel types, weather, the physics of falling trees, wind conditions and topography. Then I had to take the deciding "Pack Test," the endurance test of hiking three miles in less than 45 minutes carrying a pack loaded down with enough water to flood a small country. Then there was "Chain Saw 101." I didn't really meet the prerequisites for this class—I was never a boy who chopped wood with Dad, and I had never used an axe, let alone a chain saw. But it was a great class, complete with a slide show and a step-by-step process for felling, limbing and bucking a tree. The hardest thing for me to do, however, was simply starting the chain saw. I didn't have the upper body strength of the guys, so I was unable to stand up and pull the starter at the same time. But I was determined to wield my new-found power to end photosynthesis, so I invented my own way of bending down so that I could use my whole body to pull the starter with one furious yank. From knowing nothing about a chain saw but the noise, I progressed to felling a tree 18 inches in diameter. That was a great day—I screamed and all the guys cheered when the tree came crashing down.

As long as the fire was raging, it was not unusual to work 16 to 20   10
hours a day. Sometimes we worked with intense action to quench a fire's roaring character, but other teasing fires demanded more patience. There were nights when we slept on the fire line, and took turns waking up every

hour to check on a burning snag that was in danger of falling across the line. Layers of thick tape tried to remedy the blisters and annoying rub of my heavy black boots. In a matter of four days, my painted toenails and soft, moisturized feet seemed to be an extension of the slashing and burning. My morning routine included talking to Evan while he massaged and bandaged my suffering feet. We discussed everything from Florida trailer parks to philosophy to the Civil War. Whenever he took out the Band-Aids from his monogrammed first-aid pack, I saw a more compassionate, caring side of a man who had not yet been completely hardened by fire.

Of the 95 people working at the fire, five were girls. Most of the guys 11 on the fire satisfied Evan's idea of the macho pyromaniac, or "23-year-old brain donor." This was a guy who lived only for beer, Copenhagen and the prospect of single-handedly smothering the blaze. I always laughed at Evan's stories, but never really believed that such a mindless male creature existed.

Then I met Dave. He was a tall kid from Colorado and, from outward 12 appearances, looked like he and his hair came straight out of a rock band. With his Pulaski, Dave would rip through burning wood like a maniac, and one time a chain saw almost severed his arm when he barged in front of the whirling destruction. He would attempt to lift heavy chunks of wood that should take two people to lift, his face turning into a grimace of bulging eyes and popping veins. Dave frequently tried to fill a silence with his own profound thoughts, but once spoken, they materialized as pure ignorance. I couldn't count the number of times he asked me, "Have you seen the girl with the beer cart?"

After we spent innumerable days on a fire, the Incident Commander— 13 the biggest of the fire bosses—called the fire "under control." Of course, the lightning that had caused the fire seemed to strike only in the middle of the wilderness, so fire crews were guaranteed to have a marathon hike back to civilization at the end of each fire. On one occasion, the nearest road was 16 miles away, so we packed our gear and left the dying wisps of smoke behind. My crew guys trekked out at a pace that shouldn't be possible while carrying a heavy pack. I worked to keep up with them, running at times—up mountains, down embankments—and finally stopping near a dry lake for lunch. I sat down to eat with Jake and Evan, but when Dave saw me, he took a long drag of his cigarette and said, "Girl, you kept up with us? You're pretty damn burly."

Even though I thought Dave intended that to be a compliment to my 14 endurance, I was furious. I finished the hike by myself. At the end of the day, I was dead-tired, but at the same time, I was proud of the work that both united and separated me from the guys on my crew. It had been a never-ending summer of trying to act like a girl while working like a man. I didn't want any favors or easy jobs just because I had to work harder to keep up. I wanted the guys to respect me, to laugh with me and to count on me. It wasn't easy. Sometimes it wasn't fun. But no matter how much my feet hurt, how thirsty I was or how badly I wanted to drench my hair in fruity conditioner, I loved working hard and being in the woods. It felt great because I was covered with layers of sticky sweat, black smoke, dried tears and the sense of accomplishment.

That summer, the inferno raged and the smoke swirled, but the girl 15 smothered the red-eyed monster.

■ ■ ■

AFTER YOU READ

■ **THINK** about the author's motivation for working as a firefighter for the Forest Service. Why do you think this job appealed to her?

■ **EXAMINE** the author's ambivalent feelings about wanting to be "one of the guys" but at the same time wanting her male colleagues to think of her as a female. How did this job as a firefighter help her to define herself?

■ **EXAMINE** also the word *burly,* which means heavy, muscular, and husky. In your opinion, why didn't Smith like to be called burly?

■ **WRITE** an essay in which you argue that gender should or should not be a consideration for a job or profession. Be sure to use specific reasons and examples to support your argument. (See pp. 372–378 at the end of Unit Six for help with writing a persuasive essay.)

One Man's Kids

■ ■ ■

DANIEL MEIER

Like Sarah Jeanette Smith, author of "Girl in an Oven," Daniel Meier knows what it is like to be part of a profession that is usually associated with the opposite gender. In Meier's case, he chose to become an elementary school teacher—a career that is usually considered "woman's work." Meier has a master's degree from Harvard's Graduate School of Education and is now an assistant professor of elementary education at San Francisco University. He is the author of *Scribble Scrabble—Learning to Read and Write; The Young Child's Memory for Words;* and *Learning in Small Moments: Life in an Urban Classroom.* In this essay, which first appeared in *The New York Times Magazine,* Meier describes his experience as a first-grade teacher in an urban classroom.

BEFORE YOU READ

■ **THINK** about the teachers you had in elementary school. Were any of them male? If so, was it unusual to have a male teacher? What was your reaction to this teacher? Do you think that it is becoming more or less common for men to choose elementary teaching as a profession? Why or why not?

■ **EXAMINE** the italicized words in the sentences below as well as their definitions:

1. "As my students groan, laugh, shudder, cry, *exult,* and wonder, I do too" (paragraph 6). To *exult* means to "rejoice greatly, to feel jubilant or triumphant."
2. "Possibly, men would have more to say to me, and I to them, if my job had more of the *trappings* and benefits of more traditional male jobs" (paragraph 12). In this sentence, *trappings* mean "characteristic accessories or signs."

■ **WRITE** a journal entry in which you describe an experience you had that involved the reversal of traditional gender expectations—for example, an experience with a male teacher in elementary school, a female police officer, a male nurse, or a female executive or politician. In what ways were your expectations different from the reality of this experience? What was your response to this person in terms of his or her vocation?

AS YOU READ

Notice how Meier responds to the children he teaches, to the school administrators who hire him, and to the friends and acquaintances who know he teaches first grade. Notice also how these people respond to him. Indicate these responses in the margins.

■ ■ ■

I teach first graders. I live in a world of skinned knees, double-knotted   1
shoelaces, riddles that I've heard a dozen times, stale birthday cakes,
hurt feelings, wandering stories, and one lost shoe ("and if you don't
find it my mother'll kill me"). My work is dominated by 6-year-olds.

It's 10:45, the middle of snack, and I'm helping Emily open her milk   2
carton. She has already tried the other end without success, and now
there's so much paint and ink on the carton from her fingers that I'm not
sure she should drink it at all. But I open it. Then I turn to help Scott clean
up some milk he has just spilled onto Rebecca's whale crossword puzzle.

While I wipe my milk-and-paint-covered hands, Jenny wants to know   3
if I've seen that funny book about penguins that I read in class. As I hunt
for it in a messy pile of books, Jason wants to know if there is a new seating arrangement for lunch tables. I find the book, turn to answer Jason,
then face Maya, who is fast approaching with a new knock-knock joke.
After what seems like the tenth "Who's there?" I laugh and Maya is
pleased.

Then Andrew wants to know how to spell "flukes" for his crossword.   4
As I get to "u," I give a hand signal for Sarah to take away the snack. But
just as Sarah is almost out the door, two children complain that "we
haven't even had ours yet." I stop the snack mid-flight, complying with
their request for graham crackers. I then return to Andrew, noticing that
he has put "flu" for 9 Down, rather than 9 Across. It's now 10:50.

My work is not traditional male work. It's not a singular pursuit.   5
There is not a large pile of paper to get through or one deal to transact. I
don't have one area of expertise or knowledge. I don't have the singular
power over language of a lawyer, the physical force of a construction
worker, the command over fellow workers of a surgeon, the wheeling and
dealing transactions of a businessman. My energy is not spent in pursuing,
climbing, achieving, conquering, or cornering some goal or object.

My energy is spent in encouraging, supporting, consoling, and praising   6
my children. In teaching, the inner rewards come from without. On any
given day, quite apart from teaching reading and spelling, I bandage a
cut, dry a tear, erase a frown, tape a torn doll, and locate a long-lost
boot. The day is really won through matters of the heart. As my students
groan, laugh, shudder, cry, exult, and wonder, I do too. I have to be soft
around the edges.

A few years ago, when I was interviewing for an elementary-school   7
teaching position, every principal told me with confidence that, as a male,
I had an advantage over female applicants because of the lack of male teachers. But in the next breath, they asked with a hint of suspicion why I
chose to work with young children. I told them that I wanted to observe
and contribute to the intellectual growth of a maturing mind. What I really
felt like saying, but didn't, was that I loved helping a child learn to write
his name for the first time, finding someone a new friend, or sharing in the
hilarity of reading about Winnie the Pooh getting so stuck in a hole that
only his head and rear show.

I gave that answer to those principals, who were mostly male, because   8
I thought they wanted a "male" response. This meant talking about intellectual matters. If I had taken a different course and talked about my interest in helping children in their emotional development, it would have been
seen as closer to a "female" answer. I even altered my language, not once
mentioning the word "love" to describe what I do indeed love about teaching. My answer worked; every principal nodded approvingly.

Some of the principals also asked what I saw myself doing later in my   9
career. They wanted to know if I eventually wanted to go into educational
administration. Becoming a dean of students or a principal has never been
one of my goals, but they seemed to expect me, as a male, to want to climb
higher on the career stepladder. So I mentioned that, at some point, I
would be interested in working with teachers as a curriculum coordinator.
Again, they nodded approvingly.

If those principals had been female instead of male, I wonder whether   10
their questions, and my answers, would have been different. My guess is
that they would have been.

At other times, when I'm at a party or a dinner and tell someone that I   11
teach young children, I've found that men and women respond differently.
Most men ask about the subjects I teach and the courses I took in my
training. Then, unless they bring up an issue such as merit pay, the conversation stops. Most women, on the other hand, begin the conversation on a
more immediate and personal level. They say things like "those kids must
love having a male teacher" or "that age is just wonderful, you must love
it." Then, more often than not, they'll talk about their own kids or ask me
specific questions about what I do. We're then off and talking shop.

Possibly, men would have more to say to me, and I to them, if my job   12
had more of the trappings and benefits of more traditional male jobs. But
my job has no bonuses or promotions. No complimentary box seats at the
ball park. No cab fare home. No drinking buddies after work. No brief-
case. No suit. (Ties get stuck in paint jars.) No power lunches. (I eat peanut
butter and jelly, chips, milk, and cookies with the kids.) No taking clients
out for cocktails. The only place I take my kids is to the playground.

Although I could have pursued a career in law or business as several of   13
my friends did, I chose teaching instead. My job has benefits all its own.
I'm able to bake cookies without getting them stuck together as they cool,
buy cheap sewing materials, take out splinters, and search just the right

trash cans for useful odds and ends. I'm sometimes called "Daddy" and even "Mommy" by my students, and if there's ever a lull in the conversation at a dinner party, I can always ask those assembled if they've heard the latest riddle about why the turkey crossed the road. (He thought he was a chicken.)

■ ■ ■

AFTER YOU READ

- ■ **THINK** about Meier's attitude toward his job and toward other people's reactions to his holding a job that has traditionally been considered a female profession. How would you describe his attitude? Does his attitude differ depending on the person with whom he is dealing? How does Meier's attitude differ from Sarah Jeanette Smith's attitude?

- ■ **EXAMINE** the details Meier includes in describing his work and his interactions with his students. What do these details suggest about the type of teacher he is? Do you think Meier is less masculine because he is nurturing and interested in how small children learn? Why or why not?

- ■ **WRITE** an essay in which you compare the advantages and disadvantages of working in a job that is traditionally associated with the opposite gender. You may want to use the essays by Meier and Smith as sources. If so, you will find it helpful to consult "Responding to a Text" on pages 244–247 at the end of this unit.

The Psychic Satisfactions of Manual Work

■ ■ ■

MATTHEW B. CRAWFORD

Matthew B. Crawford holds a PhD in political philosophy from the University of Chicago, where he was also a postdoctoral fellow on its Committee on Social Thought; he is currently a fellow at the Institute for Advanced Studies in Culture at the University of Virginia. However, he has also done manual work as an electrician and a motorcycle mechanic. Even now, he owns and operates the small motorcycle repair shop Shockoe Moto in Richmond, Virginia. The following essay, an excerpt from Crawford's highly acclaimed book *Shop Class as Soulcraft: An Inquiry into the Value of Work* (2009), can be compared and contrasted with ideas in the first essay in this unit by Mike Rose and with the attitudes toward work expressed in the later essays by Braaksma and Russert.

BEFORE YOU READ

■ **THINK** about the title of the selection. How can manual work (work done by hand) be satisfying? How is this satisfaction "psychic" or mental?

■ **EXAMINE** the following italicized words and their definitions from the essay:

1. "gang of *conduit*" (paragraph 2): tube enclosing electrical wires or cable
2. "*aesthetic* demands" (paragraph 2): artistic; tasteful
3. "*manifesting* oneself" (paragraph 3): revealing; making clear
4. "*vindicate* his worth" (paragraph 3): to justify or prove; to clear of blame
5. "*gratuitous* self-esteem" (paragraph 3): unearned; unjustified

■ **WRITE** a journal entry in which you describe your attitude to manual labor, such as repairing the car, mowing the lawn, chopping wood, or mopping a floor.

AS YOU READ

Underline phrases that show Crawford's attitude toward manual labor.

■ ■ ■

I started working as an electrician's helper shortly before I turned four-   1
teen. I wasn't attending school at the time and worked full-time until
I was fifteen, then kept the trade up during the summers while in high
school and college, with steadily increasing responsibility. When I couldn't
get a job with my college degree in physics, I was glad to have something
to fall back on, and went into business for myself, in Santa Barbara.

I never ceased to take pleasure in the moment, at the end of a job,   2
when I would flip the switch. "And there was light." It was an experience
of agency and competence. The effects of my work were visible for all to
see, so my competence was real for others as well; it had a social currency.
I was sometimes quieted at the sight of a gang of conduit entering a large
panel in an industrial setting, bent into nestled, flowing curves, with varying offsets, that somehow all terminated in the same plane. This was a skill
so far beyond my abilities that I felt I was in the presence of some genius,
and the man who bent that conduit surely imagined this moment of recognition as he worked. As a residential and light-commercial electrician, most
of my work got covered up inside walls. Still, I felt pride in meeting the
aesthetic demands of a workmanlike installation. Maybe another electrician would see it someday. Even if not, I felt responsible to my better self.
Or rather, to the thing itself—craftsmanship has been said to consist simply
in the desire to do something well, for its own sake. If the primary satisfaction is intrinsic and private in this way, there is nonetheless a sort of self-
disclosing that takes place. As the philosopher Alexandre Kojève writes,

> The man who works recognizes his own product in the World that has
> actually been transformed by his work: he recognizes himself in it, he sees
> in it his own human reality, in it he discovers and reveals to others the
> objective reality of his humanity, of the originally abstract and purely
> subjective idea he has of himself.

The satisfactions of manifesting oneself concretely in the world through   3
manual competence have been known to make a man quiet and easy. They
seem to relieve him of the felt need to offer chattering *interpretations* of himself to vindicate his worth. He can simply point: the building stands, the car
now runs, the lights are on. Boasting is what a boy does, because he has no
real effect in the world. But the tradesman must reckon with the infallible
judgment of reality, where one's failures or shortcomings cannot be inter-
preted away. His well-founded pride is far from the gratuitous "self-
esteem" that educators would impart to students, as though by magic.

■ ■ ■

AFTER YOU READ

■ **THINK** about how Crawford's ideas about manual work compare to those of Mike Rose in "Work, Mind, and Identity." Make a list of similar ideas in the two essays.

■ **THINK** also about Crawford's statement in paragraph 1 that when he "couldn't get a job with [his] college degree in physics, [he] was glad to have something to fall back on." In today's economy, do you worry that you might not be able to get a job in your field immediately after graduating from college? Crawford had his electrician's license to keep him working. What, if anything, would you have to "fall back on"?

■ **EXAMINE** Crawford's statement that when he flipped on the electrical switch "And there was light," he was always pleased. Do you recognize that Crawford's allusion is to the Bible? The book of Genesis, Chapter 1, verse 3 reads: "And God said, 'Let there be light': and there was light." How does this allusion suggest Crawford's pride in his work?

■ **EXAMINE** also the inset quotation by Alexandre Kojève in paragraph 2. Paraphrase this quotation in your own words. Be sure to look up the words *objective* and *subjective* so that you can distinguish their meanings.

■ **WRITE** an essay in which you both describe and analyze your attitude toward manual, or physical, labor. First, describe or explain how you feel about such work; then analyze, or give reasons for, why you feel this way. Also be sure to use specific examples to support your reasons.

W-O-R-K

■ ■ ■

B R I A N   B R A A K S M A

In contrast to Matthew B. Crawford in the previous essay, Brian Braaksma dislikes manual labor immensely. He describes vividly his experience working on a family farm in northwest Iowa, where winters are severe and work is taken seriously. At the time he wrote this essay, Braaksma was a senior at Texas Christian University and planning to become a doctor. In his essay, he recounts a time when his father expected him to do hard manual labor even on the coldest days.

BEFORE YOU READ

■ **THINK** about a time when you did hard manual labor. What did you learn from this experience? Do you consider manual labor more difficult than mental labor? Why or why not?

■ **EXAMINE** the reference to the "difference between work and real work" that Braaksma makes in his opening sentence. How would you define "real work"? What is the difference between "work" and "real work"?

■ **EXAMINE** also the following phrases, especially the italicized words and their definitions:

1. "*excruciating* manual labor" (paragraph 1): intensely painful
2. "*rancid* stench of pig" (paragraph 4): sour; sour smelling
3. "dust-*saturated* sweat" (paragraph 6): soaked; filled to capacity
4. "*putrid* dust" (paragraph 7): rotten; foul-smelling

■ **WRITE** a list of different work experiences you have had and what you learned from each.

AS YOU READ

Notice Braaksma's use of specific details to describe the work on his family's farm. Underline the details that communicate to you most vividly what this experience was like for him.

■   ■   ■

G rowing up on a family farm in northwest Iowa, I learned many 1
things, the most important of which was the difference between
work and real work. There is the kind of work that my friends
would continuously complain about: homework, cleaning their rooms, or
passing Super Mario Brothers 3. I was familiar with their kind of
"work," but the work I was more accustomed to was the hard, excruciating, manual labor of farmwork.

"W-O-R-K!" This word was my wake-up call every morning for 2
twelve years. It started when I was old enough to handle a grain shovel at
the age of six, and if I had not left for college three years ago at the age of
eighteen, I am sure that this morning would be no exception. My father
turned on every light in the house at five thirty in the morning, waking
up each of my three brothers and me in turn by chanting "W-O-R-K." I
would try to ignore him, but with his six-foot-four-inch, two hundred and
sixty-pound body looming over me, I knew resistance was futile. So every
day, just like clockwork, the Braaksma brothers would roll out of bed at
the crack of dawn to do farmwork. The type of work to be done on any
given day depended on the season and the day of the week, but we could
always count on two things: getting dirty and doing physical labor.

One such morning was Friday, December 12, 1992. The day before, 3
there was a terrible snowstorm that dropped twelve inches of snow over
our area, and school had been canceled. All the kids at school were ecstatic
about this fortunate turn of events and were busy planning an exciting day
of sleeping in, watching television and sledding. Yet my brothers and I had
a very different outlook on the situation—we knew we had a long day of
strenuous work ahead of us.

The day started out like any other; Dad woke us up at five thirty 4
chanting what has become the family motto: "W-O-R-K!" I reluctantly
got up and looked outside. What my friends saw as prime packing snow
for snowballs, I saw as a foot of wet, heavy snow that I was going to
have to scoop by hand. After eating a quick bowl of Lucky Charms for
breakfast, I ran barefoot across the freezing cold floor of our garage to
get my "pig clothes" that I had to wear. My pig clothes were multiple
layers of clothing that needed to be worn to defend myself against the
cold while working outside on the farm in the arctic temperatures of Iowan
winter. The pig clothes were kept outside because after being worn for only
a single day of chores in the pigpen, the smell of them was so rank that the
mere presence of them would fill the house with the rancid stench of pig.
Similarly, it would be senseless to wash them after chores because the very
next day chores would need to be done again, and the clothes would
promptly be soiled. Consequently, they were always ice-cold and dirty.

I shivered as I slid into my frigid long johns and cringed as I put on 5
crusty sweat pants and coverall—stiff with dried and frozen pig manure.
As I expected, as soon as we were dressed, Dad ordered my brothers and
me to march out to the barn and commence cleaning. The pigs were almost

large enough to sell, and at that size, they can produce an unbelievably large amount of manure. Consequently, we had the pleasure of removing their poop every week, usually on Saturday, but since we didn't have school, Dad knew he had a captive audience, and decided to clean the buildings that Friday instead. When I opened the door to the barn, a wall of dense, moist, dusty, rank air hit me. The stench was so penetrating that it took my breath away. Ammonia, formed when urine and manure mix, burns the nose and mouth and stings the eyes. I immediately closed the door, thinking about hiding to delay the torture, but at the same time I knew that the work needed to be done and wasting time would only perpetuate the suffering, so like lemmings my brothers and I filed into the barn.

Inside the barn, no matter the time of day, it was always dark due to dust particles and steam in the air from sweaty pigs, making the air too thick for the light to travel through. It was impossible to see the length of the fifty-yard barn, and cobwebs hung from the ceiling heavy and thick from a coating of dust. While breathing the filthy, unhealthy dust into my lungs, I began scooping. The task at hand was tremendous—to totally rid the building of manure, while at the same time fighting off aggressive pigs continually trying to bite us. To make matters worse, dad was a slave driver who was never satisfied. We could always be scooping faster or working harder, and he would let us know. As he barked out orders, his teeth were white against his face now black from dust-saturated sweat, but soon his teeth too would be black; nothing could escape being covered by filth. 6

Four hours later, we were finished. As soon as Dad gave permission to leave, I ran out of the barn, wanting only to breathe clean air again. I trudged back to the house exhausted and covered inside and out with a film of putrid dust. Inside the house, I tried to clean up. After thirty minutes in the shower rubbing my hands raw with industrial strength soap, my fingers still smelled as if I had just pulled them out of a steaming pile of dung. The stench seemed to seep into my pores. It consumed me, and stayed with me as a constant reminder of the work I had done. The smell of the barn remained in my nostrils for days, and for a week I blew black mucus from my nose. This was the kind of work I did, week in and week out, but that morning, I decided that I did not want to do manual labor all my life. I did not want to become a retired farmer with bones and muscles aching from years of strenuous work, lungs black with soot. I had tasted what real work was like, and I did not like it. I decided that I would much rather live my life working with my mind instead of my muscle. 7

■ ■ ■

AFTER YOU READ

■ **THINK** about Braaksma's use of a single illustration to communicate what working on his family's farm was like. Would it have been more effective if he had recounted a series of examples or just a general description of the work rather than focusing on this single event? (See Lesson 6 on the *Interactions,* eighth edition, student website for an explanation about and instructions for writing essays supported by examples or an extended illustration.)

■ **THINK** also about the difference between Braaksma's attitude toward work and that of his father. How are they different, and how are they alike? Do you think that Braaksma's attitude toward work was influenced by his father? If so, how?

■ **EXAMINE** Braaksma's last sentence: "I decided that I would much rather live my life working with my mind instead of my muscle." Does this statement suggest that Braaksma does not have a strong work ethic? Why or why not? Can mental work be as rigorous and demanding as physical work? Why or why not?

■ **WRITE** an essay in which you describe a single work experience you have had. You may include what you learned from this experience either by stating the lesson explicitly (as Braaksma does in his essay) or by simply implying the lesson you learned. Try to include the same type of vivid sensory details that Braaksma does in his essay.

Big Russ and Me

■ ■ ■

TIM RUSSERT

Tim Russert, who died suddenly of a heart attack in June 2008 at 58 years of age, was senior vice president and Washington bureau chief of NBC News. However, he is perhaps best remembered as the long-time managing editor and moderator for *Meet the Press*, a popular Sunday morning television program devoted to discussions of political issues and events. He was also the author of two books—*Big Russ and Me* (2004) and *Wisdom of Our Fathers* (2006), both of which were *New York Times* #1 bestsellers. In the following reading from *Big Russ and Me*, Russert describes how hard his father worked to provide for his family.

BEFORE YOU READ

■ **THINK** about and discuss with your classmates whether you think each generation produces people with similar work ethics or whether people of past generations had stronger work ethics than those of your own generation.

■ **THINK** also about someone in your own family who has worked hard all of his or her life.

■ **EXAMINE** the words *labor* (paragraph 1), *toil* (paragraph 1), and *work* (paragraph 5). What connotations does each of these words have? Can you think of other words that mean essentially the same thing? Notice that each of these terms can be used as either a noun or a verb.

■ **EXAMINE** also the first two paragraphs of the essay. How does Big Russ's attitude toward work differ from Braaksma's? How would you compare Big Russ's attitude to work to that of Braaksma's father? (Answer these questions in more detail after you have read Russert's essay.)

■ **WRITE** a journal entry in which you explore the different connotations of the words *work, labor,* and *toil.*

AS YOU READ

Underline each different job that Big Russ held during his life.

■ ■ ■

All through my childhood, and well beyond it, Big Russ held down two demanding jobs. But as hard as he labored and as long as he toiled, we never heard a single complaint about his heavy workload or the sacrifice he was making. He didn't talk about it; he just got it done. And if he had had to take a third job to support his wife and four kids, he would have done that, too. He could never understand why people filed for bankruptcy, or why some families remained on welfare for a generation or more. A temporary setback was one thing—"Hey, it happens"—but welfare as a way of life? Incomprehensible.

Like so many members of the strong, silent generation of men who grew up during the Great Depression and went off to war, he had learned long ago that life was hard and nothing was handed to you. In fact, Dad considered it a sign of success, and even a blessing, that he was able to hold down two jobs. He could remember a time when a man considered himself fortunate to have even one.

In South Buffalo, having two jobs was not unusual. When I was growing up in the 1950s and '60s, most of my friends' fathers had a "second front," as we called it. The cop down the street worked nights as a security guard. My Uncle Sonny, a fireman, was also a maintenance man at Mercy Hospital. Another fireman who lived on our block ran a small insurance business on the side. Jack Horrigan, a sportswriter for the *Buffalo Evening News,* supplemented his income by writing under other names for various magazines. Tucker Reddington, the head football coach at St. Joseph's Collegiate Institute, owned a funeral home. Francis Reedy drove a school bus during the day and a city bus at night. Many of the men who worked at Bethlehem Steel in Lackawanna, or the Ford stamping factory, where parts of cars were put together before they were sent to the final assembly plant, either worked overtime whenever they could or did painting, plumbing, or handyman work on weekends. The primary obligation of a husband and a father was to provide for his family, and if that meant working two jobs, that was what you did.

Dad's main job was with the Sanitation Department. He could have made more money at the steel plant, or doing construction work, but his father, who had also worked for the city, had encouraged his two sons, Francis and Timothy, to apply for civil service jobs, rather than higher paying work in industry, because the public sector offered security. That advice suited Dad fine; he believed that slow and steady wins the race. "One day the heyday will be over," he would say, and that certainly proved true in Buffalo during the 1970s, when the economy tanked and thousands of people in private industry were laid off. By working for the city, Dad was choosing payday over heyday.

He started out as a lifter on the back of a garbage truck, and gradually worked his way up to driver. Later, when he took a test to become foreman, his high score earned him a promotion and a raise. A foreman was responsible for supervising and checking up on the various crews in a neighborhood, and for making sure there were enough men each day to complete the job. When I was young, I often woke up at 5:45 A.M. to the sound of Dad on the telephone: "What do you mean you can't come to work? Roy, you can't be doing this. You gotta give me some *notice!* How the hell am I going to find a man—yeah, I know you don't feel well. Listen, I don't feel so hot myself. Do me a favor, will you, Roy? Next time you're sick, could you call me the night before so I can get a man who wants to work? This is brutal!" Slam went the phone.

Maybe Roy really was sick. Or maybe it was snowing too hard, or he   6 had stayed out a little too late the night before. Either way, Dad had a problem that had to be solved, because if even one truck was a man short, it was awful for everyone. He had a list of substitutes—day hires, they were called, and he'd start calling around, waking these men up and trying to cajole them into work. "Come on, Jerry, I really need you to come in." It often took some persuading to pry Jerry out of his warm bed on a cold winter morning when he hadn't been expecting to get up early.

A few years after he became a foreman, Dad took the test to become a   7 superintendent, which meant he would oversee several of the foremen. He did well on the test, and by law, the Commissioner of the Streets Department had to appoint as superintendent someone who had finished in the top three places. We were excited about this, because Dad might get a big promotion, and the superintendent job came with a car and, of course, a raise. One day, three strangers appeared at our house, which was very unusual, because the only people who ever came to our door were friends, neighbors, or family. "You kids go outside," Dad said, and of course we obeyed. After about twenty minutes, the men got back in their car and drove away. When I asked Dad about the visitors, he said, "Oh, they're just some guys I know from work."

Years later, we were talking about his work and I said, "Dad, what-   8 ever happened to that superintendent job?"

"It just didn't work out."   9

"What happened?"   10

As I suspected, there was more to the story than I knew, and the three   11 visitors had something to do with it. "They wanted me to sign off the superintendent list," he said. "If they could get the guys with the highest scores to sign off, they could appoint the candidate they wanted, who didn't do so well on the test."

"What did you tell them?" I asked.   12

"I said no," he answered.   13

"And what did they say?"   14

"They weren't happy. They said that if I changed my mind, they would   15 make it worthwhile."

"What does that mean?" I asked. Like some politicians I have inter-   16 viewed, Dad doesn't volunteer much information. You have to ask.

"They offered to sweeten the deal."   17

"What did you tell them?"   18

"I told them I couldn't do it. I know what I could have done with the money, but I also knew what that money would do to me. I told them I didn't want any part of it." 19

"Do you remember how you said it?" 20

"I said, 'You've got the wrong guy.' They said, 'Why don't you think about it?' I said, 'I've thought about it. I'll see you later.'" 21

"Were you tempted to take the money?" 22

"Like I said, it wasn't the right thing to do. And how could I tell you kids to do the right thing if I ever did something like that?" 23

The story means the world to me. At the time, Dad was sending two or three kids to parochial school, paying the mortgage, and working two jobs, but he held his ground. Others didn't do the right thing, and Dad didn't get the promotion, but he kept his honor. 24

DAD LEFT FOR WORK AT DAWN, and when his shift was over, he went over to his second job, where he drove a delivery truck for the *Buffalo Evening News*. Later, when the Sanitation Department made him foreman of the downtown district, he started working nights because trash collection was too disruptive to be done while stores and businesses were still open. This new schedule was fine with him, because now he could drive full-time for the *News*. He'd come home from his day job around 5:30 and eat a quick supper. Then he'd sprawl out diagonally across the bed for a short nap before heading out for the night shift. We had to be quiet during his nap, and stay off the telephone when he was home in case one of the workers was trying to reach him. 25

Dad didn't have much time off, but when he wasn't working for pay, he was working around the house—changing the storm windows, cutting the grass, resealing the driveway, or taking care of his car. There was a public golf course at the end of our street, but Dad never went there. "Some of my friends picked up golf," he once said to me, "but I never had the time." There may have been a note of regret in that comment, but it was far from a complaint. 26

Dad talked as little about his work as he did about the war, so for years I didn't know much about either of his jobs. A couple of years ago, an old friend from South Buffalo told me that when he was a boy, he resented the fact that his father, who worked at the steel plant, used to spend every Friday night getting drunk in a bar. My friend served as an infantry squad leader during some of the bloodiest fighting of the Vietnam War, and when his tour was over, he took a summer job in the same factory where his father had worked all those years. "It was awful," he told me. "I lasted exactly three days, and my respect for my father went up exponentially. He went into that awful place every day, and worked overtime to support his family. All was forgiven. Vietnam was depressing, but the steel plant was worse." 27

I had some idea of what he was talking about. I had always known that Dad worked hard, but I didn't really appreciate what he went through every day until I did it myself. When I was in college, I spent just about every school vacation doing exactly what Dad had done, and was still 28 doing—working on garbage trucks and delivering bundles of newspapers for the *Buffalo Evening News*. Every morning I lifted heavy garbage cans, just as Dad had done when he was starting out. It was good, tough, honest work, and I knew it would be hard. But I hadn't expected it would be *that* hard.

The lifter is the man who picks up the cans and empties them into the 29 packer, or compacting truck, where a sweeping bar comes over the top and pushes the trash into the interior of the vehicle, where it is compacted. Each packer carried three men—a driver and two lifters. But sometimes one of the packers broke down and we had to use the old-fashioned fantail truck, which was nothing more than a dump truck piled high with trash. On a packer, the lifter emptied the cans into an opening about three feet off the ground. But on the older trucks, the lifters—and there were always two of us—had to hold full cans of garbage above our heads and pass them to the shaker, who emptied the cans, built the load, and covered the growing pile with canvas so the garbage wouldn't fall into the street. For obvious reasons, the job of lifter was always awarded to the youngest, most inexperienced member of the team. That would be me. And if an old fantail truck had to be pressed into service, you can guess where the college boys were sent.

There was no overtime on this job: you worked until you finished your 30 route, and if, for some reason, your route took longer than usual, that was your problem. Sometimes, especially on Friday, when everyone wanted to finish early, the driver would get out of the cab and give you a hand. On the other side of the ledger, you might be teamed up with Walter "Take a Leak" Scott, who insisted on stopping for a bathroom break every ten minutes. It took me a week or so to realize that he was really going off to take another nip.

When Dad had started out as a lifter, compacting trucks hadn't come 31 in yet. He must have lifted heavy cans above his head every day for years. In his day, incidentally, residents of Buffalo had full garbage service: Before the garbage truck came to your house, a team of rollers would bring your trash cans out to the front. After the truck had taken the trash, the rollers came back and returned the empty cans.

The routes I worked on were full of two-family houses, so there were 32 as many as ten or twelve garbage cans for each one. In winter, on dark, freezing mornings, we had to work our way around high snowdrifts and dangerous patches of ice. Christmas week was especially hard, with all that extra packaging from gifts and all those empty bottles. (This was long before recycling.) Summer presented a different set of challenges, such as picking up trash from a couple of raw clam stands. Take my word for it; there is *nothing* quite like the stench of two-day-old clam shells on a hot, humid day in August. That's an aroma that lingers on your clothes, and in your memory.

Barbara Ehrenreich has written that there is really no such thing as un- 33 skilled labor. One of the first lessons I learned on the garbage detail was the proper way of removing a lid from a metal can. It's not complicated, but you had to make sure to pull the lid back toward your chin, using it as a shield to protect your throat in case a rat jumped out at you. Rats were part of the landscape, and we saw them every day. Sometimes I rode shotgun when we drove a load of trash to the dump, which looked like a scene from a horror movie with packs of rats swarming over the garbage.

I soon understood why Dad was so meticulous when it came to throw- 34 ing things out. He always put the kitchen grease in a coffee can and let it settle and harden, because he knew what it felt like to pick up a bag and have the bottom fall out. He also knew—and I learned the hard way—that some people threw their garbage right into the can, without even bagging it. When they did that, we'd have to smell it, and wear it, for the rest of the day. Others, especially in the Polish neighborhoods, wrapped their garbage so neatly and carefully that you almost expected them to put a ribbon on it. As soon as we picked up their trash, they'd be out there with a hose, rinsing out the empty cans.

Well before I had any hands-on experience, Dad had taught me how to 35 wrap garbage. Part of it was his passion for doing things correctly. "Do it right the first time," Big Russ would say, "and you won't have to do it again." He was also being considerate. If you got into the habit of thinking about the other guy, including the person who picked up your trash, and you realized that you were just one household out of many stops along his route, you could make life a little easier for this father, this uncle, this brother, or this son. To this day I put our garbage out with real care and attention, because I remember what it's like to pick it up.

After a day of lifting garbage cans, my arms and shoulders would be 36 aching, and I still have a problem with my toe from the time I dropped a heavy can on it. But it wasn't all pain and suffering. One summer I was teamed up with a shaker named Willie, a black man with a wonderful sense of humor who liked to sing on the job. Willie loved pizza, and we were sharing one for lunch one day when a well-dressed woman happened to walk by. "My, oh my," said Willie, in a voice just loud enough to be overheard. "Here's a pizza pie that doesn't look more than a day or two old." It worked: the woman yelled at us for eating garbage. But Willie hadn't counted on the possibility that she might call City Hall to report us. When the foreman came by to check on us, we explained that, No, we hadn't been eating any garbage, and where would that poor lady ever get *that* idea? When I told Dad about it, he said that in his day they'd take an apple, polish it, and pretend they had found it in the garbage. "Work is tough," he'd say, "but there's no law against having a good laugh."

Friday was payday. I had to move on to my second job, but most of 37 the crew would repair to a tavern for lunch and stay there for hours. Once, when I joined them for a sandwich, I watched as one man cashed his paycheck at the bar. The bartender gave him half the money in an envelope, which the customer put in his back pocket "for the little woman." The other half stayed with the bartender, and I realized that this man was planning to drink his way through half a paycheck's worth of booze. Dad loved to have a couple of cold ones, but he would never even think of doing something like that. Now I was grateful not only for all that he did for us, but also for the things he didn't do.

"Now I got you this job," Dad reminded me, "so don't embarrass me, 38 okay?" He was never embarrassed about being a garbageman, and even when his title was Foreman of the Streets Division, everybody knew what that meant. Because he was proud of his work, I was proud of him for doing it. He took pride in a job well done, and he wanted to be sure that I measured up. I knew that, of course; I took the job seriously and worked hard. I was aware that Dad had called in a favor or two to get me this job, and he didn't want to hear any complaints about me from his buddies, or even worse, his bosses. One time, my foreman on the garbage route saw Dad on the street and called out to him.

"Hey Tim!"   39

"Yeah?"   40

"He's a good kid."   41

Big Russ took the cigar out of his mouth and said, "Thanks, Whitey. 42 That means a lot."

Dad never mentioned this exchange, but he didn't have to—I witnessed 43 it, and I felt like I had won a medal. There's nothing worse than disappointing your parents, and nothing better than making them proud. Here and there I had pleased him in other ways, mostly at school, in church, or on the playground, but this was different. This was his world, and I had done my job—his job, actually—with some degree of competence.

The money was good and I'm glad I did it, but I had no desire to con- 44 tinue lifting garbage cans. Today, when I see Dad with arthritis in his joints, I picture him hanging off the back of a truck and lifting all those loads. On my last day on the job, I told Phil, the driver, that I was finished. "I'm out of here," I proclaimed. "I've got my college degree, and I'm hoping to go to law school."

"Yeah, they all say that. You'll be back."   45

"No, Phil, I'm telling you, this is it." With a flourish, I took off my 46 headband, my boots and my gloves, threw them into the packer, and pushed down the blade. Then I got into my car and started putting on my sneakers.

"What did you do?" Phil called to me.   47

"Everything is in the truck. It's over, pal."   48

"You'll be back," he said again. Phil, who fancied himself a singer, 49 proceeded to serenade me with an old Peggy Lee song, "Is That All There Is?" Many years later, when I was living in New York, I read in the paper that Peggy Lee was performing in a Sunday matinee. My wife, Maureen, and I went to see her, and when she sang "Is That All There Is?" I was grinning from ear to ear. Phil turned out to be wrong about my coming back, although there were a couple of times along the way when I feared he might be right.

But I don't regret my time on the trucks, and I couldn't have put my- 50 self through college without a good summer job. Despite the smells, the cold, the heat, and my aching arms, being a garbageman was an invaluable experience. After that, no job has ever seemed too difficult.

I learned a few things, too. That there is no substitute for getting up in 51 the morning, reporting to work on time, and putting in an honest day's work for an honest day's pay. That everybody has a job to do and a contribution to make, and that no matter how small that job may seem in the larger scheme of things, if it's worth doing at all, it's worth doing well. That the person who litters, or doesn't bother to wrap his trash, or doesn't show up to work, makes life a little harder for everyone else. I learned, too, that having a certain job at one point in your life doesn't mean you'll be doing it forever. But most of all, I learned how hard Big Russ had worked to support us.

■   ■   ■

AFTER YOU READ

■ **THINK** about the task of collecting garbage, which Big Russ did before he became a foreman and which Russert did in summers and on other school vacations. Explain the process and difficulties of this work as Russert describes it in paragraphs 28–32.

■ **EXAMINE** and discuss the author's own satisfaction and enjoyment of his work (see paragraphs 34–38) and his obvious pride in his father and what he learned from Big Russ (see the last paragraph). What is Big Russ's work ethic—his attitude and convictions about work—and how does he pass down this work ethic to his son?

■ **EXAMINE** the statement from Barbara Ehrenreich that Russert quotes: "there is really no such thing as unskilled labor." How does this statement relate to the earlier readings by Mike Rose, Matthew B. Crawford, and Brian Braaksma? How does Russert's description of the skill required to be a garbageman relate to Rose's description of his mother's skill as a waitress? How do Russert's and Big Russ's feelings about their physical work compare or contrast to Crawford's feelings about his own manual labor? How do these feelings compare or contrast to those of Braaksma?

■ **WRITE** a character sketch or profile about someone you know who has a strong work ethic. You may want to interview this person before writing about him or her.

■ **OR WRITE** an essay about a job you have (or have had) to help pay for your college education. How does your motivation for an education relate to your attitude toward your job?

FOCUS: PROCESS

Regular Work for an Irregular Economy

■ ■ ■

CARMEN MARTINO AND
DAVID BENSMAN

Carmen Martino is the director of the Latino Occupational Safety and Health Initiative (LOSHI) at the Rutgers School of Management and Labor Relations, where she is also a strategic researcher. A professor of labor studies and employment relations at Rutgers University, David Bensman is also the author of *The Practice of Solidarity: American Hatters in the Nineteenth Century* and the coauthor of *Rusted Dreams: Hard Times in a Steel Community*. This essay appeared in the October 2008 issue of *American Prospect*.

BEFORE YOU READ

■ **THINK** about the title of this essay. How is our economy "irregular" for those seeking employment? How difficult is it to get regular, full-time work? Have you, or has anyone you know, lost a job? Have you, or has anyone you know, sought or had temporary employment? How do you feel about temporary employment? About the agencies that offer such work?

■ **EXAMINE** the first two paragraphs, which explain that the situation being described here is found in the particular city of Brunswick, New Jersey. As you read the essay, see if this New Jersey situation sounds familiar. Are similar situations occurring in other parts of the country? Explain.

■ **EXAMINE** also the phrases "filling *pallets*" (paragraph 6) and "*exploitive* businesses" (paragraph 9). In this context, a pallet is a portable platform (usually wooden) for moving or storing freight. An exploitive or exploitative business is one that makes unethical or selfish use of its workers.

■ **WRITE** in your journal two lists, one giving reasons for and the other giving reasons against having a temporary employment agency of some kind (not necessarily like the one described above) in your town or city.

AS YOU READ

Be aware that although this essay has some qualities of a narrative, it is actually a process essay because it describes the experience not just of one person on one day but also of every person who seeks work at this agency on any day. That is, the process is repeated many times.

■   ■   ■

I magine that you are a young person trying to find your first full-time   1
job in New Brunswick, New Jersey, a small city about 35 miles southwest of New York. You don't want to work in a restaurant or a fast-
food joint, because they won't give you enough hours to make a living, and
they don't provide benefits. There aren't many full-time opportunities in
your neighborhoods, because most factories and warehouses have left
town for the suburbs. Commuting to suburban regions where there are
more employers is impractical; mass transit is inadequate, you can't afford
a decent car, and fuel prices are high.

If you are a Latino worker, your only option is to register at one of the   2
labor agencies that have flocked to your neighborhood in recent years. One is
probably within walking distance, with a big sign saying, "Workers wanted."
Most of these labor agencies are organized along racial and ethnic lines. If
you're African American, chances are there won't be a labor agency for you
nearby. These firms locate where desired workers live; most employers request
Latinos, who are promoted as reliable, compliant—and often desperate.

If you are serious about finding work, you arrive at the temp office at   3
6 A.M. and begin your wait. At 7, the boss begins issuing work orders; if
you're lucky, you'll be told the name of the company where you'll work
that day. Nothing's in writing: not your assignment, not your pay rate,
not the length of your contract.

For most jobs, you'll be paid the minimum wage, and you can forget   4
health insurance or other benefits. The pay is not only low; it's unpredictable. You don't know whether you'll have six hours of work or eight, and
you don't know whether you'll be paid the advertised rate or less, without
explanation. The agency issues you a separate check for each job you work
that week, and somehow, when your hours for all the jobs are added up,
you're never paid the overtime rate.

This system is also costly to you. The agency—or the business that   5
rents space at the agency office—charges you $1 to $2 to cash each check,
and since your neighborhood has no bank where you can open an account,
you have to pay. For your transportation, the agency deducts $7 per day,
regardless of how far you are going and no matter how long you have to
wait for the van to pick you up before and after work or how many stops
it makes on the way to the workplace. Many of the vans are overcrowded,
old, and unsafe; their drivers may be unqualified or unlicensed; and they're
still getting into well-publicized accidents, despite the "van safety" law
passed by the New Jersey legislature.

When you get to the workplace—it makes little difference whether it's   6
a well-known company's warehouse or the backroom of a local grocery
store—you will receive little training or instructions. Whether you are un-
loading trucks, filling pallets, digging a ditch, or cleaning a bathroom, your

chances of working with dangerous materials are high, but you're not told about any hazards to which you may be exposed. If you are injured, you won't be paid for your time out of work, regardless of whether or not the agency has paid its workers'-compensation insurance. And more than likely, you won't know your rights under the state's laws, because no one has told you what they are.

At the end of the day, you wait for the van to take you back to the   7 agency office. You may have to wait an hour or two, for which you won't be paid, and if the van never shows, you'll have to walk home or pay for a cab. Whatever the case, your van fee will still be deducted from your paycheck, and after the fees for check cashing and transportation have been deducted, more than a third of your earnings are gone.

Next week won't be any better; there are no job ladders in the   8 temporary-labor industry, no pay increases, no paths to permanent employment. (You have to sign a form agreeing not to go to work for the agency's client.) When you tire of the temp agency and you go back out on job market, you'll find once again that few full-time jobs are available at any wage rate.

And street-corner day labor also feeds into ethnic stereotypes and fuels   9 anti-immigrant feelings. It is in the interest of everyone—except exploitive businesses—to regularize these employment relations.

■   ■   ■

AFTER YOU READ

■ **THINK** about the uncertainty that the workers described in this essay must feel every day that they go to work. Make a list of the things that they do not know or cannot predict about their work day. How would this uncertainty make you feel?

■ **EXAMINE** the essay to identify the process that the worker follows throughout the day. Mark each of the three separate stages of the day that Martino and Bensman discuss. Note that the authors also take the process into the "next week," suggesting that this process is—or seems to be—unending.

■ **WRITE** an essay in which you discuss some of the problems faced by temporary workers or some of the reasons that individuals might seek temporary employment. In either case, use your own experiences, ideas, and observations as well as ideas from this reading.

■ Or **WRITE** an essay discussing the process of applying for a job. Divide your essay into chronological stages and include all of the details, definitions, and transitions necessary to make the process clear to your reader. See Lesson 4 on the *Interactions,* eighth edition, student website at www.cengagebrain.com for help with writing a process essay.

Easy Job, Good Wages

■ ■ ■

JESUS COLON

Born in Puerto Rico in 1901, Jesus Colon immigrated to the mainland as a boy by stowing away on a ship bound for New York City. To survive he worked at various menial jobs that made him aware of the exploitation of unskilled workers, especially those who did not know English. He soon became a champion for their cause, speaking and writing about the immigrant experience. Although he published only one book, a collection of essays entitled *A Puerto Rican in New York and Other Sketches,* he was politically active throughout his life and shared his views in newspaper articles and speeches. As a result, he has had a significant influence on Americans' perception of Puerto Ricans. In this essay, Colon describes one of his early experiences as a young man looking for a job and the lesson he learned from that experience.

BEFORE YOU READ

■ **THINK** about the process of looking for a job. If you have looked for a job, what tools and strategies did you use? Which were the most useful?

■ **THINK** also about how the process of finding a job has changed in recent years. Is it easier or harder to find a job now than it was in the past? Explain.

■ **EXAMINE** the following italicized words and their definitions:

1. "*galvanized* tubs half filled with water" (paragraph 2): substance made of sheet metal and covered with zinc
2. "transparent *mucilage* used to attach the label" (paragraph 4): a sticky substance from certain plants often used as glue, especially for paper
3. "*tenaciously* fastened to the bottles" (paragraph 4): holding or clinging very firmly

■ **WRITE** a journal entry in which you describe an experience you had while looking for a job or working at a certain job.

AS YOU READ

Notice Colon's description of the work he was asked to do. Does he criticize the job and working conditions, or does he simply describe how he felt and responded?

■   ■   ■

This happened early in 1919. We were both out of work, my 1
brother and I. He got up earlier to look for a job. When I woke
up, he was already gone. So I dressed, went out and bought a
copy of the *New York World,* and turned its pages until I got to the
"Help Wanted Unskilled" section of the paper. After much reading and rereading the same columns, my attention was held by a small advertisement.
It read: "Easy job. Good wages. No experience necessary." This was
followed by a number and street on the west side of lower Manhattan.
It sounded like the job I was looking for. Easy job. Good wages. Those
four words revolved in my brain as I was traveling toward the address
indicated in the advertisement. Easy job. Good wages. Easy job. Good
wages. Easy...

The place consisted of a small front office and a large loft on the floor 2
of which I noticed a series of large galvanized tubs half filled with water
out of which I noticed protruding the necks of many bottles of various
sizes and shapes. Around these tubs there were a number of workers,
male and female, sitting on small wooden benches. All had their hands in
the water of the tub, the left hand holding a bottle and with the thumbnail
of the right hand scratching the labels.

The foreman found a vacant stool for me around one of the tubs of 3
water. I asked why a penknife or a small safety razor could not be used
instead of the thumbnail to take off the old labels from the bottles. I was
expertly informed that knives or razors would scratch the glass thus depre-
ciating the value of the bottles when they were to be sold.

I sat down and started to use my thumbnail on one bottle. The water 4
had somewhat softened the transparent mucilage used to attach the label to
the bottle. But the softening did not work out uniformly somehow. There
were always pieces of label that for some obscure reason remained affixed
to the bottles. It was on those pieces of labels tenaciously fastened to the
bottles that my righthand thumbnail had to work overtime. As the minutes
passed I noticed that the coldness of the water started to pass from my
hand to my body, giving me intermittent body shivers that I tried to conceal with the greatest of effort from those sitting beside me. My hands became deadly clean and tiny little wrinkles started to show especially at the
tip of my fingers. Sometimes I stopped a few seconds from scratching the
bottles to open and close my fists in rapid movements in order to bring
blood to my hands. But almost as soon as I placed them in the water they
became deathly pale again.

But these were minor details compared with what was happening to the 5
thumb of my right hand. For a delicate, boyish thumb, it was growing by the
minute into a full-blown tomato-colored finger. It was the only part of my
right hand remaining blood red. I started to look at the workers' thumbs.
I noticed that these particular fingers on their right hands were unusually
developed with a thick layer of cornlike surface at the top of their right
thumb. The nails on their thumbs looked coarser and smaller than on the

other fingers—thumb and nail having become one and the same thing—a primitive unnatural human instrument especially developed to detach hard pieces of labels from wet bottles immersed in galvanized tubs.

After a couple of hours I had a feeling that my thumbnail was going to 6 leave my finger and jump into the cold water of the tub. A numb pain imperceptibly began to be felt coming from my right thumb. Then I began to feel such pain as if coming from a finger bigger than all of my body.

After three hours of this I decided to quit fast. I told the foreman so, 7 showing him my swollen finger. He figured I had earned 69 cents at 23 cents an hour.

Early in the evening I met my brother in our furnished room. We 8 started to exchange experiences of our job hunting for the day. "You know what?" my brother started, "early in the morning I went to work where they take labels off old bottles—with your right-hand thumbnail.... Somewhere on the west side of lower Manhattan. I only stayed a couple of hours. 'Easy job ... Good wages ...' they said. The person who wrote that ad must have had a great sense of humor." And we both had a hearty laugh that evening when I told my brother that I also went to work at that same place later in the day.

Now when I see ads reading, "Easy job. Good wages," I just smile an 9 ancient, tired, knowing smile.

■ ■ ■

AFTER YOU READ

■ **THINK** about the working conditions in the first part of the 1900s. Were there laws about hiring minors? Were working conditions and hours regulated by the government? Was there a minimum wage? How and why have working conditions changed in this country in the last century? What other changes do you think need to be made?

■ **EXAMINE** paragraph 2, which emphasizes that all workers were doing the same task. The narration that follows is, thus, a *process narrative* describing the process that all workers go through rather than an individual experience.

■ **EXAMINE** also the conclusion of this essay, in which Colon reveals the lesson he learned from his experience. Put that lesson into your own words. Do you think there are other lessons to be learned from this essay? If so, what are they?

■ **WRITE** an essay describing an experience you have had in trying to find a job or working at a job. You may use the experience from your journal entry, or you can use a different one. In either case, try to conclude your essay by stating or suggesting a lesson you learned from your experience.

Salvaging an Interview

■ ■ ■

TAMEKIA REECE

A Houston-based freelance writer, Tamekia Reece has published articles in *Woman's Day, Parenting, Seventeen, Real
Health, Health & Fitness Sports,* and various other magazines.
Her articles on heart disease have earned her several awards. In
the following essay, which appeared in the May–June 2009 issue of *Career World,* Reece gives advice on how to salvage an
interview "when the worst that could happen does."

BEFORE YOU READ

■ **THINK** about an interview you had to apply for a scholarship, to be admitted to a college, to get a job, or even just to discuss a grade with a
teacher. Did the interview go well? If so, what do you think made it
successful? If the interview did not go well, what went wrong? What
do you think you could have done to improve the interview?

■ **EXAMINE** the word *salvage* in the title. You have probably heard this
word used in the context of salvaging cargo from a ship or reusable
parts from a wrecked car. But the word simply means "to save." You
may also need to know that in paragraph 1, *attire* means clothes and
that in paragraph 7, *prospective* means a possible future employer.

■ **WRITE** a journal entry in which you describe the interview you thought
about for the THINK questions above. What made it successful, or
what could have made it better?

AS YOU READ

Identify and number the four "worst" interview situations that Reece
identifies.

■ ■ ■

I f you had your way, job interviews would be a breeze. Your attire 1
would be clean and professional, you'd arrive early, and you'd have
brilliant answers for every question, and the interviewer would be so
amazed, you'd be hired on the spot.

Here's how to salvage your chances of landing the job when the worst 2
that could happen does.

The worst: You got directions off the Web and planned to arrive 15 min- 3
utes before the appointed time. Instead, you find yourself lost, sitting on the
side of the road with a flat tire, or waiting for a bus that's extremely late.

Salvage it: "Be on time." It's a job search tip that's repeated over and 4
over. So if you're going to be late, what should you do? What you
shouldn't do is show up late without calling in advance or assume that because you're tardy there's no point in showing up at all. Those things are
inexcusable, and they show a lack of courtesy or respect for the employer's
time, says Rachelle Canter, author of *Make the Right Career Move.*

"If you're running late, the best thing is to call and give advance notice 5
and make sure the employer doesn't want to reschedule," advises Canter. If
the employer does wish to reschedule, apologize and be sure you're early
next time. "If you're given permission to come in late, apologize again—
briefly!—when you get there, and then focus your efforts on making the
best impression in the interview that you can," Canter says.

The worst: When she called about the interview, the manager specifi- 6
cally said, "Bring a résumé." So you typed one up, proofed it, had others
look it over, made corrections, and then printed two clean, crisp copies the
morning of the interview. However, three blocks from the building, you
realize you left your résumé at home.

Salvage it: What many people, especially prospective bosses, respect 7
more than anything else is integrity, says Nancy Irwin, a Los Angeles-
based psychotherapist who offers counsel on career direction. "Be honest
and straightforward and simply say, 'I don't have my résumé on me. May I
e-mail it to your assistant, or would you prefer I drop it off or mail it to
you directly?'" she suggests. Don't repeatedly apologize, get into a long explanation, or state how dumb you feel. If you do, the manager may not
hire you for fear you'll crumble under even the smallest amount of on-
the-job stress. "It's not about your feeling bad or like an idiot," Irwin
says. "It's about recovering and moving on to get hired."

A strategy for safeguarding against this issue is saving your résumé on 8
a small USB flash drive. Keep the drive in your bag or on your key chain. If
you forget your résumé, the interviewer can plug the drive into his or her
computer and print a copy.

The worst: You're the total package: neat, clean, and well-groomed. 9
But minutes before entering the building, you're splashed with mud, you
spill coffee on your shirt, or your pen explodes in your pocket.

Salvage it: No time to borrow or buy a new outfit? Try to get rid of 10
the stain, or hide it with a sweater. If that doesn't work, it doesn't mean
your chances are shot. Laugh at yourself to lighten the situation, suggests
Catherine Palmiere, president of Adam Personnel and an adjunct instructor
at Grace Institute, a business training school, both in New York. "Go into
the interview just as you are, look at the recruiter, chuckle a bit, and say
'I was clean until 10 minutes ago,'" she says. Then apologize and briefly
explain what happened.

Or, use the stain to your advantage. "Simply point out the stain, laugh, 11
and say something like: 'I was not about to let *this* stop me from meeting

you and learning more about the company," Irwin says. That little tidbit of information shows the employer you really want the job and won't let minor setbacks stop you from going after and achieving your goals.

The worst: You studied the company's Web site and prepared answers 12 **for the most common job interview questions. Once in the interview, though, you draw a blank or you're asked a question you have no idea how to answer.**

Salvage it: If you don't understand the question, ask the interviewer to 13 clarify or rephrase it. Nothing still? "It's OK to ask for a minute to think about the question and then compose your thoughts," Canter says. If you're still stuck, she recommends you ask whether you can have more time to think about it and call or e-mail your answer later that day or the next. That shows the employer you won't simply give up if there's something you don't know or understand on the job. It also gives you a reason to follow up and stay on the recruiter's radar.

Although your goal is to go in and slam-dunk the interview, things do 14 happen. Employers understand that. "When recruiters have a job to fill, they're looking for reasons to hire people, not reasons to not hire them," Palmiere says. So as long as you haven't committed too big of a blunder, if you're apologetic and sincere, odds are you'll be given a chance to redeem yourself.

■ ■ ■

AFTER YOU READ

- ■ **THINK** about the method of development that Reece uses for her essay. Even though the essay focuses on interviewing, which is a process, Reece actually gives examples of four of the worst situations that could happen in an interview situation. For instruction on using brief or extended examples in your writing, see Lesson 6 of the *Interactions,* eighth edition, student website, at www.cengagebrain.com.

- ■ **THINK** also about, and list for class discussion, the four worst interview situations that Reece describes. Have you ever been in one of these situations? Explain. Which of these situations do you think is the worst of the worst?

- ■ **EXAMINE** Reece's advice for salvaging each of the bad interview situations that she describes. Which section of advice do you think would be the most effective for the situation? Why? Which do you think would be the least effective? Why?

- ■ **WRITE** a process essay in which you give instructions to a job applicant about how to complete a successful job interview. For suggestions about how to write a good process essay, see Lesson 4 of the *Interactions,* eighth edition, student website, available at www.cengagebrain.com.

The Way We Worked

■ ■ ■

TOM BROKAW

Tom Brokaw's face and voice are familiar to millions of television viewers because for over 20 years he was the anchor and managing editor of *NBC's Nightly News*. But he is also the author of several books, including *The Greatest Generation* (1998), in which he praises the generation that not only fought and won World War II but also survived the Great Depression; and *Boom! Voices of the Sixties: Personal Reflections on the '60s and Today* (2007). In this article, based on *The Greatest Generation*, Brokaw points out that one of the defining characteristics of the people of this generation was their great capacity for work.

BEFORE YOU READ

■ **THINK** about the attitude of your own generation toward work. Do you value work for itself or for what it can provide you? Are you aware of differences between your perceptions of work and those of your parents or grandparents? What are these differences?

■ **EXAMINE** the term *work ethic*, which appears in this essay. What does it mean to have a work ethic? (See page 201.) Are all work ethics the same?

■ **EXAMINE** also the words *flamboyant*, meaning "showy"; *gratification*, meaning "pleasure, satisfaction, or even indulgence"; and *mélange*, meaning "a mixture." You will encounter these words in Brokaw's essay.

■ **WRITE** in your journal a definition of your own work ethic.

AS YOU READ

Underline details that pertain to the work ethic of the generation Brokaw is describing.

■ ■ ■

When my father, Anthony "Red" Brokaw, was preparing to retire, all of us in the family were supportive and relieved. After all, he had been working for almost 50 years, since he was a husky ten-year-old driving a team of horses for a Swedish homesteader on the plains of South Dakota.

However, as his retirement date drew near, he became uncharacteristi- 2
cally emotional at the thought of not having a job to go to every day. He
was almost poetic as he described his love of plowing snow after a harsh
blizzard. "Tom," he'd say, "it's the most beautiful thing when the sun
catches the snowflakes as they come off the big blade of my plow. I would
really miss that."

So we weren't surprised when he postponed his retirement for another 3
year. When he did finally quit, though, we had another worry: What would
he do now?

Work defined him in every way. It was how he made his living and it 4
was his favorite leisure-time activity. When he wasn't plowing snow or
building parks and campsites along the Missouri River for the U.S. Army
Corps of Engineers, he was in his basement workshop restoring antique
furniture or in his garage tuning up the family car. One Father's Day
when I came home from college, he spent that Sunday changing the brake
pads on my car. For him, it was the perfect way to spend the day.

In his generation, he was not unusual. As I researched the lives of the 5
men and women who came of age in the Great Depression, went through
World War II, and built the country we know today, I was struck by how
many of them went to work in their early teenage years. They had to work
because their families needed the extra income for food, for clothing, to
meet that month's rent.

Al Neuharth, the flamboyant publisher who founded USA Today 6
when he was CEO of Gannett, worked as a butcher's assistant and soda
jerk when he was a teenager, to help his widowed mother. As a teenager,
Charles Briscoe, who later helped build the first long-range B-29 bombers
during World War II, made a deal with a local dentist: He would clean his
offices in exchange for the dental work Briscoe's mother required. When
Bob Bush returned from the war with the Congressional Medal of Honor,
he found a partner and they started a building-supply business. They both
worked seven days a week; every other week each man would work a full
24-hour cycle so they could add a day to their workload.

Dorothy Haener left her poor Michigan family to work on Ford's as- 7
sembly lines during the war. When she lost her job to returning vets, she
became a labor activist to ensure that women got equal opportunity and
pay. "I didn't go to work to find myself," she says. "I needed the
money."

When my mother, Jean, graduated from high school, she went to work 8
at the post office for a dollar a day because she couldn't afford the college
tuition of $125 a year.

Lifelong work habits for this generation were formed by more than the 9
bleak economics of the Depression, however. In the '30s and '40s, America
was a much more rural society and there were very few of the labor-saving
devices that we normally take for granted today. The daily chores of even
middle-class homes required shoveling coal into the furnace, carrying
heavy baskets of wet laundry outside to hang on the clothesline, washing
and drying dishes, canning fruits and vegetables from the large garden,

mending socks, and cutting patterns and sewing them into homemade dresses, blouses, and shirts.

Many of the farms of the '30s and '40s had no indoor plumbing. 10 Water was heated atop wood-burning stoves. Cows were milked by hand. Tractors and motorized combines were available, but they were primitive compared with the mechanized wonders of the modern farm; many a young farm boy got tough fast by lifting heavy bales of hay all day long in the hot sun.

As a result of its early experience of developing a work ethic out of 11 necessity, that generation was uniquely ready for the rigors of WWII. Young men off the farm showed up for basic training already in peak physical condition. Women who went to work on assembly lines were already used to working with their hands. Nursing was a popular way out of hard times for many of them, so when the Army suddenly needed thousands of nurses, it had a ready supply of women who knew how to cope with difficulties.

When the war ended, that same generation rushed into the task of 12 building modern America: The suburbs became sprawling landscapes of new homes, Detroit hummed with automobile production after turning out tanks and jeeps and other military equipment during the war years, and the interstate highway system laced the country together with great ribbons of pavement.

The rewards of work in the postwar years went well beyond the meager 13 returns of the '30s. Families were buying new homes, new cars, and modern appliances, as well as saving for their children's college education. It was an unheard of experience for many of the WWII generation—to actually have more than they needed.

Still, they remembered the bad old days, and there was always an un- 14 derlying anxiety that the Depression could return at any moment. In the small towns of South Dakota where I grew up, my parents and their friends managed their new prosperity very carefully.

In the '50s, before credit cards, they paid cash for everything. They 15 made sure there was always a direct connection between what they earned and what they spent.

If we were going on a family trip to, say, Minneapolis, my father 16 would go to the bank and get one $100 bill to mix in with the fives, tens, and 20s in his wallet.

He told us it was his insurance against running short. When we asked, 17 he would let me and my brothers have a peek at it, then he'd tuck it away again. I don't think he ever actually spent one of those $100 bills, but he did have a certain pride in knowing that he'd reached a stage where he could have $100 all in one banknote.

Sometimes that conditioning from the dark days of the '30s would 18 seem a little excessive to those of us who were their offspring. The children of the WWII generation, by and large, have never known really hard times. The American economy has been expanding since the war ended and that, in turn, has given birth to a long run of instant gratification in American society.

Buy now, worry later. Don't like your job? Quit and get another one. 19 Tired of working so hard? Take off for three months to "find yourself."

It is an approach to life that those of the WWII generation, now in 20 their 70s and 80s, cannot fathom. How many have visited their kids' homes, walked through the yard, garage, and living quarters, and mentally added up all the luxuries and what they must have cost? How many have said in a bewildered tone, "He had a good job—but he quit because he had to work too many Saturdays"?

Every generation is a reflection of the times it has lived through. Mod- 21 ern America is a mélange of experiences, from the extremes of deprivation to the comforts of material wealth. However, as those of the WWII generation pass on and the personal memories of the Depression fade away, we will lose a tempering influence on our common experience of work and its rewards.

■ ■ ■

AFTER YOU READ

■ **THINK** about Brokaw's statement about his father: "Work defined him in every way." Do you know someone who is defined by work? What does it mean to be defined by work? Do you think it is desirable to define yourself in terms of the work you do? Why or why not?

■ **EXAMINE** the following sentence from the essay:

As a result of its early experience of developing a work ethic out of necessity, that generation was uniquely ready for the rigors of WWII.

In this statement, Brokaw clearly suggests that a strong work ethic is an important attribute for citizens. Do you agree with this statement? Why or why not? This statement also suggests that Brokaw idealizes the World War II generation, believing it to be superior to other generations. Do you think that entire generations can be characterized in this way? Is it accurate to generalize about generations and to attribute specific characteristics to them? Why or why not?

■ **WRITE** an essay in which you describe or define your own generation's work ethic, comparing it to and contrasting it with that of an earlier generation—perhaps that of your parents or grandparents.

The Future of Work

■ ■ ■

ROBERT B. REICH

Robert Reich, a political economist, is the Maurice B. Hexter Professor at Brandeis University. He has also served three national administrations in various capacities, most recently as secretary of labor in President Bill Clinton's administration. Reich's articles have appeared in *The New Yorker, Atlantic Monthly, Harper's, The New York Times,* and *The Wall Street Journal.* He has also published more than a dozen books, including *The Future of Success* (2000); *Reason: Why the Liberals Will Win the Battle for America* (2005); and *Aftershock: The Next Economy and America's Future* (2010). Whereas the previous essay by Tom Brokaw focuses on the work ethic of a past generation, this essay, which was published in *Harper's* magazine, focuses on the future, predicting which careers and occupations will expand in the future and suggesting how to prepare for them.

BEFORE YOU READ

■ **THINK** about your plans for the future. Have you decided on a career? If so, how did you reach that decision? What do you think is the best way to prepare for future success?

■ **EXAMINE** Reich's tone in the first paragraph. Notice his use of humor and his directness (including the use of *you* when he addresses his readers). Is his tone what you would expect of an economist and professor? What is your response to his informal, direct tone? Is it appropriate for this essay? Is it effective?

■ **EXAMINE** also the following words and their definitions from Reich's essay:

1. *extrapolation* (paragraph 6): to estimate from known values or information
2. *lucrative:* (paragraph 6): profitable
3. *attrition:* (paragraph 8): gradual reduction
4. *cumulative* (paragraph 14): enlarging or increasing by successive addition

■ **WRITE** a journal entry in which you predict which careers or occupations Reich will select as the most promising ones for the future.

AS YOU READ

Identify Reich's predictions about the nature of work in the future and indicate those you think are accurate. Also underline Reich's definitions of *complex services* and *person-to-person services*.

■   ■   ■

I t's easy to predict what jobs you *shouldn't* prepare for. Thanks to the   1
wonders of fluoride, America, in the future, will need fewer dentists.
Nor is there much of a future in farming. The federal government
probably won't provide long-term employment unless you aspire to work
in the Pentagon or the Veterans Administration.... The real wages of university professors have been declining for some time, the hours are bad,
and all you get are complaints.

Moreover, as the American economy merges with the rest of the   2
world's, anyone doing relatively unskilled work that could be done more
cheaply elsewhere is unlikely to prosper for long. Imports and exports
now constitute 26 percent of our gross national product (up from 9 percent
in 1950), and barring a new round of protectionism, the portion will move
steadily upward. Meanwhile, ten thousand people are added to the world's
population every hour, most of whom, eventually, will happily work for a
small fraction of today's average American wage.

This is good news for most of you, because it means that you'll be able   3
to buy all sorts of things far more cheaply than you could if they were
made here (provided, of course, that what your generation does instead
produces even more value). The resulting benefits from trade will help off-
set the drain on your income resulting from paying the interest on the nation's foreign debt and financing the retirement of aging baby boomers like
me. The bad news, at least for some of you, is that most of America's traditional, routinized manufacturing jobs will disappear. So will routinized
service jobs that can be done from remote locations, like keypunching of
data transmitted by satellite. Instead, you will be engaged in one of two
broad categories of work: either complex services, some of which will be
sold to the rest of the world to pay for whatever Americans want to buy
from the rest of the world, or person-to-person services, which foreigners
can't provide for us because (apart from new immigrants and illegal aliens)
they aren't here to provide them.

Complex services involve the manipulation of data and abstract symbols.   4
Included in this category are insurance, engineering, law, finance,
computer programming, and advertising. Such activities now account for
almost 25 percent of our GNP, up from 13 percent in 1950. They already
have surpassed manufacturing (down to about 20 percent of GNP). Even
within the manufacturing sector, executive, managerial, and engineering
positions are increasing at a rate almost three times that of total

manufacturing employment. Most of these jobs, too, involve manipulating symbols.

Such endeavors will constitute America's major contribution to the rest   5
of the world in the decades ahead. You and your classmates will be exporting engineering designs, financial services, advertising and communications advice, statistical analyses, musical scores and film scripts, and other creative and problem-solving products. How many of you undertake these sorts of jobs, and how well you do at them, will determine what goods and services America can summon from the rest of the world in return, and thus—to some extent—your generation's standard of living.

Work involving securities and corporate law has been claiming one-   6
quarter of all new private sector jobs in New York City and more than a third of all the new office space in that industrious town. Other major cities are not too far behind. A simple extrapolation of the present trend suggests that by 2020 one out of every three American college graduates will be an investment banker or a lawyer. Of course, this is unlikely. Long before that milestone could be achieved, the nation's economy will have dried up like a raisin, as financiers and lawyers squeeze out every ounce of creative, productive juice. Thus my advice: Even if you could bear spending your life in such meaningless but lucrative work, at least consider the fate of the nation before deciding to do so.

Person-to-person services will claim everyone else. Many of these jobs will   7
not require much skill, as is true of their forerunners today. Among the fastest growing in recent years: custodians and security guards, restaurant and retail workers, day-care providers. Secretaries and clerical workers will be as numerous as now, but they'll spend more of their time behind and around electronic machines (imported from Asia) and have fancier titles, such as "paratechnical assistant" and "executive paralegal operations manager."

Teachers will be needed (we'll be losing more than a third of our entire   8
corps of elementary and high-school teachers through attrition over the next seven years), but don't expect their real pay to rise very much. Years of public breast-beating about the quality of American education notwithstanding, the average teacher today earns ... only 3.4 percent more, in constant dollars, than he or she earned fifteen years ago.

Count on many jobs catering to Americans at play—hotel workers, re-   9
creation directors, television and film technicians, aerobics instructors (or whatever their twenty-first century equivalents will call themselves). But note that Americans will have less leisure time to enjoy these pursuits. The average American's free time has been shrinking for more than fifteen years, as women move into the work force (and so spend more of their free time doing household chores) and as all wage earners are forced to work harder just to maintain their standard of living. Expect the trend to continue.

The most interesting and important person-to-person jobs will be in   10
what is now unpretentiously dubbed "sales." Decades from now most

salespeople won't be just filling orders. Salespeople will be helping customers define their needs, then working with design and production engineers to customize products and services in order to address those needs. This is because standardized (you can have it in any color as long as it's black) products will be long gone. Flexible manufacturing and the new information technologies will allow a more tailored fit—whether it's a car, machine tool, insurance policy, or even a college education. Those of you who will be dealing directly with customers will thus play a pivotal role in the innovation process, and your wages and prestige will rise accordingly.

But the largest number of personal-service jobs will involve health care, 11 which already consumes ... [a large] percent of our GNP, and that portion is rising. Because every new medical technology with the potential to extend life is infinitely valuable to those whose lives might be extended—even for a few months or weeks—society is paying huge sums to stave off death. By the second decade of the next century, when my generation of baby boomers will have begun to decay, the bill will be much higher. Millions of corroding bodies will need doctors, nurses, nursing-home operators, hospital administrators, technicians who operate and maintain all the fancy machines that will measure and temporarily halt the deterioration, hospice directors, home-care specialists, directors of outpatient clinics, and euthanasia specialists, among many others.

Most of these jobs won't pay very much because they don't require 12 much skill. Right now the fastest growing job categories in the health sector are nurse's aides, orderlies, and attendants, which compose about 40 percent of the healthcare work force. The majority are women; a large percentage are minorities. But even doctors' real earnings show signs of slipping. As malpractice insurance rates skyrocket, many doctors go on salary in investor-owned hospitals, and their duties are gradually taken over by physician "extenders" such as nurse practitioners and midwives.

What's the best preparation for one of these careers? 13

Advice here is simple: You won't be embarking on a career, at least as 14 we currently define the term, because few of the activities I've mentioned will proceed along well-defined paths to progressively higher levels of responsibility. As the economy evolves toward services tailored to the particular needs of clients and customers, hands-on experience will count for more than formal rank. As technologies and markets rapidly evolve, moreover, the best preparation will be through cumulative learning on the job rather than formal training completed years before.

This means that academic degrees and professional credentials will 15 count for less; on-the-job training, for more. American students have it backwards. The courses to which you now gravitate—finance, law, accounting, management, and other practical arts—may be helpful to understand how a particular job is *now* done (or, more accurately, how your instructors did it years ago when they held such jobs or studied the people who held them), but irrelevant to how such a job *will* be done. The intellectual equipment needed for the job of the future is an ability to define problems, quickly assimilate relevant data, conceptualize and reorganize the information, make deductive and inductive leaps with it, ask hard questions about it, discuss findings with colleagues, work collaboratively to find solutions, and then convince others. And *these* sorts of skills can't be learned in career-training courses. To the extent they can be found in universities at all, they're more likely to be found in subjects such as history, literature, philosophy, and anthropology—in which students can witness how others have grappled for centuries with the challenge of living good and productive lives. Tolstoy and Thucydides are far more relevant to the management jobs of the future, for example, than are Hersey and Blanchard (*Management of Organizational Behavior,* Prentice-Hall, 5th edition, 1988).

■ ■ ■

AFTER YOU READ

- ■ **THINK** about the advice Reich gives his readers (generally young people about to launch a career). Because he wrote this article a few years ago, you should be able to judge whether Reich's predictions seem to be on target. Which of his predictions have thus far proved accurate? Are there some that have not proved accurate?

- ■ **EXAMINE** Reich's prediction that "hands-on experience will count for more than formal rank" in the future and that "on-the-job training" will count for more than "academic degrees and professional credentials." Do you agree with this viewpoint? Why or why not? Do you think Reich's intention is to discourage young people from going to college? Why or why not?

- ■ **EXAMINE** also the names Tolstoy and Thucydides. Tolstoy was a great nineteenth-century Russian novelist, and Thucydides was a fifth-century Greek historian.

- ■ **WRITE** an essay in which you make your own predictions about "the future of work."

- ■ Or **WRITE** an essay in which you respond to one of Reich's predictions by arguing that it is either accurate or inaccurate. (See "Responding to a Text" on pages 244–247).

UNIT FOUR
■ ■ ■
Critical Thinking, Reading, and Writing

■ RESPONDING TO A TEXT

Throughout your college career, you will frequently be asked to respond to what you read either in a journal entry or in a more formal assignment. Often this type of assignment is called a *response essay*. Whether you are responding to an essay, an article, or even a book, the process is much the same. Although a response essay usually begins with a brief summary, it is not just a summary. Nor is it the same as a review or report, which focuses on the text being reviewed and on the audience for whom it was written. A response essay, in contrast, focuses on you and your response, or reaction, to what you have read. What you have read is an important source in a response essay, but it functions primarily as a springboard for your own ideas.

BEFORE YOU WRITE

Obviously, the first step in writing a response to something you have read is to read the text itself carefully, annotating it as you read. In addition to identifying main ideas, words you don't know, questions you have, and so on, your annotations should also focus on identifying passages or features of the text that you find especially interesting in some way. Be sure to mark anything with which you especially agree or disagree, anything you question, anything you would like to explore further, and anything that prompts a particular reaction or response from you.

For example, the essay "What You Do Is What You Are" by Nickie McWhirter in Unit Four argues that "Americans ... tend to define and judge everybody in terms of the work they do, especially work performed for pay." As you read this essay, you might decide that the author's argument is invalid because in your hometown people are defined by the family or church to which they belong. Or, if you are an international student, you may realize that in your culture people are not defined by the work they do but on some other basis. Or perhaps you have had some experience yourself that validates or contradicts the author's argument. In general, keep the following guidelines in mind as you read:

1. Look for areas of agreement or disagreement.
2. Mark any passage that prompts a question or provokes a response.
3. Be alert for ideas that are related to your own experience.

After you finish reading and annotating the text but before you begin to write your response, review your annotations and then make a list of possible topics for your response paper. In addition, you may want to write a journal entry in which you respond to the text you have just read. Often, once you begin to write, ideas will come to you that did not occur to you before. Then reread your journal entry to see if it includes possible topics for your response essay. What you need is a topic that is introduced or suggested by the author of the text (not necessarily the main argument) and with which you have some personal experience.

Example
Below is a response essay based on McWhirter's essay. Notice that the writer summarizes McWhirter's essay first and then responds to it by establishing her own thesis.

The McDonald Image

When I was a junior in high school, I went to work at the local   1
McDonald's for a year. The money was good and the hours convenient, so I couldn't figure out why I hated that job so much. However, when I read Nickie McWhirter's essay "What You Do Is What You Are," it was suddenly clear to me. McWhirter argues that Americans tend to define one another by what they do—their job or profession. She also questions whether we should judge people in this way because America is supposedly a "class-less society." However, in my case, it wasn't that other people defined me in a certain way because of my job at McDonald's but that I defined myself as a fast-food employee because I worked there. I was, in fact, stereotyping myself. **This realization forced me to examine why being associated with McDonald's had such negative connotations for me.**

The other people I worked with at McDonald's were from a variety of   2
economic and ethnic backgrounds. There was Greg, a high school senior who was working to make money for college. He wanted to go to Auburn University to study animal science. And Amy, whose father had been killed in an automobile accident, was working there to help out with expenses at home. Carlos, in contrast, was attending a local community college and hoped to move up McDonald's corporate ladder to become a manager some day. Habib was the most recent employee. A Middle Eastern immigrant, he spoke little English but was able to work in the kitchen and seemed pleased to be not only working but also learning English. And, finally, our manager, Mrs. Johnson, had worked for several fast-food places in the past and was pleased to have a position at last that enabled her to support her four small children.

Unlike me, these people did not complain about the irregular hours,   3
the rude customers, or the pervasive odor of fried food. They were grateful to have jobs and optimistic about their futures. I, on the other hand, could not get beyond my feeling that I was too good to dish up French fries and flip hamburgers. I was working at McDonald's because I had lost my previous job and could find nothing better. And every day when I came to work I felt as if I were lowering myself in some way.

Gradually, however, as I began to know Mrs. Johnson, Habib, Carlos,   4
Greg, and Amy better, I realized that they all had aspirations and hopes just as I did but were grateful to have a decent job that enabled them to

work toward their dreams for the future. Little by little, I began to enjoy bantering with our regular customers and to feel a sense of belonging
with the other members of my crew. I never gave up my desire for a better
job and never stopped hating the odor of fried food, but I did learn to
respect my fellow employees and to realize that honest labor is always
respectable.

————————

The writer of the essay above refers briefly to the thesis of the essay by
Nickie McWhirter in the first paragraph but quickly moves on to her own
experiences and ideas. Although she acknowledges that the McWhirter essay provided her with the idea for her own essay, she clearly indicates in
this introduction that the essay she is writing will focus on her own experiences. In the second paragraph, she introduces her fellow workers and describes each briefly. In the third paragraph, she contrasts herself to those
with whom she worked. And in the final paragraph, she concludes by explaining what she learned from this experience and by briefly describing
the change that took place in her own attitude.

Assignments

Read the following assignments, and select the one to which you want to
respond:

1. Read the essay by Brian Braaksma, which focuses on the author's reac-
    tion to his chores; then respond to it in an essay of your own.

2. Select a reading selection from Unit Four that is related to some work
    experience you have had and write a response to it.

3. Read "The Way We Worked" by Tom Brokaw or "Big Russ and Me"
    by Tim Russert and write a response that focuses on your experience
    with the work ethic of someone from an earlier generation.

AS YOU WRITE

After you have chosen and read the reading selection to which you want to
respond and determined the focus for your response, you are ready to begin writing. As you write, keep in mind the guidelines below:

- Summarize briefly the text to which you are responding. Be sure to identify the author and title of the source material. (See "Summarizing a
  Text," pages 186–188 of Unit Three.)

- Clearly indicate your own topic and thesis. (See "Writing a Personal
  Essay," pages 128–133 of Unit Two.)

- Develop your own thesis, using your own experiences, ideas, and
  knowledge. You may refer to the text to which you are responding
  throughout your response, or you may want to limit these references to
  the introduction and conclusion. Keep in mind that your own ideas
  should be the focus of your response.

AFTER YOU WRITE

In addition to receiving comments on your draft from your instructor, you may want to share your rough draft with one or more of your classmates to get further suggestions. As you prepare to revise your response, keep in mind the following guidelines:

- Reread the summary you have included to be sure it accurately reflects the author's main idea(s) and is not too long.

- Reread your entire essay, focusing on whether your own arguments, experiences, and ideas dominate (as they should).

- Revise for readability (are your sentences clear and easy to read?) and development (is your own thesis well developed and adequately supported?).

Finally, edit and proofread your essay before making a final copy to submit to your instructor.

■ EXPLORING IDEAS TOGETHER

1. Several essays, especially the ones by Rose and Crawford, discuss the role of the mind in manual labor. With a group of your classmates, answer the question "How mental is physical labor?" Be sure to discuss particular types of physical labor, such as carpentry, farming, hairdressing, and so on.

2. With a group of your classmates, discuss the role of gender in today's workplace. Do you think gender is still a factor in hiring and promotion decisions? Why or why not? Do you think it is less of a factor than it once was? Why or why not? Consider the essays by Rose, Smith, and Meier in your discussion.

3. McWhirter argues in her essay "What You Do Is What You Are" that Americans tend to be defined by their jobs or careers. Which of the other essays in this unit support her argument? Do you think her argument is more or less valid today than it was in the past? Explain.

4. Discuss the current employment situation. Is it getting better or worse? Are people taking temporary work or going without jobs? Or are more full-time jobs becoming available? Why do you think the employment situation is moving in the direction that it is going?

5. Several authors of readings in this unit write about hard work—times when they or someone they knew worked long hours doing something that required significant physical labor. Often this type of hard work is associated with earlier generations rather than present ones. With a group of your classmates, discuss whether people of your generation work as hard as people did in the past. Consider also whether work that does not require physical labor can be defined as "hard work," and compare the effects of physical and mental labor on people. You may want to refer to the reading selections by Rose, Braaksma, Russert, Colon, and/or Brokaw.

■ EXPLORING THE INTERNET

You can find Internet links for the following exercises at the *Interactions*, eighth edition, student website, at www.cengagebrain.com:

1. Using a search engine such as Google (or the link on the Related Websites section of the student website), look up the current *Occupational Outlook Handbook* from the Bureau of Labor Statistics. This site includes helpful links for the following topics: (1) Where to Learn about Job Openings, (2) Job Search Methods, (3) Applying for a Job, (4) Job Interview Tips, and (5) Evaluating a Job Offer. Work in small groups so that some students look up and study each of these links. Share the information you gain with the rest of the class.

2. Look up the page for "Hottest Careers for College Graduates" on the College Board website, available as a link on the "Related Websites" section of the *Interactions* student site. What careers have the most job openings for graduates with two-year degrees? What occupations have the most openings for college graduates with bachelor's degrees? What other helpful information can you find on the link "Majors & Careers Central"?

3. Using the sites identified in Items 1 and 2 of this section, "Exploring the Internet," and a search engine of your choice (for example, Google or Yahoo), research a career in which you are interested. Try to find out what preparation, experience, and skills are required; what types of positions are available and how much competition exists for these positions; what the usual salary range is; and what the working conditions are. The purpose of your research should be to form a realistic idea of the pros and cons of this career in terms of your own interests, abilities, and so on. Take notes on your research or print out copies of the sources you find especially helpful. Be sure to identify each source and the date you accessed it.

■ WRITING ESSAYS

1. Using the information you gathered about a career you are considering (see item 3 under "Exploring the Internet"), write an essay in which you share the information you have collected with other college students who are interested in the same career. In addition to the information you gathered from your Internet research, you might interview someone who is working in that field.

2. Write an essay in which you explore the effect(s) of some aspect of work and/or a career on a particular person's life—your own or someone else's (whom you might interview). Consider such issues as the effects of working too hard or too much, of not being able to find a job, or of facing the stereotypical attitudes that some people have toward certain professions. (See Lesson 5 on the *Interactions*, eighth edition,

student website, at www.cengagebrain.com, for information about writing cause and effect essays.)

3. Write an essay in which you discuss the relationship between mental and physical work. You might argue, as Rose does, that a good mental capacity is necessary for physical work, especially for skilled labor (see pages 372–378 for guidelines for "Writing a Persuasive Essay"). Or you might compare and contrast two related but different jobs, showing that one is more mental and one is more physical. (See Lesson 7 on the *Interactions*, eighth edition, student website for help with writing comparison and contrast essays.)

4. In response to one of the essays in this unit, write an essay in which you argue that an individual's work does or does not define that person in our society. (See "Responding to a Text" on pages 244–247 at the end of this unit.)

5. Write an essay in which you describe how the roles of men and women in the work force have changed in recent years. The reading selections by Smith and Meier should be helpful to you.

6. The type of work that Americans do has changed dramatically in the last 50 years. Focusing on one type of work or career, write an essay in which you describe the changes that have occurred and identify the factors responsible for these changes. You may want to refer to one or more of the essays by Smith, Meier, Brokaw, and Reich.

7. Write an essay in which you compare and contrast the problems your generation faces in selecting and establishing careers with those faced by earlier generations. You may want to interview someone from an earlier generation, but you will also find information and ideas on this topic in the reading selections by Russert, Colon, and Brokaw.

A DIVERSE SOCIETY

Mark Wilson/ Reportage /Getty Images

Observe the people in the photograph above. How many different races, ethnicities, ages, genders, and so forth can you see? What does the presence of American flags suggest about the relationships of this diverse group of people?

■ ■ ■

P erhaps more than any nation on earth—today or at any time in history—the United States is known for its diversity. In this country, people from all over the world live and work together in relative harmony and are considered equal in the sight of the law. Never before has a nation accepted such a wide variety of people and given those people an *opportunity to become citizens with equal rights and privileges. And never before has a nation made a strength and virtue of diversity. The United States is, in one sense, a great experiment in multiculturalism. And most people today view the experiment as a success. Our nation is known around the world for successfully melding a rich variety of cultures into a single society. For this, we can all be proud.*

But the struggle to live together in peace and harmony has not been easy. If we are not watchful, our diverse society can become a divisive society, with each group fighting for its own causes. One of the most effective remedies for divisiveness is learning more about one another. This unit focuses on and celebrates the diversity that has made us unique. But it also recognizes that prejudice and discrimination have been, and continue to be, serious threats to the ideals of diversity and equality. Some selections highlight different ethnic groups within our society, while others discuss explicitly some of the problems and solutions associated with a diverse society.

Interactions with specific individuals—even your own family and friends—can be complicated and difficult, but your relationship with society—with all the diverse people who exist in this country—is even more complex. Because our society is made up not only of different individuals but also of individuals from many different backgrounds, the task becomes enormous. As a member of such a diverse society, you are called upon to make decisions about people who are very different from you; who live in different parts of the country; who have different religious and ethnic backgrounds; who are of a different gender, age, ability, or sexual orientation; and who have different social and economic conditions. Although such diversity is clearly a strength, giving the American culture a special texture and energy, it can also be a challenge.

Before you begin this unit, think about the rights and privileges of citizenship in this country and ask yourself these questions:

- *Can a society such as ours endure if some groups do not have a voice?*
- *Which groups in our society enjoy the greatest privileges?*
- *What rights should every member of a society have?*
- *What tensions are created by the fact that some segments of society enjoy a much better lifestyle than do others?*
- *Can problems be solved without understanding the people who have these problems?*
- *How can our society protect its citizenry and yet continue the tradition of opening our doors to newcomers?*
- *How will increasing populations of different ethnic groups affect our future society?*
- *Is our society more or less integrated than it once was?*

A Passion for Diversity

■ ■ ■

ANN POMEROY

In the following essay from the March 2008 issue of *HR Magazine,* senior writer Ann Pomeroy profiles the life of Deborah Dagit, the chief diversity officer at Merck and Company. In her essay, Pomeroy not only gives insight into Dagit's challenges as a disabled women but also reveals how Dagit has used her own "passion for diversity" to promote the rights of the disabled and other diverse groups worldwide.

BEFORE YOU READ

■ **THINK** about the concept of diversity. How does diversity—different ages, genders, races, ethnicities, abilities, and sexual orientations—create challenges for our society? How does it contribute to the richness of our society?

■ **EXAMINE** the title "A Passion for Diversity." How do you think someone would show a passion for diversity? Do you have such a passion? Why or why not?

■ **WRITE** a journal entry about how someone might show a "passion for diversity."

AS YOU READ

Underline phrases and sentences that show Dagit's support of diversity.

■ ■ ■

D eborah Dagit, chief diversity officer at Merck & Co's Whitehouse   1
Station, N.J., headquarters, stands just 4 feet tall, but she has a
large presence in the diversity community. Dagit played a key
role in passing the Americans with Disabilities Act in 1990, working with
then-Rep. Norman Mineta, a Democrat from California, to prevent efforts
to weaken this important legislation. She also co-founded the Conference
Board's first Workforce Council on Diversity in 1993 and works regularly
with other thought leaders in the field.

Dagit's passion for diversity "permeates her life," says Jeanne Stahl, a   2
Merck executive on loan from the manufacturing division to work on

global diversity with Dagit. "Deb is such a visionary. She [has the] ability to pull people into that future place."

Stahl co-chairs the pilot women's group Dagit launched in May 2007. As vice president for global diversity innovations during the startup phase, Stahl works closely with the diversity head on the first of 10 "global constituency teams" made up of senior leaders representing Merck business units and world markets. The remaining teams, to launch in early 2008, are Asians; blacks; Latinos; men; indigenous peoples; lesbian, gay, bisexual and transgendered; generational; interfaith; and differently able.   3

Members of the women's team want to identify effective ways to develop local female leaders in each country and market to diverse female populations. The other teams will do the same for their segments of the global marketplace.   4

Stahl says they have been encouraged to find that women around the world share more similarities than differences....   5

FROM THOUGHT TO DIVERSITY LEADER

Dagit originally planned to be a psycho-therapist. After earning a Bachelor of Science degree in psychology and then completing the coursework for a master's degree in clinical psychology, she began working with patients dealing with family issues such as marriage and childbirth.   6

That's when she changed course.   7

"At age 24, I was working on issues I had not yet experienced in my own life," says Dagit. Deciding that she "needed some life experience," Dagit shifted her career sights to an area she knew plenty about through personal experience—handling disabilities.   8

Dagit was born with osteogenesis imperfecta, or brittle bone disease, a condition that can cause short stature and a high susceptibility to broken bones. During her 48 years, she has broken 60 bones and undergone 25 operations—"I have a lot of hardware in my legs"—but it's clear that she has never allowed the disease to hold her back.   9

In 1987, she founded and managed Bridge-to-Jobs, a job placement organization, and personally placed 400 people with disabilities during a four-year period.   10

Insisting that people with disabilities must be included in the diversity arena along with people of differing races, ages, ethnicities, genders and sexual orientations, Dagit quickly became a leader in the field.   11

After holding diversity management positions at Silicon Valley companies Sun Microsystems Inc. and Silicon Graphics, Dagit was invited to become Merck's first chief diversity officer in 2001.   12

In addition to implementing the company's affirmative action and employee relations programs, including dotted-line responsibility for labor relations, Dagit has integrated diversity into the culture of the organization worldwide. She has also demonstrated by example that disability accommodations are no different from flexible work arrangements for single   13 mothers, long-distance commuters or members of any other group with individual needs.

Dagit sometimes works from home. In the office, her chair has been 14 modified to fit her size and she carries a cane. "Merck [executives have] not been concerned about where I work, just about the outcome," she says. "What I like is that they don't expect something less of me. I'm seen as a positive representative for the company who is held to the same standards as other Merck employees."

DISABILITY: SPECIAL GIFT, CHALLENGE

"As a person with a visible disability, I have a special gift and a unique 15 challenge," says Dagit. Because of "my packaging, and because there are not many people with disabilities who do the work I do," Dagit says she has been given opportunities she might otherwise not have had. "Having a disability is a tool in my toolbox," she explains.

Dagit says her work is "difficult and complex, but it's also interesting 16 and fun." As she looks for visible signs of progress, "I see the destination, not the finish line."

Increasing the representation of others like her in diversity organiza- 17 tions remains a daily challenge. Although the U.S. Census Bureau reports that 51.2 million Americans have some level of disability, Dagit says she rarely sees people with visible disabilities when she goes to diversity conferences.

"There is no gathering of my tribe," she laments. And so, Dagit chal- 18 lenges members of every minority group to "ask themselves if their tribe includes people with disabilities."

As Stahl says, "Deb is always thinking about diversity. It's her life's 19 work."

AFTER YOU READ

- **THINK** about Dagit's personal challenges as a disabled person. What is her disability? In your opinion, what are her biggest challenges? How has she met these challenges? Do you think you would have been able to accomplish what she has if you had "broken 60 bones and undergone 25 operations" (paragraph 9)? Explain.

- **EXAMINE** paragraph 3. How many different groups has Dagit identified for encouraging global diversity? What are these groups? Can you think of other groups that are part of our society's diversity? Which group(s) do you think are in most need of recognition and support? Why do you think that Dagit started with gender—with the role of women? And what are the implications of her discovery that "women around the world share more similarities than differences" (paragraph 5)?

- **EXAMINE** also paragraphs 13–15. How has Dagit been able to work at Merck without accommodations that are different from those for other workers? How does she feel about being held to "the same standards as other Merck employees"? How does having a disability actually help her in her work?

■ **WRITE** an essay in which you argue for more recognition and job opportunities for the disabled (or for another group identified by Pomeroy in paragraphs 3 and 11). You may want to read the explanation on "Writing a Persuasive Essay" on pp. 372–378 of Unit Six.

Getting to Know about You and Me

■ ■ ■

CHANA SCHOENBERGER

Currently Chana Schoenberger is a Tokyo-based freelance foreign correspondent. Between 1999 and 2009 she was on the staff of *Forbes* magazine, where she rose to become associate editor. With a B.A. from Harvard and a master's in journalism from Columbia University, she has published in *The Washington Post, The New York Times,* and *The Wall Street Journal* and has appeared on the *Forbes on Fox* news show. Written when she was a high school student, the following essay, which first appeared in *Newsweek,* tells of her experience during a summer scholarship program when she encountered a group of people who knew nothing about Judaism or her Jewish background. In this essay, Schoenberger describes how it feels to be the victim of stereotyping—to be defined on the basis of, in this case, religion.

BEFORE YOU READ

- ■ THINK about a time when you felt stereotyped, when someone judged you on the basis of your race, religion, class, gender, ethnic background, or appearance. How did this experience make you feel?

- ■ EXAMINE the first paragraph of this essay, which serves as the introduction. How does Schoenberger introduce her subject? On the basis of this introduction, do you want to read the essay? From just reading this first paragraph, do you think you know what the author is going to focus on in the essay and what her thesis will be? What focus and main point do you expect?

- ■ EXAMINE also the word *commemorates* in the first paragraph of the essay. To commemorate is to ceremonially honor the memory of an event or person, just as Passover "commemorates the [Jewish] Exodus from Egypt."

- ■ WRITE a journal entry in which you describe a time when you felt you were stereotyped—judged as a member of a group rather than as an individual. The group can be religious or political, social or economic, racial or ethnic, or a group such as smokers, commuters, pickup truck owners, hunters, athletes, or beauty contestants.

AS YOU READ

Discover what scared Schoenberger most about her experience and what she believes caused the problems she faced. Underline and indicate in the margin those sentences or paragraphs that focus on the cause (C) of her problems as well as on the stereotyping that resulted—the effects (E).

■   ■   ■

A s a religious holiday approaches, students at my high school who will be celebrating the holiday prepare a presentation on it for an assembly. The Diversity Committee, which sponsors the assemblies to increase religious awareness, asked me last spring if I would help with the presentation on Passover, the Jewish holiday that commemorates the Exodus from Egypt. I was too busy with other things, and I never got around to helping. I didn't realize then how important those presentations really are, or I definitely would have done something.   1

This summer I was one of 20 teens who spent five weeks at the University of Wisconsin at Superior studying acid rain with a National Science Foundation Young Scholars program. With such a small group in such a small town, we soon became close friends and had a good deal of fun together. We learned about the science of acid rain, went on field trips, found the best and cheapest restaurants in Superior and ate in them frequently to escape the lousy cafeteria food. We were a happy, bonded group.   2

Represented among us were eight religions: Jewish, Roman Catholic, Muslim, Hindu, Methodist, Mormon, Jehovah's Witness and Lutheran. It was amazing, given the variety of backgrounds, to see the ignorance of some of the smartest young scholars on the subject of other religions.   3

On the first day, one girl mentioned that she had nine brothers and sisters. "Oh, are you Mormon?" asked another girl, who I knew was a Mormon herself. The first girl, shocked, replied, "No, I dress normal!" She thought Mormon was the same as Mennonite, and the only thing she knew about either religion was that Mennonites don't, in her opinion, "dress normal."   4

My friends, ever curious about Judaism, asked me about everything from our basic theology to food preferences. "How come, if Jesus was a Jew, Jews aren't Christian?" my Catholic roommate asked me in all seriousness. Brought up in a small Wisconsin town, she had never met a Jew before, nor had she met people from most of the other "strange" religions (anything but Catholic or mainstream Protestant). Many of the other kids were the same way.   5

"Do you all still practice animal sacrifices?" a girl from a small town in Minnesota asked me once. I said no, laughed, and pointed out that this was the 20th century, but she had been absolutely serious. The only Jews she knew were the ones from the Bible.   6

Nobody was deliberately rude or anti-Semitic, but I got the feeling that 7
I was representing the entire Jewish people through my actions. I realized
that many of my friends would go back to their small towns thinking that
all Jews liked Dairy Queen Blizzards and grilled cheese sandwiches. After
all, that was true of all the Jews they knew (in most cases, me and the only
other Jewish young scholar, period).

The most awful thing for me, however, was not the benign ignorance 8
of my friends. Our biology professor had taken us on a field trip to the
EPA field site where he worked, and he was telling us about the project
he was working on. He said that they had to make sure the EPA got its
money's worth from the study—he "wouldn't want them to get Jewed."

I was astounded. The professor had a doctorate, various other degrees 9
and seemed to be a very intelligent man. He apparently had no idea that he
had just made an anti-Semitic remark. The other Jewish girl in the group
and I debated whether or not to say something to him about it, and
although we agreed we would, neither of us ever did. Personally, it made
me feel uncomfortable. For a high-school student to tell a professor who
taught her class that he was a bigot seemed out of place to me, even if he
was one.

What scares me about that experience, in fact about my whole visit to 10
Wisconsin, was that I never met a really vicious anti-Semite or a malig-
nantly prejudiced person. Many of the people I met had been brought up
to think that Jews (or Mormons or any other religion that's not mainstream Christian) were different and that difference was not good.

Difference, in America, is supposed to be good. We are expected—at 11
least, I always thought we were expected—to respect each other's traditions. Respect requires some knowledge about people's backgrounds. Singing Christmas carols as a kid in school did not make me Christian, but it
taught me to appreciate beautiful music and someone else's holiday. It's
not necessary or desirable for all ethnic groups in America to assimilate
into one traditionless mass. Rather, we all need to learn about other cultures so that we can understand one another and not feel threatened by
others.

In the little multicultural universe that I live in, it's safe not to worry 12
about explaining the story of Passover because if people don't hear it from
me, they'll hear it some other way. Now I realize that's not true
everywhere.

Ignorance was the problem I faced this summer. By itself, ignorance is 13
not always a problem, but it leads to misunderstandings, prejudice and
hatred. Many of today's problems involve hatred. If there weren't so
much ignorance about other people's backgrounds, would people still
hate each other as badly as they do now? Maybe so, but at least that
hatred would be based on facts and not flawed beliefs.

I'm now back at school, and I plan to apply for the Diversity Commit- 14
tee. I'm going to get up and tell the whole school about my religion and the
tradition I'm proud of. I see now how important it is to celebrate your heritage and to educate others about it. I can no longer take for granted that

everyone knows about my religion, or that I know about theirs. People who are suspicious when they find out I'm Jewish usually don't know much about Judaism. I would much prefer them to hate or distrust me because of something I've done, instead of them hating me on the basis of prejudice.

■ ■ ■

AFTER YOU READ

■ **THINK** about Schoenberger's argument that ignorance causes prejudice and stereotyping. Do you agree or disagree with her argument? Explain your belief and the reasons for it.

■ **THINK** also about the structure of a cause and effect essay. In writing such an essay, an author can identify an effect and then analyze various causes. Or, as Schoenberger does, a writer can identify a cause (ignorance; see paragraphs 8–10) and then develop the essay by discussing or giving examples of the effects. What specific effects of ignorance about other people's religions does Schoenberger provide?

■ **EXAMINE** Schoenberger's solution to the problem of ignorance and its stereotypical effects. What does she plan to do personally to eradicate the ignorance that she believes is at the root of prejudice and stereotyping? What larger, more systematic, efforts might be implemented to solve this problem?

■ **WRITE** an essay in which you begin with a brief anecdote about a time when you were the victim of stereotyping. Then analyze the causes of the stereotyping and/or some of its secondary effects. For more instruction on writing cause and effect essays, see Lesson 5 on the *Interactions*, eighth edition, student website, available at www.cengagebrain.com.

FOCUS: CAUSE AND EFFECT

Mother Tongue

■ ■ ■

AMY TAN

The daughter of Chinese immigrants, Amy Tan was born and raised in California. She is the author of five novels—*The Joy Luck Club* (1989), *The Kitchen God's Wife* (1991), *The Hundred Secret Senses* (1993), *The Bonesetter's Daughter* (2001), and *Saving Fish from Drowning* (2005)—all of which were *New York Times* bestsellers. She has also published numerous short stories and essays. The following essay, like much of her work, deals with the relationship between Chinese American mothers and daughters—in this case, with Tan and her own mother.

BEFORE YOU READ

■ **THINK** about the language—the English—that you use with your family, with your friends, at work, and at college. How many different Englishes (or languages) do you use, and how do they differ according to your situation and the people you are with?

■ **EXAMINE** the title of the essay. *Mother tongue* usually refers to the language a person learned as a child. In reading Tan's essay, look for other possible meanings for this phrase.

■ **EXAMINE** also the following italicized words, their context, and their definitions:

1. "*evoke* an emotion" (paragraph 2): to call forth
2. "*empirical* evidence" (paragraph 9): based on observation or experiment
3. "*impeccable* broken English" (paragraph 13): without flaw or weakness
4. "*hone* my talents" (paragraph 19): to sharpen
5. "mental *quandary*" (paragraph 20): dilemma; state of uncertainty
6. "*nascent* state" (paragraph 20): new and emerging; state of being born

■ **WRITE** a journal entry describing the different English languages you use with different people in different situations.

AS YOU READ

Underline and number the descriptions of the different Englishes that Tan describes in her essay. Also, identify in the margins the causes (C) and Effects (E) of these different Englishes.

■ ■ ■

I am not a scholar of English literature. I cannot give you much more than personal opinions on the English language and its variations in this country and others.

I am a writer. And by that definition, I am someone who has always loved language. I am fascinated by language in daily life. I spend a great deal of my time thinking about the power of language—the way it can evoke an emotion, a visual image, a complex idea, or a simple truth. Language is the tool of my trade. And I use them all—all the Englishes I grew up with.

Recently, I was made keenly aware of the different Englishes I do use. I was giving a talk to a large group of people, the same talk I had already given to half a dozen other groups. The nature of the talk was about my writing, my life, and my book, *The Joy Luck Club*. The talk was going along well enough, until I remembered one major difference that made the whole talk sound wrong. My mother was in the room. And it was perhaps the first time she had heard me give a lengthy speech, using the kind of English I have never used with her. I was saying things like, "The intersection of memory upon imagination" and "There is an aspect of my fiction that relates to thus-and-thus"—a speech filled with carefully wrought grammatical phrases, burdened, it suddenly seemed to me, with nominalized forms, past perfect tenses, conditional phrases, all the forms of standard English that I had learned in school and through books, the forms of English I did not use at home with my mother.

Just last week, I was walking down the street with my mother, and I again found myself conscious of the English I was using, the English I do use with her. We were talking about the price of new and used furniture and I heard myself saying this: "Not waste money that way." My husband was with us as well, and he didn't notice any switch in my English. And then I realized why. It's because over the twenty years we've been together I've often used that same kind of English with him, and sometimes he even uses it with me. It has become our language of intimacy, a different sort of English that relates to family talk, the language I grew up with.

So you'll have some idea of what this family talk I heard sounds like, I'll quote what my mother said during a recent conversation which I videotaped and then transcribed. During this conversation, my mother was talking about a political gangster in Shanghai who had the same last name as her family's, Du, and how the gangster in his early years wanted to be adopted by her family, which was rich by comparison. Later, the gangster became more powerful, far richer than my mother's family, and one day showed up at my mother's wedding to pay his respects. Here's what she said in part.

"Du Yusong having business like fruit stand. Like off the street kind.   6
He is Du like Du Zong—but not Tsung-ming Island people. The local people call putong, the river east side, he belong to that side local people. That man want to ask Du Zong father take him in like become own family. Du Zong father wasn't look down on him, but didn't take seriously, until that man big like become a mafia. Now important person, very hard to inviting him. Chinese way, came only to show respect, don't stay for dinner. Respect for making big celebration, he shows up. Mean gives lots of respect. Chinese custom. Chinese social life that way. If too important won't have to stay too long. He come to my wedding. I didn't see, I heard it. I gone to boy's side, they have YMCA dinner. Chinese age I was nineteen."

You should know that my mother's expressive command of English   7
belies how much she actually understands. She reads the *Forbes* report, listens to *Wall Street Week,* converses daily with her stockbroker, reads all of Shirley MacLaine's books with ease—all kinds of things I can't begin to understand. Yet some of my friends tell me they understand 50 percent of what my mother says. Some say they understand 80 to 90 percent. Some say they understand none of it, as if she were speaking pure Chinese. But to me, my mother's English is perfectly clear, perfectly natural. It's my mother tongue. Her language, as I hear it, is vivid, direct, full of observation and imagery. That was the language that helped shape the way I saw things, expressed things, made sense of the world.

Lately, I've been giving more thought to the kind of English my mother   8
speaks. Like others, I have described it to people as "broken" or "fractured" English. But I wince when I say that. It has always bothered me that I can think of no other way to describe it other than "broken," as if it were damaged and needed to be fixed, as if it lacked a certain wholeness and soundness. I've heard other terms used, "limited English," for example. But they seem just as bad, as if everything is limited, including people's perceptions of the limited English speaker.

I know this for a fact, because when I was growing up, my mother's   9
"limited" English limited *my* perception of her. I was ashamed of her English. I believed that her English reflected the quality of what she had to say. That is, because she expressed them imperfectly her thoughts were imperfect. And I had plenty of empirical evidence to support me: the fact that people in department stores, at banks, and at restaurants did not take her seriously, did not give her good service, pretended not to understand her, or even acted as if they did not see her.

My mother has long realized the limitations of her English as well. When   10
I was fifteen, she used to have me call people on the phone to pretend I was she. In this guise, I was forced to ask for information or even complain and yell at people who had been rude to her. One time it was a call to her

stockbroker in New York. She had cashed out her small portfolio and it just so happened we were going to go to New York the next week, our very first trip outside California. I had to get on the phone and say in an adolescent voice that was not very convincing, "This is Mrs. Tan."

And my mother was standing in the back whispering loudly, "Why he   11 don't send me check, already two weeks late. So mad he lie to me, losing me money."

And then I said in perfect English, "Yes, I'm getting rather concerned.   12 You had agreed to send the check two weeks ago, but it hasn't arrived."

Then she began to talk more loudly. "What he want, I come to New   13 York tell him front of his boss, you cheating me?" And I was trying to calm her down, make her be quiet, while telling the stockbroker, "I can't tolerate any more excuses. If I don't receive the check immediately, I am going to have to speak to your manager when I'm in New York next week." And sure enough, the following week there we were in front of this astonished stockbroker, and I was sitting there redfaced and quiet, and my mother, the real Mrs. Tan, was shouting at his boss in her impeccable broken English.

We used a similar routine just five days ago, for a situation that was   14 far less humorous. My mother had gone to the hospital for an appointment, to find out about a benign brain tumor a CAT scan had revealed a month ago. She said she had spoken very good English, her best English, no mistakes. Still, she said, the hospital did not apologize when they said they had lost the CAT scan and she had come for nothing. She said they did not seem to have any sympathy when she told them she was anxious to know the exact diagnosis, since her husband and son had both died of brain tumors. She said they would not give her any more information until the next time and she would have to make another appointment for that. So she said she would not leave until the doctor called her daughter. She wouldn't budge. And when the doctor finally called her daughter, me, who spoke in perfect English—lo and behold—we had assurances the CAT scan would be found, promise that a conference call on Monday would be held, and apologies for any suffering my mother had gone through for a most regrettable mistake.

I think my mother's English almost had an effect on limiting my possi-   15 bilities in life as well. Sociologists and linguists probably will tell you that a person's developing language skills are more influenced by peers. But I do think that the language spoken in the family, especially in immigrant families which are more insular, plays a large role in shaping the language of the child. And I believe that it affected my results on achievement tests, IQ tests, and the SAT. While my English skills were never judged as poor, compared to math, English could not be considered my strong suit. In grade school I did moderately well, getting perhaps B's, sometimes B-pluses, in English and scoring perhaps in the sixtieth or seventieth percentile on achievement tests. But those scores were not good enough to override the opinion that my true abilities lay in math and science, because in those areas I achieved A's and scored in the ninetieth percentile or higher.

This was understandable. Math is precise; there is only one correct 16 answer. Whereas, for me at least, the answers on English texts were always a judgment call, a matter of opinion and personal experience. Those tests were constructed around items like fill-in-the-blank sentence completion, such as, "Even though Tom was___, Mary thought he was___." And the correct answer always seemed to be the most bland combinations of thought, for example, "Even though Tom was shy, Mary thought he was charming," with the grammatical structure "even though" limiting the correct answer to some sort of semantic opposites, so you wouldn't get answers like, "Even though Tom was foolish, Mary thought he was ridiculous." Well, according to my mother, there were very few limitations as to what Tom could have been and what Mary might have thought of him. So I never did well on tests like that.

The same was true with word analogies, pairs of words in which you 17 were supposed to find some sort of logical, semantic relationship—for example, "*Sunset* is to *nightfall* as ___ is to ___." And here you would be presented with a list of four possible pairs, one of which showed the same kind of relationship: *red* is to *stoplight*, *bus* is to *arrival*, *chills* is to *fever*, *yawn* is to *boring*. Well, I could never think that way. I knew what the tests were asking, but I could not block out of my mind the images already created by the first pair, "Sunset is to nightfall"—and I would see a burst of color against a darkening sky, the moon rising, the lowering of a curtain of stars. And all the other pairs of words—red, bus, stoplight, boring—just threw up a mass of confusing images, making it impossible for me to sort out something as logical as saying: "A sunset precedes nightfall" is the same as "a chill precedes a fever." The only way I would have gotten the answer right would have been to imagine an associative situation, for example, by being disobedient and staying out past sunset, catching a chill at night which turns into feverish pneumonia as punishment, which indeed did happen to me.

I have been thinking about all this lately, about my mother's English, 18 about achievement tests. Because lately I've been asked, as a writer, why there are not more Asian Americans represented in American literature. Why are there few Asian Americans enrolled in creative writing programs? Why do so many Chinese students go into engineering? Well, these are broad sociological questions I can't begin to answer. But I have noticed surveys—in fact—just last week—that Asian students, as a whole, always do significantly better on math achievement tests than in English. And this makes me think that there are other Asian-American students whose English spoken in the home might also be described as "broken" or "limited." And perhaps they also have teachers who are steering them away from writing and into math and science, which is what happened to me.

Fortunately, I happen to be rebellious in nature and enjoy the chal- 19 lenge of disproving assumptions made about me. I became an English major my first year in college, after being enrolled as pre-med. I started writing nonfiction as a freelancer the week after I was told by my former boss that writing was my worst skill and I should hone my talents toward account management.

But it wasn't until 1985 that I finally began to write fiction. And at   20 first I wrote using what I thought to be wittily crafted sentences, sentences that would finally prove I had mastery over the English language. Here's an example from the first draft of a story that later made its way into *The Joy Luck Club*, but without this line: "That was my mental quandary in its nascent state." A terrible line, which I can hardly pronounce.

Fortunately, for reasons I won't get into today, I later decided I should   21 envision a reader for the stories I would write. And the reader I decided upon was my mother, because these were stories about mothers. So with this reader in mind—and in fact she did read my early drafts—I began to write stories using all the Englishes I grew up with: the English I spoke to my mother, which for lack of a better term might be described as "simple"; the English she used with me, which for lack of a better term might be described as "broken"; my translation of her Chinese, which could certainly be described as "watered down"; and what I imagine to be her translation of her Chinese if she could speak in perfect English, her internal language, and for that I sought to preserve the essence, but neither an English nor a Chinese structure. I wanted to capture what language ability tests can never reveal: her intent, her passion, her imagery, the rhythms of her speech and the nature of her thoughts.

Apart from what any critic had to say about my writing, I knew I had   22 succeeded where it counted when my mother finished reading my book and gave me her verdict: "So easy to read."

■   ■   ■

AFTER YOU READ

- ■ **THINK** about how society judges people by their language. How do the negative prejudgments of Mrs. Tan's language cause problems in her daily life? How does her daughter help solve her problems? How and why is she able to accomplish what her mother can't? Give examples.
- ■ **THINK** also about the way Tan develops her essay by analyzing and describing the effects of the various English languages (causes) that she identifies, especially the effects of her mother's "broken" English on both her mother's life and her own life. What are these effects? What other causes and effects did you identify as you read this essay?
- ■ **EXAMINE** paragraphs 6 and 7. First, describe and analyze the English that Mrs. Tan uses in paragraph 6, being as specific as you can. (But be sure that you are also respectful of Mrs. Tan's language.) Then, note that Tan points out in paragraph 7 that her mother's reading

language is quite different from her oral language. How are Mrs. Tan's two Englishes different?

■ **EXAMINE** also paragraph 21, in which Tan lists the Englishes that she uses in her writing. What qualities in her mother's English does Tan want to capture in her own writing? Discuss whether or not this essay has these qualities.

■ **WRITE** an essay in which you discuss the effect(s) that someone's language—probably their "English"—has had on you and your language. For help with writing cause and effect essays, see Lesson 5 on the *Interactions*, eighth edition, student website, at www.cengagebrain.com.

Black Men and Public Space

■ ■ ■

BRENT STAPLES

Awarded a Danforth Fellowship for graduate study, Brent Sta-
ples earned a Ph.D. in psychology at the University of Chicago.
After teaching for a while, he became a reporter for the *Chicago
Sun-Times*. In 1983 he moved to New York and began working
for *The New York Times,* where he is currently an editorial
writer and a member of the editorial board. Staples won the
Anisfield-Wolff Book Award for his autobiography *Parallel
Time: Growing Up in Black and White* (1994) and has published numerous articles in periodicals such as *The New York
Times* and *New Republic.* The following essay was published
in *Harper's* in 1987, although an earlier version of it was published in *Ms. Magazine* the preceding year.

BEFORE YOU READ

■ **THINK** about how you feel when you are out alone at night. Are you nervous and fearful if you encounter a stranger? Is your fear greater if the
stranger is a member of a race or ethnic group different from yours? If so,
do you think this fear is unfair or justified? Why do you feel as you do?

■ **EXAMINE** the title and the first sentence of this selection. From the title
and this first sentence, what do you expect the rest of the paragraph and
the essay to be about? Then read the entire first paragraph. What different views do you think Staples and the woman have of the distance
between them—of what Staples calls "public space"? What do you
think could have created these different viewpoints?

■ **EXAMINE** also the following italicized words in their context and the
definitions provided for you:

1. "*affluent* neighborhood in an otherwise mean, impoverished section"
   (paragraph 1): wealthy
2. "*vulnerable* to street violence" (paragraph 5): unprotected from danger
3. "the *lethality* nighttime pedestrians attributed to me" (paragraph 6): ability
   to cause death
4. "fearsomeness ... has a *perilous* flavor" (paragraph 8): dangerous
5. "*labyrinthine* halls" (paragraph 8): complicated, as in intricately connected
   passages (The word derives from the labyrinth, or maze, in which the
   ancient Cretan Minotaur—half man, half bull—was confined by the
   craftsman Daedalus.)
6. "late-evening *constitutionals*" (paragraph 12): walks, or exercise, taken
   regularly for health reasons

■ **WRITE** a journal entry describing an unexpected encounter in which you were frightened or frightened someone else.

AS YOU READ

Underline words and phrases that suggest space or distance.

■ ■ ■

My first victim was a woman—white, well-dressed, probably in her late twenties. I came upon her late one evening on a deserted street in Hyde Park, a relatively affluent neighborhood in an otherwise mean, impoverished section of Chicago. As I swung onto the avenue behind her, there seemed to be a discreet, uninflammatory distance between us. Not so. She cast back a worried glance. To her, the youngish black man —a broad six feet two inches with a beard and billowing hair, both hands shoved into the pockets of a bulky military jacket—seemed menacingly close. After a few more quick glimpses, she picked up her pace and was soon running in earnest. Within seconds, she disappeared into a cross street. 1

That was more than a decade ago. I was twenty-two years old, a graduate student newly arrived at the University of Chicago. It was in the echo of that terrified woman's footfalls that I first began to know the unwieldy inheritance I'd come into—the ability to alter public space in ugly ways. It was clear that she thought herself the quarry of a mugger, a rapist, or worse. Suffering a bout of insomnia, however, I was stalking sleep, not defenseless wayfarers. As a softy who is scarcely able to take a knife to a raw chicken— let alone hold one to a person's throat—I was surprised, embarrassed, and dismayed all at once. Her flight made me feel like an accomplice in tyranny. It also made it clear that I was indistinguishable from the muggers who occasionally seeped into the area from the surrounding ghetto. That first encounter, and those that followed, signified that a vast, unnerving gulf lay between nighttime pedestrians—particularly women—and me. And I soon gathered that being perceived as dangerous is a hazard in itself. I only needed to turn a corner into a dicey situation, or crowd some frightened, armed person in a foyer somewhere, or make an errant move after being pulled over by a policeman. Where fear and weapons meet—and they often do in urban America—there is always the possibility of death. 2

In that first year, my first away from my hometown, I was to become thoroughly familiar with the language of fear. At dark, shadowy intersections, I could cross in front of a car stopped at a traffic light and elicit the *thunk, thunk, thunk* of the driver—black, white, male, or female—hammering down the door locks. On less traveled streets after dark, I grew accustomed to but never comfortable with people crossing to the other side of the street rather than pass me. Then there were the standard unpleasantries with policemen, doormen, bouncers, cabdrivers, and others whose 3 business it is to screen out troublesome individuals *before* there is any nastiness.

I moved to New York nearly two years ago and I have remained an   4 avid nightwalker. In central Manhattan, the near-constant crowd cover minimizes tense one-on-one street encounters. Elsewhere—in Soho, for example, where sidewalks are narrow and tightly spaced buildings shut out the sky—things can get very taut indeed.

After dark, on the warrenlike streets of Brooklyn where I live, I often   5 see women who fear the worst from me. They seem to have set their faces on neutral, and with their purse straps strung across their chests bandolier-style, they forge ahead as though bracing themselves against being tackled. I understand, of course, that the danger they perceive is not a hallucination. Women are particularly vulnerable to street violence, and young black males are drastically overrepresented among the perpetrators of that violence. Yet these truths are no solace against the kind of alienation that comes of being ever the suspect, a fearsome entity with whom pedestrians avoid making eye contact.

It is not altogether clear to me how I reached the ripe old age of twenty-   6 two without being conscious of the lethality nighttime pedestrians attributed to me. Perhaps it was because in Chester, Pennsylvania, the small, angry industrial town where I came of age in the 1960s, I was scarcely noticeable against a backdrop of gang warfare, street knifings, and murders. I grew up one of the good boys, had perhaps a half-dozen fist-fights. In retrospect, my shyness of combat has clear sources.

As a boy, I saw countless tough guys locked away; I have since buried   7 several, too. They were babies, really—a teenage cousin, a brother of twenty-two, a childhood friend in his mid-twenties—all gone down in episodes of bravado played out in the streets. I came to doubt the virtues of intimidation early on. I chose, perhaps unconsciously, to remain a shadow—timid, but a survivor.

The fearsomeness mistakenly attributed to me in public places often has   8 a perilous flavor. The most frightening one of these confusions occurred in the late 1970s and early 1980s, when I worked as a journalist in Chicago. One day, rushing into the office of a magazine I was writing for with a deadline story in hand, I was mistaken for a burglar. The office manager called security and, with an ad hoc posse, pursued me through the labyrinthine halls, nearly to my editor's door. I had no way of proving who I was. I could only move briskly toward the company of someone who knew me.

Another time I was on assignment for a local newspaper and killing time   9 before an interview. I entered a jewelry store on the city's affluent Near North Side. The proprietor excused herself and returned with an enormous red Doberman pinscher straining at the end of a leash. She stood, the dog extended toward me, silent to my questions, her eyes bulging nearly out of her head. I took a cursory look around, nodded, and bade her good night.

Relatively speaking, however, I never fared as badly as another black   10 male journalist. He went to nearby Waukegan, Illinois, a couple of summers ago to work on a story about a murderer who was born there.

Mistaking the reporter for the killer, police officers hauled him from his car at gunpoint and but for his press credentials would probably have tried to book him. Black men trade tales like this all the time.

Over the years, I learned to smother the rage I felt at so often being taken   11 for a criminal. Not to do so would surely have led to madness. I now take precautions to make myself less threatening. I move about with care, particularly late in the evening. I give a wide berth to nervous people on subway platforms during the wee hours, particularly when I have exchanged business clothes for jeans. If I happen to be entering a building behind some people who appear skittish, I may walk by, letting them clear the lobby before I return, so as not to seem to be following them. I have been calm and extremely congenial on those rare occasions when I've been pulled over by the police.

And on late evening constitutionals I employ what has proved to be an   12 excellent tension-reducing measure: I whistle melodies from Beethoven and Vivaldi and the more popular classical composers. Even steely New Yorkers hunching toward nighttime destinations seem to relax, and occasionally they even join in the tune. Virtually everybody seems to sense that a mugger wouldn't be warbling bright, sunny selections from Vivaldi's *Four Seasons*. It is my equivalent to the cowbell that hikers wear when they know they are in bear country.

■   ■   ■

AFTER YOU READ

■ **THINK** about how Staples must have felt when he first realized that the woman in the park (paragraph 1) was afraid of him because she was alone and he was black. What other similar experiences has he had since that one? How has he learned to deal with such experiences?

■ **EXAMINE** the words and phrases referring to space and distance that you underlined in Staples's essay. How is the concept of public space central to his essay? How and why is his freedom to move about in public space limited? In paragraph 5, Staples admits that he understands the fear that women who are "vulnerable to street violence" have when they encounter "black males [who] are drastically overrepresented among the perpetrators of that violence." In your opinion, how reasonable or unreasonable is this fear? In spite of Staples's understanding of this fear, how does it unfairly alienate him from society?

■ **WRITE** an essay in which you tell about an incident in which your intentions were misunderstood. Explain what happened, why you think your intentions were misunderstood, how the misunderstanding made you feel, and how the incident was resolved.

■ Or **WRITE** an essay suggesting ways to make public space more open for people of all backgrounds.

Indian Education

■ ■ ■

S H E R M A N   A L E X I E

A prolific writer, Sherman Alexie was born in Spokane, Washington. He was one of the first members of his tribe to earn a university degree, graduating from Washington State University. Alexie is the author of novels, stories, poems, and a screenplay, *Smoke Signals* (1998), which was made into a successful film. He is perhaps best known, however, for his books of poetry and stories. To date, he has published four collections of stories: *The Toughest Indian in the World* (2000), *Ten Little Indians* (2003), *The Lone Ranger and Tonto Fistfight in Heaven* (2005), and, most recently, *War Dances* (2009). In the following selection from *Ten Little Indians,* as in most of his work, Alexie focuses on his experiences as a Native American and the conflicts that Native Americans face as they struggle to live in two very different cultures.

BEFORE YOU READ

■ **THINK** about how an "Indian" education might differ from the education that other students receive in public schools. Why do you think Alexie uses the term *Indian* rather than *Native American* in this title?

■ **EXAMINE** the format of this reading selection, noting especially the headings that divide it into different segments. What is the effect of these headings?

■ **EXAMINE** also Alexie's reference to his "HUD house" in paragraph 26 and later paragraphs. The U.S. Department of Housing and Urban Development (HUD) provides low-income housing for those who cannot afford their own housing. Why do you think Alexie mentions his HUD house several times? How does living in a HUD house make him feel?

■ **EXAMINE** also the following italicized words and their definitions:

1. *symmetrical* (paragraph 5): balanced
2. *scrawny* (paragraph 11): gaunt, bony
3. *intercepted* (paragraph 18): interrupted; stopped and perhaps kept
4. *confiscated* (paragraph 18): seized by authorities
5. *ultimately* (paragraph 45): at last; eventually

6. *anorexia* (paragraph 50): eating disorder resulting in loss of appetite and desire to lose weight with intense dieting or fasting
7. *bulimia* (paragraph 50): eating disorder characterized by binge eating followed by guilt and depression and then extreme attempts to lose weight, as in fasting and regurgitation
8. *commodities* (paragraph 53): in this context, groceries provided by the government
9. *valedictorian* (paragraph 69): student with highest academic rank
10. *stoic* (paragraph 70): apparently indifferent

■ **WRITE** a journal entry in which you write one sentence for each of your 12 years in school. Label your sentences as *First Grade, Second Grade,* and so on, and try to remember one "true thing" about each of the years you were in school.

AS YOU READ

Underline the term *Indian* (or indian) and circle the term *Native American.* Try to determine when and why Alexie uses one term or the other. Identify also the conflicts that Alexie describes or to which he alludes in this selection. Number each conflict.

■   ■   ■

FIRST GRADE

My hair was too short and my U.S. Government glasses were horn-rimmed, ugly, and all that first winter in school, the other Indian boys chased me from one corner of the playground to the other. They pushed me down, buried me in the snow until I couldn't breathe, thought I'd never breathe again.

They stole my glasses and threw them over my head, around my outstretched hands, just beyond my reach, until someone tripped me and sent me falling again, facedown in the snow.

I was always falling down; my Indian name was Junior Falls Down. Sometimes it was Bloody Nose or Steal-His-Lunch. Once, it was Cries-Like-a-White-Boy, even though none of us had seen a white boy cry.

Then it was a Friday morning recess and Frenchy SiJohn threw snowballs at me while the rest of the Indian boys tortured some other *top-yogh-yaught* kid, another weakling. But Frenchy was confident enough to torment me all by himself, and most days I would have let him.

But the little warrior in me roared to life that day and knocked Frenchy to the ground, held his head against the snow, and punched him so hard that my knuckles and the snow made symmetrical bruises on his face. He almost looked like he was wearing war paint.

But he wasn't the warrior. I was. And I chanted *It's a good day to die, it's a good day to die,* all the way down to the principal's office.

SECOND GRADE

Betty Towle, missionary teacher, redheaded and so ugly that no one ever   7
had a puppy crush on her, made me stay in for recess fourteen days
straight.

"Tell me you're sorry," she said.   8

"Sorry for what?" I asked.   9

"Everything," she said and made me stand straight for fifteen minutes,   10
eagle-armed with books in each hand. One was a math book; the other
was English. But all I learned was that gravity can be painful.

For Halloween I drew a picture of her riding a broom with a   11
scrawny cat on the back. She said that her God would never forgive me
for that.

Once, she gave the class a spelling test but set me aside and gave me a   12
test designed for junior high students. When I spelled all the words right,
she crumpled up the paper and made me eat it.

"You'll learn respect," she said.   13

She sent a letter home with me that told my parents to either cut my   14
braids or keep me home from class. My parents came in the next day and
dragged their braids across Betty Towle's desk.

"Indians, indians, indians." She said it without capitalization. She   15
called me "indian, indian, indian."

And I said, *Yes, I am. I am Indian. Indian, I am.*   16

THIRD GRADE

My traditional Native American art career began and ended with my very   17
first portrait: *Stick Indian Taking a Piss in My Backyard.*

As I circulated the original print around the classroom, Mrs. Schluter   18
intercepted and confiscated my art.

Censorship, I might cry now. *Freedom of expression,* I would write in   19
editorials to the tribal newspaper.

In third grade, though, I stood alone in the corner, faced the wall, and   20
waited for the punishment to end.

I'm still waiting.   21

FOURTH GRADE

"You should be a doctor when you grow up," Mr. Schluter told me, even   22
though his wife, the third grade teacher, thought I was crazy beyond my
years. My eyes always looked like I had just hit-and-run someone.

"Guilty," she said. "You always look guilty."   23

"Why should I be a doctor?" I asked Mr. Schluter.   24

"So you can come back and help the tribe. So you can heal people."   25

That was the year my father drank a gallon of vodka a day and the   26
same year that my mother started two hundred different quilts but never
finished any. They sat in separate, dark places in our HUD house and wept
savagely.

I ran home after school, heard their Indian tears, and looked in the   27
mirror. *Doctor Victor,* I called myself, invented an education, talked to
my reflection. *Doctor Victor to the emergency room.*

FIFTH GRADE

I picked up a basketball for the first time and made my first shot. No. I   28
missed my first shot, missed the basket completely, and the ball landed in
the dirt and sawdust, sat there just like I had sat there only minutes
before.

But it felt good, that ball in my hands, all those possibilities and   29
angles. It was mathematics, geometry. It was beautiful.

At that same moment, my cousin Steven Ford sniffed rubber cement   30
from a paper bag and leaned back on the merry-go-round. His ears rang,
his mouth was dry, and everyone seemed so far away.

But it felt good, that buzz in his head, all those colors and noises. It   31
was chemistry, biology. It was beautiful.

Oh, do you remember those sweet, almost innocent choices that the   32
Indian boys were forced to make?

SIXTH GRADE

Randy, the new Indian kid from the white town of Springdale, got into a   33
fight an hour after he first walked into the reservation school.

Stevie Flett called him out, called him a squawman, called him a pussy,   34
and called him a punk.

Randy and Stevie, and the rest of the Indian boys, walked out into the   35
playground.

"Throw the first punch," Stevie said as they squared off.   36

"No," Randy said.   37

"Throw the first punch," Stevie said again.   38

"No," Randy said again.   39

"Throw the first punch!" Stevie said for the third time, and Randy   40
reared back and pitched a knuckle fastball that broke Stevie's nose.

We all stood there in silence, in awe.   41

That was Randy, my soon-to-be first and best friend, who taught me   42
the most valuable lesson about living in the white world: *Always throw the
first punch.*

SEVENTH GRADE

I leaned through the basement window of the HUD house and kissed the   43
white girl who would later be raped by her foster-parent father, who was
also white. They both lived on the reservation, though, and when the head-
lines and stories filled the papers later, not one word was made of their
color.

Just Indians being Indians, someone must have said somewhere and   44
they were wrong.

But on the day I leaned through the basement window of the HUD   45
house and kissed the white girl, I felt the good-byes I was saying to my
entire tribe. I held my lips tight against her lips, a dry, clumsy, and ultimately stupid kiss.

But I was saying good-bye to my tribe, to all the Indian girls and   46
women I might have loved, to all the Indian men who might have called
me cousin, even brother.

I kissed that white girl and when I opened my eyes, she was gone from   47
the reservation, and when I opened my eyes, I was gone from the reservation, living in a farm town where a beautiful white girl asked my name.

"Junior Polatkin," I said, and she laughed.   48

After that, no one spoke to me for another five hundred years.   49

EIGHTH GRADE

At the farm town junior high, in the boys' bathroom, I could hear voices   50
from the girls' bathroom, nervous whispers of anorexia and bulimia. I
could hear the white girls' forced vomiting, a sound so familiar and natural
to me after years of listening to my father's hangovers.

"Give me your lunch if you're just going to throw it up," I said to one   51
of those girls once.

I sat back and watched them grow skinny from self-pity.   52

Back on the reservation, my mother stood in line to get us commodi-   53
ties. We carried them home, happy to have food, and opened the canned
beef that even the dogs wouldn't eat.

But we ate it day after day and grew skinny from self-pity.   54

There is more than one way to starve.   55

NINTH GRADE

At the farm town high school dance, after a basketball game in an over-   56
heated gym where I had scored twenty-seven points and pulled down thirteen rebounds, I passed out during a slow song.

As my white friends revived me and prepared to take me to the emer- 57
gency room where doctors would later diagnose my diabetes, the Chicano
teacher ran up to us.

"Hey," he said. "What's that boy been drinking? I know all about 58
these Indian kids. They start drinking real young."

Sharing dark skin doesn't necessarily make two men brothers.   59

TENTH GRADE

I passed the written test easily and nearly flunked the driving, but still 60
received my Washington State driver's license on the same day that Wally
Jim killed himself by driving his car into a pine tree.

No traces of alcohol in his blood, good job, wife and two kids.   61

"Why'd he do it?" asked a white Washington State trooper.   62

All the Indians shrugged their shoulders, looked down at the ground. 63

"Don't know," we all said, but when we look in the mirror, see the 64
history of our tribe in our eyes, taste failure in the tap water, and shake
with old tears, we understand completely.

Believe me, everything looks like a noose if you stare at it long enough. 65

ELEVENTH GRADE

Last night I missed two free throws which would have won the game 66
against the best team in the state. The farm town high school I play for is
nicknamed the "Indians," and I'm probably the only actual Indian ever to
play for a team with such a mascot.

This morning I pick up the sports page and read the headline: 67
INDIANS LOSE AGAIN.

Go ahead and tell me none of this is supposed to hurt me very much. 68

TWELFTH GRADE

I walk down the aisle, valedictorian of this farm town high school, and my 69
cap doesn't fit because I've grown my hair longer than it's ever been. Later,
I stand as the school board chairman recites my awards, accomplishments,
and scholarships.

I try to remain stoic for the photographers as I look toward the future. 70

Back home on the reservation, my former classmates graduate: a few 71
can't read, one or two are just given attendance diplomas, most look

forward to the parties. The bright students are shaken, frightened, because they don't know what comes next.

They smile for the photographer as they look back toward tradition.   72

The tribal newspaper runs my photograph and the photograph of my   73
former classmates side by side.

POSTSCRIPT: CLASS REUNION

Victor said, "Why should we organize a reservation high school reunion?   74
My graduating class has a reunion every weekend at the Powwow Tavern."

■ ■ ■

AFTER YOU READ

■ **THINK** about how Alexie portrays himself in this story. How would you describe him? Have you known students like him?

■ **THINK** also about the two schools in this story. How would you describe them? How are they similar to or different from each other? How are they similar to or different from schools you attended?

■ **THINK** also about the pressure that Alexie's society put on him to assimilate—to take on the customs and values of the society as a whole rather than to preserve and feel pride in his own Native American heritage. How did his teachers contribute to this process? Who else contributed to this process, and how did they do it?

■ **EXAMINE** the structure of the selection. Each separate section presents a narrative anecdote from a particular year of Alexie's public school education. Notice also that each of these sections ends with a sentence or phrase that comments on and in some way interprets the theme, or truth, of the previous anecdote. Work in pairs to study these final sentences, and discuss how they explain or perhaps even change the effect of the anecdote itself.

■ **EXAMINE** also the conflicts that Alexie describes and that you annotated. Compare those you identified with those your classmates or group members identified. Which conflicts were physical? Which were with peers? Which were with school authorities? Which were conflicts in cultures? Were there also internal conflicts? Explain.

■ **WRITE** an essay in which you describe one or more years of your elementary and/or high school education. The experience (or experiences) you describe should focus on a single idea or theme that you want to convey about your education. You may state this theme explicitly (either in your introduction or your conclusion), or—like Alexie—you may just imply this theme, allowing your reader to reach his or her own conclusion.

■ Or **WRITE** an essay about the pressure to assimilate that society brings to bear on individuals who are part of a particular racial or ethnic group. Have you observed or experienced such pressure? If so, include your experience in your essay. In your introduction and/or conclusion, comment on the positive and/or negative effects of this pressure to assimilate. (For more information about writing cause and effect essays, see Lesson 5 on the *Interactions*, eighth edition, student website, at www.cengagebrain.com.)

People Like Us

■ ■ ■

DAVID BROOKS

David Brooks, who was born in Canada and graduated from
the University of Chicago, writes social commentary. Brooks
wrote for *The Wall Street Journal* from 1986 to 1985, and he
was senior editor for *The Weekly Standard* from 1995 to 2003,
when he became a columnist for *The New York Times*. He is a
frequent commentator and guest on National Public Radio and
various television shows, and a regular guest on PBS's *The
NewsHour with Jim Lehrer*. A prominent voice of moderate
conservative politics, Brooks has authored several books,
including *On Paradise Drive: How We Live Now (and Always
Have) in the Future Tense* (2004). He has also been a contributing editor to the *Atlantic Monthly*, in which this essay
appeared in 2003.

BEFORE YOU READ

■ **THINK** about the epigraph that preceded the following essay when it
was originally published in *The Atlantic Monthly*: "We all pay lip service to the melting pot, but we really prefer the congealing pot." What is
the difference between a melting pot and a congealing pot? Why is the
United States often called a *melting pot*? What would a "congealing
pot" look like? What do you think Brooks is suggesting by this
statement?

■ **EXAMINE** the following sentence: "The United States might be a diverse
nation when considered as a whole, but block by block and institution
by institution it is a relatively homogeneous nation" (paragraph 4). In
this sentence Brooks is stating his thesis, or argument. Restate this argument in your own words, keeping in mind that *homogeneous* means
"similar, alike in nature."

■ **WRITE** a journal entry in which you react to the epigraph that preceded
this essay, "We all pay lip service to the melting pot, but we really prefer
the congealing pot."

AS YOU READ

Notice the different factors (wealth, race, education, etc.) that Brooks cites
to support his argument that Americans segregate themselves voluntarily.
Note each of these factors in the margins of the essay. Also, circle

unfamiliar words; after you finish reading the essay, add these words and their definitions to your vocabulary journal.

■   ■   ■

Maybe it's time to admit the obvious. We don't really care about diversity all that much in America, even though we talk about it a great deal. Maybe somewhere in this country there is a truly diverse neighborhood in which a black Pentecostal minister lives next to a white anti-globalization activist, who lives next to an Asian short-order cook, who lives next to a professional golfer, who lives next to a postmodern-literature professor and a cardiovascular surgeon. But I have never been to or heard of that neighborhood. Instead, what I have seen all around the country is people making strenuous efforts to group themselves with people who are basically like themselves.

Human beings are capable of drawing amazingly subtle social distinctions and then shaping their lives around them. In the Washington, D.C., area Democratic lawyers tend to live in suburban Maryland, and Republican lawyers tend to live in suburban Virginia. If you asked a Democratic lawyer to move from her $750,000 house in Bethesda, Maryland, to a $750,000 house in Great Falls, Virginia, she'd look at you as if you had just asked her to buy a pickup truck with a gun rack and to shove chewing tobacco in her kid's mouth. In Manhattan the owner of a $3 million SoHo loft would feel out of place moving into a $3 million Fifth Avenue apartment. A West Hollywood interior decorator would feel dislocated if you asked him to move to Orange County. In Georgia a barista from Athens would probably not fit in serving coffee in Americus.

It is a common complaint that every place is starting to look the same. But in the information age, the late writer James Chapin once told me, every place becomes more like itself. People are less often tied down to factories and mills, and they can search for places to live on the basis of cultural affinity. Once they find a town in which people share their values, they flock there, and reinforce whatever was distinctive about the town in the first place. Once Boulder, Colorado, became known as congenial to politically progressive mountain bikers, half the politically progressive mountain bikers in the country (it seems) moved there; they made the place so culturally pure that it has become practically a parody of itself.

But people love it. Make no mistake—we are increasing our happiness by segmenting off so rigorously. We are finding places where we are comfortable and where we feel we can flourish. But the choices we make toward that end lead to the very opposite of diversity. The United States might be a diverse nation when considered as a whole, but block by block and institution by institution it is a relatively homogeneous nation.

When we use the word "diversity" today we usually mean racial integration. But even here our good intentions seem to have run into the brick wall of human nature. Over the past generation reformers have tried heroically, and in many cases successfully, to end housing discrimination. But recent patterns aren't encouraging: according to an analysis of the 2000 census data, the 1990s saw only a slight increase in the racial integration of neighborhoods in the United States. The number of middle-class and upper-middle-class African-American families is rising, but for whatever reasons—racism, psychological comfort—these families tend to congregate in predominantly black neighborhoods.

In fact, evidence suggests that some neighborhoods become more segregated over time. New suburbs in Arizona and Nevada, for example, start out reasonably well integrated. These neighborhoods don't yet have reputations, so people choose their houses for other, mostly economic reasons. But as neighborhoods age, they develop personalities (that's where the Asians live, and that's where the Hispanics live), and segmentation occurs. It could be that in a few years the new suburbs in the Southwest will be nearly as segregated as the established ones in the Northeast and the Midwest.   6

Even though race and ethnicity run deep in American society, we should in theory be able to find areas that are at least culturally diverse. But here, too, people show few signs of being truly interested in building diverse communities. If you run a retail company and you're thinking of opening new stores, you can choose among dozens of consulting firms that are quite effective at locating your potential customers. They can do this because people with similar tastes and preferences tend to congregate by ZIP code.   7

The most famous of these precision marketing firms is Claritas, which breaks down the U.S. population into sixty-two psycho-demographic clusters, based on such factors as how much money people make, what they like to read and watch, and what products they have bought in the past. For example, the "suburban sprawl" cluster is composed of young families making about $41,000 a year and living in fast-growing places such as Burnsville, Minnesota, and Bensalem, Pennsylvania. These people are almost twice as likely as other Americans to have three-way calling. They are two and a half times as likely to buy Light'n'Lively Kid Yogurt. Members of the "towns & gowns" cluster are recent college graduates in places such as Berkeley, California, and Gainesville, Florida. They are big consumers of Dove Bars and *Saturday Night Live*. They tend to drive small foreign cars and to read *Rolling Stone* and *Scientific American*.   8

Looking through the market research, one can sometimes be amazed by how efficiently people cluster—and by how predictable we all are. If you wanted to sell imported wine, obviously you would have to find places where rich people live. But did you know that the sixteen counties with the greatest proportion of imported-wine drinkers are all in the same three metropolitan areas (New York, San Francisco, and Washington, D.C.)? If you tried to open a motor-home dealership in Montgomery County, Pennsylvania, you'd probably go broke, because people in this ring of the Philadelphia suburbs think RVs are kind of uncool. But if you traveled just a short way north, to Monroe County, Pennsylvania, you would find yourself in the fifth motor-home-friendliest county in America.   9

Geography is not the only way we find ourselves divided from people   10
unlike us. Some of us watch Fox News, while others listen to NPR. Some
like David Letterman, and others—typically in less urban neighborhoods—
like Jay Leno. Some go to charismatic churches; some go to mainstream
churches. Americans tend more and more often to marry people with education levels similar to their own, and to befriend people with backgrounds
similar to their own.

My favorite illustration of this latter pattern comes from the first, non-   11
controversial chapter of *The Bell Curve*. Think of your twelve closest
friends, Richard J. Herrnstein and Charles Murray write. If you had chosen them randomly from the American population, the odds that half of
your twelve closest friends would be college graduates would be six in a
thousand. The odds that half of the twelve would have advanced degrees
would be less than one in a million. Have any of your twelve closest
friends graduated from Harvard, Stanford, Yale, Princeton, Caltech, MIT,
Duke, Dartmouth, Cornell, Columbia, Chicago, or Brown? If you chose
your friends randomly from the American population, the odds against
your having four or more friends from those schools would be more than
a billion to one.

Many of us live in absurdly unlikely groupings, because we have orga-   12
nized our lives that way.

It's striking that the institutions that talk the most about diversity often   13
practice it the least. For example, no group of people sings the diversity
anthem more frequently and fervently than administrators at just such
elite universities. But elite universities are amazingly undiverse in their
values, politics, and mores. Professors in particular are drawn from a
rather narrow segment of the population. If faculties reflected the general
population, 32 percent of professors would be registered Democrats and
31 percent would be registered Republicans. Forty percent would be evangelical Christians. But a recent study of several universities by the conservative Center for the Study of Popular Culture and the American
Enterprise Institute found that roughly 90 percent of those professors in
the arts and sciences who had registered with a political party had registered Democratic. Fifty-seven professors at Brown were found on the
voter-registration rolls. Of those, fifty-four were Democrats. Of the forty-
two professors in the English, history, sociology, and political-science
departments, all were Democrats. The results at Harvard, Penn State,
Maryland, and the University of California at Santa Barbara were similar
to the results at Brown.

What we are looking at here is human nature. People want to be   14
around others who are roughly like themselves. That's called community.
It probably would be psychologically difficult for most Brown professors to
share an office with someone who was pro-life, a member of the National
Rifle Association, or an evangelical Christian. It's likely that hiring com-
mittees would subtly—even unconsciously—screen out any such people
they encountered. Republicans and evangelical Christians have sensed that
they are not welcome at places like Brown, so they don't even consider

working there. In fact, any registered Republican who contemplates a career in academia these days is both a hero and a fool. So, in a semi-self-selective pattern, brainy people with generally liberal social mores flow to academia, and brainy people with generally conservative mores flow elsewhere.

The dream of diversity is like the dream of equality. Both are based on 15 ideals we celebrate even as we undermine them daily. (How many times have you seen someone renounce a high-paying job or pull his child from an elite college on the grounds that these things are bad for equality?) On the one hand, the situation is appalling. It is appalling that Americans know so little about one another. It is appalling that many of us are so narrow-minded that we can't tolerate a few people with ideas significantly different from our own. It's appalling that evangelical Christians are practically absent from entire professions, such as academia, the media, and filmmaking. It's appalling that people should be content to cut themselves off from everyone unlike themselves.

The segmentation of society means that often we don't even have argu- 16 ments across the political divide. Within their little validating communities, liberals and conservatives circulate half-truths about the supposed awfulness of the other side. These distortions are believed because it feels good to believe them.

On the other hand, there are limits to how diverse any community can 17 or should be. I've come to think that it is not useful to try to hammer diversity into every neighborhood and institution in the United States. Sure, Augusta National should probably admit women, and university sociology departments should probably hire a conservative or two. It would be nice if all neighborhoods had a good mixture of ethnicities. But human nature being what it is, most places and institutions are going to remain culturally homogeneous.

It's probably better to think about diverse lives, not diverse institu- 18 tions. Human beings, if they are to live well, will have to move through a series of institutions and environments, which may be individually homogeneous but, taken together, will offer diverse experiences. It might also be a good idea to make national service a rite of passage for young people in this country: it would take them out of their narrow neighborhood segment and thrust them in with people unlike themselves. Finally, it's probably important for adults to get out of their own familiar circles. If you live in a coastal, socially liberal neighborhood, maybe you should take out a subscription to *The Door*, the evangelical humor magazine; or maybe you should visit Branson, Missouri. Maybe you should stop in at a megachurch. Sure, it would be superficial familiarity, but it beats the iron curtains that now separate the nation's various cultural zones.

Look around at your daily life. Are you really in touch with the broad 19 diversity of American life? Do you care?

■   ■   ■

AFTER YOU READ

■ **THINK** about the arguments about diversity put forth by Brooks. State his primary arguments in your own words. Which one do you find most convincing? Is Brooks arguing *for* segregation or merely pointing out that it is what has occurred? Also think about the last paragraph of the essay (paragraph 19) in which he asks his reader, "Are you really in touch with the broad diversity of American life?" and "Do you care?" How would you respond to his questions?

■ **THINK** about the different types of diversity that Brooks discusses. How many—and which ones—can you identify in the essay? Which of these types of diversity, such as educational or economic differences, are relatively new to this unit? How important are these kinds of diversity in our society?

■ **EXAMINE** the following sentences: "The dream of diversity is like the dream of equality. Both are based on ideals we celebrate even as we undermine them daily" (paragraph 15). Do you agree with Brooks that the qualities of diversity and equality are merely dreams rather than reality in the United States today? Why or why not? Do you think Brooks is saying that Martin Luther King Jr.'s dream of equality has not really been fulfilled? Explain your opinion, using support from the essay.

■ **EXAMINE** also the suggestions that Brooks makes in paragraph 18. Notice that one of his suggestions is to make "national service a rite of passage for young people in this country" so that they would be forced to associate with "people unlike themselves." What is your reaction to this suggestion? To the other solutions that Brooks proposes in this paragraph?

■ **WRITE** an essay in which you argue for your own view of what the United States is like today in terms of diversity and/or segregation. You can find suggestions for writing a persuasive essay on pages 372–378 of Unit Six.

Mongrel America

■ ■ ■

GREGORY RODRIGUEZ

Gregory Rodriguez is a senior fellow at the New America Foundation and a contributing editor for the *Los Angeles Times* opinion section. His book *Mongrels, Bastards, Orphans, and Vagabonds: Mexican Immigration and the Future of Race in America* was listed by *The Washington Post* as one of the Best Books of 2007. In this essay, which appeared in the *Atlantic Monthly* (2003), Rodriguez argues that "the most important long-term social fact in America may be the rising rates of intermarriage among members of ethnic and racial groups."

BEFORE YOU READ

■ **THINK** about the title of this essay. What is a mongrel? To what is the term usually applied? Does the term have positive or negative connotations for you? Can you guess why the author uses this word to describe the United States?

■ **EXAMINE** the following italicized words, their context, and their definitions:

1. "the *ensuing polemics* will only *obscure* the more fundamental question" (paragraph 1): The phrase *ensuing polemics* means "following arguments"; *obscure* means "to conceal or obstruct."
2. "thirty-six years after the Supreme Court struck down *antimiscegenation* laws, young African-Americans are considerably more likely than their elders to claim mixed heritage" (paragraph 2): The prefix *anti-* means "against," while *miscegenation* means a "mixture or marriage involving persons of different races"; thus the term *antimiscegenation* means opposition to marriage between people of different races.
3. "the growth of the Mexican-American mestizo population has begun to challenge the Anglo-American *binary* view of race" (paragraph 9). The prefix *bi* usually means "two" (as in words like *bicycle*). The word *binary* means "characterized by two parts or components," so a binary view of race is one that is limited to two components, in this case black and white.

■ **WRITE** a journal entry in which you describe someone you know who derives from more than one ethnic group. This person could be you.

AS YOU READ

Try to determine whether Rodriguez's essay counters the arguments set forth by Brooks in the preceding essay. Write a "B" in the margin to indicate statements by Rodriguez that refute or contradict arguments made by Brooks.

■ ■ ■

Are racial categories still an important—or even a valid—tool of government policy? In recent years the debate in America has been between those who think that race is paramount and those who think it is increasingly irrelevant, and in the next election cycle this debate will surely intensify around a California ballot initiative that would all but prohibit the state from asking its citizens what their racial backgrounds are. But the ensuing polemics will only obscure the more fundamental question: What, when each generation is more racially and ethnically mixed than its predecessor, does race even mean anymore? If your mother is Asian and your father is African-American, what, racially speaking, are you? (And if your spouse is half Mexican and half Russian Jewish, what are your children?)

Five decades after the end of legal segregation, and only thirty-six years after the Supreme Court struck down antimiscegenation laws, young African-Americans are considerably more likely than their elders to claim mixed heritage. A study by the Population Research Center, in Portland, Oregon, projects that the black intermarriage rate will climb dramatically in this century, to a point at which 37 percent of African-Americans will claim mixed ancestry by 2100. By then more than 40 percent of Asian-Americans will be mixed. Most remarkable, however, by century's end the number of Latinos claiming mixed ancestry will be more than two times the number claiming a single background.

Not surprisingly, intermarriage rates for all groups are highest in the states that serve as immigration gateways. By 1990 Los Angeles County had an intermarriage rate five times the national average. Latinos and Asians, the groups that have made up three quarters of immigrants over the past forty years, have helped to create a climate in which ethnic or racial intermarriage is more accepted today than ever before. Nationally, whereas only eight percent of foreign-born Latinos marry non-Latinos, 32 percent of second-generation and 57 percent of third-generation Latinos marry outside their ethnic group. Similarly, whereas only 13 percent of foreign-born Asians marry non-Asians, 34 percent of second-generation and 54 percent of third-generation Asian-Americans do.

Meanwhile, as everyone knows, Latinos are now the largest minority group in the nation. Two thirds of Latinos, in turn, are of Mexican heritage. This is significant in itself, because their sheer numbers have helped Mexican-Americans do more than any other group to alter the country's old racial thinking. For instance, Texas and California, where Mexican-Americans are the largest minority, were the first two states to abolish affirmative action: when the collective "minority" populations in those states began to outnumber whites, the racial balance that had made affirmative action politically viable was subverted.

Many Mexican-Americans now live in cities or regions where they are   5
a majority, changing the very idea of what it means to be a member of a "minority" group. Because of such demographic changes, a number of the policies designed to integrate nonwhites into the mainstream—affirmative action in college admissions, racial set-asides in government contracting—have been rendered more complicated or even counterproductive in recent years. In California cities where whites have become a minority, it is no longer clear what "diversity" means or what the goals of integration policies should be. The selective magnet-school program of the Los Angeles Unified School District, for example, was originally developed as an alternative to forced busing—a way to integrate ethnic-minority students by encouraging them to look beyond their neighborhoods. Today, however, the school district is 71 percent Latino, and Latinos' majority status actually puts them at a disadvantage when applying to magnet schools.

But it is not merely their growing numbers (they will soon be the   6
majority in both California and Texas, and they are already the single largest contemporary immigrant group nationwide) that make Mexican-Americans a leading indicator of the country's racial future; rather, it's what they represent. They have always been a complicating element in the American racial system, which depends on an oversimplified classification scheme. Under the pre–civil-rights formulation, for example, if you had "one drop" of African blood, you were fully black. The scheme couldn't accommodate people who were part one thing and part another. Mexicans, who are a product of intermingling—both cultural and genetic—between the Spanish and the many indigenous peoples of North and Central America, have a history of tolerating and even reveling in such ambiguity. Since the conquest of Mexico, in the sixteenth century, they have practiced *mestizaje*—racial and cultural synthesis—both in their own country and as they came north. Unlike the English-speaking settlers of the western frontier, the Spaniards were willing everywhere they went to allow racial and cultural mixing to blur the lines between themselves and the natives. The fact that Latin America is far more heavily populated by people of mixed ancestry than Anglo America is the clearest sign of the difference between the two outlooks on race.

Nativists once deplored the Mexican tendency toward hybridity. In the   7
mid-nineteenth century, at the time of the conquest of the Southwest, Secretary of State James Buchanan feared granting citizenship to a "mongrel race." And in the late 1920s Representative John C. Box, of Texas, warned his colleagues on the House Immigration and Naturalization Committee that the continued influx of Mexican immigrants could lead to the "distressing process of mongrelization" in America. He argued that because Mexicans were the products of mixing, they harbored a relaxed attitude toward

interracial unions and were likely to mingle freely with other races in the United States.

Box was right. The typical cultural isolation of immigrants notwith- 8
standing, those immigrants' children and grandchildren are strongly oriented toward the American melting pot. Today two thirds of multiracial and multiethnic births in California involve a Latino parent. *Mexicanidad,* or "Mexicanness," is becoming the catalyst for a new American cultural synthesis.

In the same way that the rise in the number of multiracial Americans 9
muddles U.S. racial statistics, the growth of the Mexican-American mestizo population has begun to challenge the Anglo-American binary view of race. In the 1920 census Mexicans were counted as whites. Ten years later they were reassigned to a separate Mexican "racial" category. In 1940 they were officially reclassified as white. Today almost half the Latinos in California, which is home to a third of the nation's Latinos (most of them of Mexican descent), check "other" as their race. In the first half of the twentieth century Mexican-American advocates fought hard for the privileges that came with being white in America. But since the 1960s activists have sought to reap the benefits of being nonwhite minorities. Having spent so long trying to fit into one side or the other of the binary system, Mexican-Americans have become numerous and confident enough to simply claim their brownness—their mixture. This is a harbinger of America's future.

The original melting-pot concept was incomplete: it applied only to 10
white ethnics (Irish, Italians, Poles, and so forth), not to blacks and other nonwhites. Israel Zangwill, the playwright whose 1908 drama *The Melting Pot* popularized the concept, even wrote that whites were justified in avoiding intermarriage with blacks. In fact, multiculturalism—the ideology that promotes the permanent coexistence of separate but equal cultures in one place—can be seen as a by-product of America's exclusion of African-Americans from the melting pot; those whom assimilation rejected came to reject assimilation. Although the multicultural movement has always encompassed other groups, blacks gave it its moral impetus.

But the immigrants of recent decades are helping to forge a new Amer- 11
ican identity, something more complex than either a melting pot or a confederation of separate but equal groups. And this identity is emerging not as a result of politics or any specific public policies but because of powerful underlying cultural forces. To be sure, the civil-rights movement was instrumental in the initial assault on racial barriers. And immigration policies since 1965 have tended to favor those immigrant groups—Asians and Latinos—who are most open to intermarriage. But in recent years the government's major contribution to the country's growing multiracialism has been—as it should continue to be—a retreat from dictating limits on interracial intimacy and from exalting (through such policies as racial set-asides and affirmative action) race as the most important American category of being. As a result, Americans cross racial lines more often than ever before in choosing whom to sleep with, marry, or raise children with.

Unlike the advances of the civil-rights movement, the future of racial   12
identity in America is unlikely to be determined by politics or the courts
or public policy. Indeed, at this point perhaps the best thing the government can do is to acknowledge changes in the meaning of race in America
and then get out of the way. The Census Bureau's decision to allow Americans to check more than one box in the "race" section of the 2000 Census
was an important step in this direction. No longer forced to choose a single
racial identity, Americans are now free to identify themselves as mestizos—
and with this newfound freedom we may begin to endow racial issues with
the complexity and nuance they deserve.

■ ■ ■

AFTER YOU READ

■ **THINK** about Rodriguez's suggestion that "at this point perhaps the best
thing the government can do is to acknowledge changes in the meaning
of race in America and then get out of the way" (paragraph 12). Do you
agree that the government should get out of the way of racial issues in
this country? What if the government had never intervened in this issue?
Would every U.S. citizen now have the right to vote and would public
schools be integrated? Without government intervention in the past,
would we now live in a country in which interracial marriages are
increasingly accepted and are beginning to erase racial barriers? What
is your reaction to interracial marriage as a solution for racial divisions?
Why do you feel as you do?

■ **EXAMINE** the following three words, which all mean essentially the
same thing:

Mongrel	*A cross between different breeds, varieties, or groups (especially a dog of mixed breed); of mixed character or origin*
Mestizo	*A person of mixed racial ancestry, in particular of mixed European and Native American ancestry* (mestiza *is the feminine form of the word)*
Hybrid	*The offspring of genetically dissimilar parents; something or someone of mixed origin or composition*

Although all these words have essentially the same denotative meaning, each word has a slightly different connotation. Discuss the connotations each of these words has for you. Now go back to the question you
answered before reading the essay: why did Rodriguez choose to use the
word *mongrel* in his title? Do you have a clearer idea now about why he
may have chosen this particular word?

■ **WRITE** an essay in which you argue for or against Rodriguez's argument that intermarriage offers this country its best hope of eradicating racial divisions. You may also want to use ideas or information from the selection by Brooks in your essay. (If so, be sure to cite his essay as a source. If you need help with citing sources parenthetically, consult Purdue University's Online Writing Lab Website, listed on the "Related Websites" section of the *Interactions*, eighth edition, student site, available at www.cengagebrain.com.)

Two Ways to Belong to America

■ ■ ■

BHARATI MUKHERJEE

Born in Calcutta, India, to wealthy and highly respected parents, Bharati Mukherjee attended college at the University of Iowa, where she met and married American-born novelist Clark Blaise, with whom she has two sons. Currently a professor of English at the University of California, Berkeley, Mukherjee has published seven novels as well as short stories and nonfiction. She won the National Book Critics Circle Award for *The Middleman and Other Stories* (1988). *Desirable Daughters* (2002) and *The Tree Bride* (2004) are the first two novels of a trilogy focusing on a Calcutta-born protagonist who also has ties to the States. As in all of her work, Mukherjee focuses on identity in the following essay, praising universal qualities that bind people of different cultures together rather than on particular cultural elements that can separate people.

BEFORE YOU READ

■ **THINK** about what it would be like to attend college in another country and then decide to stay. If you had come from India to get an education in the United States, do you think you would want to get your degree, work a while, and then return home, or would you want to stay permanently in the United States? This is the dilemma that both Mukherjee and her sister faced.

■ **EXAMINE** the title and the first sentence of this essay. How do they emphasize differences, or contrasts, between the two sisters?

■ **EXAMINE** also the word *mongrelization* (paragraph 5), which is based on the word *mongrel* that you studied in the previous selection. Mukherjee uses this word to mean the process of intermarrying and having children with people of different ethnic and cultural backgrounds. You should also know that an *expatriate* (paragraphs 9 and 15) is a person who is exiled—usually self-exiled—from his or her native land on a temporary or permanent basis and that *divergence* (paragraph 11) means going in different directions.

■ **WRITE** a journal entry explaining why you think you would want to stay or return home after getting an education in another country, such as England or France.

AS YOU READ

Write a B beside sentences and paragraphs that describe Bharati Mukherjee's actions and attitudes, and an M beside those that describe her sister Mira's.

■   ■   ■

I OWA CITY—This is a tale of two sisters from Calcutta, Mira and   1
Bharati, who have lived in the United States for some 35 years, but
who find themselves on different sides in the current debate over the
status of immigrants. I am an American citizen and she is not. I am moved
that thousands of long-term residents are finally taking the oath of citizenship. She is not.

Mira arrived in Detroit in 1960 to study child psychology and pre-   2
school education. I followed her a year later to study creative writing at
the University of Iowa. When we left India, we were almost identical in
appearance and attitude. We dressed alike, in saris; we expressed identical
views on politics, social issues, love and marriage in the same Calcutta
convent-school accent. We would endure our two years in America, secure
our degrees, then return to India to marry the grooms of our father's
choosing.

Instead, Mira married an Indian student in 1962 who was getting his   3
business administration degree at Wayne State University. They soon
acquired the labor certifications necessary for the green card of hassle-free
residence and employment.

Mira still lives in Detroit, works in the Southfield, Mich., school sys-   4
tem, and has become nationally recognized for her contributions in the
fields of pre-school education and parent-teacher relationships. After 36
years as a legal immigrant in this country, she clings passionately to her
Indian citizenship and hopes to go home to India when she retires.

In Iowa City in 1963, I married a fellow student, an American of   5
Canadian parentage. Because of the accident of his North Dakota birth, I
by-passed the labor-certification requirements and the race-related "quota"
system that valued the applicant's country of origin over his or her merit.
I was prepared for (and even welcomed) the emotional strain that came with
marrying outside my ethnic community. In 33 years of marriage, we have
lived in every part of North America. By choosing a husband who was not
my father's selection, I was opting for fluidity, self-invention, blue jeans and
T-shirts, and renouncing 3,000 years (at least) of caste-observant, "pure culture" marriage in the Mukherjee family. My books have often been read as
unapologetic (and in some quarters overenthusiastic) texts for cultural and
psychological "mongrelization." It's a word I celebrate.

Mira and I have stayed sisterly close by phone. In our regular Sunday   6
morning conversations, we are unguardedly affectionate. I am her only
blood relative on this continent. We expect to see each other through the

looming crises of aging and ill health without being asked. Long before Vice President Gore's "Citizenship U.S.A." drive, we'd had our polite arguments over the ethics of retaining an overseas citizenship while expecting the permanent protection and economic benefits that come with living and working in America.

Like well-raised sisters, we never said what was really on our minds,   7
but we probably pitied one another. She for the lack of structure in my life, the erasure of Indianness, the absence of an unvarying daily core. I, for the narrowness of her perspective, her uninvolvement with the mythic depths or the superficial pop culture of this society. But, now, with the scapegoating of "aliens" (documented or illegal) on the increase, and the targeting of long-term legal immigrants like Mira for new scrutiny and new self-consciousness, she and I find ourselves unable to maintain the same polite discretion. We were always unacknowledged adversaries, and we are now, more than ever, sisters.

"I feel used," Mira raged on the phone the other night. "I feel manip-   8
ulated and discarded. This is such an unfair way to treat a person who was invited to stay and work here because of her talent. My employer went to the I.N.S. and petitioned for the labor certification. For over 30 years, I've invested my creativity and professional skills into the improvement of this country's pre-school system. I've obeyed all the rules. I've paid my taxes. I love my work, I love my students, I love the friends I've made. How dare America now change its rules in midstream? If America wants to make new rules curtailing benefits of legal immigrants, they should apply only to immigrants who arrive after those rules are already in place."

To my ears, it sounded like the description of a long-enduring, comfortable   9
yet loveless marriage, without risk or recklessness. Have we the right to demand, and to expect, that we be loved? (That, to me, is the subtext of the arguments by immigration advocates.) My sister is an expatriate, professionally generous and creative, socially courteous and gracious, and that's as far as her Americanization can go. She is here to maintain an identity, not to transform it.

I asked her if she would follow the example of others who have   10
decided to become citizens because of the anti-immigration bills in Congress. And here, she surprised me. "If America wants to play the manipulative game, I'll play it too," she snapped. "I'll become a U.S. citizen for now, then change back to Indian when I'm ready to go home. I feel some kind of irrational attachment to India that I don't to America. Until all this hysteria against legal immigrants, I was totally happy. Having my green card meant I could visit any place in the world I wanted to and then come back to a job that's satisfying and that I do very well."

In one family, from two sisters alike as peas in a pod, there could not   11
be a wider divergence of immigrant experience. America spoke to me—I married it—I embraced the demotion from expatriate aristocrat to immigrant nobody, surrendering those thousands of years of "pure culture,"

the saris, the delightfully accented English. She retained them all. Which of us is the freak?

Mira's voice, I realize, is the voice not just of the immigrant South Asian community but of an immigrant community of millions who have stayed rooted in one job, one city, one house, one ancestral culture, one cuisine, for the entirety of their productive years. She speaks for greater numbers than I possibly can. Only the fluency of her English and the anger, rather than fear, born of confidence from her education, differentiates her from the seamstresses, the domestics, the technicians, the shop owners, the millions of hard-working but effectively silenced documented immigrants as well as their less fortunate "illegal" brothers and sisters.   12

Nearly 20 years ago, when I was living in my husband's ancestral homeland of Canada, I was always well-employed but never allowed to feel part of the local Quebec or larger Canadian society. Then, through a Green Paper that invited a national referendum on the unwanted side effects of "nontraditional" immigration, the Government officially turned against its immigrant communities, particularly those from South Asia.   13

I felt then the same sense of betrayal that Mira feels now. I will never forget the pain of that sudden turning, and the casual racist outbursts the Green Paper elicited. That sense of betrayal had its desired effect and drove me, and thousands like me, from the country.   14

Mira and I differ, however, in the ways in which we hope to interact with the country that we have chosen to live in. She is happier to live in America as expatriate Indian than as an immigrant American. I need to feel like a part of the community I have adopted (as I tried to feel in Canada as well). I need to put roots down, to vote and make the difference that I can. The price that the immigrant willingly pays, and that the exile avoids, is the trauma of self-transformation.   15

■ ■ ■

AFTER YOU READ

■ **THINK** about the two different immigrant experiences that Mukherjee describes. Do you agree or disagree with Mukherjee's sister Mira that noncitizen immigrants should be able to stay and work in the United States and receive the same benefits as a citizen? Or do you think that immigrants should be required to become citizens to receive these benefits? Do you agree or disagree that immigrants—legal or illegal—should be allowed to become citizens? Explain.

■ **EXAMINE** the annotations that you made as you read the essay—the B's that you wrote in the margins to identify sentences and paragraphs that describe Mukherjee's attitudes, beliefs, and actions and the M's that focus on Mira's. The pattern of your annotations shows that Mukherjee has written an effective comparison and contrast essay. (You may want to review comparison and contrast in Lesson 7 of the *Interactions*, eighth edition, student website, available at www.cengagebrain.com.) What similarities does Mukherjee point out? What major differences, or contrasts, does she discuss? How does she organize her information? Does she give all the details about one sister and then all the details about the other? Or does she alternate details about various issues for one sister and then the other? Give specific examples.

■ WRITE an essay in which you respond to Mukherjee's last sentence: "The price that the immigrant willingly pays, and that the exile avoids, is the trauma of self-transformation." Define the phrase *self-transformation* early in your essay, and then use reasons and examples to show both the trauma and the ultimate "self-transformation" of truly becoming an American. (You may want to review the guidelines for "Responding to a Text" on pp. 244–247.)

Anonymous Victims of Dreams and a River

■ ■ ■

Victor Landa

This essay focuses on the attempts of illegal immigrants, whom Mukherjee briefly discusses in paragraph 12 of the previous essay, to enter the United States. In the following article, Victor Landa, a contributing columnist for the *San Antonio Express-News*, remembers when he was a young journalist, living and working on the Rio Grande border between Texas and Mexico. The tone of his essay is reflective and poetic, but it also includes some hard facts about the number of immigrants who die each year attempting to cross the Rio Grande River.

BEFORE YOU READ

■ **THINK** about what compels people to leave the place of their birth and come to a new country. What would motivate you to leave your home and go to a strange land?

■ **EXAMINE** the title of the essay. Why are the victims described as anonymous? How can someone be a victim of a dream? What kind of dreams do you think these people had?

■ **EXAMINE** also the following italicized words: *cadavers* (paragraph 2), meaning dead bodies; *"pauper's graves"* (paragraph 3)," meaning graves provided by public charity to poor or unknown people; and *macabre* (paragraph 11), meaning gruesome, ghastly.

■ **WRITE** a journal entry in which you explain what it would take to convince you to immigrate into a new country.

AS YOU READ

Identify the passages that are clearly poetic by underlining them and those that are clearly informative by bracketing them.

■ ■ ■

There are rivers that we shouldn't cross. There are places where we shouldn't go, not because it's prohibited but because we're not prepared. Because it is the end. 1

When I was a young journalist in Laredo, cadavers would regularly   2
appear on the Rio Grande. We called them "floaters" out of a sharp
sense of cynicism that protected us from the cold reality of death.

They seldom had identification, and if they did, it was of no use. Their   3
names were entered in some official ledger, and the bodies were buried in
paupers' graves, marked by simple wooden crosses in a remote corner of
the city cemetery.

They came from small towns, farming communities, forgotten enclaves   4
of industrial centers—they came from families, from homes that saw them
leave and never heard from them again.

The official reports always read the same: Dead for two or three days,   5
death by drowning.

The Rio Grande is a dangerous river. The current is tricky. One slip   6
and you lose control. The water pulls you; it suffocates and kills.

The bodies sink to the bottom and stay there until gases form inside   7
them—gases lighter than water that eventually make the corpses rise to
the surface. The same currents that took their lives deposit them among the
green rushes on the river's edge.

Boys would come on their bicycles from the nearby neighborhoods.   8
People would emerge from everywhere. Women in housecoats carrying
babies on their hips would arrive, like moths drawn to a light—attracted
by the police, by the television cameras, by the fascination with death.

Death is a part of the risk, the losing end of the gamble. When you   9
travel among the shadows, death is a constant companion.

Between 1993 and 1996, according to the U.S. Immigration and Nat-   10
uralization Service, more than 1,000 of these travelers died trying to cross
the border between the United States and Mexico. From San Ysidro, Calif.,
to Brownsville, almost 400 die every year now. More than one a day. Most
of them in Texas.

The agents in charge of the macabre count travel to every town along   11
the border, endure bureaucracies, speak with policemen, coroners, cemetery keepers. They comb through registers and record books, looking for
details. And the final result is a simple number. In the end, they are all the
same.

Their efforts, though, should mean something. The impulse to leave   12
everything behind obeys the promise of a light much brighter than the
darkness they came from. They gambled for very human reasons, and the
tragedy of their death is a very human event.

Since I was a young journalist on the border so many years ago, there   13
have been tens of thousands of dreams that have ended floating in the current, among the rushes. And in all those years, I still haven't been able to
understand the misery of the river's end.

All I know is that there are places where we shouldn't go, places that   14
will take your life and your name in a cruel exchange for an empty dream.

■   ■   ■

AFTER YOU READ

■ **THINK** about Landa's representation of the Rio Grande. How does he describe it? Is it the river's fault that the immigrants drown while trying to cross it? Landa does not refer to the people who die in the river as illegal immigrants, but obviously they are illegal or they would be crossing the river on the bridges at the legal immigration entry points. Why do you think he avoids this term?

■ **THINK** also about Landa's thesis, which is implicit rather than explicit. Although he does not state his thesis, the essay's purpose is ultimately persuasive. Try to state his thesis in your own words.

■ **EXAMINE** Landa's statement that "the impulse to leave everything behind obeys the promise of a light much brighter than the darkness they came from." This statement implies that people immigrate to a new land not only because of the problems that characterize their lives in the place where they live but also because of their dreams of what is possible in the new land. Do you agree or disagree with this statement? Explain.

■ **WRITE** an essay in which you argue for or against stronger enforcement of immigration laws or propose new immigration laws for Mexicans entering the United States.

I Have a Dream

■　■　■

MARTIN LUTHER KING, JR.

Throughout his all-too-brief career, the African American civil rights leader Martin Luther King, Jr. worked with the Southern Christian Leadership Conference to gain for African Americans the freedom and justice promised all Americans in the Constitution but denied for many years to its nonwhite citizens. King was assassinated in Memphis in 1968, but his speeches and writings have become important documents in the ongoing struggle for civil rights. The following version of King's "I Have a Dream" speech was based on the King papers project at the Martin Luther King, Jr. Research and Education Institute at Stanford University.

BEFORE YOU READ

■ THINK about what life was like for African Americans in 1963 when this speech was made. What kind of dreams did King and other civil rights leaders have then? To what extent have their dreams been realized? How does the success of King's dream compare and contrast with the unfulfilled dreams to which Landa refers in the previous essay?

■ EXAMINE the first two paragraphs of King's speech. In his first paragraph, he states the purpose of the rally and of his speech. What is this purpose? Notice that King begins paragraph 2 with the phrase "Five score years ago." This phrase recalls Abraham Lincoln's famous Gettysburg Address, which begins "Four score and seven years ago our fathers brought forth on this continent a new nation, conceived in liberty and dedicated to the proposition that all men are created equal." By using a phrase similar to the one Lincoln used, King reminds his hearers and readers of the promises—or at least assumptions—in Lincoln's speech that all people are equal and that liberty and justice belong to all humankind.

■ EXAMINE also King's use of the word *Negro* to refer to African Americans. This usage was common during the civil rights era but is seldom employed today. What other terms does King use to designate African Americans?

■ EXAMINE also the following italicized words and their definitions, with which you may not be familiar: *degenerate* (paragraph 8), meaning "to deteriorate; go down"; *interposition* (paragraph 17), meaning "separation; segregation"; *nullification* (paragraph 17), meaning "negation, invalidation"; and *prodigious* (paragraph 21), meaning "enormous."

■ **WRITE** a journal entry about your own personal dream for the future of the United States.

AS YOU READ

Remember that you are reading a speech rather than an essay. Make notes in the margins to indicate passages that you think would be especially effective if you were listening to rather than reading this speech.

■   ■   ■

I am happy to join with you today in what will go down in history   1 as the greatest demonstration for freedom in the history of our nation.

Five score years ago, a great American, in whose symbolic shadow we   2 stand today, signed the Emancipation Proclamation. This momentous decree came as a great beacon light of hope to millions of Negro slaves who had been seared in the flames of withering injustice. It came as a joyous daybreak to end the long night of their captivity.

But one hundred years later, the Negro still is not free. One hundred   3 years later, the life of the Negro is still sadly crippled by the manacles of segregation and the chains of discrimination. One hundred years later, the Negro lives on a lonely island of poverty in the midst of a vast ocean of material prosperity. One hundred years later, the Negro is still languished in the corners of American society and finds himself an exile in his own land. And so we've come here today to dramatize a shameful condition.

In a sense we've come to our nation's capital to cash a check. When   4 the architects of our republic wrote the magnificent words of the Constitution and the Declaration of Independence, they were signing a promissory note to which every American was to fall heir. This note was the promise that all men, yes, black men as well as white men, would be guaranteed the "unalienable Rights of Life, Liberty, and the pursuit of Happiness." It is obvious today that America has defaulted on this promissory note in so far as her citizens of color are concerned. Instead of honoring this sacred obligation, America has given the Negro people a bad check; a check which has come back marked "insufficient funds."

But we refuse to believe that the bank of justice is bankrupt. We refuse   5 to believe that there are insufficient funds in the great vaults of opportunity of this nation. And so we've come to cash this check, a check that will give us upon demand the riches of freedom and the security of justice.

We have also come to this hallowed spot to remind America of the   6 fierce urgency of now. This is no time to engage in the luxury of cooling off or to take the tranquilizing drug of gradualism. Now is the time to make real the promises of democracy. Now is the time to rise from the dark and desolate valley of segregation to the sunlit path of racial justice.

Now is the time to lift our nation from the quicksands of racial injustice to the solid rock of brotherhood. Now is the time to make justice a reality for all of God's children.

It would be fatal for the nation to overlook the urgency of the moment. This sweltering summer of the Negro's legitimate discontent will not pass until there is an invigorating autumn of freedom and equality. Nineteen sixty-three is not an end, but a beginning. And those who hope that the Negro needed to blow off steam and will now be content will have a rude awakening if the nation returns to business as usual. There will be neither rest nor tranquility in America until the Negro is granted his citizenship rights. The whirlwinds of revolt will continue to shake the foundations of our nation until the bright day of justice emerges. 7

But there is something that I must say to my people, who stand on the worn threshold which leads into the palace of justice. In the process of gaining our rightful place, we must not be guilty of wrongful deeds. Let us not seek to satisfy our thirst for freedom by drinking from the cup of bitterness and hatred. We must forever conduct our struggle on the high plain of dignity and discipline. We must not allow our creative protests to degenerate into physical violence. Again and again, we must rise to the majestic heights of meeting physical force with soul force. The marvelous new militancy which has engulfed the Negro community must not lead us to a distrust of all white people, for many of our white brothers, as evidenced by their presence here today, have come to realize that their destiny is tied up with our destiny. And they have come to realize that their freedom is inextricably bound to our freedom. We cannot walk alone. 8

And as we walk, we must make the pledge that we shall always march ahead. We cannot turn back. There are those who are asking the devotees of Civil Rights, "When will you be satisfied?" 9

We can never be satisfied as long as the Negro is the victim of the unspeakable horrors of police brutality. We can never be satisfied as long as our bodies, heavy with the fatigue of travel, cannot gain lodging in the motels of the highways and the hotels of the cities. We cannot be satisfied as long as the Negro's basic mobility is from a smaller ghetto to a larger one. We can never be satisfied as long as our children are stripped of their selfhood and robbed of their dignity by signs stating "for whites only." We cannot be satisfied as long as the Negro in Mississippi cannot vote and a Negro in New York believes he has nothing for which to vote. No! No, we are not satisfied and we will not be satisfied until "justice rolls down like waters and righteousness like a mighty stream." 10

I am not unmindful that some of you have come here out of great trials and tribulations. Some of you come fresh from narrow jail cells. Some of you have come from areas where your quest for freedom left you battered by the storms of persecution and staggered by the winds of police brutality. You have been the veterans of creative suffering. Continue to work with the faith that unearned suffering is redemptive. Go back to Mississippi. 11

Go back to Alabama. Go back to South Carolina. Go back to Georgia. Go back to Louisiana. Go back to the slums and ghettos of our Northern cities, knowing that somehow this situation can and will be changed. Let us not wallow in the valley of despair.

I say to you today, my friends, so even though we face the difficulties 12 of today and tomorrow, I still have a dream. It is a dream deeply rooted in the American dream.

I have a dream that one day this nation will rise up and live out the 13 true meaning of its creed, "We hold these truths to be self-evident, that all men are created equal."

I have a dream that one day on the red hills of Georgia, sons of former 14 slaves and the sons of former slave owners will be able to sit down together at the table of brotherhood.

I have a dream that one day even the state of Mississippi, a state swel- 15 tering with the heat of injustice, sweltering with the heat of oppression, will be transformed into an oasis of freedom and justice.

I have a dream that my four little children will one day live in a nation 16 where they will not be judged by the color of their skin, but by the content of their character. I have a dream today.

I have a dream that one day down in Alabama—with its vicious 17 racists, with its Governor having his lips dripping with the words of interposition and nullification—one day right there in Alabama, little black boys and black girls will be able to join hands with little white boys and white girls as sisters and brothers. I have a dream today.

I have a dream that one day "every valley shall be exalted, and every 18 hill and mountain shall be made low; the rough places will be made plain, and the crooked places will be made straight; and the glory of the Lord shall be revealed, and all flesh shall see it together."

This is our hope. This is the faith that I go back to the South with. 19 With this faith we will be able to hew out of the mountain of despair a stone of hope. With this faith we will be able to transform the jangling discords of our nation into a beautiful symphony of brotherhood. With this faith we will be able to work together, to pray together, to struggle together, to go to jail together, to stand up for freedom together, knowing that we will be free one day. This will be the day, this will be the day when all of God's children will be able to sing with new meaning:

> My country 'tis of thee, sweet land of liberty, of thee I sing.
> Land where my father died, land of the pilgrim's pride,
> From every mountain side, let freedom ring!

And if America is to be a great nation, this must become true. 20
So let freedom ring from the prodigious hilltops of New Hampshire. 21
Let freedom ring from the mighty mountains of New York. 22
Let freedom ring from the heightening Alleghenies of Pennsylvania. 23
Let freedom ring from the snowcapped Rockies of Colorado. 24
Let freedom ring from the curvaceous slopes of California. 25
But not only that: Let freedom ring from Stone Mountain of Georgia. 26
Let freedom ring from Lookout Mountain of Tennessee. 27

Let freedom ring from every hill and mole hill of Mississippi. 28

"From every mountainside, let freedom ring." 29

And when this happens, when we allow freedom to ring, when we let 30
it ring from every village and every hamlet, from every state and every city,
we will be able to speed up that day when all of God's children, black men
and white men, Jews and Gentiles, Protestants and Catholics, will be able
to join hands and sing in the words of the old Negro spiritual:

> Free at last! Free at last!
> Thank God Almighty, we are free at last!

■ ■ ■

AFTER YOU READ

■ **THINK** about the words and phrases that King frequently repeats in his
speech. What word does King use most often? What other words or
phrases are repeated frequently?

■ **EXAMINE** King's use of parallel structure to emphasize important
points. For example, in paragraph 3 King repeats four times the introductory phrase "One hundred years later, the Negro is ..." King follows
each repeated phrase with a different point, but the drum-like—almost
poetic—repetition of the similar statements emphasizes the fact that the
life of African Americans had not changed appreciably in the 100 years
between Emancipation and the time in which King was speaking.
Reread King's essay carefully, identifying other places where he effectively uses repeated structures to emphasize a point.

■ **WRITE** an essay in which you argue for your own dream for America as
it exists today. You can elaborate on the dream you identified in your
journal entry or select a new one. Your dream need not be limited to
racial concerns or issues.

UNIT FIVE

■ ■ ■

Critical Thinking, Reading, and Writing

■ ANALYZING A TEXT

To analyze means to take something apart and figure out how the parts work together to make the whole. We often associate analysis with a science lab, where people in white lab coats work with chemicals and test tubes. But analysis also applies to texts. Any time you read something, you use analytical skills. For example, you may question the author's qualifications or the reason a certain word is used. We inevitably analyze certain elements of a text as we read it. But, as a college student, you will often be asked to make a more formal, written analysis of a text—to analyze a text not just by explaining the overall effect or your general impression of the whole but also by identifying specific elements of a text and explaining their function. Thus, analyzing a text is another important reading and writing skill that you should master.

There are many ways to analyze a text. A rhetorical analysis focuses on the appeals that an author uses to convince a reader. A linguistic analysis focuses on the language that the author uses. However, one of the most useful types of analysis simply focuses on the writer's audience and purpose. This lesson will give you basic guidelines for analyzing a text in this way.

BEFORE YOU WRITE

Any type of analysis requires a careful reading of the text. Thus, you should begin by reading and annotating the text you are analyzing. Your annotations will focus, as usual, on the thesis of the text and the writer's supporting arguments and evidence. However, as you read, you should also note any clues that will help you identify the writer's audience and purpose. Essentially, you will read to determine *why* the writer is writing and *to whom* the writer is writing. In most cases, you will find that the answers to these two questions are related.

These general guidelines will be useful as you read and annotate the text you are analyzing:

- Pay particular attention to the introduction of the text because the writer's purpose and audience are often indicated in the introduction.

- Do not assume that the writer's stated thesis is the same as his or her purpose. The two are usually related but are not necessarily the same.

- Because writers seldom explicitly identify their audience, you will have to infer their intended readers from clues in the text. You will probably not be able to determine the intended audience precisely; however, if you read carefully, you should be able to figure out the general audience for whom the writer is writing. For example, in "Getting to Know about You and Me," Chana Schoenberger is writing not only to the general audience of *Newsweek*, where the essay was published, but also to students and adults everywhere who do not understand and respect religious differences.

- Be sure that you also annotate the text in the usual ways—noting questions and comments in the margins, underlining or highlighting important ideas, identifying words that are unfamiliar to you, and so on.

Example

An Analysis of Audience in Martin Luther King's "I Have a Dream" Speech

When Martin Luther King, Jr. delivered his now famous "I Have a Dream" speech on the steps of the Lincoln Memorial in 1963, he was speaking primarily to a particular audience—the hundreds of thousands of supporters who had gathered in Washington, D.C. to protest for an end to racial segregation in public schools and for more meaningful Civil Rights legislation. **However, an analysis of King's speech reveals that he was speaking to multiple audiences.** Although physically he was addressing the throngs gathered on this particular day to hear him, King was, in reality, speaking not only to the people in this audience but also to Civil Rights workers and sympathizers across the nation, to others across the nation who did not sympathize with his goals, to African Americans across the nation, and, finally, to future generations—those people in the future who would read or listen to his speech. An awareness of all of these audiences is important to an understanding and appreciation of King's speech.

Primarily, of course, King was speaking to throngs who were assembled in front of him on the Mall in Washington, D.C.—those who had struggled for many years to bring about meaningful Civil Rights legislation. These people were gathered not only in protest but also to celebrate the progress that had been made. And King's speech reflects his awareness of this audience and his desire not only to reward them with praise for what they had already accomplished but also to spur them on to additional victories. For example, King begins his speech by addressing those who stood before him specifically: "I am happy to join with you today in what will go down in history as the greatest demonstration for freedom in the history of our nation." And repeatedly, throughout his speech, King speaks directly to those gathered to hear him that day, congratulating them as well as encouraging them to continue the struggle.

However, beginning with his second sentence (paragraph 2), King broadens his audience by addressing black people of the past and present specifically, not just those gathered on the mall in

Washington that day. He speaks here especially to those who have been victims of the "withering injustice" of slavery, discrimination, and segregation throughout our history. And again in paragraph 8, King states that "there is something that I must say to my people...." Although King knows only too well that his audience is both black and white, throughout his speech he clearly feels the need at times to address his fellow African Americans specifically.

Then, beginning with the last sentence in paragraph 9, King speaks directly to those who disagree with him, those who are not even sympathetic to the goals of Civil Rights for which he has struggled, by stating that "There are those who are asking the devotees of Civil Rights, 'When will you be satisfied?'" And he warns these people that the Civil Rights movement will continue until "justice rolls down like waters and righteousness like a mighty stream."

4

Finally, it is clear that King was also addressing those who would read or listen to recordings of his speech in the future. In paragraph 11, King speaks of the "difficulties of today and tomorrow" and states for the first time, "I still have a dream." He repeats this refrain again and again in the final paragraphs of his speech. And in his final paragraph, he refers to that day "when all of God's children, black men and white men, Jews and Gentiles, Protestants and Catholics, will be able to join hands and sing in the words of the old Negro spiritual: 'Free at last. Free at last. / Thank God Almighty, we are free at last.'" It was as if King knew, even then, that his speech was not just for that time and place but would survive long after he was gone.

5

King's speech is effective and memorable for many reasons—its poetry, its effective use of historical references, its passion, and its rhetorical effectiveness. But one of its strengths, then and now, is clearly King's sense of audience—his awareness that he was speaking to multiple audiences, not just those assembled before him on that day in Washington, D.C.

The writer of the essay above begins by placing King's speech in context—telling when and where and why it took place. He then quickly moves to establish the purpose of his essay, which is to analyze the audiences whom King was addressing. Next, at the end of the first paragraph, he clearly states the thesis of his essay and in paragraph 10 he warns: "An awareness of all of these audiences is important to an understanding and appreciation of King's speech."

In paragraphs 2 through 5, the writer discusses each of these different audiences. He not only identifies each but also points out specific places in the speech that support the idea that King was deliberately addressing different audiences. These supporting paragraphs are important for any analysis because they are the "proof" that the writer is presenting to support his or her thesis.

Finally, in his last paragraph the writer of this essay concludes by returning to King's speech as a whole and providing reasons why it is memorable. He then reinforces his thesis by repeating his argument that King's awareness of speaking to multiple audiences helped to shape his speech and contributed to its success.

Assignments

1. Read, or reread, "Indian Education" by Sherman Alexie, and identify his purpose and audience. Then write an essay analyzing one or both of these aspects of the selection.

2. Read and annotate "Anonymous Victims of Dreams and a River" by Victor Landa. Then write an essay in which you analyze the author's audience and/or purpose in this text about illegal immigration along the Texas–Mexico border.

3. Locate a website that you are interested in, and analyze it to determine its audience and purpose. Write an essay in which you identify the audience and purpose of the website and explain how the visual and verbal elements of the site reflect its purpose and the audience for whom it is intended.

AS YOU WRITE

The paper you write will reflect the results of your analysis. For example, your thesis will, in effect, summarize your conclusions about the text's audience and/or purpose. The rest of your paper will support your conclusions. You will need to convince your reader that your conclusions about the writer's audience and purpose are accurate by identifying and explaining the "clues" or "evidence" you found in the text itself. In general, your purpose in this type of analysis is to go beyond the text as it appears on the printed page—to read between the lines, to discern what was in the writer's mind. Although this is not an easy task, the following guidelines will be useful to you as you write this essay:

• In your introduction, you will need to identify and *briefly* summarize the text you are analyzing. You will also want to include in your introduction your own thesis—the conclusion you have reached about the writer's audience and/or purpose.

• In the remainder of your essay, you will support your thesis by explaining how you reached your conclusions and by presenting evidence from the text itself.

• In your conclusion, you should address the significance of your findings by answering one or more of these questions: How do the audience and/or purpose you have identified affect your understanding of the text?

How do these conclusions shed new light on the writer and/or the text? Why is it significant that the writer was addressing a certain audience or writing for a certain purpose? How do your conclusions differ from other possible assumptions about the audience and purpose of this text?

AFTER YOU WRITE

After you have written a draft of your essay, you will need to revise it. If possible, allow some time to elapse before you begin your revision. Before beginning your revision, reread your draft and answer the following questions:

- Have you identified the author and title of the text you are analyzing?
- Does your introduction include a brief summary of the text you are analyzing?
- Have you stated your own thesis clearly?
- Do you support your thesis adequately with evidence from the text?
- Do you make clear in your conclusion why your analysis is significant in terms of understanding the text?

■ EXPLORING IDEAS TOGETHER

1. Our country is enriched by many kinds of diversity. Select one kind of diversity (differently abled, age, religion, gender, race, ethnicity, etc.) and discuss what contributions various members or subcategories of this type of diversity have made to our society. In your discussion, consider ideas from at least two readings.

2. Discuss with your classmates ways in which our society can protect its citizenry and yet continue to open its doors to newcomers. The selections by Brooks, Rodriguez, Mukherjee, and Landa can contribute to your discussion.

3. The selections by Schoenberger and Alexie focus on school experiences. Discuss the special challenges that face students who are not members of the mainstream culture. What types of problems do they encounter? What compromises must these students make? How can they educate other students about their religion or culture? What could schools do to accommodate these students?

4. Compare the dreams discussed by Landa and King. Define each of the dreams, and then discuss how they are alike and how they are different.

5. Discuss with your classmates the role of language in shaping attitudes, especially prejudice. The reading selections by Schoenberger, Tan, and Alexie will help you frame your discussion and identify issues.

■ EXPLORING THE INTERNET

You can find more information to help you with the following exercises at the *Interactions*, eighth edition, student website, at www.cengagebrain.com.

1. Sherman Alexie is a Spokane/Coeur D'Alène Indian whose own life has been as interesting and dramatic as the stories he writes. To learn more about Alexie, author of "Indian Education," you can read a biography of him on his official website, which is listed in the "Related Websites" section of the *Interactions* student site.

2. Martin Luther King, Jr. has become one of our national heroes. His remarkable life is now commemorated by a national holiday, and his voice is one that almost everyone, even those born long after his death, recognizes. You can learn more about the life of Martin Luther King, Jr. and listen to audio excerpts from his speeches by searching for The Martin Luther King, Jr. Research and Education Institution on the Internet. (Or you can use the link on "Related Websites.")

3. The process of coming to the United States as an immigrant is more difficult today as a result of the September 11, 2001, attacks, but people continue to flock to our shores. To learn more about the process and experience of immigrating to the United States, both now and in the past, explore the Ellis Island website, which you can find in the list of "Related Websites" on the *Interactions* site.

■ WRITING ESSAYS

1. Write an essay in which you argue that our diversity either strengthens or weakens our society. To prepare for this essay, list both the problems that result from having a diverse population and the strengths that result from this diversity. Support your thesis with specific examples from your reading, observations, and experience.

2. Not only are many different languages spoken in our country, but also—as Amy Tan shows us—each of us speaks different languages with different people and in different situations. Write an essay about the different languages you speak with different people and different situations. Conclude by explaining which language(s) define you the most clearly.

3. Write an essay in which you describe one or more of the problems (effects) that have been caused by immigration and then propose a solution (or solutions) for the problem(s). You will find the selections by Landa and Rodriguez useful as sources. (effects) (You may want to refer to Lesson 5 on cause and effect essays on the *Interactions*, eighth edition, student website, available at www.cengagebrain.com.).

4. Write an essay about how the position and rights of one particular ethnic group have changed for the better or worse. If you are writing about African Americans, for example, you may want to incorporate

ideas and quotations from the readings by Staples and King into your essay along with your own ideas; if you are writing about Mexican Americans, review the selections by Landa and Rodriguez.

5. Write an essay in which you describe your own hopes and dreams for the United States. To develop your essay, you may want to refer to several of the reading selections from this unit, especially those by Rodriguez, Mukherjee, Landa, and King.

6. Write a poem or essay about yourself, celebrating your own diversity— how you are different or unique in some way.

NATURE AND ENVIRONMENT

UNIT **SIX**

Examine this photograph closely. If you block off the upper two-thirds of it, you can see peaceful—if shaded—farmland, broken into a checkerboard pattern of roads and crops. Then look carefully at the tornado slashing across this land. What details show its power and potential destructiveness? Is your final impression one of beauty or horror?

■ ■ ■

Including all living—both human and animal—and nonliving things, our natural environment extends from the close surroundings of our homes and workplaces to the distant reaches of the entire world.

Although the top of a distant mountain or the middle of an inaccessible wilderness may seem to be pristine natural landscapes, human activity and the natural processes taking place in these remote locations are actually interrelated. You as an individual, therefore, are inextricably connected to nature and to the environment.

As shown by the readings in this unit, the environment may be personal or distant, friendly or hostile, beautiful or ugly, awe-inspiring or frightening. As you read you will think about your own sense of nature and the environment—your own "sense of place." You will read about the annual cycle of the seasons in a rural area of the Dakotas; the green sky, forked lightning, and rumbling thunder that accompany a midwestern funnel cloud; and the drenching rains and powerful winds of Hurricane Katrina. In addition, you will examine different points of view about the use and treatment of our natural resources, and you will analyze the continuing debate about climate change. In making decisions about how we interact with nature and our environment, we as human beings can think primarily of ourselves and our time, or we can think about future generations and their world. In our own lives, we can make ourselves aware of and responsible for our physical and natural environment, or we can impoverish our lives and the lives of others by ignoring it or damaging it.

To prepare to read these selections, use one of the following sets of questions to write a journal entry about the natural environment.

1. *What is the most beautiful natural place you have ever seen or heard about? What makes this place so lovely? Have you visited it, or would you like to do so? Explain.*
2. *In what physical place do you feel most at home? Do you have a true "sense of this place" from memory and experience? How has this place affected you?*
3. *What kind of personal environment do you enjoy most? Do you like to be outside or inside? Do you prefer a rural or urban environment? What kind of weather do you enjoy? What kind bothers or frightens you?*
4. *In what ways do you interact with your natural environment? Do you like to go on scenic drives? Do you like to walk, jog, hike, or mountain bike? Explain.*
5. *Do you ever worry about the future of the environment? Are you concerned about the depletion of natural resources, endangered species, pollution, waste disposal, or climate change? What possible danger to the environment disturbs you the most?*
6. *How should we balance the welfare of human beings with that of the environment so that both are protected?*

After you have written your journal entry, meet with a group of classmates who responded to the same questions and discuss your responses. Also, as you read these selections, write your questions and reactions in the margins.

A Sense of Place

■ ■ ■

GEORGE J. DEMKO

A respected scholar and scientist, George J. Demko has served as director of the U.S. Office of Geography, has edited several scholarly books on social and political geography, and is currently a professor of geography at Dartmouth College in Hanover, New Hampshire. In his book *Why in the World: Adventures in Geography,* however, Demko shows that his real interest is in people and how they are affected by the geographical environments—or places—in which they live. In this selection from his book, Demko encourages you to take a geographical adventure by exploring your own personal place.

BEFORE YOU READ

■ **THINK** about your own "sense of place." Demko believes, "When we give ourselves to a place, we put it on, the surroundings included, as if it were our very own clothing. We are truly 'in place.'" Have you given yourself to a particular place, or have you moved so much that you do not identify with one single place?

■ **EXAMINE** the word *geography,* which occurs in the title of Demko's book. This word was created from the Greek *geo,* meaning "earth," and *graph,* meaning "write." Therefore, geography is a written record of the earth, including its changing boundaries, physical formations, oceans, weather, cities, countries, and people.

■ **EXAMINE** also the third paragraph, in which Demko writes, "Few of us in the West envy the peoples of Third World countries, their hardships and often-hostile environments." When you think of the West, you probably think of the western United States or of cowboys associated with the Old West. However, Demko uses the word to mean the Western Hemisphere, which includes all of Europe and both North America and South America. Poor and underdeveloped countries are often referred to as *Third World* sites; the term initially meant countries that were not aligned with or supported by either the Communist or non-Communist worlds.

■ **WRITE** a journal entry about your sense of place, or lack of it.

AS YOU READ

Underline passages that define the phrase "a sense of place." Also look for and bracket the specific examples that Demko gives of a sense of place.

■   ■   ■

Every place on Earth is unique. Each has characteristics distinguish- 1
ing it from all other places. Geographers usually describe places by
their characteristics, both human and physical. Sometimes they
group places that are somewhat similar, thereby "creating" regions, such
as "the Corn Belt," or the "American South," which is a cultural region
that is changing rapidly. Regions can be created from any set of places
with something in common.

It is hard to think of any place that is untouched by human contact, even 2
the cruelest, most hostile environments, such as the glaciers of Antarctica and
the broiling, waterless Sahara. All places bear the imprimatur of human visits
and habitation, or the vestiges of such connections.

Few of us in the West envy the peoples of Third World countries, their 3
hardships and often-hostile environments. But these peoples are usually in
touch with their indigenous places in a very real, a very physical sense.
Changes in locales, whether in vegetation and agricultural methods or
available building materials, come slowly. These peoples rarely leave their
corners of the world. Neither are they uprooted by choice or necessity, as
are so many Westerners. (The average American moves his residence
18 times in his lifetime.) They remain relatively unaware of the variety of
places that lie outside their borders. Billions of people have never heard
of the United States.

People often say of their childhood, "We were poor, but we didn't 4
know it." They may not be exaggerating. But what they are really saying,
I think, is that they knew who they were, they had the security of belonging somewhere. Why else do so many of us want to go home again? When
we give ourselves to a place, we put it on, the surroundings included, as if
it were our very own clothing. We are truly "in place."

Too many Westerners, in their getting and spending and laying waste, 5
have lost their understanding of place in any meaningful sense. Oh, we
may remember our hometowns, the house we grew up in, the schools
we went to, where we went to college, where we got inducted into the
armed services, where we proposed marriage and spent our honeymoon.
We may be swept away on a tide of memory if we revisit these scenes, recol-
lecting beloved faces and good times long ago. But we do not have that
sense of the totality of place that is the essence of geography. We have static
images of places frozen in time.

"One place comprehended," Eudora Welty remarks, "can make us 6
understand other places better. A sense of space gives equilibrium, a sense
of direction."

All places change. They change in themselves and they change relative 7 to other places, and they may cause change in other places. We may imagine there are certain places magically untouched by time or change. But we have to turn to literature to find Shangri-la and Brigadoon.

Maps can conjure up images of strange and enchanting landscapes, 8 unintelligible languages, and rainbow-hued peoples. Tweakings of the imagination are the magic of geography, a magic that stays with some of us forever, enriching our lives as we travel, observe, work, and dream.

Places and their contents, and the processes that continually change 9 places and their contents, are the wondrous ingredients of geography and the seductive potion that excites minds and imaginations. All places, even after they have been found, described, and added to maps, can still thrill us in their rediscovery and reexploration.

We can search for an understanding of why places are continually 10 changing and try to predict how they will change. There can be no doubt that the Germany east of the former Berlin Wall and barbed-wire boundary is a different place now than it was in 1989. The spatial processes bombarding the former East Germany—migration, the flow of capital, the flow of ideas—are transforming its towns, villages, and cities, farms, landscapes, population, and industry. They will require new explorations by all of us to know it again.

I don't believe anyone has written more sensitively about the sense of place 11 and the inevitability of change than the novelist Willa Cather. In *My Antonia*, two characters reminisce about their childhood in a town in Nebraska. They recall the burning summers with everything green and billowy under a brilliant sky and the smell of heavy harvests and the ferocious winters when the whole country was bare and gray as sheet iron. "We agreed that no one who had not grown up in a little prairie town could know anything about it," one of the characters remarks. "It was a kind of freemasonry, we said."

Civilization, as we know it, is the poorer when we lose the sense of 12 place. Every piece of space is unique. Processes over space and time keep them so. A sense of place is central to our very comprehension of the world, "this spherical universe wrapped layer around layer with the cunning of nesting dolls."

■　■　■

AFTER YOU READ

■ **THINK** about Demko's favorite example of a strong sense of place, Willa Cather's novel *My Antonia*. Reread his description of the two characters' memories of their Nebraska home town (paragraph 11). What natural images do these characters, who are riding in a train through a vastly changed landscape, recall from their childhood? How effective are these images? Do you agree with Demko that Cather wrote about place with great sensitivity? A writer may, like Demko, use one strong example to prove his point, or, as you will discover in later readings by Kathleen Norris and Michael Grunwald, may base an entire essay on several well-chosen examples.

■ **THINK** also about how place and change are related. Why do changes in physical and social geography come more slowly in Third World countries? Why do places change more rapidly in developed countries like the United States?

■ **EXAMINE** paragraphs 7 and 10 to determine Demko's attitude toward how places change. Paragraph 7 suggests that, to him, only literary places such as Shangri-la and Brigadoon escape time and change. (Shangri-la and Brigadoon are both exotic and imaginary places. Brigadoon is the subject of a 1947 musical written by Alan Jay Lerner and Frederick Loewe. Shangri-la, the setting of James Hilton's 1930s novel *Lost Horizons,* is an imaginary land of youth and peace in the mountains of Tibet that has become a symbol of an ideal place of refuge.) In paragraph 10, what example does Demko give of a place that has undergone major changes in "spatial processes"? What specific changes have occurred there? What other countries are currently undergoing major changes in physical and cultural geography?

■ **WRITE** an essay in which you discuss a physical environment, or place, that has given you a sense of identity—of who you are. This place may be a location from your childhood or a place that has more recently become important to you. Use the following plan to structure your essay:

1. In your introduction, explain the importance of this particular place, or environment, to your life.
2. Describe the place, using vivid, specific details that appeal to your reader's senses.
3. If this place has changed over time, explain how and why change has taken place.
4. Conclude with a brief discussion about how your personal sense of this place has changed or remained the same.

FOCUS: EXAMPLES

Weather Reports

■　■　■

KATHLEEN NORRIS

Award-winning writer Kathleen Norris has published eight volumes of poetry and ten nonfiction books, including the spiritual memoirs *The Cloister Walk* (1996), *Amazing Grace: A Vocabulary of Faith* (1998), and—more recently—the compelling *Acedia & Me: A Marriage, Monks, and a Writer's Life* (2008), an examination of the particularly painful type of depression she experienced after her husband's death. In the mid-1970s, Norris and her husband moved to a small town on the border between North and South Dakota to live in a house built by her grandparents. Here she explored not only the isolated, elemental landscape of the region but also the values, customs, and faith of this land from which her family had come. The result was her first nonfiction book, *Dakota: A Spiritual Geography* (1993), from which this selection is taken. Interspersed between the chapters of the book are short pieces called "Weather Reports." Read in sequence, these reports form a poetic and spiritual narrative of one of the years she spent in this small North Dakota town.

BEFORE YOU READ

■ **THINK** about the information we get from weather reports. What do weather reports tell us about a region and the people who inhabit it? What do they not tell us?

■ **EXAMINE** the dates of these reports. At what intervals were they written, and what period of time do they span?

■ **EXAMINE** also the words *canticle* (paragraph 9), which means a chant or song from a biblical text; *lefse* (paragraph 21), which is a soft Norwegian flatbread; and *vespers* (paragraph 26), which are evening prayers.

■ **WRITE** in your journal an objective description of the weather you are currently experiencing.

AS YOU READ

As you read the following selection with its "weather reports," underline details that provide a strong sense of both time and place. Also highlight, or underline, passages that suggest the changing of the seasons during this year of Norris's life.

■   ■   ■

We hold on to hopes for next year every year in western Dakota: hoping that droughts will end; hoping that our crops won't be hailed out in the few rainstorms that come; hoping that it won't be too windy on the day we harvest, blowing away five bushels an acre; hoping (usually against hope) that if we get a fair crop, we'll be able to get a fair price for it. Sometimes survival is the only blessing that the terrifying angel of the Plains bestows. Still, there are those born and raised here who can't imagine living anywhere else. There are also those who are drawn here—teachers willing to take the lowest salaries in the nation; clergy with theological degrees from Princeton, Cambridge, and Zurich who want to serve small rural churches—who find that they cannot remain for long. Their professional mobility sets them apart and becomes a liability in an isolated Plains community where outsiders are treated with an uneasy mix of hospitality and rejection.

When my husband and I moved nearly twenty years ago from New York to ... [my deceased grandparents' farm and small] house in South Dakota, only one wise friend in Manhattan understood the inner logic of the journey. Others, appalled, looked up Lemmon, South Dakota ... in their atlases and shook their heads. How could I leave the artists' and writers' community in which I worked, the diverse and stimulating environment of a great city, for such barrenness? Had I lost my mind? But I was young, still in my twenties, an apprentice poet certain of the rightness of my returning to the place where I suspected I would find my stories. As it turns out, the Plains have been essential not only for my growth as a writer, they have formed me spiritually. I would even say they have made me a human being.

WEATHER REPORT: JANUARY 17

Encircled. The sea that stretched out before me in Maili, on the Waianae coast of Oahu, as this month began, has been transformed into the plains of North Dakota. I am riding a Greyhound bus to the small town where I'll be teaching writing to schoolchildren for the next two weeks. Snow in the fields has crusted over; wind-lines, restless as waves, flash like the ocean in sunlight.

"Never turn your back on the sea," is Hawaii's wisdom, "Or the sky," we Plains folk might add. Like sailors, we learn to read cloud banks

coming from the west. We watch for sundogs and count rings around the
moon.

I have turned with the circle: away from gentle air and birdsong, the   5
Waianae Range unfolding like a fan in mist, toward a wind gritty with
spent soil burning my tongue, a freezing rain that stings my hands and
face.

In the schoolyard, a snow angel's wings are torn, caught in grass   6
exposed by the sudden thaw. In the stuffy classroom, a little girl, restless
and distracted, probably a bad student, becomes White Buffalo Calf
Woman, speaking of a world in which all people are warm in winter and
have enough to eat.

"They sing, 'the rain is new,'" she writes, "'the rain is always new.'"   7

WEATHER REPORT: FEBRUARY 10

I walk downtown, wearing a good many of the clothes I own, keeping my   8
head down and breathing through several thicknesses of a wool scarf. A
day so cold it hurts to breathe; dry enough to freeze spit. Kids crack it on
the sidewalk.

Walking with care, snow barely covering the patches of ice, I begin to   9
recall a canticle or a psalm—I can't remember which—and my body keeps
time:

Cold and chill, bless the Lord

Dew and rain, bless the Lord

Frost and chill, bless the Lord

Ice and snow, bless the Lord

Nights and days, bless the Lord

Light and darkness, bless the Lord.

Another line comes to mind: "at the breath of God's mouth the waters   10
flow." Spring seems far off, impossible, but it is coming. Already there is
dusk instead of darkness at five in the afternoon; already hope is stirring at
the edges of the day.

WEATHER REPORT: MARCH 25

Mud and new grass push up through melting snow. Lilacs in bud by my   11
front door, bent low by last week's ice storm, begin to rise again in today's
cold rain. Thin clouds scatter in a loud wind.

Suddenly, fir trees seem like tired old women stooped under winter   12
coats. I want to be light, to cast off impediments, and push like a tulip
through a muddy smear of snow. I want to take the rain to heart, let it
move like possibility, the idea of change.

WEATHER REPORT: JUNE 30

I get started early, before six. It promises to be a good laundry day: a   13
steady wind but not too strong. I come by my love of laundry honestly:
my earliest memory is of my mother pulling clothes in from the sky on a
line that ran out our apartment window in Washington, D.C.

Hanging up wet clothes while it is still cool, I think of her. Though   14
she's lived in Honolulu for more than thirty years, she's a plainswoman
at heart; her backyard clothesline is a dead giveaway. The challenge of drying clothes in a tropical valley agrees with her; mountain rains sweep down
at least once a day, and she must be vigilant.

Here no rain is likely, unless, as so often happens, our most beautiful   15
summer days turn dark and violent in late afternoon, thunderstorms pelt-
ing us with rain or hail. I think of a friend who was dying, who had saved
up all her laundry for my visit. "I can't trust my husband with it," she
whispered conspiratorially. "Men don't understand that clothes must be
hung on a line."

She was right. Hanging up wet clothes gives me time alone under the   16
sky to think, to grieve, and gathering the clean clothes in, smelling the sunlight on them, is victory.

WEATHER REPORT: JULY 3

Rains came late in June and haying was delayed. But today it was   17
65 degrees by six A.M., and that means a hot day, 100 degrees or more;
it means haying can't wait.

It's one of the miracles of nature that this empty-looking land can be   18
of such great use, that cattle can convert its grasses to milk and meat.

I know that the brome and wheatgrass will lose its value as feed if it   19
isn't hayed soon, but ever since I moved to Dakota I've felt a kind of grief
at haying time. I hate to see the high grass fall.

Alfalfa and clover still stand tall by the road, smelling sweet and clean,   20
like a milkfed infant's breath. In a few days these vigorous plants will be
coffin-size heaps in the ditch.

WEATHER REPORT: OCTOBER 2

"When my third snail died," the little girl writes, sitting halfway in, half-   21
way out of her desk, one leg swinging in air, "I said, 'I'm through with
snails.'" She sits up to let me pass down the aisle, the visiting poet working
with the third grade: in this dying school, this dying town, we are writing
about our lives. I'm hungry, looking forward to the lefse I bought for lunch
at the Norwegian Food Festival sponsored by the Senior Citizen Center,
one of the few busy places on Main Street. That and the post office, the
café, the grocery. The other buildings are empty.

The teacher's writing too. Yesterday she told me that when I asked the kids to make silence and the room was suddenly quiet, she thought of her mother. "She's been dead for years," she said, adding almost apologetically, "I don't know why I thought of her. But then I just had to write." She told me about the smells, how this time of year the lingering scent of pickling spices in the house would gradually give way to cinnamon, peppermint, cloves, the smells of Christmas baking. "It was the candy I loved most," she wrote, "nut fudge, caramels, divinity."

The sunsets here have been extraordinary, blazing up like distant fire in the window of the old boarding house where the school has put me. Last night I was reading when the light changed: I looked up and gasped at the intensity of color, a slash of gold and scarlet on the long scribble of horizon.

I was reading one of the old ones who said, "One who keeps death before his eyes conquers despair." The little girl calls me, holding up her paper for me to read:

When my third snail died, I said,

"I'm through with snails."

But I didn't mean it.

WEATHER REPORT: NOVEMBER 2

Wind prowled the monastery grounds, giving night silence an increased air of watchfulness. Glass shook in the window frames and sleep was slow in coming.

We had prayed at vespers for the deceased members of the community, from Isidore who died in 1898 to Michael who died last year. We sang of "the narrow stream of death," as if the distance were not so far. I woke to find the ground dusted with snow, the Killdeer Mountains looming white on the horizon, a distance of forty-five miles.

All Souls', blustery and chill. I hear them before I see them, six lines scribbling across the white sky. I look up at the tiny crosses beating above me. The pain is new each year, and I'm surprised, even though I expect it: the sudden cold, the geese passing over.

■ ■ ■

AFTER YOU READ

■ **THINK** about the main idea(s) expressed in this reading selection; identify Norris's thesis in paragraph 2 and restate it in your own words. Consider also how the author changed and grew, as suggested by her thesis, during the year described in these reports.

■ **THINK** also about ways in which this reading selection provides a strong understanding of and sympathy with the place where Norris is living. What passages reveal this sense of place most effectively? What did she learn about this place and about herself from her experiences?

■ **EXAMINE** the structure of the reading selection. After two introductory paragraphs and the thesis, the remainder of the selection consists of separate, dated weather reports, each a sample report narrating the events of a day with special significance for Norris. The reports, which are similar in length and structure, serve as examples supporting Norris's thesis that although the weather in this little Dakota town is often problematic, this place has helped her to find herself spiritually and as a writer.

■ **EXAMINE** also the events recorded in the final weather report (November 2). Describe the tone of this report and compare or contrast it to that of previous reports. Finally, identify the weather images the author includes. How do these images reinforce the tone?

■ **WRITE** a weather report similar to those included in this selection. Describe current weather conditions but include subjective as well as objective details. Use vivid images that appeal to your reader's senses. Begin or end your report with an account of a single event that is related in some way to the weather conditions and the place you are describing. Also include a main idea about the significance of the report.

Storm Country

■ ■ ■

PAUL CRENSHAW

A graduate of the master of fine arts writing program at the University of North Carolina, Paul Crenshaw has published essays and stories in *The North American Review, South Dakota Review, North Dakota Quarterly,* and *Southern Humanities Review.* The title essay of a recently completed collection, "Storm Country" was originally published in *Southern Humanities Review* and was selected for *The Best American Essays 2005.* Crenshaw teaches English at Elon University in Elon, North Carolina.

BEFORE YOU READ

■ **THINK** about the storms you have experienced. Have you ever experienced a bad rainstorm, thunderstorm, windstorm, hailstorm, ice storm, tornado, or hurricane? What did you see, hear, and feel?

■ **EXAMINE** the first paragraph to get a sense of Crenshaw's descriptive style and powerful use of language. Underline specific details that help you sense the experience that Crenshaw describes. Notice especially Crenshaw's effective use of verbs (or verb forms) such as *marching, braying,* and *snap.* (As you read, circle effective verbs and verb forms that you find.)

■ **EXAMINE** also the following words, their context, and their definitions:

1. "*sepia* photograph" (paragraph 8): brown tinted
2. "tornadoes could *spawn*" (paragraph 8): produce, develop
3. "clouds looked *ominous*" (paragraph 11): foreboding, threatening

■ **WRITE** a journal entry in which you describe an experience you have had with some type of weather. Describe what you saw, heard, and felt.

AS YOU READ

Notice the movement in the essay from the writer's general experience of his first storms to his meteorological explanation and finally to the specific experience of his first tornado. Number and label each section in the margins.

■ ■ ■

When the storms came in the spring, we went underground. This was western Arkansas, not far from the Oklahoma line, and all afternoon, as the radio gave reports of thunderstorms marching east across the windblown prairie, my father would alternate between listening to the radio and watching the sky, the radio braying static in the flashes of lightning. My mother opened windows, worrying about the curtains. My brother and I got out candles, a flashlight, in case the power went out. Outside, the air was heavy and still, the leaves on the trees listlessly hanging as the storm moved closer and the nasal voice on the radio told of a line of severe storms from Tulsa to Muskogee, moving east at thirty-five miles per hour, bringing high winds and hail, lightning, the possibility of tornadoes. My father would go outside and stand in the yard, scanning the western horizon, and at some point, usually when the first black clouds appeared over the purple hills, or even earlier, when the late afternoon light looked like it was seen through yellow glass, my father would snap off the radio.

"Let's go," he would say, and we would rush out through the beginning rain or an unusually warm afternoon or a hot night lit up by lightning, coloring the world white so that the darkness seemed greater when it returned. The trees swayed in a hostile wind, brown grasses rippling out across the fields. Leaves and branches and scraps of paper lifted in the wind, hovering in air. My father held me tight to his chest, one hand on the back of my head as we climbed in his truck and drove up the hill to my grandfather's house, where the men of my family gathered outside the storm cellar. When they saw us coming up the road they rushed to the truck, taking my brother and me, ushering my mother inside, out of the wind and rain. My father would stay outside, accept a cup of coffee and a cigarette, join the other men in keeping an eye on the developing storm.

The cellar was built away from the house, a small structure of cinderblocks about the size of an outhouse. The door stood upright, opening on a sharp descent of concrete steps that were always crossed by spiderwebs that would wrap around my face as I hurried down. A small window was cut into the cinderblocks just above ground level, so you could walk a few steps down the stairs and still see what was forming in the air outside.

Inside, the cellar smelled of damp and earth. While my father and uncles and grandfather watched the storm, my mother herded my brother and me down the stairs where, in a little room at the bottom, my grandmother and aunts and cousins sat quietly in the light of a kerosene lamp, their shadows thrown large on the wall. Their eyes were dark and silent. In the room there were only four cots with damp quilts and a small table holding the kerosene lamp, a twelve-volt flashlight, some candles, and the Bible. Outside, the storm was gathering strength, and to quiet the children, my grandmother would tell stories or sing songs in a deep voice, and only occasionally would her eyes flicker to the door. Late at night, if the storm was a long one, or if we'd been woken up in the middle of the night and torn from our beds to be taken to the cellar, my brother and I would fall asleep in our mother's lap, closing our eyes to the movement of shadows on the wall, soft voices above the sound of the wind and rain outside telling us all was safe.

Sometimes I'd stand near the door at the bottom of the stairs, peeking through the crack and craning my head up to watch my father. When the rain and wind hit, the men would step inside the door. They'd stay on the stairs, though, instead of coming down, watching the storm through the window cut at ground level for that purpose. They smelled of coffee and cigarettes and the rain that sometimes blew in the little window if it had been opened to hear the storm better. Sometimes they nodded toward a cloud off over the hills that might uncoil at any moment into a tornado. They scanned the skies, judging the weather, when it might be safe to return home.

Throughout the evening the radio would give reports, telling where tornadoes had touched down and where power lines had fallen and where golfball-sized hail had been seen. Sometimes the radio reported that the storms were losing intensity, or that they had all moved through and passed on, and sometimes we slept in the cellar, waking up in the morning to the smell of moldy quilts and kerosene, climbing the stairs to emerge into a bright world after the storms had passed, the spring grass glistening with the rain from the night and all around leaves and branches and debris from the storm littering the ground. We'd climb in the truck and drive around, surveying the damage. Sometimes trees would be blocking the road, or an old barn would have fallen from the wind. Sometimes there'd be hail covering the ground as if it had snowed, and as the day warmed, the hail would steam as it evaporated, a low mist hanging over the fields.

Other times there would be no sign that any storm had ever come through but for a light rain that patterned the dirt, but when we got home and watched the news we would learn that the next town over had been hit, that people were dead and homes were destroyed, that anyone wishing to donate food or clothing or blood could call this number on the screen. On these days I'd walk out under the clear sky, trying to recall the night in the cellar, the way it smelled and felt and tasted, the way the storm looked when it passed, at what point the men decided it was over. After the storms I always felt unmoored and adrift, as if something had passed that I didn't quite understand.

In March in Arkansas the Gulf Stream sucks up moisture from the Gulf of Mexico to collide with cold air from up north, lingering remnants of winter meeting the warmth of spring. The clash of opposite air masses sends lines of tornadoes spinning out over the prairies of Kansas and Oklahoma and Texas, into the hills of Arkansas. In the late afternoon, they color the day like an old sepia photograph as they roll in, shading the light. At night, you can see funnel clouds in the flashes of lightning, or low-hanging spikes from which—my father would tell me as I got older—tornadoes could spawn.

Long before storm-chasing became an excursion for the rich or foolhearted, my father and grandfather watched tornadoes from the stairs of our cellar, judging when they might drop, how big they might be, if we were in danger. They judged clouds as some men judge the stock market, wondering if it might rise or fall, as all through spring and into summer the storms in Tornado Alley rolled up out of the west, advancing in lines extending from thirty miles south of Broken Bow, Oklahoma, to fifteen miles north of De Queen, Arkansas. I learned the counties of Arkansas— Logan and Sequoia and Crawford and Sebastian and Scott, Franklin and Johnson and Washington and Pope and Polk—through radio reports of tornado warnings or sightings, my geography formed of radio static in lightning, late nights in a storm cellar. I learned to judge the movement of storms across a TV screen, how a storm moving north-northeast through Scott County might end up in my own Logan, or how long it might take a tornado in Sebastian County to reach my house if it was moving at thirty-five miles an hour. I learned to recognize at a glance my own county and the counties surrounding it, because when tornado watches or warnings were issued, in the bottom right part of the TV screen would be a map of Arkansas with certain counties flashing red. On these nights I lay awake in bed, red bands of heavy storms moving across computer-drawn counties in my mind, reciting the path of storms: LeFlore, Sebastian, Crawford, Logan, knowing that at some time in the night I would be awakened, either by my father or the storm outside. I would be wrapped in a blanket, hurried through the rain and into the truck and up the hill, to the flickering kerosene images of aunts and cousins, sleepy-eyed like myself, their shadows large on the wall, as outside the storm raged on.

My grandfather could tell by the way leaves hung on the trees if it would   10
rain that day or not—an old-time meteorologist who watched the seasons and the sky simply because they were there.

"See there?" he said once. We were standing outside the cellar as the   11
first storms began to fire up in the heat of late afternoon. Low green clouds hung silent in the distance, and I have since learned that when clouds turn green, one should take cover. A point hung from the clouds, a barb that looked ominous as the clouds passed on and we watched them go, and always after I have looked for low barbs hanging from dark green clouds, for silent formations that might spawn destruction. He knew, standing on the cellar stairs watching through the little window, when a tornado might drop from the clouds. He knew the feel of the air, the presence that announces a heavy storm.

Sometimes it will stop raining when the funnel falls. Sometimes the   12
wind stops and the trees go still and the air settles on you as everything goes quiet. Then, faint at first as the storm gathers speed, you can hear the force as it spins itself into existence, touching earth, whirling out into the day or night. It sounds like rusted sirens, howling dogs, the call of a freight train on a long trip across the plains somewhere in the western night, pushing speed and sound before it, lonely and forlorn on its midnight ride.

I've seen tornadoes drop from a clear blue sky. I've seen barns and houses   13
and fields wiped out, cattle thrown for a distance to lie in the rain bawling with broken legs. Once I watched as a three- or four-hundred-pound cut

of sheet metal floated across the highway, touched down once, then lifted off again, light as air. I've seen towns wrecked by tornadoes in November, houses swept away, all that was left of a church roof lying on the ground, unscathed but for a few shingles missing at one corner. One time I was almost struck by a bullet of hail the size of my fist. It crashed through the window and landed on our living room floor. We all looked at it for a moment. My mother tried to protect the curtains as the rain came in, but my father herded us toward the cellar up the hill at my grandfather's house.

I know the sound of storms, the low growl of thunder that means storms 14 in the distance, the loud quick clap that means storms overhead. I've blinked in the afterglow of forked lightning, watched flash lightning light the hills as night turns into day. I've seen the remains of exploded houses, nothing left of the house but kindling, from when the tornado drops and the air pressure changes and the air inside the house has to get out.

I've seen storms come with no warning, boiling up out of a western 15 sky rimmed with the red rays of the last sun, lightning flickering in the twilight, the air gone heavy and still. I've seen them sweep through with hardly a ripple but the wind in your hair, passing to other places and other times. I've huddled in hallways and bathtubs and cellars listening to tornadoes pass overhead, and when I see on television the remnants of a town destroyed by the force of storms, I always offer, however briefly, a thanks that it was not my people or my town.

The first tornado I can remember was when I was eight. The storm came in 16 the afternoon, as many storms do. It was early in March—a month that, as the saying goes in Arkansas, enters like a lion, leaves like a lion. My father was watching a basketball game on TV when the sound disappeared, followed by the steady beep that meant an announcement was coming. Thunderstorms are moving through the area, the announcement ran at the bottom of the screen. Tornadoes possible. Take shelter. When the announcement disappeared, the state of Arkansas appeared on the screen, the western counties lit like radiation. My father went out to study the sky and came back in at a run.

"Let's go," he said. 17

The trees were dancing as we ran to the truck, leaves and small 18 branches swirling in the wind and falling all around. At the road up the hill to my grandfather's house a dust devil danced before my father ran his truck through it, dispersing the dust. A line of rain moved toward us through the fields. The clouds in the distance were green.

By the time we reached the top of the hill the wind was rocking the 19 truck and the first drops of rain were hitting the hood, big and loud and hard. The curtain of rain reached us, going from a few drops to a downpour in an instant. The wind ripped the truck door from my father's hand. My grandfather ran out from the cellar door, where he'd been watching for us, waiting. He took my brother, my father took me. We couldn't see the cellar in the rain. Thunder rumbled the hills, and lightning stabbed down, sharp and quick, splitting the rain, everything quiet for an instant before the thunder struck.

We splashed through the rain and into the cellar. I was wet, plastered to my father's chest. My mother took us down the stairs. My father and grandfather stood peering through the window at the rain. The day had gone dark. 20

Downstairs, my grandmother was telling stories to my two younger cousins, who were flinching in the sharp crashes of each thunder. The room smelled of kerosene, of earth and wind and rain. My skin was wet, hair cold, as my mother wrapped me in a quilt. In the brief silences between thunderclaps, we could hear the rain and my father and grandfather on the stairs. I peered through the door and heard my father say, "There it is." 21

He turned and saw me standing at the bottom of the stairs and motioned me up. The rain had slowed and was falling lightly now; the wind settled down in the trees. I stood on the steps with my father as he pointed into the distance, where a dark funnel coiled downward from the black clouds, like smoke, or wind taking shape and color. At the base of the tornado, dust and debris hovered, circling slowly, and I heard the sound of storm for the first time. It grew out of air, out of wind. It seemed as silent as noise can be, a faint howling that reached us over the rain, almost peaceful from a distance. But then it would hit a line of trees or a fence, shooting trees and fence posts and barbed wire into the air. It crossed over a pond, and water turned it almost white for an instant. It hit an old barn like a fist, smashing boards and metal, slinging the debris about. 22

We watched, not speaking, as the tornado moved over the empty fields in the distance, leaving a swath of devastation in its wake. After a time it folded itself back into the underbelly of the clouds, rising silently, dispersing like smoke in the wind, the sound gone and the air still once again. 23

"It's over," my father said, but I could still see in my mind the black funnel dropping from the clouds, twisting across the landscape, throwing trees and dirt and anything in its path, tearing tracts of land as it went on its way. Before me was the result, the path of the tornado, cut through the hills. And, for no reason it seemed, it faded away, gone as surely as it had come. 24

We stood there for a long time after it was over, silent, watching the clouds roll on through, speeding swiftly toward night. After a time—an hour or three or four—the clouds peeled back, revealing bright stars flung across the sky. 25

My father and my grandfather had watched other tornadoes before, just like that one, had seen them and knew what they could do. I had thought that they were standing guard through the night, watching until it was safe for us to come out, putting themselves between us and the danger that lurked outside. But as we turned and went down the stairs together, I realized they watched from the window to see the terrible beauty of the storm rolling across the hills, hail falling from the sky, 26 streaks of lightning in the jagged edges of the storm, the twisting funnel of clouds that held such power.

■ ■ ■

AFTER YOU READ

■ **THINK** about how Crenshaw's focus moves from the general to the specific—from a general description of tornadoes to a specific description of the first tornado he saw. Do you believe this is an effective structure for the essay? If so, why do you think so? (Interestingly, Crenshaw's general-to-specific order is also similar to the structure of a tornado, which funnels down from a wide base in the clouds to a more narrow tip that skims along the ground.)

■ **EXAMINE** the four different sections of the essay and the following description of each of these sections:

- Section 1 sets the scene of the storm cellar.

- Section 2 provides a scientific description of the formation of tornadoes and a brief narrative of the Crenshaw family's watching both the sky and the television's factual list of nearby Oklahoma and Arkansas counties affected by tornadoes.

- Section 3 describes the general experiences that the writer's grandfather and the writer himself have had with tornadoes.

- Section 4 is an extended example, or an illustration, that describes the writer's first experience of a tornado.

What differences in style occur in these four sections? What stylistic qualities remain similar throughout the essay?

■ **EXAMINE** also the last paragraph of the essay. What discovery does Crenshaw make about his father and grandfather after the tornado has passed on? How has the entire essay prepared for the realization not only of the destruction of the storm but also of its "terrible beauty"?

■ **WRITE** an essay in which you describe an experience that you have had with a storm of some kind—a rainstorm, thunderstorm, tornado, hurricane, or the like. Begin by describing what you were doing or what was happening before the storm, then describe in detail what happened and how you felt during the storm, and conclude by explaining how you felt or what you learned after the storm. Be sure to include, as Crenshaw does, details that help your reader see, hear, and feel your experience. (For help with writing description, see Lesson 2 on the *Interactions*, eighth edition, website, at www.cengagebrain.com.)

Dispatch from the Edge: Katrina

■ ■ ■

ANDERSON COOPER

On Sunday, August 29, 2005, Anderson Cooper found himself, like Paul Crenshaw in the previous selection, on the edge of a storm. But unlike the tornado in "Storm Country," whose swath of destruction crossed empty barns and fields, the hurricane Cooper witnessed caused immense destruction and loss of life on the Louisiana and Mississippi coastlines. Formerly an ABC news correspondent, Cooper joined CNN in December 2001 and currently anchors the wide-ranging news program *Anderson Cooper 360*. Cooper has won several awards, including the National Headliners Award for his tsunami coverage and four Emmy Awards, including one in 2006 for his reporting on New Orleans's Charity Hospital during the aftermath of Katrina. The following essay is taken from his book *Dispatches from the Edge: A Memoir of War, Disasters, and Survival* (2006).

BEFORE YOU READ

■ **THINK** about the danger and devastation associated with hurricanes, especially with Hurricane Katrina. As you probably know, hurricanes are categorized on a 1–5 scale based on wind strength: category 1 (74–95 mph), category 2 (96–110 mph), category 3 (111–130 mph), category 4 (131–155 mph), and category 5 (more than 155 mph). Hurricane Katrina made landfall as a strong category 3 storm, with estimated 125 mph winds, but it had just weakened from a category 4 storm. At the time it hit, the hurricane was the third strongest recorded hurricane to hit the United States.

■ **EXAMINE** the word *dispatch* in the title. A report or a letter, a dispatch is particularly associated with the reports of war correspondents during conflict. Please note also the following italicized words and their definitions:

1. "make the evacuation *mandatory*" (paragraph 5): required, compulsory
2. "conditions *deteriorate* rapidly" (paragraph 14): get worse
3. "memories *obliterated* in a gust of wind" (paragraph 19): destroyed, wiped out

■ **WRITE** a journal entry describing what you remember about Hurricane Katrina, or another, more recent hurricane. Then meet with a small group of your classmates to share your memories.

AS YOU READ

Notice how Cooper's reporting gradually changes from an objective and factual style to a more subjective and emotional one. Mark the place where the biggest change occurs.

■   ■   ■

I t begins as a breeze, barely noticed, brushing the land where man was born. A bush pilot flying out of Kisangani might have found himself buffeted by a surprisingly strong current of air, or a farmer on a rocky Rwandan slope stretching his back as he stood could have felt the cool wind on his face. But it's not until the third week of August 2005 that meteorologists take note of a powerful tropical wave of wind and water moving slowly off the coast of West Africa. It crosses the Atlantic and feeds off the warm waters of the Bahamas, growing in size and strength. On August 24 it becomes a tropical storm, and automatically is assigned the next name on a list created by the National Hurricane Center: Katrina.

I'm on a boat with friends off the coast of Croatia, sailing in the crisp blue waters of the Adriatic. This is my second attempt this year to have a vacation, after cutting short my trip to Rwanda in July to go to Niger. I've resisted checking my e-mails for several days, but my BlackBerry is on and when it begins to ring, I know it's not good.

"Sorry, buddy, but you need to come back," David Doss, my executive producer, tells me.

Katrina becomes a hurricane on Thursday, August 25, and that evening it hits southern Florida. Twelve people die. Over land, the storm weakens, but once it returns over water, this time the Gulf of Mexico, it begins to re-form.

Saturday morning, I fly out of Dubrovnik, bound for Houston. In Louisiana, New Orleans mayor Ray Nagin and Governor Kathleen Blanco hold a press conference, asking city residents to leave. Nagin and Blanco don't, however, make the evacuation mandatory. That evening, Max Mayfield of the National Hurricane Center calls the mayor to warn him personally of the seriousness of the storm. It's only the second time he's called a politician to do that.

New Orleans' emergency plan requires authorities to provide buses to evacuate the one hundred thousand residents without access to transportation. No buses, though, are organized to get people out of the city. On Sunday, over the central Gulf of Mexico, Katrina turns northwest as expected, becoming a monstrous category 5 hurricane. Sustained winds 175 miles per hour. The mayor and governor finally declare a mandatory evacuation.

I arrive in Houston late Sunday and drive to Baton Rouge. I get there around 1:00 A.M. on Monday, just as the outer bands of rain are beginning to hit. It's another hour-and-a-half drive to New Orleans, but when I call into my office, they tell me that the roads are closed. I am furious with myself for getting there late, but it turns out that CNN has pulled its satellite trucks from New Orleans because they anticipate flooding. Even if I were able to get there, I couldn't broadcast during the storm, so I decide to ride it out in Baton Rouge, then head to New Orleans as soon as it's over.

Katrina is the sixth major hurricane I've covered in the last fifteen   8
months, the second one this year. I never used to understand people's fascination with the weather. One of the great joys of living in New York is that I'm able to ignore what little bit of sky I ever see. Since covering Hurricane Charley in 2004, however, I've continually volunteered to report on hurricanes. It's not just the storm itself that I find compelling, but also the hours before and after. There is a stillness, quietness. Stores are shut, homes boarded up. In many ways it feels like a war zone.

A few hours before Hurricane Charley made landfall, I checked into a   9
waterfront hotel in Tampa, Florida. The manager, a large woman with a small parrot perched on her head, agreed to let me stay if I signed a waiver absolving the hotel of any responsibility for my safety. As I signed the paper, the parrot defecated on the woman's shoulder.

"She's just a little nervous about the s-t-o-r-m," the woman said, spell-   10
ing the word out, worried the parrot would hear.

Reporting on a hurricane, you depend on your skills for survival; it's   11
all in your hands. You rent an SUV, load it up with water, food, whatever supplies you can buy; gas cans, coolers, and ice are always the hardest to find. In a war, you head to the front; in a hurricane you head to water. You pick your location as if you're planning an ambush. You want a spot near the water, so you can see the storm surge, but you need to be on high ground so you don't get flooded when the water rises. You don't want too many trees or signposts near you, because they can become airborne and turn into flying missiles in high winds. You also need several fallback positions so that as the storm intensifies, you can retreat to ever more secure locations.

In Baton Rouge, a team of CNN engineers has already found a river-   12
front location on a pier. There's a big building several hundred yards away that can protect the satellite truck. As long as the satellite dish works, you can broadcast, so keeping it safe is essential. The problem is, the dish acts as a sail. It can get picked up by a strong wind, causing the truck it's attached to to flip over. You have to find a spot where the satellite truck is protected by a building on at least two sides. That way even when the hurricane winds shift, the dish will not be directly hit.

After covering several hurricanes, you start to know what to expect. At   13
first the winds just pick up gently. Then it starts to rain. Your fancy Gore-Tex clothing keeps you dry for about thirty minutes; then the water starts to seep in. Within an hour you're completely wet. Your feet slosh around in your boots, and your hands are wrinkled and white. If you've ever wondered what your skin will look like when you're eighty-five, try standing in a hurricane for a few hours.

Katrina comes ashore at 6:10 A.M., on Monday near Buras, Louisiana. 14
The sustained winds are estimated to be 125 miles per hour, a category 3
hurricane. In Baton Rouge, conditions deteriorate rapidly. What seemed
like high winds just a few hours ago now seem calm by comparison. The
electricity goes out, transformers explode, lighting up the darkened sky
with greenish blue flares. I can't see any debris flying through the air; I can
only hear it; the snap of tree branches, the twisting of signs, aluminum roofs
ripping loose. You can't tell where the noise is coming from or where the
debris is headed.

Between live shots I sit inside my SUV, dripping in steamy darkness. As 15
the storm intensifies, other reporters' transmissions get knocked off the air,
so the network starts coming back to me more and more—live shot after
live shot. Chris Davis, my cameraman, can barely see through his view-
finder, but he keeps working, steadying himself against the railing of the
pier. After a while I'm just repeating myself: "It's really blowing now . . .
and the rain, it's torrential." There's really not much else to say. It's
water and it's wind. How many ways are there to describe them?

You see weird stuff in a storm: floating Coke machines, boats washed 16
up on roads. During Hurricane Frances, two guys in a brand-new Humvee
with HURRICANE RESEARCH TEAM printed on the side pulled into the
marina where we were working. From their matching yellow raincoats, I
assumed they were scientists, but it turned out they were just two guys
with a storm fetish. I last saw them around 1:00 A.M. They were hooting
and hollering and videotaping each other getting tossed around by 110-
mile-per-hour gusts of wind.

It's easy to get caught up in all the excitement, easy to forget that while 17
you are talking on TV, someone is cowering in a closet with their kids, or
drowning in their own living room.

After Hurricane Charley, I drove around Punta Gorda, Florida, survey- 18
ing the damage. There was aluminum siding wrapped around trees, shockingly silver in the morning sun; a family's photo album lay in the street;
a sofa sat on top of a car. A relief official mistakenly said that there were
a dozen or more bodies at one trailer park, and all the morning-show
reporters in mobile news vans crisscrossed the small town searching for
the dead. They'd slow down and ask local residents if they knew of a
nearby trailer park where "something" had happened. (No one wanted to
come right out and ask, "Seen any dead people around here?")

In the end, the real power of a hurricane isn't found in its wind speed. 19
It's in what it leaves behind—the lives lost, the lives changed, the memories
obliterated in a gust of wind. Anyone who does hurricane reporting for
any length of time knows all too well that standing in the aftermath of a
storm is much more difficult than standing in the storm itself, no matter
how hard the winds blow.

■   ■   ■

AFTER YOU READ

■ **THINK** about the potential problems in New Orleans that Anderson notes in his opening paragraphs—the lack of an early mandatory evacuation, the fact that buses had not been organized, and the anticipation of flooding. What other problems in planning showed up on all governmental levels in the aftermath of the hurricane?

■ **THINK** also about the sights that Cooper has seen or imagined during hurricanes. Those that he describes in paragraph 16 have a dreamlike quality, but other images are heart-wrenching. What images in paragraphs 17 and 18 are particularly sad and moving?

■ **EXAMINE** Cooper's statement that in the "hours before and after" a hurricane, an endangered area "feels like a war zone." Then analyze Cooper's extension of this comparison in paragraph 11. What other comparisons can you make between an area hit by a hurricane and a war zone?

■ **EXAMINE** also Cooper's last paragraph. Where is the real power of a hurricane felt? How is "standing in the aftermath of a storm ... much more difficult than standing in the storm itself"?

■ **WRITE** an essay in which you analyze some aspect of the "aftermath" of Hurricane Katrina or of a more recent disaster—a hurricane, a flood, an earthquake, a tsunami, or a wildfire. You might focus on economic, environmental, or political effects; you might focus on the effects on a particular city or geographical area; or you might focus on the effects on a particular group of people, perhaps even on someone you know. Use descriptive details where they are appropriate. (See Lesson 2 on description on the *Interactions*, eighth edition, student website, at www.cengagebrain.com.)

Rescuing Oiled Birds

■ ■ ■

JOHN FLESHER AND
NOAKI SCHWARTZ

On April 20, 2010, an explosion on the Deepwater Horizon oil rig killed eleven men and ripped a huge hole in a pipe a mile below the ocean surface, allowing oil to gush into the water and eventually to reach shorelines all along the Gulf Coast. After several failed attempts to stop, or even appreciably limit, the huge leak, British Petroleum used a specially designed cap to reduce the flow in mid-July, and in early August was able to stop the leak by completing the process called "static kill," which pumped mud and cement into the well from above. On September 19 a relief well, called "bottom kill," was successfully completed. The region seems to be recovering, but before the oil flow was stopped, over 200 million gallons of oil had surfaced, virtually halting tourism, boating, and fishing for the entire Gulf Coast area and costing not only millions of dollars but also the livelihoods of many citizens of the coast. Not least among the costs of the spill is the damage done to the environment—the Gulf's shores and marshes as well as birds, marine life, and other wildlife. The following Associated Press article, posted on June 10, describes the debate over rescuing oiled birds.

BEFORE YOU READ

■ **THINK** about what you have read or heard on the news about the Gulf oil spill, which is the worst environmental disaster our country has ever experienced. In your opinion, what are the worst consequences of the spill? How long do you think it will take the region to recover from this spill? Is it possible that—in some ways—this area will never fully recover?

■ **THINK** also about the connection between the Gulf oil spill and Hurricane Katrina, which hit the same region just a few years earlier. How are the two events similar? How are they different? In your opinion, which event caused the most damage? Explain.

■ **EXAMINE** the following sentence, which was used as a subtitle for this article: "Poignant, but is it futile?" What is your position on cleaning oiled birds? Do you think the rescue efforts are worth the time and money they cost? Why or why not?

■ **EXAMINE** also the following italicized words and their definitions:

1. "animal care *initiative*" (paragraph 6): an introductory movement
2. "*rehabilitation* techniques" (paragraph 11): restoration to good condition or health
3. "hungry, *dehydrated* and exhausted" (paragraph 20): excessive loss of water from the body

■ **WRITE** a journal entry in which you explain your position on cleaning oiled birds.

AS YOU READ

Put a check mark to the left of paragraphs that support rescuing oiled birds; put a check mark to the right of paragraphs that provide arguments against rescuing these birds.

■ ■ ■

ORT JACKSON, La.—Rescuers gently washing the goo from pelicans make for some of the few hopeful images from the disaster on
the Gulf of Mexico, yet some scientists contend those efforts are
good for little more than warming hearts.   1

Critics call bird-washing a wasteful exercise in feel-good futility that   2
simply buys doomed creatures a bit more time. They say the money and
man-hours would be better spent restoring wildlife habitat or saving
endangered species.

In the seven weeks since oil began erupting from a mile-deep well after   3
a drilling rig explosion in the Gulf of Mexico, more than 150 pelicans,
gulls, sandwich terns and other birds have been treated at a rehabilitation
center 70 miles south of New Orleans.

A total of 473 birds in the Gulf region have been collected alive with   4
visible oil; 117 oiled birds have been found dead. More are on the way, as
oil slicks assault beaches and marshes that serve as breeding areas for
many species.

The victims are scrubbed clean and held a week or more to recover.   5
Then a Coast Guard plan flies them to Tampa Bay in Florida for release—
far enough away, workers hope, that the birds won't return to the oiled
waters and get soaked again. Birds treated from this disaster have been
tagged, and none has been spotted in oil again.

It's all part of a broader animal care initiative overseen by federal   6
agencies and operated largely by nonprofit groups, with funding from BP
PLC. Other centers focus on turtles and marine mammals.

"All of us here taking care of the wildlife feel it's important," said   7
Rhonda Murgatroyd of Wildlife Response Services in Houma, La. "We
can't just leave them there—somebody had to take care of them."

A noble sentiment, said Ron Kendall, director of the Institute of 8
Environmental and Human Health at Texas Tech University. But the hard
reality is that many, if not most, oiled creatures probably won't live long
after being cleansed and freed, he said.

"Once they've gone through that much stress, particularly with all the 9
human handling and confinement, it's very difficult," Kendall said. "Some
species might tolerate it better than others, but when you compare the benefits to the costs ... I am skeptical."

The arm of the federal government that nominally oversees offshore 10
rigs agrees with Kendall, and has for some time.

"Studies are indicating that rescue and cleaning of oiled birds makes 11
no effective contribution to conservation, except conceivably for species
with a small world population," the U.S. Minerals Management Service
said in a 2002 environmental analysis of proposed Gulf oil drilling projects. "A growing number of studies indicate that current rehabilitation
techniques are not effective in returning healthy birds to the wild."

Fewer than 10 percent of brown pelicans that were cleaned and 12
marked for tracing after a 1990 spill in Southern California were
accounted for two years later, while more than half the pelicans in a control group could be found, three scientists with the University of California,
Davis, reported in a paper published in 1996. The formerly oiled birds also
showed no signs of breeding.

Dan Anderson, a professor emeritus of conservation biology at the 13
University of California at Davis who led the study, said last week he still
questions how well the rescue missions succeed but doesn't oppose them.
"If nothing else, we're morally obligated to save birds that seem to be save-
able," Anderson said.

Besides, bird rehabilitation groups have improved their methods the 14
past couple of decades, he said.

A 2002 study by Humbolt State University scientists found that gulls 15
treated after a California spill survived just as well as gulls that were not
oiled. Rescue supporters also point to data showing high survival rates for
penguins receiving care from a South African foundation that has handled
more than 50,000 oiled seabirds since 1968.

Rescue missions can convey a false impression that damage from oil 16
spills can be fixed, said Jim Estes, an ecologist at the University of California,
Santa Cruz, who worked on the federal effort to save animals after the
Exxon Valdez spill in 1989.

"Oil may be doing a species considerable harm, but rehabilitation 17
won't change that," Estes said. "It will just help a relatively small number
of individuals from suffering and dying."

At the Fort Jackson warehouse, where shivering pelicans huddled inside 18
pens awaiting their turn to be cleansed, such criticisms are shrugged off.

"What do you want us to do? Let them die?" said Jay Holcomb, exec- 19
utive director of the International Bird Rescue Research Center, who has
aided oiled animals for 40 years.

Most birds arrive at rescue centers hungry, dehydrated and exhausted, 20
having neglected eating in the frantic struggle to clean themselves. Once a

bird is strong enough, two workers cover it in warm vegetable oil to remove the sticky oil, then apply dish soap and scrub parts of its head with a toothbrush.

It's time-consuming and expensive. Cleaning a single pelican can   21 require 300 gallons of water. After the Exxon Valdez, some studies estimated that $15,000 had been spent for each marine bird treated, a figure others said was exaggerated. Scientists with the Marine Wildlife Veterinary Care and Research Center in California said it costs them $600 to $750 to clean a bird.

James Harris, a senior wildlife biologist with the U.S. Fish and Wildlife   22 Service helping care for birds sullied by the current spill, said critics also forget that many rescued animals will produce offspring—especially brown pelicans, which were taken off the federal endangered list only last year.

"It may be one pelican to me," he said, "but it could represent a cou-   23 ple dozen pelicans to my children and could be in the tens of hundreds for my grandchildren."

■ ■ ■

AFTER YOU READ

■ **THINK** about Rhonda Murgatroyd's statement in paragraph 7: "We can't just leave them there—somebody has to take care of them." If you saw a bird or another creature whose life was endangered and you could help it, would you feel the same way? Explain.

■ **EXAMINE** paragraph 4. By mid-June of 2010, how many seabirds were in the process of being rescued? How many had been found dead? How many birds do you think were eventually rescued from the oil spill? How many do you think died from the oil? (You might find some relevant statistics on the Internet.) Then look at James Harris's comments in the last two paragraphs. If he is right, what effect might "rescuing oiled birds" have on various species?

■ **EXAMINE** also the check marks you made to identify arguments for and against rescuing oiled birds. Are the arguments in the article rather evenly divided? If not, which argument receives more space? What conclusions can you draw about the opinion of the Associated Press writers?

■ **WRITE** an essay in which you argue for or against rescuing oiled birds. You may want to use more recent information from the Internet as well as support from this essay. In either case, be sure to credit your sources and to put in quotations any phrases and sentences that you borrow. You will find guidelines for writing persuasive essays on pp. 372–378 at the end of this unit.

ANWR: The Great Divide

■ ■ ■

SCOTT WALLACE

The nearly 20 million acres of the Arctic National Wildlife Refuge (ANWR) has been a source of conflict between conservationists and oil developers for over 50 years. The region first came under federal protection in 1960; in 1980 an additional 1.5 million acres of coastal plain—the 1002 area—was added, with the stipulation that congressional approval was necessary for drilling in this area. Democrats and Republicans disagree vehemently over the best use of this area. But the political-environmental debate is only one of the conflicts about this region. The other conflict, as described by Scott Wallace in this essay from *Smithsonian* (2005), is the conflict between the ways of life of the two native groups who inhabit this area: the traditional Gwich'in Indians in the southern part of ANWR, who depend on the indigenous caribou for their subsistence, and the Inupiat Eskimos on the northern edge, who have used oil money to bring modern improvements to their village.

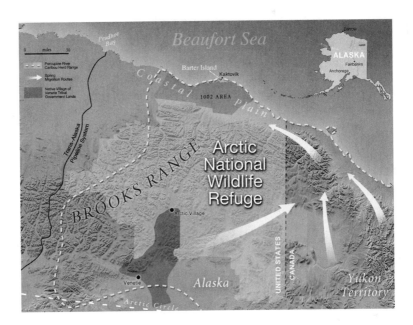

BEFORE YOU READ

■ **THINK** about what you know about the Arctic National Wildlife Reserve (ANWR) and about Wallace's description of it as "The Great Divide," a title that implies the conflicts associated with the region. Which do you think is more important—preserving a pristine wilderness and its wildlife, including the caribou, or providing oil to the country at a reasonable price? Which is more important—preserving a group's ancient and traditional way of life, or providing sanitary conditions such as bathrooms and running water for a village?

■ **EXAMINE** the map on page 325, locating (1) the area of ANWR itself, (2) the Coastal Plain and the 1002 area, (3) the Inupiat village of Kaktovik, (4) the Gwich'in villages of Arctic Village and Venetie, and (5) the migration routes of the caribou. Having a visual image of these locations will help you to understand the essay.

■ **EXAMINE** also the word *tundra,* which occurs several times in the essay. Lying between the northernmost arctic tree line and the ice cap, the tundra has a permanently frozen subsoil but low-growing vegetation and bushes.

■ **WRITE** a journal entry in which you take a side on either the conflict between conservationists and oil developers or between the traditional Gwich'in and the more modern Inupiat.

AS YOU READ

Write a "G" in the margin beside discussion of the Gwich'in and an "I" beside discussion of the Inupiat. Note the contrasts that Wallace makes between these two groups.

■ ■ ■

"Hear that howling out there?" Charlie Swaney asked, cocking an ear and shifting the weight of the rifle slung on his shoulder. The cry of a lone wolf echoed in the distance. "That's a good sign. When there's wolf around, that means they're following the caribou."   1

It was just after 4 a.m., and the Arctic sky was smeared with orange rippled clouds that hung low over the mountains to the north. Songbirds greeted the dawn with riotous chirping from the tops of spindly spruce trees, whose black silhouettes rose straight around us.   2

Half Gwich'in and half Ahtna Indian, Swaney, 47, has lived all of his life in the boreal forests of the Alaskan north. On this chilly morning in early May, he wore a hat made from a wolverine he trapped years ago pulled down tight on his thick salt-and-pepper hair.   3

The night before, we had sat drinking coffee at his kitchen window, 4
looking out on the mountains blanketed in snow as he dispensed tidbits
of Native wisdom. If you see wolves digging in the snow, most likely an
avalanche has buried a group of caribou there. If you kill a crow for no
good reason, the weather will turn bad. "It's true," he insisted when he
saw my raised eyebrow. "I've seen it happen."

What is certain is that when Swaney and his fellow Gwich'in hunters 5
bring back fresh caribou to their homes in Arctic Village, they bring joy as
well ... especially to the children. "Their attitude changes," he said. "You
can see it in their faces. They know they're going to be eating good."

Our hunt would begin at dawn with five other men. The caribou had 6
been sighted two days earlier by bush pilots out on the tundra south of
Arctic Village. The animals were probably from the Porcupine River caribou herd, the unlikely focus of one of the most intractable and divisive
environmental debates in our nation's history: whether the Artic National
Wildlife Refuge, or ANWR, should be opened up for oil exploration.

Down in the lower 48, the tangle between oil industry proponents and 7
environmentalists, between Republicans and Democrats and between conservatives and liberals over ANWR centers on issues of energy self-
sufficiency versus preservation of a pristine wilderness. But here, above
the Arctic Circle, the debate is less abstract, with two Native Alaskan peoples locked in a complex dispute over oil development on the coastal
tundra.

On one side are the militantly traditionalist Gwich'in—7,000 people 8
living in 15 settlements scattered along the caribou's migration route
between northeastern Alaska and the Canadian Yukon. On the other are
roughly 9,000 Inupiat Eskimo, whose once-ramshackle coastal villages
have been transformed into modern communities with schools, clinics,
and indoor plumbing since oil started flowing from Alaska's North Slope
in the late 1970s.

The Gwich'in fear that drilling in ANWR will put an end to their exis- 9
tence as subsistence caribou hunters, while the Inupiat worry that without
development of ANWR's gas and oil reserves the money to support their
modern comforts will disappear. To most Gwich'in, the Inupiat are motivated by greed and have sold out their traditional culture for the lure of oil
dollars; to many Inupiat, the Gwich'in are hopeless romantics, living voluntarily in squalor to cling to a way of life that is bound to disappear.

Though ANWR's coastal plain hosts a dazzling abundance of wildlife— 10
the largest concentration of land-denning polar bears in Alaska; enormous
flocks of migratory birds; wolves, wolverines, musk, ox, Artic fox and
snowy owls—the caribou remain the symbol of the fight over the refuge.
It's the one animal that moves through the full range of Arctic and subarctic
ecosystems: barrier islands, coastal plain, mountain talus, boreal forest
and alpine tundra. Even the boundaries of ANWR were largely determined
by the range of the Porcupine River herd.

Some of the herd, which numbered 123,000 when last counted in 11
2001, migrate nearly 3,000 miles each year, zigzagging to and from their

calving grounds on a long, narrow strip of coastal plain some 150 miles north of Arctic Village. Though the plain takes up a relatively small corner of the 19.6 million-acre refuge, conservationists describe it as ANWR's most important and environmentally sensitive area. The Gwich'in call it the "sacred place where life begins." An idyllic nursery for the nearly 40,000 caribou calves born here each year, it provides protection from wolves and grizzlies, while offering a diet of nutritious grasses for the calves' lactating mothers. The plain also happens to sit atop what is believed to be billions of barrels of untapped oil. . . .

[The Gwich'in] fear that the caribou could shift their migration routes 12 away from Native villages or even cease to exist as a migratory herd if oil development begins in the refuge. While the Gwich'in hunt other game, such as moose and ptarmigan, they call themselves the "People of the Caribou" and say the blood of the animal flows in their veins. The caribou figures in all of their rituals, traditional dances and stories, and nothing marks their annual calendar like the comings and goings of the Porcupine herd. More prosaically, the caribou is the Gwich'in's major source of food. "If it's gone," said Swaney, "what are we going to do?"

The Inupiat Eskimo village of Kaktovik, Alaska, is on Barter Island, just 13 offshore from the mainland. Once a trading center for whalers and hunters who plied the frigid waters along the Arctic coast, today Kaktovik is a village of prim, oil-heated houses, wide, gravel streets, a large, fully-staffed school, a police station and a power plant. All of it has been made possible by tax revenues generated from the Prudhoe Bay oil fields, about 100 miles to the west, during the past three decades of oil production on the North Slope.

Just a stone's throw south of town lies ANWR's coastal plain—1.5 14 million acres of tundra potentially available for oil exploration, hemmed in between the slopes of the Brooks Range and the Arctic shore. The tract is called the "1002" area (universally referred to as "Ten-Oh-Two") for a clause in the 1980 federal legislation that expanded the refuge to include much of the U.S. range of the caribou herd while, at the same time, setting aside the coastal plain for possible future oil and gas development.

Most of Kaktovik's 300 residents are shareholders in two Native natu- 15 ral resource companies—the Kaktovik Inupiat Corporation and the Arctic Slope Regional Corporation, or ASRC. Respectively, the companies own the surface and subsurface rights to 92,000 acres within the 1002 area and stand to reap a windfall if there's a major oil strike on ANWR's coastal plain.

The Gwich'in of Arctic Village and neighboring Venetie chose not to 16 participate in the land distribution under the act and also declined the seed money that the rest of Alaska's Natives have used to improve, in many cases dramatically, their standard of living. Instead, the Gwich'in held on to their land—almost two million acres of spruce taiga, rolling foothills, twisting, braided rivers and vast stretches of alpine tundra bordering ANWR's southern flank. Now they have their homeland and its abundance of fish and wildlife, but they enjoy few of the creature comforts the Inupiat have on the North Slope.

Carla Sims Kayotuk, 38, is torn. She was raised in Kaktovik, and 17 today her family owns one of the village's two grocery stores. Although she worries that unsightly oil pipelines, the high-pitched scream of winches and the clatter of helicopters will forever mar the tranquil landscape close to her village, she also worries about declining oil production in the Prudhoe Bay fields. "If we don't have the oil development," she says, "where are we going to get our money from?"

As I walked around Kaktovik's windblown streets, a small car pulled 18 up beside me. Crammed into the compact was Robert Thompson, a burly 58-year-old Inupiat wilderness guide. He offered me a tour of the island, where—despite the oil money—many people still derive much of their diet and cultural identity from subsistence hunting and whaling. We cruised slowly past Kaktovik's tidy modular houses, out past the large aluminum hangar that serves as the town's airport.

Thompson says he finds the Gwich'in's defense of their cultural values 19 "admirable," adding that the prospect of oil development on the nearby tundra has opened a rift among local residents. We passed an SUV idling at a stop sign amid a cloud of exhaust and vapor. As if to prove Thompson's point, a local Eskimo official, sitting impassively behind the wheel, responded to Thompson's wave with an icy stare. "He used to wave," Thompson shrugged. "But now he doesn't."

This past spring, nearly one-third of Kaktovik's voting-age adults 20 signed a petition opposing oil development in ANWR—fearing, according to Kayotuk, that onshore oil drilling would lead to offshore leasing, endangering the annual bowhead whale hunt, the core of the Eskimo culture across the North Slope.

Still, most Kaktovik residents support oil development in the 1002, 21 though they would agree with Karl Francis, a pro-oil adviser retained by Kaktovik's city council to serve as a buffer between local authorities and the outside world. It must be done "responsibly," he says, with minimal impact on the environment, hunting and whaling to ensure the long-range survival of the people and their traditions. Those who favor drilling, he acknowledged, also hope that outside corrosive effects, such as drugs and alcohol, can be kept at bay even after the road needed to develop the oil fields reaches Kaktovik.

"This is a little village living on a time bomb," Francis said. "We're 22 sitting on top of a huge pool of oil, and the people here need to have a say about how it's developed. We're trying to strategize how this town will be around 200 years from now with everyone happy and healthy."

■ ■ ■

AFTER YOU READ

- **THINK** about what it would be like to live in either a Gwich'in or Inupiat village. What makes the Gwich'in way of life special? Do you think you would be willing to live as the Gwich'in live? Why or why not? Do you understand why the Inupiat have taken the oil money to improve their villages? Do you think this group made the right choice? Why or why not?

- **EXAMINE** the annotations that you made identifying passages about the Gwich'in and the Inupiat groups. Did the author devote as much space to one group as to the other? Do you think his presentation of these two groups and their ways of life is fair and evenhanded? Support your opinion. With which group do you identify more? Which group do you admire more? Explain.

- **EXAMINE** the last paragraph of the essay. How is the little village of Kaktovik sitting, metaphorically, "on a time bomb"? How might it be different in ten years? Twenty years? Fifty years? What about the Gwich'in villages? Do you think they will be able to remain as they are? What changes do you think might take place in their culture?

- **WRITE** an essay in which you argue for the position taken by either the Gwich'in or the Inupiat. See "Writing a Persuasive Essay" (pages 372–378) at the end of this unit for help with your essay.

FOCUS: EXAMPLES

Seven Myths about Alternative Energy

■　■　■

MICHAEL GRUNWALD

The winner of several journalism awards, Michael Grunwald has been a reporter for *The Washington Post* but is currently a senior correspondent at *Time* magazine. His articles on the environment have appeared in several journals, including *Audubon, New Republic*, and *U.S. News & World Report*; his book *The Swamp: The Everglades, Florida, and the Politics of Paradise* was published in 2006. The following essay is from the September–October 2009 issue of *Foreign Policy.*

BEFORE YOU READ

■ **THINK** about the title, "Seven Myths about Alternative Energy." What is a myth? How many different kinds of alternative energy can you name? Based on this title, what do you think Grunwald will say about alternative energy?

■ **EXAMINE** the structure of the essay. How many sections does it have? How does each section begin? What do the first sentences of each section have in common?

■ **WRITE** in your journal a list of as many different kinds of alternative energy as you can think of.

AS YOU READ

Determine whether your original prediction about Grunwald's attitude toward alternative energy was accurate or inaccurate. Also, circle and make a list of unfamiliar words. (You will work with these later.)

■　■　■

As long as there have been dominant forms of energy, people have been searching for alternatives to them. Coal became popular in the 16th century as Europeans looked to replace increasingly scarce wood. Nineteenth-century Americans facing "peak" whale oil turned to petroleum to fuel their lamps. Inventor Alexander Graham Bell thought that the world's supplies of coal and oil were already running out in 1917 and called for a switch to ethanol made from corn. Today, the race is on to find alternatives to the fossil fuels that are seen as poisoning the atmosphere and pumping up petrostates.

But when it comes to energy, nothing is as fraught with myths, misperceptions, and outright flights of fancy as the conversation about oil's successors. As the world looks around anxiously for an alternative to oil, energy sources such as biofuels, solar, and nuclear seem like they could be the magic ticket. They're not.   2

1. "We Need to Do Everything Possible to Promote Alternative Energy."

Not exactly. It's certainly clear that fossil fuels are mangling the climate   3
and that the status quo is unsustainable. There is now a broad scientific consensus that the world needs to reduce greenhouse gas emissions more than 25 percent by 2020—and more than 80 percent by 2050. Even if the planet didn't depend on it, breaking our addictions to oil and coal would also reduce global reliance on petrothugs and vulnerability to energy-price spikes.

But though the world should do everything sensible to promote alter-   4
native energy, there's no point trying to do everything possible. There are financial, political, and technical pressures as well as time constraints that will force tough choices; solutions will need to achieve the biggest emissions reductions for the least money in the shortest time. Hydrogen cars, cold fusion, and other speculative technologies might sound cool, but they could divert valuable resources from ideas that are already achievable and cost-effective. It's nice that someone managed to run his car on liposuction leftovers, but that doesn't mean he needs to be subsidized.

Reasonable people can disagree whether governments should try to pick   5
energy winners and losers. But why not at least agree that governments shouldn't pick losers to be winners? Unfortunately, that's exactly what is happening. The world is rushing to promote alternative fuel sources that will actually accelerate global warming, not to mention an alternative power source that could cripple efforts to stop global warming.

We can still choose a truly alternative path. But we'd better hurry.   6

2. "Renewable Fuels Are the Cure for Our Addiction to Oil."

Unfortunately not. "Renewable fuels" sound great in theory, and agricul-   7
tural lobbyists have persuaded European countries and the United States to enact remarkably ambitious biofuels mandates to promote farm-grown alternatives to gasoline. But so far in the real world, the cures—mostly ethanol derived from corn in the United States or biodiesel derived from palm oil, soybeans, and rapeseed in Europe—have been significantly worse than the disease.

Researchers used to agree that farm-grown fuels would cut emissions   8
because they all made a shockingly basic error. They gave fuel crops credit for soaking up carbon while growing, but it never occurred to them that fuel crops might displace vegetation that soaked up even more carbon.

It was as if they assumed that biofuels would only be grown in parking lots. Needless to say, that hasn't been the case; Indonesia, for example, destroyed so many of its lush forests and peat lands to grow palm oil for the European biodiesel market that it ranks third rather than 21st among the world's top carbon emitters.

In 2007, researchers finally began accounting for deforestation and other land-use changes created by biofuels. One study found that it would take more than 400 years of biodiesel use to "pay back" the carbon emitted by directly clearing peat for palm oil. Indirect damage can be equally devastating because on a hungry planet, food crops that get diverted to fuel usually end up getting replaced somewhere. For example, ethanol profits are prompting U.S. soybean farmers to switch to corn, so Brazilian soybean farmers are expanding into cattle pastures to pick up the slack and Brazilian ranchers are invading the Amazon rain forest, which is why another study pegged corn ethanol's payback period at 167 years. It's simple economics. The mandates increase demand for grain, which boosts prices, which makes it lucrative to ravage the wilderness.

Deforestation accounts for 20 percent of global emissions, so unless the world can eliminate emissions from all other sources—cars, coal, factories, cows—it needs to back off forests. That means limiting agriculture's footprint, a daunting task as the world's population grows—and an impossible task if vast expanses of cropland are converted to grow middling amounts of fuel. Even if the United States switched its entire grain crop to ethanol, it would only replace one fifth of U.S. gasoline consumption.

This is not just a climate disaster. The grain it takes to fill an SUV tank with ethanol could feed a hungry person for a year; biofuel mandates are exerting constant upward pressure on global food prices and have contributed to food riots in dozens of poorer countries. Still, the United States has quintupled its ethanol production in a decade and plans to quintuple its biofuel production again in the next decade. This will mean more money for well-subsidized grain farmers, but also more malnutrition, more deforestation, and more emissions. European leaders have paid a bit more attention to the alarming critiques of biofuels—including one by a British agency that was originally established to promote biofuels—but they have shown no more inclination to throw cold water on this $100 billion global industry.

3. "If Today's Biofuels Aren't the Answer, Tomorrow's Biofuels Will Be."

Doubtful. The latest U.S. Rules, while continuing lavish support for corn ethanol, include enormous new mandates to jump-start "second-generation" biofuels such as cellulosic ethanol derived from switchgrass. In theory, they would be less destructive than corn ethanol, which relies on tractors, petroleum-based fertilizers, and distilleries that emit way too much carbon. Even first-generation ethanol derived from sugar cane—which already provides half of Brazil's transportation fuel—is considerably greener than corn ethanol. But recent studies suggest that any biofuels requiring good agricultural land would still be worse than gasoline for global warming. Less of a disaster than corn ethanol is still a disaster.

Back in the theoretical world, biofuels derived from algae, trash, agricultural waste, or other sources could help because they require no land or at least unspecific "degraded lands," but they always seem to be "several" years away from large-scale commercial development. And some scientists remain hopeful that fast-growing perennial grasses such as miscanthus can convert sunlight into energy efficiently enough to overcome the land use dilemmas—someday. But for today, farmland happens to be very good at producing the food we need to feed us and storing the carbon we need to save us, and not so good a generating fuel. In fact, new studies suggest that if we really want to convert biomass into energy, we're better off turning it into electricity. 13

Then what should we use in our cars and trucks? In the short term ... gasoline. We just need to use less of it. 14

Instead of counterproductive biofuel mandates and ethanol subsidies, governments need fuel-efficiency mandates to help the world's 1 billion drivers guzzle less gas, plus subsidies for mass transit, bike paths, rail lines, telecommuting, carpooling, and other activities to get those drivers out of their cars. Policymakers also need to eliminate subsidies for roads to nowhere, mandates that require excess parking and limit dense development in urban areas, and other sprawl-inducing policies. None of this is as enticing as inventing a magical new fuel, but it's doable, and it would cut emissions. 15

In the medium term, the world needs plug-in electric cars, the only plausible answer to humanity's oil addiction that isn't decades away. But electricity is already the source of even more emissions than oil. So we'll need an answer to humanity's coal addiction, too. 16

4. "Nuclear Power Is the Cure for Our Addiction to Coal."

Nope. Atomic energy is emissions free, so a slew of politicians and even some environmentalists have embraced it as a clean alternative to coal and natural gas that can generate power when there's no sun or wind. In the United States, which already gets nearly 20 percent of its electricity from nuclear plants, utilities are thinking about new reactors for the first time since the Three Mile Island meltdown three decades ago—despite global concerns about nuclear proliferation, local concerns about accidents or terrorist attacks, and the lack of a disposal site for the radioactive waste. France gets nearly 80 percent of its electricity from nukes, and Russia, China, and India are now gearing up for nuclear renaissances of their own. 17

But nuclear plants cannot fix the climate crisis. The first reason is timing. The West needs major cuts in emissions within a decade, and the first new U.S. reactor is only scheduled for 2017—unless it gets delayed, like every U.S. reactor before it. Elsewhere in the developed world, most of the talk about a nuclear revival has remained just talk; there is no Western country with more than one nuclear plant under construction, and scores of existing plants will be scheduled for decommissioning in the coming 18 decade, so there's no way nuclear could make even a tiny dent in electricity emissions before 2020.

The bigger problem is cost. Nuke plants are supposed to be expensive to 19 build but cheap to operate. Unfortunately, they're tuning out to be really, really expensive to build; their cost estimates have quadrupled in less than a decade. Energy guru Amory Lovins has calculated that new nukes will cost nearly three times as much as wind—and that was before their construction costs exploded for a variety of reasons, including the global credit crunch, the atrophying of the nuclear labor force, and a supplier squeeze symbolized by a Japanese company's worldwide monopoly on steel-forging for reactors. A new reactor in Finland that was supposed to showcase the global renaissance is already way behind schedule and way, way over budget. This is why plans for new plants were recently shelved in Canada and several U.S. states, why Moody's just warned utilities they'll risk ratings downgrades if they seek new reactors, and why renewables attracted $71 billion in worldwide private capital in 2007—while nukes attracted zero.

It's also why U.S. nuclear utilities are turning to politicians to supple- 20 ment their existing loan guarantees, tax breaks, direct subsidies, and other cradle-to-grave government goodies with new public largesse. Reactors don't make much sense to build unless someone else is paying; that's why the strongest push for nukes is coming from countries where power is publicly funded. For all the talk of sanctions, if the world really wants to cripple the Iranian economy, maybe the mullahs should just be allowed to pursue nuclear energy.

Unlike biofuels, nukes don't worsen warming. But a nuclear expansion— 21 like the recent plan by U.S. Republicans who want 100 new plants by 2030—would cost trillions of dollars for relatively modest gains in the relatively distant future.

Nuclear lobbyists do have one powerful argument: If coal is too dirty 22 and nukes are too costly, how are we going to produce our juice? Wind is terrific, and it's on the rise, adding nearly half of new U.S. power last year and expanding its global capacity by a third in 2007. But after increasing its worldwide wattage tenfold in a decade—China is now the leading producer, and Europe is embracing wind as well—it still produces less than 2 percent of the world's electricity. Solar and geothermal are similarly wonderful and inexhaustible technologies, but they're still global rounding errors. The average U.S. household now has 26 plug-in devices, and the rest of the world is racing to catch up; the U.S. Department of Energy expects global electricity consumption to rise 77 percent by 2030. How can we meet that demand without a massive nuclear revival?

We can't. So we're going to have to prove the Department of Energy 23 wrong.

5. "There Is No Silver Bullet to the Energy Crisis."
Probably not. But some bullets are a lot better than others; we ought to 24 give them our best shot before we commit to evidently inferior bullets. And one renewable energy resource is the cleanest, cheapest, and most

abundant of them all. It doesn't induce deforestation or require elaborate security. It doesn't depend on the weather. And it won't take years to build or bring to market; it's already universally available.

It's called "efficiency." It means wasting less energy—or more precisely, using less energy to get your beer just as cold, your shower just as hot, and your factory just as productive. It's not about some austerity scold harassing you to take cooler showers, turn off lights, turn down thermostats, drive less, fly less, buy less stuff, eat less meat, ditch your McMansion, and otherwise change your behavior to save energy. Doing less with less is called conservation. Efficiency is about doing more or the same with less; it doesn't require much effort or sacrifice. Yet more efficient appliances, lighting, factories, and buildings, as well as vehicles, could wipe out one fifth to one third of the world's energy consumption without any real deprivation.   25

Efficiency isn't sexy, and the idea that we could use less energy without much trouble hangs uneasily with today's more-is-better culture. But the best way to ensure new power plants don't bankrupt us, empower petrodictators, or imperil the planet is not to build them in the first place. "Negawatts" saved by efficiency initiatives generally cost 1 to 5 cents per kilowatt-hour versus projections ranging from 12 to 30 cents per kilowatt-hour from new nukes. That's because Americans in particular and human beings in general waste amazing amounts of energy. U.S. electricity plants fritter away enough to power Japan, and American water heaters, industrial motors, and buildings are as ridiculously inefficient as American cars. Only 4 percent of the energy used to power a typical incandescent bulb produces light; the rest is wasted. China is expected to build more square feet of real estate in the next 15 years than the United States has built in its entire history, and it has no green building codes or green building experience.   26

But we already know that efficiency mandates can work wonders because they've already reduced U.S. energy consumption levels from astronomical to merely high. For example, thanks to federal rules, modern American refrigerators use three times less energy than 1970s models, even though they're larger and more high-tech.   27

The biggest obstacles to efficiency are the perverse incentives that face most utilities; they make more money when they sell more power and have to build new generating plants. But in California and the Pacific Northwest, utility profits have been decoupled from electricity sales, so utilities can help customers save energy without harming shareholders. As a result, in that part of the country, per capita power use has been flat for three decades—while skyrocketing 50 percent in the rest of the United States. If utilities around the world could make more by helping their customers use less power, the U.S. Department of Energy wouldn't be releasing such scary numbers.   28

6. "We Need a Technological Revolution to Save the World."

Maybe. In the long term, it's hard to imagine how (without major advances) we can reduce emissions 80 percent by 2050 while the global   29 population increases and the developing world develops. So a clean-tech Apollo program modeled on the Manhattan Project makes sense. And we do need carbon pricing to send a message to market makers and innovators to promote low-carbon activities; Europe's cap-and-trade scheme seems to be working well after a rocky start. The private capital already pouring into renewables might someday produce a cheap solar panel or a synthetic fuel or a superpowerful battery or a truly clean coal plant. At some point, after we've milked efficiency for all the negawatts and negabarrels we can, we might need something new.

But we already have all the technology we need to start reducing emissions by reducing consumption. Even if we only hold electricity demand flat, we can subtract a coal-fired megawatt every time we add a wind-powered megawatt. And with a smarter grid, green building codes, and strict efficiency standards for everything from light bulbs to plasma TVs to server farms, we can do better than flat. Al Gore has a reasonably plausible plan for zero-emissions power by 2020; he envisions an ambitious 28 percent decrease in demand through efficiency, plus some ambitious increases in supply from wind, solar, and geothermal energy. But we don't even have to reduce our fossil fuel use to zero to reach our 2020 targets. We just have to use less. 30

If somebody comes up with a better idea by 2020, great! For now, we should focus on the solutions that get the best emissions bang for the buck. 31

7. "Ultimately, We'll Need to Change Our Behaviors to Save the World."
Probably. These days, it's politically incorrect to suggest that going green will require even the slightest adjustment to our way of life, but let's face it: Jimmy Carter was right. It wouldn't kill you to turn down the heat and put on a sweater. Efficiency is a miracle drug, but conservation is even better; a Prius saves gas, but a Prius sitting in the driveway while you ride your bike uses no gas. Even energy-efficient dryers use more power than clotheslines. 32

More with less will be a great start, but to get to 80 percent less emissions, the developed world might occasionally have to do less with less. We might have to unplug a few digital picture frames, substitute teleconferencing for some business travel, and take it easy on the air conditioner. If that's an inconvenient truth, well, it's less inconvenient than trillions of dollars worth of new reactors, perpetual dependence on hostile petrostates, or a fricasseed planet. 33

After all, the developing world is entitled to develop. Its people are understandably eager to eat more meat, drive more cars, and live in nicer houses. It doesn't seem fair for the developed world to say: Do as we say, not as we did. But if the developing world follows the developed world's wasteful path to prosperity, the Earth we all share won't be able to accommodate us. So were going to have to change our ways. Then we can at least say: Do as we're doing, not as we did. 34

■   ■   ■

AFTER YOU READ

■ **THINK** about Grunwald's attitude to each of the seven myths and to alternative energy in particular. Although he rejects many of these "myths" as immediate cures for our problems, he does identify several ideas that he thinks will help reduce our energy usage and carbon emissions and that will therefore help with the problem of global warming. Identify as many of these good ideas as you can. What are his two most important suggestions?

■ **EXAMINE** again the structure of the essay, focusing this time on the type of content included in each section. Each of the seven sections gives an *example* of one "myth" about alternative energy. Notice that these myths and the discussion of them could have been arranged in a different order. In a narrative, the organization is generally chronological; that is, the content, or events, are usually arranged in the order in which they occurred. In an exemplification essay, the examples can be arranged in several different orders—as long as the order is logical. Can you identify a logical order in these seven myths—perhaps from lesser important to more important ones? Notice also that, just as each section provides one example of a myth, Grunwald gives more specific examples about each myth. Divide the class into seven groups, with each group focusing on a different section, and identify some of these examples. (Note: An essay like this in which examples are numbered is sometimes called an *enumeration essay*.)

■ **EXAMINE** also, in your same groups, the vocabulary in your section, including the words you circled while reading. Identify from three to five words in the section that are unfamiliar to some students in your group, and—using context, word parts, or a dictionary—define these words. Your teacher may want each group to share their vocabulary words with the rest of the class. Add any words that are new to you to your vocabulary journal.

■ **WRITE** a collaborative summary of Grunwald's essay. Work in the same groups as in earlier activities, with each group focusing on and writing a one-paragraph summary of your assigned section. Then, using a computer, combine your individual summaries into a complete summary of the essay. Begin your group summary by identifying the author, the name of the essay, and its thesis. (See "Writing a Summary," pages 186–188.)

■ Or **WRITE** an essay in which you give and develop three or four examples of ways to conserve energy. See Lesson 6 on the *Interactions*, eighth edition, student website, at www.cengagebrain.com, for more instructions on writing example essays.

The True Cost of Carbon

■ ■ ■

AL GORE

Al Gore served as a congressman and senator from Tennessee before being elected as vice president of the United States in 1992. Gore has been a supporter of the environment for many years, helping to pass environmental legislation as a congressman and focusing on the health of the national ecosystem as vice president. His first major environmental book was the bestselling *Earth in the Balance: Ecology and the Human Spirit* (1992, 2000), which explained the ecological problems of global warming, overpopulation, deforestation, and acid rain and proposed global solutions. In 2006 he continued his environmental focus with *An Inconvenient Truth*, which was initially available as a documentary and won an Oscar for the best documentary feature of the year. The following selection is taken from his most recent environmental publication, *Our Choice: A Plan to Solve the Climate Crisis* (2009). Gore was awarded the Nobel Peace Prize in 2007 for his efforts to draw worldwide attention to the dangers of global warming.

BEFORE YOU READ

■ **THINK** about the most widely accepted explanation for climate change: that human emitted carbon is the primary cause of global warming that exists on Earth and that this climate change has "the potential to end human civilization as we know it" (paragraph 2). Do you agree or disagree with this explanation? Why do you feel as you do?

■ **EXAMINE** the title of the selection. Explain the double meaning of this title.

■ **WRITE** a journal entry stating your position on climate change, particularly on global warming. Do you agree or disagree that global warming is human caused and potentially disastrous for both human beings and the planet? Explain why you hold this position.

AS YOU READ

Underline passages that comment on the cost or pricing of carbon. Also, circle unfamiliar words. Select several of these words to look up in a dictionary and add to your vocabulary journal.

■ ■ ■

Human civilization and the earth's ecological system are colliding, and the climate crisis is the most prominent, destructive, and threatening manifestation of this collision. It is often lumped together with other ecological crises, such as the destruction of ocean fisheries and coral reefs; the growing shortages of freshwater; the depletion of topsoil in many prime agricultural areas; the cutting and burning of ancient forests, including tropical and subtropical rain forests rich in species diversity; the extinction crisis; the introduction of long-lived toxic pollutants into the biosphere and the accumulation of toxic waste from chemical processing, mining, and other industrial activities; air pollution; and water pollution.

These manifestations of the violent impact human civilization has on the earth's ecosystem add up to a worldwide ecological crisis that affects and threatens the habitability of the earth. But the deterioration of our atmosphere is by far the most serious manifestation of this crisis. It is inherently global and affects every part of the earth; it is a contributing and causative factor in most of the other crises; and if it is not quickly addressed, it has the potential to end human civilization as we know it.

For all its complexity, however, its causes are breathtakingly simple and easy to understand.

All around the world, we humans are putting into the atmosphere extraordinary amounts of ... different kinds of air pollution that trap heat and raise the temperature of the air, the oceans, and the surface of the earth.

These ... pollutants, once emitted, travel up into the sky quickly. But all ... of them eventually come back down to earth, some quickly, others very slowly. And as a result, the oft-cited aphorism "What goes up must come down" will work in our favor when we finally decide to solve the climate crisis.

Indeed, the simplicity of global warming causation points toward a solution that is equally simple, even if difficult to execute: we must sharply reduce what goes up and sharply increase what comes down. ...

The biggest global warming cause by far—carbon dioxide—comes primarily from the burning of coal for heat and electricity, from the burning of oil-based products (gasoline, diesel, jet fuel) in transportation, and from the burning of coal, oil, and natural gas in industrial activity. Carbon dioxide produced in the burning of these fossil fuels accounts for the single largest amount of the air pollution responsible for the climate crisis. That is why most discussions of how to solve the climate crisis tend to focus on producing energy in ways that do not at the same time produce dangerous emissions of CO_2.

At this point, however, the burning of coal, oil, and natural gas is not only the largest source of CO_2 but also far and away the most rapidly increasing source of global warming pollution.

After fossil fuels, the next largest source of human-caused CO_2 pollution— almost a quarter of the total—comes from land-use changes—predominantly deforestation, the burning of trees and vegetation. Since the majority of forest burning is in relatively poorer developing countries and the majority of industrial activity is in relatively wealthier developed countries, the negotiators of proposed global agreements to solve the climate crisis generally try to strike a balance between measures that sharply reduce the burning of fossil fuels on the one hand and sharply reduce deforestation on the other.

There's good news and bad news about CO_2. Here is the good news: if we stopped producing excess CO_2 tomorrow, about half of the man-made CO_2 would fall out of the atmosphere (to be absorbed by the ocean and by plants and trees) within 30 years.

Here's the bad news: the remainder would fall out much more slowly, and as much as 20 percent of what we put into the atmosphere this year will remain there 1,000 years from now. And we're putting 90 million tons of CO_2 into the atmosphere every single day!

The good news should encourage us to take action now, so that our children and grandchildren will have reason to thank us. Although some harmful consequences of the climate crisis are already under way, the most horrific consequences can still be avoided. The bad news should embolden us to a sense of urgency, because—to paraphrase the old Chinese proverb—a journey of a thousand years begins with a single step.

. . .

Carbon dioxide, the most important source of global warming pollution, is invisible, tasteless, and odorless. It is largely invisible to market calculations as well. And when something's not recognized in the marketplace, it's much easier for government, business, and all the rest of us to pretend that it doesn't exist. But what we're pretending doesn't exist is destroying the habitability of the planet. We put 90 million tons of it into the atmosphere every 24 hours, and the amount is increasing decade by decade.

The easiest, most obvious, and most efficient way to employ the power of the market in solving the climate crisis is to put a price on carbon. The longer we delay, the greater the risk the economy faces from investments in high-carbon-content assets and activities. The artificial value placed on such investments ignores the reality of the climate crisis and its consequences for business. As Jonathan Lash, president of the World Resources Institute, recently said, "Nature does not do bailouts."

There are three options available to us for fixing the flawed signals in the marketplace:

- A CO_2 tax that internalizes the true environmental cost of coal and oil.
- The use of a cap and trade system, which accomplishes the same result indirectly by restricting the amount of CO_2 that can be produced and allocating it through a market-based trading system.
- Direct regulation of CO_2 emissions under laws such as the Clean Air Act.

I have long advocated the first option—a CO_2 tax that is offset by equal reductions in other tax burdens—as the simplest, most direct, and most efficient way of enlisting the market as an ally in saving the ecosystem of the planet. However, one of the first casualties of the ascendance of market fundamentalism in the United States was in its success in creating massive opposition in the Congress to any new taxation—even taxation offset by reductions in other tax areas. The coal and oil companies, assisted by coal-burning utilities, have provided political contributions, massive lobbying resources, and aggressive public advertising with corporate funds to buttress opposition by many elected officials to anything that these companies feel might hurt their profits.

It is possible that these attitudes may change over time as the merits of   17 a revenue-neutral CO_2 tax become more widely understood—and as recognition of the unthinkable consequences of failing to solve the climate crisis begins to play a bigger role in our assessment of what is right and what is wrong.

In the last few years, some who used to oppose a CO_2 tax have come   18 out in favor of it. For example, Arthur Laffer, a conservative Republican who was one of the architects of President Reagan's initial tax-reduction plan, joined with a Republican Congressman from South Carolina, Bob Inglis, to support my proposal for a CO_2 tax in a *New York Times* column they wrote in 2008.

For the foreseeable future, however, it is only prudent to assume that   19 the U.S. political system is incapable of making such a bold and controversial decision. This could change, but I vividly remember what happened in 1993 when I persuaded President Clinton and his economic team to include a version of the CO_2 tax (at that time called a BTU—British Thermal Unit—tax) in our economic plan. With great effort, we were able to persuade the House of Representatives to adopt the measure, but the Senate refused and watered it down to the point where it was worse than nothing at all.

Confronted with the unlikelihood of gaining sufficient support for a   20 CO_2 tax, most thoughtful advocates have concentrated instead on option two, the cap and trade system. Indeed, virtually all of the bills introduced in Congress by members of both political parties have featured a cap and trade system as their preferred mechanism for including the hidden costs of carbon-based fuels in our market calculations. This approach is also the centerpiece of President Obama's strategy for reducing CO_2 emissions, and the centerpiece of the global negotiation in Copenhagen at the end of 2009.

In my opinion, the real solution would include both a CO_2 tax and a   21 cap and trade system, and I believe that will eventually be our choice. Several countries, mostly in Europe, have already enacted both approaches. Sweden, often considered the country with the most advanced strategy for reducing CO_2, has enacted both measures. Recently it increased the CO_2 tax, after an initial experience that was overwhelmingly positive.

The third option for fixing the mistaken signals in the market for   22 carbon-based fuels involves government regulation of CO_2 emissions. In concert with a CO_2 tax and/or a cap and trade system, direct regulation of CO_2 is a very effective approach. Moreover, in early 2007, the conservative-dominated U.S. Supreme Court formally ruled that the Environmental Protection Agency was required under the Clean Air Act to go forward with a formal consideration of whether or not to regulate

CO_2 as an air pollutant covered by the law. Since CO_2 is obviously the most dangerous form of air pollution we face, most assumed that this court decision would inevitably lead to regulation. And early in 2009, the new head of the EPA under President Obama, Lisa Jackson, initiated formal proceedings that may result in regulation.

Another form of regulation that promises to accelerate the transition to renewable energy comes in the form of a legally required mandate to producers and sellers of electricity that they obtain a large and growing percentage of their electricity from renewable sources. This approach has already been enacted by the state of California and several other states and has already resulted in a surge of new investment for windmills and solar plants that would not have been built without the legal mandate. If this approach is codified in national law—as appears likely—this surge in renewable-energy investment will grow rapidly. 23

■ ■ ■

AFTER YOU READ

- ■ THINK about the idea of "put[ting] a price on carbon" (paragraph 14). Is this a good idea or a bad idea? Support your opinion.

- ■ EXAMINE the three ideas that Gore gives for pricing—and hopefully reducing—carbon in the United States. In your opinion, which of these ideas is the best idea? Which is the worst idea? Or do you like or dislike all of these ideas? Explain your reasoning.

- ■ EXAMINE also the persuasive structure of Gore's essay. In paragraphs 1–12, he provides his background argument, explaining the problem of global warming and that carbon is its greatest cause. Then, in paragraph 13, Gore gives reasons why carbon hasn't been viewed as a greater threat, and in paragraph 14 he states his primary argument that we must "employ the power of the market in solving the climate crisis." Finally, he argues for three possible economic-based solutions for reducing carbon and potentially solving the climate crisis.

- ■ WRITE an essay in which you argue for or against one or more of Gore's suggestions for reducing carbon in our country. See "Writing a Persuasive Essay" at the end of this unit, pages 372–378.

Is Humanity Losing the Global Warming Debate?

■ ■ ■

S. Fred Singer and Dennis T. Avery

An expert on geophysics, atmospheric science, weather, and the environment, S. Fred Singer has taught and researched at Princeton and Johns Hopkins University and is currently professor emeritus of environmental sciences at the University of Virginia. The author and editor of numerous books, Singer founded in 1989 the conservative Science and Environmental Policy Project, of which he is the director and president. The author of *Saving the Planet with Pesticides and Plastic: The Environmental Triumph of High-Yield Farming* (2000), Dennis T. Avery is currently the editor of *Global Food Quarterly* and the director of the Center for Global Food Issues at the Hudson Institute. Singer and Avery coauthored *Unstoppable Global Warming: Every 1,500 Years* (2007), from which this selection is taken.

BEFORE YOU READ

■ **THINK** about the title of this essay. Relying not only on the previous essays by Grunwald and Gore but also on your own general knowledge, describe the global warming debate going on today. What are some of the arguments of each side of this debate? How might humanity "lose" this debate? Is there more than one way for humanity to lose in this debate? Explain.

■ **EXAMINE** the first paragraph of the essay. In what way do Singer and Avery agree with Al Gore in the previous reading? In what ways do they disagree?

■ **EXAMINE** also the terms *ice-core* and *sediment cores* in the bulleted list found in paragraph 5. *Sediments* are deposits of materials on the bottom of a surface, such as the sea; a *core* is the center or heart of an object. In this context, both types of cores are scientific samples bored out of a substance that has been filling up for hundreds of thousands of years.

■ **WRITE** a brief journal entry in which you predict how Singer and Avery will answer the question posed in their title.

AS YOU READ

Look for and underline the different 1,500-year cycles of warming and cooling that scientists have identified.

■ ■ ■

The Earth is warming but physical evidence from around the world 1 tells us that human-emitted CO_2 has played only a minor role in it. Instead, the mild warming seems to be part of a natural 1,500-year-climate cycle (plus or minus 500 years) that goes back at least one million years.

The cycle has been too long and too moderate for primitive peoples 2 lacking thermometers to recount in their oral histories. But written evidence of climate change does exist. The Romans had recorded a warming from about 200 B.C. to A.D. 600, registered mainly in the northward advance of grape growing in both Italy and Britain. Histories from both Europe and Asia tell us there was a Medieval Warming that lasted from about 900 to 1300; this period was also known as the Medieval Climate Optimum because of its mild winters, stable seasons, and lack of severe storms. Human histories also record the Little Ice Age, which lasted from about 1300 to 1850. But people thought each of these climatic shifts was a distinct event and not part of a continuing pattern.

This began to change in 1984 when Willi Dansgaard of Denmark and 3 Hans Oeschger of Switzerland published their analysis of the oxygen isotopes in the first ice cores extracted from Greenland (Dansgaard et al. 288–98). These cores provided 250,000 years of the Earth's climate history in one set of "documents." The scientists compared the ratio of "heavy" oxygen-18 isotopes to the "lighter" oxygen-16 isotopes, which indicated the temperature at the time the snow had fallen. They expected to find evidence of the known 90,000-year ice ages and the mild interglacial periods recorded in the ice, and they did. However, they did not expect to find anything in between. To their surprise, they found a clear cycle—moderate, albeit abrupt—occurring about every 2,550 years running persistently through both. (This period would soon be reassessed at 1,500 years, plus or minus 500 years.)

By the mid-1980s, however, the First World had already convinced 4 itself of the Greenhouse Theory and believed that puny human industries had grown powerful enough to change the planet's climate. There was little media interest in the frozen findings of obscure, parka-clad Ph.D.s in far-off Greenland.

A wealth of other evidence has emerged since 1984, however, corrob- 5 orating Dansgaard and Oeschger's natural 1,500-year climate cycle:

- An ice core from the Antarctic's Vostok Glacier—at the other end of the world from Iceland—was brought up in 1987 and showed the same 1,500-year climate cycle throughout its 400,000-year length.

- The ice-core findings correlate with known advances and retreats in the glaciers of the Arctic, Europe, Asia, North America, Latin America, New Zealand, and the Antarctic.
- The 1,500-year cycle has been revealed in seabed sediment cores brought up from the floors of such far-flung waters as the North Atlantic Ocean and the Sargasso Sea, the South Atlantic Ocean and the Arabian Sea.
- Cave stalagmites from Ireland and Germany in the Northern Hemisphere to South Africa and New Zealand in the Southern Hemisphere show evidence of the Modern Warming, the Little Ice Age, the Medieval Warming, the Dark Ages, the Roman Warming, and the unnamed cold period before the Roman Warming.
- Fossilized pollen from across North America shows nine complete reorganizations of our trees and plants in the last 14,000 years, or one every 1,650 years.
- In both Europe and South America, archaeologists have evidence that prehistoric humans moved their homes and farms up mountainsides during the warming centuries and retreated back down during the cold ones.

The Earth continually warms and cools. The cycle is undeniable, 6 ancient, often abrupt, and global. It is also unstoppable. Isotopes in the ice and sediment cores, ancient tree rings, and stalagmites tell us it is linked to small changes in the irradiance of the sun.

The temperature change is moderate. Temperatures at the latitude of 7 New York and Paris moved about 2 degrees Celsius above the long-term mean during warmings, with increases of 3 degrees or more in the polar latitudes. During the cold phases of the cycle, temperatures dropped by similar amounts below the mean. Temperatures change little in lands at the equator, but rainfall often does.

The cycle shifts have occurred roughly on schedule whether CO_2 levels 8 were high or low. Based on this 1,500-year cycle, the Earth is about 150 years into a moderate Modern Warming that will last for centuries longer. It will essentially restore the fine climate of the Medieval Climate Optimum.

The climate has been most stable during the warming phases. The "lit- 9 tle ice ages" have been beset by more floods, droughts, famines, and storminess. Yet, despite all of this evidence, millions of well-educated people, many scientists, many respected organizations—even the national governments of major First World nations—are telling us that the Earth's current warming phase is caused by human-emitted CO_2 and deadly dangerous. They ask society to renounce most of its use of fossil fuel-generated energy and accept radical reductions in food production, health technologies, and standards of living to "save the planet."

We have missed the predictive power of the 1,500-year climate cycle. 10

Will the fear of dangerous global warming lead society to accept dra- 11 conian restrictions on the use of fertilizers, cars, and air conditioners?

Will people give up the scientific and technological advances that have 12 added thirty years to life expectancies all over the globe in the last century?

Massive human sacrifices would be required to meet the CO_2 stabiliza- 13
tion goals of the Kyoto Protocol. The treaty's "introductory offer" is a tiny
5 percent reduction in fossil fuel emissions from 1990 levels, but that
would do almost nothing to forestall greenhouse warming of the planet.
Saving the planet from man-made global warming was supposed to wait
on Kyoto's yet-unspecified second stage, scheduled to begin in 2012.

In 1995, one U.S. environmentalist assessed the outlook: "According 14
to the [United Nations] Intergovernmental Panel on Climate Change, an
immediate 60 to 80 percent reduction in emissions is necessary just to sta-
bilize atmospheric concentrations of CO_2—the minimum scientifically
defensible goal for any climate strategy. Less-developed nations, with their
relatively low emissions, will inevitably increase their use of fossil fuels as
they industrialize and their populations expand. Thus heavily polluting
regions like the [United States] will have to reduce their emissions even
more [than 60 to 80 percent] for the world as a whole to meet this goal"
(Ryan).

Humans use eighty million tons per year of nitrogen fertilizer to nour- 15
ish their crops. The nitrogen is taken from the air (which is 78 percent N_2)
through an industrial process generally fueled by natural gas. In 1900,
before industrial nitrogen fertilizer, the world could support only 1.5 billion people, at a far lower standard of living, and was clearing huge tracts
of forest to get more cropland.

Suppose the world went all-organic in its farming, gave up the man- 16
made fertilizer, and cleared half of the world's remaining forests for more
low-yield crops. It's reasonable to expect that half the world's wildlife species would be lost in the land clearing and one-fourth of the world's people
would succumb to malnutrition. What if research then confirmed that the
climate was warming due to the natural cycle instead of CO_2? Is that a no-
regrets climate insurance policy?

What if the Kyoto treaty or some similar arrangement prevented the 17
Third World from moving away from using wood for heating and cooking? How much additional forest would then be sacrificed for firewood in
the developing countries over the next fifty years?

The stakes in the global warming debate are huge. Humanity and wild- 18
life may both be losing the debate.

Works Cited

Dansgaard, W., et al. "North Atlantic Climatic Oscillations Revealed by
     Deep Greenland Ice Cores." In *Climate Processes and Climate Sensitiv-
     ity*. Ed. F. E. Hansen and T. Takahashi. Geophysical Monograph 29.
     Washington, D.C.: American Geophysical Union, 1984.
Ryan, John C. "Greenhouse Gases on the Rise in the Northwest." North-
     west Environment Watch, 1995. <www.northwestwatch.org> 12 Feb.
     2004.

AFTER YOU READ

■ **THINK** about the theory of 1,500-year warming and cooling cycles that Singer and Avery believe have taken place on Earth for the past 400,000 years. Does this theory make sense to you or not? Which theory seems more logical to you—the theory described in this selection or the theory of extreme global warming in which Al Gore and many other environmentalists believe?

■ **EXAMINE** carefully the supporting evidence that Singer and Avery give for their theory of continual, but moderate, warming and cooling in paragraph 5. What evidence seems the strongest to you? What seems the weakest? Explain.

■ **EXAMINE** also paragraphs 11–18 in which Singer and Avery list negative consequences that they believe can happen from overreaction to a belief in extreme global warming and its potentially negative—even devastating—effects. How disastrous could the possible effects of overreaction to global warming be? Which of the possible effects listed by Singer and Avery would, in your opinion, be the most disastrous? How do these effects compare to those Al Gore thinks will occur if the manmade global warming in which he believes is allowed to continue?

■ **WRITE** an essay in which you take and argue for a position on the seriousness of global warming and its impact on human beings, wildlife, and the Earth itself. Refer to this essay as well as to the previous essay by Al Gore, agreeing or disagreeing with selected points relevant to your argument. (See the guidelines for "Writing a Persuasive Essay" at the end of this unit, pages 372–378.)

Waste

■ ■ ■

WENDELL BERRY

Although Wendell Berry has written several novels and short stories, he is known primarily as a poet and essayist; his most recent collection of essays is *Imagination in Place* (2010). Berry currently lives on the Kentucky farm that was also the home of his parents, grandparents, and great-grandparents. As a writer and an organic farmer, he is deeply concerned about the environment, and his goal is to live in harmony with nature. In the following selection from *What Are People For,* Berry describes the contamination of our countryside with trash and explores the relationship between the waste of physical items and what he views as the related decline in human potential and achievement.

BEFORE YOU READ

■ **THINK** about the amount of waste or trash that you produce each day. How much of this trash is organic—vegetable peelings, leftover food, and so on? How much is inorganic—paper, metal, plastic? Do you throw away cans, bottles, Styrofoam containers, old toasters or radios, or other appliances? How do you dispose of this trash? Do you ever think about what happens to the trash that you throw away?

■ **EXAMINE** the following italicized words and their definitions:

1. *ubiquitous* (paragraph 3): widespread, everywhere
2. *symbiosis* (paragraph 5): the practice of two or more organisms or ideas existing together
3. *ecological* (paragraph 5): relates to *ecology,* which is the study of relationships between organisms and their environment.

■ **WRITE** a journal entry in which you list all the items you throw away in a particular day. Subdivide your list into organic and inorganic materials. If possible, further subdivide these groups. (For example, you can probably subdivide inorganic materials into three groups—paper products, metal products, and plastic products.)

AS YOU READ

Underline examples and details of the trash that Berry found on or near his farm. Also think about what *you* can do to reduce the problem of waste disposal.

■   ■   ■

A s a country person, I often feel that I am on the bottom end of the   1
waste problem. I live on the Kentucky River about ten miles from its entrance into the Ohio. The Kentucky, in many ways a lovely river, receives an abundance of pollution from the Eastern Kentucky coal mines and the central Kentucky cities. When the river rises, it carries a continuous raft of cans, bottles, plastic jugs, chunks of Styrofoam, and other imperishable trash. After the floods subside, I, like many other farmers, must pick up the trash before I can use my bottomland fields. I have seen the Ohio, whose name (*Oyo* in Iroquois) means "beautiful river," so choked up with this manufactured filth that an ant could crawl dry-footed from Kentucky to Indiana. The air of both river valleys is seriously polluted. Our roadsides and roadside fields lie under a constant precipitation of cans, bottles, the plasticware of fast food joints, soiled plastic diapers, and sometimes whole bags of garbage. In our county we now have a "sanitary landfill" which daily receives, in addition to our local production, fifty to sixty large truckloads of garbage from Pennsylvania, New Jersey, and New York.

Moreover, a close inspection of our countryside would reveal, strewn   2
over it from one end to the other, thousands of derelict and worthless automobiles, house trailers, refrigerators, stoves, freezers, washing machines, and dryers; as well as thousands of unregulated dumps in hollows and sink holes, on streambeds and roadsides, filled not only with "disposable" containers but also with broken toasters, television sets, toys of all kinds, furniture, lamps, stereos, radios, scales, coffeemakers, mixers, blenders, corn poppers, hair dryers, and microwave ovens. Much of our waste problem is to be accounted for by the flimsiness and unrepairability of the labor-savers and gadgets that we have become addicted to.

Of course, my sometime impression that I live on the receiving end of   3
this problem is false, for country people contribute their full share. The truth is that we Americans, all of us, have become a kind of human trash, living our lives in the midst of a ubiquitous damned mess of which we are at once the victims and the perpetrators. We are all unwilling victims, perhaps; and some of us even are unwilling perpetrators, but we must count ourselves among the guilty nonetheless. In my household we produce much of our own food and try to do without as many frivolous "necessities" as possible—and yet, like everyone else, we must shop, and when we shop we must bring home a load of plastic, aluminium, and glass containers designed to be thrown away, and "appliances" designed to wear out quickly and be thrown away.

I confess that I am angry at the manufacturers who make these things. 4
There are days when I would be delighted if certain corporation executives
could somehow be obliged to eat their products. I know of no good reason
why these containers and all other forms of manufactured "waste"—solid,
liquid, toxic, or whatever—should not be outlawed. There is no sense and
no sanity in objecting to the desecration of the flag while tolerating and
justifying and encouraging as a daily business the desecration of the country for which it stands.

But our waste problem is not the fault only of producers. It is the fault 5
of an economy that is wasteful from top to bottom—a symbiosis of an
unlimited greed at the top and a lazy, passive, and self-indulgent consump-
tiveness at the bottom—and all of us are involved in it. If we wish to correct this economy, we must be careful to understand and to demonstrate
how much waste of human life is involved in our waste of the material
goods of Creation. For example, much of the litter that now defaces our
country is fairly directly caused by the massive secession or exclusion of
most of our people from active participation in the food economy. We
have made a social ideal of minimal involvement in the growing and cooking of food. This is one of the dearest "liberations" of our affluence. Nevertheless, the more dependent we become on the *industries* of eating and
drinking, the more waste we are going to produce. The mess that sur-
rounds us, then, must be understood not just as a problem in itself but as
a symptom of a greater and graver problem: the centralization of our economy, the gathering of the productive property and power into fewer and
fewer hands, and the consequent destruction, everywhere, of the local
economies of household, neighborhood, and community. This is the source
of our unemployment problem, and I am not talking just about the unemployment of eligible members of the "labor force." I mean also the unemployment of children and old people, who, in viable household and local
economies, would have work to do by which they would be useful to
themselves and to others. The ecological damage of centralization and
waste is thus inextricably involved with human damage. For we have, as
a result, not only a desecrated, ugly, and dangerous country in which to
live until we are in some manner poisoned by it, and a constant and now
generally accepted problem of unemployed or unemployable workers, but
also classrooms full of children who lack the experience and discipline of
fundamental human tasks, and various institutions full of still capable old
people who are useless and lonely.

I think that we must learn to see the trash on our streets and roadsides, 6
in our rivers, and in our woods and fields, not as the side effects of "more
jobs" as its manufacturers invariably insist that it is, but as evidence of
good work *not* done by people able to do it.

■   ■   ■

AFTER YOU READ

■ **THINK** again about the waste in our society. Do you agree or disagree with Berry that we cause as well as suffer from waste? Berry further suggests that our throw-away society pays a price in a "waste of human life." Explain further what Berry means by this phrase; then discuss why you agree or disagree with Berry.

■ **EXAMINE** the examples and details of waste that Berry found on or near his farm (see your underlining). What are some of the examples that he gives? How would you categorize these examples? Have you seen items of trash similar to these on the highway or near your home? How does this sight make you feel?

■ **WRITE** an essay in which you explain what you can do personally to decrease the problem of trash and waste disposal in your home or in the area surrounding your home. Be sure to give specific examples and details.

It's Inconvenient Being Green

■ ■ ■

LISA TAKEUCHI CULLEN

Born in Kobe, Japan, Lisa Takeuchi Cullen came to the United States for a university education. She graduated from Rutgers College with a B.A. in 1988 and from Columbia University Graduate School of Journalism in 1998. She married and stayed in the United Stated as a journalist, writing first for *Money* magazine and then for *Time*. She has published one book, *Remember Me: A Lively Tour of the New American Way of Death* (2006). The following essay appeared in *Time* magazine in December 2007.

BEFORE YOU READ

■ **THINK** about the title of this selection. Do you recognize the writer's allusion to Al Gore's 2006 book (and documentary), *An Inconvenient Truth*? What does Cullen's title lead you to expect in her essay?

■ **EXAMINE** the first paragraph, paying particular attention to Cullen's tone. Is it serious or light? Solemn or humorous? Does it have a touch of satire—of wit or irony drawing attention to what Cullen views as exaggerated attempts at "being green"? Support your opinion from the paragraph itself.

■ **EXAMINE** also paragraph 3 to see if it includes any words that are unfamiliar to you. Composed of two word parts, the new term *eco-anxiety* means being anxious, worried, or uneasy about humanity's relationship to the environment. *Etymology* is the origin and historical development of a word, and an *imperative* is a command or obligation.

■ **WRITE** a journal entry in which you agree or disagree with Cullen that "It's Inconvenient Being Green."

AS YOU READ

Underline passages that you think are particularly humorous.

■ ■ ■

My condition began when I read of a couple in New York City 1 who had vowed to live a whole year without toilet paper. They were conducting an experiment in environmentally low-impact living as research for a book, they said. For a year they would eschew transportation that emits carbon dioxide, shun foods wrapped in plastic packaging and, most dramatically, conduct the elimination of their waste without the aid of wasteful paper products. I mull the logistics of paperless hygiene as I load a family-size pack of Charmin Ultra Soft into my Subaru Forester. According to the plastic packaging, each roll contains 569 sq. ft. (or 52 square metres, which sounds a lot better) of murdered tree. Like the bear in the commercial, I squeeze it tight. I like my toilet paper. I like it a lot.

I am not particularly eco-conscious. But I am increasingly eco-anxious.   2
Every day, it seems, I hear of some new way the world around me is going aggressively green. Workers in Portland, Ore., are cycling to the office. Ireland has slapped a tax on plastic bags. Incoming freshmen at California colleges are asked to keep their Red Bulls in thermoelectric fridges. David Duchovny says he recycles, has solar power and drives an electric car. Now every time I purchase a single-serving water bottle, I hear the opening theme from *The X-Files*.

So it was with some relief that I learned that eco-anxiety is a diagnos-   3
able condition. A so-called eco-therapist in Santa Fe, N.M., reportedly sees up to 80 patients a month who complain of panic attacks, loss of appetite, irritability and what she describes as some sort of a twitchy sensation in their cells. Eco-anxiety is not new—the etymology website WordSpy found it mentioned in a 1990 Washington *Post* article—but it's only now becoming widespread. Environmental consciousness is no longer just another lifestyle choice, like open marriages or joining the circus; it has been upgraded to a moral imperative. That forces Americans to add environmentalism to their already endless checklist of things to fret about. Did I remember to turn out the kitchen light? Couldn't I memorize the directions to my job interview instead of printing them out? Why, for the love of Pete, did I use a napkin to wipe my mouth when I have a perfectly good sleeve?

Recently I have spent considerable time considering my environmental   4
failings, if not actually doing much about them. Like the average American household, we own two cars. Between my husband and me, we drive 13,000 miles (21,000 km) a year, making our country 520 gal. (2,000 L) of gas more dependent on foreign suppliers. The thermostat in our 2,200 sq. ft. (200 sq m) house is set at 70° F (21° C). It takes 6,960 Kw-h a year to power our computers, halogen lights and plasma TV. My child went through an industry-calculated average of 4.4 diapers a day for 34 months, which amounts to 4,488 soiled Huggies in some landfill. So far this year, I have travelled 34,574 miles (or 55,636 km, which sounds a lot worse) by air. According to the calculator on ClimateCrisis.net, my household produces 15 tons of carbon dioxide a year. The average is 7.5. Mine is the Sasquatch of carbon footprints.

Anxiously I ponder the ways I might reduce my shoe size. I have seri-   5
ously considered banning Christmas gifts this year to avoid the senseless consumption of sheer stuff, but I don't want my kid to say she saw

Mommy dissing Santa Claus. I could theoretically ride a bicycle to work, but I am concerned that somewhere along the eight miles of highway, I will have a seizure. I have looked into yurts, but they are not a popular housing alternative in New Jersey.

The reasons for not going green usually boil down to one, so elegantly 6 put by a frog who had no choice in the matter: It's not easy being green. It's easier to toss the leftovers into the 13-gal. (50 L) Hefty bag than figure out how to use the compost bin that sits just outside. It's easier to drive to the grocery store than to plant my own vegetable garden. It's easier to keep my job writing for a magazine that prints 3.25 million copies a week than it is to start over in a new career designing suburban yurts.

Yes, the truth is inconvenient. But I'm trying. I am attempting to 7 reverse my eco-unconsciousness, if only to assuage the twitchy sensation in my cells. I have installed the low-energy lights I bought at Home Depot, even though they make my living room look like a gas-station toilet. I look for products at the grocery store with the green recycling thingy on the package and then place my purchases in reusable burlap bags. I potty-trained my kid. When I die, I plan to be placed au naturel in a shallow hole and become fertilizer for a dogwood tree. But there's one thing I won't give up. If he wants my toilet paper, Al Gore himself will have to pry it from my cold, biodegradable hands.

■   ■   ■

AFTER YOU READ

■ **THINK** about the ideas that Cullen has for reducing her "shoe size" (i.e., her "carbon footprint") and becoming more "green." Which of these ideas are really good ones? Which does she propose "tongue-in-cheek"?

■ **EXAMINE** the humorous details that you underlined and compare the passages you thought were funny with those identified by some of your classmates. Do you think the exaggerated statistics in paragraph 4 are humorous or satirical? What statements are the most humorous to you? Do you think that Cullen's intention was simply to be entertaining and humorous? Or do you think she intends to gently satirize the green movement? Support your answer with specifics from the essay.

■ **WRITE** an essay in which you agree or disagree with Cullen that "It's Inconvenient Being Green." If you believe that there are inconveniences associated with being ecoconscious, explain whether or not you think these inconveniences are justified. If you believe that they are justified, explain how worthwhile the effects of this awareness and of "being green" are to humanity and the environment.

UNIT SIX

■ ■ ■

Critical Thinking, Reading, and Writing

■ WRITING A PERSUASIVE ESSAY

Persuasive essays differ from other essays primarily in purpose. Whereas other types of essays may entertain or inform their readers, the writer of a persuasive essay attempts to convince readers to agree with his or her viewpoint on a subject and, perhaps, to take some action in support of that viewpoint. Because we encounter persuasive writing daily, we need to be aware of the techniques that other writers use to persuade us. Political speeches, editorials, and advertisements are all persuasive in nature as are many of the articles that you read for your English, history, or sociology classes. As a writer, you also need to know how to promote effectively your own viewpoint about issues that matter to you.

BEFORE YOU WRITE

Your subject, purpose, and audience are important in any essay that you write, but these elements are especially important in persuasive essays. In addition, an effective persuasive essay requires a more complex organization than a personal or informative essay.

Subject, Purpose, and Audience

In writing a persuasive, or argumentative, essay, you should select a subject that can be disputed and one that matters to you. You know initially that your general purpose is to persuade your audience. However, you also need to determine your specific purpose and suggest this idea in your thesis statement. In this section's sample essay ("Dice or Doves?"), Cindy Camburn hopes to persuade her readers that the casinos on the Mississippi Gulf Coast are causing real harm to bird life. Camburn clearly states her thesis as follows:

> The Casinos have changed the entire face of the Coast; in particular, they have changed the habitat of one of the coast's greatest attractions: its flocks of birds.

Camburn hopes to persuade her readers of the truth of her thesis. However, this essay—like many other persuasive works—also encourages readers to act on their new convictions.

Subject, purpose, and audience are all closely related. Thus, while a writer's overall persuasive purpose remains the same, she may focus on different aspects of her subject or vary her thesis statement depending on the audience she is addressing. Thus, if you were arguing for or against the use of pesticides to a Third World audience, you would need to keep in mind that Third World countries are usually poverty-stricken areas where many people—even children—go hungry daily. You would, therefore, be likely to have a sympathetic audience if you argued for the use of pesticides that would improve crop production. However, if you wanted to argue against the use of certain pesticides, such as DDT, you would need to explain clearly why you believe the long-range dangers outweigh the short-term benefits to poor countries. To convince this audience, you would also need to recognize the problem of hunger in these countries and propose an alternate solution.

Depending on your purpose and audience, you may use one of three basic appeals. A writer may appeal to the audience's emotions, reason, or sense of character. For example, Anderson Cooper appeals to his readers' emotions during Hurricane Katrina when he describes a family's photo album lying in the street and searchers looking for the dead; Michael Grunwald appeals to his readers' reason when he tells us that the cost of building a nuclear plant has "quadrupled in less than a decade" and that for more short-term reductions in energy use and carbon emissions, we must conserve energy usage; and Al Gore uses the character appeal through his status of being a former vice president of the United States and a Nobel Peace Prize winner and his dedication to preserving the planet. You may combine two or more of these appeals, but you should be careful to use appeals that will be effective for your chosen audience.

Organization

A persuasive essay, like any other kind of essay, follows the overall structural pattern of an introduction, a body, and a conclusion. However, persuasive essays often employ the following structural elements (although not necessarily in this order):

1. Introduction: statement of the problem and thesis (or purpose) statement

2. Background information

3. Recognition and refutation of the opposing argument

4. Evidence to support the writer's argument

5. Conclusion and possible call for action

Example

To help you write your own persuasive essay, read the following selection by Cindy Camburn:

Dice or Doves?

One of my earliest memories of growing up on the Mississippi Gulf   1
Coast is waking every morning to the sounds of birds in the trees around the feeder. The types of birds varied with the season, but the most common visitors were a pair of doves with distinctive markings. Some mornings the doves would not be there, but they always eventually reappeared. I would watch them walk slowly around the deck, one bird pecking at the

seeds which had fallen from the feeder while the other bird stayed alert for danger. At breakfast on these mornings, my mother would always say, "My doves are back." I was constantly surprised that the birds were hers because I felt they had returned for me.

When I went home from college to visit beginning in the mid-1990s, however, I always closed the blinds before I went to bed. Even so, I was aware of a beam of light that washed across the back yard, penetrated the closed blinds, and bounced off my mirror every thirty seconds. That beam came from the laser show at Palace Casino, ten miles across the bay from my home. The Palace was then one of fifteen casinos which sat on the twenty-six-mile stretch of coast, creating an economic boom for the area. "Things couldn't be better," stated George Lammons, editor of the *Coast Business Journal*. The Coast, he explained, was "enjoying robust economic growth. The biggest reason for our turnaround and one of the biggest reasons for the expectation of a good, long-term outlook is probably our newest industry—casino gambling." Lammons added that the casinos had "put smiles on the faces of coastians" (4).

If Lammons had looked a little more closely, he would have found that many coastians were not smiling. Even before Katrina hit the area in August of 2006, Gulf Coast citizens felt—as they still feel—that the casinos were destroying their quality of life. These casinos turned the coast highway into a perpetual construction project and traffic jam. Their employees dumped trash and waste water into the Mississippi River sound. Their six-story parking garages replaced the palm trees and shrimp fleets and blocked the views of the beach. **The casinos changed the entire face of the Coast; in particular, they changed the habitat of one of the coast's greatest attractions, its flocks of birds.**

According to Becky Gillette in the *Coast Business Journal*, the Wildlife and Nature Preservation Center has cited large increases in orphaned and injured wildlife due to habitat destruction created by the rapid growth caused by the rise of the casino industry (31). In a *National Geographic* article entitled "Silence of the Songbirds," Les Line puts the problem in a larger perspective, declaring that "when Rachel Carson wrote of 'a spring without voices' and the silence of the dawn without the chorus of robins, catbirds, doves, jays, and wrens, we thought the culprit was TOXINS. Now," he adds, "we know that habitat destruction is an even greater threat" (79–80). He also explains:

> Each spring, from mid-March to mid-May, [the birds] come north across the Gulf of Mexico in great waves, riding flows of warm humid air on a flight launched shortly after sunset from staging areas like the Yucatán Peninsula. Under the best conditions the . . . larger, faster fliers . . . will reach the coast by mid-morning after a 600-mile journey; smaller birds . . . lag behind. The travelers' goal is to make a rest stop in the first line of extensive forest on the mainland, perhaps 30 miles inland. But if they are

buffeted by head winds or storms enroute, they will drop exhausted into remnant scrub woodlands along the coast. . . . (72)

When the rest and recovery areas of forests and shrubs have been replaced by buildings and concrete parking areas, many exhausted birds die. Without a place to rest on the coast, many of the surviving birds are unable to reproduce, so the population is dwindling. In the early '60s, "Thirty thousand [migrating birds] would cross a given mile of coast . . . every hour for five hours" every day during the peak season in April. Today, however, those numbers have already been reduced by more than forty percent (Line 73-74).

In addition to losing their natural resting and nesting areas, birds 5 arriving on the Mississippi Gulf Coast face another hazard, the casinos' laser lights. According to Gillette, the Palace Casino's lights are considered to be hazardous within 2,000 feet because they cause "temporary flash blindness and/or permanent retina damage" (1). As Gillette further reports, local wildlife specialists feel that the threat to birds is even greater. Judith Toups, a local ornithologist, says any strong beam of light is a major hazard for migrating birds, especially in foggy or stormy weather, because birds "get disoriented and head toward the light." Janet Miller, president of the Mississippi Gulf Coast Audubon Society, adds, "We end up with migrating birds being attracted to the bright lights of the casinos and then having their eyesight damaged by the laser shows" (31).

Although Hurricane Katrina shut down area casinos when it ravaged the 6 Gulf Coast in late August of 2005, the casinos—including the Palace Casino—are again up and running, and Stephen Richer, the executive director of the Mississippi Gulf Coast Convention and Visitors Bureau, believes their "potential is higher than ever" and there may be as many as twenty casinos on the coast by the end of the decade (Shattuck 1). The casino industry did do some good by continuing to pay its workers for several months after the hurricane (Mohr D3), but that philanthropy doesn't change the basic situation. Of course, casino officials have always been quick to defend the lasers that are now as bright as ever. As these officials explained, the laser shows, which can be seen as far as fifty miles away, draw people to the casino. Officials further stated that they have received many compliments and have had "few complaints" (Gillette 31-32).

I am complaining. The laser shows and the economic boom the casinos 7 represent do not put a smile on my face. If the unrestrained development continues, the Mississippi Gulf Coast will have to depend on the lasers to produce holographs of birds. Then the casino officials can receive compliments on how real the holographic birds look. I do not want the laser versions. I want my (and my mother's) birds, particularly doves, to keep reappearing.

Works Cited

Gillette, Becky. "Will It Harm the Birds? Will It Harm Planes?" *Coast Business Journal* 1 Aug. 1994: 1, 31+. Print.

Lammons, George. "State of the Coast: Taking Off after Tough Times." *Coast Business Journal* 15 Feb. 1993: 4. Print.

Line, Les. "Silence of the Songbirds." *National Geographic* June 1993: 68-92. Print.

Miller, Janet. Personal interview. 22 April 2007.

Mohr, Holbrook. "Casino Workers Lose Post-Katrina Benefits." *St. Louis Post-Dispatch* 8 Dec. 2005: D3. Gale Infotrac Custom Newspapers. Web. 22 March 2007.

Shattuck, Harry. "Mississippi: A New Beginning." *The Houston Chronicle* 17 Sept. 2006: 1. Gale Infotrac Custom Newspapers. Web. 22 March 2007.

Toups, Judith. Personal interview. 20 April 2007.

■   ■   ■

Camburn's persuasive essay includes all the major structural elements outlined on page 373. However, she varies her structure by reversing the order of the background information and statement of the problem and by delaying her thesis statement until the third paragraph. Thus, her first paragraph captures audience attention by providing background information about the writer's youth on the Mississippi coast, whereas the second paragraph introduces some of the problems caused by area casinos and acknowledges the opposing viewpoint about economic growth. In her third paragraph Camburn refutes the opposing point of view and states her thesis that the casinos have changed the habitat of birds on the coast. She provides evidence for her thesis in paragraphs 4 and 5, summarizes the opposition in paragraph 6, and concludes in paragraph 7 by restating her own position and implicitly calling for action from her audience.

Camburn also employs all three of the major persuasive appeals. She initially appeals to readers' emotions, first by describing her early memories of birds near her home and second by explaining that the casinos and their lights are killing these birds. Next, Camburn appeals to her audience's reason by using documented evidence to show the extent of the destruction to the birds of the Gulf Coast. Third, both Camburn's personal experiences and her research—which employs sources that appear to be trustworthy— suggest an honest, caring, sympathetic, and careful writer.

Notice also that Camburn cites her sources clearly and accurately in both the text of her essay and her Works Cited list. Her essay as a whole is clear, well organized, well supported, and ultimately persuasive.

Assignments

1. Cindy Camburn focuses on doves that have been harmed or reduced in numbers because their habitats have been changed by human interference. Select another animal that is threatened or endangered because of human or natural changes to the environment, and write a persuasive essay for a particular audience arguing for protection of this animal. Use at least two or three sources.

2. Write a persuasive essay arguing for or against drilling in the Arctic National Wildlife Refuge. Use at least two sources in addition to the essay in this unit by Scott Wallace.

3. Write a persuasive essay suggesting to your neighbors and townspeople how to solve a local environmental problem.

AS YOU WRITE

Once you decide on your subject, purpose, and audience, you need to gather information for your essay. For either of the first two assignments, you will probably need to do research in the library or on the Internet. If you are writing about an environmental problem near your home, you will certainly use your own experiences and observations, but you may also want to interview others who have special knowledge about the issue. Be sure to keep a careful and accurate record both of the information you gather and of your sources.

When you begin drafting your essay, remember to follow these guidelines:

- State clearly both the problem and your thesis.
- Provide necessary background information.
- Recognize and refute the opposing argument.
- Provide supporting evidence for your argument.
- Conclude the essay effectively and perhaps call for action from your readers.

As you write, remember to employ the appeals of emotion, reason, and/or character. If you use any sources other than your own ideas, be sure to identify quoted material by introducing it and by enclosing it in quotation marks if it is four lines or fewer or by indenting it one inch if it is more than four lines. Also, credit borrowed wording or borrowed ideas by putting your sources in parentheses in your paper and listing them in a Works Cited. (You may use Camburn's essay as a starting model for your citations, but see the link to the *Modern Language Association Documentation Style Guide from Purdue University's Writing Lab* on the *Interactions,* eighth edition, student website at www.cengagebrain.com for more

information on using Modern Language Association style in your paren-
thetical references and Works Cited.)

AFTER YOU WRITE

After you complete a draft of your persuasive essay, reread it carefully to
see if it includes each of the following:

- The basic elements of a persuasive essay listed on pages 373 and 377.
- A logical organization of these elements
- The appeal(s) most likely to convince your audience
- Clear documentation of sources in your essay and in a Works Cited
  section

After you evaluate your essay, add, delete, or rearrange information to
improve your organization and development.

You may also want to meet with a partner or a small group of your
classmates to evaluate one another's essays. First, identify and evaluate
each of the major persuasive elements to see if one or more sections need
further revision. Second, identify the appeal(s) used in each essay and
determine whether the writer needs to adjust his or her appeal for the
intended audience. Third, be sure that outside sources are documented correctly in the essay and in the Works Cited.

After you—and perhaps a peer group—have evaluated your essay, edit
it to eliminate problems in grammar, usage, sentence structure, and style.
Finally, proofread your essay carefully before submitting it to your
instructor.

■ EXPLORING IDEAS TOGETHER

1. Do you enjoy spending time in a natural environment? What natural
   areas or scenes do you most enjoy? What do you enjoy about these
   areas? What activities do you like to do in nature? Compare your preferences with those of a group of your classmates.

2. Many people in our country believe that our climate is warming, that
   the warming is caused by human beings (primarily by carbon emissions), and that this warming may cause disastrous results. However,
   this debate is ongoing, and new information on the topic is coming
   out every day. Discuss this topic with a group of classmates, comparing and contrasting your ideas about it.

3. With a group of your classmates, discuss the effects of some recent natural phenomenon on the environment and its people. Have you had a
   forest fire, a drought, a flood, a blizzard, an ice storm, a wind storm, a
   tornado, or a hurricane in your area recently? Have you read about
   such events in other areas of the country? What were the effects? You

may even want to bring newspaper accounts to share with your group members.

4. As suggested by Cindy Camburn's essay on pages 373–376, a vigorous debate exists about how to protect both the environment and property rights. In class, debate this issue, with one group arguing for the rights of property owners and another group arguing for the protection of the environment, perhaps specifically for endangered species. Is it possible for our society to respect both the environment and property rights? How?

■ EXPLORING THE INTERNET

Several of the following resources are listed on the Related Websites section of the *Interactions*, eighth edition, student website, available at www.cengagebrain.com.

1. You may go to the Arctic National Wildlife Refuge's website listed as a link on the "Related Websites" section of the *Interactions* student website to find out more about this geographical area, its inhabitants, and its wildlife—including the caribou. This site is managed by the U.S. Fish and Wildlife Service. You may also want to Google *ANWR* for different points of view about drilling in this area.

2. Recommended sites for information on renewable energy are "Learning about Renewable Energy," managed by the National Renewable Energy Laboratory (NREL), and the private site, "Alternate Energy Sources." See the "Related Websites" page of the *Interactions* student website for links to these sites.

3. For additional information on the global warming debate represented in this unit by the readings by Al Gore and by S. Fred Singer and Dennis Avery, you may go to the site "An Inconvenient Truth," based on Gore's book of the same name, and to a PBS interview with Singer. You may access these sites at "Related Websites" on the *Interactions* student site.

■ WRITING ESSAYS

1. Write an essay describing a natural location that you enjoy visiting or observing. What do you enjoy about this particular area, and why do you enjoy it?

2. Norris and Crenshaw both describe a natural rural environment, but many individuals enjoy an urban environment. Write an essay in which you compare rural life with city life. What are the advantages of each environment? What are the disadvantages? Which do you ultimately prefer and why?

3. The essays by Norris, Crenshaw, and Cooper focus on how the weather affects the environment and the people in it. Write an essay

in which you discuss how you have been affected by the weather—either by the changing of the seasons as in "Weather Reports" or by one or more specific weather events as in the essays by Crenshaw and Cooper.

4. Write an essay in which you give examples of three types of alternative energy (energy other than that derived from fossil fuels). Briefly describe each type of energy you are discussing, and then give additional examples of how this kind of energy can be used effectively and efficiently. (See Lesson 6 on the *Interactions* student website at www. cengagebrain.com, for help with writing exemplification essays.)

5. Write a narrative describing some possible effects of global temperatures rising to a dangerous level. Use your imagination as well as sources such as the film *An Inconvenient Truth* to describe how climates might change in certain areas.

6. Write an essay in which you try to persuade your readers that global warming is—or is not—a real and imminent danger and that they should (or should not) begin to take immediate action to prevent the problem from becoming even more serious. (Refer back to "Writing a Persuasive Essay" on pages 372–378.)

7. Identify a local environmental issue (water usage, waste management, some type of pollution, etc.) that you know about or can investigate. Then write a persuasive essay to a particular audience advocating a specific solution to the problem. You may want to interview local citizens or officials about the issue. (See pages 372–378 for help with writing persuasive essays.)

8. Write an essay in which you respond to *one* of the reading selections in this unit, agreeing or disagreeing with the author's position. Begin by summarizing briefly the selection to which you are responding (be sure to identify the title and author in your summary), then provide your own thesis statement, and finally develop supporting ideas and examples for your thesis. For help with writing a response essay, see pages 244–247.

TECHNOLOGY & MEDIA

What are the students in this photograph doing? When an individual uses more than one kind of technology at a time, we say that he or she is multitasking. How many different kinds of technology do you see represented in this photograph? Do you think students can study effectively while 'multitasking'? Explain.

■ ■ ■

Our interaction with technology and the media affects not only us as individuals but also our families, our personal relationships with friends and mates, and our roles at work and in society. In *its most general and basic form, technology can be traced to the invention of simple machines—of wheels, levers, and other devices used to achieve a particular task. During the Industrial Revolution of the nineteenth century, machines were developed to save time and effort in farming, the textile industry, and many other areas.*

By the early 1900s, however, many machines and gadgets had been invented to make everyone's lives easier and more pleasant. Today, an alarm clock or radio wakes you each morning, a coffeemaker brews your coffee, a dishwasher washes your mug, a hair dryer styles your hair, a washing machine launders your clothes, a microwave cooks your dinner, and a car or bus or truck transports you to school or work. A radio or stereo or iPod keeps you company during the day, a television entertains you in the evening, and a VCR, DVD, or TiVo even records programs for you while you sleep. Not only do computers perform many routine tasks that you once did manually, but you can even take along a wireless laptop and cell phone to stay connected. Although you do not relate to technology in the same way you relate to people, some machines may evoke an emotional response from you. For example, you may have a special feeling for your first car, or you may get particularly frustrated with a computer that continually freezes up.

Although the print media of books and newspapers have been around for centuries, the rapid development of technology—especially the development of the "high technology" of electronics and computers—in the twentieth century brought about an astounding increase both in the types of media used to transmit information and entertainment and in individual media sources. The radio dominated the first half of the century, but by the 1950s nearly every household had a television. News that we once only read or heard came right into our living rooms by the power of the camera and, later, satellite technology. The personal computer revolution began about 1975, and the Internet was developed during the 1980s. However, it wasn't until the early 1990s that the advent of the World Wide Web and decreased prices for PCs made these new resources readily available on college campuses and in most homes. We can now research a medical condition, check the news and weather, and read political and entertainment commentary in the comfort of our homes at any time of the day. In fact, we have become so used to these technological conveniences and to easy and immediate access to media sources that it is hard to remember when we did not have them.

The readings in this unit explore not only technology and the media but also the relationship between them. Various authors explore both the benefits and the abuses of various personal technologies such as cell phones, television, and the Internet. Other writers investigate how the Internet is changing both the way we read and learn and the way news and opinion are disseminated. One writer asserts that technology has almost become a religion while another writer encourages us to "live with less" technology.

FOCUS: COMPARISON AND CONTRAST

Literacy Debate Online:
R U Really Reading?

■ ■ ■

Motoko Rich

Born in Los Angeles, California, Motoko Rich graduated from Yale University in 1991 with a degree in history and then, on a Mellon Fellowship, attended Cambridge in the United Kingdom. She has been a reporter for the *Financial Times* in London and, for six years, for *The Wall Street Journal.* Since 2003 she has worked for *The New York Times,* where she has recently been assigned the book news section of the paper. Like the three essays that follow it, this essay focuses on the relationship between technology and education.

BEFORE YOU READ

■ **THINK** about the concept of literacy—of being able to read and write and of doing both well. How effective are you as a reader and a writer? Do you consider yourself to be truly "literate"? Besides class assignments, what do you read? Do you read books, magazines, newspapers, and Internet articles? What else do you read? How much do you read? Do you enjoy reading? Explain.

■ **EXAMINE** the title and the two subheadings. Why do you think Motoko spelled "Are You" as she did? What "debate" do you think will be described in this essay? On which side of the debate do you think you will be? Why?

■ **EXAMINE** also paragraph 13, which has at least three words that may be unfamiliar to you. Something that is *cryptic* is unclear, hidden, and mysterious. *Argot* is a specialized vocabulary known only to a particular group of people, in this case Internet writers. And a *cornucopia* is a horn of plenty, typically a goat's horn overflowing with grains and fruits. (The term is derived from the horn of the goat that fed the Greek god Zeus in his infancy.)

■ **WRITE** a journal entry in which you describe your literacy development—when and how you learned to read and write and the literacy that you have achieved at this point in your life.

AS YOU READ

Identify arguments from both sides of the debate by writing a "B" (for books) in the margins besides sentences and paragraphs that discuss and argue for books as the best source of literacy and an "I" (for Internet) beside those sentences and paragraphs that argue for the Internet.

■ ■ ■

BEREA, Ohio—Books are not Nadia Konyk's thing. Her mother, hoping to entice her, brings them home from the library, but Nadia rarely shows an interest.

Instead, like so many other teenagers, Nadia, 15, is addicted to the Internet. She regularly spends at least six hours a day in front of the computer here in this suburb southwest of Cleveland.

A slender, chatty blonde who wears black-framed plastic glasses, Nadia checks her e-mail and peruses myyearbook.com, a social networking site, reading messages or posting updates on her mood. She searches for music videos on YouTube and logs onto Gaia Online, a role-playing site where members fashion alternate identities as cutesy cartoon characters. But she spends most of her time on quizilla.com or fanfiction.net, reading and commenting on stories written by other users and based on books, television shows or movies.

Her mother, Deborah Konyk, would prefer that Nadia, who gets A's and B's at school, read books for a change. But at this point, Ms. Konyk said, "I'm just pleased that she reads something anymore."

Children like Nadia lie at the heart of a passionate debate about just what it means to read in the digital age. The discussion is playing out among educational policy makers and reading experts around the world, and within groups like the National Council of Teachers of English and the International Reading Association.

As teenagers' scores on standardized reading tests have declined or stagnated, some argue that the hours spent prowling the Internet are the enemy of reading—diminishing literacy, wrecking attention spans and destroying a precious common culture that exists only through the reading of books.

But others say the Internet has created a new kind of reading, one that schools and society should not discount. The Web inspires a teenager like Nadia, who might otherwise spend most of her leisure time watching television, to read and write.

Even accomplished book readers like Zachary Sims, 18, of Old Greenwich, Conn., crave the ability to quickly find different points of view on a subject and converse with others online. Some children with dyslexia or other learning difficulties, like Hunter Gaudet, 16, of Somers, Conn., have found it far more comfortable to search and read online.

SETTING EXPECTATIONS

Few who believe in the potential of the Web deny the value of books. But 9
they argue that it is unrealistic to expect all children to read "To Kill a
Mockingbird" or "Pride and Prejudice" for fun. And those who prefer
staring at a television or mashing buttons on a game console, they say,
can still benefit from reading on the Internet. In fact, some literacy experts
say that online reading skills will help children fare better when they begin
looking for digital-age jobs.

Some Web-evangelists say children should be evaluated for their profi- 10
ciency on the Internet just as they are tested on their print reading comprehension. Starting next year, some countries will participate in new
international assessments of digital literacy, but the United States, for
now, will not.

Clearly, reading in print and on the Internet are different. On paper, 11
text has a predetermined beginning, middle and end, where readers focus
for a sustained period on one author's vision. On the Internet, readers
skate through cyberspace at will and, in effect, compose their own beginnings, middles and ends.

Young people "aren't as troubled as some of us older folks are by 12
reading that doesn't go in a line," said Rand J. Spiro, a professor of educational psychology at Michigan State University who is studying reading
practices on the Internet. "That's a good thing because the world doesn't
go in a line, and the world isn't organized into separate compartments or
chapters."

Some traditionalists warn that digital reading is the intellectual equiva- 13
lent of empty calories. Often, they argue, writers on the Internet employ a
cryptic argot that vexes teachers and parents. Zigzagging through a cornucopia of words, pictures, video and sounds, they say, distracts more than
strengthens readers. And many youths spend most of their time on the
Internet playing games or sending instant messages, activities that involve
minimal reading at best.

Last fall the National Endowment for the Arts issued a sobering report 14
linking flat or declining national reading test scores among teenagers with
the slump in the proportion of adolescents who said they read for fun.

According to the Department of Education data cited in the report, 15
just over a fifth of 17-year-olds said they read almost every day for fun in
2004, down from nearly a third in 1984. Nineteen percent of 17-year-olds
said they never or hardly ever read for fun in 2004, up from 9 percent in
1984. (It was unclear whether they thought of what they did on the Internet as "reading.")

"Whatever the benefits of newer electronic media," Dana Gioia, the 16
chairman of the N.E.A., wrote in the report's introduction, "they provide
no measurable substitute for the intellectual and personal development initiated and sustained by frequent reading."

Children are clearly spending more time on the Internet. In a study of 17
2,032 representative 8- to 18-year-olds, the Kaiser Family Foundation

found that nearly half used the Internet on a typical day in 2004, up from just under a quarter in 1999. The average time these children spent online on a typical day rose to one hour and 41 minutes in 2004, from 46 minutes in 1999.

The question of how to value different kinds of reading is complicated   18
because people read for many reasons. There is the level required of daily life—to follow the instructions in a manual or to analyze a mortgage contract. Then there is a more sophisticated level that opens the doors to elite education and professions. And, of course, people read for entertainment, as well as for intellectual or emotional rewards.

It is perhaps the final purpose that book champions emphasize the   19
most.

"Learning is not to be found on a printout," David McCullough, the   20
Pulitzer Prize-winning biographer, said in a commencement address at Boston College in May. "It's not on call at the touch of a finger. Learning is acquired mainly from books, and most readily from great books."

. . .

BUT THIS IS READING TOO

Web proponents believe that strong readers on the Web may eventually   21
surpass those who rely on books. Reading five Websites, an op-ed article and a blog post or two, experts say, can be more enriching than reading one book.

"It takes a long time to read a 400-page book," said Mr. Spiro of   22
Michigan State. "In a tenth of the time," he said, the Internet allows a reader to "cover a lot more of the topic from different points of view."

Zachary Sims, the Old Greenwich, Conn., teenager, often stays awake   23
until 2 or 3 in the morning reading articles about technology or politics—his current passions—on up to 100 Websites.

"On the Internet, you can hear from a bunch of people," said Zachary,   24
who will attend Columbia University this fall. "They may not be pedigreed academics. They may be someone in their shed with a conspiracy theory. But you would weigh that."

Though he also likes to read books (earlier this year he finished, and   25
loved, "The Fountainhead" by Ayn Rand), Zachary craves interaction with fellow readers on the Internet. "The Web is more about a conversation," he said. "Books are more one-way."

The kinds of skills Zachary has developed—locating information   26
quickly and accurately, corroborating findings on multiple sites—may seem obvious to heavy Web users. But the skills can be cognitively demanding.

Web readers are persistently weak at judging whether information is   27
trustworthy. In one study, Donald J. Leu, who researches literacy and technology at the University of Connecticut, asked 48 students to look at a spoof Website (http://zapatopi.net/treeoctopus/) about a mythical species

known as the "Pacific Northwest tree octopus." Nearly 90 percent of them missed the joke and deemed the site a reliable source.

Some literacy experts say that reading itself should be redefined. Inter- 28 preting videos or pictures, they say, may be as important a skill as analyzing a novel or a poem.

"Kids are using sound and images so they have a world of ideas to 29 put together that aren't necessarily language oriented," said Donna E. Alvermann, a professor of language and literacy education at the University of Georgia. "Books aren't out of the picture, but they're only one way of experiencing information in the world today."

■ ■ ■

AFTER YOU READ

- ■ **THINK** about the thesis of Rich's essay and formulate it in your own words. (Hint: Look at paragraph 5.)
- ■ **EXAMINE** the general structure of the essay, which compares and contrasts reading books with reading on the Internet. Comparison and contrast essays can be organized by the subject-by subject (block) method or by the point-by-point (alternating method), as illustrated below:

Subject by Subject (Point)	Block by Block (Alternating)
Subject A: Books	Point 1
Point 1	Subject A: Books
Point 2	Subject B: Internet
Subject B: Internet	Point 2
Point 1	Subject A: Books
Point 1	Subject B: Internet

These two methods can also be combined in a comparison and contrast essay. Examine closely the B's and I's that you wrote in the margins as you read the essay. Then decide what you think is the primary organizational method of the essay. Discuss your opinion with your instructor and classmates.

- ■ **EXAMINE** also certain paragraphs in each of the two main subsections. (1) In paragraphs 14–17 of "Setting Expectations," what are the findings of the U.S. Department of Education about teenagers' reading habits? What "sobering report" did the National Endowment for the Arts issue recently about students' reading scores? Do you see a possible link between these two pieces of information? (2) Review "But This Is Reading Too" (paragraphs 21–29) to determine the possible advantages and disadvantages of reading on the Internet. Does the value of one kind of reading—in books or on the Internet—negate the value of the other kind of reading? Discuss.

■ **WRITE** your own literacy autobiography, reviewing your journal entry for this selection before you begin. When did you first learn to read and write? How did you learn these skills? Was learning to read and write easy or difficult for you? Was it enjoyable or stressful? How has your literacy developed in the years between then and now? What and how much do you read? In what media format do you do most of your reading? Have your literacy skills prepared you well for your college work, or do you still have trouble with some kinds of reading and writing? How do you think you can improve your literacy more? (Remember that we all continue to develop our literacy throughout our lives.)

■ Or **WRITE** a comparison and contrast essay debating the advantages and disadvantages of writing in a notebook or journal with those of writing on a computer word-processing program. Organize your essay either subject by subject or point by point. You may want to read the additional instructions for writing comparison and contrast essays on Lesson 7 of the *Interactions*, eighth edition, student website available at www.cengagebrain.com.

Games and Literacy

■ ■ ■

LIZ DANFORTH

Liz Danforth is best known as a freelance artist of maps and illustrations in science fiction and fantasy games, but she has also been a game developer, scenario designer, writer, and editor in the gaming industry. In 1995 she was selected to be a member of the Academy of Gaming Arts and Design's Hall of Fame. More recently, she has been working with the American Library Association on a million-dollar grant project that studies how gaming can improve literacy and problem-solving skills.

BEFORE YOU READ

■ **THINK** about the history of games. What do you think were some of the earliest games played by human beings? How have you seen games change and develop in your lifetime? (Paragraph 2 provides a brief description of the history of gaming, but you should be able to add ideas from your own experience.)

■ **EXAMINE** the title and the first paragraph, which link games with literacy. Have you ever connected games with literacy yourself? How does one need to be literate to play certain games? How important is visual literacy as well as verbal literacy in our culture and in the world of gaming in particular? Explain. Think of at least three different games that you like to play and, with a group of your classmates, discuss the literacy required for each game.

■ **EXAMINE** also the following italicized words and definitions:

1. *cogitations* (paragraph 8): serious thoughts and reflections
2. *wikis* (paragraph 9): websites that let users employ their web browsers to add and update content on the site
3. *hypothesizing* (paragraph 9): conjecturing based on known data
4. *optimize* (paragraph 9): to make the most effective use of something
5. *credibility* (paragraph 11): reliability.

For the most part, Danforth explains in context the specialized terms that she uses.

■ **WRITE** a journal entry in which you discuss the literacy skills required to play one of your favorite games.

AS YOU READ

Underline Danforth's descriptions of the increasing levels of literacy required to play the various games that she discusses.

■   ■   ■

"Games and literacy? That's a stretch." So said a school librarian last year when I broached the American Library Association's (ALA) "Libraries, Literacy, and Gaming" initiative.

It's a surprisingly common sentiment. Many consider games faddish despite their proven longevity: board-game playing goes back to the dawn of time, miniatures wargaming starts with H. G. Wells's *Little Wars* (1913), and console games have been around since the 1970s, the same time that role-playing games (RPGs) exploded. In the future, I expect, we won't be asking ourselves "What were we thinking?" so much as "Why all the fuss about gaming in libraries?"

Games and literacy—which I'll here define as the ability to read and write—go hand in hand. (Games and literature are actually old friends. . . .)

READING INSIDE/OUTSIDE THE GAME

At the very least, video game players need to be able to read well enough to set up a game and get it running. Even for a game like **RockBand**, they have to choose the player mode (single player, multiplayer) and be able to read the list of songs; while the songs load, they can read a short snippet about rock music history. A more elaborate example is the real-time strategy game **Warcraft III**, which features cinematics and "cut scenes," with text mirroring the dialog like subtitles.

Additionally, RPGs, massively multiplayer online role-playing games (MMORPGs), and tabletop games require players to read about the nature of their quests, assignments, or missions—to know what to look out for and where to go, to learn the characteristics of items in their inventory, and to discover tips on strategy. With such games, reading comprehension is a requirement for success.

Without stepping far outside the game, video game players have manuals and strategy guides, cheats, and walkthroughs. Manuals are often quite short and mean little until the player has spent time exploring the game to achieve contextualization. Strategy guides and walkthroughs, step-by-step descriptions of how to find and solve every element of a game, can be pretty dense reading, often single-spaced fine print going on for dozens of pages. After finishing a game, players might also use these guides to go back and see what they might have overlooked, or how a different story line might have unfolded.

READING WELL BEYOND THE GAME

People invested in gaming as their hobby spend a lot of time reading and 7
writing about games, even games they're not presently playing. Games are
reviewed in print and online; players weigh in about the relative merits of
this game or that in community forums and discuss upcoming game
releases with all the anticipatory fever they would a best-selling author's
next release or a summer blockbuster.

There are countless blogs on games, too. They might be hosted by a 8
top-drawer panel of experts and scholars talking about virtual worlds
(terranova.blogs.com), or they might be the cogitations of a 15-year-old
playing **World of Warcraft** (wowkid.thestorythusfar.com).

It's the theorycrafting websites that require most from players (e.g., 9
elitistjerks.com or any of the game wikis at www.wikia.com/wiki/big_
wikis). Theorycrafting refers to the in-depth analysis and hypothesizing of
how to optimize one's game. One recent study (tinyurl.com/WoWstudy)
broke down the threaded discussions on these theorycrafting sites and
found that they follow the framework of systematic scientific methodologi-
cal analysis. On these sites, people write thoughtfully at considerable
length.

There are also forums in which players discuss the lore of a game, a 10
character's latest achievements (sometimes as fictional diaries, e.g., www.
pathofahero.com), why the game is or isn't balanced, and how the writer
might propose to fix it. Some players even write as their gaming personas
on sites like Twitter.

Not only is the ability to read such a discussion "literacy," but the dis- 11
cussion itself promotes structured critical thinking skills and written communication excellence. And it's being done in the name of fun, which cuts
down the resistance and increases the motivation to push through a difficult passage, to hunt down the meaning of the work, to compare assertions
and assess credibility. And aren't these the very approaches to learning our
profession deems valuable? Don't doubt the worth of games to support literacy in all its manifestations.

■   ■   ■

AFTER YOU READ

- ■ **THINK** about the games that you like to play. Which ones challenge
  your literacy and require you to work hard to understand how the
  games function and how to be successful at them? Has any game motivated you to develop your literacy—verbal as well as visual? Explain.

- ■ **EXAMINE** the titles of Danforth's subsections: "Reading Inside/Outside
  the Game" and "Reading Well beyond the Game." These subtitles suggest that there are different levels of literacy required for playing games.

What are the different levels that Danforth discusses? How is each level more challenging than the one before? Look also at the last paragraph. According to Danforth, how do these different levels increase literacy motivation?

■ **EXAMINE** also the websites on gaming that Danforth cites in her essay. Select the one that interests you the most, look it up, and report back to the class on its contents and its contribution to literacy.

■ **WRITE** an essay in which you discuss the different levels of literacy required to play a game that you play, like, or know about. You may base your essay on your earlier journal entry if you wish.

Fraternities of Netheads:
Internet Addiction on Campus

■ ■ ■

KIMBERLY S. YOUNG

After teaching psychology for many years, Kimberly S. Young
is currently a faculty member in the School of Business at
St. Bonaventure University. She is also the executive director of
the Center for Internet Addiction Recovery (located at Bradford,
Pennsylvania), which provides consultations to educational institutions, mental health facilities, and corporations. Young has
spoken about Internet abuse on network news programs and
published articles on the subject in *The Wall Street Journal, The
New York Times,* and *U.S. News and World Report.* She has
published *Tangled in the Web: Understanding Cybersex from
Fantasy to Addiction* (2001), and *Internet Addiction: A Handbook and Guide to Evaluation and Treatment* (2010). In the following selection from her 1998 book *Caught in the Net: How to
Recognize the Signs of Internet Addiction—and a Winning Strategy for Recovery,* Young discusses broad-scale Internet addiction
on college campuses.

BEFORE YOU READ

■ **THINK** about the problem of Internet addiction, of being "caught in the
net," as Young phrases it. An addiction is a compulsive commitment to
a particular substance or activity; hence, Internet addiction is compulsive use of the Internet. Do you think Internet addiction is a serious
problem on college campuses? Do you spend large blocks of time
online? Do you have friends or classmates who are frequent Internet
users? Would you consider yourself, or anyone you know, to be
"addicted" to the Internet?

■ **EXAMINE** the description of the party in the first paragraph of the
essay. How is this party like other parties you have experienced or
heard about? Then examine both paragraphs 1 and 2 to see how this
party differs from most late-night campus socials. Can you guess what
type of party Young is describing?

■ **EXAMINE** also the reference to MUDs in paragraph 11. *MUD* stands
for multiple-user dimensions, dialogues, or dungeons, in which users
assume the identity of computerized characters.

■ **WRITE** a journal entry in which you describe Internet use on your campus. How do most students use the Internet? Do they spend time

sending personal or academic e-mail messages, participating in chat rooms, playing games, ordering merchandise, or doing research for their classes? How much time do most students spend on these activities? How much time do you spend?

AS YOU READ

Number the factors that contribute to Internet overuse and think about which of these factors are present on your campus.

■　■　■

I t's after midnight at an upstate New York university, and there's a   1
party on—lots of food and drink, lively conversation, juicy gossip,
boyfriends and girlfriends retreating to private corners to pour out
their affections. New friendships are forming between students who delight in learning of the many interests and beliefs they share despite coming from separate states or even different countries. The lights stay on at this campus hot spot all night, and by dawn most partygoers slink bleary-eyed back to their dorm rooms. Vampires, some call them. And when darkness descends the next day, they're back. The party cranks up again.

Let's take a closer look at this party, symbolic of what's fast becoming   2
the most popular college activity of the late '90s. While the chips and cookies might resemble the same munchies of parties in decades past, we see that instead of beer, the drink of choice tends to be the nonalcoholic Jolt, selected because of its extra dose of caffeine to keep participants awake and alert. We also notice how this party is eerily quiet—no blaring music, no outrageous dancing, no shouting or singing to keep other students awake or arouse the suspicions of campus security making late-night rounds.

In fact, these party animals seldom leave their seats. No, they're not   3
passing joints around, either. Usually, they don't interact with their fellow partygoers seated beside them at all. That lively conversation, juicy gossip, secret romancing, and new bonds with friends from afar—it's all happening through their individual computer terminals. This is, after all, a gathering of a typical fraternity of netheads, those Internet-obsessed students who every night fill the large computer labs sprinkled throughout campus. Seated in row upon row of terminals all hooked up to the Internet, these busy young men and women are taking advantage of their free and unlimited on-line access—their ticket to one continuous, semester-long party.

The parties aren't happening only in the computer labs. During the last   4
several years, the demand for instant Internet availability has spread so rapidly that many colleges with crowded computer labs now ship hundreds of additional terminals and modems into newly created computer residence halls. These designated lounges are stationed right inside the dormitories, so students need no longer even walk across campus to plug into their

favorite chat room. Some colleges even provide a modem and free Internet access in students' individual rooms. Most computer residence halls have replaced TV lounges or other open meeting spaces, but few students protest. As we near the dawn of a new century, TV is out. The Net is in.

"Staying up late at night on the Internet is the best time I have at school," reveals Kim, a sophomore physics major and regular attendee of the kind of party we just witnessed. "After awhile, it was all I wanted to do, all I thought about. It was all so fascinating. In the chat rooms, I met a woman from Ottawa, Canada, who was a physics major at a university there. I don't see many women physics majors where I am. And I became close friends with a guy living in England, who was actually an exchange student from California. We connected over everything in life!"

Kim got so engrossed in her Net world that she ignored her studies. A former math and science whiz in high school with serious career ambitions, she allowed her grades to crash before recognizing that her new obsession was sabotaging her goals. When we met Kim . . . she just had tried and failed to quit the Internet cold turkey before understanding the power of this addiction. Now she's seeking help through a campus counselor and . . . recovery strategies. . . .

At least Kim recognized the problem. Most netheads, sadly, do not. And as their numbers continue to soar, colleges may be becoming the major breeding ground of Internet addiction. For example, when the dropout rate at Alfred University in Alfred, New York, more than doubled recently, Provost W. Richard Ott wanted to find out why. He couldn't see any logical explanation for why so many students who had arrived in college with SAT scores of 1,200 or higher would fail so quickly. An in-house survey revealed that 43 percent of these dropouts had been staying up late at night logged on to the Internet. "It's ironic," Ott said, "we've put all this money in for an educational tool, and some students are using it for self-destruction." Connie Beckman, director of Alfred's computing services, said "through educational programs designed to increase awareness of the danger of Net abuse, heavy pattern use dropped to 19 percent in this year's freshman class."

Here's a quick look at the contributing factors to such rampant Internet overuse:

• Free and unlimited Internet access.

When freshmen register today, they get a student ID card, a meal card, and most important, a free personal e-mail account. They've got no on-line service fees to pay, no limits to their time logged on, and computer labs open for their convenience round-the-clock. It's an Internet user's dream.

• Huge blocks of unstructured time.

Most college students attend classes for 12 to 16 hours per week. The rest of the time is their own to read, study, go to movies or parties, join clubs, or explore the new environment outside their campus walls. Many forget all those other activities and concentrate on one thing: the Internet.

• Newly experienced freedom from parental control.

Away from home and their parent's watchful eyes, college students long   11
have exercised their new freedom by engaging in pranks, talking to friends
to all hours of the night, sleeping with their boyfriends and girlfriends, and
eating and drinking things Mom and Dad would not approve of. Today,
they utilize that freedom by hanging out in the MUDs and chat rooms of
cyber-space, and no parent can complain about on-line service fees or their
refusal to eat dinner with the family or help out with chores.

• No monitoring or censoring of what they say or do on-line.

When they move on to the job world, college students may find suspicious   12
bosses peeking over their shoulder or even monitoring their on-line time
and usage. Even e-mail to coworkers could be intercepted by the wrong
party. In college, no one's watching. Computer lab monitors tend to be
student volunteers whose only responsibility is to assist anyone who needs
help understanding how to use the Internet, not tell them what they can or
cannot do on it.

• Full encouragement from faculty and administrators.

Students understand that their school's administration and faculty want them   13
to make full use of the Internet's vast resources. Abstaining from all Net use is
seldom an option; in some large classes, professors place required course
materials solely on the Net and engage in their only one-on-one contact with
students through e-mail! Administrators, of course, want to see their major
investments in computers and Internet access justified.

• Adolescent training in similar activities.

By the time most kids get to college, they will have spent years staring at   14
video game terminals, closing off the world around them with Walkmans,
and engaging in that rapid-fire clicking of the TV remote. Even if they
didn't get introduced to the Internet in high school, those other activities
have made students well suited to slide into aimless Web surfing, skill-
testing MUDs, and rat-a-tat-tat chat-room dialogue.

• The desire to escape college stressors.

Students feel the pressures of making top grades, fulfilling parental expec-   15
tations, and, upon graduation, facing fierce competition for good jobs. The
Internet, ideally, would help make it easier for them to do their necessary
course work as quickly and efficiently as possible. Instead, many students
turn to their Net friends to hide from their difficult feelings of fear, anxiety,
and depression.

• Social intimidation and alienation.

With as many as 30,000 students on some campuses, students can easily   16
get lost in the crowd. When they try to reach out, they often run into
even tighter [cliques] than the in crowds of high school. Maybe they

don't dress right or look right. But when they join the faceless community of the Internet, they find that with little effort they can become popular with new "friends" throughout the United States and in England, Australia, Germany, France, Hungary, Japan, New Zealand, and China. Why bother trying to socialize on campus?

• A higher legal drinking age.

With the drinking age at 21 in most states, undergraduate students can't openly drink alcohol and socialize in bars. So the Internet becomes a substitute drug of choice for many: no ID required and no closing hour!   17

With so many signs on campus pointing toward heavy reliance on the Internet, it's little wonder that when respondents to my Internet addiction survey were asked to name their main complications from excess online usage, academic problems ranked No. 1. When I asked respondents to identify which problem areas they would rate severe, 58 percent mentioned academic woes. Fifty-three percent referred to relationship issues, 52 percent cited Internet-related financial burdens, and 51 percent said their jobs were impacted. Internet addiction, clearly, has hit college students especially hard.   18

■   ■   ■

AFTER YOU READ

■ **THINK** about the factors identified in this report that contribute to Internet overuse. What can students and college administrators do to reduce the number of factors leading to Internet overuse and abuse?

■ **EXAMINE** paragraphs 5 and 6, which describe Kim's struggle with Internet addiction. What were the major causes of Kim's getting "caught in the net"?

■ **EXAMINE** also the last paragraph of the selection, which discusses the complications that students experience from excessive Internet use. What are the major problems caused by spending too much time online?

■ **WRITE** a report about Internet use on your campus. In your report, focus on one of these questions:

1. For what purpose(s) do most students use the Internet? How beneficial or harmful to students are these purposes?

2. What are the positive and negative effects of Internet use on your campus? Which effects are more dominant?

3. Is Internet addiction a problem on your campus? If so, what are the major reasons? What are some potential solutions?

Before writing your essay, you may want to interview three or four students—perhaps students who are actually working in a computer lab on your campus. Use the questions above and the information in Young's essay to help you formulate your interview questions. (See also pages 441–447 at the end of this unit for guidelines for writing reports.)

We ALL Pay for Internet Plagiarism

■ ■ ■

ELLEN LAIRD

Like the previous essay by Kimberly S. Young, Ellen Laird focuses on the abuse of the Internet by college students. Laird is a faculty member in English at Hudson Valley Community College in Troy, New York. Part of the State University of New York (SUNY) system, Hudson Valley Community College enrolls approximately 11,000 students each semester. About 80 percent of these students come from the local region, with the other 20 percent coming from various other states and countries. Laird's commitment to providing her students with the help they need to write effective essays is shown by the guidelines and resources that she provides on her home page. The following essay was originally published in *The Chronicle of Higher Education* in July 2001, and then republished in condensed form by *Education Digest* that November.

BEFORE YOU READ

■ **THINK** about plagiarism. How do you define *plagiarism*? Have you ever deliberately plagiarized by using the words or ideas of someone else without giving appropriate credit to your source? Do you think that you may have plagiarized without realizing it? Do you think that having sources on the Internet has made plagiarism more tempting to many students? If so, how and why?

■ **EXAMINE** the title of the essay: "We ALL Pay for Internet Plagiarism." How do you think all students are harmed by Internet plagiarism? Who else is hurt by such plagiarism? Explain.

■ **WRITE** a journal entry in which you speculate about who is harmed most by Internet plagiarism and how these individuals are harmed.

AS YOU READ

Try to determine why Chip and other students plagiarize from the Internet and why such plagiarism "costs us all." Also, circle words you do not know, look them up in a dictionary, and add them to your vocabulary journal.

■ ■ ■

When I first read Chip's essay, I was ecstatic. He had clearly absorbed class lessons on specificity, readership, and organization in writing. In fact, he had shown he could write a clever thesis and select examples perfectly suited to the topic. My enthusiasm darkened to suspicion upon a second reading, however. Chip was an A student in the course, but his essay seemed a bit too mature in content and focus, compared with his previous work. His rhetorical voice was deeper than what I had come to expect of his prose.

A 60-second AltaVista search brought me to the full essay. A Dave Barry–like piece at BigNerds.com, the text was filtered through life experience that Chip, at 18, would be lacking. I was crushed. Like so many problems, this was supposed to happen only to others.

Except for a small number of individuals over the years, my students don't intentionally plagiarize. In both our actual and virtual English-composition class meetings, I am a witness to their writing process, not just a reader of their written products. I keep their rhetorical fingerprints—their in-class writing samples—in my file cabinet. And I teach them what it means to be honest in college.

Last year, I reinforced my instruction with a repertoire of stories— about dethroned and dishonored college presidents and seven-figure damage awards—to demonstrate the price paid, even by the high and mighty, for the theft of words and ideas. And after sculpting a lesson on academic honesty, based on an article by an English professor, Richard Fulkerson, in *The Writing Instructor,* I pointed out my bold-faced attribution on the handout. I explained, "Even in the relaxed setting of this class, I must tell you whose idea this lesson was originally. Fulkerson owns it; I borrowed it."

Yet, the day after the Fulkerson-based lesson, Chip submitted as his own an essay from the Internet. Not for a researched essay or an important course grade, but for a portfolio piece he could have chosen to leave ungraded.

TENSE IN THE PRESENT TENSE

Chip committed his academic felony in April 2000, but he and his essay remain for me in the present tense. Surely, with all my harping and haranguing, he knew better. His act had none of the fuzziness of what might be called unintentional plagiarism—unattributed text too close to the spirit and structure of the original. His was a clear-cut point, click, and save theft.

I am struggling to understand what happened. Which of the usual explanations for academic dishonesty apply in this instance? Pressure to succeed? Not Chip, and not this assignment. Lack of clarity about plagiarism in our learning environment? Not in the English department at Hudson Valley Community College. Lack of a clear position on the instructor's part? Not with this fanatic teaching the course. An assumption that I lacked Web savvy? Not with a Website, linked syllabus, online discussion of readings, and interactive lessons for the course. Lack of personal connection in a large institution? Chip and I had just seen each other at a local event over the weekend, and he had introduced his mother to me.

To save face with myself, I must assume that Chip understood that 8 downloading an essay and submitting it as his own was an egregious act. Why, then, did he do it?

Chip explained he had been "mentally perturbed" the weekend before 9 the paper was due, and the essay he wrote failed to meet his high standards. But I sensed that Chip felt he had made a choice akin to having a pizza delivered. He had procrastinated on an assignment due the next day, had no time to prepare from scratch, and had to get on to those pressing matters that shape the world of an 18-year-old. He dialed his Internet service provider, ordered takeout, and had it delivered.

Twenty-some years of teaching in two-year colleges have taught me 10 that cheating on research papers is fairly straightforward. Most of my plagiarists (a tiny pool to begin with), despite lessons like that mentioned earlier, borrow words and ideas too often, with too little attribution, from sources in their "Works Cited." The result is criminal; the intent clearly is not.

A few omit citations or fail to indicate quoted material is quoted. The 11 final 1%—class felons all—submit papers written by friends or professionals on unapproved topics switched 10 minutes before the deadline. Such theft most often is an act of desperation: "I won't be able to play football if I fail your course."

PLAGIARISM AS DELIVERED PIZZA

Chip's cheating feels different. The assignment, specific to the class and 12 based on an essay in our reading materials, did not require the rigor of a typical freshman research paper. Students should have been able to complete it comfortably within a relatively short time, with careful thought but without research or hand-wringing. Like delivered pizza, Chip's download was an act of expediency, not desperation. And here, the metaphor fails. Ordering takeout prose is not an acceptable alternative to composing, but I wonder if Chip even flinched.

My sense is that Internet plagiarism is becoming more dangerous than 13 we realize. In a student's home or dorm room, questions of ethics may be coming to seem academic only. From his own bedroom, Chip has access to an unprecedented wealth of resources. He is not sitting in a library, which might, like a church, prompt behavior worthy of the setting.

Might Chip's download be related to a certain slipperiness, only partly 14 Internet fueled, that characterizes our culture? I think of runners, myself included, arriving mid-pack at the finish line of a recent 5K Race for a Cause. A table has water, juice, fruit, and all the energy bars one could want. Race etiquette, if not regulation, instructs us to take only what we will consume on the spot. But most of us squirrel away rations for family on the sidelines, next week's school lunches, or next month's ski trip. Such bounty, free for the taking, seduces us to step over the line of self-regulation.

Students have now reached the food table, taking what is there, with-   15
out regard for whether they can handle it, need it, even know what it is.
They copy, paste, and wallpaper their academic existences. This used to
seem wrong, but now I wonder whether we all have become inured to the
concept of ownership, as we enhance our PowerPoint notes or Websites.

The allure of and easy access to abundance, and the absence of the   16
cues physical settings provide, work with another factor. In most cases,
Internet cheating, while surprisingly easy to trace, is dishearteningly
tricky to spot. The majority of papers plagiarized from the Internet are
devoid of the professional gloss—an instant tip-off—of the products of
research-paper mills. Writing of all kinds is taken from student and class
Websites, where text has been shared and "published" for laudable purposes. Text that students download from the Web is written by students
just like them, so it appears student written—exactly what we instructors
want it to be.

In addition, the limits of a library's physical collection no longer signal   17
possible problems. Seemingly limitless sources for the researched writing
published online are collected in electronic databases available to most students who have a college I.D. card. Thus, those sources on a "Works
Cited" page raise no red flags, making the plagiarism even more convincing. And the sheer volume of online material and the sophistication of
search tools mean that the casual plagiarist can finish his or her "work" in
seconds.

TEACHING AND LEARNING PROFOUNDLY ALTERED

A chance meeting with my friend Jane, a high-school English teacher, at   18
the local supermarket confirmed my sense that teaching and learning are
being profoundly altered, and that Internet plagiarism may be gathering
sufficient force to become an academic hurricane. Jane explained that she
now has to conduct an Internet search before she selects required reading.
She then listed works she will no longer assign to her Advanced Placement
English class, because of the ease with which students download chat content, journal entries, chapter notes, and essays.

Sylvia Plath's "Mirror" and David Guterson's *Snow Falling on Cedars*   19
were the latest cross-outs on her list. Students must complete assignments
on classic texts like *The Great Gatsby* and *The Grapes of Wrath* in front
of Jane, in class, in longhand.

Like Jane, I found myself hesitating over an essay or two on my read-   20
ing list while preparing my last batch of syllabuses. I fear that academic
takeout will soon begin to drive course content. I worry that these new
student practices will shape our reading lists right down to the individual
poems we select.

In years past, plagiarists suffered loss in learning, if not in grades. After 21 entering his guilty plea, Chip received an F where his A might have been and forfeited his stature in the class. To his credit, he tried to mend our academic friendship. But the consequences of cheating like Chip's ripple far beyond a transcript or a conscience. This new taking, which costs student-thieves neither time nor money, will cost us all.

■ ■ ■

AFTER YOU READ

■ **THINK** about Laird's disappointment when she realized Chip had plagiarized his essay. What caused her to suspect that one of her best students had committed plagiarism? How easy was it to confirm her suspicions of Internet plagiarism? According to Chip, why had he plagiarized his essay? What more complex reasons might lie behind Chip's actions?

■ **THINK** also about the difference between intentional and unintentional plagiarism as explained by Laird. How does she describe unintentional plagiarism? What instruction had Laird given her class to be sure her students knew how to avoid such unintentional plagiarism? Do you agree or disagree with Laird's conclusion that "the result [of unintentional plagiarism] is criminal; the intent clearly is not" (paragraph 10)? How do you think unintentional plagiarists should be punished? Do you agree or disagree that intentional plagiarists are "felons all" (paragraph 11)? How do you think intentional plagiarists should be punished?

■ **EXAMINE** paragraphs 13–15. Why does Laird believe that "Internet plagiarism is becoming more dangerous than we realize"? How might such plagiarism be related to a serious ethical crisis in our culture?

■ **EXAMINE** also the last sentence of the essay. Although Laird says that plagiarism "costs student-thieves neither time nor money," what does it cost students? What does it cost "us all"—other students, instructors, and society in general?

■ **WRITE** an essay in which you briefly identify the cause(s) of increased Internet plagiarism and then explain in more detail the effects—the costs—of such plagiarism (For guidelines for writing cause-and-effect essays, see Lesson 5 on the *Interactions*, eighth edition, student website, at www.cengagebrain.com.).

Facebook in a Crowd

■ ■ ■

HAL NIEDZVIECKI

The cofounder and editor of *Broken Pencil* magazine and a correspondent for the Canadian Broadcasting Corporation, Hal Niedzviecki is a Canadian writer of both fiction and nonfiction. His books of social criticism—including *We Want Some, Too: Underground Desire and the Reinvention of Mass Culture; Cyborg: Digital Destiny and Human Possibility in the Age of the Wearable Computer* (coauthored); and *Hello, I'm Special: How Individuality Became the New Conformity*—focus on culture and technology. His latest book is *The Peep Diaries: How We're Learning to Love Watching Ourselves and Our Neighbors* (2009). This essay was published in *The New York Times Magazine* in 2008.

BEFORE YOU READ

■ **THINK** about the social-networking world. Are you registered on Facebook or on another social-networking site? If so, how many online "friends" do you have? How many of these friends did you know before "friending" them online? How many new online friends have you met personally? How much confidence do you have in online friends becoming real-life friends? Explain your reasoning.

■ **EXAMINE** the title of the selection. "Facebook in a Crowd" is a play on the phrase "just a face in a crowd," which suggests being lost and lonely in a crowd of people.

■ **EXAMINE** the word *rationalization* (paragraph 13), which is basic to an understanding of the essay. In the context of this essay, a rationalization is an inaccurate but self-assuring reason for one's situation or behavior. You may also need to know that "the Masons" (paragraph 2) belong to the Masonic Lodge, an ancient fraternal order that has many chapters across the country; that being *beneficent* (paragraph 10) is being good-willed and kind; and that a *vigil* (paragraph 13) is a watch or period of observation.

■ **WRITE** in your journal a list of reasons why many people rely on Facebook or other social-networking sites as a source for "friends."

AS YOU READ

Underline phrases that show Niedzviecki's excitement before the Facebook event and circle phrases that show his disappointment during and after the event.

■ ■ ■

One day this past summer, I logged on to Facebook and realized 1
that I was very close to having 700 online "friends." Not bad,
I thought to myself, absurdly proud of how many cyberpals, connections, acquaintances and even strangers I'd managed to sign up.

But the number made me uneasy as well. I had just fallen out with a 2
friend I'd spent a lot of time with. I'd disconnected with a few other ones
for the usual reasons—jobs in other cities, family life limiting social time.
I was as much to blame as they were. I had a 2-year-old kid of my own at
home. Add to that my workaholic irritability, my love of being left alone
and my lack of an office environment or mysterious association with the
Masons from which to derive an instant network of cronies. I had fewer
friends to hang out with than I'd ever had before.

So I decided to have a Facebook party. I used Facebook to create an 3
"event" and invite my digital chums. Some of them, of course, didn't live
in Toronto, but I figured, it's summer and people travel. You never know
who might be in town. If they lived in Buffalo or Vancouver, they could
just click "not attending," and that would be that. Facebook gives people
the option of R.S.V.P.'ing in three categories—"attending," "maybe
attending," and "not attending."

After a week the responses stopped coming in and were ready to be 4
tabulated. Fifteen people said they were attending, and 60 said maybe.
A few hundred said not, and the rest just ignored the invitation altogether.
I figured about 20 people would show up. That sounded pretty good to
me. Twenty potential new friends.

On the evening in question I took a shower. I shaved. I splashed on my 5
tingly man perfume. I put on new pants and a favorite shirt. Brimming
with optimism, I headed over to the neighborhood watering hole and
waited.

And waited. 6

And waited. 7

Eventually, one person showed up. 8

I chatted with my new potential friend, Paula, doing my best to pre- 9
tend I wasn't dismayed and embarrassed. But I was too self-conscious to
be genuine. I kept apologizing for the lack of attendance. I looked over
my shoulder every time the door opened and someone new came in.
Paula was nice about it, assuring me that people probably just felt shy
about the idea of making a new friend. She said she herself had almost
decided not to come.

"And now you have me all to yourself," I said, trying to sound benefi- 10
cent and unworried. We smiled at each other awkwardly.

We made small talk. I found out about her job, her boyfriend, her soc- 11
cer team. Paula became my Facebook friend after noticing I was connected
to a friend of hers. She thought it would be interesting to drop by and
meet me.

Eventually we ran out of things to say. Anyway, she had to work in   12
the morning. I picked up the tab on her Tom Collins and watched as she
strode out into the night, not entirely sure if our friendship would grow.

After she left, I renewed my vigil, waiting for someone to show. It was   13
getting on 11 o'clock and all my rationalizations—for example, that people
needed time to get home from work, eat dinner, relax a bit—were wearing
out.

I would learn, when I asked some people who didn't show up the next   14
day, that "definitely attending" on Facebook means "maybe" and "maybe
attending" means "likely not." So I probably shouldn't have taken it personally. But the combination of alcohol and solitude turned my thoughts to
self-pity. Was I really that big of a loser? Or was it that no one wants to
get together in real life anymore? It wasn't Facebook's fault; all those digital pals were better than nothing. For chipping away at past friendships
and blocking honest new efforts, you really have to blame the entire modern world. People want to hang out with you, I assured myself. They just
don't have the time.

By now it was nearing midnight. My head was clouded by drink, and   15
it was finally starting to sink in: no one else was coming. I'd have to think
up some other way to revitalize my social life. I ordered one more drink.

The beer arrived, a British import: Young's Double Chocolate Stout.   16
I raised my glass in a solitary toast and promised myself I'd spend less
time online. Then I took a gulp: the beer was delicious but bittersweet.
Seven hundred friends, and I was drinking alone.

■ ■ ■

AFTER YOU READ

- ■ **THINK** about the main point, or thesis, of this essay; then write this thesis in your own words. As you consider this task, pay particular atten-
  tion to the title and the last paragraph.
- ■ **EXAMINE** the details that you underlined. Which details show
  Niedzviecki's excitement before the event most clearly?
- ■ **EXAMINE** also the details that you circled. Which of these details show
  most clearly Niedzviecki's disappointment during and after the event?
  What rationalizations does he give in paragraphs 13 and 14 for the disappointing turnout at the event?
- ■ **WRITE** an essay in which you take a position on whether or not a
  person can find a real friend on Facebook or another networking site.
  Remember to use personal experiences and observations to support
  your point of view.

Bad Connections

■ ■ ■

CHRISTINE ROSEN

Christine Rosen is a senior editor of *The New Atlantis: A Journal of Technology and Society* and has been a fellow at the Ethics and Public Policy Center in Washington, D.C. She is the author of *Preaching Eugenics: Religious Leaders and the American Eugenics Movement* (2004) and *My Fundamentalist Education: A Memoir of a Divine Girlhood* (2005) and the coauthor (under the name of Christine Stolba) of two books in women's studies. Rosen has also appeared on National Public Radio (NPR), CNN, Fox News, and ABC News. In the following essay from *The New York Times Magazine,* Rosen criticizes the inappropriate use of personal technologies such as the cell phone and the digital video recorder (DVR).

BEFORE YOU READ

■ **THINK** about the use of cell phones and iPods or other music players in public places. Do you think such use of these personal technologies is rude? Have you been bothered or distracted by others involved in private—and perhaps loud—conversations on their cell phones? Have you encountered any problems because individuals were "tuned out" to their surroundings because they were listening to their iPods or other music players? How do you think users should handle such private technologies in public places?

■ **EXAMINE** the title of the essay. Do you think that cell phones and digital video recorders (DVRs), such as TiVos, are "bad connections" or "good connections"? Why do you feel as you do?

■ **EXAMINE** also the following italicized words and their definitions:

1. *proliferated* (paragraph 1): increasing rapidly
2. *provoked* (paragraph 3): to stir to anger, resentment, or action
3. *facile* (paragraph 3): superficial, easy
4. *gratification* (paragraph 6): state of being pleased or satisfied
5. *ambivalence* (paragraph 10): mutually conflicting feelings

■ **WRITE** a journal entry in which you state and support your view about cell phones or DVRs. Are these devices primarily good or bad?

AS YOU READ

Identify and underline Rosen's arguments that cell phones and DVRs have negative effects on individuals and society.

■ ■ ■

I n the 16th century, Venetian and French glassmakers perfected a tech-   1
nique of coating glass with an alloy of silver to produce an effective mirror. Mirrors soon proliferated in public spaces and private homes, and owning a pocket or hand mirror became a marker of status. The mirror, you might say, was an early personal technology—ingenious, portable, effective—and like all such technologies, it changed its users. By giving us, for the first time, a readily available image of ourselves that matched what others saw, it encouraged self-consciousness and introspection and, as some worried, excesses of vanity.

By the 19th century, it was the machines of the Industrial Revolution—   2
the power loom, the motor, the turbine—that prompted concern about the effects of technology on the person. Karl Marx argued that factory work alienated the worker from what he was toiling to produce, transforming him into "a cripple, a monster." Men were forced to become more like machines: efficient, tireless and soulless.

Today's personal technologies, particularly the cellphone and the   3
digital video recorder, have not provoked similar worries. They are marvels of individual choice, convenience and innovation; they represent the democratization of the power of the machine. Our technologies are more intuitive, more facile and more responsive than ever before. In a rebuke to Marx, we have not become the alienated slaves of the machine; we have made the machines more like us and in the process toppled decades of criticism about the dangerous and potentially enervating effects of our technologies.

Or have we? The cellphone, a device we have lived with for more than   4
a decade, offers a good example of a popular technology's unforeseen side effects. More than one billion are in use around the world, and when asked, their owners say they love their phones for the safety and convenience they provide. People also report that they are courteous in their use of their phones. One opinion survey found that "98 percent of Americans say they move away from others when talking on a wireless phone in public" and that "86 percent say they 'never' or 'rarely' speak on wireless phones" when conducting transactions with clerks or bank tellers. Clearly, there exists a gulf between our reported cellphone behavior and our actual behavior.

Cellphone users—that is to say, most of us—are both instigators and   5
victims of this form of conversational panhandling, and it has had a cumulatively negative effect on social space. As the sociologist Erving Goffman

observed in another context, there is something deeply disturbing about people who are "out of contact" in social situations because they are blatantly refusing to adhere to the norms of their immediate environment. Placing a cellphone call in public instantly transforms the strangers around you into unwilling listeners who must cede to your use of the public space, a decidedly undemocratic effect for so democratic a technology. Listeners don't always passively accept this situation: in recent years, people have been pepper-sprayed in movie theaters, ejected from concert halls and deliberately rammed with cars as a result of rude behavior on their cellphones.

Recently, when hackers gained access to Paris Hilton's T-Mobile Sidekick, news organizations had no trouble finding pictures of her talking and typing into the device to illustrate their stories; Hilton, like most wireless users, spends a great deal of time in public engaged in private communications. Why? The cellphone, like the mirror, also offers a great deal of gratification to our egos. By making us available to anyone at any time, it serves as a "publicization of emotional fulfillment," as the French sociologist Chantal de Gournay has argued. Answering the phone and entering into conversation immediately informs everyone around us that we are in demand by someone, somewhere. Like a security blanket, the cellphone and other wireless devices serve as a form of connection when we are alone—walking down the street, standing in line—and connection is our contemporary currency.   6

So is control, and enthusiasts of DVR's like TiVo ecstatically praise the amount of it the device gives them: they can skip commercials, record hundreds of hours of their favorite shows, pause live television and be pleasantly surprised by recommendations, based on stored preferences, of other programs they might like to watch. In one TiVo subscriber survey, 98 percent of TiVo owners reported that they "couldn't live without" the device.   7

Fewer Americans will in the years to come. According to Forrester Research, 41 percent of American homes will have a DVR within the next five years. Given that the only two things we do more than watch television are sleep and work, the DVR is, it seems, a perfect technological solution for controlling viewing habits. Yet, as a recent study by Next Research found, DVR users end up watching five to six hours more television per week than they did before they owned the device. Rather than freeing them to watch less television by eliminating waste, the DVR encourages them to watch greater amounts of television by making it a thoroughly personalized experience.   8

The near future promises even more of these ego-casting technologies, which offer us greater control and encourage the individualized pursuit of personal taste. Soon we'll carry cellphones that double as credit cards, toll passes, televisions and personal video cameras. At home, we'll merge the functions of these many technologies into a single streamlined machine that will respond to the sound of our voice, like the multimodal browser   9 being developed by I.B.M. and Opera. This expansion of choice and control will foster the already prevalent expectation that we can and should be able to have anything we want on demand.

This is not a world without costs. Having our every whim satisfied at   10
the touch of a button might encourage a childish expectation of instant gratification and could breed intolerance for the kinds of music, film and literature that require patience to enjoy fully. As we use these technologies to increase the pace and quantity of our experiences, we might find that the quality of our pursuits declines. Nevertheless, whatever ambivalence we might feel toward these technologies, we end up buying and using them anyway, not only because they make life more convenient but also because everyone else uses them and so we must as well. The traveling businessman without a cellphone will not have a business for long.

Although there is no obvious political solution to the unintended   11
problems created by our personal technologies—we wouldn't want the government taxing our TiVo use—there are possibilities for nonpartisan agreement about changing our use of them. Conservatives like to complain about the content of popular culture and yet champion an unregulated market that thrives on creating and supplying new wants. Liberals herald the power of individual choice yet fret about the decline of community and the power corporations often exercise over our politics and culture. Both might agree, then, that it is a good thing if parents discourage children from watching too much television. Both might find something beneficial in private entities enforcing civility in discrete spaces, like restaurants and theaters that ban cellphones, and an increase in public transportation providers who offer cell-free spaces, like the "quiet car" that Amtrak offers.

As a society, we need to approach our personal technologies with a   12
greater awareness of how the pursuit of personal convenience can contribute to collective ills. When it comes to abortion or Social Security, we avidly debate the claims of individual freedom against other goods. Why shouldn't we do the same with our private technologies? In the end, it does matter if we watch six more hours of television every week, and it does affect our broader quality of life if hollering into our cellphones makes our daily commute a living hell for our fellow citizens on the bus or a danger to other drivers on the road. Rather than turning on, tuning in and dropping out, we might perhaps do better, individually and socially, to occasionally simply turn our machines off.

■ ■ ■

AFTER YOU READ

■ **THINK** about, and explain, how Rosen relates cell phones to the idea of "connection" and DVRs to the idea of "control." Do you think that these associations could be reversed, with cell phones related to control?

Explain. Do you believe cell phone connections are good, bad, or both? Do you think the ability that DVRs give users to control their television usage is good, bad, or both? Ultimately, do you agree or disagree with Rosen that "we might perhaps do better, individually and socially, to occasionally simply turn our machines off"? Explain your viewpoints.

■ **EXAMINE** Rosen's analysis of the mirror as one of the first personal technologies (paragraph 1). How did the mirror, in Rosen's opinion, change its users? Then examine paragraph 6 to see how Rosen compares the early technology of the mirror to the modern cell phone. According to Rosen, how are these technologies similar in their effect on users and their egos? How are these effects negative? Do you believe Rosen is correct or incorrect in her analysis? Explain.

■ **WRITE** an essay in which you enumerate and discuss either the positive or negative effects of one type of personal technology (cell phones, DVRs, iPods, etc.). If you wish, you may use Rosen's essay as a starting point to which your essay is a response. (See "Responding to a Text" on pages 244–247, and Lesson 5 on writing cause and effect essays on the *Interactions,* eighth edition, student website, at www.cengagebrain. com.)

Buckle Up and Stop Texting:
One Teen's Legacy

■ ■ ■

MARGIE JACINTO

Today, cell phones are used, especially by young people, as much for texting as for voice calls. The following essay recounts the story of one of many personal tragedies that have resulted from texting while driving. The website "Distraction.Gov" reports that in 2008 alone almost 6,000 people died and more than half a million people sustained injuries from wrecks caused by individuals texting while driving. According to the same site, using a cell phone—hand-held or hands-free, affects a driver's reactions "as much as having a blood alcohol concentration at the legal limit of .08 percent." This story, with these details, appeared in *Texas Heritage for Living* in the summer of 2010. A regular writer for the magazine, Margie Jacinto lives in Dallas, Texas.

BEFORE YOU READ

■ **THINK** about the popularity of texting today, especially among young people. Do you text? How much do you text? Have you ever texted while driving or performing some other potentially dangerous activity?

■ **EXAMINE** both the title and the first three paragraphs of the essay. Has someone told you before to "Buckle up and stop texting"? In your opinion, how important is this advice? Based on your examination of the first three paragraphs, what happened to Alex Brown on November 10, 2009? Can you guess why this happened?

■ **WRITE** a journal entry about the phenomenon of texting. What, in your opinion, has made texting so popular, especially among young people? Why do people text while driving even though they know it is dangerous?

AS YOU READ

Look for the reason Alex Brown died and for her "legacy"—for the effect her life and death had on others.

■ ■ ■

W hen Alex Marie Brown didn't show up for high 1
school one autumn morning, her mother went looking for
her.

Jeanne Brown teaches at the same school, so she retraced her 17-year-old 2
daughter's route. Along an old country road, she found Alex, lying next to
her mangled pickup. She had veered off the road.

Despite being airlifted to a medical facility, Alex died. On that day, 3
Jeanne and Johnny Mac Brown's world changed forever.

"She was not supposed to take that road to school," Jeanne says. "It is 4
a dangerous road, especially for an inexperienced driver. We also discovered that she went down that road often."

Alex wasn't wearing her seat belt that day, and they learned that she 5
had been texting while driving. Bright and popular, she was the kind of
girl who would light up the room whenever she entered. "Alex was an outstanding student," her mother adds, "salutatorian of her class and on her
way to being valedictorian. Her dream was to become the next Megyn
Kelly on Fox News."

As friends and family struggled to adjust, they realized that life would 6
never be the same. "So many things we had looked forward to will never
happen . . . Alex's graduation and college, planning her wedding and baby
showers—it's all gone."

But one thing the Browns have is support. Justin Bennett, their Texas 7
Farm Bureau Insurance agent, threw the term "business hours" out the
window. "Justin was available whenever and wherever we needed him.
He checks on our family regularly and always offers encouragement. He
has been a wonderful blessing throughout this tragedy," Jeanne says.

Today, the Wellman residents are on a mission to educate others about 8
the dangers of driving distracted and unbuckled. "Texting and driving is
never safe," Jeanne says. "All it takes is a couple of seconds for the road
ahead to change—if you are focused on your text, there is no time to react
to avoid a wreck."

Alex's accident prompted Pete Christy, a sportscaster with KCBD 9
NewsChannel 11 in Lubbock, to develop a program to educate youth and
adults of dangers associated with texting and driving. Called BUST—
Buckle Up & Stop Texting—the program was embraced by the Browns,
who now share their story as a warning to others.

The Browns travel throughout the state, bringing along what's left of 10
Alex's white truck. Earlier this spring, their story was also featured on the
Oprah Winfrey Show's No Phone Zone Day.

"Now, instead of going to work each day, we travel most days to 11
schools and visit with students and adults about the danger of texting and
driving, and how on just a normal day, our lives were shattered because of
what seems like a small, insignificant choice."

Before her untimely death, Alex had written a very poignant post on 12
her MySpace page: "I'm going to change the world, or die trying."

Jeanne reveals, "That was her entire spirit—to make a difference in 13
this world because of the life she lived."

■ ■ ■

AFTER YOU READ

■ **THINK** about the effects of Alex's death, both on those who knew her and on many who did not know her. What effect did her death have on her parents? On her friends and family? What did this tragedy cause sportscaster Pete Christy to create? How have Alex's parents become involved with the program that Christy developed? How might this program save the lives of other young people?

■ **EXAMINE** the post Alex had written on her MySpace page before her death (see paragraph 12). How has her death become a "legacy" that is making a difference in her state and in the world? Go to the BUST website (www.bust2day.org) and read the BUST challenge. Whether you live in Texas or some other state, are you willing to take this pledge? Why or why not? In your opinion, how many of your friends and family would be willing to take this pledge?

■ **WRITE** a letter to young people—perhaps members of your own generation—urging them to wear their seat belts and not to text (or do another dangerous activity, such as drinking) while driving. Be as persuasive as you can. (See "Writing a Persuasive Essay" on pages 372–378.)

FOCUS: COMPARISON AND CONTRAST

The Real Digital Divide

■ ■ ■

SHARI CAUDRON

A prolific and award-winning freelance writer and columnist, Shari Caudron has published over 500 articles on business, lifestyle, travel, and other subjects in national newspapers and magazines, including *USA Today, Reader's Digest, The Christian Science Monitor, Sunset Magazine,* and *Workforce Magazine.* She has also written two books, *What Really Happened When God Came Down* (2005) and *Who Are You People? A Personal Journey into the Heart of Fanatical Passion in America* (2006). In the following essay, which originally appeared in *Workforce* in July 2002, Caudron describes what she learned about different types of computer users when she decided to create her own website.

BEFORE YOU READ

■ **THINK** about how you and the people you know interact with computers. Do most people use a computer in the same way, or do different people use different ways to manipulate computers or to surf the web? For example, are some people more likely to rely on icons, whereas others use the keys more frequently? Are some people more likely to click on the reverse, or "go-back," icon, whereas others are more likely to "close out" a page to return to a previous site? Do you think that using certain computer techniques reveals something about the personality of the computer user? If so, how?

■ **EXAMINE** the title of this essay, "The Real Digital Divide." What was your first thought when you saw this title? Caudron argues that the digital divide occurs between web users who "go back" to pages and those who "close out" pages. Do you view this particular division as the "real digital divide" in computer use, or can you think of another way to distinguish between computer users?

■ **EXAMINE** also the words *introvert* and *extrovert* in paragraph 18. An introvert is one whose thoughts and interests are turned inward; an extrovert is a person whose thoughts and interests are directed outward, more toward other people.

■ **WRITE** a journal entry in which you speculate on what your computer techniques reveal about your personality.

AS YOU READ

Insert brackets in the left margin beside Caudron's descriptions of "go-backs" and in the right margin beside her descriptions of "close-outs."

■ ■ ■

Two months ago, I decided to create a Website. I made this decision   1
with the same breezy indifference I use in selecting my morning
coffee cup, as in: Today, I'll use the blue mug I bought in Mendocino.
Next Tuesday, I'll create a Website. Simple, right?

Actually, it was fairly simple—when I was working alone to gather the   2
material for the site. But once I hired a Web designer, things grew to a
staggering level of complexity. For the sake of this story, let's call the
Web designer Like Totally, for that seemed to be one of his favorite
expressions.

About two weeks into the process, Like Totally called to tell me that a   3
rough draft of my site was on the Web. I logged on, began to navigate my
way through the site, and quickly discovered that whenever I clicked onto
a new page I could not click back to where I began. I called the Web
designer.

"The site looks great," I explained. "But when I reach certain pages, I   4
can't go back."

"Go back?" he asked, plainly mystified by my question. "Like, why   5
would you want to do that? All you have to do is close out the page."

"Close out?" I didn't know what he was talking about.   6

"Yes, just close out the page and you'll get where you were   7
previously."

"But I never navigate the Web that way," I protested. "Closing out is   8
far too risky. What if I can't get back to where I started?"

Mr. Totally started to chuckle. "Wow," he said. "You must be naïve   9
and unsophisticated and like totally inept at Web navigation. Go
back!!!???" His laughter grew in intensity, and I swear I could hear him
slapping the armrest of his chair and saying, "That's a good one!"

Okay, maybe these weren't his exact words, but you get the idea.   10

Over the next few days, I conducted an informal poll among friends   11
and discovered that the world does indeed consist of two kinds of people:
go-backs and close-outs. It was information I could not readily accept. For
me, hitting the back button is such a natural, no-brainer way to traverse
the Internet that I couldn't believe there might be other, equally effective
ways to move around in cyberspace.

As I thought about it, I realized that Web navigation is something most 12 of us teach ourselves according to some intuitive sense of order and direction. Given that, I began to wonder what a person's navigational preference might say about his or her personality.

Go-backs, it seemed to me, would be people who like having links to 13 the past and probably have many long-term friendships. Go-backs are probably impulsive Web users, the kind of people who start out looking for research on the consumer-confidence index and end up on a site about the Whirling Dervishes of southern Turkey. Because go-backs are also insecure about technology, they need a digital handrail to guide them back to where they started. In the world of the Internet, go-backs are the impetuous kindergartners who climb over the schoolyard fence, get into trouble, and then beg the teacher to give them a second chance. Go-backs are my people.

Now, let's talk about close-outs. People who shut down Web pages 14 when done with them are clearly more decisive and confident than go-backs. They're forward thinkers who gather data, make decisions, and emphatically stand by them. They don't dawdle, which makes them reliable, but they may have a tendency to be a bit brash. Close-outs scare me.

In conducting my poll, I was pleased to discover that the writers and 15 editors I work best with are just like me. They like to go back. Like Dorothy, we believe there's no place like home. I was, however, astonished to learn that I live with a close-out, which actually helps to explain some of our arguments. "Honey, let's go back to when you first got upset," I might say to my beloved close-out, whose initial response typically is: "No. It's over, I'm not talking about this anymore."

Now, I've taken just about every personality assessment known to 16 humankind. The Myers-Briggs tells me I'm an INFP. On the Strong Interest Inventory, I'm an ASE. In astrology, I'm a Taurus. In numerology, I'm a five. Furthermore, I've written extensively about diversity and I know— on an intellectual level—that people have different experiences and viewpoints according to their gender, skin color, sexual orientation, religion, occupation, income, and whether they subscribe to *Martha Stewart Living* or *Atlantic Monthly*. Still, I was completely dumbstruck to learn that people also differ in how they navigate the Web. Do the differences never end?

Then it hit me that all the assessments, evaluations, and tests that 17 promise to reveal our true personality type and how to use that knowledge to relate to others are all saying the same thing: We're different— and the best way to get along with others is to understand how we're different.

Well, that's great. In theory. But the fact is that there are so infinitely 18 many potential areas of difference between people that it often doesn't even occur to us that a difference might exist. (Don't we like how I've switched to the third person all of a sudden?) Maybe, in addition to trying to understand and embrace the big distinctions—i.e., introvert versus extrovert, young versus old, black versus white—it might make sense to be alert for the small differences as well. "You check your e-mail at the end of the day? Tell me more." Heck, we wouldn't even need personality assessments if we went into every situation assuming that differences would have to be accommodated.

Unfortunately, when it came to my Website, Like Totally was not able   19
to accommodate both close-outs and go-backs. The difficulty had something to do with browser liposuction and HTML backsplash—or some such thing. However, knowing there were different ways of navigating the Web, I was able to research what worked best for my particular audience and design the site accordingly. As you might expect, every article is now accompanied by a soothing little back button that helps users find their place in the world.

■   ■   ■

AFTER YOU READ

■ **THINK** about the comparison and contrast organization of this essay shown by the brackets you inserted beside Caudron's descriptions of "go-backs" and "close-outs." As explained on page 387 of Motoko Rich's essay, elements to be compared can be arranged subject by subject, point by point, or in some combination of the two. How does Caudron organize her comparison and contrast essay?

■ **THINK** about the experience Caudron had with the web designer. Have you ever tried to learn something about a computer—or, indeed, about any other type of technology—from someone whose methods were so different from your own that you were unable to follow the explanation? Describe this experience and how it made you feel.

■ **EXAMINE** the descriptions of "go-backs" and "close-outs" that you bracketed as you read Caudron's essay. Would you classify yourself as either a "go-back" or a "close-out"? Do you agree or disagree with Caudron's descriptions of these two types of computer users? Do you believe, as she does, that the way one uses a computer can yield insights into one's personality? (You may want to look up Caudron's homepage on the Related Websites section of the *Interactions*, eighth edition, student site to see how the site works and how it reflects her personality.)

■ **EXAMINE** also the sentence "Like Dorothy, we believe there's no place like home" (paragraph 15). Dorothy is the main character in L. Frank Baum's book *The Wonderful Wizard of Oz* (1900), which was made into a movie in 1939. From the time a cyclone first carries her to Oz, Dorothy's greatest desire is to return home to Kansas.

■ **WRITE** an essay in which you classify or compare and contrast computer users into groups based on how they use their computers. For example, you could classify users according to their expertise as beginners, intermediate users, and advanced users; or you could compare and contrast them according to whether they use their computers for work or for entertainment. Be sure to include specific examples to depict each type of computer user. If possible, try to show, as Caudron does, what the different methods of using computers illustrate about the personalities of the users. (For instructions on writing classification essays, see Lesson 3 on the *Interactions,* eighth edition, student website, available at www.cengagebrain.com; for instructions on writing comparison and contrast essays, see Lesson 7 on the same website.)

The Distorting Mirror of Reality TV

■ ■ ■

SARAH COLEMAN

Sarah Coleman, a freelance journalist and fiction writer, was
born in London and studied English at Cambridge University
before moving to the United States. She earned a master of
fine arts degree at Columbia University in 1993 and has lived
in both New York and San Francisco. Her work has appeared
in a number of different publications, including *New York,
Newsday, Salon, World Press Review,* the *San Francisco Bay
Guardian,* and the *San Francisco Chronicle.* In the following
essay, Coleman examines and critiques reality television.

BEFORE YOU READ

■ **THINK** about the concept of reality television. How long do you think
this concept has been around? Do you enjoy watching reality shows, or
do you dislike them? Why do you feel as you do?

■ **EXAMINE** the title of Coleman's essay. The word *distort* literally means
"to twist apart, or to change the true picture or meaning." Reality television is supposed to reflect, or mirror, the real world. How could this
mirror—or reflection of reality—be distorting or distorted? Based on her
title, do you think that Coleman likes or dislikes reality TV?

■ **EXAMINE** also the names Mahatma Gandhi and Nelson Mandela from
paragraph 5. Gandhi was an early twentieth-century spiritual and political leader of India; Mandela, who won the Nobel Peace Prize in 1993,
served as the first black president of South Africa.

■ **WRITE** a journal entry in which you explain your attitude toward reality television and why you feel as you do.

AS YOU READ

First, determine Coleman's attitude toward reality television. Second,
underline and number in the margins the reasons she feels as she does.

■ ■ ■

T ake ten people. Put them (a) on an island, (b) in a locked house, or
(c) in a desert. Turn on some television cameras, give them strange
tests to perform as a group, and ask them to vote one person out

1

of the group each week. In between, watch them fight, lie, eat, wash, fall in love. The last player left will win a big pot of money. This is the basic premise of a popular form of entertainment called "reality television."

The idea of watching people behave spontaneously on television isn't a 2 new one. MTV's hugely successful show *The Real World* debuted in 1992, and way back in the television dark ages of the 1940s, Allen Funt's *Candid Camera* began using hidden cameras to catch ordinary people reacting to strange events. No doubt there exists some ancient civilization in which entrepreneurs knocked holes in their neighbors' wall and called their friends together to peep. But the new crop of reality shows seems different somehow: meaner, tougher, and less connected with reality than ever before.

Let's start with the contestants. Most producers of reality TV shows 3 would like you to believe they've picked a group of people who span a broad spectrum of human diversity. But if you took the demographics of the average reality show and applied them to the population at large, you'd end up with a society that was 90 percent white, young, and beautiful. In fact, though reality TV pretends to hold up a mirror to society, its producers screen players in much the same way as the producers of television commercials and Hollywood movies screen their actors. For ethnic minorities, old people, the unbeautiful, and the disabled, the message is harsh: even in "reality" you don't exist.

Nor do stereotypes disappear once a contestant makes it into the cast 4 of a reality show. Players who can't wait until they appear on television as themselves are often surprised to find that viewers see only one side of their personality. To make the shows more dramatic, it helps if viewers can easily identify each player as a particular type of person, so producers find cast members' most obvious traits and accentuate them through careful editing. The hunk, the girl next door, the know it all, and the flirt: these are all popular recurring "characters" on reality shows. With this kind of simplification, the complexity that makes real people so interesting is gone; instead, these "real" people are no more profound than the average soap opera character.

Reality shows' view of human potential is similarly diminished. In 5 movies and soaps, evil characters often capture our imagination, but their badness is effective because it contrasts with other characters' goodness. In reality TV, every character is a villain. Since the shows are set up as contests with a single winner, naked self-interest is the force motivating each contestant. To walk away with the jackpot, players must be wily and calculating. They must charm other players into letting them stick around, but be ready to crush anyone who stands in the way of their success. What we see here is really a refined form of mud wrestling. Cynics might argue that it is nothing more than real life with the gloves off—but if humans are that ruthlessly self-interested, how do we account for inspirational figures from Mahatma Gandhi to Nelson Mandela? Real people are capable of nobility to differing degrees, but reality TV gives us a world where nobody can be trusted and where manipulation and backstabbing are rewarded with big cash prizes.

This eat-or-be-eaten mentality is often underscored by the shows' exotic locations. Crystal-clear water cascades over craggy rocks, a red cardinal's feathers are lit by the setting sun, but we see that even amid all this natural beauty people are still petty and conniving. No wonder one show continually showed shots of crocodiles poking their snouts out of murky river water: the producers wanted us to remember that every paradise has its poison-filled serpent, every jungle its tiger.

6

In other ways, reality shows are less reminiscent of movies and mud wrestling than of another form of popular entertainment: the ancient Roman fight to the death between gladiators and lions. By eliminating one contestant each week, the shows offer us a symbolic form of public execution (one show even used that term to describe the way it dispatches its losers). We enjoy the suspense of seeing who will be eliminated, and perhaps we enjoy the loser's humiliation (after all, it's not "us"). The "executions" also offer the fantasy that annoying people can be banished from our lives. This is a place where irritating, self-absorbed types usually get their comeuppance, unless they make themselves useful to the group by hunting or cooking. Of course, real life is never that convenient: annoying people have a habit of sticking around, and they usually don't bring you fish.

7

Flimsy people in search of money and glory: Is that what we humans are all about? Reality TV puts forward a dark view of humanity in the guise of light entertainment. While it's fun to see "real" people (however reduced) on television—and to gossip about them the next day—it's depressing to think that their decency and ours is being hijacked in the name of entertainment. Nor are the shows' producers the only cynics in this game. With winners appearing everywhere from *Playboy* to lip-salve commercials, and sore losers suing producers for alleged results-fixing, it seems everyone is exploiting everyone here. Andy Warhol once predicted, "In the future everyone will be world-famous for fifteen minutes." Could he have foreseen how ugly people would make themselves for their moment in the spotlight?

8

■ ■ ■

AFTER YOU READ

■ **THINK** about the description of reality shows that Coleman provides in her first paragraph. How many reality shows can you name that fit this description? Explain how one or more of these shows conforms to Coleman's description. Can you think of any reality shows that do not fit this format? If so, give one or more examples and explain the difference.

■ **EXAMINE** the last sentence of paragraph 2: "But the new crop of reality shows seems different somehow: meaner, tougher, and less connected with reality than ever before." Then examine carefully the reasons Coleman provides to support this statement—reasons that you were asked to underline and number as you read the selection. In your own words, what are these reasons?

■ **WRITE** an essay in which you argue for or against the idea that reality television is a distortion of reality itself. Refer not only to Coleman's essay, agreeing or disagreeing with it, but also to one or more specific reality shows. (See "Responding to a Text" on pages 244–247 and "Writing a Persuasive Essay" on pages 372–378.)

YouTube: The People's Network

■ ■ ■

LEV GROSSMAN

Lev Grossman, who holds a bachelor's degree from Harvard and a master's degree from Yale, is a book critic and technology writer for *Time* magazine and *Time Digital*. Grossman has contributed articles to *The New York Times*, *The Wall Street Journal*, *Salon*, and the *Village Voice*. He has also written three novels—*Warp* (1997), *Codex* (2004), and *The Magicians* (2009)—the last of which was a *New York Times* bestseller. In the following article from *Time*, Grossman introduces and comments on the reality of the Internet phenomenon YouTube, which he calls "The People's Network."

BEFORE YOU READ

■ **THINK** about the concept behind YouTube—which *Time* magazine named as its Invention of the Year for 2006. Through sharing amateur videos on the Internet, YouTube has, as Grossman states in paragraph 3, "created a new way for millions of people to entertain, educate, shock, rock, and grok one another on a scale we've never seen before." What do you think about this idea? Have you viewed videos on YouTube? What different kinds of videos do you find on the site? What kind of videos do you enjoy the most? What kind of videos do you dislike?

■ **EXAMINE** the title of the essay and the YouTube site itself (see "Related Websites" on the *Interactions* website). How is YouTube really a "people's network"? Who creates videos for the site? Who watches these videos? How do these videos differ from "professional" videos? In your opinion, what is more, or less, enjoyable about these videos than professional ones?

■ **EXAMINE** also the names mentioned in paragraph 11. You probably recognize the celebrity Paris Hilton and the rapper P. Diddy, but you may not recognize the references to actor Michael J. Fox and Senator George Allen. During the 2006 senatorial campaign, Fox, who suffers from Parkinson's disease, made a political advertisement for the Missouri Democratic senatorial candidate who supported stem cell research, and Allen lost his own senatorial race in Virginia in part because he called one of his opponent's staff members *macaca*, a term that is a racial slur against African immigrants.

■ **WRITE** a journal entry about the type of videos you enjoy—or would enjoy—watching on YouTube.

AS YOU READ

Identify and underline the various reasons Grossman gives for the success of YouTube.

■ ■ ■

Meet Peter. Peter is a 79-year-old English retiree. Back in WW II he served as a radar technician. He is now an international star.

One year ago, this would not have been possible, but the world has changed. In the past 12 months, thousands of ordinary people have become famous. Famous people have been embarrassed. Huge sums of money have changed hands. Lots and lots of Mentos have been dropped into Diet Coke. The rules are different now, and one website changed them: YouTube.

It's been an interesting year in technology. Nintendo invented a video game you control with a magic wand. A new kind of car traveled 3,145 miles on a single gallon of gas. A robot learned to ride a bike. Somebody came up with a nanofabric umbrella that doesn't stay wet. But only You-Tube created a new way for millions of people to entertain, educate, shock, rock and grok one another on a scale we've never seen before. That's why it's TIME's Invention of the Year for 2006.

But if YouTube is the Invention of the Year, who exactly invented it?

Let's be clear: we know who started it. That would be three twenty-something guys named Steve Chen, Chad Hurley and Jawed Karim. At a Silicon Valley dinner party one night in 2004 they started talking about how easy it was to share photos with your friends online but what a pain it was to do the same thing with video.

So they did something about it. They hacked together a simple routine for taking videos in any format and making them play in pretty much any Web browser on any computer. Then they built a kind of virtual video village, a website where people could post their own videos and watch and rate and comment on and search for and tag other people's videos. Voilà: YouTube.

But even though they built it, they didn't really understand it. They thought they'd built a useful tool for people to share their travel videos. They thought people might use it to pitch auction items on eBay. They had no idea they had opened a portal into another dimension.

The minute people saw YouTube they did its creators a huge favor: they hijacked it. Instead of posting their home movies, they posted their stand-up routines and drunken ramblings and painful-looking snowboarding wipeouts. They uploaded their backyard science projects, their delivery-room footage and their interminable guitar solos. They sent in eyewitness footage from the aftermath in New Orleans and the war in Baghdad—from both sides. They promulgated conspiracy theories. They sat alone in their basements and poured their most intimate, embarrassing secrets into their webcams. YouTube had tapped into something that appears on no business plan: the lonely, pressurized, pent-up video subconscious of America. Having started with a single video of a trip to the zoo in April of last year, YouTube now airs 100 million videos—and its users add 70,000 more—every day.

What happened? YouTube's creators had stumbled onto the intersection of three revolutions. First, the revolution in video production made possible by cheap camcorders and easy-to-use video software. Second, the social revolution that pundits and analysts have dubbed Web 2.0. It's exemplified by sites like MySpace, Wikipedia, Flickr and Digg—hybrids that are useful Web tools but also thriving communities where people create and share information together. The more people use them, the better they work, and more people use them all the time—a kind of self-stoking mass collaboration that wouldn't have been possible without the Internet. 9

The third revolution is a cultural one. Consumers are impatient with the mainstream media. The idea of a top-down culture, in which talking heads spoon-feed passive spectators ideas about what's happening in the world, is over. People want unfiltered video from Iraq, Lebanon and Darfur—not from journalists who visit there but from soldiers who fight there and people who live and die there. 10

The videos may not be slick, but they're real—and anyway, slick is overrated. Slick is 2005. The yardstick on YouTube is authenticity. That's why celebrities like Paris Hilton and P. Diddy can compete with a cute sleepy kitty and a guy doing a robot dance—and lose. That's why Peter's crusty, good-natured reminiscences have made him the all-time second-most-subscribed-to uploader on YouTube. That's why Michael J. Fox let his Parkinson's tremors show. That's why politicians have suddenly started to act like real human beings in their campaign ads, and why some—like Senator George Allen of "Macacagate" fame—have been busted for getting a little too real. 11

Less than a year after its launch, YouTube has become a media giant in its own right. Last month the company moved out of its 30-person office above a pizzeria in San Mateo, Calif., and into an office building in nearby San Bruno. Oh, and on Oct. 16 Hurley and Chen sold the company to Google for $1.65 billion. 12

With that kind of money behind it, YouTube has to start conducting itself with a little more legal and financial gravitas. That means making money—mostly through advertising—and convincing the TV, movie and music executives who find copyrighted material on YouTube that it's a revenue opportunity and not grounds for litigation. The learning curve is still steep. "The people marketing content see it as a great new platform, but the legal side of the business doesn't know how to react," Hurley says. "We have instances where someone within the company uploaded something, and the other side's asking you to take it down." 13

But YouTube isn't Napster. It already has partnerships with NBC, 14
CBS, Universal Music, Sony BMG and Warner Music. And come on—it's
the one place on the Net where people willingly, knowingly click on ads,
like Nike's legendary clip of sharpshooting soccer star Ronaldinho. If you
can't find money on YouTube, you're in the wrong economy, buddy.

YouTube is ultimately more interesting as a community and a culture, 15
however, than as a cash cow. It's the fulfillment of the promise that Web
1.0 made 15 years ago. The way blogs made regular folks into journalists,
YouTube makes them into celebrities. The real challenge old media face
isn't protecting their precious copyrighted material. It's figuring out what
to do when the rest of us make something better. As Hurley puts it,
"How do you stay relevant when people can entertain themselves?" He
and his partners may have started YouTube, but the rest of us, in our basements and bedrooms, with our broadband and our webcams, invented it.

■ ■ ■

AFTER YOU READ

■ **THINK** about the different kinds of videos Grossman describes in paragraph 8. Of those that he mentions, which are created for entertainment? Which are made to record history? And which simply record life
experiences? Do you think there is a connection between the popularity
of YouTube and the success of reality television? In your opinion, which
is more truly "real"?

■ **EXAMINE** paragraphs 9 and 10, in which Grossman explains the three
revolutions that he believes came together in the creation and success of
YouTube. What are these three revolutions? Why does Grossman think
the "cultural" revolution is the most important? Do you agree that
many people are displeased with the "top-down" political and media
culture and want "unfiltered" video of current events? What do you
think has led to this desire? Do people trust the "filtered" versions of
reality portrayed by politicians and the media? Why or why not?

■ **WRITE** an essay in which you discuss why people (and you in particular) want, or do not want, to see unfiltered videos like those posted on
YouTube. Be sure to include examples of specific videos (or types of
videos).

The Blogs Must Be Crazy

■ ■ ■

PEGGY NOONAN

A columnist for *The Wall Street Journal*, Peggy Noonan is the author of several books, including *The New York Times* bestseller *When Character Was King: The Story of Ronald Reagan*, and, more recently, *John Paul the Great: Remembering a Spiritual Father* (2005) and *Patriotic Grace: What It Is and Why We Need It Now* (2008). Noonan has also published in *Time, Newsweek, Forbes, The Washington Post*, and *The New York Times*. Recently she has served as a consultant for the television drama *The West Wing*, and earlier in her career she wrote news specials for *CBS News*. In the following editorial from *The Wall Street Journal Online*, Noonan emphasizes the positive effects of Internet blogs, a revolutionary news media format that, as Grossman asserts in the previous essay, has "made regular folks into journalists."

BEFORE YOU READ

- **THINK** about your view of the "mainstream" media as represented in network news and specials as well as in traditional newspapers. In your opinion, how effective are the mainstream media in presenting information to the public? Do you believe these sources remained dignified as well as accurate, careful, and thorough in their reporting? If you have heard of blogs, what is your opinion of these sources of information? To what extent do you respect or trust blogs? Why do you feel as you do? Support your opinion with examples.

- **EXAMINE** the abbreviations *MSM* (mainstream media) and *J-schools* (journalism schools) as well as the word *blogs* and related terms. *Blogs* (*web* + *logs*) are online journals or newsletters that state their writers' opinions, are frequently updated, and are often linked to other websites. Some variations of *blog* that Noonan uses are *bloggers* (people who write blogs) and *blogosphere* (a community of bloggers).

- **EXAMINE** also the first three paragraphs of the selection. How do these paragraphs capture your attention? Are you surprised by the source of the name calling in paragraph 1? Why or why not?

- **WRITE** a journal entry in which you compare and contrast your opinions about blogs and the mainstream media *before* you read Noonan's essay.

AS YOU READ

Underline passages in paragraphs 4–7 that suggest Noonan's thesis. Also be aware that this selection is in part an analytic report in which Noonan devotes a section to each of seven power sources of blogs. Underline the key sentence or passage in each of these sections. Also, circle words that you do not know, look them up in a dictionary, and add them to your vocabulary journal.

■ ■ ■

"Salivating morons." "Scalp hunters." "Moon howlers." "Trophy 1 hunters." "Sons of Sen. McCarthy." "Rabid." "Blogswarm." "These pseudo-journalist lynch mob people."

This is excellent invective. It must come from bloggers. But wait, it was 2 the mainstream media and their maidservants in the elite journalism reviews, and they were talking about bloggers!

Those MSMers have gone wild, I tell you! The tendentious language, 3 the low insults. It's the Wild Wild West out there. We may have to consider legislation.

When you hear name-calling like what we've been hearing from the 4 elite media this week, you know someone must be doing something right. The hysterical edge makes you wonder if writers for newspapers and magazines and professors in J-schools don't have a serious case of freedom envy.

The bloggers have that freedom. They have the still pent-up energy of 5 a liberated citizenry, too. The MSM doesn't. It has lost its old monopoly on information. It is angry.

But MSM criticism of the blogosphere misses the point, or rather 6 points.

Blogging changes how business is done in American journalism. The 7 MSM isn't over. It just can no longer pose as if it is The Guardian of Established Truth. The MSM is just another player now. A big one, but a player.

The blogosphere isn't some mindless eruption of wild opinion. That 8 isn't their power. This is their power:

1. They use the tools of journalists (computer, keyboard, a spirit of 9 inquiry, a willingness to ask the question) and of the Internet (Google, LexisNexis) to look for and find facts that have been overlooked, ignored or hidden. They look for the telling quote, the ignored statistic, the data that have been submerged. What they are looking for is information that is true. When they get it they post it and include it in the debate. This is a public service.

2. Bloggers, unlike reporters at elite newspapers and magazines, are 10 independent operators. They are not, and do not have to be,

governed by mainstream thinking. Nor do they have to accept the directives of an editor pushing an ideology or a publisher protecting his friends. Bloggers have the freedom to decide on their own when a story stops being a story. They get to decide when the search for facts is over. They also decide on their own when the search for facts begins. It was a blogger at the World Economic Forum, as we all know, who first reported the Eason Jordan story. It was bloggers, as we all know, who pursued it. Matt Drudge runs a news site and is not a blogger, but what was true of him at his beginning (the Monica Lewinsky story, he decided, is a story) is true of bloggers: It's a story if they say it is. This is a public service.

3. Bloggers have an institutional advantage in terms of technology and   11
    form. They can post immediately. The items they post can be as
    long or short as they judge to be necessary. Breaking news can be
    one sentence long: "Malkin gets Barney Frank earwitness report."
    In newspapers you have to go to the editor, explain to him why the
    paper should have another piece on the Eason Jordan affair, spend a
    day reporting it, only to find that all that's new today is that
    reporter Michelle Malkin got an interview with Barney Frank.
    That's not enough to merit 10 inches of newspaper space, so the
    Times doesn't carry what the blogosphere had 24 hours ago. In the
    old days a lot of interesting information fell off the editing desk in
    this way. Now it doesn't. This is a public service.

4. Bloggers are also selling the smartest take on a story. They're selling   12
    an original insight, a new area of inquiry. Mickey Kaus of Kausfiles
    has his bright take, Andrew Sullivan has his, InstaPundit has his.
    They're all selling their shrewdness, experience, depth. This too is a
    public service.

5. And they're doing it free. That is, the *Times* costs me a dollar and   13
    so does the *Journal,* but Kausfiles doesn't cost a dime. This too is a
    public service. Some blogs get their money from yearly fund-raising,
    some from advertisers, some from a combination, some from a sal-
    ary provided by *Slate* or *National Review.* Most are labors of love.
    Some bloggers—a lot, I think—are addicted to digging, posting,
    coming up with the bright phrase. OK with me. Some get burned
    out. But new ones are always coming up, so many that I can't keep
    track of them and neither can anyone else.

    But when I read blogs, when I wake up in the morning and go   14
    to About Last Night and Lucianne and Lileks, I remember what the
    late great Christopher Reeve said on "The Tonight Show" 20 years
    ago. He was the second guest, after Rodney Dangerfield. Danger-
    field did his act and he was hot as a pistol. Then after Reeve sat
    down Dangerfield continued to be riotous. Reeve looked at him,
    gestured toward him, looked at the audience and said with grace
    and delight, "Do you believe this is free?" The audience cheered.
    That's how I feel on their best days when I read blogs.

That you get it free doesn't mean commerce isn't involved, for it 15
is. It is intellectual commerce. Bloggers give you information and
point of view. In return you give them your attention and intellectual energy. They gain influence by drawing your eyes; you gain
information by lending your eyes. They become well-known and
influential; you become entertained or informed. They get something from it and so do you.

6.   It is not true that there are no controls. It is not true that the blo-   16
gosphere is the Wild West. What governs members of the blogosphere is what governs to some degree members of the MSM, and
that is the desire for status and respect. In the blogosphere you lose
both if you put forward as fact information that is incorrect, spe-
cious or cooked. You lose status and respect if your take on a story
is patently stupid. You lose status and respect if you are unprofes-
sional or deliberately misleading. And once you've lost a sufficient
amount of status and respect, none of the other bloggers link to you
anymore or raise your name in their arguments. And you're over.
The great correcting mechanism for people on the Web is people on
the Web.

There are blogs that carry political and ideological agendas. But 17
everyone is on to them and it's mostly not obnoxious because their
agendas are mostly declared.

7.   I don't know if the blogosphere is rougher in the ferocity of its per- 18
sonal attacks than, say, Drew Pearson. Or the rough boys and girls
of the great American editorial pages of the 1930s and '40s. Bloggers are certainly not as rough as the splenetic pamphleteers of the
18th and 19th centuries, who amused themselves accusing Thomas
Jefferson of sexual perfidy and Andrew Jackson of having married a
whore. I don't know how Walter Lippmann or Scotty Reston would
have seen the blogosphere; it might have frightened them if they'd
lived to see it. They might have been impressed by the sheer digging
that goes on there. I have seen friends savaged by blogs and winced
for them—but, well, too bad. I've been attacked. Too bad. If you
can't take it, you shouldn't be thinking aloud for a living. The blogosphere is tough. But are personal attacks worth it if what we get
in return is a whole new media form that can add to the true-
information flow while correcting the biases and lapses of the
mainstream media? Yes. Of course.

I conclude with a few predictions.   19

Some brilliant rising young reporter with a growing reputation at the 20
Times or *Newsweek* or *Post* is going to quit, go into the blogging business,
start The Daily Joe, get someone to give him a guaranteed ad for two
years, and become a journalistic force. His motive will be influence, and
the use of his gifts along the lines of excellence. His blog will further legiti-
mize blogging.

Most of the blogstorms of the past few years have resulted in outcomes   21
that left and right admit or bray were legitimate. Dan Rather fell because his
big story was based on a fabrication, Trent Lott said things that it could be
proved he said. But coming down the pike is a blogstorm in which the bloggers turn out to be wrong. Good news: They'll probably be caught and
exposed by bloggers. Bad news: It will show that blogging isn't nirvana,
and its stars aren't foolproof. But then we already know that, don't we?

Some publisher is going to decide that if you can't fight blogs, you can   22
join them. He'll think like this: *We're already on the Internet. That's how
bloggers get and review our reporting. Why don't we get our own bloggers
to challenge our work? Why don't we invite bloggers who already exist
into the tent? Why not take the best things said on blogs each day and
print them on a Daily Blog page? We'd be enhancing our rep as an honest
news organization, and it will further our branding!*

Someone is going to address the "bloggers are untrained journalists"   23
question by looking at exactly what "training," what education in the art/
science/craft/profession of journalism, the reporters and editors of the
MSM have had in the past 60 years or so. It has seemed to me the best
of them never went to J-school but bumped into journalism along the
way—walked into a radio station or newspaper one day and found their
calling. Bloggers signify a welcome return to that old style. In journalism
you learn by doing, which is what a lot of bloggers are doing.

Finally, someday in America the next big bad thing is going to happen,   24
and lines are going to go down, and darkness is going to descend, and the
instant communication we now enjoy is going to be compromised. People
in one part of the country are going to wonder how people in another part
are doing. Little by little lines are going to come up, and people are going
to log on, and they're going to get the best, most comprehensive, and ultimately, just because it's there, most heartening information from . . . some
lone blogger out there. And then another. They're going to do some big
work down the road.

■   ■   ■

AFTER YOU READ

- **THINK** about Noonan's thesis. Then express this thesis in your own
  words.

- **THINK** also about the seven elements of a blogger's power that Noonan
  lists in paragraphs 9–18. Which of these elements do you think contributes the most to the power of the blogosphere? Explain.

- **EXAMINE** the predictions that Noonan makes about blogs in paragraphs 20–24. Which of these predictions do you think is most likely
  to come true? Why?

■ EXAMINE also the following explanations of several names in Noonan's essay with which you may not be familiar. Award-winning journalist Eason Jordan resigned as chief news executive of CNN in February 2005 because of the controversy generated by his comment that American troops in Iraq were targeting journalists; talk radio host and Internet journalist Matt Drudge initially broke the Monica Lewinsky–Bill Clinton story on the *Drudge Report* website in 1998 (paragraph 10). Michelle Malkin is a conservative American columnist and television commentator, whereas Barney Frank is the liberal Democratic and openly gay congressman representing Massachusetts' Fourth District (paragraph 11). Mickey Kaus is a political journalist whose blog is featured on Slate.com, and Andrew Sullivan is a journalist who writes for *Time* magazine and serves as an advocate for gay rights (paragraph 12). In the entertainment world, Christopher Reeve reached stardom with the leading role in the 1978 *Superman* movie and its sequels before his tragic accident, paralysis, and death, and Rodney Dangerfield was a successful comedian before his death in 2004 (paragraph 14). Andrew Russell "Drew" Pearson (1897–1869), Walter Lippmann (1889–1974), and James Barrett "Scotty" Reston (1909–1995) were all legendary journalists (paragraph 18). How many of these people had you heard about before reading the essay? What did you know about them?

■ EXAMINE also Noonan's home page, available as a link on the *Interactions*, eighth edition student website, at www.cengagebrain.com. This site provides more information about Noonan as a person and a journalist as well as other recent opinion pieces published by her in *The Wall Street Journal*.

■ WRITE an analytic report on one particular blog (perhaps one mentioned in Noonan's essay) or media source (a newspaper, a news program, or a political or cultural television commentary). Who is (are) the main reporter(s) or analyst(s)? What are the major parts of the site or the show? How effective is each part? How informative, thought-provoking, or entertaining is the site or show in general? (See pages 441–447 for instruction on writing reports and pages 305–309 for help with analyzing texts.)

In iPad We Trust

■ ■ ■

Daniel Lyons

A journalist focusing on technology issues, Daniel Lyons was a senior editor for *Forbes* magazine from 1998 to 2008, when he became a technology columnist for *Newsweek*. In addition to the book of short stories *The Last Good Man* (1993) and the novel *Dog Days* (1998), Lyons has written a fictional biography, *Options: The Secret Life of Steve Jobs, a Parody* (2007). Under the pseudonym "Fake Steve Jobs," he also writes a blog called *The Secret Diary of Steve Jobs,* which parodies Jobs. Lyons's interest in Jobs and all Apple products continues in the following column from the February 8, 2010, issue of *Newsweek*.

BEFORE YOU READ

■ **THINK** about the question in Lyons's first sentence. Why *do* we have so much hope for new technology? What do we, as a nation, think it can do for us? What do you, personally, think it can do for us? Do you think our hope is justified? Explain.

■ **EXAMINE** the title of Lyons's essay, which is an allusion to our national motto "In God We Trust." This phrase was first stamped on a coin in 1864 and was adopted by Congress as the national motto in 1956. Today it is printed on both coins and paper money. What attitude does this title, which introduces the connection between technology and religion in his essay, express toward both religion and technology? Do you agree or disagree with this attitude? Explain.

■ **EXAMINE** also the italicized words in this sentence: "Our iPhones not only play music and make phone calls, but they have also become *totemic* objects *imbued* with techno-voodoo" (paragraph 6). In this context, *totemic* refers to a highly respected emblem or symbol; *imbued* means inspired, filled, permeated.

■ **WRITE** a journal entry answering the question in Lyons's first sentence.

AS YOU READ

Underline passages that relate technology—especially the iPad—to religion.

■ ■ ■

W hy do we invest so much hope in new technology? What do we   1
expect these devices will do for us, and why are we so disappointed when the Next Big Thing turns out to be just a new
computer? This is what I'm asking myself after Apple's latest overhyped
product introduction. This time around the Next Big Thing is called an
iPad. It's basically an oversize iPod Touch, and it will be great for watching
movies, reading books, and browsing the Web.

Yet for some of us who sat in the audience watching Steve Jobs introduce the device, the whole thing felt like a letdown. The iPad is a perfectly   2
good product. It's reasonably priced, and after spending a few minutes
with one, I'm pretty sure I'll buy one for myself and probably a second
one for my kids so they can watch movies on road trips.

So why did I feel disappointed? As a friend at Apple put it, "Did you   3
think it was going to cure cancer or something?" The thing is, rumors
about an Apple tablet have been floating around for months, and during
that time a lot of us started dreaming up a list of amazing things that it
might do.

Some said the tablet would save newspapers and magazines by creating   4
a platform where publishers could charge readers for digital subscriptions.
Others said Apple would offer TV subscriptions so we wouldn't need to
have cable TV anymore.

At the very least, we had hoped a tablet from Apple would do something new, something we've never seen before. That's not the case. Jobs   5
and his team kept using words like "breakthrough" and "magical," but
the iPad is neither, at least not right now. It might turn out to be magical
for Apple, because what Jobs is really doing here is trying to replace the
personal computer with a closed application that runs software only from
Apple's online App Store. So instead of selling you a laptop and never
hearing from you again, Apple gets an ongoing revenue stream with iPad
as you keep downloading more apps. That really is "magical"—for Apple's
bottom line, anyway.

And that's fine. What's wrong, or at least interesting, is why some of us   6
expected so much more from a new gadget. I suspect this is because for
some people, myself included, technology has become a kind of religion.
We may not believe in God anymore, but we still need mystery and wonder.
We need the magic act. Five centuries ago Spanish missionaries put shiny
mirrors in churches to dazzle the Incas and draw them to Christianity. We,
too, want to be dazzled by shiny new objects. Our iPhones not only play
music and make phone calls, but they also have become totemic objects,
imbued with techno-voodoo. Maybe that sounds nuts, but before the iPad
was announced, people were calling it the "Jesus tablet."

Our love affair with technology is also about a quest for control.   7
We're living in an age of change and upheaval. There's an overwhelming
sense of powerlessness. But technology gives us the illusion of control, a
sense of order. Pick up a smart phone and you have a reliable, dependable
device that does whatever you tell it to do. You certainly can't say that
about your colleagues or families. And no wonder a lot of folks in the

media wanted to believe that a new device from Apple could stop the decline of our industry. Newspapers and magazines are struggling to adapt to the Internet, and no one has any idea what our business will look like when we get to the other side of this wrenching period. We just have blind faith that technology ultimately will make our business better, not worse. In one example of that blind faith, David Carr of *The New York Times* wrote recently that Apple's tablet would be nothing less than "the second coming of the iPhone, a so-called Jesus tablet that can do anything, including saving some embattled print providers from doom."

He may even be right—eventually. My friend Richard Ward, the vice president of innovation at HIS Inc., a research firm, imagines deals in which you'll get an iPad free, or at a very low price, when you sign up for a two-year subscription to one or more news publications. No doubt there will be loads of partnerships and new uses coming. 8

The thing about any new platform, including the iPhone and now the iPad, is that its real power is never apparent on day one. What Apple delivered last week is a simple product that does a few things very well. And whatever disappointment we might have felt says more about us than about Apple. 9

■ ■ ■

AFTER YOU READ

- ■ **THINK** about—and list—the reasons that Lyons believes our culture expects so much from technology. With which of his reasons do you agree? With which do you disagree? Explain.

- ■ **EXAMINE** the passages connecting technology and religion that you underlined while reading the essay. Analyze the connection(s) Lyons makes between technology and religion. How is it logical? How is it ridiculous? What does this connection suggest about today's culture and its values? Explain.

- ■ **EXAMINE** also Lyons's web blog "The Secret Diary of Steve Jobs," by Googling it. How well do you think Lyons's understands Jobs's personality and accomplishments? Do you find the site to be humorous or offensive? Do you think Lyons really admires Jobs? Explain.

- ■ **WRITE** an essay explaining why you think people today expect so much from technology. In your conclusion, evaluate these expectations. Do you think they are good or bad? (You may want to refer to your earlier journal entry.)

Could You Live with Less?

■ ■ ■

STEPHANIE MILLS

In contrast to Daniel Lyons and many of the earlier writers in
this unit, Stephanie Mills rejects the use of advanced technologies. Instead, her career and writings reflect her dedication to
environmental and ecological issues. A winner of a 1987
award from the Friends of the United Nations Environment
Program, Mills was the vice president of the Earth First!
Foundation from 1986 to 1989 and is currently a Fellow of
the Post Carbon Institute. She is the author of *Whatever Happened to Ecology?* (1989); *In Service of the Wild: Restoring and
Reinhabiting Damaged Land* (1995); *Epicurean Simplicity*
(2003); *Tough Little Beauties* (2007); and *On Gandhi's Path:
Bob Swann's Work for Peace and Community Economics*
(2010). She explains her concern about the relationship between
technology and the environment in the following essay from
Glamour magazine.

BEFORE YOU READ

■ **THINK** about the amount of technology with which you live daily. Do
you really need all of the technological gadgets and machines that you
have?

■ **EXAMINE** the question posed in the title. Which of your technological
machines and gadgets could you live without?

■ **EXAMINE** also the following italicized words, their contexts, and their
definitions:

1. "*monastically* simple life" (paragraph 1): reclusive and solitary, like
   monks
2. "at the *periphery* rather than at the center" (paragraph 4): outer-
   most edge
3. "as a *condiment* rather than as a staple" (paragraph 4): seasoning,
   such as mustard
4. "purchasing treadmill of planned *obsolescence*" (paragraph 4): state
   of being obsolete; outmodedness

   Notice that the context gives clues to the meanings of most of these
   words.

■ **WRITE** a journal entry in which you answer Mills's question, "Could
You Live with Less?"

AS YOU READ

Underline the technological products or services that Mills has chosen to live without.

■ ■ ■

Compared to the lifestyle of the average person on Earth, my days are lush with comfort and convenience: I have a warm home, enough to eat, my own car. But compared to most of my urban American contemporaries, I live a monastically simple life.

Since 1984 I've made my home outside a small city in lower Michigan, where the winters are snowy but not severely cold. My snug 720-square-foot house is solar- and wood-heated. No thermostat, just a cast-iron stove. There's electric lighting, indoor plumbing, a tankless water heater, a second refrigerator and range—but no microwave oven, no dish-washer, no blow-dryer, no cordless phone. My gas-sipping compact station wagon has 140,000 miles on it and spreading patches of rust. I've never owned a television set. My home entertainment center consists of a thou-sand books, a stereo system, a picture window, and two cats.

Part of the reason I live the way I do is that as a freelance writer, my income is unpredictable and at best fairly unspectacular. Thus it behooves me to keep in mind the differences between wants and needs. Like all human beings, I have some needs that are absolute: about 2,000 calories a day, a half a gallon of water to drink, a sanitary means of disposing of my bodily wastes, water to bathe in, something muscular to do for part of the day and a warm, dry place to sleep. To stay sane I need contact with people and with nature, meaningful work and the opportunity to love and be loved.

I don't need, nor do I want, to complicate my life with gadgets. I want to keep technology at the periphery rather than at the center of my life, to treat it like meat in Chinese cuisine—as a condiment rather than as a staple food. Technology should abet my life, not dominate it or redefine it. A really good tool—like a sharp kitchen knife, a wheelbarrow or a baby carrier, all of which have been with us in some form for thousands of years—makes a useful difference but doesn't displace human intelli-gence, character or contact the way higher technologies sometimes do. Working people need the tools of their trade, and as a writer, I do have a fax, but I've resisted the pressure to buy a personal computer. A manual typewriter has worked well for me so far. Noticing that the most computer-savvy people I know are always pining for more megabytes and better software, I've decided not to climb on the purchasing treadmill of planned obsolescence.

Doing with less is easier when I remember that emotional needs often get expressed as material wants, but can never, finally, be satisfied that way. If I feel disconnected from others, a cellular phone won't cure that. If I feel like I'm getting a little dowdy, hours on a tanning bed can't eradicate self-doubt.

Why life in a snowy region when I don't use central heat? I moved here for love several years ago, and while that love was brief, my affection for this place has grown and grown. I like the roots I've put down; living like Goldilocks, moving from chair to chair, seems like not much of a life to me. 6

Being willfully backward about technology suits my taste—I like living this way. Wood heat feels good, better than the other kinds. (Central heating would make my home feel like it was just anywhere.) Fetching firewood gets me outdoors and breathing (sometimes gasping) fresh air in the wintertime when it's easy to go stale. It's hard, achy work to split and stack the 8 or 12 cords of stove wood I burn annually. I've been known to seek help to get it done. But the more of it I do myself, the more I can brag to my city friends. 7

My strongest motivation for living the way I do is my knowledge, deep and abiding, that technology comes at a serious cost to the planet and most of its people. Burning fossil fuels has changed the Earth's climate. Plastics and pesticides have left endocrine-disrupting chemicals everywhere—in us and in wildlife, affecting reproductive systems. According to Northwest Environment Watch in Seattle, the "clean" computer industry typically generates 139 pounds of waste, 49 of them toxic, in the manufacture of each 55-pound computer. 8

I refuse to live as if that weren't so. In this, I'm not unique. There are many thousands of Americans living simply, questioning technology, fighting to preserve what remains of nature. We're bucking the tide, acting consciously and succeeding only a little. Yet living this way helps me feel decent within myself—and that, I find, is one luxury worth having. 9

■ ■ ■

AFTER YOU READ

■ **THINK** about Mills's distinction between needs and wants. What does she consider necessary to sustain a healthy and happy life? What technological products has she decided she can live without? What does she consider unnecessary wants? What products of technology do you "need" in your own life? Which ones do you "want"?

■ **EXAMINE** paragraph 8, which reveals Mills's "strongest motivation" for living the way she lives. What is this motivation? Do you agree with her belief that "technology comes at a serious cost to the planet and most of its people"? What are the human and environmental "costs" of some technologies? In your opinion, what technologies are most "costly" to humanity and the environment? On the other hand, do you believe that some technologies make vital contributions to human and environmental "needs"? What are some technologies that contribute to life's essential needs?

■ WRITE an essay in which you describe what your life (and that of your family) would be like with little or no technology. How would it be better? How would it be worse? In your essay, you may want to use ideas from the journal entry you wrote before reading this selection.

UNIT SEVEN

■ ■ ■

Critical Thinking, Reading, and Writing

■ WRITING A REPORT

Reports are informative accounts of problems, procedures, actions, responses, situations, or results. Colleges and universities create reports about students' reasons for attending or leaving college and about their success or failure while in college. Businesses use reports of their sales and profits to make management decisions. And Congress frequently calls for an investigative report on some individual or event. As a student, you may be asked to write a report of an observation, an experiment, or a project.

BEFORE YOU WRITE

A report can be viewed as a variation of an essay. A well-written report, like an essay, should have a clear purpose. The purpose of an essay may be to entertain, inform, or persuade; the primary purpose of a report is usually to inform, although a secondary purpose may be to persuade or entertain. Whereas Kimberly S. Young ("Fraternities of Netheads: Internet Addiction on Campus") presents an objective account of the problem of Internet addiction on campus, Ellen Laird ("We ALL Pay for Internet Plagiarism") reports on problems of academic integrity in an effort to convince students to avoid plagiarism of any kind, especially Internet plagiarism.

Types of Reports

Depending on the assignment and your own purpose for writing, you may write one of several different types of reports. Three of the most common types of reports assigned in college classes and written in the workplace are **problem/solution reports, investigative reports,** and **analytic reports.**

1. **A problem/solution report.**
   A problem/solution report identifies and explains a particular problem and then provides solutions for the problem. This type of report can focus on either the problem or the solution(s). An example of a problem/solution report in this unit is Kimberly S. Young's "Fraternities of Netheads: Internet Addiction on Campus." In her report, Young focuses on the problem of Internet addiction and its causes. However, she could have stated the problem only briefly and concentrated on the solutions. In preparing a problem/solution report, you may want to gather information in the form of interviews and observations, just as Young did.

2. **An investigative report.**

In an investigative report the writer employs field research (observation or interviews), library research, and/or Internet research. In her investigative report "We ALL Pay for Internet Plagiarism," Ellen Laird analyzed and researched online the essay her student Chip had submitted, interviewed Chip to confirm her suspicion of Internet plagiarism and discover why he had cheated, and finally interviewed a local high school English teacher about her experiences with Internet plagiarism.

3. **An analytic report.**

An analytic report divides an issue into various aspects and then explains each aspect. The term *analytic report* is a general designation that includes reports focusing on causes or effects of a situation, but **analysis,** or dividing a problem or situation or issue into its various parts, is also relevant to both problem/solution and investigative reports. Examples of analytic reports in Unit Seven are Sarah Coleman's "Reality Television" and Peggy Noonan's "The Blogs Must Be Crazy." Coleman analyzes the situations and characters (types, stereotypes, potential, and motivation) on reality shows, whereas Noonan analyzes the power sources and potential effects of bloggers. (See also "Analyzing a Text" on pages 305–309.)

As you are selecting your subject, you also need to consider whether you want to develop it through a problem/solution, investigative, or analytic approach. Then gather information for your report from library and Internet sources as well as field sources such as observations, interviews, and perhaps short questionnaires. Besides reviewing your notes, you may want to do some additional freewriting and planning before you begin to write (see the "Introduction" on pages 7–10).

Organization

A report generally follows the overall pattern of an essay: an introduction, a body, and a conclusion. However, reports may also use the more structured format outlined here:

1. Introduction: background and thesis (or purpose) statement

2. Description of the problem, situation, or first part of analysis

3. Discussion of problems, solutions, methods, findings, or additional parts of analysis

4. Conclusion, solutions, and/or recommendations

Although these are the basic elements you will include in your report, you may vary the order in which they occur, perhaps introducing the problem before explaining the background. If your report is persuasive (see "Writing a Persuasive Essay" on pages 372–378), you may want to recognize the opposing point of view.

In addition, you may not actually compose these sections in the order listed or in the order they are eventually presented in your report. For example, you may want to write your discussion before writing your introduction.

Whatever type of report you write, you should clearly indicate quoted material with quotation marks (for quotations four lines or less) or a one-inch indentation (for longer quotations), credit all borrowed material parenthetically, and cite all sources in a Works Cited in Modern Language Association format.

Example

Tammy Holm used information from an audiology course to help her write the following problem/solution report about how technology has both hurt and helped people with hearing impairments.

Technology and the Hearing Impaired

By the end of the twentieth century, 22 million Americans had lost   1
some or all of their hearing. Some of this hearing loss is due to genetic defects, damage to the developing fetus, infections, physical problems, and the natural process of aging, but more and more cases of hearing loss are due to the loud noises to which Americans' ears are exposed daily.

Diesel trucks, loud music, and factory machinery are all examples of   2
noises we hear daily that cause damage to our hearing. The noises travel to the middle ear via the ear canal. Located in the middle ear are the eardrum and a number of tiny bones that convey the vibrations of the noise to the cochlea. The cochlea is a spinal canal in the inner ear that is lined with thousands of cells with microscopic hairs. The response of the cells to the noise causes the hairs to vibrate. These hairs are the stimulant of the auditory nerves. When the nerves are stimulated, they send the message to the areas of the brain that are responsible for sound perception. The loud noises we expose our ears to damage the tiny hairs. When these hairs are damaged, the high frequencies are not sensed, and the auditory nerve is not stimulated. This lack of stimulation stops the message of high frequencies from arriving at the brain. The damage may be immediate, or it may develop slowly. It may also be temporary or permanent. Repeated exposure to loud noises may enhance the hearing loss associated with age.

Even though technological advances indirectly cause some hearing   3
loss, they can also be the cure or at least a source of improvement for
hearing loss. Technological advances have been used to develop a more advanced hearing aid called the Phoenix. New improvements in technology have also led to the development of a cochlear implant. Other advancements include the use of computers to help hearing-impaired people learn to speak and make phone calls and the development of closed caption for television viewing purposes.

First, the Phoenix hearing aid helps a hearing-impaired person hear   4
higher frequencies such as some consonants in speech. With hearing aids
developed before the Phoenix, a person would hear lower frequencies such
as an air conditioner and the quiet conversation of other patrons in a
restaurant over the spoken words of the person's companion. The difference between the Phoenix and other hearing aids is that the Phoenix has a
computer circuitry which analyzes the incoming sounds to determine their
frequency, rhythms, and loudness. Then it suppresses background noise
and enhances speech by using the results from the analysis. Even though
the Phoenix costs more and is bulkier, it works better than regular hearing aids.

If a person's hearing loss is so great that a digital hearing aid such   5
as the Phoenix does not improve hearing, the person may want to consider
a cochlear implant. A cochlear implant is a small electronic device
implanted in the inner ear that acts as a substitute for hair cells that
have been damaged by loud noises or other causes. As explained by
Philipos C. Loizou, all cochlear implant devices include

> a microphone that picks up the sound, a signal processor
> that converts the sound into electrical signals, a transmiss-
> ion system that transmits the electrical signals to the
> implanted electrodes, and an electrode or an electrode array
> (consisting of multiple electrodes) that is inserted into the
> cochlea by a surgeon. ("Introduction")

Various frequencies of sound stimulate different electrodes, which
actually function like hairs, protruding out of the cells and stimulating
the auditory nerves, which in turn causes the brain to perceive the
"sounds." These sounds may be distorted, but with training most people
report improvement in hearing.

Hearing-impaired individuals—especially those who begin to lose   6
the ability to hear at a young age—may also have trouble with speaking.
With the help of the cochlear implant, people whose speech becomes
impaired along with their hearing may also improve their speaking
abilities by the use of sensors and computers. A hearing-impaired person is fitted with sensors that are placed on the nose and inside the
mouth. A speech pathologist is fitted with the same type of sensors. The
sensors are hooked to a computer that generates an image on a video
screen which illustrates the vibration of the speech pathologist's
nose, the tongue position within the mouth, and the intensity of the
speech pathologist's voice when he or she speaks sounds or words. The
hearing-impaired person then tries to duplicate the items on the video
screen.

Once hearing-impaired people learn to speak, or improve their speak-   7
ing ability, they can communicate via telephone with the use of a keyboard that allows messages to be sent over the telephone lines to a small
video screen or a printer. The T.D.D. (telecommunication device for the
deaf), also known as a TTY (text telephone), is similar in size to a small

laptop computer, has a QWERTY keyboard, and an LCD screen that electronically shows text that has been sent over a telephone line. Relay services also allow a hearing or speech disabled person to communicate over a regular voice phone with the help of a human operator ("Telecommunications").

Another technological advancement is closed caption, the process of displaying dialogue on a television screen. A digital code, activated by a computer chip, prints the words of the television show on the screen. Closed caption has become more available in the past 20 years due to the Television Decoder Circuitry Act, passed by Congress in 1990. The act stated that by July 1, 1993, any television set with a screen larger than 33 centimeters (13 inches) must have a built-in closed caption decoder. After this time, any production without the decoder would be declared illegal (Television Decoder Circuitry Act). 8

By reducing the noises we hear to under ninety decibels or by taking simple precautions such as wearing ear plugs when working around loud equipment, we can prevent damage to our hearing. The inconveniences of hearing loss far outweigh the inconveniences of prevention. The sense of hearing is important for survival and should be taken care of just as we take care of our lives. More and more advances are being developed every year to improve hearing problems that could have been prevented, but they are expensive and do not always cure the problem. Prevention is the only one hundred percent cure for hearing impairments. 9

Works Cited

Loizou, Philipos. "Introduction to Cochlear Implants." *IEEE Signal Processing Magazine* Sept. 1998: 101–130. Web. 24 Mar. 2007.

"Telecommunications Device for the Deaf." *Wikipedia Encyclopedia*. 1 Mar. 2007. Web. 24 Mar. 2007.

Television Decoder Circuitry Act of 1990. Web. 24 Mar. 2007.

■   ■   ■

Holm's report generally follows the basic structure outlined on page 442. However, she varies the basic structure by describing the problem of hearing loss in her first paragraph before providing background about causes of the problem and an explanation of how the ear works, and she delays until the third paragraph her thesis that technology can cure or improve problems in hearing loss. The body of Holm's report (paragraphs 4–8) focuses on technological solutions for hearing loss: the Phoenix hearing aid, a cochlear implant, sensors and computers, T.D.D. or TTY, and closed captioning. Her final paragraph concludes that although prevention is the best way to avoid hearing problems, new improvements in technology can treat or minimize the effects of hearing loss. The essay as a whole is clear, concise, informative, and well organized—displaying all of the characteristics of an effective report.

Assignments

1. Write a report in which you explain how a particular type of technology has been used to solve a problem—perhaps an environmental problem or a health problem as shown in Holm's report.

2. Write a report analyzing either the positive or negative effects of computers as educational tools. You may find some helpful information in the essays by Rich, Young, and Laird.

3. Write a report in which you discuss the problem of addiction to some form of technology, such as television, video or computer games, or the Internet. Then propose one or more potential solutions to this problem. (You may want to focus your report more on the problem or the solution.) To gather information for your report, you might do field research in the form of interviews and observations. The report by Young, which is based primarily on interviews and questionnaire results, is an excellent example of a problem/solution report based on field research.

AS YOU WRITE

After selecting the topic of your report, research your subject in the library, on the Internet, and/or through field research, being sure to take careful notes. Use the guide on page 442 to plan and perhaps outline your report, adapting the plan as necessary for your material and the type of report you are writing (problem/solution, investigative, or analytic). Then use your plan and your notes to draft your report, being sure to cite any outside sources you use, both in the text of your report and in a Works Cited section. (See the *Modern Language Association Documentation Style Guide* from Purdue University's Writing Lab in the "Related Websites" section of the Interactions, eighth edition, website, at www.cengagebrain.com, for help with documenting your report.)

AFTER YOU WRITE

After you complete a draft of your report, reread it to be sure it includes each of the elements of an effective report listed on page 442. In fact, you might identify the purpose of each of your paragraphs and label them, just as we have identified the purpose of each of Holm's paragraphs on page 445. Then reread each paragraph to be sure it achieves its purpose clearly and that you have provided each of the following elements:

- Background information
- A statement of the problem (or situation)

- A clear thesis statement
- Relevant and specific support
- A logical conclusion
- Clear recommendation(s)
- Accurate and complete citation of outside sources in your text and in a Works Cited section

After you analyze the content and development of your report, edit it for problems in grammar, usage, sentence structure, and style. Then proofread your report and submit the final draft to your instructor.

■ EXPLORING IDEAS TOGETHER

1. Working with a group of your classmates, write a brief technical definition of a simple machine, describing it, identifying its function, and telling how it differs from other machines with similar functions. For example, you might define a hammer, a stapler, nail clippers, a pair of scissors, or a screwdriver. Be as factual and objective as possible in this definition. Then exchange your group's definition with that of another group and critique one another's work. Begin your definition by writing that "The _____ is a tool (or hand tool, or machine) that. . . ." Then distinguish it from other tools (hand tools, machines, etc.)

2. Some fantasy and science fiction writers often *personify* machines. That is, they give the machines the attributes and characteristics of a human. Work with a group of your classmates to write a brief narrative or description of a common machine (such as a computer, car, vending machine, alarm clock, or microwave oven), personifying it by giving it a name and other human characteristics. Exaggerate your narrative for humorous effect.

3. Discuss with a small group of your classmates the effects of technology on individuals as opposed to its effects on society as a whole. Is it possible that a certain technology or machine may benefit an individual yet harm society? For example, cars make life easier on individuals but create problems (pollution, dependency on oil-producing nations, deteriorating highways, and so on) for our society. Make a list of different technologies and machines, and decide whether each benefits both individuals and society or just (or primarily) individuals.

4. Discuss the influence that the media have on you and your classmates. How do the media affect what you buy, which movies and television shows you watch, which candidates you support, and what you think about certain events? Be sure to include specific examples in your discussion.

■ EXPLORING THE INTERNET

You can find links for most of the following exercises at the *Interactions*, eighth edition, student website, available at www.cengagebrain.com.

1. In her essay "Games and Literacy," Liz Danforth lists several gaming websites that she recommends for additional information about gaming (see pages 389–392). If you are a gamer yourself, select one of these sites, review it, and evaluate it.

2. An excellent educational site about the media is the MEF: Media Education Foundation site, available as a link on the *Interactions* student website. The MEF site provides educational assignments and printable handouts as well as news and articles. We particularly recommend the educational assignments under "Handouts & Downloads," one of which is "Substances as Stress Relievers: Deconstructing Advertisements." Divide your class into three groups, with each group working on one of the topics and the accompanying advertisement provided in the assignment: Advertising Food, Advertising Cigarettes, or Alcohol Advertising. (This site also includes other good assignments such as "War Games: Thinking Critically about Video Games That Play at War" and "Deconstructing an Alcohol Advertisement." However, you will have to provide your own alcohol advertisement for the latter assignment.)

3. Work in small groups of three or four, with each member giving a brief investigative report on a new technological discovery or application that she or he has read about on the web. To prepare for your group discussion, go to the *MIT Technology Review* website (you might try the "Expanded List" of articles) or to the technology section of one of these sources: *Time* (look up "Techland"), *Newsweek* (look up "Technology"), or *CNN Technology Page*. These websites are all available as links on the *Interactions* student website, but you may be able to access only abstracts of some recent articles.

4. Although most media websites and news organizations purport to be unbiased in their reporting, it is difficult for any organization or individual to be completely objective. Explore the websites of the Media Research Center and FAIR: Fairness and Accuracy in Reporting, both of which are media groups, to identify liberal and conservative reporting. (See the "Related Websites" section of the *Interactions* student website.) You may want to divide into small groups, with each group comparing how the two websites treat a single topic. Then compare your results and conclusions with those of the rest of the class.

■ WRITING ESSAYS

1. Imagine that the machines and technology on which you depend were suddenly destroyed or inoperative. Write an imaginative narrative

describing what a typical day in your life would be like if this were to happen.

2. Write a humorous essay about a time when you were frustrated by a certain machine (for example, when your car would not start, a vending machine would not give you your selection or return your money, your smoke alarm kept going off, or your microwave burned your dinner).

3. Write an essay about a time when you skillfully operated a machine. How did you overcome the challenges of the task, and how did you feel during and after the process?

4. Write an essay in which you argue that the effects of a particular type or use of technology—such as television, cell phones, TiVos, computers, or the Internet—are either positive or negative. You may use support from readings in this unit that are relevant to your topic, and you may do additional research on the Internet by using a search engine such as Google. (For help with writing persuasive essays, see pages 372–378 of Unit Six.)

5. Write an essay in which you argue for or against the idea that men are more fascinated by machines and technology than women are. Before you write, decide whether you are writing for an audience of males, females, or both. (For help with writing persuasive essays, see pages 372–378 of Unit Six.)

6. Write an essay in which you discuss how the Internet has changed—and will continue to change—our lives. You might focus on its use in one of these activities: shopping, keeping up with the news, entertainment, or socializing. In this particular area of life, is the effect of the Internet primarily positive or negative? Why? (You may want to review some of the essays in this unit—particularly those by Rich, Young, Laird, Niedzviecki, Caudron, and Grossman—before writing your essay. See also pages 372–379 for instructions on writing persuasive essays.)

7. Write an essay in which you identify the type of media that you think represents the news most truthfully, and argue for the effectiveness of this medium in comparison with others. (See pages 372–378 of Unit Six for help with writing persuasive essays.)

8. Write an essay in which you compare and contrast the coverage of a recent event by one or more Internet blogs with reports by one or more mainstream media sources (newspapers, magazines, broadcast news, etc.). For help in citing your sources for this assignment and for any of the other assignments in this unit, you may refer to Purdue University's Writing Lab website, which includes a helpful section on using Modern Language Association documentation style. You will find this website listed in the "Related Websites" section of the *Interactions* website.

HEROES AND
ROLE MODELS

Look carefully at the photograph above and imagine a storyline to go with it. What has happened—and what is happening—in the background? What is the fireman directing others to do? What does the expression on the fireman's face tell you about the danger of the situation? Are this fireman and others working with him heroic?

M ost of us have heroes or at least role models—*people whom we admire because they have done something we consider noble, brave, or generous. Traditionally, heroes were male figures who performed remarkable feats of bravery. These traditional heroes slew dragons, fought in battles, embarked on exciting adventures, or went on long, difficult quests.*

During the last quarter of the twentieth century, however, political scandals and the media's close scrutiny of public figures took a heavy toll on society's belief in contemporary heroes and role models. Simultaneously, historians and teachers began calling attention to the human faults of traditional heroes such as Christopher Columbus, George Washington, and Thomas Jefferson. In searching for people to admire, people have increasingly focused on celebrities, such as models, movie stars, and sports figures. As a result, before the events of September 11, 2001, we were in danger of becoming a nation without heroes.

The many heroic responses to the devastation created by the terrorists who transformed fuel-filled passenger planes into lethal weapons against the Pentagon and the World Trade Center have forever changed the way we view heroes. The brave individuals who responded to this attack— including firefighters, police officers, paramedics, ordinary citizens, and (perhaps most notably) the passengers who crashed their plane into the Pennsylvania countryside rather than allow it to be used as another missile—have restored and enlarged our faith in heroism. In the aftermath of the terrorist attacks we recognize heroes not just on the battlefield but also in our daily lives. Quiet and unassuming, many heroes today are displaying a courage that is moral and emotional as well as physical.

In this unit you will read about male and female heroes, about heroes and role models, about traditional heroes and nontraditional heroes, about real heroes and inflated heroes. You will consider how society's view of its heroes is affected by the media, and you will discover that heroes can be ordinary as well as extraordinary. Finally, you will turn your focus back to yourself as a potential hero, considering yourself in the context of the heroes and heroic acts you have read about.

Before reading the selections in this unit, consider the following questions, perhaps responding to one or more in your journal or discussing selected questions with a group of your classmates:

1. *How do you define a hero? What qualities does a hero have? Is a hero the same as a role model or something quite different? Explain.*
2. *Are heroes born or made? Are heroes discovered or developed? Is character a qualification for heroes, or is the act of heroism the issue?*
3. *Are heroes perfect or imperfect? Have you ever been disappointed with or disillusioned by someone you considered a hero? How?*
4. *How do the media portray heroes? Do the media confuse heroes with celebrities and role models? Explain.*
5. *Do you define male and female heroes in the same way? Does our society have more male heroes than female heroes? Why or why not? Does this situation reflect the basic heroism of men and women or the beliefs and traditions of our society? How?*

6. *Do you believe that our society has more or fewer heroes today than in the past? Why or why not? Have your ideas about heroes and heroism changed recently—especially since September 11, 2001? If so, how?*
7. *Have you ever witnessed a heroic act? What was this act and why was it heroic? What do heroic acts have in common?*
8. *Who is your favorite hero? Why did you select this person?*
9. *Have you ever been a hero? Do you think you could be? Why or why not?*

As this unit shows, heroes and role models influence our beliefs and goals and even shape the people that we become, showing us the potential for goodness that lies within us all. Ultimately, heroes teach us as much about who we are as about who they are. Clearly, we still need heroes.

FOCUS: DEFINITION

Larger Than Life

■   ▦   ■

PHILIP TOSHIO SUDO

Philip Sudo was a Japanese American musician, black-belt martial artist, and author of four books, including *Zen Guitar* and *Zen 24/7*. After working as a journalist in New York, Sudo spent 12 years in Japan studying Zen, a branch of Buddhism focusing on individual potential to achieve enlightenment, and five years on the island of Maui writing and raising a family. Sudo died of cancer in June 2002. The following essay, written while Sudo was managing editor of *Scholastic*, defines the word *hero* and argues that we can learn about the values of a society from its heroes.

BEFORE YOU READ

■ **THINK** about your own heroes. That is, think about the men and women you look up to as heroes. Do you admire these people because they are attractive, famous, or wealthy? Or do you look up to them because they have performed some great good, not for themselves but for humanity?

■ **EXAMINE** the title "Larger Than Life." What does this title suggest about Sudo's view of heroes? Examine also Sudo's first paragraph and subheadings. What do they suggest about Sudo's definition of a hero?

■ **WRITE** a journal entry listing some living men and women whom you consider to be heroes.

AS YOU READ

Underline Sudo's definitions of *hero*.

■   ▦   ■

The word "hero" comes from the Greek word *heros*, meaning to protect or to serve. Originally, the term applied only to mythical figures—gods or semidivine beings, such as Hercules and Perseus, who excelled in battle and embodied such values as courage and loyalty. The ancient Greeks developed an entire tradition of literature around such heroes; in classic epics like the *Iliad* and the *Odyssey,* Homer spun tales of

1

the brave Odysseus and other warriors, whose adventures were first passed down orally, then later through the written word.

The notion of heroes was not unique to the West. Other early societies, 2 such as China and India, developed similar traditions, around heroes such as Kuan Ti and epics like the *Mahabharata.*

Over time, historians began to look upon real people as heroes—Simón 3 Bolívar, Sun Yat-sen, George Washington—larger-than-life individuals who founded countries or dedicated their lives to liberation. These were the rare men and women who embodied, as one historian wrote, "the perfect expression of the ideal of a group, in whom all human virtues unite."

Learning the tales of these greats helps forge values and a cultural identity. 4 When you read the story of George Washington cutting down a cherry tree and saying, "I cannot tell a lie," you learn the value of honesty in American society. In Japan, when schoolchildren read the tale of the 47 *Ronin,* a band of samurai who stick together through years of hardship to avenge their master's death, they learn the value of loyalty and group togetherness. . . .

In this country, some educators believe our heroes are too one-sided. 5 U.S. history books, they say, are filled with the accomplishments of white European males to the exclusion of women and minorities.

In fact, many Americans today are beginning to question the very defi- 6 nition of a "hero." These days, we bestow the honor mainly on sports figures, movie stars, musicians, and comedians. "The word 'hero' is a debased word," says Michael Lesy, a professor at Hampshire College in Amherst, Mass., and author of the . . . book *Rescues.* It has become confused with "celebrity," "role model," and "idol," he says. . . .

WHAT MAKES A HERO?

But if there is argument over what constitutes a "hero," few among us fail 7 to admire heroic acts. Thwarting a robbery, rescuing a drowning man, pulling a child from a burning house—these are all unquestionable acts of heroism. And while the brave souls who perform them may never become famous or reap rewards, they are certainly heroes.

In fact, the one trait of heroes that transcends all cultural boundaries, 8 Lesy says, is the willingness to risk one's life for the good of others. "It's not an American trait, it's not Japanese, it's not Iraqi, it's the bottom-line of the human species," he says.

Consider the words of Nelson Mandela: "I have cherished the idea of a 9 democratic and free society. It is an ideal which I hope to live for and to achieve. But if needs be, it is an ideal for which I am prepared to die."

And these words from slain civil rights leader Martin Luther King, Jr.: 10 "If a man hasn't found something he will die for, he isn't fit to live."

POTENTIAL WITHIN US ALL

We hail these men as heroes because their courage gives us strength, their 11 ideals give us vision, and their spirit enlarges our own. But keep in mind that, extraordinary as these heroes may seem, they are still human beings like you and me. And as such, they demonstrate that within all of us, there is the potential to become heroes ourselves.

Look around you, at your friends, your family, your school. Is there   12
someone among them that you'd call a hero? Probably so.

Now take a look in the mirror. What do you see?   13

What do you *want* to see?   14

■ ■ ■

AFTER YOU READ

■ **THINK** about the last section of Sudo's reading, noting particularly his statement that we all have "the potential to become heroes ourselves." Although Sudo didn't ever call himself a hero, many of his friends who observed his brave battle against cancer did consider his actions to be heroic. To get a sense of Sudo's courageous personal struggle and his unselfish values, read sections of his online "Cancer Journal." (See "Related Websites" on the *Interactions* student site, at www.cengagebrain.com.)

■ **THINK** also about the last section of Sudo's reading, subtitled "Potential within Us All." Do you see a potential hero when you look in the mirror? How do you think you could become more heroic? Would you have to save someone's life to become a hero, or could you perform heroic acts and make heroic decisions in your daily life?

■ **EXAMINE** how Sudo develops his definition of a hero. Like most definition essays, this one also uses several other methods of development, including examples, comparison and contrast, and cause and effect. Find examples of each of these methods of development in the essay. (You may find that you have already underlined passages exhibiting these methods of development.)

■ **EXAMINE** also the specific qualities that, according to Sudo, make a hero. Sudo gives a formal definition when he places a *hero* in the larger group of "real people" and then distinguishes heroes from other "real people" by describing them as "larger-than-life individuals" who are willing to risk their lives for "the good of others" (paragraphs 3 and 8). As you read definitions of *hero* by other writers in this unit, compare these definitions with Sudo's.

■ **WRITE** an essay giving your own definition of *hero*. Before you write your definition, review the list of heroes that you wrote before reading the selection. What qualities do these people have in common? How is your definition similar to or different from Sudo's definition? (See Lesson 8 on the *Interactions*, eighth edition, student website at www.cengagebrain.com for instructions on writing definition essays.)

Risking Your Life for Another

■ ■ ■

JOHN QUIÑONES

Although he is a fifth-generation San Antonian, John Quiñones did not learn English until he started to school. Nevertheless, he was able to graduate not only with a bachelor's degree from St. Mary's University but also with a master's degree from the Columbia University School of Journalism. While attending college, Quiñones worked for local radio stations, but his real success began when he started working for *ABC News* in 1982. The winner of several awards, including seven Emmy awards, Quiñones has appeared on *20/20, PrimeTime,* and ABC's *World News Tonight.* The following selection comes from his 2008 book, *Heroes Among Us: Ordinary People, Extraordinary Choices.*

BEFORE YOU READ

■ **THINK** about what you would do if you saw one or more people in trouble or in danger and had the ability to help. What would you do if you realized that helping these people would also put you in danger?

■ **EXAMINE** the title and first paragraph of this essay. How does the title relate to Philip Sudo's definition of a hero in the previous essay? How does the first paragraph capture your attention? What questions do you have after reading this paragraph?

■ **EXAMINE** also the word *corrosion,* reading its surrounding context in paragraph 10. What clues to the meaning of this word do you find? It might also help to know that this word derives from the Latin *corrōdere,* meaning "to gnaw to pieces." If you are still unsure of the word's meaning, look it up in a dictionary.

■ **WRITE** a journal entry telling about a time when you helped someone who was in trouble or in danger.

AS YOU READ

Write a C beside paragraphs that describe possible causes of the bridge collapse; write an E beside those paragraphs that describe effects of that collapse.

■ ■ ■

Twenty-year-old Jeremy Hernandez wasn't feeling at all spectacular   1
on the sunny day when fate called him to risk his life for the sake
of another—actually, make that fifty others, all of them children.
Instead, he was sleeping in the back of the bus.

It was August 1, 2007, a typical day of a typical Midwestern summer   2
in Minneapolis. Jeremy was the gym coordinator for a group of kids ranging in age from kindergarten to high school at Waite House Neighborhood
Day Camp. His job was to play games with the kids and help with the
swimming classes. He loved it even though most days he came home
completely exhausted.

Jeremy spent that morning giving swimming lessons to fifty-two kids,   3
which would be enough to wear out even the hardiest person. The bus
driver, a woman named Kim Dahl, was taking them back to the camp's
home base at Waite House when traffic slowed to a crawl. The eight-lane
bridge they were taking across the Mississippi River was being repaired,
with several lanes closed, so the rush-hour traffic had to squeeze into a
tight space.

The work had been going all summer, as huge crews of more than a   4
dozen guys with jackhammers pounded away at the concrete. So the traffic
wasn't a surprise. But the bridge collapsing was. It fell right out from under
them and into the Mississippi River.

Thirteen people died in the tragedy, and nearly a hundred, including   5
twenty-two children, were treated at hospitals. There could easily have
been fifty more casualties, all of them kids. But there weren't, thanks in
great part to Jeremy.

What a way to wake up.   6

Bridge 9340, as it was officially known, was built between 1964 and   7
1967 to carry highway I-35W across the Mississippi River in Minneapolis,
and just below St. Anthony's Falls' lock and dam. The 1,907-foot bridge
had fourteen spans, including three long main spans that rose over the
rough waters downstream from the falls. The structure wasn't what you
would call a work of art, like the Brooklyn Bridge or the Golden Gate
Bridge, but it was well used. Before Bridge 9340 collapsed, about
140,000 cars crossed it on a typical day. If you lived in the Twin Cities,
you'd have used it. There's no other option.

Minneapolis and its sister city, St. Paul, suffer incredibly cold and icy   8
winters. Whenever I'm there between November and March, I long for the
healing warmth and sunshine of Miami or points farther south. But most
Minneapolitans seem to love their winters, and they do a lot to adapt to
them. Up there, people even plug in their cars during the coldest months
to keep the oil in the crankcase from getting too sluggish. The locals are
tough, and they're used to hazardous conditions. Even so, Bridge 9340
was known as a danger zone.

One year it was named the most treacherous cold-weather stretch of   9
freeway in the Twin Cities. That's because some combination of how it

was constructed, the wet wind of St. Anthony's Falls, and other factors made it common for a layer of thin black ice to form on the roadway when the temperature dropped below 30 degrees, which is often. Cars routinely spun out on the black ice and collided with one another.

To counter this, in 2000 the Minnesota Department of transportation 10 installed temperature-activated nozzles to spray the surface with a de-icer when it dropped below freezing. Some people think this chemical might have weakened the bridge. Apparently, there were cracks and corrosion visible on the underside of the bridge. And perhaps the weight of the cars and workers, and the jackhammering, had weakened the bridge more than anyone imagined.

Whatever the cause, at 6:05 p.m., the long central span shook and 11 there was a huge rumbling. But it wasn't like the famous video of Galloping Gertie, the bridge that in 1940 started swaying in gale force winds over the Tacoma, Washington, narrows, until it undulated like a ribbon in the wind before collapsing. No, the Minneapolis bridge just fell in one flat piece, like a cracker falling from your hand to the floor. The entire middle section went into the river in one awful moment, sending shock waves of water high into the air. One driver said he felt the road bend and twist, and then suddenly all the cars ahead just vanished. Behind him, the broken roadway went downhill until it connected with the riverbank. He backed down it to the end. Looking through his windshield, he saw the cars farther up sliding toward him. They crashed into a pile nearby.

A video of the collapse shows the whole thing happening in a matter of 12 seconds. Suddenly, there were cars in the water, trucks dangling off the edge, cars stranded on chunks of concrete. There were people swimming. People fleeing. Others were running to help. On land, terrified people screamed. In the water, victims tried to claw their way out of cars. Frantic men and women shouted into cell phones everywhere, overwhelming the 911 switchboards.

There were many heroes that day—civilians making 911 calls, the di- 13 vers braving the treacherous currents, the police, the firefighters—but Jeremy stands out.

It was Wednesday, the kids at Waite House had gone to a big water 14 park, and everyone was worn-out from the sun and fun. Headed toward home base, Kim, the driver, downshifted into the bumper-to-bumper traffic. They were running late. Her own two kids were with her on the trip that day, but she worried that the other parents might start to worry.

As they inched along a section of the bridge that spanned the riverbank 15 with a good view of the waterfall upstream, one of the kids woke Jeremy. So much for his nap. He looked out the window at the waterfalls below. Then the concrete turned to Jell-O. The span bent, and the bus careened downhill as if it was on skis.

"I thought I was dreaming," Jeremy said.   16

The section they were on split from the roadway and dropped about 17 twenty feet, sending the bus careening to the side.

Jeremy Hernandez was wide awake now.   18

"It was almost like a wave happened and the whole bridge went   19
down," Kim said. "I mean we were just going straight down, not knowing
what was happening, just scared to death."

The bus fell with the roadway.   20

I can't even imagine.   21

The bus and its section of roadway fell until one end crashed into the   22
riverbank and the other end dangled from broken bridge parts above.

"It felt like we were on a roller-coaster ride at Valley Fair and my   23
stomach was in my chest and I was waiting for it to stop," said Jeremy.

Kim slammed on the brakes, not knowing what else she could do. The   24
bus slammed against the guardrail, a truck, who knows. There was broken
glass everywhere. The bus came to a stop at the railing, finally. The railing
held firm. They were not going to tumble off the bridge.

Kim realized she couldn't feel anything in her legs. She was injured.   25
But the kids were her first priority. What a relief, then, to have Jeremy
Hernandez on board—even though he still didn't know he was about to
become a hero.

Dust filled the air. A semi nearby burst into flames. The kids started   26
screaming. One teenager used her cell phone to call her mom. She got
voicemail.

"Mom, answer the phone, it's me," she cried into the phone.   27
"Momma. Momma."

Jeremy was scared, but he didn't have time to think. As the dust set-   28
tled, the view got clearer and he could see the disaster: rebar sticking up
from chunks of concrete, twisted steel, smashed cars, people wandering the
bridge.

"We're going to go in the river, we're going to go into the river," some   29
kids screamed.

When some others heard that, they started screaming, too.   30

"We're going in the river!"   31

"I looked over the water and my heart started beating fast," Jeremy   32
said. The bus felt like it was still moving. He didn't want to die on this
bus. And he didn't want to fall into the river. He'd swum in the Mississippi
before, and he knew it was powerful. It was at this point that he made a
courageous decision.

In some ways, it wasn't even a decision. It was just instinct.   33

"I jumped over the seats, and I opened the emergency door and kicked   34
the coolers that were blocking it out of the way."

He could have jumped out and run for his life, saved himself and to   35
hell with the others. But he didn't.

The possibility didn't cross his mind. Not with all the kids on the bus.   36

"They're like my brothers, my little sisters. I've been working here for   37
years, I feel like they're a part of me. Every day, I come, I come to see 'em,
their smiles," he said.

Not to mention the other counselors. And poor Kim, the bus driver,   38
who was hurt.

The kids surged toward the open door. A man came to the back of the 39
bus and Jeremy started handing kids off to him. Throwing them really. He
was that desperate to save them. The kids lined up together along the edge
of the bus. Jeremy could still feel the bridge shaking. Who knew if it would
collapse further?

"You got to get off the bridge, you got to get off the bridge," he 40
shouted at the kids.

More people ran up and Jeremy kept handing kids to them. Ten, 41
twenty, thirty, the kids just kept on coming.

"I just remember grabbing one and then putting them down, grabbing 42
and then putting them down," said Jeremy. "It felt like it went on forever."

The children were screaming and clutching any adult they could reach. 43
They were sure they were going to die.

"It was terrifying," said one of Jeremy's fellow counselors. "But our 44
bus was one of the lucky ones. People died in that collapse. It felt like it
was a miracle we didn't."

Jeremy says he was just glad to be able to help. And lucky to be alive 45
to see another day.

After he got all the kids safely off the bus, along with the counselors 46
and the driver, Jeremy took a careful look around to be sure none of the
kids had strayed from the group. He looked at the semi that burned uncontrollably nearby. He looked at the block of cement that had fallen on another vehicle. He looked down toward the river where rescue workers were
struggling against the current to find survivors. He felt blessed.

Jeremy stayed at the disaster until every single child was either reunited 47
with their parents or taken to the hospital. When he got home, he realized
how much his own hip and leg hurt. But other than that, he was fine.

A hero? He didn't think about it, but I have. And I'm here to say that 48
he is. I'm proud to breathe the same air as this guy.

■   ■   ■

AFTER YOU READ

■ **THINK** about how Jeremy must have felt when he was jolted awake
after the collapse of the bridge and looked out of the window (paragraphs 6 and 15). What were his initial reactions (paragraphs 16–23,
28)? What decision does he make (paragraphs 32 and 33)? Why do
you think he made this decision?

■ **EXAMINE** the marginal notations you made indicating the causes and
effects of the bridge collapse. What were some possible causes of the disaster? What were some of the major effects? Your class might break
into several groups, with one group finding and discussing the causes,
another group discussing the immediate effects on the bridge itself,

another discussing the effect on the bridge's occupants (except Jeremy), and a fourth group discussing the effects on Jeremy and his actions.

■ **EXAMINE** also the last paragraph of the essay. Do you agree that Jeremy was an exceptional hero on August 1, 2007? Explain why or why not.

■ **WRITE** an essay explaining how and why you helped someone who was in danger or trouble—or in which you describe the actions of someone you know, have heard about, or read about who helped someone in a dangerous or troublesome situation. In your conclusion, state whether you think your actions or the actions of the helper you are writing about were truly heroic or simply kind and thoughtful.

My Right Hand

■ ■ ■

MICHAEL WEISSKOPF

A senior correspondent for *Time* magazine, Michael Weisskopf has won many awards, including the Goldsmith Award for Investigative Reporting, the National Headliners Award, and the Daniel Pearl Award for Courage and Integrity in Journalism. While riding in an open Army Humvee in Baghdad with photographer James Nachtwey and soldiers Private Orion Jenks and Private First Class Jim Beverly on December 23, 2003, Weisskopf threw out a grenade that had landed in their vehicle, losing a hand in the process. In his award-winning book *Blood Brothers* (2006), he wrote about his experience and the experiences of three soldiers he met in the amputee ward of Walter Reed Medical Center. The following excerpt from the book was published in *Time* on October 6, 2006.

BEFORE YOU READ

- ■ **THINK** about the conflicts in Iraq, Afghanistan, and anywhere else in the world where American soldiers and journalists are in danger. Do you believe these people display heroism in their jobs and their daily lives? If possible, describe a particular act of heroism by a soldier or a journalist.

- ■ **EXAMINE** the first two paragraphs in which Weisskopf describes the background setting for his injury. What specific details help you to visualize this setting? (You may not know the word *byzantine*, which refers to the complex architecture and politics developed in the 1,000-year-long empire founded by Constantine in 330 A.D. at Byzantium, the natural transit point between Asia Minor and Europe that was renamed Constantinople.) Then read the third paragraph. How does Weisskopf build suspense and make you want to continue reading?

- ■ **EXAMINE** also the word *prostheses* (paragraph 16), which means artificial limbs or other artificial parts of the body. A *prosthetist* (paragraph 15) is one who makes, fits, and attaches a prosthesis.

- ■ **WRITE** a journal entry about the heroism of a particular soldier or journalist you know or have heard about.

AS YOU READ

Look for passages that show changes in Weisskopf's attitude toward his heroism and his resulting disability.

■ ■ ■

The Army convoy rattled through Al-Adhamiya like a carnival roller coaster, each turn as blind as the next. Not that the soldiers could see much anyway. Night had fallen on the old Baghdad quarter, a byzantine maze lit only by kerosene lamps flickering from rugged stone houses. We moved warily in the darkness, patrolling for insurgents in blind alleys custom-made for ambushes and narrow passages perfect for concealing roadside bombs. It was anyone's bet who faced a more dire risk, the hunted in terrorist cells or the hunters in humvees, along with whom I was riding under a half-moon. I was in Iraq to profile the American soldier as "Person of the Year" for TIME magazine. It was a dream assignment, a chance to escape Washington and work in exotic environs on a big story.

We emerged into Al-Adhamiya's main marketplace, a large treeless square that was host to what looked like a block party in full swing. Old men, rocking back and forth on tiny stools, shuffled dominoes. Boys volleyed soccer balls. Women veiled in black fed their children from stalls of roasted chickens and *shashlik*. No one seemed to notice the foreign invaders passing by.

At first I thought it was a rock, the specialty of street urchins—a harmless shot against an armored humvee. I gazed down and spotted an object on the wooden bench 2 ft. away. The dark oval was as shiny and smooth as a tortoiseshell, roughly 6 in. long and 4 in. wide. None of my fellow passengers seemed to notice. I confronted the intruder alone, a journalist caught in a military moment. Something told me there was no time to consult the soldiers.

I rose halfway, leaned to the right, and cupped the object. I might as well have plucked volcanic lava from a crater. I could feel the flesh of my palm liquefying. Pain bolted up my arm like an electric current. In one fluid motion, I raised my right arm and started to throw the mass over the side of the vehicle, a short backhand toss. Then everything went dark.

The humvee bed was cold and hard, an inhospitable place to awaken. I struggled to sit up and fell back. My right leg burned from knee to hip. Blood was oozing from it; my right arm felt heavy and numb. Was I having a nightmare? The hollow, faraway sound of voices was dreamlike. I shook my right arm, trying to wake it up. Still no response. I elevated it to see why.

My wrist looked like the neck of a decapitated chicken. The wound was jagged, the blood glistening in the light. My mouth was dry, my brow soaked in sweat; my heart beat quickly and weakly, little dings in my chest.

All sound and sight dimmed, as my thoughts turned inward. This is 7
not how I pictured my life ending; futilely and unglamorously, on the frigid
floor of a truck, thousands of miles away from anyone I loved.

After medic Billie Grimes stopped the bleeding with an elastic cord, I was 8
rushed in the humvee to a nearby brigade clinic and then medevacked to a
U.S. Army hospital elsewhere in Baghdad for surgery to clean what was
left of my arm and the shrapnel wounds in my right thigh. There, I learned
that everyone else in the back of the humvee had survived, though Jenks
had serious leg wounds, Beverly had knee and hand injuries and Nachtwey
had taken shrapnel in his knees and abdomen. The next morning, a
middle-aged nurse with blond highlights approached my bed.

"You're a hero," she said. "You lost a hand and saved lives."   9

Hero? I was feeling anything but valiant. Mangled. Pitiful. Disoriented. 10
Scared. I was anxious about my ability to work again with one hand and
to parent my children, who lived with me half-time in Washington. My son
Skyler was 11 years old, the same age I had been when my father, a work-
aholic community newspaper publisher, dropped dead of a heart attack.
Olivia was 8, roughly as old as my sister had been. I couldn't bear to think
I might let such wrenching family history repeat itself.

Mostly, however, I was angry at myself for getting in the wrong hum- 11
vee, releasing the grenade too slowly, even grabbing it in the first place.
Nothing would have happened if I hadn't picked it up. Why had I been
acting like a cowboy? Why hadn't I just left the damn thing alone?

"It was an impulsive act," I told the nurse. "If I hadn't picked it up, I'd 12
still have a hand."

"You probably wouldn't have had a life," she retorted. "You and 13
everyone else in the vehicle would have died. It wasn't an impulse; it was
an instinct to survive."

Dec. 10 marked the passing of a year since my injury. I knew I'd never 14
regain what I had lost in penmanship, tennis, home repair, lovemaking,
freedom from pain and dexterity. Even putting on a tie remained a challenge, one fraught with danger. Rushing to a TV appearance a few weeks
earlier, I tried to knot one in the backseat of a taxi. I gripped the short end
with my prosthetic hand, which began to spin uncontrollably, almost
strangling me before I managed to extricate myself.

Despite occasional disasters, however, I was adjusting to a fake arm— 15
thanks to certain modifications by prosthetist John Miguelez's team. Ralph
[the name I had given my unsuccessful myoelectric arm] had bit the dust,
replaced by a more tapered, slightly lighter shell made of carbon fiber and
acrylic resin. The modifications improved my range of motion and ward-
robe—I could now button a dress shirt. But I was hardly wearing a second
skin. The rigid shell chafed my forearm and got so hot in the summer that
sweat dripped out of a small hole used to put it on.

Before Iraq, the technology of arm prostheses hadn't changed much 16
since World War II. The tiny population of amputees created little market

incentive. Miguelez used the burst in demand from Walter Reed to lean on manufacturers for progress. Before long, he was outfitting Iraq war amputees with an electronic hand that opened and closed 2 1/2 times faster and could be programmed to function at different speeds and grip strength.

The cosmetic arts also had improved. I received a silicone hand that was   17
so lifelike it passed for real in social settings. But Pretty Boy, as I called it, kept tearing and afforded the precision of a boxing glove. It was too spongy to grasp anything small and too slippery to hold most objects for long.

Function was only part of the problem. The idea of trying to pass had   18
begun to trouble me. It made me feel as if I had something to hide or be ashamed of. When I started to go bald, I shaved my head. No comb-overs, transplants or toupees for me. So why try to conceal a handicap? I was now proud of how I had lost my hand. The stump had a story to tell, regardless of my motivations for grabbing a grenade. Why not draw attention to it?

No one could miss my disability now. I put on a hook for Thanksgiv-   19
ing dinner and never took it off. It twisted into the end of my myoelectric prosthesis and turned 360° like an electronic hand. Only it worked better. Two silver talons opened like forceps, locked on to items and could pick a dime off the floor. Occasionally I screwed on a plastic, clawlike device known by the German word for grabber—*Greifer*—to move heavy objects, and I contemplated the long list of attachments—garden tools, spatulas, hammers and pool-shooting bridges—that were available by special order. I usually sported the hook, however, even if it aroused more fear than friendship among people I passed on the street. Some kids cowered. Friends accepted it and greeted me with a high-two. Rebekah, who had agreed to marry me several months earlier, thought my choice impudent but sexy and advised me on clothing to complement it—black was obviously best.

Half a year after I dismissed the suggestion from a Walter Reed doctor,   20
the hook had become my trademark. It was brash, straightforward and pragmatic, virtues I cherished. I had left a lot of me behind in the Baghdad grenade attack. By its first anniversary, I was starting to reclaim it.

On July 3, Rebekah and I flew to Rancho Mirage, Calif., to celebrate my   21
stepfather's 90th birthday. My mother hosted a party in the main ballroom of a swank hotel, the Lodge, for more than 60 family members and friends. Inevitably, when the subject of my accident came up and led to admiring comments, I felt a familiar twinge of guilt and embarrassment. I still couldn't embrace the notion of my so-called heroism.

Lying awake that might, I was reminded of a conversation I'd had with   22
Hal Wain, a psychologist at Walter Reed. I had sought him out a few months earlier to discuss why I had grabbed the grenade. Wain said I had one overriding objective: self-preservation. "That's what all heroes are made of," he said. "I have learned from guys coming back that the instinct to survive, the instinct to take care of oneself or others, is incredibly potent. I really don't care if you did it for your needs or for others; you did it. The end result would have been the same—you saved people's lives."

Wain defined heroism as quick response to a changing environment, 23
like a driver who swerves into another lane for the purpose of avoiding
an oncoming car and, in the process, saves the life of his passenger.
"That wasn't his intent," he said. "But being flexible and shifting is a
higher level of intelligence. The people who can't change die."

I expressed my frustration that such a major ordeal had seemed to have 24
so little effect on me—I was still the same impatient, competitive and self-
critical person I'd always been. If I had acted so nobly, why didn't I feel
more content? Wain's response struck me at the time as somewhat facile: the
good deed, he said, had left me angry at myself. "You're thinking you could
have done the same thing and didn't have to lose the hand. You love a perfect
win and didn't get that perfect victory that you wanted and maybe deserved."

As I tossed and turned in the early hours of Independence Day, the 25
simple truth of the psychologist's words hit me. It was true: I was mad at
myself for failing to pull off a clean sweep. And it was that anger that was
preventing me from savoring the achievement of a lifetime: saving my own
skin and that of three others. My failure to get rid of the grenade before it
exploded was only the first in a long list of wrongs I would have to pardon
before I could finally put the ordeal behind me.

I had gone to Iraq for adventure and glory, discounting the interests of 26
family and friends.

I had blithely ridden into danger with little to gain journalistically.   27

I had focused more on the loss of my hand than on the higher impor- 28
tance of preserving life.

The shortcomings were tough to swallow. But I was resolved to begin 29
the process, keeping in mind Hal Wain's definition of heroism: self-
preservation. By that standard, I had scored a perfect win after all.

The prize was the rest of my life.   30

■   ■   ■

AFTER YOU READ

■ **THINK** about how Weisskopf first reacted to his injury. How does this
reaction change over time? What people and experiences contribute to
his changing attitude and personal growth? What important truths
does he realize, as stated in the last six paragraphs of the essay?

■ **EXAMINE** the definitions of a hero by the nurse (paragraphs 9–13) and
the psychologist Hal Wain (paragraphs 22–23). Do you agree or disagree with the nurse's assessment? Explain. Do you agree with Wain's
belief that the "overriding objective" of a hero is "self-preservation,"
or "the instinct to take care of oneself or others"? Why do you feel as
you do? Does taking care of oneself always coincide with taking care of
others, or are the two goals sometimes in opposition? Does Wain's definition describe or contradict the actions of those who risked or sacrificed their lives on September 11, 2001, to save others or Jeremy

Hernandez's decision in "Risking Your Life for Another" to go back to try to save the children in the bus on the collapsing bridge? Explain.

■ **EXAMINE** also the language of paragraph 4, especially the verbs. Weisskopf uses strong active verbs (such as *cupped, plucked,* and *bolted*) that vividly describe the events. Try to use this technique in your own writing.

■ **EXAMINE** also the term *high-two* in paragraph 19. Discuss with your classmates the significance of this phrase and of friends greeting Weisskopf with a "high-two" instead of a "high-five."

■ **WRITE** an essay about the heroism of a soldier or a journalist. You may write about someone you know, or you may focus on someone about whom you have heard or read. You may need to research this subject online or in the library. (Assignment 1 of "Exploring the Internet" provides one good source.)

Ferguson

■ ■ ■

MICHAEL NORMAN

Having been a professional writer and journalist for over 35 years, Michael Norman is currently a professor of journalism at New York University. Coauthored with his wife Elizabeth M. Norman, his latest book, *Tears in the Darkness: The Story of the Bataan Death March and Its Aftermath* (2010), received a starred review from *Booklist*. But the following essay derives from his Viet Nam experience, which he has previously described in *These Good Men: Friendships Forged from War* (1991). Norman's personal essay about the soldier "Ferguson," published in *The New York Times Magazine* in May 2008, certainly describes a brave and "good" man.

BEFORE YOU READ

■ **THINK** about Norman's statement in paragraph 1 that he's "not home yet." Since he is clearly physically home from Viet Nam, what does he mean here? How does the remainder of the paragraph help explain Norman's feelings in Viet Nam, soon after he returned to the States, and even now?

■ **EXAMINE** the phrase "toll the knell" in paragraph 2. To *toll* is to sound at regular intervals; *knell* is the slow, solemn, mournful sound of a bell. How much more effectively does this phrase indicate grief than the term "ring the bell"?

■ **WRITE** a journal entry in which you tell about an instance in which it took you a long time to get back "home." Your journal could include discussion about a physical journey—although it doesn't have to, but it should go beyond the physical experience to discuss the kind of emotional and psychological homecoming to which Norman refers.

AS YOU READ

Underline words, phrases, and sentences that refer specifically to Ferguson.

■ ■ ■

A colleague dropped by on a recent day to tell me that it was the third anniversary of her son's coming home from Iraq. That stopped me. It's been 40 years since I stepped off the battlefield, 1 and I'm not home yet. I can still feel the muck of rice paddies pulling on my boots, still hear the jungle hiss and snap in the dark. Even after the night dreams and day drifts have stopped and the loud noises no longer startle, you still press your chin against your shoulder and look back.

In those days, we had no time for the dead: Jim Payne from Glendale, Calif., Tommy Gonzales from Beeville, Tex. It was hard losing those good men, hard watching them fall. But we were too busy to grieve or to toll the knell. We wrapped the bodies in muddy ponchos, tossed them like sacks of rice into a helicopter and moved on.   2

We couldn't cry for them until we came home, and then we couldn't stop crying. I cried because they were dead and I was alive, and I could not shake the feeling that I had somehow purchased my life at their expense. I wanted to tell them how sorry I was for living when they could not, sorry for my beautiful wife, for my sweet sons, my wonderful career. For a long time, I lived my life for my fallen comrades. For Worley and Parsons and Ferguson. Ferguson? I knew him all of a minute.   3

We were on some barren, wind-swept mound of dirt, and the enemy had been raining mortar and artillery fire on us daily. Here came this replacement walking up the road as if he were out for a Sunday stroll. I was sitting on a wall of sandbags next to my fighting hole with Squeaky Williamson of Oklahoma.   4

"Hey, marine," the replacement said, stopping in front of me, "where's the company first sergeant?" I tilted my head in the right direction. "I'm Ferguson," he said. And just at that moment, as Ferguson was about to lean his rifle against the sandbag wall and shake my hand, I heard the soft *phft phft phft* of enemy mortars going off on the far slope of the hill opposite ours. "Incoming!" someone yelled. Squeaky flew into the hold first, I landed on top of him and Ferguson landed on top of me. The attack went on for two, three minutes, then there was quiet.   5

Squeaky, in the bottom of the hole, with the two of us on top of him, was yelling now for us to move, but Ferguson just lay there. "Tell that new [expletive] to get up," Squeaky yelled. I thought Ferguson was paralyzed with fear, so I jammed my elbow hard in his ribs and rolled him slightly up and off me. I could feel my shirt clinging to my back—fear makes the sweat pour out of you—and when I finally pulled myself out of the hole, I was covered in sweat and blood.   6

I rolled him back over and instantly saw the wound: shrapnel. He'd gotten hit diving into the hole on top of me and had been lying there on my back, dead, during the attack. Squeaky and I dragged the body out of the hole and laid it in the dirt beside the sandbags.   7

"Who the hell is that?" a sergeant said, checking for casualties.   8

"Said his name was Ferguson," I said. "Just got here."   9

"Well, since you're the only one who can put a name to a face, you get to go to the morgue and ID the body."   10

"But I don't know him," I protested.   11

"Yeah, well, you're it," the first sergeant said.   12

The morgue in Danang was a refrigerated Quonset hut by the main 13
airstrip. A pasty-faced corporal sat at a desk filling out forms. Behind him
were racks of shelves holding scores of green body bags. "This way," he
said. Ferguson was on a shelf in the back. The corporal unzipped the bag.
I gave a quick look. "That's him," I said.

"You can't see his face," the corporal insisted. And with both hands he 14
reached into the bag and tried to turn Ferguson's head toward me. Rigor
mortis had set in, and the corporal kept trying to jerk the head around in
my direction. "I'm telling you—that's him," I said.

When I got back, Squeaky was sitting on the sandbags around the 15
hole. "What was that guy's name again?" he asked.

"Ferguson," I said, setting my rifle down and taking off my helmet.   16

So I took Ferguson home with me. Who else was going to remember 17
him? Who else among us "knew" him and could carry his good name, his
reputation, the memory of him as a marine? Remembering was part of the
bargain we all made, the reason we were so willing to die for one another.

■　■　■

AFTER YOU READ

- ■ **THINK** about, and look back at, the words, phrases, and sentences that
  you underlined about Ferguson. What did Norman find out about him
  in the "minute" that he knew him? What does his "walking up the road
  as if he were out for a Sunday stroll" (paragraph 4) suggest about his
  character? Why do you think Ferguson was the last to jump into the
  fighting hole and thus the one to be shot and killed? Do you think,
  even in these few seconds, Ferguson acted bravely, even heroically?

- ■ **EXAMINE** carefully the passages that describe Norman's brief relationship with Ferguson and his feelings after Ferguson's death. What are his
  first reactions, immediately after discovering that Ferguson is dead, and
  upon being questioned by his sergeant? What are his reactions in the
  morgue where he has to identify Ferguson?

- ■ **EXAMINE** also paragraphs 2, 3, and 17. Why and how have Norman's
  feelings for his fallen comrades—and especially for Ferguson—changed
  over the years? According to Norman, what responsibility does he have
  toward these "good men" who were not able to return home themselves? Do you agree with Norman about his responsibility? Do you believe that this responsibility should also be shared by others? If so, why?
  And by whom?

- ■ **WRITE** an essay in which you discuss how a person whom you knew
  for only a brief period of time affected your life. Why do you still remember that person? Why did you take him or her "home" with you
  to keep in your memory?

September 11, 2001: Answering the Call

■ ■ ■

BILL MOON

On September 11, 2001, the members of an interdisciplinary class on the topic of heroes in ancient and modern society gathered to begin their discussion of Joseph Campbell's *The Hero with a Thousand Faces* while the shock and grief of the morning's terrorist attacks on the Pentagon and the World Trade Center were still fresh on their minds. Over the next several weeks the students discussed developing events, constantly relating them to their reading of Campbell. Out of that experience Bill Moon developed the following essay, which primarily expresses his own feelings and reactions to the tragedy but also reflects some ideas expressed by the class as a whole, especially by his fellow students Gina Allemang and Denise Bryson-Hurley. Moon, an English major, was a junior at Texas A&M University–Commerce when he wrote the essay.

BEFORE YOU READ

■ **THINK** about what you know about the September 11, 2001, attacks on the World Trade Center and the Pentagon. If you are old enough to remember these events well, where were you when you first heard about the attacks or saw them on television? What were your first thoughts? How did you adjust to the news as it kept pouring in? If you were a child at the time, what have you seen, heard, and read about these events as you grew older? Has your knowledge of these attacks affected you in any way? If so, how?

■ **EXAMINE** the title of the selection. In your opinion, what was the "call" issued on September 11, 2001? Who do you think answered this call most heroically? Why do you consider these individuals to be heroic? Are individuals still answering the call issued on that day? How?

■ **EXAMINE** also the words *transfiguration* (paragraph 2), which means a radical transformation or glorification; and *regeneration* (paragraph 8), which means renewal or restoration.

■ **WRITE** a journal entry in which you describe where you were and how you reacted when you first heard of—or really understood about—the terrorist attacks of September 11.

AS YOU READ

Identify the individuals who, according to Moon, answered the call to heroism most effectively on September 11.

■ ■ ■

When the Pentagon was seriously damaged and the twin towers   1
of the World Trade Center were physically leveled by the terrorist attack on September 11, 2001, I was emotionally leveled myself. My fellow students and I had believed that the terrorism that occurs on a daily basis in many places could not happen here, and we were outraged to hear that terrorists had flown fuel-filled passenger planes into these buildings. As Americans, we are not accustomed to being on the defensive. We pick and choose our battles, deciding when and where we will have a confrontation. But we didn't have that option on that fateful Tuesday.

In spite of the initial shock, or perhaps because of it, this tragic event   2
has become an enormous opportunity for the renewal of heroism, patriotism, and unity in our nation. Indeed, the events surrounding those first shocking moments have helped us all see not only the heroic actions of our fellow citizens but also the heroic potential within ourselves. In his book *The Hero with a Thousand Faces*, Joseph Campbell describes the pattern of heroic action—a pattern that begins with a call to action, a "summons [that] may be to live . . . or to die," but one that "rings up the curtain, always, on a mystery of transfiguration—a rite, or moment, of spiritual passage, which, when complete, amounts to a dying and a rebirth" (51). The attacks on America were indeed a call to action on the part of our nation. Those involved—from the firefighters to the police officers to the passengers on Flight 93—had a choice between accepting or refusing the call. An amazing number of individuals answered the call, and the reactions of these many heroic individuals are an inspiration to all of us as we continue to attempt to understand exactly what occurred and why.

Many of the heroes of September 11 are nameless faces on the pages of   3
weekly news magazines and local newspapers: people who donated blood, money, or water for the victims and workers; the doctors and nurses who worked around the clock to provide medical attention for those who needed it most; and the crews who dug for weeks to clear away the smoldering razor-sharp debris and recover the remains of the dead. The very wise author Anonymous once said, "Character is made up of small duties faithfully performed—of self-denials, of self-sacrifices, of kindly acts of love and duty." On that horrible day the most memorable heroic responses came from two particular groups who indeed sacrificed themselves for love and duty—the firefighters and rescue personnel of the cities involved and the passengers on United Airlines Flight 93.

On that terrible day, firefighters and rescue personnel rushed to the   4
scenes at the Pentagon and the World Trade Center, but it was at the
WTC where the most lives—almost 3,000—were lost. Two of the over
300 firefighters who lost their lives at what has come to be known as
"Ground Zero" were Ray Downey and the Rev. Mychal Judge. The chief
of special operations in New York City, 63-year-old Downey was in the
first tower trying to save those still trapped inside when the second tower
collapsed and he disappeared. Downey had a history of being a hero: in
1993 he answered the call at the first World Trade Center bombing; in
1995 he was in Oklahoma City answering the call there; and in 1996 he
had responded to the TWA Flight 800 explosion. He stepped into the
crumpled Trade Center on September 11 knowing full well what potential
danger lay ahead, but he also knew that there were people in the building
who needed to be rescued ("Facing" 75). He answered the call. The Rev.
Mychal Judge also responded to the call to heroism on September 11.
When a fellow Franciscan monk told him about the attack, he immediately
rushed to where he could be of most service. Eyewitnesses say that he was
administering last rites and comforting the wounded when he was killed by
falling rubble ("Courage" 40–41). He, too, answered the call.

Another group of individuals called into action on September 11 were   5
the passengers on United Airlines Flight 93, who apparently rushed hijackers who had also taken over their plane with intentions to use it as another
missile. We don't know—and may never know—exactly what went on
during those few minutes before the plane slammed into a rural Pennsylvania field. However, we can be fairly sure that a few courageous passengers
saved the lives of hundreds of potential terrorist targets—many of whom
may have been government officials—and perhaps preserved an American
landmark such as the White House. In phone calls to relatives, Jeremy
Glick, Tom Burnett, and Mark Bingham all revealed their plans to rush
the hijackers ("Facing" 68), and Todd Beamer was heard on an onboard
phone call giving the signal, "Let's roll." These men also answered the call,
sacrificing their lives in the process.

After accepting the call to service, the potential hero undergoes a rig-   6
orous challenge. The firefighters literally had to go through what Campbell describes as "dark and devious ways" (21) as they climbed through
the ruins of the Pentagon and the World Trade Center. Because they had
more time to think about their decision, the passengers of Flight 93 must
have traveled the hero path that Campbell says is "fundamentally inward
rather than outward." But all of these heroes left their comfort zones, giving their lives unselfishly, unswervingly. They pressed on into dark,
frightening places. Some crawled through black, billowing smoke and
falling debris into tight airless passages to pull out victims; others grappled both physically and psychologically with crazed and determined terrorists, wrestling them and therefore the plane itself to the ground. All
faced death.

In the traditional hero tale, the successful adventurer returns to his   7
or her society with a "boon" of some kind—either physical treasure or

spiritual knowledge. The stories of many of the heroes of September 11 do not have happy endings for the individuals involved, for in giving of themselves, many gave the ultimate sacrifice of their lives. However, the gift they bestowed on society is far greater than anything they could have lived for. Drawing on their own inner resources, these heroes revived the heroic potential in all of us and made it available for "the transfiguration of the world" (Campbell 29). Even though they died in the process, these heroes live on in our memories, in the lives of those they saved, and in the renewed sense of patriotism our nation has experienced.

Indeed, those individuals who answered the call on September 11 have renewed our belief in heroism itself. Campbell believes that the hero of the fairy tale "prevails over his personal oppressors" whereas the hero of myth "brings back from his adventure the means for the regeneration of his society as a whole" (38). As countless numbers of quiet heroes continue to sift through the ashes of the World Trade Center and as Americans throughout the country give of their blood, tears, and prayers, we need both kinds of heroes. Our country must prevail over our attackers, and our citizens must have the courage, diligence, and faith to continue the process of regeneration our society has already begun.   8

Works Cited

Campbell, Joseph. *The Hero with a Thousand Faces,* 2nd ed. Bollingen Series 42. Princeton, NJ: Princeton UP, 1968. Print.

"Courage Under Terrible Fire." *U.S. News and World Report, Special Issue* 24 September 2001: 40–43. Print.

"Facing the End." *Time, Special Issue* 24 September 2001: 68–77. Print.

■   ■   ■

AFTER YOU READ

■ **THINK** about the two different groups of heroes that Moon identifies in paragraph 3: the firefighters and the passengers on United Airlines Flight 93. What qualities did these heroes have in common? What was unique and special about each group?

■ **EXAMINE** Moon's claim in paragraph 7 that "drawing on their own inner resources, these heroes revived the heroic potential in all of us and made it available for 'the transfiguration of the world'" (Campbell 29). On what inner resources do you think the heroes of September 11 relied? Do you agree that the heroic response to the attacks "transfigured" American society? If so, how? Has this change lasted? Why or why not?

- **WRITE** an essay in which you describe what you believe to have been the most heroic response to the terrorist attacks.
- Or **WRITE** an essay in which you discuss the effects that terrorist attacks, such as—but not limited to—those of September 11 have had on *either* (1) the values of our society or (2) our society's view of heroes.

Hero Inflation

■ ■ ■

Nicholas Thompson

Whereas the previous essay focuses on the heroism associated with September 11, Nicholas Thompson questions whether the word *hero* has been used too frequently and too loosely since the terrorist attacks. A Phi Beta Kappa graduate of Stanford University with degrees in political science, earth systems, and economics, Thompson is a fellow at the New America Foundation. He has published *The Baobab and the Mango Tree: Africa, the Asian Tigers and the Developing World* (2001); and *The Hawk and the Dove: Paul Nitze, George Kennan, and the History of the Cold War* (2009), as well as articles in periodicals such as *The Washington Monthly*, *Chicago Tribune*, *The New York Times*, and *The Washington Post*. The following essay appeared in *The Boston Globe* in January 2002.

BEFORE YOU READ

■ **THINK** about the way the use of the word *hero* has changed since September 11, 2001. For a number of years before September 11, the word was used infrequently and often ironically. In fact, many individuals in our society did not seem to recognize or even believe in heroes. In contrast, how often have you seen or heard the words *hero* and *heroic* applied to individuals since September 11? Do you think that everyone who has been called a hero qualifies as a true hero? Explain your position on this issue.

■ **EXAMINE** the title "Hero Inflation." To inflate something is to increase it beyond its normal or natural size, as in inflating or blowing up a balloon. In his essay Thompson uses the term *hero inflation* to describe the practice of overusing the words *hero* and *heroic*, especially in reference to individuals and situations that do not really qualify for the designation. Look also at these words and their definitions: a *pantheon*, meaning "the gods of the people," in paragraph 11; *incorrigibly*, meaning "not capable of reform," in paragraph 15; and *paragons*, meaning "models of excellence," in paragraph 15.

■ **EXAMINE** also the name Oskar Schindler from paragraph 6. If you saw the movie *Schindler's List,* you already know that Schindler (1908–1974) was a German industrialist who saved many Jews from Nazi concentration camps by hiring them as workers in his factories.

■ WRITE a journal entry in which you describe the use of the word *hero* as you have observed it since September 11, 2001. Also include in your journal your response to how this word and the idea of heroism have been used recently. Do you think they have been used appropriately in most instances? Why or why not?

AS YOU READ

Underline the changing definitions of a hero that Thompson provides.

■ ■ ■

Since September 11, America has become a nation of heroes. Paul   1
McCartney, Willie Nelson, and Bruce Springsteen played a "tribute to heroes" that raised $150 million for victims of the attacks. Firefighters and rescue workers have earned acclaim for heroism, but so has nearly everyone who directly suffered on that horrible morning.

"The fatalities of that day are all heroes and deserve to be honored as   2
such," said Thomas Davis, a Republican congressman from Virginia, while successfully working to obtain a full burial plot in Arlington National Cemetery for the former National Guardsman who piloted the plane that crashed into the Pentagon.

The victims of the terrorist attacks deserve tremendous sympathy.   3
They died tragically and often horrifically. But not all died in a way that people have previously described as heroic. And even the heroism attributed to the rescue workers stems as much from the country's needs in responding to the disaster as from what actually happened in the collapsing buildings.

It is long overdue that Americans appreciate their public servants. It is   4
also necessary to honor those who died simply for being in America. But changing the definition of hero to accommodate tragic victims may actually weaken us by diminishing the idea of role models who perform truly extraordinary acts.

To the ancient Greeks, "heroes," such as Hercules or Odysseus,   5
performed great deeds, frequently challenged the gods, and were immortalized after death. Heroes lived in times and realms halfway between gods and men and often were deemed to have brought prosperity to the people who praised them.

That definition gradually evolved in this country as Americans adapted   6
it to the people most respected here. Heroes won that standing by courageously transforming the world—Martin Luther King Jr. or Mother Teresa, for example. Or heroes could earn that title simply for incredible acts of bravery several steps above the call of duty—Oskar Schindler, a young girl who plunges into a dangerous icy river and saves a stranger's life, or maybe someone from battle such as Henry Johnson who fought

off twenty Germans with a knife and a couple of hand grenades in World War I.

Roughly speaking, American heroes first needed bravery. But bravery   7
is not sufficient because evil people can be brave, too. So, the second trait in American historical lore is nobility. Heroes must work toward goals that we approve of. Heroes must show ingenuity. Lastly, they should be successful. Rosa Parks wouldn't have been nearly as much of a hero if she hadn't sparked a boycott that then sparked a movement. Charles Lindbergh wouldn't have been nearly as heroized if the *Spirit of St. Louis* had crashed into the Atlantic, or if scores of other people had made the flight before.

Recently though, a fourth trait—victimhood—seems to have become as   8
important as anything else in determining heroic status. Today heroes don't have to do anything; they just need to be noble victims.

For example, if J. Joseph Moakley was known at all nationally, it was   9
as a hard-working Massachusetts congressman who almost always followed the Democratic Party line. But when he was stricken with leukemia, he became a national hero, earning praise from the president and seemingly everyone else in Washington. He was cited from the balcony, traditionally the spot reserved for heroes, by President Bush during the State of the Union message. (This paper [the *Boston Globe*] even wrote about a letter received at his house addressed simply to "Joe Moakley, Hero.") His death earned almost as much newspaper coverage as the death this year of the ninety-eight-year-old Mike Mansfield, a giant of the U.S. Senate who served as majority leader longer than anyone in history and initiated the Senate Watergate Committee.

But that shouldn't surprise us. Books about overcoming adversity clog   10
the bestseller lists, and perseverance during illness—any illness—is grist for the heroic mill. If John F. Kennedy wanted to run for president today, he might constantly mention his struggle against Addison's disease as opposed to emphasizing his exploits on his PT boat in the Pacific.

Of course, victimhood hasn't completely eclipsed action in our   11
national selection of heroes. The biggest heroes have many of the virtues of traditional heroes but also are victims—for example, the 350 firefighters who died in the World Trade Center and who now stand atop our national pantheon. These men have been honored everywhere from the current cover of *Sports Illustrated* to a recent best-selling comic book that makes them into superheroes. They even inspired thousands of Halloween costumes.

But although the firemen who died in the Trade Center bravely fought   12
the flames and led the evacuation, they did so as workers doing the best they could in their jobs—people trained by the city to rush into buildings and save others. Firefighters choose a very worthy line of work, but to die while doing it isn't completely different from, say, the computer programmers who stayed in the Trade Center and perished while desperately trying to preserve the data backing people's financial portfolios. Just after Christmas, a New

Bedford policeman carried a woman out of a burning building. "I'm not a hero," he said upon emerging outside. "I'm just a worker."

There were no doubt some unconditional individual heroes on September 11, including some of the people on United Flight 93 who fought the hijackers[,] and individual firefighters and police who went well beyond the requirements of the job, but most of the other people who died in the attacks were simply victims, much like the tens of thousands of innocent people killed in home fires, or on highways, every year.   13

They deserve our grief and their families and communities merit great sympathy. But it's time for a little more perspective when Congress almost unanimously passes a bill called the "True American Heroes Act" awarding Congressional Gold Medals—the highest honor that body can give—to every government official who died in the attacks, including Port Authority employees who were killed in their World Trade Center offices.   14

Of course, some of the hero-making is born of necessity. In the aftermath of the attacks, we needed to turn the narrative away from the horror of the images on television and our clear vulnerability. As soon as the buildings came down, we needed to build the victims up. It also helped to reclassify everyone on the opposing side as incorrigibly demonic and everyone on our side as paragons of virtue. After the 11th, the first part was easy and the second part took a little bit of work.   15

That wasn't of course a wholly bad thing. The inflation of the heroism of September 11 surely helped the nation recover and pull together. Moreover, America probably didn't have enough heroes. An August *U.S. News & World Report* poll revealed that more than half of all Americans didn't consider a single public figure heroic. Right before the attacks, Anheuser Busch planned an ad campaign titled "Real American Heroes" that, among other things, saluted the inventor of the foot-long hot dog.   16

But just because the sometimes false focus on heroism helped the nation salve its wounds doesn't make such attitudes wholly good either. Heroes often end up as role models, a task not well suited for victims. Moreover, by lowering the bar for heroism, we cheapen the word and, in some ways, the exploits of people who have earned the right to be called that in the past.   17

Finally, when people earn classification as heroes, those acting in their names often try to take it a step too far. Last month, for example, the federal government announced plans to disburse about as much money this year to families of attack victims as the entire international aid community has slated to give to Afghanistan over the next decade—and that money will come in addition to incredible amounts of charitable aid also already raised. Nevertheless, a spokesman for a victims' lobby group immediately dissented, demanding more. "We are exploring our legal options and lining up attorneys," he said. Almost no criticism could be found in response.   18

Emerson once wrote that "every hero becomes a bore at last." Well, at least their lawyers and lobbyists do.   19

■ ■ ■

AFTER YOU READ

■ **THINK** about Thompson's description of the way our definition of a hero has changed over the centuries. How did the ancient Greeks define a hero? What qualities have modern Americans usually sought in heroes? Since September 11, what new trait is often used to identify and define heroes? Do you agree or disagree with Thompson that this last trait—being a victim—is not a legitimate heroic quality? If you agree with Thompson on this last point, explain the difference between victims and true heroes.

■ **THINK** also about the various effects of what Thompson calls our "false focus on heroism" (paragraph 17). What positive effects have resulted from this focus on heroism? What negative effects have resulted—or could result—from this focus on heroism, particularly on the idea of victims as heroes?

■ **EXAMINE** paragraphs 12 and 13, in which Thompson distinguishes between actions that he considers heroic and those that he believes are simply in the line of duty. Paragraph 12 concludes with a quotation from a police officer who had just carried a woman out of a burning building: "'I'm not a hero,' he said upon emerging outside. 'I'm just a worker.'" Do you believe that the officer's actions were any less heroic because he was expected to perform such actions in his job? Do you agree or disagree with Thompson that, although some individuals "went well beyond the requirements of the job" in the response to the September 11 attacks, most firefighters and police officers who were killed in the aftermath of the attacks were simply doing their jobs in much the same way as "the computer programmers who stayed in the Trade Center and perished while desperately trying to preserve the data backing people's financial portfolios"? Is it ultimately possible to distinguish between the heroes and the victims of September 11? If so, how can—or should—we make this distinction?

■ **WRITE** an essay in which you respond to Thompson's ideas about hero inflation. You may agree or disagree with Thompson, or you may take a position somewhere in the middle. Decide on a clear main point or thesis, and then develop that thesis with quotations and references from Thompson's essay as well as your own ideas and examples. (See "Responding to a Text" on pages 244–247.)

Giving Students the Heroes They Need

■ ■ ■

PETER H. GIBBON

The author of numerous articles in professional journals and publications such as *The New York Times, The Washington Post*, and *The Los Angeles Times* and a senior research fellow at Boston University's School of Education, Peter H. Gibbon spent many years talking with high school students across the country about the concept of heroism. He published the results of his research in his book *A Call to Heroism: Renewing America's Vision of Greatness* (2002). Gibbon argues in the following selection that a hero can be imperfect and still be great. This excerpt is taken from an article that was originally published in *American Educator* and then republished in *Education Digest*.

BEFORE YOU READ

■ **THINK** about the idea that heroes are not perfect. Can you think of examples of public figures from the past or present who are viewed as heroic despite personal flaws? How do you reconcile the weaknesses of these individuals with their being viewed as heroes?

■ **EXAMINE** the title of the essay. Do you believe that students need heroes to admire and perhaps imitate? Why or why not? Do you think society as a whole needs heroes? Why or why not?

■ **EXAMINE** also the words *apathy* and *nihilism* from the first paragraph. *Apathy* is a lack of interest, feeling, or emotion; *nihilism* is the belief that nothing exists or is worthwhile and that there are no moral values.

■ **WRITE** a journal entry in which you discuss an individual whom society considers to be a hero in spite of one or more personal flaws. Identify the flaw(s) of this individual, and then explain why you do (or do not) believe that this person is a hero. If you view this person as a hero, what heroic qualities and deeds do you (or others) believe outweigh the flaws?

AS YOU READ

Underline the passages in which Gibbon defines the word *hero*.

■ ■ ■

Human beings are deeply divided, eternally torn between apathy 1
and activity, nihilism and belief. We wage a daily battle between
a higher and lower self. The *hero* stands for our higher self. To
get through life and permit the higher self to prevail, we depend on public
models of excellence, bravery, and goodness.

During the last 40 years in America, such models have been in short 2
supply. Except among politicians and advertising firms, the word *hero*
has been out of fashion since the late 1960s to describe past or present
public figures. We are reluctant to use it this way, doubtful if any one person can hold up under the burden of such a word.

After the September 11 terrorist attacks, *hero* was resurrected to de- 3
scribe the firefighters and police officers who lost their lives in the World
Trade Center, rescue workers who patiently picked their way through the
rubble, passengers who thwarted terrorists on a hijacked airplane, and soldiers who left on planes and ships. In difficult times, we turn to the word
hero to express our deepest sorrow, our highest aspiration, and our most
profound admiration.

I have plugged *hero* into every available database; read hundreds of 4
biographies and books on heroism; traveled the country talking to Americans about heroes; and interviewed educators, historians, journalists, min-
isters, politicians, scientists, and writers, asking questions that shaped my
book, *A Call to Heroism:* How did we lose our public heroes? Why does
it matter? Where do we go from here?

As a historian, I have been tracing the changing face of the American 5
hero, researching what has happened to the presentation of heroes in history books, and analyzing ways revisionist historians have shaped teachers'
attitudes, which in turn shape the way students respond.

The most rewarding part of this odyssey has been the five years I spent 6
talking to students about heroes. Most of my audiences have been in high
schools—from a thousand students sitting on gym bleachers to small classes in history and literature.

In these talks, I challenge that they are too old, too jaded, or too cyni- 7
cal for heroes. I quote Ralph Waldo Emerson, another true believer in heroes and a writer most students will know: "Go with mean people and you
think life is mean" and "with the great, our thoughts and manners easily
become great."

In spirited debate, they agree, disagree, challenge, and probe. "Is Mal- 8
colm X a hero? John Brown? Why is Hitler worse than Columbus?" They
ask about celebrities, athletes, historical figures, politicians, and rescuers,
and about personal heroes: parents, teachers, friends.

MORAL ASPECT

For most of human history, *hero* has been synonymous with *warrior*. 9
Although we often link these words today, we do have an expanded,

more inclusive definition of *hero* than the Greeks'. Modern dictionaries list three qualities in common after *hero:* extraordinary achievement, courage, and the idea (variously expressed) that the hero serves as a "model" or "example"—that heroism has a moral component.

The moral component of heroism—and, I believe, the most important   10 one—is elusive. *The Oxford English Dictionary* cites "greatness of soul," which I believe to be a mysterious blend of powerful qualities summarized by Shakespeare in *Macbeth* as "king-becoming graces": "justice, verity, temp'rance, stableness, bounty, perseverance, mercy, lowliness, devotion, patience, courage, fortitude."

The greatest burden *hero* carries today is the expectation that a hero   11 be perfect. In Greek mythology, even the gods have flaws. They are not perfect but rather hot-tempered, jealous, and fickle, taking sides in human events and feuding among themselves.

In America today we define the person by the flaw: Thomas Jefferson   12 is the president with the slave mistress, Einstein the scientist who mistreated his wife. We need a more subtle, complex definition of *hero,* one that acknowledges weaknesses as well as strengths, failures as well as successes—but still does not set the bar too low.

Some Americans reject the word *hero* outright and insist on *role*   13 *model,* which is less grandiose, more human. I like author Jill Ker Conway's distinction: "Women should have heroines, not role models." Women, she said, are as physically brave and as daring as men, and the routine use of *role model* to describe outstanding women conceals their bravery and diminishes their heroism. Conway's distinction argues that *heroine* is a more powerful word than *role model* and that heroism is a reach for the extraordinary.

The definition of *hero* remains subjective. What is extraordinary can   14 be debated. Courage is in the eye of the beholder. Greatness of soul is elusive. How many and what kinds of flaws can one have and still be considered heroic?

Nevertheless, today we are reluctant to call past or present public fig-   15 ures heroic. The twentieth-century assumption of a hero as perfect has made many Americans turn away from the word—and the concept—altogether. The contemporary preference for *role model* and the shift from recognition of national to local heroes are part of the transformation of *hero* in the second half of the twentieth century.

There is something appealing about a society that admires a range of   16 accomplishments and celebrates as many people as possible. But making *hero* more democratic can be carried to an extreme, stripping it of all sense of the extraordinary and leading to an ignorance of history, a repudiation of genius, and an extreme egalitarianism disdainful of high culture and unappreciative of excellence.

We need role models and local heroes; but limiting our heroes to   17 people we know restricts our aspirations. Public heroes—imperfect people of extraordinary achievement, courage, and greatness of soul whose reach is wider than ours—teach us to push beyond ourselves and our neighborhoods for excellence models, enlarging our imagination, teaching us to think big, and expanding our sense of the possible.

■   ■   ■

AFTER YOU READ

■ **THINK** about the relationship between heroism and democracy that Gibbon discusses in paragraph 16. Gibbon suggests that our society believes in an "extreme egalitarianism," which views all citizens as "equal" regardless of their ideas, accomplishments, or contributions to society. How is this shift related to the increasing emphasis on role models and local rather than public heroes? Gibbon further implies that the democratization of heroes can keep us from recognizing the greatness, or heroism, in certain individuals. Do you believe Gibbon's concern is valid? Explain.

■ **EXAMINE** the definitions of the word *hero* that you underlined in Gibbon's essay. According to Gibbon, how has our definition of *hero* changed over the years? According to Gibbon, what essential qualities do heroes have, and what is the most important quality for heroes of either gender? Why do he and Jill Ker Conway, whom he quotes in paragraph 13, prefer the term *heroine* to *role model?* Explain Gibbon's belief that an individual can be flawed and still be a hero. Finally, explain how your own definitions of a hero and a heroine compare to those of Gibbon.

■ **EXAMINE** also Gibbon's website, "Heroes in America," available as a link on the *Interactions* website. On this site you will find a biography of Gibbon as well as articles by and about him and a list of quotations about heroes and heroism.

■ **WRITE** an essay in which you compare and contrast Gibbon's definition of a hero with Phil Sudo's (see "Larger Than Life," pages 454–456). Conclude your essay by evaluating the definitions provided by these two authors. (See Lesson 7 on the *Interactions*, eighth edition, student website at www.cengagebrain.com for help with writing a comparison and contrast essay.)

■ Or **WRITE** an essay in which you argue that a particular individual is (or is not) a hero without regard to recognized personal flaws.

Rosa Parks Through a New Lens

■ ■ ■

PAUL ROGAT LOEB

Social and political activist Paul Rogat Loeb is currently an af-
filiate scholar at Seattle's Center for Political Leadership. Loeb
has lectured at more than 300 college campuses; has been inter-
viewed on various radio and television stations such as National
Public Radio, NBC, and CNN; and has published his work in
numerous newspapers and magazines, including *The New York
Times*, *The Washington Post*, *The Los Angeles Times*, *The
Chronicle of Higher Education*, *Psychology Today*, *Mother
Earth News*, and *Mother Jones*. The most widely known and
influential of his five books are *Soul of a Citizen: Living with
Conviction in a Cynical Time* (1999); and the award-winning
*The Impossible Will Take a Little While: A Citizen's Guide to
Hope in a Time of Fear* (2004). In the following essay, Loeb
argues that a heroic act, such as the stand for civil rights that
Rosa Parks made in 1955 when she refused to give her bus
seat to a white man, can be truly understood only in its fuller
context.

BEFORE YOU READ

■ THINK about the terms *hero*, *heroine*, and *role model* that Gibbon discusses in the previous essay. From what you know about Rosa Parks
(1913–2005) and her role in the civil rights movement, how would you
classify her? Why do you view her as you do? Do you think she dis-
played the moral component of heroism that Gibbons calls "greatness
of soul"? Explain.

■ THINK also about the distinction between public and local heroes that
Gibbon makes (pages 483–485). Do you think the fact that Parks is
clearly a public hero makes her heroism more important than that of a
local or even an unknown hero? How does her public renown make her
heroic act more influential on society?

■ EXAMINE the title of the essay as well as the word *context* in paragraph
4. In his essay, Loeb portrays Parks's stand for civil rights in a new
way, through the context or the circumstances surrounding her action.
That is, he suggests that a socially or politically heroic figure such as
Rosa Parks represents not only her own admirable actions but also
those of her teachers, coworkers, and followers. To provide you with
an even fuller context for Parks's heroic act, you may look up her
official website (available as a link on the *Interactions* website at

www.cengagebrain.com), which provides photographs of Parks and an "Events Timeline" in the biographical section.

■ **WRITE** a journal entry in which you explain why you think the heroism of public figures such as Rosa Parks is, or is not, more important than the heroism of local or personal heroes.

AS YOU READ

As you read, find and underline passages in which Loeb explains the importance of background information in understanding and appreciating heroism.

■ ■ ■

We learn much from how we present our heroes.   1

A few years ago, on Martin Luther King Jr. Day, I was inter-   2
viewed on CNN. So was Rosa Parks, by phone from Los Angeles.
"We're honored to have her," said the host. "Rosa Parks was the   3
woman who wouldn't go to the back of the bus. She wouldn't get up and
give her seat in the white section to a white person. That set in motion the
yearlong bus boycott in Montgomery. It earned Rosa Parks the title of
'mother of the Civil Rights movement.'"

I was excited to hear Parks' voice and to be part of the same show.   4
Then it occurred to me that the host's description—the story's standard
rendition and one repeated even in many of her obituaries—stripped the
Montgomery boycott of all of its context.

Before refusing to give up her bus seat, Parks had been active for 12   5
years in the local NAACP chapter, serving as its secretary.

The summer before her arrest, she had attended a 10-day training ses-   6
sion at Tennessee's labor and civil rights organizing school, the High-
lander, where she'd met an older generation of civil rights activists, such
as South Carolina teacher Septime Clark, and discussed the recent Supreme
Court decision banning "separate-but-equal" schools.

During this period of involvement and education, Parks had become   7
familiar with previous challenges to segregation. A bus boycott in Baton
Rouge, La., won limited gains two years before Parks was arrested, and
the previous spring, a young Montgomery woman had also refused to
move to the back of the bus, causing the NAACP to consider a legal challenge until it turned out that the woman in question was unmarried and
pregnant and therefore a poor symbol for a campaign.

In short, Parks didn't make a spur-of-the-moment decision. She didn't   8
single-handedly give birth to the civil rights efforts—she was part of an existing movement for change at a time when success was far from certain.

We all know Parks' name, but few of us know about Montgomery   9
NAACP head E. D. Nixon, who served as one of her mentors and first

got Martin Luther King involved. Nixon carried people's suitcases on the trains and was active in the Brotherhood of Sleeping Car Porters, the union founded by legendary civil rights activist A. Philip Randolph.

Nixon played a key role in the campaign. No one talks of him, any 10 more than they talk of JoAnn Robinson, who taught nearby at an under-funded and segregated black college and whose Women's Political Council distributed the initial leaflets after Parks' arrest.

Without the often lonely work of people such as Nixon, Randolph and 11 Robinson, Parks probably never would have taken her stand. Without their work, her action never would have had the same impact. This in no way diminishes the power and historical importance of Parks' refusal to give up her seat. But it reminds us that this tremendously consequential act, along with everything that followed, depended on all the humble and frustrating work that Parks and others had undertaken earlier. It also reminds us that Parks' initial involvement was just as courageous and crucial as the stand on the bus that all of us have heard about.

A PERILOUS PEDESTAL

People such as Parks shape our models of social commitment. Yet from 12 responses to talks I've given throughout the country, most citizens do not know the full story of her involvement. And the conventional, stripped-down retelling creates a standard so impossible to meet that it may actually make it harder for us to get involved, inadvertently removing Parks' most powerful lessons of hope.

This conventional portrayal suggests that social activists come out of 13 nowhere to suddenly take dramatic stands. It implies that we act with the greatest impact when we act alone, at least initially. And that change occurs instantly, as opposed to building on a series of often invisible actions.

The myth of Parks as a lone activist reinforces a notion that anyone 14 who takes a committed public stand, or at least an effective one, has to be a larger-than-life figure—someone with more time, energy, courage, vision or knowledge than any normal person could ever possess. This belief pervades our society, in part because the media tend not to represent historical change as the work of ordinary human beings, which it almost always is.

Once we enthrone our heroes on pedestals, it becomes hard for mere 15 mortals to measure up in our eyes. However individuals speak out, we're tempted to dismiss their motives, knowledge and tactics as insufficiently grand or heroic. We fault them for not being in command of every fact and figure, or being able to answer every question put to them. We fault ourselves as well, for not knowing every detail or for harboring uncertainties and doubts.

We find it hard to imagine that ordinary human beings with ordinary 16 flaws might make a crucial difference in worthy social causes.

Yet those who act have their own imperfections, and ample reasons to 17
hold back.

"I think it does us all a disservice when people who work for social 18
change are presented as saints—so much more noble than the rest of us,"
says Sonya Tinsley, a young African-American activist in Atlanta.

"We get a false sense that from the moment they were born they were 19
called to act, never had doubts, were bathed in a circle of light. But I'm
much more inspired learning how people succeeded despite their failings
and uncertainties. It's a much less intimidating image. It makes me feel
like I have a shot at changing things, too."

Tinsley had recently attended a talk given by one of King's Morehouse 20
professors in which he mentioned how much King had struggled when he
first came to college—getting only a "C," for example, in his first philosophy course.

"I found that very inspiring, when I heard it, given all that King achieved," 21
Tinsley said. "It made me feel that just about anything was possible."

WIDESPREAD WORK

Our culture's misreading of the Rosa Parks story speaks to a more general 22
collective amnesia in which we forget the examples that might most inspire
our courage, hope and conscience.

Apart from obvious times of military conflict, most of us know next to 23
nothing of the many battles that ordinary men and women fought to preserve freedom, expand the sphere of democracy and create a more just
society. Of the abolitionist and civil rights movements, we at best recall a
few key leaders—and often misread their actual stories.

We know even less about the turn-of-the-[twentieth-]century populists 24
who challenged entrenched economic interests and fought for a "coopera-
tive commonwealth."

Who these days can describe the union movements that ended 80-hour 25
workweeks at near-starvation wages? Who knows the origin of the Social
Security system, now threatened by systematic attempts to privatize it?
How did the women's suffrage movement spread to hundreds of communities and gather enough strength to prevail?

As memories of these events disappear, we lose the knowledge of me- 26
chanisms that grassroots social movements have used to shift public sentiment and challenge entrenched institutional power. Equally lost are the
means by which their participants managed to keep on and eventually prevail in circumstances at least as harsh as those we face today.

LOOKING THROUGH A NEW LENS

Think again about the different ways one can frame Parks' historic action. 27

In the prevailing myth, Parks decides to act almost on a whim, in iso- 28
lation. She's a virgin to politics, a holy innocent. The lesson seems to be

that if any of us suddenly got the urge to do something equally heroic, that would be great. Of course, most of us don't, so we wait our entire lives to find the ideal moment.

Parks' real story conveys a far more empowering moral. She begins   29
with seemingly modest steps. She goes to a meeting, and then another, helping build the community that in turn supported her path. Hesitant at first, she gains confidence as she speaks out. She keeps on despite a profoundly uncertain context, as she and others act as best they can to challenge deeply entrenched injustices, with little certainty of results.

Had she and others given up after her 10th or 11th year of commit-   30
ment, we might never have heard of Montgomery.

Parks also reminds us that even in a seemingly losing cause, one person   31
may unknowingly inspire another, and that person yet a third, who may then go on to change the world—or at least a small corner of it.

Rosa Parks' husband, Raymond, persuaded her to attend her first   32
NAACP meeting, the initial step on a path that brought her to that fateful day in Montgomery. But who got Raymond involved? And why did that person take the trouble to do so? What experiences shaped their outlook, forged their convictions?

The links in any chain of influence are too numerous, too complex to   33
trace. But being aware that such chains exist, that we can choose to join them and that lasting change doesn't occur in their absence, is one of the primary ways to sustain hope—especially when our actions seem too insignificant to amount to anything. Finally, Parks' journey suggests that change is the product of deliberate, incremental action, whereby we join together to try to shape a better world.

Sometimes our struggles will fail, as did many earlier efforts of Parks,   34
her peers and her predecessors. Other times they may bear modest fruits. And at times they will trigger a miraculous outpouring of courage and heart—as happened with her arrest and all that followed. For only when we act despite all our uncertainties and doubts do we have the chance to shape history.

■ ■ ■

AFTER YOU READ

■ **THINK** about Loeb's thesis that a particular heroic action can only be understood and appreciated in its broader social and historical context. After reading Loeb's essay on Parks, do you think his thesis applies to her life and her stand on the Montgomery bus? Explain also why you think this thesis is, or is not, relevant to other heroic figures or acts. Give examples to support your opinion.

■ **EXAMINE** the section entitled "A Perilous Pedestal" (paragraphs 12–21). Would Loeb agree or disagree with Sudo's definition of a hero as a "larger-than-life" figure (page 455)? Why or why not? Does Loeb agree or disagree with Gibbon that heroes can have flaws and imperfections (page 484)? Support your opinions with details from Loeb's essay. Finally, does Loeb believe that knowing the context surrounding a heroic act makes that act more or less inspirational? Why does he feel as he does? Do you agree or disagree with him? Why do you feel as you do?

■ EXAMINE also the final section, "Looking Through a New Lens" (paragraphs 27–34). According to Loeb, is an individual born with heroic traits, or can one gradually develop such qualities so that he or she is ready to act if an opportunity arises? What is your personal opinion on this question? Support Loeb's opinion with details from his essay and your opinion with examples from your experience and observation.

■ WRITE an essay on a heroic figure from one of the groups alluded to in paragraphs 23–25 (abolitionists, civil rights leaders, populists, or women's suffrage leaders). Select the group that interests you most, and then use the library or a search engine such as Google to identify and gather information on an important figure in this movement. In writing your essay, explain clearly not only why you believe this person is a hero or heroine but also the context in which this person's heroism developed. Be sure to write your paper in your own words, citing borrowed information in your text and a Works Cited section. If you use an actual phrase or sentence, put the borrowed words in quotation marks; if you cite a longer passage such as multiple sentences or a paragraph of more than four lines, indent the material one inch from the left margin. See Cindy Camburn's "Dice or Doves" (pages 373–376), Tammy Holm's "Technology and the Hearing Impaired" (pages 443–445), and Bill Moon's "September 11, 2001: Answering the Call" (pages 473–475) for models of internal citation and Works Cited.

The New Heroes and Role Models

■ ■ ■

Tyler Cowen

A professor of economics at George Mason University with a
doctoral degree from Harvard, Tyler Cowen is an associate editor of the *Southern Economic Journal* and the author of several
books on economics, including *Creative Destruction: How
Globalization Is Changing the World's Culture* (2004); and
*Discover Your Inner Economist: Use Incentives to Fall in
Love, Survive Your Next Meeting, and Motivate Your Dentist*
(2007). In the following article, adapted from his book *What
Price Fame?* (2000), Cowen explores not only the distinction
between heroes and role models but also the changing relationship between fame and merit.

BEFORE YOU READ

- **THINK** about the words *heroes* and *role models* which Cowen uses in
  his title. After reading the previous essays in this unit, how do you define a hero? How do you define a role model? How are heroes and role
  models similar? How are they different?

- **EXAMINE** the first sentence of the essay, which focuses on the deaths of
  Princess Diana and Mother Teresa. Do you consider Princess Diana to
  be a hero or a role model? Do you view Mother Teresa as a hero or a
  role model? Explain the reasons that you view each woman in the way
  that you do.

- **EXAMINE** also the terms *pseudo-events* (paragraph 2), *pace* (paragraph
  14), *doux commerce* and *bourgeois* (paragraph 20), and *farce* (paragraph 20). Used in the title of Daniel Boorstin's book *The Image: A
  Guide to Pseudo-Events in America*, the term *pseudo* means "false,
  fictional, or unreal," as in the related word *pseudonym*, which means
  "a false name or pen name." A *pseudo-event* is thus "a false event."
  As Cowen further explains, Boorstin is suggesting that the fleeting
  actions of celebrities are relatively unimportant in comparison to those
  who gain fame for meritorious or heroic deeds. The word *pace* (from the
  Latin word for *peace*) is a preposition used primarily as a courteous or
  ironic apology for a difference of opinion. The eighteenth-century political
  theory of *doux commerce* suggested that the mutual needs of society
  would allow commerce to create worldwide peace. The term *bourgeois*
  refers to the middle class, and a *farce* is a broadly satirical comedy.

- **WRITE** a journal entry in which you distinguish between a hero and a
  role model.

AS YOU READ

Underline passages that define and distinguish between heroes and role models. In addition, pay particular attention to Cowen's discussion of how the relationship between fame and merit has changed over the years.

■ ■ ■

W hat does it mean that the funeral of Princess Diana in 1997 1 attracted so much more media attention than did the funeral, the same week, of Mother Teresa? What significance should we give the appearance of such figures as Buddy Holly and Elvis Presley on recent U.S. postage stamps? Fame, it is often argued, used to reflect merit; now it reflects commercializing forces. The commercial generation of fame, according to many critics, leads to a society weak in virtue. Are such critics right?

Daniel Boorstin, the former Librarian of Congress, argued in his 1962 2 book *The Image: A Guide to Pseudo-Events in America* that the concept of transient celebrity is replacing the concept of the true hero, who serves as a role model and exhibits moral leadership. Pondering what he perceived to be the lack of giants in modern society, Winston Churchill asked in 1932, "Can modern communities do without great men? Can they dispense with hero-worship? Can they provide a larger wisdom, a nobler sentiment, a more vigorous action, by collective processes, than were ever got from Titans? Can nations remain healthy . . . in a world whose brightest stars are film stars?"

If these worries are valid, then the separation of fame and merit is 3 indeed problematic. We risk the danger that commercially successful heroes may invite dangerous forms of imitation by their fans, and fail to help their societies organize around noble ideals. Plutarch wrote nearly 20 centuries ago of great men as a kind of looking glass, in which we see how to "adjust and adorn" our own lives. The contemporary question is whether today's heroes provide a foundation for a desirable moral discourse.

THE CHANGING NATURE OF FAME

Over time, entertainers and sports figures have displaced politicians, mili- 4 tary leaders, and moral preachers as the most famous individuals in society, and in some cases, as the most admired.

An 1898 survey of 1,440 12- through 14-year-olds asked them the fol- 5 lowing question: "What person of whom you have ever heard or read would you most like to resemble?" Forty percent chose either George Washington or Abraham Lincoln. Clara Barton, Annie Sullivan (Helen Keller's teacher), Julius Caesar, and Christopher Columbus also received prominent mention. One bicycle racer and one boxer were mentioned, but otherwise sports figures accounted for few of the answers. Seventy-eight percent of the selections came from history, both contemporaneous and past, including politicians, moral leaders, and generals. No entertainers were picked (though 12 percent were characters from literature).

Another poll was conducted a half-century later, in 1948, with a com-   6
parable number of schoolchildren of similar age. The children were asked, "Which one of all these persons that you know or have read about do you want most to be like 10 years from now?" This time, only a third of the respondents chose historical figures; Franklin Delano Roosevelt topped the list for boys and Clara Barton topped the list for girls. Sports figures accounted for 23 percent, with baseball players Ted Williams and Babe Ruth heading that category. Entertainers accounted for 14 percent, with boys picking radio and movie heroes like Gene Autry and girls preferring movie figures such as Betty Grable. Characters from literature were completely absent. Religious figures fell from 5 percent in 1898 to less than 1 percent in 1948. Figures from comic strips, such as Joe Palooka, were selected much more often than Jesus Christ.

In 1986, *The World Almanac* listed the 10 figures most admired by   7
American teenagers that year, all of whom (except Ronald Reagan, a former actor) were entertainers:

1. Bill Cosby

2. Sylvester Stallone

3. Eddie Murphy

4. Ronald Reagan

5. Molly Ringwald

6. Chuck Norris

7. Clint Eastwood

8. Rob Lowe

9. Arnold Schwarzenegger

10. Don Johnson

Postage stamps from the 19th century commemorate political and mil-   8
itary leaders almost exclusively, especially George Washington. Recent U.S. postage stamps feature rock, blues, and jazz singers. Until the late 1960s, only two entertainers had made it onto U.S. postage stamps. The 1970s and 1980s combined brought a total of nine entertainers on stamps. During the first half of the 1990s, 32 entertainers appeared on stamps. The most famous such stamp featured Elvis Presley. After Elvis' death, his fans lobbied for a stamp to honor him, and bickered over whether it should feature a young, thin Elvis or an older, fat Elvis. The subsequent public vote attracted so much attention that the networks televised the press conference that announced the winning portrait.

At the beginning of this century, political biographies accounted for   9
46 percent of magazine biographies published in the United States, as measured by one extensive sample. By 1940 the figure had fallen to 25 percent.

The market share of entertainment biographies picked up most of the slack, moving from 26 percent of the market in 1900 to 55 percent of the market in 1940. In the 1901–1914 period, 77 percent of all entertainment biographies covered "serious" high art. The figure had fallen to 38 percent by the 1920s, and by 1940–41, only 9 percent of the entertainment biographies addressed high art.

COMMERCIAL MORALITY

When commerce de-links fame from merit, merit does not disappear from 10 social discourse. We can talk about merit without talking about fame in the same breath. Although separating fame and merit may be perceived by some as negative, it can also be viewed quite differently. It can be seen as the liberation of merit from fame, and from dependence on the famous for moral instruction.

Even if the fame of entertainers corrupts the realm of moral discourse, 11 moral discourse adjusts by relying less on fame. Audiences may respond to the charisma and wealth of Eddie Murphy and Madonna, but most people know that such performers are not the most virtuous individuals in society. Rather than looking to stars for moral inspiration, many turn elsewhere, to parents, relatives, or people renowned in realms where fame and merit are more closely linked than they are in popular culture.

In fact, moral discourse may operate more effectively when imperfect 12 and blemished individuals are in the public eye. Athletes, entertainers, and characters in television shows provide more complex models than do many saints, and thus they may serve as more fruitful topics of discussion.

When the meritorious and the famous are different individuals, the so- 13 cial vision of virtue rests less upon the adulation of personalities, and more on the critical analysis of personality traits. Since fans do not expect the famous to be fully moral or meritorious, they can separate the good and bad qualities of celebrities more sharply and cleanly. Thus, fans could approve of Michael Jordan's quest for excellence in sports while disapproving of his excessive gambling.

The severance of fame and merit allows us to evaluate different aspects 14 of an individual's behavior separately, rather than judging that person as uniformly good or bad. This more cautious kind of moral discourse may be more appropriate and more realistic than the uncritical elevation of moral and political leaders as heroes and heroines. Commercialized fame, by directing fame away from moral merit, frees ideas of virtue from the cult of personality. *Pace* Churchill, when it comes to working through complicated moral and ethical issues, the healthiest nations may well be those "whose brightest stars are film stars."

Heroes, by their very nature, serve as highly visible and sharply 15 focused reflections of various qualities in their societies, including morality. To the extent that such heroes dominate moral discourse, morality will be excessively black and white, some individuals will be undeservedly idolized, and personalities will be conflated with moral qualities. Because commercialization shifts moral discourse out of the realm of fame, it actually may improve moral discussions.

Role models don't automatically induce either moral or immoral behavior. Many people have already decided to act a certain way, and they seek out whichever role models will validate that behavior. Or else they interpret and reinterpret the qualities of role models in ways that support their preexisting agendas. In this way as in others, fans are not guided by the famous, they use the famous for their own purposes.   16

The original nature of a given "role model" has less influence than does the transformation of that model by fans and others. The story of Cal Ripken Jr., a very durable baseball player, has entered the public consciousness as a tale of heroism, even if Ripken is not a true hero by any exacting moral standards. Thomas Jefferson has moved from being a virtuous Founding Father to a morally ambiguous slaveholder.   17

THE TAMING OF FAME

Fame and merit have never been tightly connected, no matter what era we examine, or whether and how we define merit. Kings and queens were the best-known people of their times, but hardly worth praising in many instances. Commercialized fame, while taking relative recognition away from moral leaders, also has taken renown away from tyrants and violent rulers.   18

Many of the supposed "heroes" of the past were liars, frauds, and butchers. The association of fame with entertainers, for all its flaws, departs from earlier concepts of heroic brutality and martial virtue. Most of today's famous people have had to persuade consumers to offer their allegiance and their dollars. Nowadays fame is attained through a high-stakes game of pursuit and seduction, rather than a heroic contest or a show of force in battle. The shift in fame to entertainers is a modern extension of the Enlightenment doux commerce thesis that the wealth of the market civilizes morals and manners and supports an ethic of bourgeois virtue.   19

Cervantes was the first writer to recognize the importance of commercializing fame and the new breed of hero in commercial society. His protagonist Don Quixote seeks to create a chivalrous image that he took from the old world of medieval fame, in which the knowledge of great fighting deeds was spread by word of mouth. Cervantes portrayed this ideal of martial virtue as an ironic farce. Book 2 of *Don Quixote* showed that Don Quixote does in fact attain fame, but only by virtue of being the subject of an entertaining novel. Cervantes self-consciously presented the new world of fame achieved through commercial entertainment as displacing the older world of fame achieved through chivalry and heroism.   20

The traditions of antiquity also illustrate the essentially male nature of concepts of the heroic. Heroic standards were defined largely by males, and martial virtue was exhibited primarily by men. Women (albeit imaginary   21 ones) achieved mythological fame in their roles as goddesses, such as Aphrodite and Hera, or as mothers and wives of warriors, but they had a hard time winning fame for their independent achievements. Contemporary culture, in contrast, has erected a growing number of female icons.

CALLING PRINCESS DI

Princess Diana provided one example of the new feminine heroine ideal. [22] She embodied the quality of vulnerability, and that is one reason she attracted so much interest, especially from women. Diana struck an emotional pose, spoke openly of her feelings and her failures, and admitted her problems with depression, bulimia, and her marriage. She did not hesitate to cry in public. Nor did she hide her own fascination with fame and popular culture, so different from the prevailing aloofness of British royalty. In her 20s, Diana wanted to meet John Travolta. Compare this to earlier young European rulers, who sought their place in history by conquering other nations.

Ironically, the taming of fame also entails a growth in the number of [23] violent images. In a peaceful world, many fans seek cathartic experiences, and fame- and profit-seeking performers respond by meeting this demand. Clint Eastwood, Bruce Lee, Arnold Schwarzenegger, and many other contemporary and recent heroes represent the modern sublimation, transformation, and simulation of violent impulses. The same institutions that deglorify actual martial deeds—the entertainment businesses—end up glorifying *images* of martial deeds. In network television programming for children, each broadcast hour averages 22 simulations of acts of violence.

Modern commercial society therefore cannot fulfill the Enlightenment [24] promise of civilizing manners. While commercial society defangs fame and weakens the ethic of martial virtue, it provides new ways of experiencing violent images. Popular culture often portrays violence as fun. The same processes that lessen the status of real violent acts make simulated violence appear more glamorous and more attractive.

Yet commercialization also induces individuals to aim their glory- [25] seeking impulses toward peaceful ends. Rather than centralizing the rewards of fame in an absolutist state, or repressing fame-seeking impulses, commercialization decentralizes fame into market-based niches. In highly commercial societies, fame-seekers can achieve renown in science, sports, entertainment, and many other fields. These famous individuals cannot start wars, sway elections, or exercise coercive control over the lives of other people.

Contemporary stars are well-paid but impotent puppets. But these [26] market-based heroes are truly meritorious in one essential way: They serve their fans rather than making their fans serve them.

■   ■   ■

AFTER YOU READ

■ **THINK** about Cowen's statement that, according to Daniel Boorstin, "the concept of transient celebrity is replacing the concept of the true hero" (paragraph 2). Do you think this is an accurate observation? Why or why not? Do you consider most traditional heroes (George Washington, Thomas Jefferson, Abraham Lincoln, John F. Kennedy, Martin Luther King, Jr., General George Patton, General Colin Powell, General David Petraeus, etc.) to be true heroes? Can you think of "supposed 'heroes' of the past" who were "liars, frauds, and butchers" (paragraph 19)? Explain and give examples to support your responses to each of these questions.

■ **THINK** also about Cowen's conclusion that celebrities—"market-based heroes" in sports, entertainment, science, or other fields—"serve their fans rather than making their fans serve them" (paragraph 26). Do you agree that there are some advantages in admiring celebrities rather than more traditional military and political figures, or do you ultimately agree with Boorstin that celebrities who represent fame without merit are poor heroes and role models? Explain.

■ **EXAMINE** the section of the essay entitled "The Changing Nature of Fame" (paragraphs 4 to 9). Who were the heroes of young people in 1898? In 1948? Who were the ten most admired figures in 1986? If a national survey about heroes were taken today, who do you think would be the top ten individuals? Who are your top ten heroes?

■ **EXAMINE** also the section entitled "Commercial Morality," especially paragraphs 10 through 16, in which Cowen discusses the relationship between fame and merit. How has "the liberation of merit from fame" (paragraph 10) changed the nature of heroism and celebrity in our society? How has this change led us to look beyond famous people "for moral inspiration" (paragraph 11)? Finally, explain the possible advantages of separating fame from merit that Cowen describes in paragraphs 12 through 15. Do you believe that the greater emphasis on fame today has changed for our society Daniel Boorstin's "concept of the true hero, who serves as a role model and exhibits moral leadership" (paragraph 2)? Has the increased emphasis on fame and famous people in our society made it necessary—or even desirable—to separate a role model from a hero or celebrity, or can the same person still fill both roles? Explain why you feel as you do.

■ **EXAMINE** also paragraphs 21 and 22. Do you agree with Cowen that our society's view of heroes has been traditionally male dominated? Have you observed in recent years, as Cowen has, a "new feminine heroine ideal" (paragraph 22) in figures like Princess Diana? If so, can you identify other women who fit this ideal? Finally, do you agree or disagree with Cowen that as both men and women in our society seek to reduce actual violence, there has been an increase in the imagery of violence in films and other media (paragraph 23)? Do you believe that this trend suggests something about the relative impact of male and female heroes and role models in our society? If so, what does it suggest?

■ **WRITE** an essay in which you define and distinguish between a hero and a role model. Be sure to give specific examples of both heroes and role models.

■ Or **WRITE** a response essay in which you argue that separating fame from merit is or is not good for our society. Use specific support from Cowen's essay as well as your own ideas. (See "Responding to a Text," pages 244–247.)

I Am Not a Role Model

■ ■ ■

Charles Barkley

One of the greatest players in the history of the National Basketball Association, Charles Barkley is one of only four players to have compiled over 20,000 points, 10,000 rebounds, and 4,000 assists. Barkley, who was voted the NBA's Most Valuable Player in 1993 and elected to the Naismith Memorial Basketball Hall of Fame in 2006, was drafted by the Philadelphia 76ers in 1984, played for the Phoenix Suns from 1992 to 1996, and concluded his career with the Houston Rockets, retiring at the end of the 2000 season because of a knee injury. Throughout his career, the undersized power forward (only 6 feet 4 inches, although he was listed as 6 feet and 6 inches) outsmarted and outmaneuvered the giants in the game, but he may be even better known today for his controversial actions and comments than for his skill. The following essay, which was published in Barkley's straightforward autobiography *I May Be Wrong but I Doubt It* (2002), deals with the relative qualities of fame and merit in celebrities and role models that was discussed by Cowen in the previous essay.

BEFORE YOU READ

- ■ THINK about the idea of role models, especially of celebrities as role models. Are the best role models people you know, or can people you read about or see on the media also become effective role models? Explain your opinion.
- ■ EXAMINE the title, "I Am Not a Role Model." In 1993, Barkley made a controversial Nike commercial on this theme, saying he wasn't "paid" to be a role model and parents should be role models to their kids. (You can view this commercial on YouTube.)
- ■ EXAMINE also the words *emulate* (paragraph 5) and *mentors* (paragraph 6). To *emulate* is to imitate, striving to equal or excel. A *mentor* is a wise and trusted teacher or counselor.
- ■ WRITE a journal entry in which you explain why you believe celebrities can, or cannot be, good role models for young people. Be sure to include specific examples.

AS YOU READ

Underline passages in which Barkley explains why he is not a role model for most young people as well as the circumstances under which he believes he can be a role model.

■ ■ ■

Nike didn't come to me with the idea to do a commercial about role 1 models—I went to Nike with that idea. I talked to my friend the Nike executive Howard White about it, called him after thinking about it for a while, and said, "Howard, people have this role model thing completely screwed up. Is a role model just a celebrity that parents turn their kids over to? Damn, can't we do better than that? Is the best we can do for kids pointing them to celebrities they have no real chance of ever knowing?" I just thought we as a society need to do better in that area. So I asked, and Nike said, cool. And I thought it turned out great.

Remember, the main theme was "I am not a role model." 2

And for that, I got ripped. I'd been criticized before, of course, for 3 having my own take on social issues. But the first time I got hit really hard was for taking that stance. There were some columnists who defended me, but mostly I got killed. I'm okay with it, though, because nobody in all this time has been able to convince me that it's wrong to tell kids to listen to their parents and not a basketball player they've never met. How crazy is it to get slammed for saying, "Listen to your parents, listen to your teachers, listen to the responsible adults in your neighborhood or people who have done something with their lives." I know it's hard to get an entire message across in less than a minute. But I still believe the message was clear enough that I thought kids need to be able to look up to folks right there around them who can teach them hard work and right from wrong.

Celebrities can't teach 'em that from television. People are crazy. Or 4 maybe they're just lazy, they don't want to do the hard work, and it's easier to just turn their kids over to somebody 'cause he's famous. How stupid is that? How can you make somebody your role model when you don't know the person? All they've got most of the time is a perception of somebody off in the distance that might be totally distorted . . . or it could be the person is just misunderstood. One thing I hate is that all the general public knows about an athlete or a celebrity is what they know from the media, which is often inaccurate or incomplete. I know cases where a guy is labeled a bad guy and he's really a good guy, maybe worthy of being a role model for kids he's close to. And I know of way too many instances where the guy comes off as a good guy in the media and he's not a good guy at all. And that's a huge problem. Either way, how could that person be a legitimate role model for a kid? Because he's famous? Because he's on TV? Can he help get questions answered for you or do anything that's specific to what you need?

Television is entertainment. I love television. And in this second stage   5
of my life it pays me well. But television is entertainment, television is
celebrity. And with so few people to emulate in their neighborhoods, black
kids started fantasizing about being athletes. And having dreams is great,
but how can somebody on TV help give you any direction? That's a one-
way relationship. A ballplayer you can only see on TV may inspire you to
do great things in athletics, sure. You can look at sports all day and want
to try and do things on a court or a field like that player. But that can't
help you with your homework, or with real aspirations, or help you if
you're having problems at home. How does an athlete help you if you're
a terrible athlete but a decent student and you need encouragement to compete academically?

A role model should be among the people who can influence your   6
direction in a real-life way. The best scenario is if they can be actually in
your life. My mother and grandmother were my two biggest role models;
my dad wasn't there. It was my mother and grandmother. A role model, in
my way of thinking, is somebody who can help shape your life and what
you believe in. And it can't be somebody on television, somebody you can't
touch or go to for advice, or cuss you out when it's necessary or sit and
listen to you. It may be more important to have mentors than role models
anyway, maybe somebody you can talk to about stuff you may not feel
comfortable talking to your parents about. It needs to be somebody
who's not going to tell you exactly what you want to hear all the time.

At the time, I felt I needed to attack the subject because on the whole I   7
don't think athletics are good for black kids. I really don't. I got to this
point because every single time I go and talk to black children or teenagers
at a school or at an event, they only want to play sports. I'll ask them what
they want to do after high school or about their plans in the next few years
and it's always "I want to play pro basketball" or "I want to play in the
NFL." Every single one, it seems to me, wants to play sports for a living.
It's like there's some mental block, or they've been conditioned or brain-
washed to feel they can't do anything but play sports. And it's scary to
me. It bothers me. Obviously, I'm not against sports; I'm thankful for everything a career in professional sports has given me. But I don't know of
any other culture where the children all want to do the same thing. I've
never heard of any other situation like that.

I know this is complex and there are some real contradictions here be-   8
cause the most really influential group of black people in America is made
up of a lot of athletes. There aren't any Martin Luther Kings or Malcolm
Xs or Medgar Everses leading the black community right now. Almost everybody, among the most prominent people in our communities right now,
who has achieved any status the past twenty-five years has done so
through athletics, which in a way is really a shame. We have a lot of hard-
working people, folks doing backbreaking work. But we still don't see the
doctors and lawyers and engineers we need to see and need to have portrayed and need to treat as role models. And the ones we do have don't
have any real platform. They're not doing anything controversial enough

or scandalous enough to get profiles in the mainstream magazines. Athletes and entertainers are the only ones among us who have the platform, mostly because they're on television every day.

So when you seriously start to think about it, our kids are so limited in 9 the number of successful black people they can see or be exposed to. They see athletes and entertainers and what else? How often do they see scientists and engineers and writers? They don't. I know in my own neighborhood, I didn't know any black doctors or lawyers or professional black folks. They weren't in the projects where I grew up. I know a whole lot of these kids I'm talking to come from neighborhoods that ain't all that different from mine.

I'm not saying that poor white kids and Hispanic kids don't have sim- 10 ilar issues with this, because I suspect they do, too. And I'm not saying that only professional people can be role models. A guy working the nine-to-five cleaning the streets or running the grocery store on the corner could be a great role model. You need to see honest, hardworking people and appreciate what they're doing with their lives. And just because somebody doesn't have a college degree doesn't mean he or she can't help give some direction to a kid who can't get it anywhere else. But we also need our kids to see some professional people they can aspire to be like, and they don't see enough. Every kid can't be Michael Jordan or Will Smith, and shouldn't want to be. But this is what they see in their lives every day, because for so many of them they ain't got anything positive going on at home.

Anyway, this had been bothering me for a while and I wanted to use 11 my own platform to address it. And I never thought so many people would miss the bigger message. I found it interesting in the spring of 2002 that somebody came up with this TV campaign: "Parents, the anti-drug." Isn't that the same point I was making in the role model commercial? That campaign is a damn good reminder. But it's nothing different from what I was saying in the role model commercial. What's different about it? It doesn't say, "Athletes and celebrities, the anti-drug," does it? I wasn't supposed to have any ideas of my own or talk about anything serious?

All I was saying was your parents and your teachers, people you ought 12 to be listening to, need to be your role models. Charles Barkley the basketball player should not be your role model. Yeah, I can be a role model to my daughter and to kids I have some contact with. But that's not only Charles Barkley the basketball player, that's me as a father, or a parental figure. Those kids don't see me only on TV, there's an actual relationship there, or at least some association. How many people on TV do these kids have an association with? We all know the answer is "None."

But if it took me getting slammed to get some dialogue started on this 13 issue, then it was worth it. I'd do it again in a second.

■   ■   ■

AFTER YOU READ

■ **THINK** about Barkley's declaration that he can serve as a role model only to his "daughter and to kids [he has] more contact with" (paragraph 12). Do you agree with Barkley, or do you think Cowen is right when he asserts that "athletes, entertainers, and characters in television shows provide more complex models" and therefore "may serve as more fruitful topics of discussion" about role models for young people (page 495, paragraph 12)? Why do you feel as you do?

■ **EXAMINE** the passages you underlined in which Barkley explains why an athlete or celebrity is not a good role model for kids. What are Barkley's arguments? In his opinion, who makes the best role models? Who were his own role models, and why were they important to him?

■ **EXAMINE** also paragraphs 7–10, in which Barkley focuses on the role models admired by black youth. Why does he believe that, in general, athletes are not good role models for young black men? What kind of role models besides family members does he believe these young people need? Do you agree or disagree with Barkley? How has the election of President Barack Obama changed the role-model situation for blacks that Barkley describes? Explain and support your opinions.

■ **WRITE** an essay arguing that a particular athlete or celebrity is or is not a good role model for today's youth. (For help with writing a persuasive essay, see pages 372–378.)

True Grit

■ ■ ■

BARRY TARGAN

The award-winning author Barry Targan is a man of many interests and talents. In addition to publishing several collections
of poetry and short stories and three novels, Targan has been
a teacher, violinist, photographer, naturalist, sailor, gardener,
and potter. His stories have won several Pushcart Prizes and the
O. Henry Award and have been anthologized in *Best American
Short Stories*. In the following excerpt from a longer autobiographical essay, Targan argues that an individual's commitment
to his or her family and work is more heroic than the deeds of
legendary heroes. In so doing, Targan shows that his father was
the true role model that Barkley believes a parent should be.

BEFORE YOU READ

■ **THINK** about the title, "True Grit," which is an allusion to a 1969 John
Wayne movie. In the movie, Wayne's "true grit" is shown through
physical courage, but this term can also refer to other types of courage.
Does sacrificing for one's family also require true grit? To go to work
when one is sick or in pain? In the portion of Targan's essay that precedes the excerpt printed here, he explains that his father, who owned a
vegetable stand that he later expanded to a small grocery store in a losing battle against the supermarkets, missed only one day of work—the
painful day that he spent in bed when he had all his teeth pulled.

■ **EXAMINE** the first two paragraphs of this essay, which list several legendary heroes. Although you will recognize many of the individuals and
groups to whom Targan refers, there are some allusions that might not
be familiar to you. You will no doubt know that John Wayne was a
famous Western movie actor, and you will probably recognize the
names of John Glenn, the first U.S. astronaut to orbit the earth and later
a four-term senator from Ohio; and General Douglas MacArthur, the
popular but controversial general who commanded the Southwest
Pacific Theater in World War II, carried out the occupation of Japan,
and was dismissed as commander of the Korean War front for publicly
advocating an invasion of China.

However, you may not know that Zeus is the powerful king of the
gods in ancient Greek mythology, that Hector is the greatest of the Tro-
jan heroes in Homer's *Iliad*, that Charles Lindbergh made the first solo
nonstop transatlantic flight from New York to Paris in 1927, or that
"pulling guards" are simply the guards in football who are positioned

next to the center and who move out of position to protect the quarter-
back. Notice also the word *maybe* at the end of paragraph 2. What
effect does this word have, and what does its use lead you to expect
about the rest of the essay?

■ **EXAMINE** also the words *Excalibur* and *chimera,* as shown in context
here:

1.   "No magical *Excalibur* singing in his hand, only a small sharp knife
     with which to trim the icy lettuce" (paragraph 3). *Excalibur* was
     King Arthur's sword, which he magically pulled out of a stone to
     prove that he was the true king of England.

2.   "The worst my father could imagine befalling him was not the
     short-term robber but the long-term inability to provide for those he
     loved. Against that *chimera* guns could not prevail" (paragraph 5).
     In Greek mythology the *chimera* was a terrible monster—part lion,
     part goat, and part serpent—that terrorized the land and was killed
     by the hero Bellerophon. By referring to a chimera, Targan suggests
     that his father is a hero for successfully fighting against the fear of
     failing to provide for his family.

■ **WRITE** a journal entry in which you describe how someone you know
has shown true grit in his or her daily life.

AS YOU READ

Determine how the heroism portrayed by Targan's father differs from the
heroism of the heroes listed in Targan's first two paragraphs. Do you believe that Targan's father is a greater or lesser hero than these individuals?

■ ■ ■

There are . . . powerful . . . reasons for our "definition" of the   1
hero: we hate to fear, but even more we hate ourselves for fearing.
The "hero"—the football player, the boxer, John Glenn, General
MacArthur, John Wayne—confronts fear for us, symbolically absorbs the
danger and pain that we cannot, or would rather not. Takes the punishment. Hangs tough, or at least appears to do so. Through our champions
we live, for the moment, cleansed of some of our deepest anxieties and self-
doubts. In a ritual act of thankfulness we give ticker-tape parades to the
winner of the World Series or turn out at the airport at 3 A.M. to greet
the Victors of the NBA or of the Super Bowl. For one brief shining hour
we are those champions. Like Zeus himself, with all his/our weaknesses,
yet are we in that moment, omnipotent. Let the cannons roar, the rifles
volley, the trumpets blast their fanfares!

Hector, heavyweight champions, Lindbergh, soldiers in combat, pulling   2
guards, inner-city vigilantes, astronauts, Texas Rangers . . . heroes all. Maybe.

On the other hand, I think of my father, who arose each morning to   3
go forth compelled by no ideology or creed or belief or quest for self-glory
or the need to impose some truth upon others and certainly not by any
sense of martyrdom. He was compelled only by the beautiful necessity to
do what his life required of him. No magical Excalibur singing in his hand,
only a small sharp knife with which to trim the icy lettuce. Unlike the abstract courage embodied in the mythicized hero, my father's courage was
rooted in the truly extraordinary strength of the uncompromising love
that defends and takes personal responsibility for the lives that it creates.

That is heroic courage. It is discovered not in a single act of heroism or   4
in a victory of some sort or by demonstrations of physical bravery; truly
heroic courage might include such things, but it transcends them. Such heroic courage is determined by the quality and magnitude of what is lived
for, the worth of what is lived for. My father lived for what he loved, for
what is profoundly and fundamentally worth loving. Against such values
nothing can be compared.

I do not know if my father was a physically brave man. In his little   5
store as the neighborhood around him disintegrated and became more
and more dangerous, he refused to keep a gun under the counter. It was
not his style. But I think he understood intuitively that what defended
him was his invincible faith in his own determination. He would not give
in to A&P or to the threatening violence that began to rise around him. Or
to fear. I think he believed at some level that fear, like victory, was actually
a kind of metaphor: fear, like victory, stood for something else. If you were
afraid of someone, some entity, then you got a gun. If you strove for a
victory, it had to be a victory over someone or something, a person or a
nation or an idea or a baseball team. But my father was not afraid of
such entities, and he did not conceive of his victory in such limited terms.
The worst my father could imagine befalling him was not the short-term
robber but the long-term inability to provide for those he loved. Against
that chimera guns could not prevail. Only his effort, his work. What victories he imagined had nothing to do with such abstractions as prestige or
status or with such tangibles as an expensive car or well-cut clothing
or a vacation in Florida. The only victory my father sought was to have
"enough," even if only just enough.

Such attitudes, such values, gave him considerable advantages. My   6
father was, it seemed, entirely without envy. For businesses that succeeded
as his did not, he had only admiration. For those that failed, businesses or
people, he had always pity, an empathetic compassion. He simply did not
have the time, certainly not the psychic energy, to spend on anything that
would not create for him his requisites. Which does not mean that he was
a narrow man limited in his concerns. He had fiercely passionate political
feelings, but not so much an allegiance to party or platform. His was more
an attitude, an orientation. His stand was for humane justice, for the un-
derdog, for social equity. For a genuine freedom for people. In his youth he
had been a Wobblie, had demonstrated for Eugene Debs. A lifetime later
he had not moved much from that position.

In the last correspondence I had with him shortly before his death 7 he enclosed in the letter an editorial that had recently appeared in the *Philadelphia Bulletin.* The editorial excoriated the conduct of Judge Julius Hoffman, who was presiding at the trial of the Chicago Seven. The editorial, while coming down hard on the accused, yet was much harder on the judge, for it was he, the judge, in whose hands all our justice rested. His conduct was dangerous and inexcusable. My father had underlined in blue pencil all the good parts, the hardest condemnations, to emphasize his agreement. That was my father.

Perhaps, in the general scheme of things, there is still need for the tra- 8 ditional idealized hero—or, rather, a need to idealize in the warrior (or warrior-athlete) those virtues we still consider to be the highest, most honorable virtues. But if our human civilization is to endure—to triumph, then my father's quiet but relentless heroism, that of the uncommon man, is the heroism that ultimately and alone will sustain us.

■ ■ ■

AFTER YOU READ

■ **THINK** about people you have known who exhibit the same kind of courage shown by Targan's father. Have your parents, or parents of your friends, shown this kind of courage? Do you know other owners of small businesses who have tried to survive the modern competition of supermarkets and discount stores? Do you consider these people heroic? Why or why not?

■ **EXAMINE** Targan's definition of *courage,* or *true grit,* in paragraphs 3, 4, and 8. Rewrite this definition in your own words and then discuss it with your classmates.

■ **EXAMINE** also the references in paragraphs 6 and 7 to Wobblies, Eugene Debs, the Chicago Seven, and Judge Julius Hoffman. Eugene Debs was a sociologist who in 1905 founded the Industrial Workers of the World; members were informally known as Wobblies. The Chicago Seven were a group of radicals charged with, but cleared of, conspiring to incite riots at the 1968 Democratic National Convention in Chicago. Judge Julius Hoffman, who presided over that 1969 trial, appeared to be biased against the defendants.

■ **WRITE** an essay in which you first summarize Targan's definition of courage and then agree or disagree with it, explaining why you feel as you do. Support your essay with brief quotations from "True Grit" as well as specific examples from your personal experience. You will find guidelines for summarizing on pages 186–188 and suggestions for responding to an essay on pages 244–247.

UNIT EIGHT

■ ■ ■

Critical Thinking, Reading, and Writing

■ **WRITING A MOVIE REVIEW**

Americans love movies. We line up for hours to see a first release at a theater, we rent or buy the videocassette or DVD, and we watch reruns of old movies on late-night television. Many of these movies focus on heroic individuals; indeed, the heroes of our movies embody the qualities we value most. In an article entitled "On Heroes and the Media," Jean Picker Firstenberg explains that the heroes of our movies reflect our changing concept of the hero (this essay appeared in *Interactions*, 5th edition, pp. 514–517). The focus has moved from romantic heroes like Clark Gable in the 1930s and 1940s; to "larger-than-life" heroes portrayed by John Wayne in the 1950s; to frailer, more sensitive heroes or antiheroes of the 1960s, represented by Dustin Hoffman in *The Graduate;* to the return of powerful figures such as Superman in the 1970s and 1980s. After a flurry of action heroes in the 1990s, we have seen in recent years the return of mythic and fantasy heroes (in *The Lord of the Rings,* the *Harry Potter* series, and *Avatar*), war heroes (in *Saving Private Ryan, Black Hawk Down,* and *The Hurt Locker*), and historical heroes (in *Braveheart, Elizabeth,* and *300*), as well as re-creations of the heroism that took place on September 11, 2001 (in *United 93* and *World Trade Center*). This lesson will provide you with the instruction you need to write a **review**—an analysis and evaluation—of a classic or modern movie that focuses on a hero, a heroine, or an act of heroism.

BEFORE YOU WRITE

Your first task is to choose the movie you want to review and then to view it carefully. Because you need to look for specific information as you view the movie, you should keep in mind the various elements of a movie review (see the list on page 510) as you watch the film and as you take notes on it afterward. Thus, this preliminary stage has two parts: (1) viewing the movie and taking preliminary notes, and (2) planning your organization.

Viewing the Movie and Taking Preliminary Notes
Be sure that the movie you select includes a hero or heroine or deals with some aspect of heroism. Remember, though, that heroes aren't always larger-than-life figures and that ordinary people can perform heroic acts and live heroic lives as well.

You should take notes on the movie as soon as you can after viewing it. (If you are watching a video or a DVD, you may be able to take notes as you view the film.) It is a good idea to see the movie at least twice, reviewing your notes between viewings to determine what you need to look for the second time. Remember that you will need to record from the credits (or from the cover of the DVD or videocassette case) the names of the production studio, the director, the major performers, and—depending on the focus of your review—perhaps the scriptwriter, costume designer, music director, and/or cinematographer.

Planning Your Organization

Understanding the essential elements and the basic organization of a movie review will help you in taking your preliminary notes as well as in writing your review. Like most other types of writing, a movie review has an introduction, a body, and a conclusion. Although the length and content of movie reviews vary widely, most reviews include the following elements:

1. Introduction (background, purpose, and thesis statement)
2. Summary (plot, major points)
3. Analysis and discussion (two or three of the following elements)

   - Major characters and the actors who portray them
   - Language and dialogue
   - Costumes and setting
   - Special effects (music, sound, lighting, and animation)
   - Theme(s)

4. Evaluation (strengths and weaknesses)
5. Conclusion and perhaps recommendation

These elements are the building blocks of a good review, but no single review is likely to include a discussion of all the analysis and discussion elements. Moreover, you may want to arrange the elements of your review in a slightly different order from the one given here.

Depending on the information you have, you may include in your introduction background information on the director, on the original source if the movie is an adaptation of a book or play, or on the social or historical context of the movie's setting. Your introduction should also include the point you want to make about the movie (your thesis statement) and perhaps an explanation of the purpose and intended audience for the movie.

Your summary should be brief (no more than one paragraph), but it should provide enough information about the movie for your readers to follow your analysis (see "Writing a Summary," pages 186–188). You can selectively include details later to support points you are making in your analysis.

The longest section of your review will be your analysis. You should select for discussion the two or three elements that you believe are most important to the movie's achieving (or not achieving) its purpose. Whereas a review of *The Blind Side* would logically focus on character and performance, a review of *Star Trek* or *2012* would be more likely to focus on special effects. You may want to devote a paragraph to each of the elements you discuss. (See "Analyzing a Text" on pages 305–309.)

The last two elements of a movie review—evaluation and conclusion—are closely related. The evaluation usually occurs in a separate paragraph just before the conclusion, but the evaluation and conclusion may be combined in the same paragraph. It is also possible to include your evaluation in your earlier analysis of specific elements. If you are discussing performances and costuming in your review, for example, you might praise the performances but criticize the inaccurate costuming. Finally, you may want to include in your conclusion a recommendation about whether or not readers should spend the money and/or take the time to see the movie you have reviewed. Including a recommendation adds a persuasive element to your review.

Example

To help you write a more effective movie review, we have included here a sample review and a brief analysis of it.

Review of *Hero*

Viewing Stephen Frears's 1992 film *Hero* (Columbia Pictures) through the lenses of our nation's renewed interest in heroes gives added significance to the work and its theme. On one level, this dramatic comedy pokes fun at the overzealous media, who often care more about the story than the people involved. **More importantly, however, the film sensitively portrays two ordinary, down-on-their-luck men who become unlikely heroes and, in so doing, show us as viewers that we all have heroic potential.**   1

Produced at a time when heroes were slightly out of fashion, *Hero*   2
focuses on the disillusioned but basically kindhearted con man Bernard LaPlante, played by Dustin Hoffman, who just happens to be the closest observer of a plane crash. Initially more worried about the expensive shoe he loses than the individuals on the plane, Bernie is nevertheless drawn by cries for help from the plane—mired in the shallows of a river—and clumsily opens the jammed door, ultimately rescuing those trapped inside. While rescuing one of the passengers, reporter Gale Gayley (Geena Davis), Bernie also takes her purse. Arrested for trying to fence her credit cards, Bernie is in jail when Gayley's television network offers a reward for the mysterious hero. The award is claimed by John Bubber (Andy Garcia), a homeless man to whom Bernie has told his story and given his remaining shoe. Bubber becomes an immediate sensation, and romance seems possible for him and Gayley. The climax of the movie occurs when a guilt-ridden Bubber threatens to jump from a ledge and Bernie crawls out on the ledge to talk with him.

Characterization and performance are the most important elements of   3
this film. Hoffman is equally convincing as the bum who lifts money from his naïve young lawyer while she is trying to keep him out of jail and as the sensitive human being who is trying to reconnect with his own son and knowingly risks his own life when a boy at the crash site pleads with him

to go back into the plane to save his father. (Indeed, the surprise and horror of the crash itself are mirrored in Hoffman's expression rather than in expensive special effects.) Garcia also makes Bubber's transformation from a homeless man to a hero believable. Even though we as viewers are well aware of Bubber's deception and the motivation for it, his optimism, his concern for others, and his humility are all qualities of a true hero. Not forgetting where he came from, Bubber asks his admirers to provide blankets for the homeless, and his words of encouragement bring about the recovery of a boy in a coma. Adequate but less noteworthy is Geena Davis's portrayal of Gale Gayley, the apparently hard-nosed reporter who nevertheless longs to find true humanity in herself and in the world.

Created by screenwriter David Webb Peoples, the dialogue is a source   4
of both comedy and theme in the film. Gayley's boss, played by Chevy Chase, is full of one-liners, and LaPlante is basically a pathetic and comical character, "not the type" to be a hero, as he admits himself. In the last scene, Bubber—after actually saving LaPlante's life when he nearly falls from the ledge on which they are standing—directly states the film's theme:

> I think we're all heroes if you catch us at the right moment.
> We all have something noble and decent inside trying to get
> out, and we're all less than heroic at other times. It's the
> media that notices one person one moment and not another. I'm
> just like the next person, full of frailty with some courage
> and some decency mixed in. You think I'm a hero. To me a hero
> is just a symbol of what is good in all of us. You look at me,
> and maybe you just notice what's good in yourself.

The fact that both the articulate Bubber and the inarticulate   5
LaPlante, kind but often weak men, have the potential to be heroes underscores the somewhat sentimental truth of Bubber's statement. Indeed, the scene in which Bubber makes his statement, with LaPlante in the background, would have been an effective conclusion for the film. The final scene, in which LaPlante tries to give his son lessons in life, fails because LaPlante's true character, which is shown in his actions and his desire to remain unknown, is blurred by his quirky advice.

Even though this film is several years old, it is worth the time and   6
money it takes to see it. *Hero's* portrayal of heroism is comical, even farcical, on the surface, but the universal underlying theme about the heroic potential in ordinary human beings is presented seriously. Although the film focuses on two different heroes, its real subjects are the concept of the hero and heroism itself.

■   ■   ■

This review clearly follows the recommended guidelines. The first paragraph provides helpful background and states the thesis of the review—that we all have heroic potential—whereas the second paragraph summarizes the film's plot. The next two paragraphs analyze selected elements of the film. The major characters LaPlante (Hoffman), Bubber (Garcia), and Gayley (Davis) are discussed in paragraph 3; analysis of dialogue and recognition of the film's weaknesses are provided in paragraph 4. Finally, the concluding paragraph places the film in a larger context and restates the thesis.

Assignments

1. Many movies—those about superheroes, legendary and historical figures, and even realistic modern individuals—focus on a hero figure. Review a movie that includes a hero or heroine or that treats the subject of heroism in some way.

2. Television shows can also focus on heroism or heroic individuals. Write a review of a documentary, a made-for-television movie, or an episode from a series that focuses on a hero, heroine, or heroism.

3. Review a movie, documentary, or television episode centered on a role model.

AS YOU WRITE

Select carefully the film you want to review, being sure that it focuses on a heroic act or individual. In making your selection, pay attention to movie trailers and advertisements of current movies, spend some time reading the jackets of DVDs and videocassettes in your local movie store, and ask your family and friends about films they have seen. You may even want to watch two or three films before selecting the one you want to review.

After you have selected your film, view it carefully at least twice, taking the notes that you will need to develop the five parts of your review. Use the list of elements on page 510 as well as your notes to write an outline, which you can then develop into a draft of your review. As you write, remember to follow these guidelines:

- Provide necessary background information.

- State your thesis clearly.

- Keep your summary brief.

- Select and develop the two or three most important elements of the movie (characters, performers, language, dialogue, costumes, setting, special effects, and/or theme) in the body of your review.

- Conclude with your final evaluation and perhaps with a recommendation.

AFTER YOU WRITE

Movie reviews are usually written with a definite audience in mind: individuals who might view the movie. After you have completed a draft of your own review, meet with a group of your classmates and read your reviews aloud to one another. For each review, determine whether the author has given readers enough information to decide whether or not they would like to view the film without spoiling their pleasure in watching it. Identify the thesis of each review, and try to determine whether the writer has chosen the most appropriate elements of the movie for focused analysis.

After you have evaluated and revised the content of your review, edit it for problems in grammar, usage, sentence structure, and style. Then proofread your review carefully and submit the final draft to your instructor.

■ EXPLORING IDEAS TOGETHER

1. With a group of your classmates, make a list of all (or most) of the heroes—male and female—that you have read about in this unit. Then categorize, or group, these heroes according to basic similarities of the individuals or their situations. What categories do you have? Which qualities distinguish the heroes in each category? Into which category or categories do most heroes fit?

2. Discuss some individuals who were presented as heroes in history books in your high school and college history classes. Which of these individuals do you consider to be true heroes? Do you think the heroism of some other individuals was inflated? If so, who and why? On the other hand, do you think there has been too great a tendency recently to disregard historical and public heroes because of one or more personal flaws? Do you agree with Gibbon that our society— and young people in particular—needs heroes? Why do you feel as you do?

3. With a group of your classmates, discuss the differences between celebrities and heroes. (You may want to review the readings by Sudo and Cowen.) After you have discussed this issue with your group, write a collaborative statement explaining your position on the differences between being famous and being heroic.

■ EXPLORING THE INTERNET

Links on the *Interactions*, eighth edition, student website, at www.cengage brain.com, will help you complete the following exercises.

1. The CNN web page entitled War in Iraq has an excellent section on "Heroes of [the] War," which can be found as a link on the "Related Websites" section of the *Interactions* student website. The site includes detailed information about each hero listed. Work with a group of your classmates to select a single hero, and report to the class about this person.

2. A good website about heroes of the September 11, 2001, terrorist attacks is the America Remembers site sponsored by CNN, which is

available as a link on the "Related Websites" page of the *Interactions* website. Work with a group of your classmates to explore this website, with each group selecting one story or topic to study. After your group has read and discussed the story you have selected, prepare a brief oral report for the rest of the class on your chosen topic.

3. Look up the website entitled "Heroism Quotes" on the "Related Websites" page of the *Interactions* website. Read through several of the quotations on the site. Then select one to discuss in class or to use as a prompt for an essay on heroism.

4. To learn more about Rosa Parks, her life, and her heroism, examine her website, which is available as a link on the "Related Websites" section of the *Interactions* website.

■ WRITING ESSAYS

1. Use the discussion assignment for Item 2 of "Exploring Ideas Together" as an essay assignment in which you evaluate one or more historic or public figures—Christopher Columbus, George Washington, Thomas Jefferson, Ronald Reagan, Bill Clinton, George W. Bush, or Barack Obama, for example—who are often identified as heroic by public school teachers but perhaps later rejected as unheroic by college professors or political commentators (or vice versa). You may argue that the individual you select is or is not a true hero, but you must also recognize the opposing argument. You will find helpful guidelines for writing a persuasive essay on pages 372–378.

2. Write an essay expressing your own ideas about the true heroes of September 11 and its aftermath. You may argue for the heroism of frequently honored heroes such as the firefighters and police officers, the citizens who tried to take Flight 93 back from its captors, or the soldiers who have fought against terrorism in Afghanistan or Iraq. Or you may take a more original or controversial viewpoint, arguing for the heroism of government officials who had to do their jobs in the face of great criticism, the media whose members were put in harm's way as they sought to post stories that were often criticized back home, or groups that spoke out against the war on terrorism in some way.

3. Write an essay about a person who has performed a heroic act in war, in a natural disaster such as a flood or an earthquake, or in a local emergency, such as a fire or a car accident. Describe the event and explain how and why this person was heroic.

4. The reading selections by Loeb and Cowen focus on female heroes and role models. What woman do you personally consider a hero or role model? Write an essay about this person.

5. Several readings in this unit, including those by Sudo, Quiñones, and Loeb focus on heroes or role models from specific ethnic groups. Write

an essay about a hero or role model who has contributed to a particular culture. If necessary, do some research on the Internet or in the library about this person before writing your essay.

6. Write an essay in which you argue for or against the idea that a sports figure or an entertainer can be a true hero or role model. Be sure to use specific examples. You may want to use support from Barkley's essay as well as your own observations. (You will find helpful guidelines for writing a persuasive essay on pages 372–378 of Unit Six.)

7. In the final reading in this unit, Targan focuses on the concept of the "ordinary hero." Write an essay about an ordinary person whom you consider a hero or an important role model.

8. Write a letter (or an essay) recommending someone you know for a citation for heroism. Your purpose is to persuade the committee awarding the citation to select your nominee. Therefore, you should include specific supporting details as well as examples that will convince your audience.

9. Write an essay in which you answer the question "Are heroes born or made?" Which element is more crucial in determining whether an individual becomes a hero—the individual's existing, or developing, character or the crucial situation in which he or she is involved?

10. Write an essay in which you evaluate yourself as a potential hero (or role model). Begin by providing your definition of a hero (or role model) and then show how you do, or do not, fit that definition. In your evaluation, you may want to consider how you have lived your daily life as well as whether you have performed "heroic" actions. Whether you find heroism in your earlier life or not, do you think you have the potential for heroism? How can you further develop your heroic potential?

CREDITS

This page constitutes an extension of the copyright page. We have made every effort to trace the ownership of all copyrighted material and to secure permission from copyright holders. In the event of any question arising as to the use of any material, we will be pleased to make the necessary corrections in future printings. Thanks are due to the following authors, publishers, and agents for permission to use the material indicated. Items are arranged in the order in which they appear in the book.

INTRODUCTION

UNIT ONE

2009, pp. 44–49. Reprinted by permission of the Joy Harris Literary Agency, Inc. **Mabry, p. 31:** "Living in Two Worlds," by Marcus Mabry, *Newsweek on Campus Supplement*, April 1988. Reprinted by permission of the author. **Soto, p. 35:** "The Jacket" from *The Effects of Knut Hamsun on a Fresno Boy: Recollections and Short Essays* by Gary Soto. Copyright © 1983, 2000 by Gary Soto. Reprinted by permission of Persea Books, Inc., New York. **Raymond, p. 39:** "On Being 17, Bright, and Unable to Read" by David Raymond. *The New York Times*, April 25, 1976. Reprinted by permission of The New York Times. **Bernstein, 43:** "The Need for Achievement," from *Essentials of Psychology,* 5th edition, by Douglas A. Bernstein. Cengage/Wadsworth. **Logan, p. 48:** Logan, Paul. "Zero." From MAKING THE MOST OF YOUR LIFE: EIGHT MOTIVATIONAL STORIES AND ESSAYS, edited by John Langan. Copyright © 2008 by Townsend Press, Inc. Reprinted by permission of Townsend Press: www.townsendpress.com. **Noda, p. 55:** "Growing Up Asian" by Kesaya E. Noda. From *Making Waves by Asian Women United of California*. Published by Beacon Press. Reprinted by permission of the author.

UNIT TWO

Herrick, p. 65: "What Is This Thing Called Family" by Lee Herrick. Reprinted by permission of the author. **Strong/DeVault/Cohen, p. 69:** "Defining Family" from THE MARRIAGE AND FAMILY EXPERIENCE, 10th ed., by Bryan Strong, Christine Devault, Theodore F. Cohen. Copyright © 2008 by Wadsworth, a part of Cengage Learning, Inc. Reproduced by permission: www.cenage.com/permissions. **Angelou, p. 73:** From EVEN THE STARS LOOK LONESOME, 47–49, by Maya Angelou. Copyright © 1997 by Maya Angelou. Used by permission of Random House, Inc. **King, p. 76:** This essay from THE OLD MAN AND LESSER MORTALS is reprinted from WARNING: WRITER AT WORK, THE BEST COLLECTIBLES OF LARRY L. KING. Texas Christian University Press. Permission granted by Texhouse Corporation, Barbara S. Blaine, PC, Washington, DC, agent. **Cisneros, p. 80:** "Only Daughter," copyright © 1990 by Sandra Cisneros. First published in GLAMOUR, November 1990. By permission of Susan Bergholz Literary Services, New York, NY, and Lamy, NM. All rights reserved. **Liao, p. 84:** Sharon Liao, "A Daughter's Journey." *The Washingtonian*, January 2001. Copyright © by *The Washingtonian*; reprinted by permission. **Herman, p. 92:** "A Parent's Journey Out of the Closet," by Agnes G. Herman, *Reconstructionist*, Vol. 51, No. 2, October, 1985. Reprinted by permission. **Klagsbrun, p. 99:** "Sibling Imprints" by Francine Klagsbrun, from *Mixed Feelings: Love, Hate, Rivalry, and Reconciliation Among Brothers and Sisters,* 1992. Copyright © 1992 by Francine Klagsbrun. Reprinted by permission of the Charlotte Sheedy Literary Agency. **Lott, p. 106:** "Brothers" by "Bret Lott, *Antioch Review*, Winter 1993. Copyright © 1993 by The Antioch Review, Inc. Reprinted by permission of Antioch Review. **Fowler, p. 112:** "No Snapshots in the Attic: A Granddaughter's Search for a Cherokee Past" by Connie May Fowler, *The New York Times Book Review*, Vol. 99, May 22, 1994, p. 49–50. Reprinted by permission of the author. **Alvarez, p. 120:** "Hold the Mayonnaise" by Julia Alvarez. Copyright © 1992 by Julia Alvarez. First published in *The New York Times Magazine*, January 12, 1992. By permission of Susan Bergholz Literary Services, New York, NY, and Lamy, NM. All rights reserved. **Goodman, p. 124:** Reprinted with the permission of Simon and Schuster, Inc., from KEEPING IN TOUCH by Ellen Goodman. Copyright © 1985 by The Washington Post Company. All rights reserved. **Hartsfield, p. 130:** Student essay. Reprinted by permission of the author.

UNIT FIVE

UNIT SIX

Demko, p. 315: "A Sense of Place" by George J. Demko with Jerome Agel and Eugene Boe, 1992. Reprinted by permission of Nina Agel. **Norris, p. 319:** "Weather Reports" from DAKOTA by Kathleen Norris. Copyright © 1993 by Kathleen Norris. Reprinted by permission of Houghton Mifflin Harcourt Publishing Company. All rights reserved. **Crenshaw, p. 325:** "Storm Country" by Paul Crenshaw. Reprinted by permission of the author. **Cooper, p. 332:** Excerpt from pp. 123–127 from DISPATCHES FROM THE EDGE by ANDERSON COOPER. Copyright © 2006 by Anderson Cooper. Reprinted by permission of HarperCollins Publishers. **Flesher and Schwartz, p. 337:** "Rescuing Oiled Birds" by John Flesher and Noaki Schwartz. Originally appeared as "Rescuing oiled birds: Poignant, but is it futile?" Posted by Associated Press online on June 10, 2010, including a version without authors on al.com. Reprinted by permission of the YGS Group. **Wallace, p. 341:** "ANWR: The Great Divide" by Scott Wallace, *Smithsonian*. October 2005, Vol. 36, No. 7, pp. 50–53. Reprinted by permission of the author. **Grunwald, p. 347:** "Seven Myths about Alternative Energy" by Michael Grunwald. From FOREIGN POLICY: THE MAGAZINE OF GLOBAL POLITICS, ECONOMICS AND IDEAS. Copyright © 2009 by FOREIGN POLICY. Reproduced with permission of FOREIGN POLICY in the format Textbook via Copyright Clearance Center. **Gore, p. 355:** "The True Cost of Carbon" by AL GORE, from OUR CHOICE: A PLAN TO SOLVE THE CLIMATE CRISIS. Reprinted from OUR CHOICE by Al Gore. Copyright © 2009 by Al Gore. Permission granted by Rodale, Inc., Emmaus, PA 18098. **Singer and Avery, p. 360:** "Is Humanity Losing the Global Warming Debate?" from UNSTOPPABLE GLOBAL WARMING: EVERY 1,500 YEARS by S. Fred Singer and Dennis T. Avery, pp. 1–4, 2007. Reprinted by permission of Rowman and Littlefield Publishing Group. **Berry, p. 365:** "Waste." Copyright © 1990 by Wendell Berry from *What Are People For?* Reprinted by permission of Counterpoint. **Cullen, p. 369:** "It's Inconvenient Being Green" by Lisa Takeuchi Cullen, TIME Magazine, December 3, 2007. Copyright © 2007 by TIME INC. Reprinted by permission. TIME is a registered trademark of Time, Inc. All rights reserved. **Camburn, p. 373:** Student essay. Reprinted by permission of the author.

UNIT SEVEN

Rich, p. 383: "Literacy Debate: R U Really Reading?" by Motoko Rich. From *The New York Times*, copyright July 27, 2008 by The New York Times. All rights reserved. Used by permission and protected by the Copyright Laws of the United States. The printing, copying, redistribution, or retransmission of the Material without express written permission is prohibited. **Danforth, p. 389:** "Games and Literacy" by Liz Danforth, *Library Journal*, June 15, 2009, p. 50. Reprinted by permission of Library Journals LLC for the author. **Young, p. 393:** "Fraternities of Netheads" by Kimberly Young, from *Caught in the Net*, 1998, pp. 174–179. Copyright © 1998. Reprinted with permission of John Wiley and Sons, Inc. **Laird, p. 399:** Ellen Laird, "We ALL Pay for Internet Plagiarism," *Education Digest*, November 2001 (based on article in the *Chronicle of Higher Education*, July 13, 2001, p. 85.) Reprinted by permission of Ellen Laird, Associate Professor, English, at Hudson Valley Community College, Troy, NY. **Niedzviecki, p. 404:** "Facebook in a Crowd" by Hal Niedzviecki. From *The New York Times [Magazine]*. Copyright © October 26, 2008. The New York Times. All rights reserved. Used by permission and protected by the Copyright Laws of the United States. The printing, copying, redistribution, or retransmission of the Material without express written permission is prohibited. **Rosen, p. 407:** "Bad Connections" by Christine Rosen, *New York Times Magazine*, March 20, 2005, pp. 17–19. Reprinted by permission of the author. **Jacinto, p. 412:** "Buckle Up & Stop Texting" by Margie Jacinto, *Texas Heritage for Living*, Summer 2010, pp. 15–17. Reprinted by permission of Texas Farm Bureau. **Caudron, p. 415:** "The Real Digital Divide" by Shari Caudron, *Workforce Magazine*, July 2002. Reprinted by permission of the author. **Coleman, p. 420:** Sarah Coleman, "The Distorting Mirror of Reality TV." Reprinted by permission of the author. **Grossman, p 424:** "YouTube: The People's Network by Lev Grossman," *Time*, November 13, 2006, pp. 62–63. Reprinted by permission of the author. **Noonan, p. 428:** "The Blogs Must Be Crazy" by Peggy Noonan. *The Wall Street Journal* (Editoral Page), February 17, 2005. WALL STREET JOURNAL, EASTERN EDITION, by Peggy Noonan. Copyright © 2005 by DOW JONES & COMPANY, INC. Reproduced with permission of DOW JONES & COMPANY, INC. in the same format Textbook via Copyright Clearance Center. **Lyons, p. 434:** "In iPad We Trust" by Daniel Lyons. From *Newsweek*, copyright © February 8, 2010 by Newsweek, Inc. All rights reserved. Used by permission and protected by the Copyright Laws of the United States. The printing, copying, redistribution, or retransmission of the Material without express written permission is prohibited. **Mills, p. 437:** "Could You Live with Less?" by Stephanie Mills, *Glamour*, May 1998. Reprinted by permission of the author. **Holm, p. 443:** Student essay. Reprinted by permission of the author.

UNIT EIGHT

Sudo, p. 454: "Larger than Life" by Phil Sudo. From SCHOLASTIC UPDATE, November 1990. Copyright © 1990 by Scholastic, Inc. Reprinted by permission of Scholastic, Inc. **Quiñones, p. 457:** "Risking Your Life for Another" from pages 131–138 of HEROES AMONG US by John Quiñones. Copyright © 2009 by John Quiñones. Reprinted by permission of HarperCollins publishers. **Weisskopf, p. 463:** "My Right Hand" from BLOOD BROTHERS: AMONG THE SOLDIERS OF WARD 57 by Michael Weisskopf. Copyright © 2006 by Michael Weisskopf. Reprinted by arrangement with Henry Holt and Company, LLC. **Norman, p. 469:** "Ferguson" by Michael Norman. From *The New York Times Magazine*, copyright © May 25, 2008 by The New York Times. All rights reserved. Used by permission and protected by the Copyright Laws of the United States. The printing, copying, redistribution, or retransmission of the Material without express written permission is prohibited. **Moon, p. 472:** Student essay. Reprinted by permission of author. **Thompson, p. 477:** Nicholas Thompson, "Hero Inflation," *The Boston Globe*, January 13, 2002. Reprinted by permission of the author. **Gibbon, p. 482:** Peter H. Gibbon, "Giving Students the Heroes They Need." From Peter H. Gibbon, *A Call to Heroism: Renewing America's Vision of Greatness.* Copyright © 2002. Reprinted by permission of the author. **Loeb, p. 486:** "Rosa Parks Through a New Lens" in *The [Fort Worth] Star Telegram* "Weekly Review," November 6, 2005, pp. 1E, 6E. Excerpted from *Soul of a Citizen: Living With Conviction in Challenging Times* by Paul Rogat Loeb. St. Martin's Press 2010. Copyright © 2010 by the author and reprinted by permission of St. Martin's Press, LLC. **Cowen, p. 492:** Tyler Cowen, "The New Heroes and Role Models," *Reason*, May 2000. Reprinted by permission of the author. **Barkley, p. 500:** "I Am Not a Role Model" by Charles Barkley. From I MAY BE WRONG, BUT I DOUBT IT by Charles Barkley, copyright © 2002, 2003 by Barkley Enterprises, Inc. Used by permission of Random House, Inc. **Targan, p. 505:** From Barry Targan, "True Grit," *The Sewanee Review*, Fall 1995, Vol. CIII, No. 4.

INDEX

Abbey, Edward, 4
Abu-Jaber, Diana, 26–30
achievement, 48–53
Alexie, Sherman, 272–279
Allemang, Gina, 472
Alphonse, Lylah M., 23–25
alternative energy, 347–354
Alvarez, Julia, 120–123
American culture, 120–123
analyzing, 305–309
    defined, 305
    example of, 306–308
    guidelines for, 305–306, 308
    for revising draft, 309
Angelou, Maya, 73–75
annotations, 17–19, 305
    defined, 54
    example of, 55–58
    guidelines for, 58
    purposes of, 54
    steps for, 54–55
    types of, 54
"Anonymous Victims of Dreams and a
    River" (Landa), 297–299
"ANWR: The Great Divide" (Wallace),
    341–346
attitude, 211–213
audience, 2, 7, 128, 305–308
    analyzing, 305–308
    for personal essay, 128
    for reading, 2
Avery, Dennis T., 360–364

"Bad Connections" (Rosen), 407–411
Barkley, Charles, 500–504
"being green," 369–371

Bensman, David, 226–228
Bernstein, Douglas A., 43–47
Berry, Wendell, 365–368
"Between Two Worlds" (Abu-Jaber), 26–30
Bhalla, Archena, 167–171
"Big Russ and Me" (Russert), 218–225
"Black Men and Public Space" (Staples),
    268–271
Bliss, Elsie, 183–185
"Blogs Must Be Crazy, The" (Noonan),
    428–433
body of personal essay, 129
"Born Black, White, and Jewish" (Walker),
    20–22
"Boyhood Friendship in a Divided Valley, A"
    (Kamin), 146–148
Braaksma, Brian, 214–217
brainstorming, 9
Brokaw, Tom, 235–238
Brooks, David, 280–285
"Brothers" (Lott), 106–111
Bryson-Hurley, Denise, 472
"Buckle Up and Stop Texting: One Teen's
    Legacy" (Jacinto), 412–414

Campbell, Joseph, 472
careers, 239–243
Carter, Jimmy, 143–145
Caudron, Shari, 415–419
cause and effect, 257–260, 261–267
Cisneros, Sandra, 15–19, 80–83
civil rights, 300–304
classification, 159–162
climate change, 355–359
clustering, 9
Cohen, Theodore F., 69–72

Coleman, Sarah, 420–423
"College Friends" (Crichton), 139–142
Colon, Jesus, 229–231
comparison and contrast, 383–388, 415–419
complex services, 240
computer techniques, personal, 415–419
conclusion, 11, 129
constructing meaning, 2
Coontz, Stephanie, 163–166
Cooper, Anderson, 332–336
"Could You Live with Less?" (Mills), 437–440
courage, 505–508
Cowen, Tyler, 492–499
Crawford, Matthew B., 211–213
Crenshaw, Paul, 325–331
Crichton, Jennifer, 139–142
Cullen, Lisa Takeuchi, 369–371
culture, 23–25, 167–171

Danforth, Liz, 389–392
"Daughter's Journey, A" (Liao), 84–91
definition, 454–456
"Defining Family" (Strong, Devault,
    Cohen), 69–72
Demko, George J., 315–318
description, 106–111
descriptive passages, 202–206
descriptive phases, 107
Devault, Christine, 69–72
"Difference between Male and Female
    Friendships, The" (Goodman and
    O'Brien), 155–158
discovery draft, 11, 132
discussion, 6
"Dispatch from the Edge: Katrina"
    (Cooper), 332–336
"Distorting Mirror of Reality TV, The"
    (Coleman), 420–423
diversity, concept of, 253–256
divorce, 172–177

"Easy Job, Good Wages" (Colon), 229–231
education, 272–279
    foreign, 292–296
effective essay, 132
English languages, 261–267
environmental conservation, 341–346
environmental disasters, 337–340
essay, defined, 128. See also specific types of
ethnic groups, 286–291
ethnicity, 23–25
evaluation, 11
    of analysis essays, 309
    of personal essays, 132–133
    of persuasive essays, 378
    of reports, 446–447
    of response essays, 247
    of summaries, 188
example (exemplification), 319–324, 347–354

"Facebook in a Crowd" (Niedzviecki),
    404–406
failure, 48–53

family
    definitions of, 69–72
    notion of, 65–68
family heritage, 112–119
"Family That Stretches (Together), The"
    (Goodman), 124–127
fear of strangers, 268–271
"Ferguson" (Norman), 469–471
first draft, 10–11
Firstenberg, Jean Picker, 509
Flesher, John, 337–340
foreign education, 292–296
Fowler, Connie May, 112–119
"Fraternities of Netheads: Internet Addiction
    on Campus" (Young), 393–398
freewriting, 8
friendships, 139–158
"Future of Work, The" (Reich), 239–243

Gable, Clark, 509
"Games and Literacy" (Danforth), 389–392
gaming, literacy required for, 389–392
gathering information, 377
"Gay Marriage Looms as 'Battle of Our
    Times'" (Lampman), 178–182
"Getting to Know about You and Me"
    (Schoenberger), 257–260
Gibbon, Peter H., 482–485
"Girl in an Oven" (Smith), 202–206
"Giving Students the Heroes They Need"
    (Gibbon), 482–485
goal motivation, 48–53
Goodman, Ellen, 124–127, 155–158
Gore, Al, 355–359
"Great Expectations" (Coontz), 163–166
Grossman, Lev, 424–427
Grunwald, Michael, 347–354

helping others, 457–462
Herman, Agnes G., 92–98
hero
    defined, 454–456, 478–481, 482–485
    role models and, distinguishing between,
        482–485, 492–499
"Hero Inflation" (Thompson), 477–481
heroism, 457–462, 463–468, 472–476,
    487–491
Herrick, Lee, 65–68
Hetherington, E. Mavis, 172–177
Hoffman, Dustin, 509
"Hold the Mayonnaise" (Alvarez), 120–123
homogeneous nation, 280–285
homosexuality, 92–98
households, 70
hurricanes, 332–336

"I Am Not a Role Model" (Barkley), 500–504
identity, 15–16, 17–19, 20–22, 22–25, 26–31
    work, 193–198, 199–201
"I Have a Dream" (King, Jr.), 300–304
"I'm Just Me" (Alphonse), 23–25
immigration, 297–299
"Indian Education" (Alexie), 272–279

information retrieval methods, 3–4
"In iPad We Trust" (Lyons), 434–436
Internet addiction, 393–398
interviews, 232–234
introduction, 11
introduction of personal essay, 129
"Is Humanity Losing the Global Warming Debate?" (Singer and Avery), 360–364
"It's Inconvenient Being Green" (Cullen), 369–371

Jacinto, Margie, 412–414
"Jacket, The" (Soto), 35–38
job searching, 229–231
journal entries, 8–9
journey "home," 469–471

Kamin, Ben, 146–148
King, Larry L., 76–79
King, Martin Luther Jr., 300–304
Klagsbrun, Francine, 99–105

Laird, Ellen, 399–403
Lampman, Jane, 178–182
Landa, Victor, 297–299
"Larger Than Life" (Sudo), 454–456
learning disability, 39–42
learning goals, 44
Liao, Sharon, 84–91
literacy, 383–388
   required for gaming, 389–392
"Literacy Debate Online: R U Really Reading?" (Rich), 383–388
"Living in Two Worlds" (Mabry), 31–34
Loeb, Paul Rogat, 486–491
Logan, Paul, 48–53
Lott, Bret, 106–111
Lyons, Daniel, 434–436

Mabry, Marcus, 31–34
main ideas, 4, 5, 6, 125. See also thesis
   example of, 4–5
   importance of, 5
   supporting ideas and, differentiating between, 5
mainstream media, 428–433
mapping, 9–10
"Marriage and Divorce American Style" (Hetherington), 172–177
Martino, Carmen, 226–228
McMurtry, Larry, 2
McWhirter, Nickie, 199–201
Meier, Daniel, 207–210
Mills, Stephanie, 437–440
"Mongrel America" (Rodriguez), 286–291
Moon, Bill, 472–476
"Mother and Freedom" (Angelou), 73–75
"Mother Tongue" (Tan), 261–267
movie reviews, writing, 509–514
   elements of, 510–511
   evaluation of, 514
   example, 511–513
   guidelines for, 513

preliminary stages of, 509–510
Mukherjee, Bharati, 292–296
"My Home, My World" (Bhalla), 167–171
"My Name" (Cisneros), 15–16
"My Right Hand" (Weisskopf), 463–468

"Name Is Mine, The" (Quindlen), 17–19
names, 15–19
narration, 35–38
"Need for Achievement, The" (Bernstein), 43–47
"New Heroes and Role Models, The" (Cowen), 492–499
new technology, 434–436
Niedzviecki, Hal, 404–406
Noonan, Peggy, 428–433
Norman, Michael, 469–471
Norris, Kathleen, 319–324
"No Snapshots in the Attic: A Granddaughter's Search for a Cherokee Past" (Fowler), 112–119
notes, 446
nuclear family, 71
Nussbaum, Anna, 152–154

O'Brien, Patricia, 155–158
occupation, 239–243
"Oil and Water" (Owen), 149–151
"Old Man, The" (King), 76–79
"On Being 17, Bright, and Unable to Read" (Raymond), 39–42
"One Man's Kids" (Meier), 207–210
"Only Daughter" (Cisneros), 80–83
organization
   of movie review, 510
   of personal essay, 129
   of persuasive essay, 373
   of report, 442–443, 445
outline for reports, 446
Owen, Valerie, 149–151

paraphrases, 186
parental expectations, 80–83
"Parent's Journey Out of the Closet" (Herman), 92–98
"Passion for Diversity, A" (Pomeroy), 253–256
Pauk, Walter, 2
people, defining, 199–201
"People Like Us" (Brooks), 280–285
performance goals, 44
personal essay
   audience for, 128
   body of, 129
   conclusion of, 129
   defined, 128
   effective, 132
   evaluating, 132–133
   example of, 130–131
   introduction of, 129
   organization of, 129
   prewriting, 129, 132
   purpose of, 128
   steps to, 128–129

personal essay (*continued*)
  structure of, 129
  subject of, 128, 132
  writing, 128–133
personal technologies, 407–411
person-to-person services, 240
persuasive essays
  evaluating, 378
  example of, 373–375
  gathering information for, 377
  guidelines for, 377–378
  purpose of, 372
  reviewing, 378
  structural elements of, 372–373
  submitting, 378
  writing, 372–378
plagiarism, 399–403
Pomeroy, Ann, 253–256
prejudices, 143–145
prewriting, 7–8
  brainstorming and clustering, 9
  freewriting, 8
  journal entries, 8–9
  mapping, 9–10
  a personal essay, 129, 132
process, 226–228
process essay, 226–227
"Psychic Satisfactions of Manual Work"
  (Crawford), 211–213
purposes
  of annotations, 54
  of personal essay, 128
  of persuasive essays, 372
  of reading, 2, 3
  of reports, 441
  of summary, 186
  of writing, 7, 128

Quindlen, Anna, 17–19
Quiñones, John, 457–462

race of person, 23–25
Raymond, David, 39–42
reading
  audience, determine, 2
  information retrieval methods, 3–4
  main ideas, 4–5
  purpose of, 2, 3
  revisions, 5–6
  subject, 4
  supporting ideas, 4
  thesis, 4
  thesis statement, 4
  topic sentence, 4
  verbs, 4
"Real Digital Divide" (Caudron), 415–419
reality television, 420–423
Reece, Tamekia, 232–234
"Regular Work for an Irregular Economy"
  (Martino and Bensman), 226–228
Reich, Robert B., 239–243
reports
  defined, 441

elements of, 446–447
example of, 443–445
notes for, 446
organization of, 442–443, 445
outline for, 446
purpose of, 441
subject of, 446
types of, 441–442
writing, 441–447
rereading, 6
"Rescuing Oiled Birds" (Flesher and
  Schwartz), 337–340
respect, 84–91
response essay
  definition of, 244
  example of, 145–146
  guidelines for, 244–247
  purpose of, 244
  revising, 247
  steps to writing, 244
review, defined, 509
revisions, 5–6
  to draft, 309
  of response essay, 247
  of summary, 188
  to writing, 11
Rich, Motoko, 383–388
"Risking Your Life for Another" (Quiñones),
  457–462
RockBand, 390
Rodriguez, Gregory, 286–291
role models, 500–504
  hero and, distinguishing between, 492–499
role reversal, 73–75
"Rosa Parks Through a New Lens" (Loeb),
  486–491
Rose, Mike, 193–198
Rosen, Christine, 407–411
Russert, Tim, 218–225

"Salvaging an Interview" (Reece), 232–234
schedules
  importance of, 2–3
  purpose of, 3
  study, 2
  work, 3
Schoenberger, Chana, 257–260
Schwartz, Noaki, 337–340
sense of place, 315–318
"Sense of Place, A" (Demko), 315–318
"September 11th, 2001: Answering the Call"
  (Moon), 472–476
"Seven Myths about Alternative Energy"
  (Grunwald), 347–354
"Sibling Imprints" (Klagsbrun), 99–105
sibling relationships, 99–105, 106–111
Singer, S. Fred, 360–364
single, being, 183–185
"Small Act, A" (Carter), 143–145
Smith, Sarah Jeanette, 202–206
social networking, 404–406
Soto, Gary, 35–38
sources, 178–182